THE MILITARY ORDERS

Allocutio habita per Patrem Bernardum Demel ex Ordine Teutonico in missa de die 6. Septembris 1992 (London)

Fratres et sorores in Domino nostro Jesu Christo !

Saluto vos omnes in initio novae hebdomadae et praesertim missae, in qua commemoramus mortem et resurrectionem Salvatoris nostri.

Ante omnia debeo gratias agere Professori et nostro Praesidenti Riley-Smith et omnibus eius adiuvatoribus, quod possibilitatem habemus, profiteri fidem et spem nostram.

Nunc aliquid fit, quod – ni fallor – usque hodie numquam factum est:Nempe, quod membrum qualificatum ex Ordine Sancti Joannis Baptistae praestat servitium in sacra missa primo sacerdoti Ordinis Teutonici, qui potuit interesse scientificae conferentiae in regno Angliae.

Ista fides, quam postea in CREDO et in omnibus, quae ad sacra celebranda neccessaria sunt, iterum profitebimur, est etiam fides membrorum in ordinibus sicdictis militaribus in medio aevo et plurium postea usque hodie. Multa nova in ista nostra finienda conferentia de hac re audivimus. Hoc iterum provocat nostram gratitudinem ad omnes, qui istam possibilitatem nobis advenientibus praestabant et praestant.

Sanctus Abbas Bernardus Claravallensis in opero suo famoso "De laude novae militiae" posuit theologicam et – sit venia verbo – ideologico–sociologicam fundationem pro ista coniunctione monachi et militis cum tribus votis consuetis. Admonuit etiam Templarios, fundatus in admonitione Epistolae Sancti Pauli ad Ephesios (in Capite sexto), uti pugnent contra diabolum et omne malum in seipsis et in eiis temporibus.

Scimus, quot effectus iste abbas habuit.

Iste ordo, quem Bernardus contra oppositionem temporalem et manentem in Ecclesia stabilire potuit, ab uno Concilio Oecumenico (1312), uti omnes bene scitis, suppressus est.

Fortasse nobis historia istius Ordinis et omnium aliorum ordinum equestrium, de quibus in civitate Londoniensi nunc melius instructi sumus, est et erit magistra vitae et impetus pro nobis, quomodo nos, mutatis temporibus et circumstantiis, pugnare debemus contra nostra peccata, delicta et omissiones.

Ergo, fratres et sorores, antequam audimus verba Dei in lectionibus et celebramus sacra mysteria fidei secundum omnia, quod Jesus voluit et instituit, imploremus gratiam Domini nostri, ut apti simus ad Eucharistiam recte celebrandam.

Confiteor ...

THE MILITARY ORDERS

Fighting for the Faith and Caring for the Sick

edited by

Malcolm Barber

editorial committee
Peter Edbury, Anthony Luttrell,
Jonathan Riley-Smith

VARIORUM
1994

Published by   Variorum
                  Ashgate Publishing Limited
                  Gower House, Croft Road,
                  Aldershot, Hampshire GU11 3HR
                  Great Britain

                  Ashgate Publishing Limited
                  Old Post Road,
                  Brookfield, Vermont 05036
                  USA

ISBN 0–86078–438–X

British Library Cataloguing-in-Publication Data
Military Orders: Fighting for the Faith
and Caring for the Sick.
  I. Barber, Malcolm.
  271.05

U.S. Library of Congress Cataloging-in-Publication Data
The Military Orders: Fighting for the faith
and caring for the sick / edited by Malcolm Barber.
    p.   cm. Includes bibliographical references and index.
    1. Military religious orders—History—Congresses.
    2. Hospitalers—History—Congresses. 3. Templars—
    History—Congresses. 4. Teutonic Knights—History—
    Congresses. I. Barber, Malcolm.
    CR4701.M55 1994
    271'.05—dc20   94-17896
                                              CIP

Typeset by   Stanford Desktop Publishing Services, Milton Keynes
Printed in Great Britain at the University Press, Cambridge

Contents

Part II The Order of the Temple

Part III The Teutonic Order

List of Illustrations

List of Tables

Abbreviations

AASS	*Acta Sanctorum Bollandiana*
AHN OO.MM	Archivo Histórico Nacional, Ordenes Militares
AOL	*Archives de l'Orient latin*
ASV	Archivio di Stato, Venice
BA	*Bullarium Ordinis Militiae de Alcantara*, ed. I.J. Ortega y Cotes, J. Fernández de Brizuela and P. de Ortega Zúñiga y Aranda (Madrid, 1759)
BASMOM	British Association of the Sovereign Military Order of Malta
BC	*Bullarium Ordinis Militiae de Calatrava*, ed I.J. Ortega y Cotes, J.F. Alvarez de Baquedano and P. de Ortego Zúñiga y Aranda (Madrid, 1761)
BL	British Library
CH	*Cartulaire général de l'Ordre des Hospitalers de Saint-Jean de Jérusalem, 1100–1310*, ed. J. Delaville Le Roulx, 4 vols (Paris 1894–1906)
CT	*Cartulaire général de l'Ordre du Temple 1119?–1150. Recueil des chartes et des bulles relatives à l'ordre du Temple*, ed. Marquis d'Albon (Paris, 1913)
Cont WT	*La Continuation de Guillaume de Tyre (1184–1197)*, ed. M.R. Morgan, Documents relatifs à l'histoire des croisades, 14 (Paris, 1982)
Crusades	*A History of the Crusades*, gen. ed. K.M. Setton, 2nd edn, 6 vols (Madison, 1969–89)
DNB	*Dictionary of National Biography*
EFF	*Feet of Fines for Essex*, ed. R.E.C. Kirk (Colchester, 1899–1910)
Eracles	*L'Estoire de Eracles Empereur et la Conqueste de la Terre d'Outremer*, in *RHC Occid*, **1, 2**, (Paris, 1859)
Ernoul-Bernard	*Chronique d'Ernoul et de Bernard le Trésorier*, ed. L. de Mas-Latrie (Paris, 1871)
GC	*Gestes des Chiprois*, ed. G. Raynaud (Geneva, 1887)

Malta, Cod.	Archives of the Order of St John, National Library of Malta, Valletta
MGH SS	*Monumenta Germaniae Historica. Scriptores*
MIC	*Monumenta iuris canonici*
MVO	Museum and Library of the Most Venerable Order of St John
NLM	National Library of Malta, Valletta
OSJ	Order of St John
PC	*The Cartulary of the Knights of St John of Jerusalem in England*, prima camera, Essex
PL	*Patrologia Latina*
PPTS	Palestine Pilgrims' Text Society
Procès	*Le Procès des Templiers*, ed. J. Michelet, 2 vols (Paris, 1841)
PUTJ	*Papsturkunden für Templer und Johanniter*, ed. R. Hiestand, 2 vols (Göttingen, 1972–84)
RCHM	Royal Commission on Historical Monuments
RDAC	*Report. Department of Antiquities, Cyprus*
RHC	*Recueil des Historiens des Croisades*
Occid	*Historiens occidentaux*
Or	*Historiens orientaux*
DArm	*Documents arméniens*
RHGF	*Recueil des Historiens des Gaules et de la France*
RIS	*Rerum Italicarum Scriptores*
ROL	*Revue de l'Orient latin*
RRH	*Regesta Regni Hierosolymitani* and *Additamentum*, ed. R. Röhricht (Innsbruck, 1893–1904)
RS	Rolls Series
RSJ	*The Rule of the Spanish Military Order of St James, 1170–1493*, ed. E. Gallego Blanco (Leiden, 1971)
RT	*La Règle du Temple*, ed. H. de Curzon (Paris, 1886)
SC	*The Cartulary of the Knights of St John of Jerusalem in England*, secunda camera, Essex, ed. M. Gervers (Oxford, 1982).
SDO	*Die Statuten des Deutschen Ordens nach den ältesten Handschriften*, ed. M. Perlbach (Halle, 1890)
SRP	*Scriptores Rerum Prussicarum*, ed. T. Hirsch *et al.* (Leipzig, 1861)
SWEH	Monograph on South Witham excavation to be published by English Heritage
TDE	Tennyson d'Eyncourt papers, Lincolnshire Archives, Lincoln
WT	Guillaume de Tyre, *Chronique*, ed. R.B.C. Huygens, Corpus Christianorum, Continuatio Mediaevalis 63, 63A (Turnhout, 1986)

List of Contributors

David Allen is Lecturer in Modern History at the University of Birmingham. He began his career as a student of Stuart history, but in recent years has published several articles about the history of the Order of St John in early modern Europe, in which he has been concerned to integrate the Order's history with the better known mainstream of European history.

Udo Arnold is Professor of History at the University of Bonn and President of the International Historical Commission for Research on the Teutonic Order. He has published extensively on the Teutonic Order and on north German and Baltic history. Among his recent books is a general survey of the Order's history, *Der Deutsche Orden. Von seinem Ursprung bis zur Gegenwart* (1992) (with Marian Tumler).

Malcolm Barber is Reader in Medieval History at the University of Reading. His publications include two books on the Templars and a general survey of medieval Europe between 1050 and 1320.

Carlos Barquero Goñi is currently working on his doctoral thesis at the Autonomous University of Madrid. His special field is the history of the Hospitallers in Castile and Leon between the twelfth and the fourteenth centuries.

Karl Borchardt is Assistant Lecturer in Medieval History at the University of Würzburg. He has written books on medieval ecclesiastical institutions in Rothenburg ob der Tauber and on medieval inscriptions in Würzburg (both published in 1988). Together with Dr Anthony Luttrell he is preparing a study of the Hospitallers in Germany in the fourteenth century.

James Brundage is Ahmanson-Murphy Distinguished Professor of History at the University of Kansas. He is a leading authority on canon law in the Middle Ages on which he has published numerous books and articles. Among his best known books are *Medieval Canon Law and the Crusader* (1969) and *Law, Sex, and Christian Society in Medieval Europe* (1987). A selection of his articles was recently published under the title *The Crusades, Holy War and Canon Law* (1991).

Marcus Bull is Lecturer in Medieval History at the University of Bristol. He is working on the prehistory of the indulgence and also on the cult of Saint Faith in the tenth and eleventh centuries. He has recently published a book based upon his doctoral thesis, *Knightly Piety and the Lay Response to the First Crusade in the Limousin and Gascony, c. 970– c. 1130* (1993).

Carlos de Ayala Martínez is Professor of Medieval History at the Autonomous University of Madrid. He is director of the research project into the development of the medieval military orders in the kingdoms of Castile and León.

Bernhard Demel is Director of the Zentralarchiv des Deutschen Ordens and Rector of the Order's church of St Elizabeth in Vienna. Since 1985 he has been Secretary of the Internationalen Historischen Komission zur Erforschung des Deutschen Ordens. He has researched extensively into the Teutonic Order and into the ecclesiastical and cultural history of Moravia and Silesia.

Peter Edbury is Senior Lecturer in Medieval History at the University of Wales, Cardiff. He has published many articles on the crusades and the Latin East and edited the proceedings of the first conference of the Society for the Study of the Crusades (1985). His two most recent books are *William of Tyre: Historian of the Latin East* (1988) (with John Rowe) and *The Kingdom of Cyprus and the Crusades* (1991).

Susan Edgington is Senior Lecturer at Huntingdonshire Regional College. Her major project is a critical edition and English translation of the *Historia* of Albert of Aachen (forthcoming).

Sven Ekdahl is Lecturer in History at the University of Göteborg and Wissenschaftlich Angestellter at the Geheimes Staatsarchiv Preussischer Kulturbesitz, Berlin. He has published *Die 'Banderia Prutenorum' des Jan Długosz* (1976) and *Die Schlacht bei Tannenberg 1410. Quellenkritische Untersuchungen.* Vol. 1, *Einführung und Quellenlage* (1982) (vol. 2 is in progress), as well as many articles in German, Swedish, Polish and Lithuanian historical journals.

Jesús Espino Nuño is Research Assistant at the University of Madrid. His special field is the relation between art and the military orders in Spain, on which he has published a number of articles.

Alan Forey is Reader in History at the University of Durham. He has published many articles on the crusades and the military orders as well as a study of *The Templars in the Corona de Aragón* (1973), *The Military Orders. From the Twelfth to the Early Fourteenth Centuries* (1992) and most recently, *Military Orders and Crusades* (1994).

Michael Gervers is Professor of History at the University of Toronto. He is a leading authority on the Hospitallers in England. He has published critical editions of the Order's cartularies for Essex, as well as articles on the medieval textile industry and on medieval round and rock-cut churches.

Anne Gilmour-Bryson is Senior Lecturer in Medieval History at the University of Melbourne. She has published several articles on the Templars and, in 1982, edited the records of the trial of the Templars in the Papal States and the Abruzzi. She has a particular interest in the application of computers in the editing of medieval texts and in the analysis of historical data, and has published a number of articles and two books on this subject.

Klaus Guth is Professor of Volkskunde (European Ethnology) und Historische Landeskunde at the Otto-Friedrich University, Bamberg. He has published monographs on subjects ranging from Guibert of Nogent to the history of confession in France, as well as over seventy articles. He is currently researching the social history of minority groups in Bavaria in the nineteenth and twentieth centuries.

Kara Hattersley-Smith is editor of Early Christian and Byzantine art for Macmillan's *The Dictionary of Art*. Her book, *Byzantine Public Architecture between the Fourth and the Eleventh Centuries with Special Reference to the Towns of Macedonia*, is soon to be published. She has had extensive archaeological and field work experience in former Yugoslavia, Greece, Turkey and, most recently Rhodes, where she has been working on settlement patterns during the Hospitaller period.

Annetta Iliéva is Assistant Professor of History at the American University in Bulgaria. She has published many articles and a book, *Frankish Morea, 1205–1262* (1991), based on her doctoral thesis.

Robert Irwin was formerly Lecturer in Mediaeval History at the University of St Andrews and is now a freelance writer. He is the author of *A History of the Middle East in the Middle Ages: The Bahri Mamluk Sultanate of Egypt and Syria* (1986) and several novels.

Fotini Karassava-Tsilingiri is a practising architect and restorer. She has worked for the Greek Ministry of Culture, Historic Buildings Section, at Patras and Athens, and is currently employed by the Commission for Ancient Monuments at Attica. Her main research interest is the fifteenth-century Hospitaller hospital at Rhodes and the architecture of their hospitals in general.

Peter Lock is Senior Lecturer in Medieval History at the University College of Ripon and York St John, York. He is the author of numerous articles on

Frankish Greece and has completed a study of the Franks in the Aegean region between 1204 –1500 to be published in 1995.

Anthony Luttrell has held lectureships at Edinburgh and Malta and is a former Assistant Director of the British School at Rome. He is a leading authority on the occupation of Rhodes by the Order of St John (1306–1522) and has also published extensively on the Order's European possessions and on other Western settlements in Greece in the later Middle Ages. The most recent selection of his articles, *The Hospitallers of Rhodes and their Mediterranean World*, was published in 1992.

Victor Mallia-Milanes is Head of the Department of History at the University of Malta. His special research interest is Venice, the Order of St John, and Malta in the early modern period, on which he has published extensively. His most recent work is *Venice and Hospitaller Malta 1530–1798: Aspects of a Relationship* (1992), and he has just completed the editing of *Hospitaller Malta 1530–1798: Studies on Malta and the Order of St John of Jerusalem* (1993).

José Matellanes Merchán is working on his doctoral thesis on the Order of Santiago, 1170–1350, at the Autonomous University of Madrid and he is also a member of a team researching into the part played by the military orders in the implantation of feudalism in the western Iberian peninsular. He has written several articles on the history of the Order of Santiago.

A.H.S. (Peter) Megaw has been Director of Antiquities, Cyprus and Director of the British School of Archaeology, Athens. He has published many archaeological reports and monographs on the eastern Mediterranean in the medieval period.

Klaus Militzer is Professor of Medieval History at the University of Bochum. His publications on the military orders centre particularly upon the history of the Teutonic order in Germany, Prussia and Livonia, and include *Die Entstehung der Deutschordensballeien im Deutschen Reich* (1981).

Helen Nicholson is Lecturer in Medieval History at the University of Wales College of Cardiff and the author of *Templars, Hospitallers and Teutonic Knights. Images of the Military Orders 1128–1291* (1993), which is based upon her doctoral thesis, as well as several articles on the military orders.

Olga Pérez Monzón is Research Assistant on a group project to investigate art and the military orders directed by Professor Ruiz Mateos at the University of Madrid. She has published articles on various aspects of the artistic links of the Order of Santiago and the Order of St John, the latter of which is the subject of her doctoral thesis.

Jonathan Phillips is Lecturer in Medieval European History at Royal Holloway College, University of London. He has recently completed his doctoral thesis on relations between the Latin East and the West, 1119–1187, which will shortly be published as a book.

James M. Powell is Professor of Medieval History at Syracuse University. Among his many books and articles are *Anatomy of a Crusade, 1213–1221* (1986) and *Albertanus of Brescia: The Pursuit of Happiness in the Early Thirteenth Century* (1992).

Denys Pringle is a Principal Inspector of Ancient Monuments, Scotland. He has published many reports, monographs and articles on the archaeology of Italy, North Africa, Scotland and the Latin Kingdom of Jerusalem. Among his books is *The Red Tower (al-Burj al-Ahmar): Settlement in the Plain of Sharon at the Time of the Crusaders and Mamluks (A.D. 1099–1516)* (1986). He is currently working on a three-volume corpus of the churches of the Crusader Kingdom of Jerusalem, the first volume of which was published in 1993.

Jean Richard, former Professor of Medieval History at the University of Dijon, is a member of the Institut de France (Académie des Inscriptions et Belles-Lettres). He is the author of numerous books and articles on the crusades, the Latin settlements in the east, the military orders, the Mongols, and the Duchy of Burgundy in the Middle Ages. His study of Louis IX has recently been published in English translation as *Saint Louis: Crusader King of France* (1992).

Jonathan Riley-Smith is Dixie Professor of Ecclesiastical History at the University of Cambridge, and President of the Society for the Study of the Crusades and the Latin East. He is the author of many books and articles on the military orders, the Western settlements in Palestine, and the crusades, including *The Knights of St John in Jerusalem and Cyprus c. 1050–1310* (1967).

Pál Ritoók works for the National Board for the Protection of Historic Monuments in Budapest, and has published articles, catalogues and guides on Hungarian art and architecture. His recent work on the architecture of the Templars arose out of his award of a scholarship from the Soros Foundation, which enabled him to research in England.

Enrique Rodríquez-Picavea Matilla is Research Assistant at the Autonomous University of Madrid, where he is a member of the team investigating the military orders in the Middle Ages in the western Iberian Peninsular (1150–1350). He is preparing a doctoral thesis on the Order of Calatrava in the twelfth and thirteenth centuries.

Walter Rödel is Professor of Early Modern History at the Johannes Gutenberg University, Mainz. He has worked extensively on the Order of St John in the archives at Valletta, and is author of more than fifty publications on Hospitaller history, including *Das Grosspriorat Deutschland des Johanniter-Ordens im Übergang vom Mittelalter zur Reformation* (1972).

Aurora Ruiz Mateos is Professor of the History of Art in the University of Madrid and director of research teams working on the architecture of the military orders in Iberia.

Jürgen Sarnowsky is Lecturer in History at the Free University of Berlin. He is an authority on scholastic thought in the later Middle Ages, as well as the history of the Teutonic Order and the Order of St John. His second book, *Die Wirtschaftsführung des Deutschen Ordens in Preussen (1382–1454)*, was published in 1993.

Elizabeth Siberry is a civil servant in the Cabinet Office, Whitehall. She has published several articles on the crusades and a book, *Criticism of Crusading, 1095–1274* (1985). She is currently working on a series of articles about images of the crusade in the nineteenth and early twentieth centuries.

H.J.A. Sire is a free-lance historical writer and the author of *Gentlemen Philosophers - Catholic Higher Studies at Liège and Stonyhurst College 1774–1916* (1988) and *The Knights of Malta* (1994).

Judi Upton-Ward has just published a translation of the French Rule of the Templars (1992) and has almost completed an edition, with English translation, of the Catalan Rule of the Templars. She is working for her doctorate at the University of Birmingham.

John Walker is Part-time Lecturer, University College, Scarborough. His doctoral thesis was on the patronage of the Templars and the Order of St Lazarus in England. He is at present preparing *The Cartulary of the Hospital of St Giles, Holborn*, for the London Record Society.

Ann Williams is Senior Lecturer in Mediterranean History at the University of Exeter. She is a specialist in the hospital and charitable work of the Order of St John in the early modern period, and is about to publish *Servants of the Sick, The Convent of the Order of St John 1309–1631*.

Joan Williamson is Professor of French at Long Island University, New York. She has published articles on Old French texts, both epic and romance, and is completing an edition of *Le Livre de la vertu du sacrement de mariage* by Philippe de Mézières.

Editor's Preface

This volume contains papers from a conference held on 3–6 September 1992 at the Museum of St John, St John's Gate, Clerkenwell, London, under the auspices of the London Centre for the Study of the Crusades. The perception of the organizers that there is a growing interest in, and enthusiasm for, the study of military orders was fully borne out. Scholars from twenty countries took part and, between them, presented forty-eight papers encompassing a vast geographical spread from Lithuania to Spain and from England to the Crusader States. It was particularly pleasing to welcome colleagues from eastern Europe now able to participate much more readily than in the past.

The conference covered every period from the origins of the military orders in the eleventh and twelfth centuries down to the present day, and a large proportion of the papers has been published here, following the overall conference format in which four main papers were given, supported by shorter communications. The event culminated in a visit to the two magnificent timber-framed barns at Cressing Temple in Essex, where the whole site of the Templar preceptory is being surveyed and excavated. It is hoped that this conference will be the first of a series, to be held at four-year intervals, and that the research presented here will stimulate further work on this multifaceted subject.

All successful conferences are the consequence of a team effort; this conference had at its core a highly effective organizing committee, chaired by Jonathan Riley-Smith and administered by Rosemary Bailey, together with Peter Edbury, Tim Everard, Helen Gribble, Anthony Luttrell and Pamela Willis. They were assisted by Julia Findlater, Julia Toffolo and Jill Geser. The staff of the Museum of St John – Amanda Devonshire, Francesca Alden and Carmel Fitzpatrick – worked many long hours to ensure its smooth day-to-day running. Adrian Gibson and Tim Robey of the Archaeology Section of Essex County Council provided authoritative guidance at the Cressing Temple site. In the production of the book my personal thanks go particularly to the editorial committee, to Judi Upton-Ward who typed the manuscript and translated four of the Spanish papers, to Pamela Willis, whose skill in researching additional material has eased several editorial problems, to Ben Arnold for advice on German history and to John Smedley and Ruth Peters of Variorum. Finally, we are all extremely grateful to Michael Carey and the Honourable Henry Hankey, Trustees of The Seven Pillars of Wisdom Trust, whose generosity in providing a subvention has ensured that the book would be published.

Introduction

Jean Richard

'Fighting for the faith and caring for the sick': when considering this double vocation of the military religious orders historians usually pay more attention to the first aspect rather than to the second, even though today it is the latter which survives while the former has steadily diminished in importance. It was therefore appropriate that the conference held at St John's Gate in September 1992 should remind us that the obligations imposed upon the orders involved a combination of both activities.

Fighting for the faith: this question was thoroughly scrutinized in the course of a colloquium which met in 1989 at Passo della Mendola, the proceedings of which have appeared under the title *'Militia Christi' e crociata*. The great debate which preoccupied the participants in this conference was how to reconcile the concept of the *miles Christi*, the monk who fights every day against the forces of evil in a conflict of a spiritual nature, with that of the warrior who repels the enemies of Christ by material arms. In particular, in examining the origins of the orders, emphasis was placed on the role of the fraternities of knights which were founded, especially in the Iberian peninsula, in order to defend the borders of Christendom. In this volume, this issue is discussed in relation to the confraternity of La Sauve-Majeure, previously thought to have been an association of this type, whose aim was to defend the abbey. Here however a new examination questions whether that interpretation should be retained.

The orders created in the Holy Land in the wake of the crusades share a common origin which was founded on the idea of caring for others. Even before 1099 the task of helping sick pilgrims was imposed upon the first Hospitallers; after this date it became even more important. The first function of the Templars was to protect such pilgrims from the dangers of the road. As for the Teutonic Knights, their order was born out of the campaign hospital created for the crusaders who were besieging Acre during the Third Crusade. It is therefore pertinent to consider the nature of the care given to the wounded and the sick. As early as the First Crusade and the years that followed, even before recourse was made to oriental doctors, the rational character of this medication is striking. A search for the causes of the illness, investigation of wounds, and appropriate care, appear to have enabled cures to be found for those seriously wounded or close to death; substantial knowledge was therefore already being applied to the care of the sick.

However, the work of the conference was essentially concerned with the period after the origins of the orders, encompassing their history right up to our own times.

On the Templars the initial question to consider is the mission entrusted by King Baldwin II of Jerusalem to the first Master of the Order, Hugh of Payns, the aim of which was to solicit aid from the barons of the West in order to attempt the conquest of Damascus. This mission was decisive in establishing the Order of the Temple and assuring its expansion in Europe. The task given to the knights, to protect the pilgrim routes, led them to construct fortresses along the route to the Jordan, which are the subject of a study here. In addition, the prince of Antioch granted them the first of the strongholds around which the Order established great lordships endowed with sovereign rights. One of these was Baghras (Gaston) which, apart from the period when it was captured by Saladin and then occupied by the Armenians, was held by the Temple until the time of Sultan Baybars. In contrast with these fortresses were the simple manors which the knights established in their Western domains, notably in England; these operated as centres for the exploitation of their resources with the main aim of collecting revenues to supply the establishments created by the Order in the crusader states.

An interesting case is that of Cyprus where the Templars had been called by King Richard to take charge of the government of the island. Although they gave this up, the Order remained a power in the Lusignan kingdom, and indeed came into conflict with the Crown. Nevertheless, following the arrest of the Templars, the inquiry which took place on the island revealed the esteem in which the Order and its members were held by the Cypriot aristocracy, even those linked to the party of King Henry II which the leaders of the Order did not support. It has been shown how the Order sent its youngest knights to the Cypriot houses, doubtless with a view to engaging them in combat with the sultan. It was only much later that the image of the Templars was tarnished in Cypriot historiography.

The Hospitallers also established themselves in Cyprus; the techniques employed in building the castle of Paphos, in the early thirteenth century, suggest that they were responsible for its construction. But it is their other domains in the West which are better known and whose extent can be more fully appreciated thanks to the documentation of the fourteenth century, and this volume contains studies on England, Castile and Aragon. The nature of these possessions was very different, for the transfer of royal revenues to the knights was very important in Spain whereas it is apparent that, for the Hospital, the function of these domains was to help maintain the Convent and not to furnish a contribution to the conflict against the Saracens in the peninsula.

It is well known that Matthew Paris attributed the possession of 19,000 manors to the Hospitallers, a figure which is certainly a fantasy. It is, however, interesting to compare this with the letter – evidently forged in the same period – recommending the collectors of the Order to the faithful of Franconia, for this gives the figure of 4,000 manors corresponding with that of the 4,000 knights who had fought the infidels. Here, it seems, is evidence of a propaganda campaign which stressed the magnitude of the effort undertaken by the Order.

After the fall of Acre, the Hospital was closely associated with the preparation of a new crusade, with which Pope Clement V was personally identified. This connection is underlined by the new dating suggested for the *Devise des Chemins de Babiloine*, one of the documents produced by the Hospital for this expedition. However, when the knights were installed at Rhodes, they once more took up the hospitaller tradition of their Order, which they could no longer exercise either in their great hospital at Jerusalem nor in that at Acre; they therefore built a new hospital at Rhodes where they continued to fulfil their medical vocation to the benefit of pilgrims and travellers. When the Order was obliged to re-establish itself on Malta, the clientele of the Hospital's doctors was not the same: the *xenodochium* was replaced by an infirmary, identical to those which each convent maintained for the use of its monks. From then on the knights dedicated themselves to the policing of the seas – a role which aroused the indignation of those who traded with the Turkish world, notably the Venetians, who had to sustain the consequences of the activities of what they regarded as Hospitaller corsairs . The chaplain brothers of the Order also felt the effects of the change in the Order's functions: some became 'galley chaplains', assuming the role of almoners on board the ships where they provided the crews with some kind of sacramental life.

The military orders were so integrated in the structure of the Latin states of the East that, after the Fourth Crusade, the conquerors of the Latin Empire of Constantinople called them into Greece. Although the Teutonic Knights occupied a modest position (in Messenia), at the beginning of the thirteenth century, the Templars enjoyed an active role in the region and the Hospitallers established themselves in Thessaly; Baldwin II even made an unsuccessful appeal to the knights of Santiago in an attempt to reinforce the defences of his empire. However, in the following century the Hospital – imbued with the mission to maintain a Frankish presence in Asia Minor, at Smyrna and, after 1407, at Bodrum – concerned itself directly with the defence of Frankish Greece. Although the grandiose plan conceived by the Grand Master Heredia ended in defeat, the Order remained committed to the conflict against the Turks in Greece. This continued to be linked to its presence in Rhodes – a presence which has been related to the existence of a class of Greek proprietors on the island.

With the onset of the Reformation the knights divided between the confessions. Those from the bailiwick of Brandenburg who had taken up the

Lutheran faith intended to remain members of the Order; it was agreed that they be permitted to continue to recognize the authority of the Grand Master, but not that of the bailiff of Brandenburg *in partibus*, who was a Catholic, appointed by the Master. After the taking of Malta by Bonaparte, the king of Prussia wished to make the Hospitallers a purely Prussian order: thus, in the mid-nineteenth century, it was once again theoretically united. The example of the Brandenburg compromise was invoked in the course of the curious transactions which occurred in England, also in the nineteenth century, with a view to reviving the English *Langue* at the heart of the Order. In the course of these dealings the idea of re-establishing the knights in Rhodes with the agreement of the Greek insurgents, was also proposed. But these negotiations, which were very delicate on the confessional issue, foundered due to the involvement of dubious individuals. In the event the English *Langue* was not restored, and the English Order of Saint John was eventually established as an order of the British Crown.

These projects should not be isolated from other contemporary perspectives. Other Englishmen, notably Sir Sidney Smith, whose victory at Saint-Jean d'Acre had stimulated a great personal interest in oriental questions (he also envisaged the restoration of the Christian presence in Ottoman Syria), had formed the idea of establishing a branch of the Order of the Temple in England after it had been revived in France. In fact the romantic epoch colourfully embellished the adventures of the knights of former times, particularly those who had vowed to fight for the faith (even though Sir Walter Scott gave the role of the villain to a Templar in *Ivanhoe*) . The renewal of the chivalric ideal thus found expression in these proposals for the restoration of the military orders.

These proposals had already nourished other dreams. Authors of chivalric romances portrayed the Templars as the protectors of lovers – indeed, they were depicted as ideal lovers. However, it is particularly important to emphasize the figure of Philippe de Mézières who, more than half a century after the canvassing of the idea of a union of the Temple and the Hospital which Pierre Dubois had imagined as dependent upon the French Crown, had conceived the idea of a new and original type of order, the Order of the Passion, as the instrument of a future crusade. Such an order had nothing in common with the orders of chivalry which flourished in almost every European court, and owed little to the true military orders .

However, the knightly cause did find the opportunity to fulfil itself thanks to the third of the great orders, that of the Teutonic Knights. It is clear that this order, which grew out of 'the hospital of the Germans' at Acre was, like the hospital of Saint John before it, given a military role parallel to its hospitaller vocation. In no way did it consider its hospitaller function of secondary importance; significantly, in Franconia it was be placed under the patronage of St Elizabeth, who exemplified a life consecrated to the service of the poor and the sick. Its military vocation was first employed in Frankish Syria, where

Frederick II had sufficiently appreciated the knights and their master, Hermann of Salza, to endow them in his kingdom of Sicily; next they faced the Cumans in the kingdom of Hungary, where King Andrew II established them in Burzenland; finally they went to Prussia and then on to Livonia, where they served to defend the 'new settlements of the faith' against the renewed pagan offensive. They were equally associated with the conflict against the Mongols and, later, against the Turks, but it is the Baltic lands which have been defined as the *Ordensland*, for it was their war against the Lithuanians and, to a lesser extent against the Russians, which gave the Teutonic Knights their specific character in fourteenth- and fifteenth-century Europe.

This war against the pagans – whose adherence to Catholicism was ignored by the Order in the time of Gedimyn and especially Jagiełło, since it would have removed the legitimacy of this struggle – was not simply religious in character. The Teutonic Knights did not put conversion of the infidel at the top of their agenda; when they launched their expeditions into pagan territory, they tried to bring back captives who, reduced to slavery, provided them with human resources which could be put to valuable use on their own estates. This was little different from the knights of Malta who used captured Muslims in their galleys, nor from the Turks, who used Christian sailors as their oarsmen. It was not this, however, which brought the knights who came from all over the West to gain the spiritual privileges attached to fighting for the faith; they found themselves welcomed and feted by the grand master and his knights and associated with the *Reisen* which honoured the participants as gallant warriors. These temporary combatants thus came to complete the armies of a knighthood which was regularly reinforced with noble recruits from a variety of German-speaking territories. The Order thus realized an ideal of chivalry which transcended the national boundaries of that time.

The victory of the Poles and Lithuanians at Tannenberg put an end to this period of the Order's history. After that the Reformation crisis provoked fissures and posed problems analogous to those encountered by the Hospital, but aggravated by the secularization of the territories of the *Ordensland*. In certain countries, the knights strove to maintain the unity of the Order in the face of confessional divisions. Only in the seventeenth century, in the Low Countries, was there established an order of knights adhering to the Calvinist confession; in Austria and Bavaria, the Order maintained its Catholic form, but within the framework of the monarchies, the knights being henceforth in the service of the state. It therefore succeeded in perpetuating itself until after the Second World War by transforming itself into the new structure which typifies it today and which emphasises its charitable character.

The Order of Saint Lazarus, which also originated in Outremer, is only alluded to here in relation to its formation in England. It appears that those who allowed it to be established in the British Isles, particularly in the priory of Burton Lazars, had been crusaders who had learned of it in the East. Yet the benefactors of the knights of Saint Lazarus were not, for the most part, participants in the Crusades, a circumstance testifies to the rapidity with which the Order took root.

Within this vast panorama of orders created in the Holy Land – and it can be seen how many varied aspects were evoked during this conference – it is important to incorporate some conception of the Spanish orders of which one – that of Mountjoy – was also started in Outremer, although it did not survive for very long. The Orders of Calatrava and of Santiago were modelled on those in the Holy Land which, as we have seen, also had dependencies in the peninsula. They are presented in this volume with particular reference to their domanial possessions. Nevertheless the problem of political power – or rather the problem of successive political powers – remains for, by incorporating Alcántara into it, the Leonese monarchy wished to make Calatrava an order especially attached to the monarchy. In Castile, the knights of Calatrava held a vast domain in the *Meseta*, and they developed its stock-rearing potential there. The knights of Santiago, who had been established in the mountainous zone spanning the frontiers of the Muslim kingdoms of Murcia and Valencia, built manors and castles there which do not reflect the influence of any specific architectural model.

Attention has therefore been focused above all on the activities of these orders in so far as they were dedicated to war and to the care of the sick, but the landed property from which they drew the revenues which, together with the products of offerings and the rights of fraternity, allowed them to support the brothers and the institutions vital to their goals, has not been neglected. It should be added that, like all landed proprietors and holders of rights and privileges, the knights engaged in innumerable legal disputes. They were therefore obliged to have recourse to lawyers and consequently to maintain, in their own ranks, brothers trained in the science of law – a category which had evidently not been anticipated in their constitutions.

It has not been easy to encompass so vast a collection of issues, and the organizers of the conference should be congratulated on succeeding in maintaining the unity at the heart of such very varied activities. The papers published here leave an impression which was gradually reinforced in the course of the conference – that of the vitality of an institution which originated in the very specific context of the crusade and the great pilgrimage, and which, over time, managed to adapt itself to many different forms. It may be that the disappearance of the Temple resulted from its continuing attachment to apparently old-fashioned structures and conceptions, but this has not been demonstrated. These orders were founded to succour the sick and the poor; they took responsibility for establishments which lacked manpower, and consequently took on a military form. They were able to provide an infrastructure capable of supporting themselves in Outremer or on the frontiers of Christian lands, with significant numbers of men, with fortifications and with hospitals. Contrary to the classic image of colonies exploiting exotic countries in order to enrich the metropolis, it fell to the knights' countries of origin to supply a lifeline to the lands where they had established themselves. Although the Temple did not survive the fall of Outremer, the other orders overcame the problem by turning to new vocations.

Nor did the Reformation succeed in entirely breaking up the military orders; despite the divergence in the loyalties of their members, they appear to have been attached to the idea of the unity of the order, which is testimony to the cohesion of the aristocratic structure on which the recruitment of the orders was based. Whether Catholic or Protestant, their members continued to belong to the same world and to be wedded to the same chivalric values. Even when they were put into the service of national states – as, for example, officers in the Austrian army, in the navy of the king of France, or as ambulance personnel in the British army – they remained faithful to the knightly ideal and, whatever may have been the vicissitudes of the initiatives towards restoration in the nineteenth century, they are witness to this attachment to the same ideal. But, as well as this military ideal, the orders have continued to serve their other vocation, which is complementary to the first: to care for and assist those stricken with illness.

Siege of Rhodes and Apparition, Caoursin.
The Museum and Library of the Order of St John, Clerkenwell.

Part I

The Hospital of St John

1

Pro defensione Terre Sancte: the Development and Exploitation of the Hospitallers' Landed Estate in Essex[*]

Michael Gervers

The Hospitallers probably reached England at about the same time as the Templars and the Cistercians, around 1128.[1] The Templars and Cistercians received an immediate and overwhelming response to their call for support. By 1140, the Cistercians had received 31 per cent of all the monastic foundations which would be granted to them in the twelfth century. Similarly, the Templars had been granted 26 per cent of their administrative sites. The Hospitallers, on the other hand, had received virtually nothing, and it was not until *c.* 1145 that they were granted the site of their English priory at Clerkenwell, near London. By the end of the next decade, however, the Order was in possession of 33 per cent of its twelfth-century administrative network throughout the country, and from *c.* 1180 to the end of the century, when the Templars and especially the Cistercians had reached the limit of their administrative expansion, it continued to receive active support.

The catalyst for Hospitaller growth appears not to have been the foundation at Clerkenwell, but rather the fall of Edessa at the end of December 1144 which led to the calling of the Second Crusade by Pope Eugenius III.[2] There is some indication that shortly thereafter, in 1146, St Bernard invited the Hospitallers

---

[*] I am grateful to Mr W. R. Powell, former County Editor of the Victoria County History for Essex, and Mrs Gillian Long of the DEEDS Project in Toronto for their helpful suggestions concerning earlier drafts of this paper. I should also like to acknowledge support received from the Social Sciences and Humanities Research Council of Canada during its preparation.

[1] *Records of the Templars in England in the Twelfth Century: the Inquest of 1185*, ed. B.A. Lees. British Academy, Records of the Social and Economic History of England and Wales, 9 (London, 1935), pp. xxxviii–ix; C. Tyerman, *England and the Crusades, 1095-1588* (Chicago/London, 1988), pp. 30–31; R.A. Donkin, *The Cistercians: Studies in the geography of medieval England and Wales* (Toronto, 1978), pp. 15, 28, 29, B.D. Hill, *English Cistercian Monasteries and their Patrons in the Twelfth Century* (Urbana, 1968), p. 27.

[2] Eugenius III, pope, letter XLVIII, *Epistolae et Privilegia* in *PL*, **180** (1902), cols 1064–6.

From *The Military Orders: Fighting for the Faith and Caring for the Sick*, ed. Malcolm Barber. Copyright © 1994 by Malcolm Barber. Published by Variorum, Ashgate Publishing Ltd, Gower House, Croft Road, Aldershot, Hampshire, GU11 3HR, Great Britain.

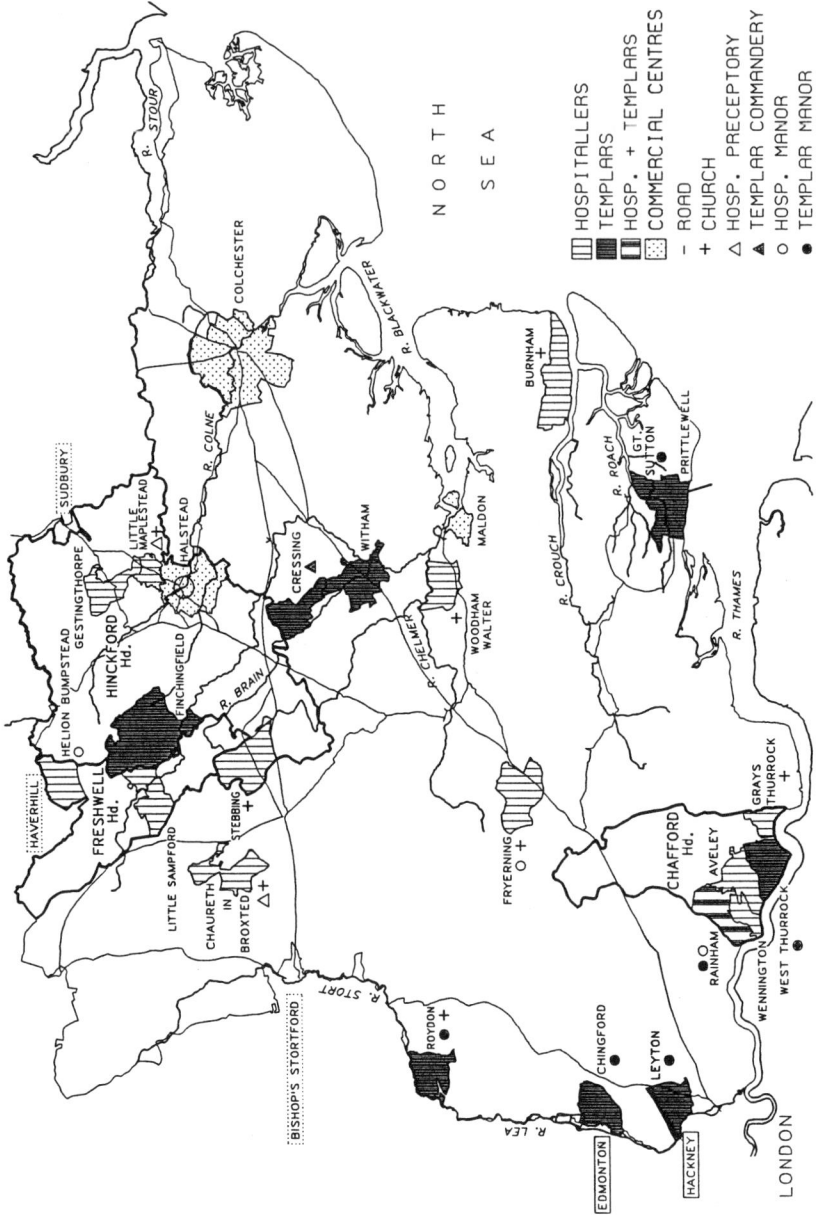

Figure 1.1 Map of Hospitaller and Templar Essex (c. 1137–1312)

Legend:

HOSPITALLERS
TEMPLARS
HOSP. + TEMPLARS
COMMERCIAL CENTRES

− ROAD
+ CHURCH
△ HOSP. PRECEPTORY
▲ TEMPLAR COMMANDERY
○ HOSP. MANOR
● TEMPLAR MANOR

NORTH SEA

COLCHESTER
R. STOUR
R. BLACKWATER
R. COLNE
R. CHELMER
R. BRAIN
R. CROUCH
R. ROACH
R. THAMES
R. LEA
R. STORT

SUDBURY
HAVERHILL
BISHOP'S STORTFORD
EDMONTON
HACKNEY
LONDON

LITTLE MAPLESTEAD
HALSTEAD
GESTINGTHORPE
HELION BUMPSTEAD
HINCKFORD Hd.
FINCHINGFIELD
FRESHWELL Hd.
LITTLE SAMPFORD
STEBBING
CHAURETH IN BROXTED
CRESSING
WITHAM
WOODHAM WALTER
MALDON
BURNHAM
FRYERNING
SUTTON
GT. SUTTON
PRITTLEWELL
ROYDON
CHINGFORD
LEYTON
RAINHAM
WENNINGTON
WEST THURROCK
GRAYS THURROCK
AVELEY
CHAFFORD Hd.

to participate in the expedition.[3] It has been proposed that the minimal material support received by the Hospitallers in England, compared to the initial rapid growth of the Templars, may be explained by the fact that the former did not constitute a military order prior to the Second Crusade (1147–49).[4] The number and chronology of English conveyances suggest a marked preference on the part of lay donors to support military involvement in the defence of the Holy Land rather than care for the weak and wounded. The Hospitallers probably responded to this preference.[5]

A common responsibility of both Hospitallers and Templars was the defence of the Holy Land, an objective which was shared by western European society as a whole during the crusading period.[6] It was obviously to the advantage of these military orders to exploit the emotional response engendered by the movement. This they accomplished in part by building copies of the rotunda, or Anastasis, of the Church of the Holy Sepulchre in Jerusalem as their prioral, and sometimes their preceptory or commandery, churches. The fact that both orders constructed rotundas simultaneously – the Templars at the New Temple in London and the Hospitallers at Clerkenwell – cannot be coincidental. Nor was it coincidental that both were consecrated by the patriarch of Jerusalem in 1185. At the time, Templars and Hospitallers alike vied to associate themselves in the public eye with the defence of the site of the Resurrection.[7]

Despite their common objective, one is more frequently struck by the differences than the similarities between the Templars and the Hospitallers. King Stephen and his Queen, Matilda, were major patrons of the Templars, granting them lands which would become the commanderies of Cressing-Witham (Essex), Eagle (Lincs.), and Temple Cowley (Oxford). They gave no

---

[3] J. Riley-Smith, *The Knights of St John in Jerusalem and Cyprus c. 1050–1310* (London, 1967), p. 58 and n. 7. A.J. Forey argues in favour of a military involvement by the Hospitallers in Syria by the mid-1130s ('The Militarisation of the Hospital of St John', *Studia Monastica*, 26 (1984), pp. 75–89 (see esp. pp. 80, 89).

[4] M. Gervers, 'Donations to the Hospitallers in England in the Wake of the Second Crusade' in *The Second Crusade and the Cistercians*, ed. M. Gervers (New York, 1992), pp. 155–61.

[5] See Forey, pp. 85–6.

[6] When confirming the grant of Sompting (Sussex) church to the Templars *c.* 1150, Theobald of Bec, Archbishop of Canterbury, addressed his confirmation 'to the religious knights of the Temple, who are fighting the enemies of the faith in defence of the Eastern Church', BL, Cotton MS Nero E VI, fol 155r–v. On the defence of the Holy Land by the Hospitaller master Gilbert of Assailly in the 1160s, see Forey, p. 87. In 1182, Henry II bequeathed 20,000 marks to the Holy Land, 5,000 of which were to be held jointly by the Templars and Hospitallers for 'the common defence of the land of Jerusalem' (Tyerman, pp. 46, 54). The defence of the Holy Land was the object of Hospitaller prayers well into the fourteenth century (*The Cartulary of the Knights of St John of Jerusalem in England*, prima camera, *Essex*, ed. M. Gervers. Forthcoming in the British Academy's Records of Social and Economic History, new ser. (Oxford), document no. 16 (cited hereafter as *PC*, followed by document no.)).

[7] M. Gervers, 'Rotundae Anglicanae', in *Actes du 22e Congrès international d'histoire de l'art*, Budapest, 1969, 1 (Budapest, 1972), pp. 359–76 (esp. pp. 363–71).

landed property to the Hospitallers, reinforcing our supposition that the Order did not, at that time, possess the military image always associated with the Templars.

The importance of royal patronage cannot be underestimated when comparing the origins and growth of the Hospitallers' estate in Essex to that of the Templars. According to the Templar Inquest of 1185, King Stephen had granted the Templars five hides in Cressing-Witham. Henry II conveyed to them a carucate[8] in Finchingfield. By 1185, an additional ninety-seven acres of land, as well as several houses and mills in twelve additional parishes, had been acquired in the region.[9] When royal extents were made of Cressing and Witham in 1309 it was reported that the accountable royal contribution in the two parishes amounted to 1,173 acres,[10] or 58 per cent of the total 2,010 acres which had accrued to the Order by that date.

Cressing-Witham was the Templar commandery in Essex from the time Stephen and Matilda made their major grants between 1137 and 1148. The closest Hospitaller equivalent, at Little Maplestead, accounted in 1338 for only 810 acres of arable, fifteen acres of meadow, thirty acres of pasture, and underwood worth 8s.[11] The net value of Cressing-Witham in 1338 was cited as 140 marks; that of Little Maplestead, only 60 marks. The Hospitallers can hardly be said to have been the Templars, rivals on the financial front.

In the absence of royal support, the Hospitallers' Essex estate grew slowly. Probably as a result of their military participation in the Second Crusade, and the efforts to mount another expedition following immediately upon its failure,[12] the Order received increasing attention from lay patrons after mid-

---

[8] The carucate is variously cited as being 80, 120 and even as much as 360 acres (J.L. Fisher, *A Medieval Farming Glossary, Latin and English* (London, 1968), p. 7; M.K. McIntosh, *Autonomy and Community: The Royal Manor of Havering, 1200–1500* (Cambridge, 1986), p. 90; K.C. Newton, *The Manor of Writtle* (London/Chichester, 1970), p. 43; W.R. Powell in *The Victoria History of the Counties of England: A History of the County of Essex*, 7 (Oxford, 1978), p. 17 (series hereafter cited as *VCH Essex*); *A Dictionary of English Weights and Measures from Anglo-Saxon times to the nineteenth century*, ed. R.E. Zupko (Madison/Milwaukee/London, 1968), p. 177. The fact that fully eight virgates of Henry's gift are stipulated as being demesne, when the virgate is generally calculated at between 20–30 acres, argues for a large carucate here.

[9] *Records of Templars*, pp. 1–12.

[10] *The Cartulary of the Knights of St John of Jerusalem in England*, secunda camera, *Essex*, ed. M. Gervers. British Academy, Records of Social and Economic History, new ser., 6 (Oxford, 1982), document nos. 83, 85 (cited hereafter as *SC*, followed by document no.). The size of the acre was based on the perch of $17\frac{1}{2}$ feet. See also *The Knights Hospitallers in England: being the Report of Prior Philip de Thame to the Grand Master Elyan de Villanova for A.D. 1338*, ed. L.B. Larking and J.M. Kemble, Camden Society Publications, 65 (London, 1857), p. 168; R.H. Britnell, 'The Making of Witham', *History Studies*, 1 (1968), 19.

[11] The actual arable cited amounts to 560 acres valued at 8d per acre. Lands at Boblow were farmed at 100s and at Abridge in Lambourne at 66s 8d per annum. At 8d per acre, these amounts translate into 150 and 100 acres respectively, giving a total acreage of 810. These round numbers may merely be approximations.

[12] B.M. Bolton, 'The Cistercians and the Aftermath of the Second Crusade' in *The Second Crusade and the Cistercians*, ed. M. Gervers (New York, 1992), pp. 131–40.

century. Most significant for the growth of the Essex estate was the conveyance by Alfred and Sibyl de Bendaville in 1151 of the church of Chaureth in the parish of Broxted, together with the land of Roger Pigot.[13] Alfred died shortly thereafter, whereupon Sibyl also granted the Order a mill in Broxted in his memory.[14]

The location of Chaureth in north-western Essex where the Hospitallers already held some land and would acquire more, and the fact that Alfred died soon after granting the Order his church there, suggests that, by then, the brethren were actively working to find suitable patrons in areas perceived to be appropriate for estate development. Around 1155 they received one-and-a-half virgates in nearby Henham.[15] At this initial stage, they supplemented grants in frankalmoin with purchases.[16]

It was not until the end of the century that the trend towards developing a centralized landed estate in north-central and north-west Essex would become definitive. The most significant of these for the future was a grant *c*. 1160, by Robert of Helion of a virgate, and various other lands comprising over forty-six acres, in Helion Bumpstead.[17] A generation later, Rose of Helion conveyed an additional thirty acres and 3s. rent in the adjoining parish of Sturmer.[18] Further grants were made by the Helion family and its tenants in the thirteenth century, with the result that the Order's manor of Boblow in Helion Bumpstead would become one of its most important holdings in the county. Boblow was rented at farm for £5 in 1338, which on the basis of land valued at 8d per acre points to a holding of 150 acres[19] put together over no less than a century. It was, one must admit, a great deal of effort for a relatively modest estate.

In the thirty-five years following the de Bendaville grant of Chaureth church, the Hospitallers acquired all or part of six other churches in the county. The chronology and topography of acquisition reflects the Order's growing awareness of developments in the local economy. Their patrons included members of the highest ranks of the nobility. Thus, *c*. 1167, Walter, son of Robert son of Richard, scion of the Fitz Walter family,[20] granted the advowson and lordship

---

[13] *PC*, 111.

[14] *PC*, 114, 152.

[15] *SC*, 334, 394.

[16] See *SC*, 334, 340, 355, 372, 416. In the middle of the thirteenth century the prior of the Hospitallers rendered annually the considerable sum of 20 marks to the prior of Ruislip *pro decimis de chauree cum pertinenciis* (*Select Documents of the English Lands of the Abbey of Bec*, ed. M Chibnall. Camden 3rd ser., **73** (London, 1951), p. 81). During the reign of William I, the Abbey of Bec upon which Ruislip depended received two-thirds of the demesne tithes of Chaureth from Garnerus, the man of Richard of Clare (M. Morgan (Chibnall), *The English Lands of the Abbey of Bec* (Oxford, 1946, repr. 1968), p. 147 and n. 12). I am indebted to Dr Chibnall for drawing my attention to these references.

[17] *SC*, 414.

[18] *SC*, 324.

[19] Larking and Kemble, p. 87. See also footnote 11 above.

[20] I.J. Sanders, *English Baronies, A Study of Their Origin and Descent, 1086–1327* (Oxford, 1960, rpt. 1963), p. 129.

of the church of Woodham Walter,[21] a parish situated on the River Chelmer. Almost simultaneously, Walter also transferred, from the Augustinian canons of Little Dunmow, the advowson and lordship of the church of Burnham situated at the mouth of the River Crouch.[22] By 1220, however, the church was back in the hands of the canons and the Hospitallers' interest therein amounted to no more than a yearly pension of 40s.[23] The granting of these two churches nevertheless suggests that the brethren sought significant holdings in parishes situated on waterways used to transport goods to the North Sea and then up the Thames to London.

Around 1170 the church of Fryerning was donated to the Hospitallers by Gilbert of Munfitchet, lord of the Essex barony of Stansted Mountfitchet.[24] The parish was conveniently situated south-west of Chelmsford on the king's highway leading from London to Colchester and to Sudbury. Later, Gilbert supplemented his original conveyance by granting the Order half of Fryerning manor.[25] His son, Richard, appears to have granted them the other half before 1199.[26] In 1293/4, they held an additional carucate of arable of Philip Burnell. The extent of the manor was therefore considerable, valued in 1338 at 40 marks[27] and clearly a going economic concern.[28] Interestingly, no mention is made in the Report of 1338 of the church, perhaps because it belonged to the prior's demesne and was accounted for separately.

A decade after the Hospitallers received the church of Fryerning they were granted two others, this time by William de Ferrières, the third Earl of Derby.

---

[21] *PC*, 37.

[22] *PC*, 39.

[23] BL, Cotton Charter XXI, 15; BL, Harley MS 662, fols 8v–9; *The Cartulary of Little Dunmow Priory*, ed. R.E. Levy, unpublished MA diss., University of Virginia (Charlottesville, 1971), p. 41 n. 9). The *CH* (1, p. clxiii) erroneously cites this charter as a confirmation to the Hospitallers by the bishop of London, William de Ste-Mère-Eglise, of the church of Little Dunmow. In fact, it is a confirmation by the same to the Augustinian canons of Little Dunmow of the church of Burnham.

[24] *PC*, 183.

[25] *PC*, 184.

[26] *Rotuli chartarum in turri Londinensi asservati, 1199–1216*, ed. T.D. Hardy (London, 1837), p. 16 (cited hereafter as *Rot. ch.*); W. Dugdale ed., *Monasticon Anglicanum: A History of the Abbies and Other Monasteries, Hospitals, Frieries, etc., in England and Wales*, new edn, ed. J. Caley, H. Ellis and B. Bandinel, 6, part 2 (London, 1830, rpt. 1846), p. 808. See also P. Morant, *The History and Antiquities of the County of Essex*, 2 (London, 1768, rpt. 1978), p. 55.

[27] Larking and Kemble, p. 94. According to the Report, the manor consisted of a messuage with a garden, 500 acres of land, pasture for 300 sheep and 20 cows, 40 acres of meadow, rents of assize worth £10 and perquisites of court

[28] While the Hospitallers received no land in Essex from royalty, Fryerning was twice the recipient of royal privileges: the right to enclose and assart their wood there in 1230 (*PC*, 188) and, in 1290, a weekly Saturday market and an annual fair on 28–30 August (*PC*, 189; *Calendar of Charter Rolls*, 2 (London: Public Record Office (PRO), 1906), p. 340). The market and fair were to be held *apud manerium suum de Gynge attestone*. Ingatestone and Fryerning, today one parish, were formerly separate (*The Place-Names of Essex*, ed. P.H. Reaney, English Place-Name Society, 12 (1935), pp. 253–4). Reference to the Hospitallers' manor in Ingatestone (*Gynge attestone*) would seem to refer to that part of the town which actually lay in Fryerning (see Morant, 2, pp. 46–7).

Of these, the church at Grays Thurrock was important because the parish was located directly on the Thames within easy reach of London. The conveyance of the church did not include any manorial lands. The tithes must have been considerable and have represented a significant source of provisions for the priory at Clerkenwell.[29] Following a dispute which was settled in 1228, the lord of the manor, Richard of Graye, agreed that the prior should have the right 'to arrive with his own ships and boats ... and to lade there his corn, etc., arising from his church in Turroc'.[30] The prior claimed, in this case, that he was wont to have access to the Thames 'to carry his victuals and to conduct them to London'.[31]

In 1181–82, probably contemporaneously with his gift at Grays Thurrock, Earl William granted the brethren his church of Stebbing in Hinckford Hundred.[32] The parish of Stebbing lies directly on Stane Street, the old Roman road and still a major transportation route running east–west between Colchester and Bishops Stortford (Herts). William's charter of conveyance is far more explicit in the case of Stebbing than it had been for Grays Thurrock; he specifies that the church is granted together with its advowson and those tithes which he owned.[33] In 1247, Pope Innocent IV granted the Order the right of appropriation of Stebbing, adding the stipulation that the church's annual value should not exceed 35 marks.[34] Here, as at Grays, the Order acquired no manorial property, although from at least the middle of the thirteenth century it held no less than fifty acres of land called War field of the fee of the monks of Hambeye for 16s annually. The field served to support the rector.[35]

During the last quarter of the twelfth century the Hospitallers obviously had their eye on the prime agricultural land of Hinckford Hundred, in which Stebbing was located.[36] It was also the centre of 'an unusually marked

---

[29] The church was attributed an estimated value of 30 marks, or £20, in 1254 (R.C. Fowler, 'Fulk Basset's Register and the Norwich Taxation', *Essex Archaeological Society, Transactions (EAST)*, new ser., **18** (1928), p. 18); £15 in 1333 (*PC*, 33); £10 in 1338 (Larking and Kemble, p. 94) and, in the sixteenth century, £7 6s 18d (*VCH Essex*, **8** (Oxford, 1983), p. 50 and n.98).

[30] *Feet of Fines for Essex*, ed. R.E.C. Kirk **1** (Colchester, 1899–1910), p. 84 n. 262 (cited hereafter as *EFF*); *VCH Essex*, **8**, p. 45; J.H. Round, 'The Thurrocks', *EAST*, new ser., **20**, (1933), p. 45.

[31] *ad carcandum victualia sua et ducendum usque ad London (Curia Regis Rolls*, **13** (London: PRO, 1959), p. 121 n.520).

[32] *PC*, 192.

[33] It was not until *c.* 1276 that the Hospitallers received the right to great tithes in Stebbing held of the Ferrières' fee by the abbey of Ste-Cathérine-du-Mont in Rouen (*PC*, 200), and in that year Prior Joseph of Chauncey purchased from the abbey of Bec-Helloin, for two marks annually, the tithes which Bec held there of the lords of Ferrières (*PC*, 203). The presence of so many alien monasteries in Stebbing is remarkable. Worth £5 annually in 1291, the vicarage was funded from various tithes, including a third of the tithe of sheaves issuing *de feodis de Colunciis et Ferariis*, the Coulonces family being tenants of the Ferrières (*PC*, 199).

[34] *PC*, 197; see also *PC*, 196 and 199.

[35] *PC*, 204; *EFF*, **1**, p.219, no. 1305.

[36] On the importance of Hinckford Hundred as an agricultural area, see L.R. Poos, *A Rural Society after the Black Death: Essex 1350–1525* (Cambridge, 1991), p. 44.

development of rural industry (especially textiles)',[37] along a corridor running between Sudbury and Halstead. Halstead lay in a favourable position on the western fringe of an economic area dominated by Colchester.[38]

The Hospitallers may have had Halstead in mind when they took over Stebbing church. However, a far better opportunity arose when, in 1187, Juliana, daughter of Robert Doisnel, who was childless, and her husband William, son of Audelin, the king's steward, granted the church and her vill of Little Maplestead to the Order.[39] Little Maplestead lies on the northern border of Halstead parish, directly on the industrial corridor leading from there to Sudbury. Juliana may have been prompted to make this gift by her husband.

William might in turn have been encouraged to do so by the king himself. In 1185, Henry II had been approached in support of the failing situation in the Holy Land by Heraclius, the Patriarch of Jerusalem, and Roger des Moulins, Grand Master of the Hospital. The king met them on 17 March at the Order's priory at Clerkenwell where, upon the advice of his barons, he agreed to provide support, but not leadership.[40] The granting of Little Maplestead may be interpreted as a tacit expression of that support. William, son of Audelin, for his part, made his grant *pro salute Henrici regis Anglie domini mei*, in London, on the eve of the anniversary of the king's visit to Clerkenwell two years before.[41] It is difficult to imagine that the Hospitallers themselves did not play the role of catalyst in this transaction. Within less than forty years, Little Maplestead would become the Order's second preceptory in Essex. By the middle of the thirteenth century, if not before, it had replaced Chaureth in that administrative role.

The Hospitallers sought to build demesne estates in the same fashion as the Templars. This objective would explain their initial flurry of activity around Chaureth, purchasing what was not immediately forthcoming in alms and undoubtedly negotiating with Sibyl de Bendaville for the mill in Broxted which she gave them soon after the death of Alfred her husband.[42] However, the mill is not heard of again; the eighty acres in Chrishall which represented the first conveyance to the Order in Essex and were certainly administered by Chaureth, were leased out *c.* 1180 for the goodly sum of one silver mark

[37] Ibid., p. 4.

[38] M. Gervers, 'The Textile Industry in Essex in the Late 12th and 13th Centuries: A Study based on Occupational Names in Charter Sources', *Essex Archaeology and History*, 3rd ser., 20 (1989), 34–73 (p. 44).

[39] *SC*, 91–4. See also J.H. Round, *The King's Serjeants and Officers of State* (London, 1911), pp. 92–3.

[40] E.J. King, *The Knights of St John in the British Empire* (London, 1934), p. 18; H.E. Mayer, *The Crusades*, trans. J.B. Gillingham (Oxford, 1972), p. 136.

[41] *SC*, 91.

[42] *PC*, 114, 152.

annually and 20s down;[43] there is no indication that the five-year lease of half a hide of land in Broxted, assumed by the Hospitallers in 1153, was ever renewed or that the land was otherwise made available to the Order.[44]

In their drive to expand, the Hospitallers seem to have run quickly into three major problems. Firstly, their numbers were too small to administer scattered territorial acquisitions. Secondly, with relatively few twelfth-century exceptions, a good deal of the land obtained in Essex came to them in small parcels spread over at least 156 parishes.[45] It was difficult to exploit such a dispersed demesne; if demesne it was, for much of what they received was customary land. Thirdly, the Hospitallers, unlike the Templars, do not appear to have had enough capital to lease or purchase extensive nucleated manors and were thus obliged to make do with what they could obtain in frankalmoin or through the purchase of small holdings.

To make up for their lack of personnel the Hospitallers began during the 1220s to employ estate agents to obtain lands as the basis for manorial growth. An appropriate choice of estate agent was someone who knew the local land market, was well respected and had no heirs. Two of the Hospitallers' three known agents in Essex met these qualifications. The first was John, son of Peter of Little Sampford, originally a tenant of Richard of Clare.[46] In 1233, John, now a tenant of the Hospitallers, granted the brethren 100 acres[47] made up of modest parcels which other charters show he had been collecting since *c.* 1220.[48] During some thirteen years, John is recorded as having paid over £85 in entry fees alone for these properties. The sum seems large for someone who does not appear to have been a member of the nobility, unless, as we suspect, the funds were being provided by his new lords, the Hospitallers.

The second estate agent was Simon of Odewell, who took his name from a manor in the parish of Gestingthorpe on the northern boundary of Little Maplestead where the Hospitallers had been granted the church and the vill in 1187.[49] Of the seven churches granted to the Order in the county, only three were conveyed with land: Chaureth, which came with the land of Roger Pigot and soon became a preceptory; Fryerning, with the land of Henry son of Alfred, was supplemented some fifteen years later with half the manor; and Little Maplestead. The combined gift of a church and land prepared the ground for the foundation of a preceptory. Fryerning was probably excluded because it was too far from the Order's growing northern agricultural estates and was under the jurisdiction of Clerkenwell. Little Maplestead seems to have

---

[43] *SC*, 219.

[44] See *SC*, 361 and above p. 7.

[45] See the list in *SC*, pp. xlix–lii and 14 others in the *PC*.

[46] For more on John, see *SC*, pp. xl–xli.

[47] *SC*, 908.

[48] *SC*, nos 918–23, 927, 928, 933.

[49] See above, p. 10.

remained dormant for some thirty-five years,[50] but *c.* 1225 X 1230, a grant of land in Gestingthorpe was made 'to the brethren [of the Hospital] at Maplestead'.[51] Once the preceptory had been founded, the Order turned to Simon of Odewell to help them build the estate. There are no grants by Simon to the Order in its great Cartulary of 1442, but his name is mentioned in 107 of the entries in that part of it reserved for Essex and known as the *secunda camera*.[52] In eighty-two of these he is cited as the recipient of rents, services, property and rights thereto in Hinckford Hundred and in Sudbury across the River Stour in Suffolk. In 1242, shortly before his death *c.* 1245, Simon and his childless wife, Margaret, are recorded in the Feet of Fines for Essex as granting to the Hospitallers 350 acres of land and $5\frac{1}{2}$ marks in rents in Hinckford Hundred and in Sudbury.[53] In exchange, the Order granted Simon and Margaret, for life, its manor at Coddenham, Suffolk, with land at Claydon, and one mark and two robes annually.[54] Simon had worked hard for the Order during at least the last decade of his life, providing it with the best it could have hoped for under the circumstances: that is, a much-fragmented estate spread over more than a dozen parishes in the neighbourhood of Little Maplestead.[55]

Undoubtedly encouraged by the success of this type of cooperative venture, the Hospitallers directed their efforts along similar lines in the southern parishes of Aveley and Wennington. Both border on the northern bank of the Thames in Chafford Hundred, somewhat to the west of Grays Thurrock where the Order held the church. It was probably not so much the church at Grays which originally attracted the brethren to the region as the fact that, during the 1180s, Gilbert de Vere, shortly to become prior of the Order in England, granted them the manor of Rainham which bounded both Aveley and Wennington to the west.[56] A century later, on 20 May 1285, John son of Geoffrey Enveyse, lord since 1281 of the manor of Enveyse in Wennington, was granted a licence from Edward I to convey in mortmain to the Hospitallers three messuages and two-and-a-half carucates of land in Aveley and Wennington.[57] This transaction is significant, because it is the only known licence to transfer property in mortmain to the Order in Essex and one of the very few for England as a whole. The circumstances behind this exceptional

---

[50] Two small grants of land and rents in the parish were made to the Order between *c.* 1215 and *c.* 1225 (*SC*, 95, 155).

[51] *SC*, 720.

[52] BL, Cotton MS Nero E VI, fols 289–467, published as *SC*, cited in n. 10.

[53] *EFF*, **1**, pp. 142–3, no. 177.

[54] *SC*, 770; see also *SC*, 769, 771.

[55] The Report of 1338 accounts for 180 acres of arable from Odewell manor (Larking and Kemble, p. 87), but even this holding was scattered. In the sixteenth century, Odewell manor lay in the parishes of Gestingthorpe, Castle Hedingham and Great Maplestead (Morant, **2**, p. 308).

[56] Dugdale, **6**, part 2, p. 808; *Rot. ch.*, p. 16.

[57] *PC*, 78.

transfer are shrouded in the uncertainties of history, but an explanation may be inferred from a series of documents in which the one recurring name is that of William Enveyse.[58] William preceded John as lord of the manor.

Of the fifty-seven entries under the Rainham *titulus*[59] of the *prima camera* in which the Aveley/Wennington documents appear, William, and occasionally members of his immediate family, are mentioned thirty-three times, mostly as recipients. The charters date from *c.* 1240 to 1269[60] and include no conveyances by William to the Hospitallers. William had three daughters,[61] but was widowed during the 1240s. It was probably at this point that he was approached by the Hospitallers to act for them as an estate agent, hence the series of documents starting *c.* 1240 in which he appears acquiring lands in the two parishes. Undoubtedly to the Order's chagrin, William remarried *c.* 1251,[62] but there is no evidence of offspring and this second wife, Matilda, is not heard of after *c.* 1255.[63] By *c.* 1265, William was married again, this time to Joan, who either brought a daughter, Emma, from a previous marriage or produced her with William.[64] By 1281 William was dead.[65]

That William, rather than John Enveyse, may be considered the original prospective donor of Enveyse lands in Aveley and Wennington is postulated from the similarities between him and the two estate agents described previously: John, son of Peter of Little Sampford, and Simon of Odewell. The absence of any gift by William to the Order suggests that he was engaged in consolidating the property to be transferred to it later in his life. The fact that the conveyance was not actually made by William can be attributed to two factors. Firstly, there were the consecutive marriages which might have complicated the eventual transfer. Secondly, and undoubtedly more significantly, there was the passage of the Statute of Mortmain in 1279.[66] As a result, grants could no longer be made to religious houses without royal permission. William died within a year of the statute's promulgation and the Order, which before 1279 would have settled the transfer directly with the conveyor in his infirmity, was left, undoubtedly in this case with some anxiety, to wait for royal favour. There is every probability that the Hospitallers worked actively behind the scenes to see that it was granted, for three messuages and two-and-a-half carucates of land represented for them a very substantial conveyance indeed.

Thus, in the second and third quarters of the thirteenth century, the Hospitallers used estate agents to augment their holdings in piecemeal fashion in

---

[58] *PC*, 46–98

[59] This is *titulus* XL on fols 185–200 of the *prima camera*, corresponding to *PC*, 44–100.

[60] *PC*, 48, 95.

[61] *PC*, 74, 76, 77.

[62] *PC*, 90; *SC*, 384.

[63] *PC*, 75.

[64] *PC*, 94, 95.

[65] *PC*, 62.

[66] For the effect of this statute on the growth of the Hospitallers' estate in Essex in general, see *SC*, pp. xlvi–xlvii.

areas designated for manorial development, that is, in Freshwell and Hinckford Hundreds in north-central Essex and in Chafford Hundred on the Thames. In many ways, the twelfth century had been more rewarding, for it was then that the Hospitallers received most of their landed patrimony in nucleated grants. On the other hand, their original hopes of exploiting the landscape like the Templars were not to be fulfilled. In the end, they opted for growth in areas of high economic potential: northern Freshwell Hundred (Helion Bumpstead and the Sampfords) in reach of Haverhill market in Suffolk; Little Maplestead in the semi-rural industrial corridor between Sudbury and Halstead; and the riverine parishes of Chafford Hundred. The preceptory at Chaureth, which had been an administrative centre for at least seventy-five years, eventually proved to be too secluded and was abandoned in that capacity by the middle of the thirteenth century.[67]

The absence of royal patronage and of sufficient capital to lease or buy large nucleated estates is, we have seen, what distinguished the landed growth of the Hospitallers from that of the Templars. The differences are emphasized in the development of the Templar estates in Essex. By 1185 the Templars had added 152 acres in small parcels, and the carucate in Finchingfield from Henry II, to the initial five hides granted to them at Cressing-Witham by Stephen and Matilda.[68] They went on to acquire six other estates of varying sizes, all of them in the southern half of the county. One of these was Roydon church and manor, located north of London on the River Stort. It was granted to them, probably in the early 1170s, by Walter, son of Robert son of Richard, who had granted the churches of Woodham Walter and Burnham to the Hospitallers.[69] Walter's son, Robert, supplemented his father's grant with an additional carucate of land shortly after Walter's death in 1198.[70] The extent of the manor is not known, but the rectory alone was valued at 20 marks in 1254,[71] and leased for 45 marks in 1313.[72]

South of Roydon on both sides of the River Lea, the continuation of the Stort, lay the Templar estate of Edmonton (Middx)-Chingford.[73] The Order acquired this holding at Easter 1270 from David of Strathbogie, eighth Earl of Atholl, and his wife Isabel, daughter of Richard of Dover, whose inheritance

---

[67] On the preceptory, see *SC*, pp. liii–lx.

[68] *Records of Templars*, pp. 1–12.

[69] *PC*, 17. The conveyance of Roydon church to the Templars has previously been attributed to Walter's son, Robert, *c*. 1198–1202 (*VCH Essex*, 8, pp. 234, 238), but the papal confirmation of a quarter century earlier clearly indicates that this cannot have been the case. Walter's grant of Roydon church would appear to coincide with his conveyances to the Hospitallers of Woodham Walter and Burnham (above pp. 7–8).

[70] *VCH Essex*, 8, pp. 234, 238.

[71] *VCH Essex*, 8, p. 238.

[72] *Calendar of Fine Rolls*, 2 (1307–19) (London: PRO, 1912), p. 180.

[73] The chief messuage consisted of 310 acres of arable, $57\frac{1}{2}$ acres of meadow, 25 acres of pasture, 100 acres of wood and a watermill. The church of Chingford, which the Templars also held, had an annual value of 17 marks (*PC*, 15).

it was. The Templars were to pay 1d per year for the first eighteen years and £18 annually thereafter.[74] By 1309, Isabel's heirs are reported to have been receiving from the Order the considerable rental of £40 annually.[75]

A third Templar holding on both sides of the same watercourse, this time only one parish north of the Thames, was at Hackney (Middx)-Ruckholt (in Leyton). The earliest evidence of the Templars there is in 1231 when they acquired the rights to six acres of land in Hackney for half a mark,[76] and in 1232 when they paid 16 marks for half a hide in the same parish.[77] In 1308, the estate was valued at just over 24 marks.[78]

Like the Hospitallers, the Templars were attracted to the parishes of Chafford Hundred on the Thames. They received a tenement and a mill at Purfleet in West Thurrock from Thomas de Briançon before 1175.[79] Little more is known before 1309, when it is recorded that their manor at Purfleet had a total income of £13 15s 9d and a net value of £8 6s $\frac{1}{2}$d.[80]

The origins of the Templars' manors in nearby Rainham are not documented, but on the manor of Berwick an enumeration of tithes made under Hospitaller administration in 1315 indicates that they held a chapel,[81] 42s in rents, 5s in pleas and perquisites of court, and 146$\frac{1}{2}$ acres of arable (including the reclaimed marsh). They also had unspecified amounts of land in fifteen other crofts and fields.[82] No valuation of the property is given. It is likely that the Templars also held the manor of Moorhall in Rainham which, in 1333, consisted of 159 acres of arable and one-and-a-half acres of meadow.[83]

The last estate which can be identified as having been built up by the Templars was at Sutton in Rochford Hundred. Sutton stands between the River Roach and the mouth of the Thames in south-eastern Essex. Produce from Templar lands there or in neighbouring parishes had easy access by water to London. The manor, which included 560 acres of land, was valued at over 62 marks in 1309.[84]

---

[74] *EFF*, 1, p. 270, no. 1608.

[75] *PC*, 15.

[76] *PC*, 3.

[77] *PC*, 2.

[78] In 1307–8 the Order held 39$\frac{1}{2}$ acres of meadow, five acres of pasture, two watermills, rents, mowing services for 12 acres of meadow and perquisites of court (*PC*, 7).

[79] *PC*, 102.

[80] The manor included a messuage, a dovecote, a watermill and 66$\frac{1}{2}$ acres of land. Rents from free tenements spread over five parishes were worth £6 6s $\frac{1}{2}$d, while perquisites of court with view of frankpledge were worth half a mark annually (*PC*, 106).

[81] *PC*, 108.

[82] *PC*, 107. This land was held by the Templars from the thirteenth century 'and perhaps earlier' according to *VCH Essex*, 7, p. 130 n. 2.

[83] *PC*, 101.

[84] *PC*, 30. The manor is described as containing a messuage, three gardens, a dovecote, 360 acres of profitable land, 130 acres of arable marshland, 15$\frac{1}{2}$ acres of mowing meadow, 50 acres of wood, a windmill, and pasture in the marsh for 440 ewes. There were rents of assize worth £6 7s 1d and other minor rents, perquisites of court worth 2s annually, a chapel, and the majority of the tithes from the demesne lands.

The origin of this manor seems to lie in a conveyance of 180 acres made by Richard of Cornard and Lucy his wife in 1227, for which the Templars paid one mark down and a modest annual rent of 12d.[85] Three years later, Richenda, wife of Robert Grapnell, sold the Templars the third part of a marsh which she claimed as dower for 40s.[86] They paid 20s for one-and-a-half acres of woodland in 1248,[87] and 50 marks to Constable Hugh of Epping in 1281 for two messuages and seventy-two acres of land.[88] They were still expanding the estate as late as 1305, when they were granted a royal licence to acquire eighty-eight acres in Great Sutton from Robert of Witham, clerk.[89] Although some property was transferred to the Templars in frankalmoin, much of it was clearly purchased.

There are a number of important points to be made from this brief consideration of the Templars' patrimony in Essex. In the first place, all of their estates were situated on major rivers permitting direct access to London. This generalization includes Cressing-Witham, with access via the Rivers Brain and Blackwater to the North Sea at Maldon which lay 10 km downstream.[90] Secondly, there is evidence, and in the cases of Edmonton-Chingford, Hackney-Ruckholt and Little Sutton ample proof, that the Templars acquired these estates largely through purchase rather than in frankalmoin. It would seem that, with the exception of Finchingfield, they exploited their own demesne. The barns at Cressing-Witham are the most obvious surviving evidence of this fact. Templar barns have not survived elsewhere, but it is known that the brethren had mills almost everywhere that they established themselves in order to grind their own corn. Their consistent approach to estate building, that is the acquisition, where necessary by purchase, of nucleated manors with access to water transportation and the London market, demonstrates their organizational skills, their strong financial backing and business acumen, and their commitment to efficient agrarian exploitation. This efficiency is confirmed by the exclusion of what to them was a landlocked holding in Finchingfield, a large carucate estimated at 240 acres of land granted to them by King Henry II.[91] By 1185, the land was leased at farm for £11 annually.[92]

The Hospitallers would have been only too delighted to receive grants like these, which the Templars considered second rate. The fact that the Hospi-

---

[85] *EFF*, **1**, p. 78, no. 203.

[86] *EFF*, **1**, p. 86, no. 276. The extent describes this land as one of three marshes, the total combined acreage of which was 130 acres (*PC*, 30).

[87] *EFF*, **1**, p. 171, no. 961.

[88] *EFF*, **2**, p. 29, no. 153A.

[89] *PC*, 29.

[90] In 1185, all Saturday carrying services were to Maldon, and *c.* 1258 to Maldon or Colchester or Chelmsford (Britnell, p. 19; *Records of Templars*, pp. 5, 6; PRO DL 43 14/1, mm. ld).

[91] *Records of Templars*, p. lxxxiii.

[92] *Records of Templars*, p. 12. 240 acres leased at £11 annually works out at lld per acre. The Report of 1338 accounts for 600 acres of arable in Cressing-Witham at 12d per acre. Other arable there was valued at 6d and 8d per acre (Larking and Kemble, p. 168).

tallers only occasionally acquired extensive estates leads to the question of how they exploited their otherwise small and fragmented property holdings. Could they, with their limited numbers, afford to manage these holdings by any other means than to lease them out? It would seem that sometimes they did, but their manors were obviously a less efficient source of income than were those of the Templars. For one thing the Hospitallers were unable to match the size and topographic unity of the Templar holdings. As a result, it would seem that, in northern Essex at least, the Hospitallers settled for supplying such local markets as Haverhill, Sudbury and Halstead, while the Templars directed much of their effort to supplying the London market. On the other hand, the Hospitallers, like the Templars in Finchingfield, readily leased out their holdings. In fact, the content of their charters suggests that most of the income they raised in Essex derived from rents.[93]

Rents notwithstanding, there is ample indication that the Hospitallers did carry on husbandry on their larger estates. The prior is cited as tilling 'with his own plough-teams [*carucis*]' in Rainham in 1219,[94] and the brethren as turning with their own plough (*cum caruga sua*) at Helion Bumpstead *c.* 1270.[95] In both cases, such ploughing would have been performed by customary tenants. Also at Helion Bumpstead, in 1254, the Order conveyed a load of wheat in recognition of a quitclaim.[96] In 1263, the Order undertook to purchase for a year the fruits of forty-two acres of land in the same parish in anticipation of acquiring the property.[97] Only once is a grant in kind recorded as having been made to the brethren in northern Essex, which further suggests that they were provided for by the fruits of their own demesne there.[98] References to rights of access, carriage and passage, and to the granting of tracks and ways, provide additional indication of exploitation. These are particularly numerous for the manor of Odewell in Gestingthorpe which was administered from the adjacent preceptory at Little Maplestead. In the earliest of these, *c.* 1220 X 1230, Gilbert, son of Walter of Odewell, conveyed to the Order four acres with a way through his land *ad faciendum cariagium suum de predicta terra usque ad publicum vicum.*[99] The public way ran between Gestingthorpe and Little Maplestead and carriage to it from the field must imply the transport of agricultural products. Even as late as 1383, the prior's right to drive *per quecumque animalia de Mapeltrestede parva*

---

[93] *SC*, p. lxix.

[94] *EFF*, **1**, p. 56, no. 57.

[95] *SC*, 139.

[96] *SC*, 451.

[97] *SC*, 488.

[98] *SC*, 144 (dated 1275), in which six quarters of grain are conveyed to the preceptor at Little Maplestead. Expenditures listed in the Report of 1338 for produce to support the household at the preceptory of Little Maplestead are probably only an accounting device to indicate the value of provender raised on an operational demesne (*SC*, pp. lxix–lxx)

[99] *SC*, 723.

versus Oddewelle is confirmed,[100] indicating that some degree of animal husbandry was carried on at Little Maplestead. In 1333 the Order leased the manor of Moor Hall in Rainham with its stock for five years.[101] Other signs of demesne development lie in the acquisition of rights to raise hedges and ditches. These also concern the area around Little Maplestead and date principally to the period *c.* 1230 to *c.* 1255 when the brethren were increasing their landed estate in the vicinity of the new preceptory.[102]

Reference has been made above to the possible existence of prioral properties, that is, holdings for which the prior rather than the General Chapter of the Order, was directly responsible. In this context we may cite Gilbert de Vere's grant of the manor of Rainham to the Hospitallers sometime in the 1180s, probably when he became a member of the Order. In view of the Order's contemporary interest in obtaining land in the riverine parishes of Chafford Hundred, there may even be a link between the gift and Gilbert's apparently meteoric rise to the priorship in 1195. No evidence concerning the details of that conveyance has survived, which is doubly unfortunate because the manor of Rainham may have been the Hospitallers' most important holding in the county and because there are indications that it was prioral property. If this were indeed the case, Gilbert would have been able, after joining the Order, to maintain a personal interest in the estate which he had donated. When he became prior, a precedent would have been set whereby subsequent priors retained a similar interest in the property. If Rainham manor were reserved for the prior from the time of Gilbert's grant, it is possible that the documents pertaining to it were kept separate from those concerning properties administered by a preceptory or by Clerkenwell itself, and that this prioral archive has been lost. It may be noted in support of this hypothesis that the properties accounted for under the Rainham heading in the Report of 1338 seem to refer to the assemblage in Aveley and Wennington attributed above to the estate agent William Enveyse, and not to the gift of Gilbert de Vere.[103]

The Hospitallers' holdings in Rainham, including the thirteenth-century acquisitions in Aveley and Wennington, and in the parish of Fryerning where they also held the church, were their only important manorial estates in the southern half of the county before the absorption of Templar lands after 1312.[104] Other properties in that region were churches appropriated by Clerkenwell, to which the churches of Chaureth and Stebbing in the north were

---

[100] *SC*, 901.

[101] The stock consisted of two cart-horses, three oxen, one bull and 20 cows, six stotts, five calves, two rams, two muttons and 133 ewes (*PC*, 101).

[102] *SC*, pp. lxxiii–lxxiv.

[103] Larking and Kemble, p. 94. The amounts of land cited in the Report and in the Enveyse conveyance are generally similar. Furthermore, there is no separate reference to lands in Aveley or Wennington in the Report.

[104] Hospitaller holdings at Abridge in Lambourne (Ongar Hd.) were administered from Little Maplestead (Larking and Kemble, p. 87).

added. The demesne lands in the parish of Fryerning and in Chafford Hundred represented the Hospitallers' response to supplying Clerkenwell, and especially the prior's table, with provisions.

It is initially surprising that there is no evidence of cooperation or collaboration between the Hospitallers and Templars in Essex, nor even a reference to one order holding property which bounded on that of the other. The two seem to have maintained entirely separate existences, their common cause notwithstanding. On the other hand, they were clearly competitors for land, income and prestige wherever they went, hence they would have wanted to make manifest their differences. Patronage in the long run, therefore, was probably determined by personal preference for one order over the other. Future research may conclude that politics played a role as well. We know already that the Templars were more favoured by royalty than were the Hospitallers. Such differences in patronage were significant for not only did they lead to the superior wealth of the Templars, but also to the way in which each order would acquire and manage its properties. The dissimilarities of their economies becomes strikingly apparent in the fact that the Templars' Essex patrimony included at least thirteen mills[105] and only three churches,[106] while the Hospitallers held seven churches and only two or three mills.[107] The Templars were staunch manorialists; the Hospitallers were predominantly farmers of rents and tithes.

When the Templars were suppressed in 1312 and the Hospitallers became heir to their estates, the Hospitallers were confronted with the management of an economy which in many ways was foreign to them. Rather than attempt, in the second quarter of the fourteenth century, to amend their established methods of exploitation and become husbandmen, the Hospitallers did what they knew best with the Templar lands: for the most part, they rented them out.[108]

---

[105] The Templars had two mills at Chingford (*PC*, 15), five at Cressing-Witham (*SC*, 83, 85), half a mill at Finchingfield (*Records of Templars*, p. 12), two at Hackney-Leyton (*PC*, 7), one at Rainham (*PC*, 107; Larking and Kemble, p. 94), one at Roydon (*PC*, 18), one at Little Sutton (*PC*, 30), and one at West Thurrock (*PC*, 105, 106; Larking and Kemble, p. 95).

[106] Chingford (*PC*, 15), Roydon (*PC*, 17, 33) and Cressing (*SC*, 1, 2).

[107] *PC*, 111; *SC*, 52, 388; *EFF*, 1, pp. 55–6, no. 57.

[108] Between 1315 and 1358 the Hospitallers were responsible for renting out property in Hackney, Middx (*PC*, 4 [1345], 5 [1349]), Chingford (*PC*, 13 and 14 [1325]), Little Sutton (Larking and Kemble, p. 170 [1338]; *PC*, 31 [1395]), at Berwick (*VCH Essex*, 7, p. 130 [fourteenth century]) and Moor Hall (*PC*, 101 [1333], 108 [1315]) in Rainham, and at Purfleet (*Calendar of Close Rolls*, Edward III, **8** (London: PRO, 1905), p. 160 [1346]) and Bayhouse (*PC*, 104 [1358]) in West Thurrock. The church of Roydon had been appropriated to Clerkenwell by 1338 (Larking and Kemble, p. 95), and the rectory was leased at term in 1390 if not before (*PC*, 18 [1390]). This accounts for all the Templar estates in southern Essex. Cressing-Witham was the exception, still being managed as a manorial estate in 1338 (Larking and Kemble, pp. 168–9) and undoubtedly until the mid 1370s when efforts by the papacy to reform the Order encouraged the leasing of all Hospitaller lands at farm (J. Glénisson, 'L'enquête pontificale de 1373 sur les possessions des Hospitaliers de Saint-Jean de Jérusalem', *Bibliothèque de l'Ecole des Chartes*, **129**, 1971, pp. 83–111 (esp. pp. 83–4)). Witham manor was clearly being leased out by the Hospitallers in 1397 (*SC*, 82).

Despite their differences, the Hospitallers held the Templars in high regard, especially after 1312. Their inheritance of former Templar properties added to their prestige, not so much because they became greater landlords but because it was an honour to follow in the footsteps of so noble a body. That they bore the Templar example as a standard is clearly exhibited in the organization of the Hospitaller archives. In the compilation of the great Cartulary of 1442, Templar documents, where they existed, were placed at the head of each topographic *titulus*, followed by the Hospitaller records.

In conclusion we may cite a case in the 1370s where the prior was accused by the Crown of illegally entering thirty acres of land and meadow in Chingford. The prior, who claimed that the property constituted his Order's rightful inheritance from the Templars, was supported by the jury. It was thereupon agreed that the Hospitallers should hold the land of the king by the same service as the Templars had previously, that is, by the sustenance of the blessed poor and by the celebration of masses for the defence of the Holy Land.[109] Spiritual defence was not what the military orders were known for, but the Hospitallers could comply while raising funds from the land in support of their continuing mission in the eastern Mediterranean.

---

[109] *PC*, 16.

2

The Character of the Hospitaller Properties in Spain in the Middle Ages

H.J.A. Sire

The Hospital of St John began to acquire properties in Spain within a few years of the First Crusade. The earliest donation known is that of a farm at Sarroca in the County of Barcelona given in 1108; it was followed by four more farms given in the next year, and by 1111 perhaps a commandery already existed in Cervera.[1] Aragon was slower to endow the Order; the royal gift of the village of Aliaga has been dated 1118, and other small bequests are recorded in the 1120s.[2] But in Castile a notable flow of royal favour begins with Queen Urraca, who in 1113 gave the Hospital the village of Paradinas near Salamanca. In 1116 she made a grant of no fewer than eleven neighbouring villages in the region of La Boveda de Toro. Her son's grant in 1126–7 of the village of Atapuerca on the road to Compostela enabled the Order to build a hospice, thus inaugurating its work of hospitality on the pilgrim route.[3]

The protection of this route was a task with which the military orders were to become closely involved, and it may be significant that shortly after the last-named grant we find the first sign of the Hospitallers' military function: a charter of Alfonso I of Aragon in 1130 gives the right to an annual dinner to two Hospitaller brethren travelling *cum suis armigeris*.[4] There is evidence that, at this time, the Hospital and the newly approved Order of the Temple were becoming associated in Spanish minds as military orders of equal standing. When

---

[1] J. Miret y Sans, *Les cases dels templers y hospitalers en Catalunya* (Barcelona, 1910), pp. 24, 29. The date interpreted as 1111 may, however, refer to 1141.

[2] S. García Larragueta, *El Gran Priorato de Navarra de la Orden de San Juan de Jerusalén*, 1 (Pamplona, 1957), p.38.

[3] C. de Ayala Martínez, 'Orígenes de la Orden del Hospital en Castilla y León (1113–1157)' (a paper kindly communicated to me by Professor Ayala in 1991 before its publication in *Homenaje al profesor D. Luis Suárez Fernández)*.

[4] *CH*, **1**, no. 89.

From *The Military Orders: Fighting for the Faith and Caring for the Sick*, ed. Malcolm Barber. Copyright © 1994 by Malcolm Barber. Published by Variorum, Ashgate Publishing Ltd, Gower House, Croft Road, Aldershot, Hampshire, GU11 3HR, Great Britain.

Four prior territories
are marked on the map
as follows:

I   Crato or Portugal
II   Castile and León
III Castellany of Amposta
IV   Sijena (convent)

○̇   *Priories*
◉   *Bailiwicks*
□   *Collegiate Churches or Communities of Priests*
△   *Nuns' Convents*
●   *Commanderies*

CATALONIA

To Catalonia

Majorca

Barcelona

CASTELLANY OF AMPOSTA

Tortosa

III Amposta

Capte..

IV

Alguaire

Saragossa

Novillas

NAVARRE

Puente la Reina

Cizur Menor

Salinas de Añana

Burgos

R. Ebro

León

Santa Sepulcro
Zamora de Toro
Tordesillas

Salamanca

CASTILE
AND
LEON

• Olmos

II Alcázar de San Juan
Consuegra
Santa María del Monte

(MURCIA)

R. Tajo

R. Guadalquivir

Lorca

Sevilla

PORTUGAL

Belver Crato
Flor da Rosa

Estremoz △

Santarém

Lisbon

R. Tejo

R. Douro

R. Guadiana

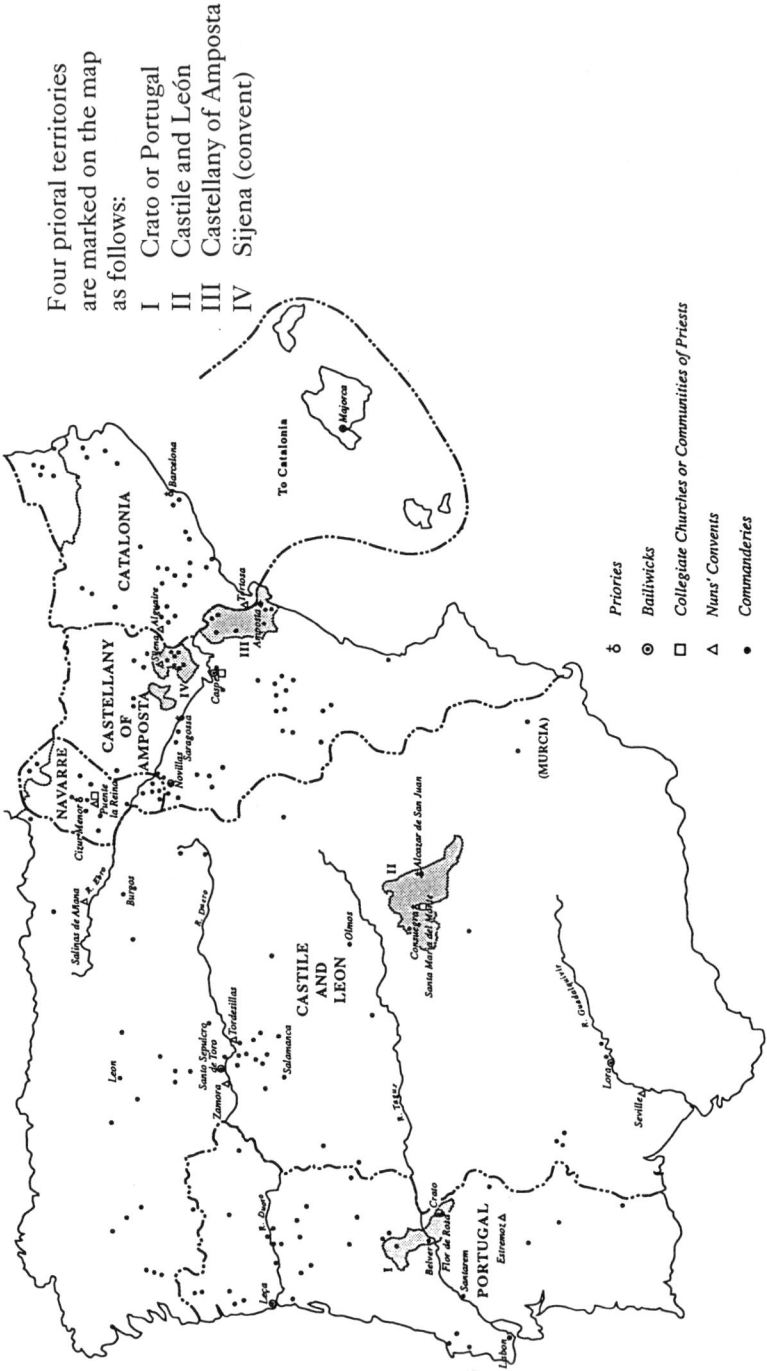

Figure 2.1   Possessions of the Order of St John in Spain and Portugal (*sixteenth century*)

Map drawn for the chapter, 'The Tongues of Aragon and Castile', in H.J.A. Sire, *The Knights of Malta* (London and New Haven: Yale University Press, 1994)

in 1133 the count of Urgell bequeathed his castle of Barberá to the Temple he erroneously described it as *hospitalis de ierusalem*.[5] The most striking instance is the singular will made by Alfonso I in 1131 for the succession to his dominions; he bequeathed these in equal parts to the Holy Sepulchre, the Hospital and the Temple.[6] The most plausible explanation for this testament by a king who had spent the thirty years of his reign fighting against the Moors is that he believed that all three orders would be capable not only of defending their territories but of pressing on with the leading role in the Reconquest with which he had himself associated them. The fact that his expectations were, in all three cases, far too sanguine ought not to cloud our appreciation of this point.

It has of course been disputed whether the bequest had a military intention, in the first place because the Holy Sepulchre was never a military order. Yet there had been a plan to attach a *Militia Sacra* to it in the earlier part of the century; Alfonso may have had some idea of assisting such a plan by the grant of one-third of his kingdom. Secondly it is urged that if the grant to the Holy Sepulchre was merely an act of piety the same could be true for the Hospital, and that of the three beneficiaries it was only the Templars whom Alfonso undeniably regarded as a military force. Nevertheless we know from his charter of the previous year that, by 1131, Alfonso was already familiar with a military element among the Hospitallers; perhaps it would be reading too much into the evidence to suggest that his spectacular generosity to the Order in 1131 is linked to the appearance of its military function, when we contrast his relatively parsimonious donations to it (at least by Castilian royal standards) in the previous years when it had figured merely as a hospitaller body.

A further point to be noted is that Alfonso's will promised the Hospital the city of Tortosa, which was then still in Muslim hands. Tortosa was an extremely powerful fortress on the lower Ebro, with a castle planted on the great rock that dominates the city. It had withstood for many years Christian efforts to conquer it and remained the only stronghold on the left bank of the Ebro still in Moorish possession when all the rest of that bank had fallen to the Christians. Alfonso must have expected that, when conquered, it would be as crucial an element in the Christian frontier defence as it had long been for the Muslim. This intended donation contrasts on the one hand with the lack of any specific enfeoffment to the Templars, and on the other with the grants to various ecclesiastical bodies of places which, though fortified, were safely behind the frontier.

---

[5] Miret y Sans, p. 24: '*Dimito hospitalis [sic] de ierusalem in omnibus castellis meis in singulis unum hominem de melioribus. Dimito ad ipsam cavalleriam de iherusalem ubicumque moriar totum meum meliorem guarnimentum cavallum scilicet atque armas. Item dimito ipsi cavallerie ipsum dominicum meum de Calcinas et ipsum decimum meum quod habeo in guardia .... Dimito item ad ipsam cavalleriam ipsum Kastrum de Barbara cum terminio suo ad proprium alodium*'. If we did not know that the count had given the castle of Barberá to the Templars the previous September, there would be no way of telling that this was not a grant to the Hospital.

[6] Text in García Larragueta, 2, no. 10.

The Aragonese case therefore provides a good test for the question of the militarization of the Order of St John. A theory that has gained favour among historians is that there was no military function at all among the Hospitallers until the grant of Bethgibelin to the Order in 1136;[7] the Hospitallers then began a process of militarization so impressive that a mere half-dozen years later they were entrusted with five castles on the frontier of Tripoli, including Crac with its incomparable strategic position. If this were true, we would expect the bequest of Alfonso I at the same period to reflect this explosive militarization. The grant of one-third of Aragon and Navarre gave both the incentive, and potentially the means, for the kind of rapid recruitment drive that characterized the Templars after the Council of Troyes. What we find is something very different: an extreme reluctance on the part of the Hospital to accept military commitments in Aragon, even at the cost of losing the king's bequest. When Raymond Berenguer of Barcelona became King of Aragon through the setting aside of Alfonso's will, he offered the Hospitallers in 1137 one-tenth of all new conquests if they came to establish themselves in the kingdom,[8] yet they still showed little willingness to take the bait. When Tortosa was finally conquered in 1148, it seems to have been with minimal Hospitaller participation. Neither the Order's role in the conquest nor its military strength in the kingdom justified fulfilling Alfonso's promise of granting the city to it. It was given instead to the Templars, together with the greater part of the territory on the other side of the Ebro conquered at the same time.

The Hospitallers' reward was reduced to the town of Amposta, given in 1153. This was the Order's first military grant under the Crown of Aragon, and it had had to wait nineteen years after Alfonso's death before receiving it. At that time Amposta was a seaport (the Ebro delta has been largely built up since the fourteenth century) and, as such, it was strongly fortified and required to be properly garrisoned, but what it was not was an important point on the new land frontier with the Muslims. The area shaded on the appended map as the territory of the Castellan of Amposta in Figure 2.1 (page 22) represents that domain as it was after 1319 (with the absorption of the Templar lands), but its western and southern border corresponds with the new Christian frontier beyond the Ebro established after 1148. The greater part of that frontier was entrusted to the Templars; the extreme south became Hospitaller territory, but not immediately. The frontier castle of Ulldecona was granted to the Hospitallers in 1178 but was promptly ceded to a lay lord and was not retroceded till the middle of the thirteenth century, when the conquest of Valencia had deprived it of its frontier status.[9] Thus, far from seeing an originally civilian

---

[7] This case has been put by R. Hiestand in 'Die Anfänge der Johanniter', in *Die geistlichen Ritterorden Europas*, ed. J. Fleckenstein and M. Hellmann (Sigmaringen, 1980). It is to be observed that Professor Hiestand did not take into account the document cited in footnote 4 above when arguing the case for late military development on the grounds of lack of earlier evidence.

[8] García Larragueta, **1**, pp 40–41.

[9] *Castells Catalans*, ed. R. Dalmau, **4** (Barcelona, *c.* 1970), article on Ulldecona.

donation developing into a military one as the Hospitallers' armed strength increased, what we seem to have on the Ebro is a grant which Alfonso I envisaged as strongly military but which was reduced to as civilian a character as it could well have had in the circumstances. To sum up, the Hospitallers' response to Alfonso's bequest in Aragon gives little support to the theory of a drive to militarize the Order in the later 1130s, while there is sufficient evidence of an armed role in the early 1130s to require the origins of that function to be pushed back at least to the previous decade.

The reluctance of the Hospital in Aragon to militarize itself is worth comparing with what was happening in Castile; for the first thirty years of the Order's presence there, all donations were located safely out of harm's way in the centre of the kingdom, and there is no evidence of any military work, unless it were the protection of pilgrims. In 1144, however, there is a change of both place and function when the Order was granted the castle of Olmos on the road leading south to Toledo.[10] Although it was not strictly a frontier castle, the proximity of the Moorish frontier to the east and the importance of the road it guarded show that the King of Castile had now begun to trust the Hospitallers with the charge of a sensitive point of the kingdom's communications. It is to be noted that the first military grant to the Hospital in Castile occurs nine years before the first in Aragon.

In the second half of the century the use of the Hospitallers as a frontier force increased. In southern Aragon the grant to them of the castle of Aliaga, which was the centre of a considerable territory, was made in 1163.[11] At the same period the Castilian Hospitallers seem to have been entrusted with a series of castles which they relinquished as the southern frontier advanced; in 1183 they received what proved to be the definitive grant of Consuegra[12] with a large territory which came to be called the Campo de San Juan, a central piece in the block of border fiefs in La Mancha which the Crown conferred on the Orders of Calatrava, St John and Santiago. The Castilian Templars had withdrawn themselves from frontier defence in 1158 and confined themselves to the protection of the route to Compostela. The castle of Consuegra became the seat of the Priory of Castile and was the most important Hospitaller castle in that kingdom.

In Portugal the first donation to the Order was made at Leça, probably in 1128.[13] There is no sign of any military role in Portugal until the last decade of the century. After the Almohads had pushed back the Christian frontier,

[10] Ayala Martínez, 'Orígenes'. The dating lacks conclusive evidence, but cf. the tentative dating in the same article of the donation of the neighbouring village of Humanes to the early 1140s.

[11] Miret y Sans, p. 206.

[12] García Larragueta, 1, p. 47.

[13] For the twelfth-century history of the Hospital in Portugal, see R. de Azevedo, 'Algumas achegas para o estudo das origens da Ordem de S. João em Portugal', *Revista Portuguesa de Historia*, 4 (1949).

reconquering as far as the Tagus, in 1194 the Portuguese Hospitallers were granted a large territory on the north bank of that river. On the river itself they built the castle of Belver to defend the frontier. Its position on the top of a small conical hill makes it almost impregnable; nevertheless, it is a much smaller and less elaborate structure that Consuegra, and supports the impression that the military resources of the Portuguese Hospitallers were much slighter than the Castilian.

Thus it seems valid to draw a picture of a very gradual militarization of the Order in Spain, starting in 1130 when the Hospital's military strength in the country may have been limited to two knights and their squires, perhaps involved in the protection of pilgrims to Compostela, and culminating in the 1190s when the Order possessed frontier castles and fiefs in Castile, Portugal and Aragon and was playing a significant part in the defence of all three kingdoms.

The Almohad advance was reversed by the battle of Las Navas de Tolosa in 1212, but in the reorganization of the new Castilian frontier the Hospitallers received almost no reward. The existing fiefs of the military orders were extended into a huge belt of territory stretching almost continuously from the Portuguese frontier to the Mediterranean, with the possessions of the Knights of Alcántara added in the extreme west alongside those of the other two Castilian orders. Yet in this distribution the Hospitaller Order received only an insignificant south-eastern appendix to the Campo de San Juan. It is clear that the Castilian Crown now preferred to patronize the native orders which it could control more directly, and that is why the distribution of the Hospitaller properties remained in the succeeding centuries almost exactly what it had been in the late twelfth century, reflecting both the kingdom's economic centre of gravity and the position of the frontier at that period.

In Portugal, however, the Crown's policy was more favourable to both the Templars and the Hospitallers, and the existing Hospitaller territory was extended in 1232 with a long tongue of land to the south of the Tagus, with its capital at Crato, which became the new prioral residence.

Two exceptions to royal neglect in Castile came in 1240, when the Hospitallers conquered and were granted a substantial property based on Lora, on the Guadalquivir, with the fortified village of Setefilla in the hills above the river, and, later under King Sancho (1284–95), whose favour may have been what encouraged the Hospitaller Prior, Ferran Perez, to transfer the capital of the Campo de San Juan from Consuegra to the town of Alcázar, and to build there, in 1287, a splendid palace of which one square tower survives today as a hint of its original greatness.

The suppression of the Templars enabled the Hospitaller and Templar properties on the lower Ebro to be consolidated into a single vast domain, while the new Hospitaller priory of Catalonia was created. Outside Aragon and Catalonia, however, the pattern of royal preference for the native military orders continued to prevail, and the Order of St John derived no benefit from the disappearance of its rival. Its subsequent progress was exhibited less in territorial acquisitions than in the consolidation of its internal life – for example, by the multiplication of the women's convents. These, whose number reached nine by the mid-sixteenth century, and whose greatest example was the sumptuously endowed royal priory of Sijena,[14] reflect the evolution of the Order to a less military character in the later Middle Ages.

---

[14] For Sijena see J. Arribas Salaberri, *Historia de Sijena* (Saragossa, 1975), and A. Ubieto Arteta, *El Monasterio Dúplice de Sijena (Cuadernos Aragoneses de Trabajo)*, 1 (Saragossa, 1986).

3

The Hospitallers and the Castilian–Leonese Monarchy: the Concession of Royal Rights, Twelfth to Fourteenth Centuries

Carlos Barquero Goñi

Relations between the Order of the Hospital and Castilian-Leonese royalty are complex and problematic, and therefore this paper will concentrate upon one facet of the development of the Order's seigneurial policy in this area of the Iberian peninsula: the Hospitallers' collection of certain royal revenues in their domains.

From the time of its first appearance in the kingdoms of Castile and León in the early twelfth century, the Order of the Hospital began to accumulate property on a large scale in a manner similar to that occurring in Aragon and Navarre.[1] Royalty played an important part in this process and several gifts granted by rulers to the Hospitallers at this time began to include exemption from some royal rights. For example, King Alfonso VII conceded such exemptions in the grants of the village of Atapuerca in 1126,[2] of an estate near Soria in 1152,[3] and of the village of Población de Campos in 1140.[4] However, the Hospitallers were not satisfied with this and, in the following years, set out to obtain a general exemption from royal rights in all their holdings. The concession of several privileges of immunity formed the basis for this.

The support received from King Alfonso VII is especially evident. As early as 1140 the king had forbidden his officers to enter the possessions of the order in order to collect certain categories of taxes (*pecho, fonsadera, homicidio,* and

---

[1] C. de Ayala Martínez, 'Orígenes de la Orden del Hospital en Castilla y León', *Hispania Sacra*, 88 (1991), pp. 775–98. S. García Larragueta, *El gran priorado de Navarra de la Orden de San Juan de Jerusalén (siglos XII–XIII)*, 1 (Pamplona, 1957), pp. 35–61.

[2] Archivo Histórico Nacional, Madrid, Ordenes Militares, (hereafter OO.MM), carpeta 577, document 17. Ed. *CH*, 1, doc. 78, pp. 73–4.

[3] Archivo de la Real Chancillería de Valladolid, Colección de Pergaminos, carpeta 107-7.

[4] AHN OO.MM, caja 7491², doc. 30 bis. Ed. J.V. Matellanes Merchán and E. Rodríguez-Picavea, 'Las Ordenes Militares en las etapas castellanas del Camino de Santiago', in *El Camino de Santiago, la hospitalidad monástica y las peregrinaciones*, ed. H. Santiago Otero (Salamanca, 1992), pp. 361–3.

From *The Military Orders: Fighting for the Faith and Caring for the Sick*, ed. Malcolm Barber. Copyright © 1994 by Malcolm Barber. Published by Variorum, Ashgate Publishing Ltd, Gower House, Croft Road, Aldershot, Hampshire, GU11 3HR, Great Britain.

mañería).[5] Some years later, in a grant dated 20 December 1152, he considerably extended these immunities through a privilege conceded to Raymond du Puy, Master of the Hospitallers,[6] although there are doubts about the authenticity of this document.[7] The king gave all the royal taxes from the Hospital's properties to the Order, exempted their inhabitants from services and again prohibited the exercise of royal justice in Hospitaller domains. The last privilege of Alfonso VII regarding the Order, given at Palencia on 20 November 1156, was a summary of these two charters and confirmed the Hospitaller immunity. He exempted the Order and its master from all taxes, duties or obligatory services in perpetuity, and ordered his officers not to enter Hospitaller villages to prosecute delinquents. Only the authorities of the Order were allowed to administer justice there.[8] The advantages which the Hospitallers received in these documents were not unusual. Leonese and Castilian kings granted very similar charters to other institutions and individuals between the ninth and thirteenth centuries.[9]

Taxes were in fact paid on the Castilian and Leonese properties of the Hospital during the thirteenth and fourteenth centuries despite the exemption given by Alfonso VII, as can be seen at Paradinas de San Juan in 1280[10] and at Población de Campos in 1332.[11] However, the brethren continued to employ a variety of methods in order either to suppress or to obtain the royal taxes for themselves in their domains. Thus the Castilian kings granted exemptions for some Hospitaller possessions newly conquered from the Muslims during the thirteenth century. This was the case in the convent of St John of Acre at Seville in 1249[12] and at Tocina in 1284.[13] On other occasions, they were conceded on older properties of the Order, as in the house of Mellid in 1201[14] or Puente de Orbigo, Villoria and Villaverde in 1257.[15]

---

[5] Archivo General del Palacio Real de Madrid, sección de Infante don Gabriel, Secretaría, legajo 760, document without number. Ed. P. Rodríguez Campomanes, *Disertaciones históricas del Orden y Caballería de los Templarios* (Madrid, 1747), pp. 246–7.

[6] AHN OO.MM, carpeta 569, doc. 35.

[7] C. de Ayala Martínez, p. 789.

[8] AHN OO.MM, caja 8077, document without number. Ed. *CH*, 1, doc. 247, pp. 186-7.

[9] C. Sánchez Albornoz, 'La potestad real y los señoríos en Asturias, León y Castilla (siglos VIII al XIII)', *Revista de Archivos, Bibliotecas y Museos*, 21, (1914), pp. 263–93. H. Grassotti, 'La inmunidad en el Occidente Peninsular del Rey Magno al Rey Santo', *Cuadernos de Historia de España*, 67–68 (1982), pp. 72–122.

[10] Archivo Catedralicio de Salamanca, caja 16, legajo 1, doc. 28, p. 43. Ed. *Documentos de los Archivos Catedralicio y Diocesano de Salamanca (Siglos XII–XIII)*, ed. J.L. Martín. Documentos y Estudios para la Historia del Occidente Peninsular durante la Edad Media (Salamanca, 1977), doc. 375, p. 473.

[11] Archivo Parroquial de Támara, Palencia, carpeta (not numbered).

[12] Archivo General de Palacio, sección de Infante don Gabriel, Secretaría, legajo 393.

[13] T. López, *Diccionario Geográfico de Andalucía: Sevilla*, ed. C. Segura (Seville, 1989), p. 152.

[14] Biblioteca de la Real Academia Española, Madrid, manuscrito 384, doc. 3.

[15] Biblioteca Nacional, Madrid, manuscrito 20.551, p. 169; D. Aguirre, *El gran priorato de San Juan de Jerusalén en Consuegra, en 1769* (Toledo, 1973), p. 177.

The Hospitallers also tried to bring up to date or to renew the immunities given by Alfonso VII, and by this means they gained some charters from kings and royal officers during the thirteenth and fourteenth centuries. The chief officer of King Ferdinand III in Galicia, Monio Fernández of Rodero, ordered his subordinates not to enter Gondrame, Friolfe, Vileiriz and Ferreiros in 1246 because the Hospitaller commander of Portomarín had royal letters which forbade it.[16] But royal officials were not always so respectful. In 1265, King Alfonso X had to order his officers not to enter villages and other properties of the Order in order to arrest malefactors, administer justice and collect tax after the Grand Commander of Spain, Gonzalo Pérez, complained about it to the king.[17] This was ineffective. In 1294 King Sancho IV again ordered his officers not to collect two taxes on vassals and commanders of the Order,[18] and in the fourteenth century King Ferdinand IV seems to have had to confirm earlier provisions exempting vassals of the Order from the payment of two taxes (*portazgo* and *castillería*).[19]

Monarchical officials were not the only ones reluctant to allow the Hospitallers these fiscal immunities on their estates; other institutions, whose tax burden grew in proportion to the immunity of the Order's possessions also tried to oppose these policies. In 1335 a judicial sentence forced the Council of Chantada to stop collecting the royal tax of *fonsadera* on properties and vassals of the Order of St John within the territory of this town and compelled the Council to return the money which it had obtained.[20]

The Order also sought papal support in order to avoid tax payments. In 1278, on the occasion of the collection of the annual tenth of ecclesiastical rents conceded by Pope Nicholas III to Alfonso X of Castile, the Hospitallers succeeded in persuading the pope to ask the king not to demand the tax from them.[21]

The pursuit of the exemption from the royal rights on the Hospital's estates was not disinterested, nor was it directed towards the greater well-being of the Order's vassals. In fact, it was an integral part of the policy developed by the Hospitallers in Castile and León with the aim of completing their power over their possessions and strengthening their exploitation by means of the appropriation of royal revenues in their lands. From some kings the brethren obtained certain concessions with this in mind. In 1224, Alfonso IX of León granted to

[16] AHN OO.MM, carpeta 578, doc. 11. Ed. *CH*, 2, doc. 2396, p. 641.

[17] AHN OO.MM, carpeta 569, doc. 35. Ed. Rodriguez Campomanes, Disertaciones históricas, pp. 247–8.

[18] Archivo General de Palacio, sección de Infante don Gabriel, Secretaría, legajo 760, *Privilegios y exempciones de la Orden de San Juan*. Ed. Rodríguez Campomanes, pp. 247–8.

[19] AHN OO.MM, Indice 176, p.21.

[20] AHN OO.MM, capeta 578, doc. 18.

[21] Archivo General de Palacio, sección de Infante don Gabriel, Secretaría, legajo 760; *Les Registres de Nicholas III (1277–1280)*, ed. J. Gay (Paris, 1898–1938), p. 57.

Prior Juan Sánchez and the brothers of the Hospital of Jerusalem a half of another royal tax, the *pedido*, from the Order's principal villages in his kingdom – namely Fresno el Viejo, Paradinas de San Juan, el Valle del Guareña and those situated in Extremadura.[22] The same ruler gave to the Order of St John his right of *maniaticum* over the property of Pelayo Yáñez and his wife, Sancha Gutiérrez, which the Hospital had bought in 1230.[23] In 1285, King Sancho IV granted his right of *acemilas* over the *bailías* of Consuegra, Olmos, Peñalver and Alhóndiga to Ferran Perez, Prior of the Hospital of St John in Castile and León, and the brethren, as well as exempting them from the taxes of *fonsadera* and *hueste*.[24] He also ordered the vassals of these *bailías* to give the royal right of *acemilas* to the Order and exempted them from the tributes of *fonsadera* and *hueste* in the same year.[25] Finally, King Ferdinand IV granted to the Hospitaller prior, Garci Perez, a half of the service and aids which were owed to the king on the Order's properties.[26]

The Hospitallers' interest in obtaining control over rents held by the king on its properties was such that, between the mid-thirteenth century and the mid-fourteenth century, they were even prepared to renounce the lordship of some places in exchange for royal revenues, or at least a share in them. Castilian and Leonese Hospitallers clearly preferred a qualitative growth of their power over their possessions rather than a simple extension of territory. There are two graphic examples of this. The first is an exchange between the Order and Alfonso X confirmed in 1281 in which the brethren gave the king the castles of Serpa, Moura and Mourao, situated on the frontier with Portugal, and the king, for his part, granted the Hospital a series of properties and, moreover, also conceded the royal rights of *martiniega* and *acemilas* on the Hospitaller properties of el Valle del Guareña, Fresno el Viejo and Paradinas de San Juan. As well as this he granted them a half of the *martiniega* paid to the king by the vassals of the Order in the *bailías* of Puente de Oibigo, Cerecinos de Campos, Santa Maria de la Horta and Vidayanes.[27] Furthermore, a confirmation of the Infante Sancho, dated 1283, shows that the number of places in which the Order had obtained the right to the royal tax of the *martiniega* was much greater than is apparent from the text of the exchange of 1281. It reveals that the Hospitallers were collecting *martiniega* in Villadecanes, San Martín de Montes, Villoria, Villaverde, Morones, San Vicente de la Lomba, Quintanilla and also in the *bailías* of Puente de Orbigo, San Juan de Benavente, Cerecinos de

---

[22] AHN OO.MM, carpeta 568, doc. 9. Ed. J. González *Alfonso IX* (Madrid, 1944), 2, doc. 447. pp. 559–60.

[23] AHN OO.MM, carpeta 568, doc. 13. Ed. J. González, 2, doc. 618, pp. 714–15.

[24] Archivo General de Palacio, sección de Infante don Gabriel, Anexo, legajo 1, doc. 39.

[25] Archivo General de Palacio, sección de Infante don Gabriel, Secretaría, legajo 564, *Visitas y Autos*, p. 5.

[26] AHN OO.MM Indice 176, p. 19; P. Guerrero Ventas, *El Archivo Prioral-sanjuanista de Consuegra. Resumen de sus fondos documentales* (Toledo, 1985), p. 101.

[27] Arquivo Nacional da Torre do Tombo, Lisbon, Gaveta 14, maço 1, doc. 9. Ed. *Diplomatario andaluz de Alfonso X*, ed. M. González Jiménez (Seville, 1991), doc. 479, pp. 502–8.

Campos, Vidayanes, Santa María de la Horta de Zamora, San Gil and Santa María de la Vega de Toro.[28] The second example is found in a bull of Pope John XXII of 1327. He authorized Ferdinand of Valbuena, prior of the Hospital in the kingdoms of Castile and León, to exchange with Alvaro Núñez of Osorio the castle of San Pedro de Latarce and the house of Villalobos, both former Templar properties, for the royal rights of the *bailías* of el Valle del Guareña, Castronuño, Villaescusa, Fresno el Viejo, Paradinas de San Juan and Cuenca.[29]

Unfortunately, there is insufficient evidence to make a full evaluation of this process of appropriation of royal revenues in the fourteenth century. However, a source exists which enables a partial judgement to be made – namely the *Becerro de las Behetrías*, written between 1351 and 1352, which gives details of seigneurial rights and those reserved for the king in many Castilian locations, although the area covered is restricted to the north-east. The *Becerro* does not list places such as Paradinas de San Juan, Fresno el Viejo or el Valle del Guareña, in all of which the Order had a special interest in obtaining royal rights. Nevertheless, the abundant references to the Order make this source an important point of departure for research.[30]

If we exclude the places in which the Hospital shared its lordship with other persons or institutions, and those in which it only held some lands or vassals, and concentrate upon those in which it held exclusive lordship, the results are as follows. According to the *Becerro*, the Hospitallers were the lords of thirty-four villages. In none of them did the brethren hold all the royal rights, nor were any of them wholly exempted from the payment of contributions to the king. In eighteen cases the Order collected no royal taxes at all.[31] However, at least sixteen places were exempted from the payment of any kind of royal tax,[32] and there were fifteen in which the Hospital had gained a share in the royal revenues.[33] It can clearly be deduced from these facts that the Hospitallers neither achieved the complete exemption from royal rights nor the collection of all of them in their lordships. Nevertheless, a significant proportion of the Order's villages paid less taxes, and the Hospital did obtain a part of some royal revenues in several places. Apparently there was no general rule but, rather, a series of local solutions.

---

[28] AHN OO.MM, carpeta 569, doc. 23.

[29] AHN OO.MM, carpeta 570, doc. 9. Ed. C. de Ayala Martínez *et al*, 'Algunos documentos sobre Ordenes Militares y fortalezas', *Castellum*, 1 (1992), doc. 12, pp. 99–100.

[30] S. Moreta Velayos, 'Los dominios de las Ordenes Militares en Castilla según el Becerro de las Behetrías', *Anuario de Estudios Medievales*, 11 (1981), pp. 125–32.

[31] *Libro Becerro de las Behetrías. Estudio y texto crítico*, ed. G. Martínez Díez. 3 vols, Fuentes y estudios de Historia leonesa, 24, 25, 26 (León, 1981), 1, pp. 166–7, 188–9, 307, 345, 413; 2, pp. 35–6, 46–7, 83, 325, 354, 399–400, 458–61, 471, 486–7.

[32] *Ibid.*, 1, pp. 162, 165, 180, 183, 184, 218, 239, 345, 413; 2, pp. 35–6, 46–7, 74, 83, 399–400, 458.

[33] *Ibid.*, 1, pp. 162, 165, 180, 181, 183, 184, 187–8, 215, 218, 221–2, 239, 327; 2, pp. 273, 458, 477.

In conclusion, the Order never obtained the seigneurial immunities that it sought from King Alfonso VII in the mid-twelfth century. In this, the situation resembles that pertaining to its ecclesiastical privileges. Here, too, the Hospital initially sought total exemption from diocesan authority – in this case by means of papal privileges[34] – but in the face of episcopal determination not to lose incomes, the Hospital reached agreements with the bishops, and a share of the income from the Hospital's churches went to the episcopate.[35]

It can be supposed that a similar process took place in the matter of royal taxes, for the collectors and lay authorities did not allow the Hospitallers to be exempt. Ultimately, the Order partially achieved its aims in that some Hospitaller lordships were exempted from certain royal rights, and the Order of St John collected a small proportion of them. Moreover, at this time, the tributes in dispute (*fonsadera*, *yantar* and *martiniega*) were starting to become archaic and their profit was diminishing, while the Castilian monarchy had full control over the new forms of taxation established by the royal treasury during the thirteenth and fourteenth centuries, and which finally proved the most productive.[36]

[34] H. Prutz, *Die geistlichen Ritterorden* (Berlin, 1908), pp. 142–94; J. Riley-Smith, *The Knights of St John in Jerusalem and Cyprus, c. 1050-1310* (London, 1967), pp. 375–420.

[35] S. García Larragueta, 1, pp. 254–7; M.L. Ledesma Rubio, *La encomienda de Zaragoza de la Orden de San Juan de Jerusalén en los siglos XII y XIII* (Saragossa, 1967), pp. 98–9; M.L. Ledesma Rubio, *Templarios y Hospitalarios en el reino de Aragón* (Saragossa, 1982), pp. 76–87.

[36] M.A. Ladero Quesada, 'Las transformaciones de la fiscalidad regia castellano-leonesa en la segunda mitad del siglo XIII (1252–1312)', in *Historia de la Hacienda Española (Epocas Antigua y Medieval). Homenaje al Profesor García de Valdeavellano* (Madrid, 1982), pp. 328–68. D. Menjot, 'L'établissement du système fiscal étatique en Castile (1268–1342)', in *Génesis medieval del Estado Moderno: Castilla y Navarra (1250–1370)* (Valladolid, 1987), pp. 149–72.

4

Catholic and Protestant Members in the German Grand Priory of the Order of St John: the Development of the Bailiwick of Brandenburg

Walter G. Rödel*

In the German-speaking area, the Order of St John did not become established until after the Second Crusade. The first donations, from which commanderies were to develop, began to be received from 1155 on, but the majority of the Order's houses were not founded until the thirteenth century. Administrative structures took shape only gradually. The year 1187 witnessed the first mention of a Prior for Germany, and there is evidence of a *magnus praeceptor sacrae domus Hospitalis Iherosolimitani in Alemania, Bohemia, Moravia et Polonia* in 1250. The Chapter General of 1301 also placed the Priories of Hungary and Dacia (that is, Scandinavia) under the German Grand Prior. This is a special case in that the priors were not directly subordinate to the head of the *Langue* as was the usual practice, but to a 'colleague' in office, namely the German Grand Prior, who in turn answered to the Grand Bailiff, the superior of the German *Langue* at the Order's headquarters. If the German *Langue* extended in practice throughout central and northern Europe, the German Grand Priory – with well over a hundred commanderies from the Netherlands to Pomerania and from Switzerland to northern Germany – comprised an enormous area which was scarcely possible for one person to administer. The Grand Prior had to delegate tasks to Vice Priors and to make a division into Upper and Lower Germany. Eventually, at the beginning of the fourteenth century, bailiwicks began to form which did not, however, achieve the firmly established status to which they had become entitled in other *Langues* of the Order. The bailiwicks concerned were Westphalia, Cologne, Utrecht, Wetterau, Franconia, Thuringia and Brandenburg, of which only the latter was able to gain an autonomous status for itself within the framework of the Grand Priory.[1]

---

* Translated by John M. Deasy.

[1] W.G. Rödel, *Der Ritterliche Order St. Johannis vom Spital zu Jerusalem. Ein Abriss seiner Geschichte,*

The bailiwick of Brandenburg had developed since the first endowment in 1160 of a church in Werben on the Elbe by Albert, Margrave of Brandenburg, who had become familiar with the Order's charitable work during a pilgrimage to the Holy Land. It included widely scattered possessions in north and east Germany, which were considerably increased as a result of the abolition of the Templars in 1312 and the transfer of Templar property to the Order of St John by Pope Clement V. Admittedly, however, the knights had to spend the considerable sum of 1,250 silver marks[2] before the margrave handed over the former Templar properties in 1318.

During this period the first efforts were made to obtain an independent position for the bailiwick within the German Grand Priory, which had, as yet, taken scant interest in the estates in north and east Germany. The eight Templar commanderies which had been taken over, thus practically doubling the Order's property, had been grouped together for administrative purposes under the charge of a preceptor. Such a solution seems the obvious one, especially as the conquest and refortification of Rhodes had thrown the Order into heavy debt which it was seeking to pay off by tightening up its administrative structures and ensuring reliable payment of its income from its individual *Langues*. The large sums which had to be paid to various European rulers in order to gain possession of the former Templar properties contributed to this critical financial situation which was accompanied by a loosening of Order's discipline.[3] The first documentary evidence of a separate administrative unit is to be found in 1323, and is followed in 1344 by a *praeceptor generalis per Saxoniam, Marchiam, Slaviam et Pomeraniam*, although it must be pointed out that this had by no means met with the approval of the German Grand Prior. When the Chapter General of the Order in Avignon in 1366 ordered the sale of the Order's houses in Pomerelia in an effort to resolve the Order's continuing dreadful financial state and these houses then passed into the hand of the Teutonic Order, fears arose among the members of the Order of St John in north-eastern Germany that their commanderies might also be sold off as outposts, especially as relations with the Order as a whole had by then become very loose. For this reason, during the period of office of Herrenmeister Bernhard von der Schulenburg (1371–97), a *rapprochement* with the German Grand Priory evolved, initially finding its expression in the appointment of

---

2nd edn (Niederweisel, 1989); *Der Johanniter-Orden – Der Malteser – Orden. Der Ritterliche Orden des Hl. Johannes vom Spital zu Jerusalem. Seine Aufgaben, seine Geschichte*, ed. A. Wienand et al., 3rd edn (Cologne, 1988); W.G. Rödel, *Das Grosspriorat Deutschland des Johanniter-Ordens im Übergang vom Mittelalter zur Reformation*, 2nd edn (Cologne, 1972).

[2] 1 mark = 248 grams of silver.

[3] W.G. Rödel, 'Reformbestrebungen im Johanniterorden in der Zeit zwischen dem Fall Akkons und dem Verlust von Rhodos (1291–1522)', in *Reformbemühungen und Observanzbestrebungen im spätmittelalterlichen Ordenswesen*, ed. K. Elm. Berliner Historische Studien, **14** (Berlin, 1989), pp. 109–29; W. Engel, 'Die Krise der Ballei Franken des Johanniterordens zur Mitte des 14. Jahrhunderts', *Zeitschrift für bayerische Landesgeschichte*, **18** (1955), pp. 279–90.

Schulenburg as Bailiff (Herrenmeister) of Brandenburg by the Grand Prior,
Conrad of Braunsberg.

In the Treaty of Heimbach (11 June 1382), relations between the bailiwick
and the Grand Priory were finally regulated on a permanent basis. It was
agreed that, in future, the bailiff would be freely elected by the commanders
of the bailiwick and merely confirmed in office by the German Grand Prior.
Although the bailiwick was still officially subject to the visitation and command
of the Grand Prior, it was in practice autonomous as the Grand Priors attempted
to exercise little influence on internal matters, and also rarely made use of their
right to send four members of the Order to participate in the administration
of the bailiwick. For his part, the Herrenmeister was obliged to appear in person
at the annual provincial chapters of the German Grand Priory, or to send a deputy.
The bailiwick paid 2,400 florins as a single settlement, and undertook to pay
an annual responsion (a tax levied by the Order) of 324 florins; in return it was
never to be subjected to special levies.[4] With this treaty, which was approved
by the Chapter General in Valence in 1383 and at the beginning of the fifteenth
century by the curia and the margrave of Brandenburg as the sovereign prince,
the bailiwick of Brandenburg had obtained a status roughly equivalent to
those priories subject to the German Grand Prior, the only exception to this
being in 1415 when, at the Emperor's command, contrary to the Order's
statutes, the Herrenmeister had to render homage to the new ruler of the Mark
of Brandenburg, Frederick of Hohenzollern.

In this way the bailiff of the Order, who had had his residence at Sonnenburg
near Küstrin since 1426, became the most exalted member of the Estates of
the Electorate. The bailiwick's autonomous position within the German Grand
Priory led to the solicitation of political backing from the sovereign prince who,
for his part, came to take on the role of a protector, protecting the bailiwick
and its possessions in the neighbouring territories (Pomerania, Mecklenburg,
Lower Lusatia, Brunswick, and the Diocese of Minden), but also exercising
an influence on the election of the Herrenmeister and the filling of positions
in the commanderies.

This development proved detrimental when the bailiwick gained a very
awkward patron in the shape of Margrave Hans von Küstrin (1535–71) as a result
of the division of the Brandenburg inheritance in 1535. As a posthumous son,
very much conscious of his princely dignity, he exercised considerable pressure
on the bailiwick – especially after his conversion to Lutheranism in 1538 – appro-
priating its available financial means (chiefly for himself) and determining the
elections of the Herrenmeister. However, he refrained from confiscating the
Order's property in the hope that the continuing existence of the bailiwick

---

[4] A. von Winterfeld, *Geschichte des Ritterlichen Ordens St Johannis vom Spital zu Jerusalem, mit besonderer Berücksichtigung der Ballei Brandenburg oder des Herrenmeistertums Sonnenburg* (Berlin, 1859), pp. 675–80; *Johanniter-Orden/Malteser-Orden*, pp. 643–5; J. von Pflugk-Harttung, 'Die Anfänge des Johanniter-Herren-Meistertums', *Historische Vierteljahrsschrift*, 2 (1899), pp. 189–210.

would afford him a growth in reputation and material advantages.[5] Herrenmeister Veit von Thümen (1527–44), although not himself a follower of the new doctrine, offered no resistance to the margrave's endeavours and allowed the commanders in the bailiwick to become Protestant and marry. The Order's headquarters, temporarily in Italy after the loss of Rhodes (1522), and then in Malta from 1530 on, were hardly in a position to combat the effects of the Reformation in the German area and the consequent seizure of commanderies, despite Imperial orders. Whereas the English *Langue* existed only on paper after the confiscation of monastic property under Henry VIII, and the commanderies of the Priory of Dacia were secularized by the kings of Denmark and Sweden, developments in the Holy Roman Empire took a somewhat different course. In the interest of their incipient territorial states, those princes who converted to the new doctrine ignored the many privileges of the Order of St John and confiscated its property within their sphere of influence. In this manner, in its German Grand Priory (excluding the bailiwicks of Utrecht and Brandenburg) the Order lost twenty-eight of its 105 houses, two-thirds of the parish churches once incorporated in it, and had to accept enormous losses in income. The number of priests in the Order dropped from 322 in 1495 to 132 in 1540; in some territories the knights of St John were even obliged to pay the salaries of Protestant pastors. The number of knights in the Order declined in the same period from 40 to 26.[6] Significantly, the Order's headquarters did not order a visitation of the German Grand Priory until 1540 and, in view of the situation described, it is even more significant that the bailiwick of Brandenburg was excluded from this.

Owing to his age (he died in 1546 aged almost 100), Grand Prior Johann von Hattstein (1512–46), who had once taken part in the defence of Rhodes against the Ottoman Turks in 1480, was no longer able to intervene personally everywhere, nor to prevent encroachments by princes and the conversion of some the Order's knights and many of its clergy to Lutheranism. In the case of the bailiwick of Brandenburg, which had adopted the new doctrine in one accord, his hands were additionally tied by the Treaty of Heimbach. Hattstein therefore advised Herrenmeister Veit von Thümen to urge the commanders to obey the Order's rules, to confiscate their commanderies in cases of disobedience and, if necessary, to take legal action at the Imperial Chamber. We know the Herrenmeister's counterargument from the instruction which he gave, in 1543, to his representative at the German provincial chapter, Sigmund von der Marwitz, the commander of Mirow.[7] In this, Thümen concealed his real

---

[5] E. Opgenoorth, *Die Balley Brandenburg des Johanniter -Ordens im Zeitalter der Reformation und Gegen-Reformation* Beihefte zum Jahrbuch der Albertus-Universität Königsberg, 24 (Würzburg, 1963); W. Hubatsch, 'Die Geschichte der Balley Brandenburg bis zur Säkularisation', in *Johanniter-Orden/Malteser-Orden*, pp. 303–11.

[6] Rödel, *Grosspriorat*, pp. 409–12; W.G. Rödel, 'Die Johanniter in der Schweiz und die Reformation', *Basler Zeitschrift für Geschichte und Altertumskunde*, 79 (1979), pp. 13–35.

[7] Opgenoorth, *Balley*, p. 67.

WALTER G. RÖDEL

attitude and followed the Lutheran argument that the marriages of commanders were permissible, as otherwise one would have to regard marriage in general as immoral. He could not, he wrote, do anything, as the sovereign princes were 'Protestant rulers in accordance with the Augsburg Confession' who would neither permit the dismissal of the commanders nor the execution of a court judgement against them. He admitted only the risk that the Order's property might pass to the commanders' heirs (something that was to be prohibited by a bailiwick chapter in 1550), and that the rulers might play a determining role in the award of commanderies.

When Margrave Hans von Küstrin declared the Herrenmeister Joachim von Arnim deposed in 1545 (although he had afforded him protection a year before) the latter escaped imprisonment by fleeing to the Grand Prior in Heitersheim, thereby confusing the position. On the one hand, the grand prior supported the bailiwick before the Emperor and Empire against the secularizing intentions of the dukes of Pomerania; on the other, he summoned the new Herrenmeister, Thomas Runge – whom he refused to recognize – to him in order to examine von Arnim's removal from office. Herrenmeister Runge did not appear and subsequently proved to be beyond the reach of the new Grand Prior, Georg Schilling von Cannstadt (1546–54), since he was under the protection of his sovereign prince, forcing the grand prior to resort to negotiations which ultimately proved fruitless. In 1551, when the Order's government in Malta described the Brandenburg knights of St John as 'rebels' against whom the grand prior should take proceedings before the Imperial Chamber, Schilling ignored this instruction and merely sent a copy of it to the Herrenmeister with the request that the married commanders should answer before him, as he wished to settle the matter amicably.[8]

This tendency towards caution on the part of the Grand Priors must always be judged against the background of the political and ecclesiastical development within the Empire. When the provincial chapter granted the members of the bailiwick of Brandenburg the right to marry in 1544,[9] the Protestant league of Schmalkalden was held in high regard. After its defeat, the Imperial–Catholic party had the upper hand, as was expressed in the Augsburg *Interim*; the princely opposition to Charles V, who had to agree to the Treaty of Passau agreements of 1552, then opened the way to the Religious Peace of Augsburg of 1555 which was to bring about a compromise within the Empire.

In Malta, the seat of the Order's government, there were admittedly more urgent problems to cope with, culminating in the great siege of the island in 1565 and the subsequent refortification. However, the 'heretical' brothers in Brandenburg were dealt with sporadically. Thus – at the instigation of the Grand

Prior – Herrenmeister Thomas Runge was admonished from Malta on 9 October 1553 at least to admit and provide for four brothers of the Order in the bailiwick in accordance with the provision of the Treaty of Heimbach.[10] Five years later, Grand Prior Georg von Hohenheim (1554–67) sent the commander of Mainz and Niederweisel, Joachim Sparr von Trampe (who came from Brandenburg) to the Herrenmeister with a request for the allocation of a commandery. Sparr had had his candidature to the dignity of Herrenmeister assigned to him in a bull from Grand Master Jean de la Valette,[11] something which became known in the bailiwick when he presented himself again in 1560. A bailiwick chapter of 20 March 1561 then rejected Sparr's request on the grounds that all the commanderies were occupied and all the candidatures had been allotted. But, it continued, 'One would be prepared in future to fulfil the provisions of the Treaty of Heimbach, if the Grand Prior were to send younger brothers'.[12] During Herrenmeister Martin, Count of Hohenstein's long period of office (1569–1609), which brought about a consolidation of the bailiwick as a whole, there was a further attempt to infiltrate Catholic brothers into the bailiwick and possibly to restore it, in this manner, to the old faith and old order. Wilhelm von Loeben, who had been born in the Mark of Brandenburg and had been in Malta and in Turkish captivity, tried in vain in 1575 to gain possession of the commandery of Wildenbruch in Pomerania, and in 1578 intervened in the dispute about the filling of the commandery of Wietersheim in the diocese of Minden. Grand Master Jean l'Evêque de la Cassière had appointed him visitor to the bailiwick and given him the task of regaining the alienated properties for the Order on the grounds that they were in the possession of people who had turned away from the true religion and were not living in accordance with the Order's rules. Loeben was indeed appointed interim administrator in Wietersheim by the bishop of Minden in 1581, but he had to give way in 1582 when the new – Protestant – administrator made a settlement in the bailiwick's favour.[13]

Various attempts to turn the Order's properties in Friedland and Schenkendorf (which were located in Lower Lusatia and formed part of the Herrenmeister's endowment) into commanderies, and to put them under the control of the Bohemian prior, also failed. In February 1580 the Emperor had notified Herrenmeister Count Hohenstein that Grand Prior Philipp Flach von Schwarzenberg had complained about him and had requested the surrender of these properties. Elector Johann Georg intervened immediately and informed the Grand Prior that he would regard measures directed against the bailiwick

---

[10] National Library of Malta, Valletta, Archives of the Order of St John (hereafter Malta, Cod.) 424, Libri Bullarum, fol. 164r.

[11] 11 January 1558. Brandenburgisches Staatsarchiv Potsdam, Rep. 9, no. 1135.

[12] Opgenoorth, *Balley*, pp. 104–5.

[13] Ibid., pp. 193–4.

as hostilities being directed against him in person, especially as the patronage over the bailiwick was a traditional right of the electors. At about the same time, in April 1580, Emperor Rudolf II declared to the elector that he wished to defend the bailiwick against the Grand Prior's encroachments. On 18 April 1580 the bailiwick chapter also responded to the Grand Prior's accusations and informed him that his predecessor, Adam von Schwalbach, had known at the time of confirming the Herrenmeister's election that the latter was married and, in addition, that married commanders had long since been tolerated. The Brandenburg knights of the Order had not, they conceded, fought against the Turks on Malta, but they had done so gloriously elsewhere. Furthermore, they had to earn their property by rendering services to their sovereign prince and were not permitted to sit around doing nothing nor be in simultaneous possession of two, three, four or even more commanderies.[14] The decision adopted unanimously by Grand Master Verdalle and the council of the Order on 9 May 1584 to transfer the two 'commanderies', Friedland and Schenkendorf, to the Prior of Bohemia *pro fidei catholicae tuitione et piis hospitalitatis operibus exercendis*, as they were being held unjustly by the bailiwick of Brandenburg, which was not operating in accordance with the rules of the Order, had no effect.[15] The attempt initiated by a Polish knight of the Order in 1603 to alienate four frontier villages in the commandery of Lagow from the bailiwick also failed.[16]

Despite these efforts to infiltrate Catholic knights of the Order into the bailiwick and to take away the bailiwick's property, a *modus vivendi* tolerating the Protestant bailiwick seems to have formed within the German Grand Priory. Yet this was once more thrown into doubt in principle when Herrenmeister Count Hohenstein, together with the Brandenburg estates, signed the *Formula Concordiae* (1577), thus officially confirming his profession of Lutheranism. Misjudging the conditions prevailing within the Empire and probably influenced by the Inquisition, which had just been established in Malta, Grand Master Jean l'Evêque de la Cassière summoned the Herrenmeister to Malta to appear before the Council of the Order. When Hohenstein let the deadline pass unheeded, the Grand Master, acting on his own authority without consulting the Council of the Order, decreed the expulsion from the Order of the members of the bailiwick of Brandenburg. This decision, which was not published in Malta, subsequently contributed there to the removal of the Grand Master from office by dissatisfied knights.[17] The German Grand Prior,

[14] Ibid., p. 199.

[15] Malta, Cod. 183, Libri Conciliorum 1583–1585, fol. 70v.

[16] E. Opgenoorth, 'Grenzkonflikte und Konfessionsprobleme zwischen Brandenburg und Polen am Anfang des 17. Jahrhunderts, dargestellt an Johanniterbesitzungen', *Zeitschrift für Ostforschung*, **18** (1969), pp. 287–98.

[17] Malta, Cod. 439, Libri Bullarum 1580–1581, fol. l99r–200v; F. de Salles, *Annales de l'Ordre de Malte ou des Hospitaliers de Saint-Jean-de-Jérusalem, Chevaliers de Rhodes et de Malte* (Vienna, 1889), pp. 141–5.

Philipp Flach von Schwarzenberg, did not even communicate this decision to the bailiwick, although he did declare his willingness in July 1581 to submit the bailiwick's defence in writing to the Order's headquarters in Malta.[18] As a result, the Order's government concluded that there was no possibility of bringing the bailiwick of Brandenburg back to the old faith nor of repealing the Treaty of Heimbach. In order not to reduce the number of grand crosses in the German *Langue*, a (Catholic) bailiff of Brandenburg was elected in Malta for the first time in May 1589 and this sinecure was retained until 1798.[19] For their part, the Herrenmeister and the members of the bailiwick of Brandenburg remained within the association of the otherwise Catholic Order, even though only loosely connected to the German Grand Priory

Finally, in 1811, the Prussian king confiscated the bailiwick's properties and in 1812 founded a Royal Prussian Order of St John in remembrance. In 1852, by an order in council, King Frederick William IV declared the bailiwick of Brandenburg restored. The eight surviving knights of the old bailiwick thereupon elected a new Herrenmeister, thus ensuring personal continuity. With reference to the Treaty of Heimbach, Herrenmeister Prince Frederick Carl Alexander of Prussia announced his election to the Deputy Grand Master, Count Colloredo-Mels, in Rome, as there had been no German Grand Prior since 1806. These are the roots of our modern *Johanniterorden*.

---

[18] Opgenoorth, 'Grenzkonflikte', p. 290.
[19] Malta, Cod. 2226, fol. 105v.

5

A Castle in Cyprus attributable to the Hospital?*

Peter Megaw

The castle in question is at Paphos, once capital of Cyprus and later a regular port of call on the route to the Holy Land. In the twelfth century it was a Byzantine outpost, guarded by a detachment of Varangians, whose establishment surrendered to Richard the Lionheart's emissaries in 1191. It was known to them as the *Castellum Baffes*, but has not survived. The remains of a second castle at Paphos were recognized by the Abbé Mariti in the mid-eighteenth century on a low hill near the harbour; they were later ploughed over and likewise forgotten. A likely site for Mariti's castle, known from its scatter of broken columns as Saranda Kolones, used to be assigned to a temple of Aphrodite,[1] but in 1957 I seized an opportunity to vindicate the learned Italian and, in excavations spread over the next thirty years, substantial remains of a compact crusader castle of concentric plan were uncovered (see Figure 5.1).[2]

The inner castle was approximately square with projecting rectangular corner towers. It was entered through an apsidal gatetower on the east side, where some of the broken columns were found in place, used as reinforcements (Figure 5.2). The accommodation was arranged in two storeys round the four sides of a small open court. It stood within a continuous outer ward, ringed by an outer wall with eight towers of various forms; that at the mid-point on the

---

* It has been suggested by John Rosser that the Hospitallers may have been influential in the design that was chosen for the new castle at Paphos, J. Rosser, 'The Lusignan Castle of Paphos called Saranda Kolones', in *Western Cyprus Connection*, ed. D.W. Rupp, SIMA, **77** (Göteborg, 1987), p. 187. In the light of Thomas Biller's subsequent study of Belvoir, that suggestion now seems fully justified, and may not have gone far enough

[1] Cf.E. Oberhummer, in Pauly-Wissowa, *Real-Encyclopädie der Classischen Altertums-Wissenschaft*, **18**, 3 (1949), s.v. 'Paphos', col. 944.

[2] Initially for the Cyprus Department of Antiquities, the excavations were subsequently sponsored by the British School at Athens, Dumbarton Oaks, Boston College and Earthwatch, with John Rosser as Associate Director from 1981.

From *The Military Orders: Fighting for the Faith and Caring for the Sick*, ed. Malcolm Barber. Copyright © 1994 by Malcolm Barber. Published by Variorum, Ashgate Publishing Ltd, Gower House, Croft Road, Aldershot, Hampshire, GU11 3HR, Great Britain.

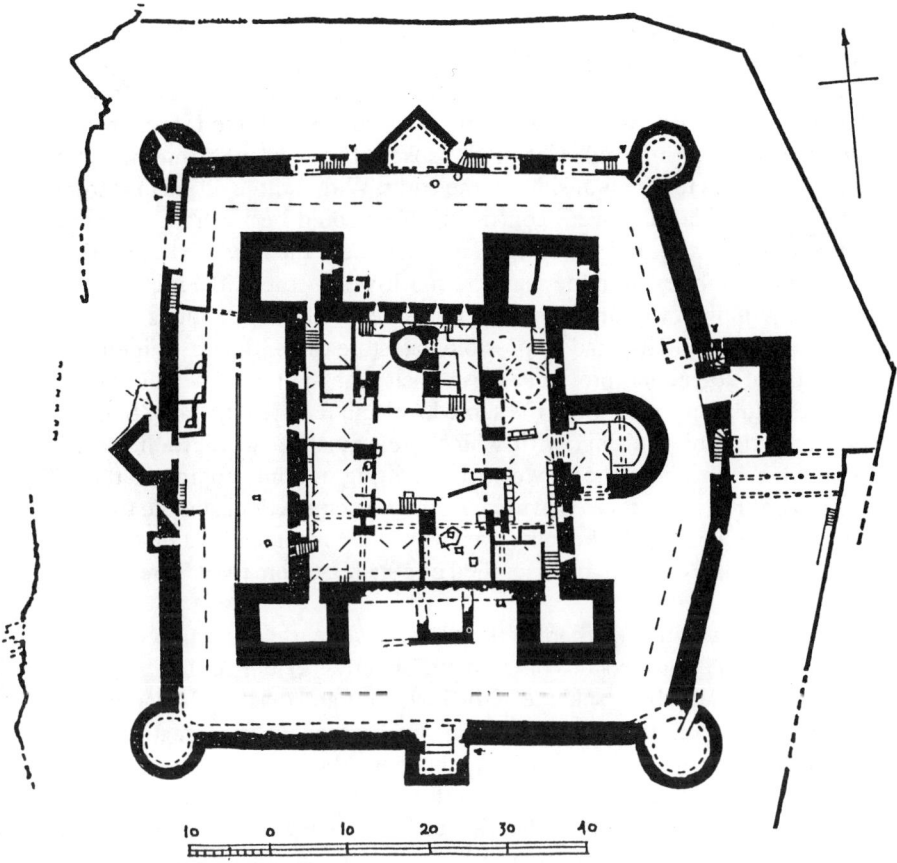

*Figure 5.1   Partly restored plan of Saranda Kolones castle
(embrasures are shown only where evidence for them has survived)*

east side contained the outer entrance. A ditch completed the defences, in part rock-cut and elsewhere limited by a masonry counterscarp; it was spanned at the entrance by a broad bridge.

Round the central court, the lower accommodation is easily identified: stables (one in the east range, another occupying the entire south-west section), a forge (south range), a mill room (north-east corner) and a bakehouse with a well preserved oven in the north range (Figure 5.3). All these are under a continuous ring of vaulting, suitably partitioned. The vaulting was carried, on the side of the court, on a series of nine massive pillars, linked (except in the entrance bay) by thin walls closing the spaces between them and providing uniform facades for the four sides of the court. Within three of the four corner pillars, pairs of latrines were contrived; these could be flushed into drains connected with a central sewer which passed under the floor of the east ditch and thence doubtless into the sea. The south-west corner pillar preserves the springings of plain vaulting ribs on all four sides, which, with others surviving on the adjoining pillars, made it possible to restore two of the ribs (Figure 5.4). They are of segmental profile and establish that the pillars were linked by separate vaults springing from the same level and rising to the same height as the outer ring of vaulting, with which they must have interpenetrated.[3] Although the height to the crown of the vaulting was only approximately 4.5 m. from ground level, there is evidence for a mezzanine floor at more than one point, notably above the bakehouse oven where there are traces of a small circular chamber, probably a steam bath, reached by a staircase from the adjoining paved area.

The vaulting carried the floor of the *piano nobile*, to which masonry staircases gave access on opposite sides of the court. There is evidence that this upper storey repeated the basic scheme of the lower one and that the flat terrace roof was carried on similar vaulting, but in this case rising to a greater height. Except for six more latrines immediately above those below, the only upper accommodation that can be located with certainty is the chapel, which is in the apsidal gatetower. From the chapel had fallen a number of moulded voussoirs from a vaulting rib, one end of which was probably supported by a foliate capital that was found nearby (Figure 5.5). A massive corbel from the west side of the court, carved on the underside with chevrons and a monster's head (Figure 5.7), probably supported an external staircase from the upper floor level to the roof terrace. The four walls of the court were crowned by a cornice supporting a parapet, which was designed to secure the maximum rainwater catchment. This was piped into an ancient cistern under the intermediate pillar of the west range.

---

[3] Their segmental form is clearest in straight-on views, e.g. G. Perbellini, 'Il Castello delle Quaranta Colonne in Paphos nell'isola di Cipro', *Castellum. Rivista dell'Instituto Italiano dei Castelli* (Rome), 25–6 (1986), 15, fig. 8.

The outer wall had survived up to the level of the outer ward at only a few places, but something remained of the barrack rooms built against it. They were of light construction, doubtless flat-roofed, and in one row of three all had corner fireplaces. Only the outer gatetower and that at the north-west corner had basements, in the latter case with embrasures raking the curtain walls. The floors of the other towers, where found, were a few steps below the outer ward level. That their upper storeys and the connected wall-walks were reached by steps in the thickness of the walls is suggested by those adjoining the pentagonal tower. Nearby, in the wall itself, is the base of the single embrasure surviving at the level of the outer ward.

Such, in brief, was the Saranda Kolones castle. As to the date of its erection, the discovery, during the early stages of its excavation, of Byzantine coins and pottery, coupled with the twelfth-century testimonia (a Byzantine *phrourion* at Paphos and the surrender of a *castellum* to Richard's men in 1191), led to the erroneous suggestion that the remains uncovered were Byzantine, at least in origin.[4] However, as the work proceeded, and once tests had been made below the castle floors, it became clear that we were dealing with a monument built *de novo* during the early years of Lusignan rule.[5]

Yet it was not the first crusader building on the site, for in the outer ward, close to the south wall of the inner castle, remains of an earlier tower of crusader masonry and a connected wall had been spared when the site was cleared and the castle built (visible in Figure 5.1). At one corner of this tower was found an associated denier of Guy of Lusignan, the first Frankish ruler of Cyprus. As Guy is known to have taken steps for the defence of his new possession, we may here have evidence for the provision of a token garrison for Paphos during his short reign. But not many years can have elapsed before what was perhaps no more than a walled encampment with a watchtower was almost totally destroyed to make way for the building of the castle. That this started around the year 1200 is attested by the seven coins found in contexts associated with the castle's construction, all of them deniers naming Guy – a type which, after his death, was not replaced before 1205.

It can hardly be doubted that the location of this sophisticated fortification at Paphos arose from the attempts of successive Byzantine emperors to recover Cyprus, both when the island was seized by Isaac Comnenus and after Richard

---

[4] Consequently early preliminary reports were misleading in this respect: A.H.S. Megaw, 'The Castle of the Forty Columns at Paphos', in *Proceedings of the VIII Meeting of the Scientific Council of the International Castles Institute* (Athens), 1969, pp. 65–70; 'Excavations at "Saranda Kolones" Paphos', *Report. Department of Antiquities*, (hereafter RDAC) (1971), pp. 117–46; 'Saranda Kolones: a Medieval Castle Excavated at Paphos', *Praktika tou protou diethnous kyprologikou synedriou*, (Nicosia), 2 (1972), pp. 173–83; 'Supplementary Excavations on a Castle Site at Paphos', Cyprus, 1970–71', *Dumbarton Oaks Papers*, 26 (1972), pp. 321–42.

[5] A.H.S. Megaw, 'Saranda Kolones: Ceramic Evidence for the Construction Date', *RDAC*, (1984), p. 337; J. Rosser, 'Excavations at Saranda Kolones, Paphos, Cyprus, 1981–1983', *Dumbarton Oaks Papers*, 39 (1985), pp. 81–97.

Figure 5.3   Saranda Kolones:
south and south-west pillars
linked by restored vaulting rib

Figure 5.2   Saranda Kolones:
column sections in position

Figure 5.4   Saranda Kolones: the bakehouse

Figure 5.5   Saranda Kolones: limestone wall-capital

Figure 5.6   Belvoir: basalt wall-capital (after Eiller)

Figure 5.7   Saranda Kolones: large limestone corbel

the Lionheart had taken it from him.[6] This menace, it was later claimed, prompted Guy's successor, Aimery of Lusignan, to obtain his crown from the Western Emperor Henry VI, who was no friend of Byzantium. Indeed, when Pope Innocent III in 1198 urged the Grand Masters of the Temple and the Hospital to assist Aimery in the defence of the young kingdom, the danger of a Byzantine assault on the island from the West must have been to the fore, for in the same year the truce with the successors of Saladin was renewed for a further five years.[7]

If the strategic role of the castle has been identified correctly, there is historical as well as archaeological support for placing its construction in the years around 1200. It would have been most unlikely for such an undertaking to have been started after the army of the Fourth Crusade occupied Constantinople in 1204. That event best explains why work on the castle was discontinued at an advanced stage and why it remained unfinished. For while the inner castle was certainly completed to the full height of its upper storey and was, to some extent, prepared for defence – to judge by the quantity of arrowheads and stone ammunition for catapults that was found during its excavation – it is clear, particularly in the outer defences, that when work was discontinued much remained to be done. For example, where the ditch had to be cut in the rock the necessary quarrying had been started, but was never completed, and a huge gap remained in the western counterscarp.

If, then, a date around 1200 for the building of the Saranda Kolones castle is not disputed, the possibility of a connection with the pope's letters to the grand masters in 1198 cannot be ignored. It is known that at some time before 1210 the Templars built a castle at Gastria on the bay of Famagusta, of which little has survived, apart from the rock-cut ditch. If Gastria castle can be regarded as a contribution of the Temple to the defences of Cyprus following Innocent III's appeal, the Hospital could well have been responsible for the building of the Paphos castle, particularly as the Hospital is known to have received estates in the neighbourhood.

That possibility can now be assessed by comparison of the remains at Saranda Kolones with those of the great Hospitaller fortress at Belvoir in Galilee, which is particularly relevant since no other crusader example of the fully concentric scheme has survived (Figure 5.8). This would not have been possible before clearance of the accumulations of later occupation by the Israeli National Parks Authority and without the careful study of the basic structure by Thomas Biller. Belvoir is about thirty years older than the Paphos

---

[6] This explanation of the location of the castle is more fully set out in A.H.S. Megaw, 'The Strategic Role of the Third Crusade Castle at Paphos', in *Proceedings of the XVIII Meeting of the Scientific Council of the International Castles Institute, 1992* (forthcoming), *passim*.

[7] For this and other cited developments affecting Cyprus at the turn of the twelfth century see P.W. Edbury, *The Kingdom of Cyprus and the Crusades, 1191–1374* (Cambridge, 1991), with references to the sources.

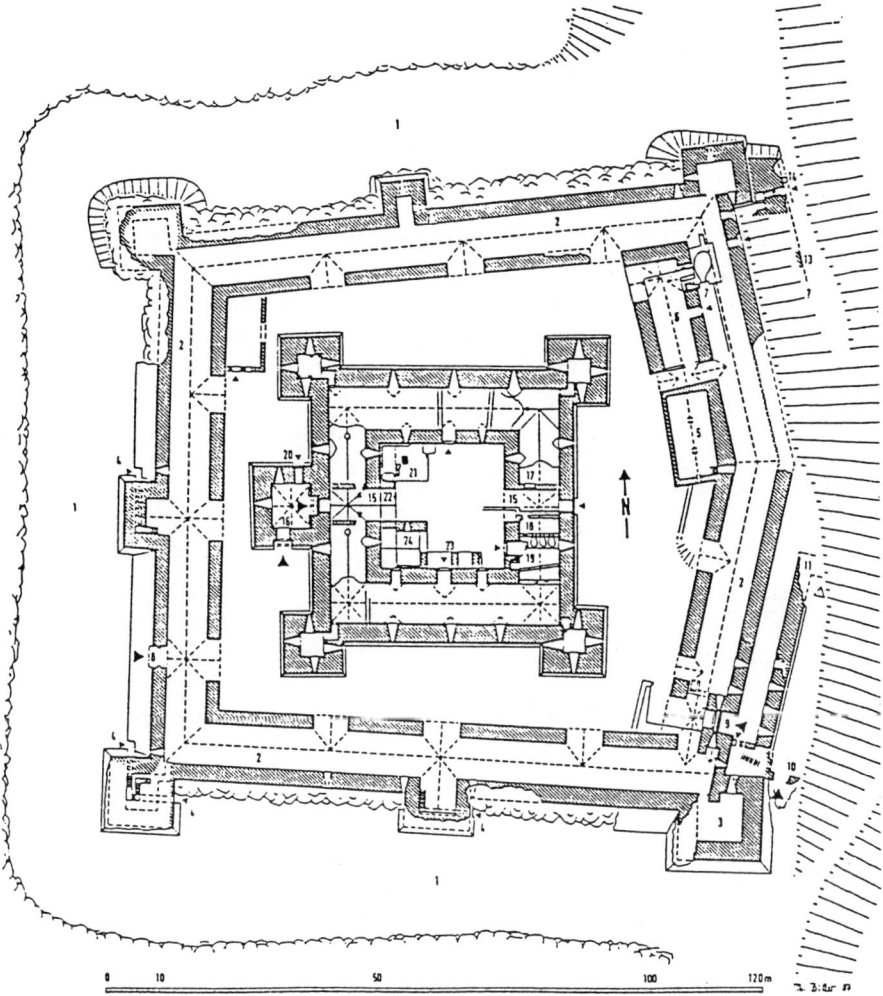

Figure 5.8   Plan of Belvoir castle (after Biller)

castle and much larger, but the similarities between them seem too close to be merely fortuitous. In the inner castles of both, the ground floor accommodation was constructed as a continuous ring of vaulting, later divided by partitions, and there is evidence in both cases that this was repeated on the upper floor. In both, the inner gatetower had two gates forming a bent entrance, above which the chapel was located. Capitals have survived from the two chapels which attest a similarity in architecture, despite the development of sculptural style during the lapse of some thirty years (see Figures 5.5 and 5.6). They are both wall-capitals of the type that supported transverse ribs of the vaulting and rested on 'bent-colonnettes', such as can be seen in position in the nave of the Hospitaller church at Abu Gosh.[8]

The outer wall at Belvoir is also lined by an almost continuous range of vaulted accommodation, to which correspond, on the smaller scale of Saranda Kolones, the remains of barrack rooms attached to the outer wall where this has survived to the level necessary to preserve them. A common feature of both castles is the surprisingly generous provision of sally-ports, which issue to the floor of the deep ditch at Belvoir at the foot of winding staircases in the substructures of three of the outer towers; there are four in the Paphos castle where the shallower ditch is reached by straight flights in the outer wall and a fifth by a spiral stair in the outer gatetower, three more having been abandoned incomplete pending quarrying the ditch to the planned level. In addition, the single postern at Belvoir, opening, at the outer ward level, on to a bridge across the west ditch, is matched by one in the flank of the pentagonal tower at Saranda Kolones, although, there, the construction of its bridge across the west ditch awaited completion of the counterscarp and the quarrying of the ditch. Such coincidences suggest that those responsible for the building of the Paphos castle, some ten years after the fall of Belvoir in 1189, included someone acquainted with that Hospitaller stronghold. Other possibilities apart, it is to be remembered that the valiance of its defenders during the eighteen-month siege so impressed Saladin that the survivors were granted safe conduct to Tyre with all their possessions.

Certainly there are features at Saranda Kolones that derive from other sources than Belvoir, notably the Byzantine multiplicity of the tower forms used in the outer wall, suggesting the participation of Cypriot castle-builders, descendants of those ordered to Tripoli by Alexius I to fortify Mont Pèlerin.[9] Even so, the historical context and the architectural links with Belvoir do seem to warrant the attribution of the Paphos castle to the Hospital, provided this is compatible with what can be established about its fate after work on it was suspended. It survived no more than eighteen years, for it was indisputably the castle reported to have been destroyed with all Paphos in the great

---

[8] Illustrated in T. Biller, 'Die Johanniterburg Belvoir am Jordan', *Architectura. Zeitschrift für Geschichte der Baukunst* (Munich–Berlin, 1989), 125 fig. 21.

[9] Anna Comnena, *Alexiad*, **XI**, 7 (2nd edn, Bonn), pp. 106ff.

earthquake of 1222.[10] Until that disaster, the inner castle remained intact, at least to the full height of the accommodation round the court, for many of the slabs and corbels from its cornice were found along the walls.[11] To judge by the equipment found, it was not only intact but occupied, as were at least some of the rooms attached to the outer wall. However, it was surely not garrisoned, for the only military equipment found in the excavations consisted of a single sword and a crushed helmet.[12] Yet at the time of the earthquake some of the castle's facilities were still in use: tools and an anvil were abandoned in the forge, and the coins found among the debris, which included recent issues from Western mints, suggest that the *piano nobile* could have served as a hospice for crusaders and pilgrims en route to and from the Holy Land. In addition, the evidence for continuing activity in the mill room and for the existence of a sugar refinery in the neighbourhood suggest that the castle could also have been used as a manorial headquarters. Lastly, the discovery of a lead seal of the reigning pope at the time of the earthquake indicates that it was still a place of some importance. So, if it is correct to attribute the building of the castle at Saranda Kolones to the Hospital, the evidence for the years after 1204 would not conflict with its retention by the Order until the end, albeit in its unfinished state.

One thing is certain: what remained of the castle after the earthquake was never repaired; instead it was ransacked and abandoned to serve as a quarry for the rebuilding of the devastated city. If, in 1204, no purpose warranted its completion, none would have been served by restoring what was left of it in 1222. Particularly so, if it had remained until then a possession of the Hospital for, well before that date, the grant to the Order of the domain of Kolossi had provided it with a more central location for the management of its many estates in the south of the island.

---

[10] Oliverus Scholasticus, *Historia Damiatina*, ed. H. Hoogeveg (Tübingen, 1894), cap. 86, p. 279. Remains of both human and animal victims of the earthquake were found during excavation of the debris.

[11] Megaw, 'Supplementary excavations', figs. 20–21.

[12] The initial garrison may have been included in the contingent of Hospitallers withdrawn from Cyprus in 1205: J. Hackett, *History of the Orthodox Church in Cyprus* (London, 1901), p. 629, quoting G. Bosio, *Storia della sacra religione di San Giovanni, Gierolimitano*, I (Venice, 1695), lib.xiii, p. 471.

6

Two Forged Thirteenth-Century Alms-Raising Letters used by the Hospitallers in Franconia

Karl Borchardt

The archives of the former Hospitaller commandery in Würzburg have preserved two strange parchments which raise several difficult questions.[1] In form and script the two parchments closely resemble charters issued in Würzburg under Bishop Hermann of Lobdeburg (1225–54). The larger parchment (known today as the Bayerisches Hauptstaatsarchiv München, Würzburger Urkunden 4828 and referred to hereafter as parchment A) purports to be a letter by the Master and the Convent of the Hospital to all ecclesiastical and secular dignitaries.

> *Frater N. dei gratia domus hospitalis Ierosolimitani magister humilis et pauperum Christi custos totusque conventus eiusdem domus [patr]iarchis, cardinalibus, archiepiscopis, episcopis, abbatibus, prepositis, prioribus, archiprespiteris, decanis et aliis ecclesiarum prelatis, gloriosissimo fratri suo Romanorum imperatori, [re]gibus, ducibus, comitibus, principibus, deinde omnibus in sublimitate constitutis salutem suamque et omnium fratrum suorum orationem cum benedictione.*

---

[1] A more comprehensive study of the two parchments is published in K. Borchardt, 'Spenden-aufrufe der Johanniter aus dem 13. Jahrhundert', *Zeitschrift für bayerische Landesgeschichte*, **56** (1993), pp. 1–61. I am very grateful to Dr Anthony Luttrell for his generous help in discussing the two charters. Parchment A is briefly mentioned and – on account of an eighteenth-century dorsal note *Rogerus primus ordinis Magister 1179* – erroneously dated 1179 May 28: *Regesta sive rerum Boicarum autographa*, 1, p. 305; parchment B, ibid., **2**, p. 257 with the unaccountable date 1236. See also J. Riley-Smith, *The Knights of St John in Jerusalem and Cyprus c. 1050–1310* (London, 1967), p. 235; W.G. Rödel, *Das Grosspriorat Deutschland des Johanniter-Ordens im Übergang vom Mittelalter zur Reformation anhand der Generalvisitationsberichte von 1494/95 und 1540/41*, 2nd ed. (Cologne, 1972), p. 172; K. Borchardt, *Die geistlichen Institutionen in der Reichsstadt Rothenburg ob der Tauber und dem zugehörigen Landgebiet von den Anfängen bis zur Reformation* (Neustadt/Aisch, 1988), pp. 118, 884 n. 18, 1126 n. 7; U. Thomas, *Die Johanniterkomture in Mainfranken: Von den Anfängen bis zum Jahre 1500*, unpubl. magisterial thesis (Würzburg, 1990), pp. 10, 90–93.

The document gives no year and has, at least nowadays, no seal; it may have had a wax seal, but not the leaden bull the Master or the Convent would usually append to charters. The document ends: '*Data Caraco per manum Rogeri summi magistri in communi omnium fratrum suorum conventu in octava Pentecostes*'. *Caraco* is Crac des Chevaliers, and the *summus magister Rogerus* could be Master Fr. Roger des Moulins (+1187), who was well known to Hospitallers from his statutes.

The smaller parchment (known today as the Bayerisches Hauptstaatsarchiv München, Würzburger Urkunden 4853/1, and referred to hereafter as parchment B) purports to be, and most probably is in reality, a letter written by a local Hospitaller commander. The place-name of the commandery *Rote* is written over an erasure and with the aid of a quartz lamp one can see that originally it was *Rodenb[ur]g*. There are several dorsal notes from later centuries – for example, *Elion sive Allianus de Villa Nova 2ter Grossmeister in Rodis*, or *Exhortatio per breve ad fratres in circa 1324*, but, according to the thirteenth-century script and for other reasons (such as the title of the issuer) the reference to Rhodes must be wrong. The place-names do not refer to Rhodes, but to Rothenburg ob der Tauber and to a small village a few miles to the north of Rothenburg, known today as Reichardsroth, but in medieval times often simply called Rode.

The Hospitallers had commanderies in both places during the thirteenth century. The text of parchment B begins:

Omnibus Christi fidelibus, ad quos presens scriptum pervenerit, frater C. commendurus et servus pauperum in Rote ceterique fratres hospitalis sancti Iohannis Iherosolim. salutem et orationes in domino.

Again, there is no date and, today, it has no seal. The parchment concludes simply:

Quoniam igitur privilegia papalia propter diversas mundi turbationes nunctiis nostris dare non possumus nec presumus, sigillo nostro hanc litteram fecimus roborari. Dat.

In short, the contents of parchment B are as follows. The faithful are expected to know papal and other privileges of the Hospital. The Hospital in Jerusalem was founded 340 years before the birth of Christ. Judas Maccabeus sent 12,000 drachmas to this Hospital. Christ himself came to the Hospital and preached there. After his resurrection he appeared there to his disciples and permitted the Apostle Thomas to touch his wounds. At Pentecost the apostles received the Holy Spirit in the Hospital. All members of the fraternity of the Hospital who do something good for it are freed from the seventh part of penances for forgotten sins [*peccata oblita*], except in cases of violence against their father or mother. If one of the members of the fraternity [*fratres*] dies in a tournament, a tavern or some other unfortunate place, he may be buried with Christian rites, except if he is personally excommunicated or a public usurer.

The *nuncii* of the Hospital who travel around to collect alms have the papal privilege to celebrate divine services once a year even in places under interdict. Those who give alms are included in the prayers of the 4,000 houses of the Order and share the spiritual merits of the 4,000 brethren of the Order who fight the infidel.

The contents of parchment A are similar, but the text is much longer. It begins with the well known twelfth-century papal arenga *Christiane fidei* and includes several quotations from the Bible. It states that Christ himself honoured the Hospital in Jerusalem with his presence while he was on earth, but now he has *ut dilectus patri filius interdum flagellatur et corripitur*, inflicted *gravem ... iacturam et casum in personis et rebus* on the Hospital. The phrase *Hec enim est sancta domus illa* then introduces a second paragraph which includes statements – similar to those in parchment B, but more detailed – on the Hospital in biblical times. Judas Maccabeus sent 12,000 drachmas to the Hospital. In this Hospital Mary Magdalene washed Christ's feet with her tears. Simon the Leper was at that time Master of the Hospital. In the Hospital Christ held the Last Supper and instituted the Eucharist. During the three days Christ lay in the Holy Sepulchre the apostles hid themselves from the Jews in this Hospital. After his resurrection Christ appeared to the apostles in the Hospital and allowed Thomas to touch his wounds. From the Hospital Christ led the apostles over the Mount of Olives to Bethany whence he ascended to Heaven. At Pentecost the apostles received the Holy Spirit in the Hospital. And afterwards the Virgin lived there for three and a half years. There her death was announced to her by the archangel Gabriel with a palm tree which *usque hodie ibi habetur et omnibus ibi videre volentibus in assumptione eius ostenditur*. The apostles came together from all over the world to the deathbed of the Virgin in the Hospital; she was then moved to Mount Sion where she died, and was finally buried in the Vale of Jehoshaphat.

The third paragraph begins:

> *Sciat itaque discretio universitatis vestre, quod non iactantie causa huius domus preconia protulimus, set pro subsequentium miseriarum diversitate, quas sine lacrimis dicere nos [recte: non] possumus. Repulit enim dominus altare suum, maledixit sanctificationi sue ...*

The text calls for support to the Christian cause in the Holy Land and could be derived from preachings for the crusade. At the end Master and Convent promise to those who give alms 1,000 masses per day to be said by the 14,130 priests of the Order in its houses throughout the world. By authority of the Apostles Peter and Paul they remit one-half of the penance for venial sins and one-seventh of the penance for capital sins.

Many, but not all, of these privileges and legends in parchments A and B are known from other sources. The legend of Judas Maccabeus, and that of Christ and the Hospital evolved from the twelfth to the fourteenth centuries. But neither in the Order's *miracula* nor in the pilgrims' guides can one find the story of the palm tree in the Hospital of Jerusalem, allegedly shown to pilgrims on the feast of Mary's assumption; only Delaville's version R mentions the palm tree, and Pope Celestine III stated, in 1191, that the Virgin had lived in the Hospital for three and a half years before she died.[2] As for the Hospital's privileges, divine services under interdict, ecclesiastical burial and remission of one-seventh of the penance were common in papal and other charters as early as the twelfth century. However, remission of one-half of the penance for venial sins and ecclesiastical burial by Hospitallers for those who died in tournaments and taverns were not common.

Since the origins and the development of the Hospital's *miracula* are not clear, they offer no help in dating parchments A and B, but palaeographical evidence suggests the first half of the thirteenth century. At that time the Hospitallers of Franconia were desperately in need of money owing to the purchase of the castle of Biebelried near Würzburg in 1244, and the more or less simultaneous construction of a huge and splendid church in Reichardsroth which was consecrated in 1254. To resolve at least part of their financial problems they apparently sent round alms collectors (*nuncii*) and it would seem reasonable to speculate that the two documents were written in this context. The erasure on parchment B could imply that, initially, the commander of Rothenburg ob der Tauber, where the Order maintained a hospital, and subsequently the commander of Reichardsroth, gave these letters to certain alms collectors. Also, because from about 1500, if not earlier, the two documents were held in the archives of the Hospitaller commandery in Würzburg (the central commandery for Franconia), the letters may have been used not only for Rothenburg and Reichardsroth but also for other commanderies such as those of Mergentheim or Würzburg itself. Indeed, in 1278 the *nuncii* of the commandery of Mergentheim were given a letter of recommendation for collecting alms by the bishop of Würzburg.[3]

A date around the first half of the thirteenth century would also fit with the situation in the Holy Land. Had the documents expressly stated that Jerusalem had been lost, that would have referred either to 1187 or to 1243–44. But the documents report merely that the Hospitallers in the Holy Land were under strong pressure. In the 1240s the Hospitallers in the Holy Land sent embassies and appeals for help to the king of Jerusalem, Conrad of Hohenstaufen, resident in southern Germany at that time. Parchment A is probably not a genuine letter of the Master and the Convent. It may have been composed with the help of a genuine letter such as Cartulaire No. 3002, now held in Spain, which Delaville dates as the mid-thirteenth century and García Larragueta, probably more correctly, dates at *c.* 1193.[4] Papal letters for collectors of alms for the Hospital were issued several times during these years; one such letter,

[2] J. Delaville Le Roulx, *De Prima origine Hospitalariorum Hierosolymitanorum*, Paris, 1885, pp. 108, 115–18; *CH*, 1, no 911, pp. 557f.

[3] *Wirtembergisches Urkundenbuch*, 8 (Stuttgart, 1903), no. 2807, pp. 121f.

[4] *CH*, 3, no. 3002, pp. 18f; S. García Larragueta, *El gran priorado de Navarra de la orden de San Juan de Jerusalén siglos XII–XIII*, 2, Colección diplomática (Pamplona, 1957), no. 73, pp. 74f.

by Pope Innocent IV, given at Lyons on 13 December 1244, was preserved in the archives of the priory of Bohemia,[5] which means that it was known in the province of Alamania at this time.

How the stories about the Hospital came to Würzburg remains an open question. Wilbrand of Oldenburg, bishop of Paderborn (+1233), incorrectly wrote that the Hospital endowed by Judas Maccabeus with 12,000 drachmas was built on Mount Sion where the Virgin died. He then added more or less the same stories contained in parchment A, with the omission of the palm tree which is, however, a common feature of legends on the Virgin's death and assumption. Wilbrand obviously transferred legends usually associated with Mount Sion to the Hospital. Wilbrand's predecessor was Oliver of Cologne, a crusader who acted as secretary to Cardinal Pelagius and who in 1225 was himself created cardinal; he died in 1227. Oliver exchanged letters with *magister Salomon*, a canon of the cathedral church in Würzburg who preached the crusade in Franconia, and these connections may have played a role in transmitting such stories to Würzburg.

As for the figures in the two documents, Matthew Paris maintains under the year 1243, that the Templars had 9,000 and the Hospitallers 19,000 manors:

> *Habent insuper Templarii in Christianitate novem milia maneriorum, Hospitalarii vero novendecim, praeter emolumenta et varios proventus ex fraternitatibus et praedicationibus provenientes, et per privilegia sua accrescentes. Quodlibet igitur manerium sine gravamine unum militem potest in subsidium Terrae Sanctae, bene et sine aliquo defectu communitum, adinvenire, etiam cum omnibus plenarie ad militem pertinentibus ...*[6]

The statements in parchments A and B that the Hospitallers had 14,130 priests, 4,000 houses and 4,000 fighting brethren continue to be an enigma – perhaps an invention of the people who drafted the two documents in Franconia some time during the second quarter of the thirteenth century.

---

[5] *Codex diplomaticus et epistolaris regni Bohemiae*, 4 (Prague, 1962), no. 341, p. 518; *CH*, 2, no. 2341, p. 623; cf. ibid., 1, no. 392, pp. 268f.

[6] Matthew Paris, *Chronica majora*, 4, ed. H.R. Luard, RS (London, 1877), p. 291.

7

How Many Miles to Babylon? The *Devise des Chemins de Babiloine* Redated*

Robert Irwin

In 1882 Count Riant published a Hospitaller document in a collection entitled *Itinéraires à Jérusalem et descriptions de la Terre Sainte, rédigés en Français aux xie, xiie & xiiie siècles*. This document, *La Devise des Chemins de Babiloine*, detailed the strengths of Mamluk armies in Egypt and Syria and gave mileages of the various routes between Cairo and the Delta ports.[1] Evidently it had been prepared as an intelligence report in preparation for some future and hypothetical crusade to be launched against Mamluk Cairo. Riant, who found the memorandum in the Vatican archives, dated it fairly precisely to between 1289 and 1291. Riant had noticed that Tripoli was listed in the *Devise* as a centre of Mamluk government, whereas Acre was not, and he deduced that the document therefore must have been drafted after Qalawun's army had taken Tripoli but before Acre had yet fallen to Qalawun's son, al-Ashraf Khalil.

Two years after Riant's publication of the document, Charles Schefer produced a study of it in *Archives de l'Orient latin*.[2] In this study scholarship and logic took a step backwards, for Schefer dated the document to the reign of the Sultan al-Zahir Baybars – that is, as he put it, sometime between the fall of Safed (1266) and the fall of Acre. (Schefer seems not have noticed that Baybars was dead by 1277, quite some years before the capture of Tripoli and Acre.) Subsequently, the document has attracted little attention and on those occasions when it is referred to in the modern literature on the crusades, Riant's dating is taken for granted. Thus the *Devise* is customarily referred to as if it were an

* I am grateful to Professor P.M. Holt and Dr Anthony Luttrell for comments made on the first version of this paper.

[1] 'La Devise des Chemins de Babiloine', ed. P. Riant, in *Itinéraires à Jérusalem et descriptions de la Terre Sainte, rédigés en Français aux xie, xiie & xiiie siécles*, ed. H. Michelant and G. Raynaud (Geneva, 1882), pp. xxxi–xxxii, 239–52.

[2] C. Schefer, 'Etude sur La Devise des Chemins de Babiloine', *AOL*, 2 1884, pp. 89–101.

unusual precursor of the *De Recuperatione Terrae Sanctae* genre of literature (that is, similar to, but earlier than, material produced by such writers as Fidenzio of Padua, Marino Sanudo, Hethoum of Armenia, William Adam and Ramon Lull).[3]

However, Riant's basis for dating the memorandum is groundless. While Tripoli did become a Mamluk province with its own *na'ib*, or governor, this provincial governorship was not set up immediately in 1289. The Christian city had been destroyed and the Muslim one was built on a new site. It is hard to be dogmatic about this but, as far as I can tell, the first Mamluk officer to be described as the *Na'ib* of Tripoli was 'Izz al-Din Aybak al-Mansuri who took charge of the city in 692/1292–93.[4] More significantly, Acre, when it fell to the Mamluks, was not elevated to the dignity of an independent *niyaba* or province, and it never became one. It never even rated a lowly *wali*, or lesser governor.[5] According to Ludolph of Suchem, who visited the place some forty years after the Mamluks' capture of Acre, the area was inhabited by peasants and patrolled by about sixty Saracen mercenaries, who supplemented whatever wages they received by selling caged birds.[6] Throughout the remaining two centuries or so of Mamluk history, Acre was usually classified as a district in the *niyaba* of Gaza. Thus Riant's *termini post* and *ante quem* are not what they seem.

So, if the *Devise* was not necessarily drafted somewhere between 1289 and 1291, is it possible to determine when it was drawn up? And on what sources did its author, or authors, draw? It is time now to examine the internal evidence and, to do this, it will be useful to quote the first part of the document in full.

> Here begins a treatise which was recently made overseas [*oultre la mer*], commissioned by the Master and the Convent of the Hospital, as well as of other worthy men, who have been overseas and who know the power of the Sultan and the Saracens and it has been done to discover how many men-at-arms the Sultan may have from all the power of the Saracens and in which places and within which days he can assemble them.
>
> By this document it may be possible to discover and know the power of the wicked Saracens who currently rule over the kingdom of Babylon [Egypt].
>
> First, the Sultan provides from his own household 1,000 cavalry, heavy and light. Then there are twenty-four great emirs, 'chieftains of the host' each of whom can field an hundred cavalry. Then there are eighty emirs of which some bring with them sixty cavalry, some fifty and some forty, and the sum total of this category amounts to 4,000 cavalry. Then there are thirty emirs, each of whom is followed

---

[3] On this sort of literature and its context see N. Housley, *The Later Crusades from Lyons to Alcazar 1274–1580* (Oxford, 1992), pp. 22–48.

[4] Al-Maqrizi, Ahmad ibn 'Ali, *Kitab al-Suluk li-Ma'rifat Duwal al-Muluk*, ed. M.M. Ziada, **1**, pt. 3 (Cairo, 1956), p. 272.

[5] M. Gaudefroy-Demombynes, *La Syrie á l'Epoque des Mamelouks d'après les Auteurs Arabes* (Paris, 1923), p. 121.

[6] *Ludolph von Suchem's Description of the Holy Land*, trans. A. Stewart, *PPTS*, **12** (London, 1895), p. 61.

by ten horsemen. Then there are seventy elmeccadem [in Arabic, *al-muqaddimun*] and each *muqaddam* brings with him forty horsemen and they are called the 'la Bahrye' [i.e. the Bahris] who are all always around the tent of the Sultan.

Then there are other *muqaddams* to the number of eighty, each of whom brings with him forty horsemen. And you should know that all the emirs can certainly produce from their mesnies approximately a further 1,000 cavalry and more. The sum total for Babylon is 14,700. And all the men-at-arms which are listed above are divided among the twenty-four chieftains also listed above. And that is the strength of Babylon.

The power of Syria: firstly at Gaza 700 cavalry, then at Safed 900 cavalry, at Damascus 4,000 cavalry, at Homs 300 cavalry, at Hama 1,000 cavalry, at Aleppo 2,000 cavalry, at Tripoli 1,000 cavalry. The sum for Syria is 9,900. The sum total of the power of the Sultan in Babylon and Syria is 24,600 men, of which at least 15,000 are so poor that they can hardly maintain their horses.[7]

The second and longer part of the document, which will not be cited in detail here, gives precise routes and distances in leagues from Gaza to Cairo, from Damietta to Cairo, a variety of routes from Rosetta to Cairo and other places, a route from Degua to Cairo and a route from Alexandria to Cairo. Garrison figures are given for both al-Fua and Alexandria. Alexandria, defended by ninety horsemen and about a hundred bedouin, must have seemed a tempting prospect for any crusade planner. The *Devise* ends abruptly with a couple of lines describing the Delta province of al-Gharbiyya.

The first thing which stands out is that the *Devise* in all its surviving versions appears to be incomplete, for in none of the three surviving manuscripts is any information given about the times and places of assembly of the Mamluk army (although this was promised at the beginning of the document). Secondly, its disparaging view of the quality of Mamluk soldiery matches that of other western observers of the Mamluk army. However, unlike other western reports on Mamluk Egypt and Syria, the *Devise* seems to have been produced by someone with objective inside knowledge of how the Mamluk system worked – from the sultan down to the lowest ranks of the *halqa*. As a report on the Mamluk system and the strength of the Mamluk army, it is in a different category from what was written by, say, William Adam in the 1320s, who airily reckoned that the Sultan had more than 40,000 mamluks, or Henry II of Cyprus who guessed that Egypt in 1311 had 60,000 horsemen of which 20,000 were good, 20,000 were mediocre and 20,000 were very poor.[8] The above are evidently subjective and unsystematically presented opinions. More soberly, Hethoum of Armenia, in *Flor des Estoires* (1307), reported that the mounted strength of Sultan al-Nasir Muhammad came to about 20,000 of which most were not of good quality.[9] (Although Hethoum's figure for Egypt is higher than that of the *Devise*,

[7] 'Devise', pp. 239–41.

[8] Guillaume Adam, 'De Modo Sarracenos Extirpandi', ed. C. Kohler, in *RHC DArm*, 2, p. 524; A.S. Atiya, *The Crusade in the Later Middle Ages* (London, 1938), p. 60.

[9] Hayton d'Arménie, 'Flor des Estoires', in *RHC DArm*, 2, pp. 222–4.

he gives only 5,000 cavalry for Syria, as against the *Devise's* 9,900.) In the
Devise the twenty-four chieftains of the host neatly match what we know to
have been the normal complement of Emirs of One Hundred and *Muqaddams*
of One Thousand. At the time of the Nasiri *Rawk* (a cadastral survey made for
military purposes) in 1315, there were exactly twenty-four of these grand
officers.[10] Similarly, all the way along the line the author(s) have a sure
knowledge of how the Mamluk army was compartmentalized between royal
manluks, emirs' mamluks and *halqa* troops.

   To be sure, it is unfortunate that numbers of troops offered by the Hospitaller
document cannot be matched by any given in the Arab sources of the period.
Baybars al-Mansuri, an emir who served under Qalawun and who certainly was
in a position to know, says that by the end of Qalawun's reign (1290) the sultan
had over 6,000 mamluks. According to the *Khitat* (a fifteenth-century source),
Qalawun had 7,000 mamluks and his son and successor, al-Ashraf Khalil, had
12,000. At the time of the Nasiri *Rawk* of 1315, when accurate figures were
made available, the army of Egypt alone numbered 24,000 horsemen, while
the Sultan could field 2,000 mamluks from his own household.[11] In both these
cases the figures are approaching double those offered by the *Devise*. On the
other hand, in 1313, according to the sultan's diploma issued to the Haman
prince Abu'l-Fida, the army of Hama amounted to 500, as against the 1,000
offered by the *Devise*.[12]

   All this is inconclusive. Turning then to the provinces listed, the *Devise*
breaks down the army estimates for Syria into seven regions which actually
correspond to the component *niyabat* or provincial governorships. The *Devise's*
list of Syrian provincial capitals agrees with that provided by the geographer
al-Dimashqi (who wrote between 1323 and 1327) with one exception.[13] The
province of Kerak does not feature among the *Devise's* list of provincial capitals.
This might suggest that the report was compiled at a time when this *niyaba* was
in abeyance. In 1293 the town was severely damaged by an earthquake and most
of the damage was not repaired until 1309. In the years 1297–99 Kerak served
as a place of exile for the once and future sultan al-Nasir Muhammad.[14] In 1309

---

[10] R. Amitai, 'The Remaking of the Military Elite of Mamluk Egypt by al-Nasir Muhammad
b. Qalawun', *Studia Islamica*, 72 (1990), p. 148; cf. D. Ayalon, 'Studies in the Structure of the Mamluk
Army, III', *Bulletin of the School of Oriental and African Studies*, 16 (1954), pp. 70–71.

[11] D. Ayalon, 'Studies on the Structure of the Mamluk Army I', *Bulletin of the School of Oriental
and African Studies*, 15 (1953), pp. 222–4; idem, 'Studies on the Structure of the Mamluk Army
III', pp. 70–71.

[12] Abu'l-Fida', *The Memoirs of a Syrian Prince, Abu'l-Fida', Sultan of Hamah (672–732/1273–1331)*,
trans. P.M. Holt (Wiesbaden, 1983), p. 65.

[13] Al-Dimashqi, *Manuel de la Cosmographie du Moyen Age, traduit de l'Arabe "Nokhbet ed-Dahr fi
Adjaib-il-Birr wal-Bahr*, trans. A.F. Mehren (Amsterdam, 1874), p. 294; cf. N.A. Ziadeh, *Urban
Life in Syria under the Early Mamluks* (Beirut, 1953), pp. 11–14.

[14] Al-Maqrizi, *Kitab al-Suluk*, 1, 3, p. 783; W. Müller-Wiener, *Castles of the Crusades* (London,
1966), p. 48.

when al-Nasir Muhammad passed through Kerak on his way to Hejaz there was no *na'ib* there to greet him, but only a humble 'castellan'.[15] A few months later Kerak became al-Nasir Muhammad's base of operations against Baybars II. It seems likely that from 1293 until 1310 at least the area had no *na'ib*.

It is unlikely that the *Devise* could have been written later than the 1340s for its author(s) imply that Homs was a *niyaba*. But, by the time al-'Umari wrote his chancery manual, the *Masalik al-Absar*, in the mid-to late 1340s, Homs had ceased to be a *niyaba* and was merely a subdistrict in the province of Damascus.[16] Homs seems to have survived as a *niyaba* until at least the 1320s, for al-Dimashqi devoted a section to it in his geography.[17] (Al-'Umari also treats Gaza as a subdistrict of Damascus,[18] but this is less significant, for the *niyaba* of Gaza flickered in and out of existence throughout the Mamluk period.[19] During the third reign of al-Nasir Muhammad, Sanjar al-Jawli was its *na'ib*.)[20]

It may be more significant that Hama is implicitly treated as if it were a province of the Mamluk sultanate. For most of the thirteenth century Hama was a principality (*mamlaka*) ruled by Ayyubid princes. When the Ayyubid prince al-Muzaffar died in August 1299 the principality was annexed and became just one of the provinces of Mamluk Syria. However, in 1310 when al-Nasir Muhammad became sultan in Egypt for the third time, he resurrected the principality and awarded it to his friend and supporter Abu'l-Fida'.[21]

When it comes to discussing routes through the Delta to Cairo, the place-names and mileages offered are eerily precise and comprehensive. When the *Devise* estimates that there are about 500 towns and villages in the Gharbiyya province of the Delta, it comes close to anticipating the figure of 476 given in the 1376 *rawk*.[22] And, as Schefer noted, the first Delta route listed follows the *barid* or mamluk courier route precisely, as that is described in Mamluk chancery manuals – [23] just as the formalized and confident setting out of the army estimates makes one think of similar expositions in works by al-'Umari, al-Qalqashandi and others.[24] In short, while I have no definite evidence and while I cannot as yet point to the source in question, I believe that the *Devise*

---

[15] Abu'l-Fida', *Memoirs*, pp. 27, 32–3, 47–51.

[16] Al-'Umari, Ibn Fadl Allah, *Masalik al-Amsar fi-Mamalik al- Amsar: Mamalik Misr wa Sham wa'l-Hijaz, wa'l-Yaman*, ed. A.F. Sayyid (Cairo, 1985), pp. 124–5.

[17] Al-Dimashqi, *Manuel*, p. 273.

[18] Al-'Umari, *Masalik*, pp. 142–3.

[19] Ziadeh, *Urban Life*, p. 12.

[20] G. Wiet, 'Les Biographies du Manhal Safi', *Mémoires de l'Institut d'Égypte*, 19 (Cairo, 1932), no. 1102, p.157 and the references provided there.

[21] Abu'l-Fida', *Memoirs*, pp. 34, 53.

[22] 'Devise', p. 252; Schefer, 'Etude', p. 101.

[23] 'Devise', pp. 241–3; Schefer, 'Etude', p. 94.

[24] On chancery manuals in the Mamluk period, see Gaudefroy-Demombynes, *La Syrie*; R. Hartmann, 'Politische Geographie des Mamlukenreiches, Kapitel 5 und 6 des Staatshandbuchs Ibn Fadlallah al-'Omari's', *Zeitschrift für Deutsches Morgenlandische Gesellschaft*, 70 (1916), pp. 1–40; W. Björkman, *Beitrage zur Geschichte der Staatskanzlei im islamischen Ägypten* (Hamburg, 1928).

is based on a partial translation of an early Mamluk administrative manual. As
to the document's date, the low figures given for both for sultan's mamluks
and for the Mamluk army as a whole, indicate a time of weakness. The failure
to mention Kerak as a province could suggest (though it certainly does not prove)
that the *Devise* drew upon data amassed during the brief reign of the Sultan
Lajin (1297–99). Indeed, some of its systematic and detailed information may
have been drawn from the data amassed by the Husami *Rawk* of 1298, which
was commissioned by the Sultan Lajin.[25] The inclusion of Hama as one of the
places furnishing troops might suggest a date between 1299 and 1310.

The Bibliothèque Nationale and Sainte Geneviève manuscripts of the
Devise have it bound in with another Hospitaller memorandum which argued
for a *passage particulier*.[26] This document was written in French but with a Latin
heading *Incipit tractus dudum habitus ultra mare per magistrum et conventum
Hospitalis et per alios probos viros qui diu steterunt ultra mare ...*[27] (The similarity
of these lines to the opening lines of the *Devise* is particularly noteworthy.) The
passage particulier memorandum (which has been published and commented
on by Benjamin Kedar and Sylvia Schein) argues against launching a major
crusade in the near future and instead puts forward proposals for a *passage
particulier* – that is for smaller forces to be sent out to the East to assist in coastal
raids and the enforcement of a naval blockade against the Mamluk lands.
However, the men who drafted the document under the direction of the
Hospitaller Grand Master, Fulk of Villaret, did envisage a landing in Egypt
and an advance against Cairo, when and if the Mongols from Oljeitu's Ilkhanate
invaded Syria. Then Egypt would be denuded of its *mamluk* soldiery and Cairo
could easily be taken and sacked.

> *Item, et se les Tartars veignent, si comme nous aveous, il convient que tout l'ost de Babiloine
> vait au Sam encontre eaus et nen laissent en tout l'Egypt nule gent a cheval. Pourquoi ceste
> gent porront monter oveuc lour galees par le flum et par terre jusques au Caire sans nul
> peril ...*[28]

The Hospitaller proposal for a *passage particulier* was drafted in the East for
the Grand Master before he travelled to the West to confer with the pope and
others. Schein and Kedar have successfully narrowed the dates for the drawing
up of this document to between September 1306 and the summer of 1307. It

---

[25] On the Husami *Rawk*, see H. Halm, *Ägypten nach den mamlukischen Lehens-registern. I. Oberägypten
und das Fayyum* (Wiesbaden, 1979), pp. 17–23; P.M. Holt, 'The Sultanate of Lajin (696–98/1286–89)',
Bulletin of the School of Oriental and African Studies, **36**, (1973), pp. 527–9; R. Irwin, *The Middle East
in the Middle Ages; The Early Mamluk Sultanate 1250–1382* (Beckenham, 1986), pp. 92–4.

[26] On this document see B.Z. Kedar and S. Schein, 'Un projet de "passage particulier" proposé
par l'ordre de l'Hôpital 1306–7', *Bibliothèque de l'Ecole des Chartes*, **137** (1979), pp. 1211–26; cf. Housley,
Later Crusades, pp. 27, 208, 214–15; A. Forey, *The Military Orders. From the Twelfth to the Early Fourteenth
Centuries* (London, 1992), pp. 96, 128, 222.

[27] Kedar and Schein, 'Un projet', pp. 211–12.

[28] Kedar and Schein, 'Un projet', p. 226.

seems most likely that the *Devise* was drawn up at exactly the same time as the document advocating a *passage particulier*. The *Devise* was then a supporting document which addressed itself to providing background information that would be needed if the Hospitallers and other crusaders were to take advantage of future hostilities between the Mongols and the Mamluks.

The *Devise* is a document of unique importance for the study of the structure and strength of the Mamluk army, but it is also of considerable importance for the light it sheds on Hospitaller policies after the fall of Acre. In the first decade of the fourteenth century the Order was, of course, primarily concerned with establishing its position on the island of Rhodes. It also had extensive interests on the island of Cyprus and in the kingdom of Cilician Armenia. In general, it was opposed to launching a major seaborne crusade. However, as both the documents it commissioned in 1306 or 1307 suggest, the Hospitallers did not entirely rule out a crusade against Egypt in the near future. In certain circumstances they were prepared to envisage a landing on the Nile Delta, and they researched the prospects for its success with great thoroughness.

8

The Hospitallers' Medical Tradition: 1291–1530

Anthony Luttrell

When the Hospitallers moved their Convent or headquarters to Cyprus after the loss of Acre and the final collapse of Latin Syria in 1291 they took with them a medical tradition which had earlier been transferred to Acre following the fall of Jerusalem in 1187. The Order of St John had grown out of a hospice in Jerusalem, and its Rule said nothing of military activities or of knighthood or nobility. It had gradually become a predominantly military institution, but even when the poor and sick were no longer of paramount concern the maintenance of its medical and charitable tradition was still of spiritual and moral significance, especially for opinion in the West. This divergence between declining tradition and active practice resulted in ambiguities. Many of the medical, liturgical and other regulations concerning hospital matters contained in the Order's statutes were applicable only in the main conventual hospital, while there was considerable terminological confusion between the poor, the sick and the sick poor; between pilgrims and other travellers; between charity and hospitality; and between medical hospitals, various types of hospice and the *infirmaria fratrum* reserved for the Hospitaller brethren. There was also a distinction between donats, who were members of the Hospital and under obedience to it, and those pensioners who could purchase or contract for board and lodging in retirement and old age.[1] The Hospitallers' original concern, reflected in their Rule, was with the poor, an involvement which was directed

---

[1] The bibliography is extensive but frequently second-hand and repetitive. Many statutes and other texts are published, with chaotic inaccuracy, in I. Pappalardo, *Storia Sanitaria dell'Ordine Gerosolimitano di Malta dalle Origini al Presente* (Rome, 1958); bibliography in W. von Ballestrem, 'Die Hospitalität des Ordens', in *Der Johanniterorden/Der Malteserorden: Der ritterliche Orden des hl. Johannes vom Spital zu Jerusalem, seine Geschichte, seine Aufgaben*, ed. A. Wienand, 3rd edn (Cologne, 1988), and B. Waldstein-Wartenberg, *Die Vasallen Christi: Kulturgeschichte des Johanniterordens im Mittelalter* (Vienna, 1988), pp. 422–3.

increasingly to those poor or pilgrims who became ill. This expressed a contemporary urge to give practical help to the suffering as an end in itself rather than as a means through which the agent of the good works might hope to secure salvation.[2]

Every religious order had some general charitable obligations, and the different military orders undertook various hospitaller functions.[3] After 1291 the Hospital's brethren were aware of their Order's Benedictine origins in Jerusalem on the eve of the First Crusade of 1099, and of the way in which some sort of association or confraternity of lay brethren had developed into a religious order serving the poor, the sick and the pilgrims. They knew of the enlargement or rebuilding, before 1156, of a true medical hospital in the Convent of which it was said, presumably with some exaggeration, that it housed 2,000 patients and that over fifty dead were sometimes carried out of it in a single day. The Hospital had a tradition of extensive alms-giving to the poor, of doctors and surgeons, of nightly prayers in the hospital for benefactors and others led by the Order's priests, of provisions for orphans and lepers, of maternity wards, and of financial support, medicines and diet, burial arrangements and the treatment of those wounded in battle.[4] The Hospitallers' medical buildings and practices in the East may well have drawn on Islamic and Byzantine models; they were less likely to have been responsible for introducing Oriental medical methods to the Latin West.[5] However, the diffusion of the texts regulating the sick, their confession, beds and food, and their treatment as lords – *quasi domini*, matters which were indeed all found in the Hospital's Rule, did not necessarily result directly from the Order's own activities, since the prayer containing them was adapted from *ritualia* long in use in the West.[6]

The Order's Jerusalem legacy included the history of the Amalfitan hospice which functioned there before 1099 and the carefully concocted legends or *miracula* which were reinterpreted after 1291 by the talented Hospitaller, William of Santo Stefano.[7] These legends invested the Hospital with the

[2] Cf. G. Lagleder, *Die Ordensregel der Johanniter/Malteser* (Saint Ottilien, 1983), pp. 76–8.

[3] Cf. C. Probst, *Der Deutsche Orden und sein Medizinalwesen in Preussen: Hospital, Firmarie und Artz bis 1525* (Bad Godesberg, 1969). The Templars took over a major hospital in Constantinople after 1204: T. Miller, 'The Sampson Hospital of Constantinople', *Byzantinische Forschungen*, **15** (1990), pp. 128–30.

[4] J. Riley-Smith, *The Knights of St John of Jerusalem and Cyprus: c. 1050-1310* (London, 1967), pp. 247–9, 332–8 *et passim*; H. Buschhausen, *Die italienische Bauplastik im Königsreich Jerusalem von König Wilhem II. bis Kaiser Friedrich II.* (Vienna, 1978), pp. 240–3/ figs 27–31; R. Hiestand, 'Die Anfänge der Johanniter', in *Die geistlichen Ritterorden Europas*, ed. J. Fleckenstein and M. Hellmann (Sigmaringen, 1980). The Jerusalem building is also known from nineteenth-century plans.

[5] The proposals in T. Miller, 'The Knights of Saint John and the Hospitals of the Latin West', *Speculum*, **53** (1978), with bibliography, should be treated with considerable caution.

[6] K. Sinclair, 'The French Prayer for the Sick in the Hospital of the Knights of Saint John of Jerusalem at Acre', *Medieval Studies*, **40** (1978).

[7] Riley-Smith, pp. 32–7.

prestige of a bogus continuity stretching back into ancient times, placing many New Testament events in its Jerusalem building and even corrupting Old Testament stories of Melchior and Judas Maccabeus in order to take the tradition of alms and service to the poor back before Christian times.[8] A rhymed Anglo-Norman translation of the Rule, possibly made at Clerkenwell in London, contained these legends which, in that version, preceded the Rule and were evidently invented before 1187, possibly between 1140 and 1160; the Anglo-Norman version was copied in England between about 1300 and 1310.[9] The *miracula*, which were also used to facilitate fund-raising in the West,[10] were being copied and translated, often in manuscripts of the Rule and statutes, during the fourteenth and fifteenth centuries.[11] A Latin version was copied at Rhodes in about 1366 into a chancery formulary in which it served as an introduction to a long list of papal privileges granted to the Hospital.[12]

Well into the fifteenth century the main hospital at Jerusalem excited the admiration of pilgrims who continued to use the enormous building; in 1395, for example, Niccolò da Martoni mentioned the great hall and separate rooms used by pilgrims.[13] Another hospital which sheltered German-speaking pilgrims and others in Jerusalem was under German management but subordinate to the Master of the Order of St John at least after 1143; it had two storeys with halls one above another and a separate church.[14] In Acre, where the Order had a hospital by 1155,[15] there was possibly a large pilgrim hospice on the east side of the Hospitallers' central courtyard and apparently a hospital for the sick a little way south of the main Hospitaller complex.[16] The Order had a number

---

[8] Selected texts, discussion and bibliography in *RHC Occid*, 5 (Paris, 1895), pp. cix–xxviii, 401–35.

[9] *The Hospitallers' 'Riwle'*, ed. K. Sinclair (London, 1984); cf. idem, 'New Light on Early Hospitaller Practices', *Revue Bénédictine*, 96 (1986).

[10] K. Borchardt, 'Two Forged Thirteenth-Century Letters for Hospitallers in Franconia', Chapter 6 above, pp. 52–6.

[11] The present author has prepared a chronological list of mss to be published in a forthcoming work on the *Miracula* by Antoine Calvet.

[12] Arxiu de la Corona d'Aragó, Barcelona, Gran Priorato de Catalunya, Armari 24, vol. 13, fols 135v–136v.

[13] S. Schein, 'Latin Hospices in Jerusalem in the Late Middle Ages', *Zeitschrift des Deutschen Palästina-Vereins*, 101 (1985).

[14] Excavation evidence in A. Ovadiah, 'A Restored Complex of the Twelfth Century in Jerusalem', in *Actes du XVe Congrès International d'Etudes byzantines*, 2 (Athens, 1981); N. von Holst, *Der Deutsche Ritterorden und seine Bauten von Jerusalem bis Sevilla von Thorn bis Narva* (Berlin, 1981), pp. 27–9, 218–19; discussion in H. Kluger, *Hochmeister Hermann von Salza und Kaiser Friedrich II.* (Marburg, 1987), pp. 126–34.

[15] *CH*, 237, 471; cf. Riley-Smith, pp. 247–8.

[16] Excavation and other data, still debatable in interpretation, in B. Dichter, *The Orders and Churches of Crusader Acre* (Acre, 1979), p. 51; Z. Goldmann, *Akko in the Time of the Crusades: the Convent of the Order of St John* (Acre, 1987), pp. 22–5 (figs 3, 11). Cf. Goldmann's plans in Wienand, pp. 107, 115; cf. Riley-Smith, pp. 247–9, and D. Jacoby, 'Les Communes italiennes et les Ordres militaires à Acre: Aspects juridiques, territoriaux et militaires (1104–1187), 1191–1291', in *Etat et*

of hospitals elsewhere in the East[17] and there was possibly an infirmary for Hospitaller brethren in the Syrian countryside;[18] they seem to have held the pilgrim hospice at Abu Gosh on the road to Jerusalem, a pilgrimage site thought to be the biblical Emmaus, where a church was added to a square Muslim courtyard building which had once been a *caravanserai*.[19] The Hospital's chapel just outside the castle entrance at Crac des Chevaliers was decorated with frescoes showing the medical saint, Pantaleon, and his miracles.[20]

The Anglo-Norman *Riwle*, possibly datable between 1140 and 1160, elaborated on the brief medical provisions in the original Rule which had probably been written by about 1140; for example, it laid down that new-born babies were to sleep in cots apart from their mothers, a provision reappearing in the medical statutes of 1182.[21] A statute of 1176 allocated the produce of the two *casalia* of *Sainte Marie* and *Caphaer* north of Jerusalem for the provision of white bread for the Jerusalem hospital.[22] Six later statutes spoke of white bread and many other foods and fruits given on medical advice, of syrups, of urine tests, of staff numbers and night duty, and of finance, and they also listed six *casalia* devoted to the production of grain, meat and other supplies for the Conventual hospital; in addition to the two mentioned in 1176, these were Mount Gabriel and Cotquinanti both unidentified, *Sareth* or *Saarethe* and *Cole* or Chola, which the Hospital acquired in 1189 and which certainly had a warehouse.[23]

Colonisation au moyen âge et à la Renaissance, ed. M. Balard (Lyon, 1989), pp. 200–4, 210–11, fig. 2 (showing side rooms?). The Hospitaller church clearly lay to the south of the main complex and the *domus infirmorum* south of that. Possibly the large vaulted building east of the main courtyard was originally the brethren's residence which became a pilgrim hospice (*hospitale*) when the brethren's residence or *auberge* (*hospitium, alberge* or *herbazium* on the maps) was moved nearer to the new walls in the suburb of Montmusard. Goldmann, p. 25, pl. XI (3), compares the facade of this presumed *domus infirmorum* with its upper and lower doorways and its staircases to those of the presumed fourteenth-century hospital at Rhodes (below, pp. 222–3) thus suggesting a continuity, but A. Gabriel, *La Cité de Rhodes: MCCCX-MDCCII*, 2 vols (Paris, 1921–1923), 2, pp. 9–10, and E. Kollias, *The Knights of Rhodes: the Palace and the City* (Athens, 1991), pp. 136–7, show that the Rhodian doorways and staircase were sixteenth-century alterations.

[17] For example, *CH*, 59, 244, 355 (Nablus); 79, 82 (Mont Pèlerin); 104 (*casale* of Turbessel); 258 (Toron); 665 (Antioch). Cf. J. Richard, 'Hospitals and Hospital Congregations in the Latin Kingdom during the First Period of the Frankish Conquest', in *Outremer: Studies in the History of the Crusading Kingdom of Jerusalem presented to J. Prawer*, ed. B. Kedar et al. (Jerusalem, 1982), pp. 90–91.

[18] For example, D. Pringle, 'Aqua Bella: the Interpretation of a Crusader Courtyard Building', in *The Horns of Hattin*, ed. B. Kedar (Jerusalem, 1992), pp. 163–7; idem, *The Churches of the Crusader Kingdom of Jerusalem: a Corpus*, 1 (Cambridge, 1993), p. 250.

[19] R. de Vaux and A-M. Steve, *Fouilles à Qaryet el- 'Enab, Abu Gôsh Palestine* (Paris, 1950), pp. 92–104; Pringle, *Churches*, 1, pp. 7–17.

[20] J. Folda, 'Crusader Frescoes at Crac des Chevaliers and Marqab Castle', *Dumbarton Oaks Papers*, 36, 1982, pp. 192–6.

[21] '*Riwle*', pp. 23–4, 57; *CH*, 627.

[22] *CH*, 494.

[23] A hitherto unnoticed fragment containing unknown statutes in Latin, probably datable post-1206, in Archives départementales des Bouches-du-Rhône, Marseilles, 56 H 4055; on Chola, see Riley-Smith, pp. 427 n. 2, 457.

The prayers of the sick in the Conventual hospital, which were to be recited by Hospitaller priests who came there every evening to pray for its benefactors and for the sick themselves, were probably composed at Acre in about 1197, but the text, in French, survives in only two manuscripts, of which the later is datable *c.* 1315; it may not have been used on Rhodes.[24] A Latin treatise, which was probably copied in about 1300 and bound with a group of Hospitaller materials including the Rule and statutes in German, the *miracula* in Latin and other documents such as papal bulls and imperial acts, discussed all sorts of matters concerning hospitals, doctors and patients. It was presumably used by Hospitallers, probably in Syria, although nothing in it indicated that it was describing the Hospitallers' hospital.[25]

When the Hospitallers established their Convent at Limassol in southern Cyprus in 1291, their resources were so low that in 1292 the complement there was fixed at a mere forty Hospitaller knights and ten sergeants-at-arms, each with two mounts, a squire and a page.[26] In March 1306 the Master explained to the Aragonese king that the Order lacked the resources to maintain the sick without borrowing at usury.[27] The military orders badly needed to present their Western public with a convincing role, and during their trials after 1307 the Templars were at pains to emphasize the extent of their alms-giving.[28] In 1297 the Hospitallers were said to be intending to build a new hospital for the sick and the poor at Limassol, and it was explicitly described as a replacement for the hospital in Acre which had formerly served needy pilgrims and the poor.[29] Statutes dating from 1300 to 1304 subsequently mentioned the Conventual hospital, the sick, the oaths of the resident doctors and surgeons, and the brethren's infirmary at Limassol.[30]

In about 1310 the Convent moved to Rhodes, and a Conventual hospital was apparently set up in an existing building somewhere near the sea walls.[31]

---

[24] L. Le Grand, 'La Prière des Malades dans les Hôpitaux de l'Ordre de Saint-Jean de Jérusalem', *Bibliothèque de l'Ecole des Chartes*, 57 (1896).

[25] An unnoticed item once in the Benedictine abbey of Bendickburen south of Munich, in Bayerische Staatsbibliothek, Munich, ms. Lat. 1245, fols 135–139; cf. *Catalogus Codicum Latinorum Bibliothecae Regiae Monacensis*, 1/2, 2nd edn (Munich, 1894), p. 218, with inaccuracies. The text awaits detailed investigation.

[26] Unpublished statutes in Marseilles, 56 H 4055; various mss of the statutes contain important and unpublished variations.

[27] Text in H. Finke, *Acta Aragonensia*, 3 (Berlin, 1922), p. 146.

[28] A. Demurger, *Vie et Mort de l'Ordre du Temple: 1118–1314*, 2nd edn (Paris, 1989), pp. 282–3.

[29] *CH*, 4336; this hospital may never have been built.

[30] *CH*, 4515 #5, 18, 4549 #19, 4612 #2, 4672 #1-4, 7, 11. The *Ospitel* and *ostel* of the *saiens* at Limassol of 1301 (ibid., 4549 #1, 10) did not refer to a hospital, the Latin translation as *in hospitio* being made at Rhodes in 1357: K. Sinclair, 'The Hospital, Hospice and Church of the Healthy belonging to the Knights of St John of Jerusalem on Cyprus', *Medium Aevum*, 49 (1980).

[31] In 1440 a *turrim que vulgariter dicebatur Turris Infirmarie Veteris* was near the walls of the *collachium* and the tower overlooking the port: Malta, Cod. 354, fol. 268, kindly communicated by Fotini Karassava-Tsilingiri and requiring further consideration.

As early as 1311 statutes referred to the *hospital dels seignors malades* at Rhodes and to a separate *enfermerie* for the brethren.[32] In 1314 the chapter general decreed the building of a proper hospital, allocating it 30,000 besants or about 6,750 florins per year from the two Rhodian *casalia* of Salakos and Apollona, with further incomes from Phileremos if those of the other two should prove insufficient.[33] An English visitor of 1345 wrote 'below the castle is the house of the hospital, mother, nurse, doctor, protector and servant to all the infirm'.[34] This may have been the two-storeyed building in the area of the arsenal close to the port on which were apparently placed the arms of Masters who ruled between 1319 and 1355, while on the adjacent building were those of Fr. Roger de Pins, Master from 1355 to 1365; with its vaulted upper floor and a chapel, it could well have been designed as a hospital.[35] In fact, a statute of 1357 decreed that the hospital, to serve both pilgrims and the 'poor sick', should continue to do so, as was the custom.[36] This task must have been accomplished, since in about 1420 Cristoforo Buondelmonti wrote of an area occupied by the *munitio* or arsenal which included the hospital which sheltered pilgrims.[37] The Conventual hospital lay within the *castrum* or *collachium* which was that part of the city reserved, in theory at least, to the Hospitaller brethren; there was no indication that it was available to the Greeks or other non-Latins.

Visitors continued to remark on the Conventual hospital. In 1395 Niccolò da Martoni reported that the Rhodian hospital had beds for pilgrims and the sick with doctors always on duty and the giving of great alms, *magna helemosina*; a few paupers were served meat and bread by the brethren and many others were given bread at the hospital.[38] In the same year the Lord of Anglure remarked that both sick and poor were received in it when ill.[39] In about 1420 Emmanuele Piloti wrote of ruined Rhodian merchants, presumably Latins, who ended their lives there in poverty.[40] More noble pilgrims also stayed in a hospice founded in 1391 outside the *collachium* but within the *borgo* by the Italian

---

[32] Biblioteca Vaticana, Vatican, ms. Vat. Lat. 3136, fols 66–68 ##2, 22.

[33] Text in Gabriel, **2**, p. 221.

[34] *Infra castrum est domus Hospitalis, mater, nutrix, medica, tutrix et ancilla infirmantibus cunctis*: text in G. Golubovich, *Biblioteca Bio-bibliografica della Terra Santa e dell'Oriente francescano*, **4** (Quaracchi, 1923), pp. 444–5.

[35] G. Jacopi, 'Monumenti di Arte Cavalleresca', *Clara Rhodos*, **1** (1923), p. 161; figs 134–6. Cf. Gabriel, **1**, pp. 9–11; **2**, pp. 34, 73; pl. XXII (i), and Kollias, pp. 136–9, pl. 115; there seems to be no published plan of this building which is now the archaeological institute.

[36] A. Luttrell, 'Rhodes Town: 1306–1350' (forthcoming).

[37] As cited in Gabriel, **2**, pp. 7, 9–10.

[38] 'Relation du Pèlerinage à Jérusalem de Nicolas de Martoni, notaire italien: 1394–1395', ed. E. Legrand, *ROL*, **3** (1895) pp. 584–5, 640.

[39] *La Saint Voyage de Jherusalem du Seigneur d'Anglure*, ed. F. Bonnardot and A. Longnon (Paris, 1878), p. 9.

[40] *Traité d'Emmanuel Piloti sur le Passage en Terre Sainte: 1420*, ed. P.-H. Dopp (Louvain and Paris, 1958), p.157.

Fr. Domenico de Alamania, and maintained by the Italian brethren who provided masses but not food.[41] The tradition of assistance to pilgrims remained strong, and in 1402–3 the Order made a potentially profitable, but ultimately abortive, agreement with the Egyptian sultan for concessions which would have allowed the Hospitallers to take pilgrims to the Syrian ports and to the holy places in and around Jerusalem.[42] In 1413 Fr. Pierre Pausedieu, Castellan of Afandou some 20 km south of Rhodes city, founded and endowed a hospice there to shelter travellers of all nations.[43] The Order's assistance was a reality to many pilgrims in the East, and on Cyprus in 1418 Nompar of Caumont stayed first in a Hospitaller house between Famagusta and Nicosia and then in the Order's 'great hostel' in Nicosia.[44] As late as the 1480s the Master of Rhodes was furnishing the old Jerusalem hospital.[45]

The Catalan Master, Fr. Antoni Fluvià, died in 1437 bequeathing 10,000 florins for a new Conventual hospital. Land was purchased and work began in 1440; after many financial difficulties the complex was finished sufficiently for the hospital to be transferred to it in 1483. On the ground level of this impressive courtyard building were stores and, facing outwards on to the street, shops to be let out for income. Medical matters were concentrated upstairs in a great open two-aisled ward with an altar or chapel in it and with curious cubicles built into the thicknesses of the walls: there was a smaller hall, refectory, kitchens, separate rooms and so on.[46] The hospital was described by the Czech pilgrim John Lord of Lobkowicz in 1493 when he and his servant were lodged there and were fed on white bread and wine:

> That house, the Infirmary, is all built of cut stone and the inside is a straight square. And windows great and broad all around, that there is little wall between these windows: but one window next to the other, so that one may look into the house, and all of it is finely painted. Now the Master of Rhodes has endowed that house, that any man being Christian, of whatever lowly or great rank, who shall come there, if he be sick and ask for it for God's sake, should at once be taken in; and there he is at once provided with medicine and other necessities, to wit food and drink and bedclothes. If an important person, he is given a room of his own; and if any lesser man, then there is a fine hall, very long, and in it made beds in double

[41] A. Luttrell, *The Hospitallers of Rhodes and their Mediterranean World* (London, 1992), **X**, pp. 192–3, 199–200; described in *Andanças e viajes de un hidalgo español: Pero Tafur (1436–1439)*, ed. M. Jiménez de la Espada et al., rev. edn (Barcelona, 1982), p. 49.

[42] Texts and discussion in Luttrell, *Mediterranean World*, **X**, pp. 194–207.

[43] Malta, Cod. 339, fols 72v–73v.

[44] A. Luttrell, 'The Hospitallers of Rhodes between Tuscany and Jerusalem: 1306–1431', *Revue Mabillon*, **64** (1992), pp. 130 *et passim*; the systematic analysis of accounts of visitors to Rhodes is an important *desideratum*.

[45] Schein, 'Latin Hospices', p. 91.

[46] Gabriel, **2**, pp. 14–36, and F. Karassava-Tsilingiri, 'The Fifteenth-century Hospital of Rhodes', Chapter 10 below; this paper has profited greatly from the unpublished work of Fotini Karassava-Tsilingiri.

row, and on some of them sick people are lying. And these beds are well made with clean white bedclothes, and on each bed there is a red cloth blanket, for there it is not as cold as [in Bohemia]. And near each of these beds a door opens upon the balcony, so that any of these sick can go out to take the air, whenever he chooses, upon that balcony; and there too he has a privy. Also in that house is a great kitchen, and in it several cooks, that prepare food for the sick. Also it is ordained, that each of these sick has a servant, that looks after him and serves him, whatever he needs. Also two doctors are ordained for this, sworn leeches, who look after the sick twice each day: once in the morning and once again in the evening. And there these doctors having in the morning examined his water, if anything from the Pharmacy be needed for him for his illness, they at once put to paper what he needs; there is next a Pharmacy endowed by the same Master. The officials appointed for this at once take this at the Pharmacy, though it be several florins' worth. And for that medicine the sick need pay nothing. Further the same doctors write a paper, what sort of dish should be given him, and when; and there the officials appointed for this must so provide this, what time these doctors write and order it. And these things are entrusted to three men: one Knight of the Order and two clerks, all of them being on oath for this. Also at that time I saw how the sick were served their meals in silver dishes, and they drink too from silver spoons. And none need pay anything for his stay there, except he freely of his goodwill gives anything to the servant that has waited upon him.[47]

Behind this activity lay a carefully organized administration. In 1440, the year in which the new building was begun, a detailed set of statutes provided probably the first major revisions of the Hospital's medical regulations since those of 1182. This and subsequent legislation controlled the inspection of stores, the oaths of officials, appointments of chaplains, confession and prayer, diet and clothing, precautions against fraud, burial, alms and bequests. The Hospitaller, a brother of the Order, remained in overall charge. There was some discussion of problems such as those arising when incurable Hospitallers occupied rooms for many months while there was no space for those who might be saved. Attention continued to be paid to symbolic matters and the maintenance of tradition. Every year on Maundy Thursday the Master's seneschal was to wash the feet of the poor, 'our lords the sick', while the Master entitled himself as 'guardian of the poor of Christ' – *pauperum Christi custos*.[48] The Master himself and his twelve companions were reported to feed twelve

---

[47] As translated in [C. von Schwarzenberg], 'What a Pilgrim saw at Rhodes', *Annales de l'Ordre Souverain Militaire de Malte*, 26 (1968), p. 104.

[48] Texts and details in Gabriel, 2, pp. 29–32, 35–6, 221–6; Pappalardo, pp. 80–81 126–7, 133–50, 162–4, 166–77, 218–23; and H. von Zwehl, *Nachrichten über die Armen- und Kranken Fürsorge des Ordens von Hospital des heil. Johannes von Jerusalem oder Souveränen Malteser-Ritterordens* (Rome, 1911), pp. 13–24. Gabriel, 2, p. 34, judges that the new hospital was exclusively reserved to the sick, but certainly there were exceptions. The *infirmarius* and the brethren's infirmary are not studied here. There seems to be no evidence for isolation wards on Rhodes.

paupers with their own hands every day.[49] It had been the custom that the responsions and other dues arriving from the West were carried before the sick in the Conventual hospital and only taken thereafter to the Treasury,[50] but that observance was in disuse by about 1340.[51]

The Conventual hospital also treated war casualties. In 1445, following Mamluk attacks on Rhodes, certificates of mutilation in war were issued so that those who, for example, had had a hand amputated in the hospital would not be regarded as criminals. In the same year the Master, somewhat exceptionally, conferred a medical degree, following lengthy examination, allowing a Jewish doctor, Jacuda Gratiano, *fisicus et professor artis medicine* who was the son of another Jewish doctor, to practise in the Conventual hospital after taking an oath on the Jewish holy scriptures. The doctors were to visit the wards twice a day, and one was to be on duty at night; there were to be two physicians paid 250 florins a year and two surgeons at 120 florins yearly. A scribe was to write down all prescriptions, and there were strict rules for the pharmacy where poisons were to be kept under lock and key.[52] The personnel included women, such as the slave Helena from Hungary who was freed in 1414 in recognition of her services to the sick, while in 1421 another slave, Jacobinus Armenus, was given his freedom in return for three years' work which he was to complete in the hospital.[53] In the fifteenth century, at least, the brethren's infirmary seems to have been within the main Conventual hospital where individual Hospitallers could have a private room.[54] In 1391 it was enacted that the commander of the lesser island of Kos was to have a garrison of twenty-

---

[49] Pero Tafur, *Andanças*, p. 49: probably written in about 1454.

[50] Riley-Smith, p. 331.

[51] Bibliothèque Nationale, Paris, ms. Lat. 4191, fol. 131v.

[52] Texts of 1440, 1445 and 1446 in Papparlardo, pp. 134–7, 142–3, 152–4, 156–7, and in R. Valentini, 'L'Infermeria degli Ospitalieri di S. Giovanni e i Minorati di Guerra', *Atti e Memorie della Accademia di Storia dell'Arte Sanitaria*, ser. 2, **16** (1950). The salaries seem low. Physicians from the West were promised a salary which, between 1385 and 1402, rose from 200 to 400 florins plus board, while in 1414 a surgeon was to be given 150 florins: Malta, Cod. 323, fol. 205; Cod. 325, fol. 174; Cod. 332, fol. 164v; Cod. 338, fol. 211v. In 1427 the Jewish doctor Vitale Gratiano received a papal licence to practise for the Hospital on Christian patients: text in *Pontificia Commissio ad Redigendum Codicem Iuris Canonici Orientalis: Fontes*, series III, 14 part 2: *Acta Martini PP. V (1417–1431)*, ed. A. Taŭtu (Rome, 1980), pp. 846–7.

[53] A. Luttrell, *Latin Greece, the Hospitallers and the Crusades: 1291–1440* (London, 1982), **V**, pp. 98–9. Nicoleta Cibo, *religionis nostre soror*, held a Rhodian vineyard before 1436, but she was of a leading Rhodian family and her case was evidently an exception: Malta, Cod. 352, fols 140–140v. The Hospitaller *soror* Margarita de Nigroponte had her own house and dispensed bread and alms in Rhodes before 1347: text in A. Luttrell, 'Emphyteutic Grants in Rhodes Town: 1347–1348', *Papers in European Legal History: Trabajos de Derecho Histórico Europeo en Homenaje a Ferran Valls i Taberner*, **5** (Barcelona, 1992), pp. 1414–15.

[54] For example, Pappalardo, pp. 146–7. From the fifteenth century the Conventual hospital was often termed the *infermaria*.

five brethren with a doctor, an apothecary and medical supplies.[55] Attention given to public health in the *borgo* included detailed regulations for doctors and apothecaries; by 1441 there was a Latin hospice of Saint Mary to maintain paupers, and by 1442 there was a Greek hospice, also for paupers. Legislation of 1509 concerned two *domini sanitatis* or health commissioners, one Latin and one Greek, who were elected annually to impose strict measures against plague which included control of landings from shipping and on occasion, forty days of isolation; there were licences for burials, segregation arrangements for lepers, and measures to keep rubbish out of the sea.[56] When a major earthquake hit Kos in 1493, the government of Rhodes immediately sent doctors, medicines and supplies in a well-organized example of sustained disaster relief.[57] The introduction of printing facilitated the dissemination of information about the Hospital's medical and charitable roles, for example through the Vice Chancellor Guillaume Caoursin's popular illustrated works and the famous *Ricordi* of Fr. Sabba da Castiglione.[58]

Overall costs would have been virtually incalculable. Roughly 6,750 florins were allocated to the Conventual hospital from incomes on Rhodes in 1314.[59] When 5,000 ducats reached Rhodes at a moment of financial crisis in 1409 some 1,450 ducats, or 29 per cent of the total, were allotted to the hospital, the pharmacy and medical salaries.[60] A very incomplete budget for the Convent's expenses, paid mainly out of European rather than Rhodian incomes, was drawn up in about 1478 and showed expenses at Rhodes on the church, the hospital, the food and pay of Hospitallers and mercenaries, the stores and so on at a total cost of 92,060 florins per year. Of this sum, 7,000 florins, or roughly 7.5 per cent, almost the same proportion as in 1314, was allotted to the Conventual hospital, its pharmacy, its doctors and surgeons, while an overall sum for expenses on grain included further unspecified expenditures on lepers, nurses, orphans and foundlings.[61] Such figures reflected the importance to the Order of its hospital on Rhodes, which constituted not only a religious obligation and a source of ideological strength, but also a show-piece to impress a visiting public which would transmit the resulting image throughout Latin Europe, thereby helping to justify the Hospitallers' extensive possessions and privileges in the West; the Conventual hospital was to some extent a public relations exercise.

---

[55] J. Delaville le Roulx, *Les Hospitaliers à Rhodes jusqu' à la mort de Philibert de Naillac: 1310–1421* (Paris, 1913), pp. 230–31.

[56] Archivio Vaticano, Reg. Lat. 384, fol. 82v; 390, fols 173–173v. On public health, see National Library of Malta, Biblioteca, ms. 740 part 1, fols 3v, 26v–28, 34v, 36v–39, 55v–56v, 57v–59v, partly published in Pappalardo, pp. 166–7, 170–72, 175–7.

[57] Malta, Cod. 77, fols 110v–115.

[58] References in Luttrell, *Latin Greece*, II, pp. 146–50; cf. Waldstein-Wartenberg, *Vasallen*, pl. 11.

[59] Above, p. 64.

[60] Malta, Cod. 339, fols 206v–207.

[61] Paris, ms. Lat. 13, 824, fols 95v–96v.

The astonishing initial success of the Order in Jerusalem after 1099 produced a great wave of donations in the West, and that involved the acquisition of property and its organization into communities of brethren grouped in priories and commanderies, as well as the sending of men and responsions to the East. These brethren had a general hospitaller obligation to the poor and sick and, more specifically, to the maintenance of hospices for pilgrims and travellers, particularly in the many places where houses were located along major routes. That development took place within a wider context. The late eleventh century had been a time of religious enthusiasm which was reflected in the reformed papacy, in new monastic movements, in the earliest crusades and in other developments which came together in the emergence of the Order of St John at Jerusalem. In the West, on the other hand, many small groupings, confraternities and individuals founded hospitals, occasionally entrusting them to the Hospitallers. Often such small hospitals and hospices had no significant endowment and little permanent organization; while founders died and enthusiasms dwindled. Thus local bishops sometimes faced a dilemma which they might solve by transferring institutions in difficulty to a well-established body such as the Hospital. By 1300, however, times were changing. While donations and testamentary bequests to the Order decreased, the loss by 1291 of all its Syrian possessions and incomes forced the Hospital to concentrate on exporting its Western resources to the East. Furthermore, welfare institutions and responsibilities were increasingly becoming the concern of municipal authorities and lay confraternities.[62] There was a particular example of this process at Hall in Swabia, where in 1249 the town council united its hospital to that of the Hospitallers, who were not however bound to receive the seriously ill, but in 1319 the authorities took the hospital back because the Hospitallers were serving the poor so badly.[63]

Strangely, none of the Hospital's medieval saints or *beati* was connected with military activity or, the founder apart, with the Convent in the East; some were holy women. There was no sign of any such medieval tradition in the Hospital's liturgical calendars, although there were genuine local cults. The professed Hospitaller sisters were often of more noble birth than the men, but they seldom, if ever, did hospital work. The crusaders found a separate female hospice attached to the Benedictines in Jerusalem in 1099, but apparently it did not depend on the men's hospital. A fourteenth-century Western chronicler made the unlikely claim that there had also been a female hospital associated with the Order's German hospital in Jerusalem. The Hospitallers had a female house of St Mary Magdalene at Acre in 1219, but there is no evidence that professed sisters did medical work there or in Jerusalem. Pious Hospitaller saints such as St Toscana, a widow who wore the Hospitaller habit and had a cell near the Order's hospital in Verona probably late in the twelfth century, and St

[62] S. Reicke, *Das deutsche Spital und sein Recht im Mittelalter*, 1 (Stuttgart, 1932), pp. 93–111.

[63] Ibid., pp. 104–5, 110–11; W. Rödel, *Das Grosspriorat Deutschland des Johanniter-Ordens im Ubergang vom Mittelalter zur Reformation*, 2nd edn. (Cologne, 1972), pp. 140–41.

Ubaldescha at Pisa, who died in about 1206, did tend the Order's sick and poor, but were probably donats rather than professed Hospitaller sisters. St Flor of Beaulieu near Cahors, who died in 1347, was of noble birth and a fully professed Hospitaller; she lived a saintly life but it was not that of a medical nurse.[64]

The Order of St John did play a leading hospitaller role in some places in the West. For example, in and near Arles, which was situated on the routes along the Rhône and where there was an early Hospitaller establishment, there were in the thirteenth century some twenty hospitals or leprosies for about 6,000 people, most of them caring for travellers or the poor rather than the sick. Easily the first and by far the largest foundation there, that of St Thomas in Trinquetaille the suburb across the Rhône, was made by the archbishop who granted it to the Hospitallers in about 1116–19; other hospitals at Arles came only after 1172. By 1338 this house at Trinquetaille was no longer functioning as a hospital but merely fed two paupers and gave some weekly alms; its buildings were destroyed by war in 1358. Yet it was not poor; in 1338 it housed two Hospitaller *milites*, two priests, four sergeants and six donats, five of them noble donats, while the former Templar house in Arles sustained six Hospitallers, one *miles*, one priest and four sergeants, plus six donats, four of them noble. The crisis had, however, come by 1373 when the two houses supported only eight Hospitaller brethren.[65]

The situation varied greatly from priory to priory and from commandery to commandery. A number of houses were situated on roads across the Alpine passes and along the Via Emilia and other routes leading to Rome or to Italian ports and embarkation points for the East; others were located along the pilgrim roads to Santiago in Galicia.[66] Hospice buildings, sometimes just a hall

---

[64] A. Luttrell, 'The Spiritual Life of the Hospitallers of Rhodes', in *Die Spiritualität der Ritterorden im Mittelalter*, ed. Z. Nowak (Toruń, 1993). F. Tommasi, 'Uomini e donne negli ordini militari di Terrasanta: per il problema delle case doppie e miste negli ordini giovannita, templare e teutonico (secc. XII–XIV)', in *Doppelklöster und andere Formen der Symbiose männlicher und weiblicher Religiosen im Mittelalter*, ed. K. Elm and M. Parisse (Berlin, 1992), p. 182, considers that the 1181 statutes and Johannes of Würzburg implied women nurses in Jerusalem; however, those texts mentioned women and maternity patients but not women nurses, let alone professed sisters. In 1219 there was a *domus Hospitalis in qua habitant sorores Hospitalis* at Acre: *CH*, 1656. L. Tacchella, *I Cavalieri di Malta in Liguria* (Genoa, 1977), p. 46, speaks of *consorelle* and *converse* serving in the Hospital at Genoa in 1251, but the document only mentions entry into the *religio* and the reception of its habit. Idem, *Le 'Donate' nella Storia del Sovrano Militare Ordine di Malta* (Verona, 1987), p. 14, claims that *donate claustrali* served the poor, the sick and pilgrims, but his source is a description (by Giacomo Bosio) of Sigena in the sixteenth century and it makes no reference to these categories.

[65] G. Giordanengo, 'Les Hôpitaux arlésiens du XIIe au XIVe siècle', in *Assistance et Charité = Cahiers de Fanjeaux*, **13** (Toulouse, 1978).

[66] Broad, if superficial, survey in E. Schermerhorn, *On the Trail of the Eight-Pointed Cross: a Study of the Heritage of the Knights Hospitaller in Feudal Europe* (New York, 1940), pp. 59–81; select details and bibliography, not here repeated, in Luttrell, *Latin Greece*, IX, pp. 369–77; idem, 'Tuscany and Jerusalem', pp. 118–21; Waldstein-Wartenberg, *Vasallen*, pp. 99–107, 128–34, 423; J. Matellanes Merchán and E. Rodríguez-Picavea Matilla, 'Las Ordenes militares en las Etapas castellanas del Camino de Santiago', in *El Camino de Santiago. la Hospitalidad monastica y las Peregrinaciones*, ed. H. Santiago-Otero (Salamanca, 1992), pp. 344–50.

and chapel, may often have been acquired rather than designed by the Hospitallers, or they may simply have been constructed in a local manner so that
there was no specifically Hospitaller hospital style. Occasionally the hospice
ward was built above the Hospitaller church as at Faenza, at Taufers in the
Tirol, at Nccharelz in Germany and at Torphichen in Scotland; however, this
disposition was not limited exclusively to Hospitaller houses.[67] Other arrangements, also not exclusive to the Hospital, involved corridors, internal doors,
windows and observation holes in the floor which permitted those in the
wards or dormitories to pass into churches or chapels to assist at services or to
attend mass without leaving their ward or bed.[68] The foundation text of 1298
for a hospice for the poor sick and pilgrims at Niederweisel in Hesse declared
that it should allow those confined to the ward to see the host at mass, and the
room, immediately above the church, did have three openings in its floor.[69]
Hospices and wards were often located in buildings physically separate from
the church or chapel. The placing of wards above, or immediately adjoining,
the chapel was doubtless a matter of convenience, yet the hospice or ward was,
in some sense, a religious place in which the inmates were associated with the
liturgy. Indulgences had been given at the Hospital's *palais de malades* in
Acre,[70] and both those who died in the hospital at Rhodes and those who visited
it benefited from various indulgences.[71]

There were hospices and poorhouses in the West, their existence or survival
often determined by local patterns of patronage and endowment. The Hospitallers occasionally maintained leprosies,[72] and in England they collected and
buried the corpses of executed felons,[73] but by the thirteenth century there
were increasingly problems with brethren dissipating charitable endowments
and failing to provide hospitality.[74] The obituary book of the Order's house
at Eskiltuna in Sweden recorded the death, probably in about 1310, of *frater
magister Arnaldus medicus*, that is a Hospitaller with some type of medical qualification, [75] but genuine Hospitaller medical hospitals were rare. Some houses
retained a doctor for a small annual fee to take some care either of the brethren
or of the poor. At Naples in 1373 there was a hospice for paupers and a *medicus*

[67] E. Grunsky, *Doppelgeschossige Johanniterkirchen und verwandte Bauten* (Düsseldorf, 1970), partly
repeated in Wienand, pp. 409–21.

[68] E. Ganter, 'Les Chapelles-Hôpitaux de l'Ordre de Saint-Jean de Jérusalem', *Annales de
L'Ordre Souverain Militaire de Malte*, **19** (1961).

[69] Wienand, pp. 419–20, 639–40, with plans and section.

[70] H. Michelant and G. Raynaud, *Itinéraires à Jérusalem et Descriptions de Terre Sainte redigés en
française au XIe, XIIe, et XIIIe siècles* (Geneva, 1882), p. 235.

[71] Pero Tafur, *Andanças*, p. 48.

[72] Schermerhorn, p. 67, without sources; on the Cologne leprosy; Rödel, pl. XIII–XIV.

[73] R. Pugh, 'The Knights Hospitallers of England as Undertakers', *Speculum*, **56** (1981).

[74] Examples in Le Grand, 325 n. 1; on alms, Schermerhorn, pp. 74–6; Waldstein-Wartenberg,
Vasallen, pp. 138–9.

[75] I. Collijn, *Ete Nekrologium fran Johanniterklostret i Eskilstuna* (Uppsala, 1929), p. 17.

who looked after its sick.[76] At Toulouse, where the Order had long had a hospital in the bourg and another in the city, there was a steady tradition of donations, often quite humble ones, made by lay folk through wills, annual gifts and burial arrangements; sometimes such people became donats of the Hospital. Toulouse was exceptional in that the Hospitaller hospital founded in the Templar house in about 1408 had nearly a hundred beds for the poor and sick when destroyed by fire in 1446.[77] In 1373 the hospital by the sea at Genoa, a major travel centre, catered for the poor and for pilgrims who fell ill, with a surgeon and a physician retained to treat them; there were separate hospitals for men, with forty beds, a salaried manager and two male attendants, and for women, with thirty-two beds and a female servant caring for the poor, the sick and foundlings, each baby having a wet nurse and the Order providing dowries to marry off its girl foundlings.[78] The Hospitallers, who also had parishes and occasionally schools, were to some extent acting like other branches of the Church in their welfare concerns.[79]

Such charitable and welfare activities were badly affected by the Great Plague and the other crises of the fourteenth century. An English inquest of 1338 showed an *Infirmaria* then containing six sick brethren at Chippenham near Cambridge, while the commandery at Skirbeck in Lancaster had twenty paupers in its hospice and 40 at its gate every day, and Carbrook fed thirteen paupers daily; but little other charitable activity was recorded in that priory.[80] In 1418 the house at Cerisiers was a centre for brethren and donats of the Priory of France who contracted leprosy.[81] In 1338 a survey of houses west of the Rhône, in the very heartland of the Hospitaller West, showed limited expenditures on alms and on doctors and medicines for the brethren, although there was a small hospice for the sick poor and for maternity cases at Monteilh and a hospital at Aix-en-Provence also for the sick poor, which had just one female

---

[76] Luttrell, *Latin Greece*, IX, p. 372.

[77] J. Mundy, 'Charity and Social Work in Toulouse: 1100–1250', *Traditio*, 22 (1966), with many examples.

[78] Archivio Vaticano, Collectorie 431 A, fols 4 and 8 suggest that the women's hospital included nine Hospitaller sisters, but fol. 6v shows that they were in a *monasterium* next to the hospital: amend Tommasi, p. 197, on this point. Cf. V. Persoglio, *Sant'Ugo cavaliere ospitaliere gerosolimitano e la Commenda di S. Giovanni di Prè: cenni storicocritici* (Genoa, 1877), pp. 356–8. No document supports claims that Hospitaller *sorores* did medical work at Genoa. The hospital and its restoration are extensively documented: Tacchella, *Cavalieri*, pp. 11–73, 159–62, and *La Commenda di Prè: un Ospedale Genovese del Medioevo*, ed. G. Rossini (Rome, 1992), with full bibliography. A pauper hospital of San Leonardo di Bisanzio, with a lay *hospitalarius* and six or eight beds in 1373 (Collectorie 431 A, fols 3, 5v, 7v), was at Cavi di Lavagna on the coast road east of Genoa: Tacchella, *Cavalieri*, pp. 52, 105–7.

[79] The social security role is studied, but mainly before 1291, in J. von Steynitz, *Mittelalterliche Hospitäler der Orden und Städte als Einrichtungen der Sozialen Sicherung* (Berlin, 1970).

[80] L. Larking, *The Knights Hospitallers in England being the Report of Prior Philip de Thame to the Grand Master Elyan de Vilanova for A.D. 1338* (London, 1857), pp. 61, 78, 82.

[81] Malta, Cod. 342, fols 17–17v.

servant and a doctor available; furthermore, three paupers were fed daily at
the very large house at Manosque and two daily at Trinquetaille across the
Rhône from Arles.[82] By 1373 things were undoubtedly worse. Thus at Bersantino
near Manfredonia in Puglia, where it was said that great sums had once been
spent, the commander was in 1373 an absentee and nothing was being expended
on *curialitas* or charity.[83] In the Priory of France eight poor were sheltered nightly
at Douai and there was an expenditure on alms at Avesne-le-Sec, but there
was no other sign of any hospice or hospital in that priory in 1373.[84] Of the
thirty houses in the diocese of Besançon in 1373 many were ruined or abandoned
and only two claimed to provide even minimum alms [85]

In some priories the commanderies were mostly small and poor; in the
Priory of Pisa, for example, there were houses in 1373 with an annual profit
of 25 florins or less, in some cases nil. Corneto was an exception, having a hospital
with twenty beds and a doctor which was managed by a married couple who
received 22 florins a year.[86] In the Priory of Bohemia, also in 1373, the poor
were given bread three times a week in Prague, while at Strakonice fourteen
paupers received bread and occasionally money as well; there were from six
to–fourteen poor at Boleslava.[87] There were hospitals of some sort at Glatz,
Zittau, Breslau and Lowenberg in Silesia, at Strakonice and Prague in Bohemia;
at Laa, Enns, Vienna and Furstenfeld in Austria; and elsewhere.[88] Shortly before
1371 the prior provided for twelve poor and sick at Prague and he constructed
and endowed a hospital at Svetla.[89] In the German priory there was also a considerable number of hospices, although there too there was little sign that they
were genuine medical hospitals.[90]

While the most profound and unprecedented economic depression plunged
welfare activity into a crisis in general, the older hospital tradition was maintained
as a result of a new development within the Order itself in which leading Hospitallers, often utilizing personal wealth, despite their vows of poverty,

---

[82] B. Beaucage, *Visites générales des Commanderies de l'Ordre des Hospitaliers dépendantes du Grand
Prieuré de Saint-Gilles: 1338* (Aix-en-Provence, 1982), pp. 68–9, 351, 354, 463–70, 595, 599 *et
passim*.

[83] Luttrell, *Latin Greece*, **IX**, p. 373.

[84] A-M. Legras, *L'Enquête pontificale de 1373 sur l'Ordre des Hospitaliers de Saint-Jean de Jérusalem*
(Paris, 1987), pp. 288, 311 *et passim*.

[85] G. Moyse, 'Les Hospitaliers de Saint-Jean de Jérusalem dans le diocèse de Besançon en 1373',
Mélanges de l'Ecole française de Rome: Moyen Age – Temps Modernes, **85** (1973), 475, 486.

[86] Luttrell, 'Tuscany and Jerusalem', p. 120 *et passim*; further detail in idem, *Latin Greece*, **IX**,
passim.

[87] V. Novotny, 'Inquisito Domorum Hospitalis S. Johannis Hierosolimitani per Pragensem Archid-
ioecesim facta anno 1373', *Historicky Archiv*, **19** (1900), pp. 22, 45, 58.

[88] B. Waldstein-Wartenberg, 'Die kulturellen Leistungen des Grosspriorates Böhmen-Osterreich
in Mittelalter', *Annales de l'Ordre Souverain Militaire de Malte*, **33** (1975), surveys a selection of the
extensive evidence.

[89] Státní Ustredí Archiv, Prague, Archives of the Hospitaller Priory of Bohemia, no. 2386.

[90] Reicke, pp. 101–6; B. Waldstein-Wartenberg, 'Donaten – Confratres – Pfründner: Die Brud-
erschaften des Ordens', *Annales de l'Ordre Souverain Militaire de Malte*, **31** (1973), p. 15.

occasionally set up individual foundations. In 1325 the Master, Fr. Hélion de Villeneuve, founded and endowed a hospice and chapel for the poor sick which was documented at Aix-en-Provence in 1338.[91] Just before 1360 Fr. Napoleone de Tibertis, Prior of Venice, apparently acting in association with various laymen, founded the hospice of Santa Caterina next to the commandery in Venice, not for the sick and pilgrims but for the poor and aged; it was managed by a married couple and in 1414 there were eight downstairs beds and further beds upstairs, but after 1451 the local confraternity of San Giorgio gradually secured control of the building.[92] In about 1408 Fr. Raymond de Lescure, Prior of Toulouse, founded a hospital in the former Templar house there both for the sick and poor and for Santiago pilgrims, endowing it with the incomes of the Hospitaller house at Garidech.[93] Most spectacularly, in about 1445 Fr. Juan de Beaumont, Prior of Navarre, endowed and established a large hospice for the poor and sick at Puente la Reina, also on the Santiago route.[94] The most famous such foundation was that made by the Master Fr. Antoni Fluvià of the new hospital at Rhodes.

The Hospitallers had another function, not strictly medical, in the provision of board and lodging, death-care facilities and posthumous prayer to single persons or couples, secular people who purchased or contracted for various forms of life pension or annuity. These newer forms of welfare generated funds which did not support the poor and sick through donations from the wealthier, but catered for individuals of some means who invested their own capital or incomes, often according to precisely worded contracts. Such arrangements were already quite common in the Toulouse area in the thirteenth century.[95] There were many pensioners in England where the unrestricted sale of pensions, sometimes to quite wealthy people, could become a business affair, but while it initially produced income the resulting expenditures had by 1328 helped to provoke a financial crisis.[96] Comparable systems were widespread in the German priory.[97] Part of the Hospital's charitable function was thus 'privatized' by being made to pay for itself.

The Order's sick constituted not a brotherhood or a formal confraternity, but rather a spiritual community with its own liturgy, its obligations such as those

---

[91] J. Raybaud, *Histoire des Grands Prieurs et du Prieuré de Saint-Gilles*, 1 (Nîmes, 1904), p. 278.

[92] Text and details in Luttrell, *Latin Greece*, IX, pp. 373–80, 328–3.

[93] Text in M. du Bourg, *Histoire du Grand-Prieuré de Toulouse* (Toulouse, 1882), appendix pp. xvii–iii (correct the date given as 1413).

[94] Luttrell, *Latin Greece*, IX, p. 370, with further bibliography; cf. L. Romera Iruela, 'La Fundación del Monasterio del Crucifijo en Puente la Reina', *Anuario de Estudios Medievales*, 11, (1981).

[95] Examples in Mundy, 'Charity and Social Work', pp. 257–74.

[96] Larking, pp. xxxvi, lix–x, 215–20 *et passim*; W. Rees, *A History of the Order of Saint John of Jerusalem in Wales and on the Welsh Border* (Cardiff, 1947), pp. 20–21, 58–9.

[97] Waldstein-Wartenberg, 'Donaten', pp. 16–18.

of making confession and testament, and its rights, such as those to treatment, burial, posthumous commemoration in prayer and so forth. After about 1300 the general trend was, despite occasional individual foundations, towards an often dramatic decline in the wealth of individual commanderies and of the number of brethren within them, so that community life and liturgy became increasingly rare, as did charity, hospitality and medical care; the sick lost their central place in the Order's life and ideology. The establishment of the hospital wards at Acre and at Rhodes in a separate building with its own chapel seemed to exemplify this detachment of the hospitaller function from the main activity of the brethren; service to the sick performed by Hospitaller knights and sergeants was replaced by treatment provided by a medical staff who, together with the Conventual hospital's own priests, came to form a separate community.[98] Yet the Conventual hospitals at Rhodes, and later on Malta, retained their importance precisely because they conspicuously maintained the ancient tradition of service to the poor and sick.

The existence there of its hospital effectively defined the Convent. When Rhodes fell to the Turks in 1522, the Master and Convent left on a small fleet carrying, *inter alia*, the Order's most precious holy relics and part of its archives. With hundreds of refugee Rhodians to support and many sick aboard ship, the medical tradition was soon in evidence. Reaching Sicily in April 1523, the Order installed its Conventual hospital in the priory building at Messina where the Master, Fr. Philippe Villiers de l'Isle Adam, went daily to feed the sick. That building overflowed with the sick and plague-stricken, and in the summer of 1523 the Conventual hospital was transferred to the galleon of the Prior of Saint-Gilles. The Master and Convent then sailed northwards, but plague kept them out of Naples harbour and so the Conventual hospital was set up in isolation at a deserted malarial spot by the shore to the west of Naples, in that part of Baia which looks westwards. The sick and healthy were installed in some ancient vaulted buildings described as 'grottos' and known as the cave of the Sibyl at Cuma, which were furnished with hangings, planks, tables and mats, and defended by ditches and artillery. Subsequently the hospital moved with the Convent to Civitavecchia, to Viterbo, to Corneto, to Villefranche, to Nice where it was installed in the commandery, to Siracusa and finally, in 1530, to Malta.[99] There a Conventual hospital was at once set up in a house in Birgu and a new hospital building was begun in 1532 and completed in 1533; by 1538 it had been decided to enlarge it.[100] The tradition was maintained and indeed,

[98] As suggested ibid., pp. 14–15; that work leans heavily on the scarcely typical German–Bohemian documentation, and (cf. Luttrell, 'Spiritual Life', 89) it confuses *confratres*, donats, the sick and others with confraternities.

[99] Pappalardo, pp. 192–202; on the Baia interlude, see J. Bosio, *Dell'Istoria della Sacra Religione et Ill.ma Militia di San Giovanni Gierosolimitano*, 3 (Rome, 1602), p. 16.

[100] A. Critien, *The Borgo Holy Infirmary now the St Scholastica Convent* (Malta, 1950), pp. 10–21; P. Cassar, *Medical History of Malta* (London, 1964), pp. 39–44; idem, 'Medical Life at Birgu in the Past', in *Birgu – a Maltese Maritime City*, ed. L. Bugeja et al., I (Malta, 1993).

the Conventual hospital continued to be governed by many of the statutes passed on Rhodes.[101]

The new city of Valletta, built after 1565, included a Conventual *infermeria*. The hospital at Birgu had not catered for pilgrims, who seldom passed through Malta, or for the Maltese population which had its own hospital at Rabat,[102] but the great hospital at Valletta and its numerous subsidiary institutions formed part of an extensive welfare apparatus designed to help placate the Catholic Maltese people.[103] That was a departure from the situation on Rhodes where the Conventual hospital had not served the Greek population. When the Order's government moved to Rome in the nineteenth century a Conventual hospital was found for it there,[104] and the Hospital, having lost its military function, continued its existence by reverting to the original hospitaller activity it had never entirely abandoned. With the enormous expansion of medical activity, modern health services have evolved in which non-governmental forms of health care are backed by compulsory national health insurance. The Order of Malta and independent national institutions, such as the St John's Ambulance Association service in Britain, and the *Malteser Hilfdienst* and the *Johanniter* in Germany have all come to play a significant role in society, building on the Hospitallers' medical tradition kept alive across some nine centuries.

---

[101] Pappalardo, p. 83.

[102] S. Fiorini, *Santo Spirito Hospital at Rabat, Malta: the Early Years to 1575* (Malta, 1989). The Rhodian surgeon Leonardo Myriti received citizenship in Malta in 1534: ibid., pp. 63–4.

[103] A. Williams, '*Xenodocium* to Sacred Infirmary: the Changing Role of the Hospital of the Order of St John, 1522–1631', chapter 11 below, pp. 100–1.

[104] Pappalardo, pp. 240–66.

9

Documentary and Archaeological Evidence for Greek Settlement in the Countryside of Rhodes in the Fourteenth and Early Fifteenth Centuries

Kara Hattersley-Smith

The topic of this paper forms part of a long-term project begun by Anthony Luttrell and Julian Chrysostomides on the Greek inhabitants of Rhodes during its occupation by the Hospitallers between 1306 and 1522.[1] The most important source of evidence are those portions of the Hospital's archive that survive in Malta.[2] They include registers beginning in 1346 which contain numerous examples of land grants naming tenants, conditions and rents, and provide topographical details and information on contiguous landholders. This evidence in turn raises questions concerning land measures, coinages, settlement in town and country, place-names and surviving architectural remains.

Clearly answers to these questions depend on detailed study not only in the archives but also in the field. It is as the field researcher that I became involved in this project, resulting so far in three trips to Rhodes: May 1990, October 1991, and November 1993.[3] On these occasions I received valuable help and advice from the Byzantine archaeological service of Rhodes. What follows is part of a preliminary report illustrating the connections between the modern toponomy of the island and those places mentioned in the Hospitaller documents that deal with land grants. On the basis of the evidence contained in these land grants it is possible to construct a picture of the towns, villages and countryside under the Hospitallers.

---

[1] A. Luttrell, 'Settlement on Rhodes, 1306–1366', in *Crusade and Settlement*, ed. P. Edbury (Cardiff, 1985), pp. 273–81; rpr. in A. Luttrell, *The Hospitallers of Rhodes and their Mediterranean World*, (Aldershot, 1992), no. V.

[2] Archives of the Order of St John, National Library of Malta, Valetta (hereafter Malta, Cod.); A. Luttrell, 'The Hospitallers at Rhodes 1306–1421', in *History of the Crusades*, 3, ed. K.M. Setton (Madison, 1975), pp. 278–313; E. Rossi, 'The Hospitallers at Rhodes, 1421–1523', in ibid., pp. 314–39.

[3] These trips have been funded by research and travel grants from: the British Federation of University Women; the British Society of Antiquaries; the Hellenic Foundation; and the Scouloudi Foundation (formerly the Twenty-Seven Foundation).

Figure 9.1   Map of Rhodes

One of the first things to emerge from my trips was that our project should for the time being exclude Rhodes town from detailed study since its history and archaeology have for some years been the focus of interest among the Greek archaeologists.[4] Another reason for concentrating on the island's smaller towns and countryside is that, although the toponomy of Rhodes has remained largely unchanged for centuries, detailed knowledge of that toponomy is disappearing.[5] As tourism attracts more and more people away from agriculture, so the names of fields, woods, vineyards and pastures around the towns and villages are forgotten. It is place-names of this kind that are preserved in the Hospitaller documents and, as our research has shown, can in many cases be plotted on the ground today.

This paper concentrates on two areas near the coast and an inland area for which there is both place-name and architectural evidence. It aims to show how the information in the registers of the fourteenth and early fifteenth centuries, referring to land grants in these areas, reflects the Hospitallers' concern for the defence of the island and how this affected their relations with the population. An assessment of the types of land grants made to the Greeks will be contrasted with the evidence for land grants made to the Latins.

The constant threat of attack from the Turks necessitated the construction and upkeep of numerous castles and towers, most of which were in view of one another and to which the rural population would flee in times of danger. One of the most impressive castles on the east side of the island is that of Archangelos (see Figure 9.1).[6] Today, Archangelos is a thriving town less than two km from the coast. It dominates a small fertile plain to the north and west, but is hidden from the sea by a cluster of hills that rise sharply to a height of 512 m to the south-east. A rocky outcrop with the ruins of the Hospitaller castle bars the only passage between the town and the coast.

Archangelos first appears in the register of 1347 as a *casale*,[7] which was an economic or agrarian unit of land. According to this entry in the register, Michaellus Culichi, the *protos* or headman of Archangelos, and his son-in-law Giorgio Philippi, were granted land in perpetual *emphyteusis* at a place called Sanctus Theodorus within the *casale* of Archangelos. The grant consisted of a *jardinum*, various trees, two fountains and seven *modiate* of land for which they paid an annual rent of one hundred aspers. This was one of the many such parcels of land granted to the Greeks in 1347 because, as is clearly stated at

---

[4] E. Kollias, *The City of Rhodes and the Palace of the Grand Master: From the Early Christian Period to the Conquest by the Turks (1522)* (Athens, 1988); idem, *The Knights of Rhodes: The Palace and the City* (Athens, 1991).

[5] Ch. Papachristodoulou, *Toponymikou Rodou* [The toponomy of Rhodes] (Rhodes, 1951); idem, *Symboli sto Toponymiko tis Rodou* [A contribution to the toponomy of Rhodes] (Rhodes, 1976).

[6] J.-C. Poutiers, 'Les établissements des Hospitaliers dans la mer Egée: villages fortifiés et bourgs maritimes', in *Ve Congrès international du Sud-Est Européen* (Belgrade, 1984).

[7] Malta, Cod. 327, fol. 248.

the beginning of this transaction, the Hospitallers did not have the manpower to cultivate the land themselves (*per domum nostram habiliter excolli non possunt*).

It seems likely that the place called Sanctus Theodorus is the same as the area about two km to the south-west of Archangelos known as Agios Theodoros and where there is a small, single-aisled church of Agioi Theodoroi.[8] This church is one of the island's few precisely dated churches from the Hospitaller period, with a donor portrait and inscription of 1372 (see Figure 9.2). The rest of the church's interior is decorated with the usual cycle of the Twelve Feasts in the nave vault, and busts and standing figures of saints and bishops on the upper and lower walls. The style of painting is Byzantine, reproducing contemporary Late Palaiologan art. It is worth noting that, until the beginning of the twentieth century, there was a settlement to the south of the church, on and below the line of the modern road. According to the local people, remnants of houses were still visible until ten to fifteen years ago when a large area was flattened to create a football pitch.

At the time the land grant was made to Michaellus Culichi in 1347, the castle at Archangelos clearly did not exist, for in early March 1399,[9] the inhabitants of Archangelos petitioned the Grand Master not to be compelled to build a castle or *fortalice*. Provision was instead made for them to take refuge in the castle of Feraklos, five km to the south. This piece of information helps to date the construction of Archangelos's castle as some time after 1399 but before 1457 when it was stormed by the Turks.[10] It also suggests that, though reluctant, the inhabitants may in the end have had to help in the construction of the castle.

On the west side of the island, further south than Archangelos and just over 2.5 km from the coast, is Apolakkia. Here, too, in 1347, the *protos* and *papas* of Apolakkia, Janni Matrigeni, was granted in perpetual *emphyteusis* a monastery together with a *jardinum*, seven beehives and an oil mill at a rent of 60 aspers per year.[11] He was also granted the monastery's twenty goats in return for an annual tithe.

In this case the exact position of the land grant is not stated in the document. However, in other cases, the boundaries of land grants are described as being contiguous to properties belonging to other Greeks or Latins, or as lying to the north, south, east or west of topographical features, such as rivers and mountains, or of conspicuous buildings such as mills. This kind of information is used to delineate the property granted, on 6 March 1359, to a Latin by the name of Antonio Cantarelli.[12] In contrast to the small land grants conveyed to

---

[8] Kollias, *The City of Rhodes*, p. 97 and fig. 45.

[9] Malta, Cod. 330, fol.121.

[10] F. Guy Sommi-Picanardi, *Itinéraire d'un Chevalier de Saint-Jean de Jérusalem dans l'Ile de Rhodes* (Lille, 1900), pp. 174–5; E. Rossi, p. 321.

[11] Malta, Cod. 317, fol. 247.

[12] Malta, Cod. 316, fols 307–307v.

Figure 9.3   Kitala: remains of the fortress

Figure 9.2   Church of Agioi 'Theodoroi':
donor portrait and inscription of 1372

the Greeks of Archangelos and Apolakkia, Antonio Cantarelli was granted a much larger tract of land, comprising the monastery of Artamiti and all its appurtenances, for his lifetime only and at a rent of fifty-five golden florins a year. The description of the property includes references to eighteen places, about a third of which are still known by the same names today, thus enabling us to gain some idea of the property's actual ground area. The first place to be mentioned is the monastery itself; today, the site is marked by a large modern church.[13] From the monastery the line of the property followed a valley with a stream which flowed from a place called Ambona, which we can reasonably assume to be a Latin's pronunciation of the Greek Embonas;[14] this town and the terraced hillsides surrounding it have long been the island's most prolific vine-growing area. In the sequence of recognizable names that then appear in the register the property is described as being contiguous with Kitala,[15] an area which lies to the north of Embonas and where, at the top of a rocky hill, there are still the remains of a fortress (see Figure 9.3). From here there are good views in all directions including an extensive stretch of the island's west coast. It seems likely that this site served both as a watchpost against marauding Turks and as a shelter for the local population, and perhaps even their livestock.

From Kitala the property extended north-eastwards to Lelo,[16] a region still so-called in the southern foothills of Profitis Elias mountain. Although several places are then listed which it has not yet been possible to locate, it is clear that the boundary line ascended the mountain at a place near Lelo and then descended to Apollona, one of the island's larger inland towns. By 1474 Apollona was the site of a Hospitaller castle of which only a segment of ruined wall survives in the town's centre.[17] From Apollona, the line of the property stretched roughly southwards back to Artamiti. A rough estimate of the total area covered by the property comes to about thirty-one sq km (c. 7,650 acres). In addition to this large area of land, Antonio Cantarelli was granted the monastery's 120 goats, a plough-team and four donkeys. A few years later, on 31 December 1365, the same property was granted to a Hospitaller for the same rent.[18]

The land grants examined in this paper reveal the great difference in size between the properties conveyed to Latins and those conveyed to Greeks. The Latin Antonio Cantarelli, and the Hospitaller after him, managed – at a rough estimate – over thirty sq km of land. By contrast, Michaellus Culichi, the Greek *protos* of Archangelos, was granted only seven *modiate* of land. The extent of the Rhodian *modiata* has yet to be quantified, but it is probably related to

[13] Papachristodoulou, *Toponymikou Rodou*, pp. 40–41.
[14] Ibid., pp. 47–8.
[15] Ibid., p. 33.
[16] Ibid., pp. 33–4.
[17] Malta, Cod. 75, fol. 70v; Papachristodoulou, *Toponymikou Rodou*, p. 40.
[18] Malta, Cod. 319, fol. 270.

the Byzantine *modios* which was between 850 and 1,000 sq m.[19] If one Rhodian *modiata* is estimated as equivalent to 1,000 sq m, then the area granted to Michaellus Culichi amounted to about 7,000 sq m (less than two acres). Although Latins were also granted small parcels of land, there are many more examples of minor grants to Greeks of anything between one and eight *modiate*.

The discrepancy in size between a grant of 7,000 sq m or less to a Greek and over 30 sq km to a Latin is to be expected in a society where the former belonged to the subject class and the latter to the ruling class. However, before any general or firm conclusions can be reached about the nature of Greek settlement on Rhodes, we have to embark on the next phase of our research in which we plan to select certain areas where the information contained in successive registers can be combined with surviving place-name and archaeological evidence to create a detailed map of the location and extent of land grants.

[19] E. Schilbach, *Byzantinische Metrologie* (Munich, 1970), pp. 76–81.

10

The Fifteenth-Century Hospital of Rhodes: Tradition and Innovation

Fotini Karassava-Tsilingiri

The Hospitallers started building a great hospital on Rhodes in 1440 following a bequest by their late Master, Fr. Antoni Fluvià (1428–1437), and by 1489 it was sufficiently advanced in construction for an inscription to be mounted commemorating its completion. The building, which now houses the town's Archaeological Museum, is the best preserved conventual hospital of the Order even after its extensive restoration by the Italians between 1914 and 1919 when its new use as a museum was established. The other conventual hospitals are either missing or greatly changed. The crusading hospital of Jerusalem is known only from a nineteenth-century plan;[1] the one at Acre is not securely identified,[2] nor is the first hospital of Rhodes, while that of Cyprus is missing altogether. We have a sound enough idea of what the first hospital of the Order at Birgu on Malta was like when it was first built,[3] as well as of the great hospital built somewhat later at Valletta.[4]

A hospital of the Order functioned on Rhodes by 1311,[5] and this was most probably replaced by a more suitable purpose-built building during the mastership of Fr. Roger de Pins.[6] This fourteenth-century hospital was by no means unusable in 1440 when the construction of the new one started, as it

[1] K. Schick, 'The Muristan, or the Hospital of St John in Jerusalem', *Palestine Exploration Fund Quarterly Statement* (London, 1902), pp. 49–53, plan 1.

[2] See Z. Goldmann, 'Die Bauten der Johanniter in Akkon' in *Der Johanniter/Der Maltesenorden: Der ritterliche Orden des hl. Johannes von Spital zu Jerusalem. Seine Geschichte, seine Aufgaben*, ed. A. Wienand, 3rd edn (Cologne, 1988), pp. 104–15, plans on pp. 107, 115.

[3] A. Critien, *The Borgo Holy Infirmary. now the Santa Scholastica Convent* (Malta, 1950).

[4] A. Critien, *Holy Infirmary Sketches* (Malta, 1950).

[5] See A. Luttrell, 'The Hospitallers' Medical Tradition: 1291–1530', Chapter 8 above, pp. 68–9. I am indebted to Dr Luttrell for letting me consult his paper in typescript and for much valuable advice.

[6] Ibid., also see A. Gabriel, *La Cité de Rhodes*, **2**, *Architecture Civile et Religieuse* (Paris, 1923), p. 73.

From *The Military Orders: Fighting for the Faith and Caring for the Sick*, ed. Malcolm Barber. Copyright © 1994 by Malcolm Barber. Published by Variorum, Ashgate Publishing Ltd, Gower House, Croft Road, Aldershot, Hampshire, GU11 3HR, Great Britain.

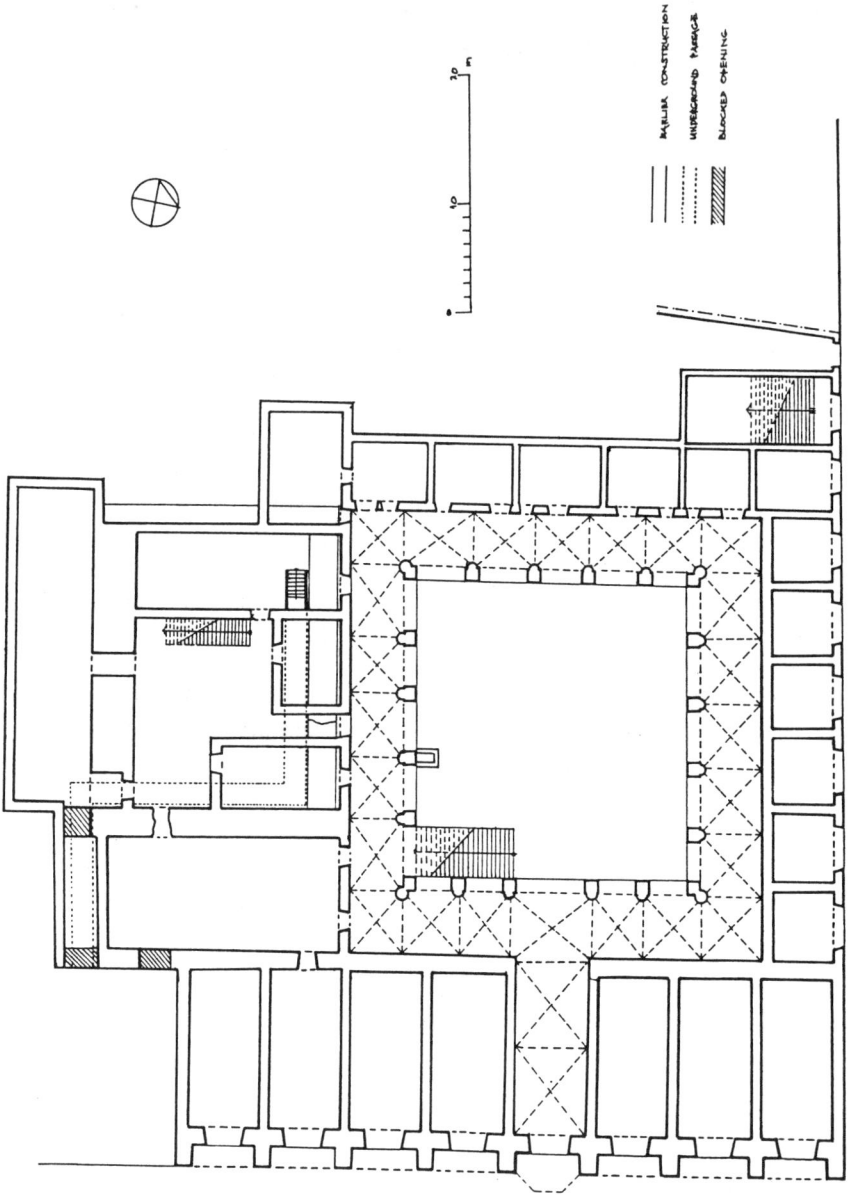

BARLUBA CONSTRUCTION
UNDERGROUND PASSAGE
BLOCKED OPENING

Figure 10.1   Hospital of Rhodes: plan of the ground floor

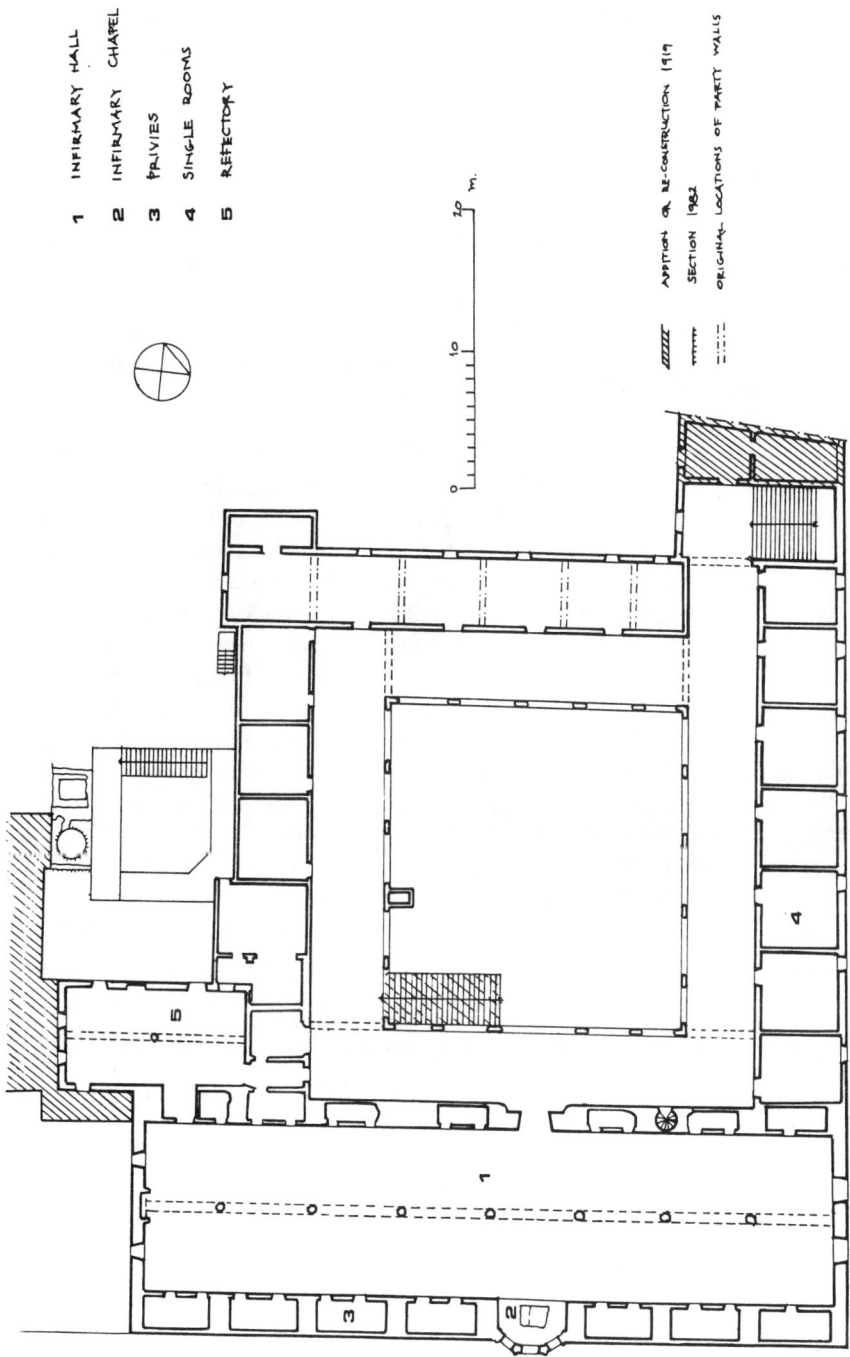

1 INFIRMARY HALL
2 INFIRMARY CHAPEL
3 PRIVIES
4 SINGLE ROOMS
5 REFECTORY

10 m.

10

0

ADDITION OR RE-CONSTRUCTION 1519
SECTION 1982
ORIGINAL LOCATIONS OF PARTY WALLS

Figure 10.2   Hospital of Rhodes: plan of the first floor

continued to be used until 1483 when the new building was at least ready to receive patients, if not actually completed.[7] The need to build a new hospital may have arisen from such factors as an increase in population or a change in hospital standards, but probably also from the Order's need of a prestigious project. During the hospital's fifty-year construction period the Order was frequently at war with the infidel and, to secure support from the West, it needed to impress the Latin Church and laity.[8] Moreover, Rhodes was being established as a pilgrimage centre in itself rather than a mere station on the road to Jerusalem, and a new grand hospital would therefore be most welcome. The first mention of a provision for this new hospital was in the will of Fr. Antoni Fluvià, the first Catalan Grand Master of the Order, in 1437.[9] Construction commenced a few years later, sometimes interrupted by financial difficulties or wars, and was completed in the decade following the Turkish siege of Rhodes and the earthquakes of 1481.

The hospital building consists of two storeys, arranged around two courtyards (Figures 10.1 and 10.2); the main courtyard is cloistered, and the entire east side of the first storey is occupied by the great hall of the infirmary. We have adequate evidence that this hall was used as the main hospital ward, housing a large number of sick; however, there were also single rooms, probably allocated to the higher officers of the Order and visiting nobility. There was probably a refectory nearby, in contact with the kitchen. There is also evidence of privies in cubicles, near the beds in the great hall.[10] The ground floor of the hospital housed mainly service rooms, but its east side was divided into eight bays, the most centrally placed of which was used as an entrance to the building, the rest being closed at the rear and rented out to provide income for the resident clergy.[11] The hospital chapel comprised a three-sided niche opening into the main ward, directly above the entrance.

The importance of the building was recognized early this century when Italian troops took possession of Rhodes.[12] Subsequently, between 1914 and 1921, the building was restored and converted into a museum.[13] The main authority

---

[7] In December 1483 a group of French brethren was ordered out of the old hospital which had recently been evacuated and its patients transferred to the new one. Malta, Cod. 76, fols 162–162v.

[8] On the founding of charitable institutions by the military orders to ensure a favourable attitude from the West, see Luttrell, Chapter 8 above, p. 73.

[9] The whereabouts of this will are unknown. The event is mentioned on the founding inscription of the hospital; text of the inscription in Gabriel, pp. 24–5. The bequest is mentioned also in Malta, Cod. 354, fol. 255. See also G. Bosia, Del' Istoria della Sacra Religione de San Giovanni Gerosolymitano, 2nd edn (Rome, 1629), 2, p. 209.

[10] C. von Schwarzenberg, 'What a Pilgrim saw at Rhodes', Annales de l'Ordre Souverain Militaire de Malte, 26 (1968), p. 104; text in Luttrell, Chapter 8 above, pp. 70–71.

[11] Cf. below, fn. 28.

[12] G. Gerola, 'I Monumenti Medioevali di tredici Sporadi', Annuario dela Regia Scuola Archeologica di Atene, 1 (1914), 169ff.

[13] Preliminary reports in G. Gerola, 'Il Restauro dello Spitale dei Cavallieri a Rodi', L'Arte (1914), and A. Maiuri, 'L'Ospedale dei Cavallieri a Rodi', Bolletine d'Arte del Ministero de Publica Istruccione (Rome, 1921).

on the Hospitaller buildings of the island at this time, the French architect Albert
Gabriel, was of the opinion that the general layout was not that of a hospital at
all, and classified it as an architectural type similar to that of an Anatolian *khan*
or caravanserai.[14] Gabriel cited the use of the Greek term *xenodochium* (hotel)
to designate the hospital on its founding inscription, as further support for the
theory that the building belonged to a wider type of hostelry. He attributed
only the main ward with the appended chapel to Western hospital design,
classifying it as a Hôtel-Dieu ward.[15] This theory was reiterated by subsequent
writers on the hospital and is more or less accepted to the present day.[16]

However, while buildings, such as hostelries, camps or monasteries designed
for the temporary or communal lodging of large groups of people, were
frequently built around a central courtyard, there is no evidence that the Hospitallers of Rhodes built their hospital on the pattern of an Anatolian road hostel.
Also, the fifteenth-century founders used the term *xenodochium* in its medieval
sense, meaning precisely a hospital. Indeed, their first hospital in Jerusalem
was designated by the same term.[17]

We know from both written and archaeological evidence, that this type of
hospital plan was often employed during the high Middle Ages. The earliest
dated example is known from a drawing: the monastic infirmary in the ideal
plan of St Gall of around 820, in which the building is arranged around one
square courtyard, with an appended chapel and services arranged close to it.
The functions of each area in the plan were very well described.[18] By the middle
of the twelfth century Cluny and Canterbury had similar infirmaries with
cloistered courtyards, remains of which still exist.[19] Hôtels-Dieu and monastic
hospitals, mainly Benedictine, very frequently followed the same planning
principle until the thirteenth century.[20] Major Byzantine hospitals also probably
followed a similar plan so far as can be deduced from their descriptions:[21]

---

[14] Gabriel, pp. 32–3. Cf. the plans of the *karavanseray* in Ch. Texier and R. Pullan, *Byzantine
Architecture* (London, 1864), pp. 130–31, pl. XXVII.

[15] Gabriel, p. 33.

[16] For example, Ch. Karuzos, *Rhodes* (Athens, 1949), p. 74; B. Waldstein-Wartenburg, 'Das Spital
der Johanniter in Rhodes in der Entwicklungsgeschichte der Kranken-hausbauten', *Artzt und Christ*,
3–4 (1977), pp. 179–96, more specifically compares it to a Seldjuk *khan*.

[17] See, for example, *CH*, 30.

[18] See T. Thompson and G. Goldin, *The Hospital, a Social and Architectural History* (London,
1975), pp. 10–12.

[19] K. Conant, *Cluny: Les églises et la maison du chef d'Ordre*, Medieval Academy of America, **17**
(Maçon, 1968), plan 1.

[20] Examples of Hôtels-Dieu in A. Erlander-Brandenburg, *La Cathédrale* (Paris, 1989), pp.
369–83 and *passim*. On monastic infirmaries, examples in U. Craemer, *Das Hospital als Bautyp des
Mittelalters* (Cologne, 1963); D. Jetter, *Geschichte des Hospitals*, 4 (Wiesbaden, 1980).

[21] Full description of a Byzantine hospital in a *typikon* of the eleventh century; text in P. Gautier,
'Le typicon du Christ Sauveur Pantocrator', *Revue d'Etudes Byzantines*, **32** (1974). See also a
description of another hospital of the same century in Constantinople in Anna Comnena, *Alexiad*,
II, *Corpus Scriptorum Historiae Byzantinae*, **1** (Bonn, 1839), pp. 345–6.

attempts at pictorial reconstructions of some of the most important ones, based on literary sources, have always pointed in this direction,[22] and there is some archaeological evidence to support this.[23]

For most of Europe, if we exclude Spain and Italy to a certain extent, this type of plan became almost obsolete by the end of the thirteenth century, roughly at the time when hospital construction was past its peak, giving way to an open-plan hospital, more suitable for extensions whenever the need should arise. Nevertheless, the open ward was still retained for many centuries, and there are cases where hospitals consist almost entirely of the open ward and the appended chapel.[24] However, the fact that the Hospitallers built such a hospital at Rhodes as late as the second half of the fifteenth century, and even later at Malta, indicates that up to the middle of the sixteenth century they had not yet abandoned the courtyard plan for their conventual hospitals. It may be significant that, when the site for the building was purchased in 1439, it already housed a square two-storeyed building with a courtyard – a palace belonging to a noble lady, as we are informed by a document of that year.[25] By the same decree the building was conceded to Helisseo Delamanna, a Latin Rhodian, to use as his family residence to prevent it from deteriorating until the infirmary was completed. Another decree of 1440 specified that the eight shops in front of the infirmary were to be rented out to provide income for the salaries of the resident clergy.[26] These documents suggest that the Hospitallers were probably initially unsure whether to re-use this building totally or in part, or to demolish it. When it was eventually pulled down, the builders of the new hospital re-used the foundations of this building in the main courtyard and eastern facade at least, as well as a portion of its walls in the auxiliary courtyard (Figure 10.1).[27] It is likely that the site's suitability as it was described in the decree, was partly related to the existence of a building with a convenient layout.

Earlier conventual hospitals of the Order probably followed the courtyard plan. A plan of the site of the hospital of Jerusalem published in 1902 suggests a courtyard but, as we do not know the exact location of the hospital in relation

[22] Pictorial representation of the Pantocrator hospital based on the *typikon* in A. Orlandos, 'I Anaparastasis tou en Konstantinoupolei Xenonos tis Monis Pantokratoros', *Epeteiris Etaireias Ellinikon Spoudon* (Athens, 1941). On the hospital of St Sampson in Constantinople, see T. Miller, 'The Sampson Hospital in Constantinople', *Byzantinische Forschungen*, **15** (1990).

[23] Ibid., also see W. Müller-Weiner, *Bildlexicon zur Topographie Istanbuls* (Tübingen, 1977), pp. 112–17.

[24] There is an extensive bibliography on Western hospitals; see examples of these smaller hospitals in Craemer, *Das Hospital*. Examples of lesser Hospitaller hospitals, usually preceptories in Europe can be found in E. Ganter, 'Les Chapelles-Hôpitaux de l'Ordre de Saint-Jean de Jérusalem', *Annales de l'Ordre Souverain Militaire de Malte*, **19** (1961) and E. Grunsky, *Doppelgeschossige Johanniterkirchen und verwandte Bauten* (Düsseldorf, 1970).

[25] Malta, Cod. 354, fol. 255.

[26] Text in I. Pappalardo, *Storia Sanitaria del' Ordine Gerosolimitano di Malta* (Rome, 1958), pp. 134, 135, 137–8, and in Gabriel, pp. 223–4.

[27] Maiuri, p. 220.

to the rest of the conventional buildings, the concept is vague.[28] At Acre, a thirteenth-century map shows a courtyard building as the *palatium infirmorum*, but the archaeological evidence published so far does not permit a definitive identification of the building.[29] We know nothing about the plans of the hospitals of Cyprus. As regards the one the Order built when it first obtained Rhodes, it is not securely identified: even if we follow its generally accepted identification of a fourteenth-century building located in the *Collachium*, the walled part of the city of Rhodes where the members of the Order lived,[30] no conclusions may be drawn as to its original layout since there have been two major alterations – one in the sixteenth century, and another in 1914 during its conversion to the Historical-Archaeological Institute of Rhodes. This design, though, was continued at Malta where the hospital built by the Grand Master, Fr. Philippe Villiers de l'Isle Adam, at Birgu, was one of two storeys and two courtyards, with a centrally placed great ward,[31] evidence which gives us reason to believe that, until their early years at Malta, the Hospitallers did not abandon the medieval architectural type of a quadrangular hospital with a courtyard, probably cloistered. It is also significant that at least some of the provincial hospitals of the Order in the Levant had quadrangular plans – for example, those at Constantinople[32] and Nablus,[33] the one at Abu Gosh[34] and a recently identified one at Aqua Bella,[35] as well as that of Espluga de Francoli in Catalonia two centuries later.[36] The hospital at Rhodes was completed in an era when, in Italy, another non-linear type was becoming popular – that of the cross-plan which, although it had existed in Italy since the thirteenth

---

[28] Plan in Schick, p. 50, plan 1.

[29] The excavator of the site, Z. Goldmann, identifies the hospital with a group of halls on Muslim foundations, but this identification is largely hypothetical. Plans in Goldmann, pp. 107 and 115. Thirteenth-century plans of the medieval city of Acre by Paulinus of Pozzuoli and Marino Sanudo the Elder published in A. Kestren, 'Acre, the Old City', in *The Maps of Acre*, ed. K. Dichter (Acre, 1973). The location of the hospital in the maps is confirmed by texts. See *CH*, 2612, 2662, *GC*, p. 152.

[30] Maiuri, p. 221; Gabriel, p. 73. The building, one of a very few datable to the fourteenth century which exist today on Rhodes, was identified on the basis of the magistral arms of Fr. Roger de Pins (1355–1365) on its facade and of a blocked pointed arch interpreted as a remains of a chapel. De Pins was associated with the completion of the hospital. See Luttrell, Chapter 8 above, p. 69.

[31] Critien, p. 14–19.

[32] On this hospital see D. Janin, *Les églises et les monasteres de Constantinople* (Paris, 1969), p. 578; description by a seventeenth-century traveller in D. d'Alessio, 'Recherches sur l'histoire de la Latinité de Constantinople', *Echos d'Orient*, **25** (1926), pp. 21–41.

[33] M. Benvenisti, *The Crusaders in the Holy Land* (New York, 1972), pp. 164–5.

[34] Plan in M. Avi-Yonah, *Encyclopedia of Excavations in the Holy Land*, **1** (Jerusalem, 1976), s.v. Abu-Gosh, plan 4.

[35] D. Pringle, 'Aqua Bella: The Interpretation of a Crusader courtyard building', in *The Horns of Ḥaṭṭin*, ed. B. Kedar (Jerusalem, 1992).

[36] For a description of this hospital see L. Martinel, 'Les Hôpitaux', in F. di Candida Gonzaga et al., *L'Architecture civile en Catalogne* (Paris, 1935), pp. 60–63.

century, was given a definitive form in the mid-fifteenth century by Filarete.[37] The adherence of the Rhodian builders to the cloistered courtyard plan thus further points to their following a tradition.

How much was new in the architecture of the hospital of Rhodes? The answer is not an easy one. The eight vaulted areas at the eastern front of the ground floor mentioned in the decree of 1440 appear to be a completely new feature in a hospital of the Order. We can conclude that these were a feature of the previous building on the site, and that their form, and probably their use, was identical in the new building. As regards latrines, it is suggested in the statutes of 1182 that, in the Jerusalem hospital at least, they were located outside the building.[38] In Rhodes they were hidden in the depth of the walls in the great hall near each bed and, if we believe a traveller of 1492, had adequate ventilation.[39] A similar solution may have existed in the infirmary of Cluny.[40] The smaller rooms at the northern and western sides of the hospital were probably a provision for brethren and noble patients. There are many cases of auxiliary courtyards in earlier hospitals, but it is not clear if they existed in previous Hospitaller hospitals. In this building the auxiliary courtyard clearly performed a service role, for it bordered on the hospital's vegetable and medicinal gardens.[41] The corresponding roles of the ground floor and first storey are not so obvious, but from what we know about the first floor it housed nursing functions, while the ground floor was probably an area for services, storerooms, and surgery. This arrangement was often followed in earlier hospitals, like that of Cluny, for reasons of hygiene.

Far from being an exotic or unusual feature in the Order's architectural history, the hospital at Rhodes had a plan which followed a well accepted and respected design principle. The layout was not a Hospitaller invention, although it was probably adopted by the Order for its hospitals very early in its history, its most likely origin being that of the Benedictine monastic *infirmariae*. Such was the Order's conservatism that it continued to follow this design principle at a time when it had been largely abandoned in the West. Its splendour, which was praised by contemporary visitors to Rhodes (perhaps with some exaggeration),[42] was achieved by incorporating into the layout some ingenious new features and finding new solutions to old problems, as well as by taking some care over the architectural decoration and tableware.

---

[37] On the evolution of this type see N. Pevsner, *A History of Building Types* (London, 1976), pp. 143–4, figs 9.10–9.13.

[38] *CH*, 627.

[39] See above n. 10.

[40] Thompson and Goldin, fig. 17; Conant, plan 1.

[41] Their location and layout were described in detail in Malta, Cod. 390, fol. 205–205v.

[42] Descriptions of contemporary travellers in R. Mitchell, *The Spring Voyage* (London, 1964); *Adanças e viajes de Pero Tafur, Por diversas Partes del mundo avidos (1435–1439)*, Colección de libros Españoles raros o curiosos, 8 (Madrid, 1878), p. 48. Pero Tafur was on Rhodes at the time of the funeral of Antoni Fluvià, but the description of the hospital was probably made on a later journey as it corresponds to the fifteenth-century hospital which did not yet exist. See a full description of the finished building in Schwarzenberg, p. 104 (see also above, pp. 70–71).

11

Xenodochium to Sacred Infirmary: the Changing Role of the Hospital of the Order of St John, 1522–1631

Ann Williams

The loss of Rhodes in 1522 sent the Convent of the Order of St John on its travels to the western Mediterranean. Removal from its strategic base close to the Ottoman empire, against which its crusading activities had been concentrated, was followed by eight years of uncertainty as to their next permanent home. In Italy in the 1520s the Knights were on the fringes of the conflict between Habsburg and Valois, and at Viterbo they were uncomfortably close to the wavering papacy and the sack of Rome in 1527. Even after the gift of Malta and Gozo had been accepted and the move made in 1530, the Order still hoped it might be given a more attractive site in Sicily, or even return to Rhodes. The Order might have been overwhelmed by these crises and turned into a tame military guard for the pope, a role which Clement VII, at least, seems to have contemplated.[1] Yet interestingly, the Order did not fall apart; rather, the years 1522–68 saw a run of important Chapters General dealing with all aspects of its activities, from its pressing financial difficulties to its religious life, its own government and the administration of the state it ruled. The hospital, of course, featured prominently in this legislation.

As Dr Luttrell has shown, the hospital commitment of the Order was strong from its very beginnings.[2] The Rhodes years saw a definition of this role, particularly in the fifteenth century with the building of the hospital there. The shape of the hospital's administration had already been set in the form it was to keep until its dissolution. The Hospitaller of the *Langue* of France was in charge of the hospital, although he remained responsible to the Grand Master and Council, and ultimately to the Chapter General for important decisions,

---

[1] Malta, Cod. Chapter General 1526, fols iiii (sic) r and v.

[2] See Chapter 8 above, pp. 64–5. See also T.S. Miller, 'The Knights of St John and the Hospitals of the Latin West', *Speculum*, **53** (1978), 719–20.

From *The Military Orders: Fighting for the Faith and Caring for the Sick*, ed. Malcolm Barber. Copyright © 1994 by Malcolm Barber. Published by Variorum, Ashgate Publishing Ltd, Gower House, Croft Road, Aldershot, Hampshire, GU11 3HR, Great Britain.

and for the confirmation of the appointment of officers below him. The
Infirmarian, also from the *Langue* of France, but a serjeant rather than a knight,
was in immediate charge of the running of the institution. He received the
sick, visited them in their beds and ensured that they received the medical
treatment recommended by the doctor. A scribe of the infirmary recorded these
details, and also recorded the testamentary wishes of the sick.[3]

Two *probi homines* or *prodomi* looked after the supplies of the hospital and
kept the accounts for the Treasury. The pharmacy was established, and a system
of checking the quality of drugs and medicaments was practised. Two doctors
and two surgeons treated the patients, and were obliged to make visits night
and morning on pain of fine for neglect. A chaplain, later the prior of the hospital,
administered the sacraments and coordinated the religious life of the community.
Limited responsibility was also accepted for the citizens of Rhodes. The
Grand Master set an example by feeding twelve poor people daily and, more
importantly, a Commissioner for the Poor saw to the destitute in the city.[4] *Domini
sanitatis* were set up in 1503 to deal with plague outbreaks, and a Guardian of
the Port supervised quarantine.

As the Order moved around the Mediterranean, it set up temporary hospitals,
for example in the Sala Grande of the Priory in Messina and in Viterbo, where
plague in 1525 and 1527 added to the problems of an already overstretched
economy.[5] The settlement in Malta meant yet another foundation but, at
first, the courtyard hospital of Rhodes was not copied. In 1533 the Grand Master
dedicated an area in the Birgu peninsula, and a number of houses were pulled
down to make a small purpose-built ward. There was an immediate need for
beds for the wounded. In 1538 more rooms were added, and this hospital
remained in use until 1574. On occasions of extreme crisis, such as the siege
in 1565, the facilities proved inadequate, and private houses were taken over,
to be used both by the Knights and the Maltese.[6]

The Order was not in an easy position in Malta. It had received the islands
from Charles V, who also committed the Knights to defend Maghribi Tripoli
– a difficult task in both manpower and supplies.[7] The local élite was not enthusiastic about exchanging the surveillance of the Viceroy of Sicily for a more
immediate ruler. The islands were poor both in population and resources, and
the arrangement made with Sicily for a corn supply kept the Knights continually
beholden to the Spanish monarch's representative in the more fertile island.
The religious life of the Maltese was already in the care of the bishop of
Malta. The gift to the Knights enshrined his position, and ensured that the
final choice in the matter of election to the See would be out of the Order's

---

[3] Malta, Cod. 282, Chapter General 1454, fols xviii v–xix r, summarizes the statutes to that time.

[4] Malta, Cod. 80, Liber Conciliorum, 11, ix. 1504, fol. 113v.

[5] Malta, Cod. 286, fol. iiv.

[6] A. Critien, *The Borgo Holy Infirmary* (Malta, 1950), pp. 14–17.

[7] Malta, Cod. 286, fols xxv r–xxviii r, April 1530.s.

hands.[8] The Order of St John itself was an exempt Order, owing direct allegiance to the papacy, and from this point of view, Malta was a bad exchange for distant Rhodes. The famous visit of Monsignor Duzzina in 1574–75 revealed the dismal state of the island's churches and chapels and added fuel to the pope's demands for a permanent inquisitor in Malta. Rumours of heresy within the Order itself and the unruly behaviour of the younger knights were other reasons for wanting this supervision. By the early 1580s another authority was established and made its home in Birgu, now Vittoriosa, after the siege.[9] The three jurisdictions of knight, bishop and inquisitor sat uneasily side by side.

The secular problems of the islands were growing too. The successful lifting of the siege in 1656 brought some respect between ruler and ruled, but also meant that the Knights finally committed themselves to staying in Malta. The decision in 1566 to build a new city, Valletta, across the harbour from the Three Cities, was a tangible proof of this.[10] The building of fortifications, public works and private houses attracted labourers from the villages and some 8,000 workers from Sicily, rapidly increasing the population of the whole urban complex. The initial blight on the Three Cities after the founding of Valletta was soon overcome, and the whole harbour area was densely settled. In 1590 there were 3,250 inhabitants in Valletta and 4,500 in the Three Cities. By 1614 the number had reached approximately 10,700 in Valletta and over 6,500 in the Three Cities. In 1632 Valletta's population had declined to 8,600 but numbers in the Three Cities' had risen to just under 10,000.[11]

The structural poverty in these cities was exacerbated by the fear and the reality of plague, war and hunger. The shifting population of a port and the presence of a very mixed group of Knights, Maltese, foreigners and slaves made matters worse. The Order itself was riven with conflict. Not confined to a *Collachio*, or separate area of the city, as they had been in Rhodes, the younger knights got into brawls with each other, with the Maltese and with people from abroad.[12] The Council records of the sixteenth century note continual disciplinary action against them.[13] The deposition of Grand Master La Cassière was partly a protest against an aged and bad-tempered individual, but was much more the culmination of a period of great adjustment to the Order's changed position, its loss of territories, and the conflicts of Church and State in the sixteenth century.

When Hugues Loubenx de la Verdalle was elected in 1582, with the blessing of the pope and the gift of a cardinal's hat, he had serious problems of recon-

---

[8] Ibid.

[9] A. Bonnici, *Storija ta'l-Inkizizzjoni ta' Malta*, 1 (Rabat and Malta, 1990), pp. 85–102.

[10] Malta, Cod. 288, Chapter General 1565, fol. 120r.

[11] B. Blouet, *The Story of Malta* (London, 1967), 174.s.

[12] Malta, Cod. 294, Chapter General 1603, fols 65v–66v, for the last debate on the importance of a *collachio*.

[13] See, for example, Malta, Cod. 89, fol. 41r, 1555 and ibid., 92, fols 159r and v, 1570.

ciliation and public order to solve in a decade and a half of plague, famine and poverty in the islands. He and his successors tackled the problem by re-emphasizing, reinterpreting and extending the hospital and charitable role of the Order. The move to the city of Valletta meant the building of new public works, like the Church of St John and the fortifications.[14] There was also a need for a bigger hospital on the new site. La Cassière himself had given the initial funds for this building. It was to be constructed on the south-east corner of Valletta, near the water, to give easy access for the wounded. Because there were similar space considerations, the plan adopted was based on that of the Hospital of Santo Spirito in Rome, not perhaps the most up-to-date model.[15]

The term for hospital in the documents up to the late sixteenth century was, commonly, *xenodochium* or *infirmaria*. The later phrase, *Sacra Infirmaria*, with capital letters, was not used. The Ordinances of the 1520 Rhodes Chapter General, recorded in Malta in 1538, do, it is true, head the hospital section, *Ordinati sopra la sacra* (lower case s) *Infirmaria*,[16] but the real change does not come until the 1580s when the new hospital expanded under Verdalle and coordinated the charitable activities of the Order, the house for exposed infants, the hospital for women and the refuge for prostitutes, as well as treatment outside the hospital for less serious diseases, and for poor law relief for the Maltese and for the Rhodians who had loyally followed the Knights.

It is always difficult to be very dogmatic about reasons for the Order's actions as its members were not given to introspection about their motives, but there are many indications to suggest that the Knights did not ignore the religious debate of the Catholic Reformation. The Vice-Chancellor Martin de Rojas attended the Council of Trent, although he later joined the inquisitorial side. Both pope and inquisitor spoke of reform, and the Chapters General of the Order emphasized it too. The assembly under Martin Garzes in 1597, counting the cost of the Order's financial commitments, stressed the supreme importance of the need

> ... to sustain the burdens and pious duties which are owed in our conventual xenodochium and Sacred Infirmary to our lords the sick and to the poor of Christ, together with the accustomed public distribution of alms, both in Malta and elsewhere.[17]

In 1612, a new oath for the *prodomi* recognized the breadth of their role for assistance both within and without the hospital, and their number was increased to four. The personal commitment of the Knights was re-emphasized by

---

[14] Q. Hughes, *The Building of Malta During the Period of the Knights of St John of Jerusalem, 1530–1795* (London, 1956), pp. 152–5.

[15] I should like to thank Michael Ellul, formerly Government Architect in Malta, who restored the Hospital of the Order in Valletta, for his generosity in lending me his drawings of the hospital and its associated buildings for the book I am writing on the hospital and the charitable work of the Order.

[16] Malta, Cod. 287, fol. 38r.

[17] Malta, Cod. 293, fol. 51r.

giving each *Langue* in turn a week's tour of duty in the hospital.[18] They were to employ such knights, serjeants and novices as were necessary for the care of the sick in the *Sacra Infirmaria* – a system that was to impress eighteenth-century travellers. This personal service was not new, but the organization in a vastly increased institution was. Similarly, the roles of doctor and surgeon were tightened up, while a collection of scribes recorded information about patients, medicines, stores and utensils. Nothing was wasted, right down to the worn-out linen which was given to elderly poor women outside the gates. The guardians of the various wards kept an eye on a very regimented system of care. Slaves carried out the domestic work and cooking for the complex.

Other institutions supported the Sacred Infirmary, an example being the creation of a Convent of St Ursula under the protection of the Order, which was needed to provide assistance in caring for women. Its Rule did not match that of the Ursuline Order word-for-word, but the nuns were to follow the prayers of the best reformed Order in Italy.[19]

They kept a house for women, initially in Vittoriosa and then, after 1592, in Valletta. In 1618 Germina Vella, née Ciantar, bequeathed her property to the Confraternity of Our Lady of Charity in the church of St Paul Shipwrecked for the support of girls from the Ciantar family, or poor girls from Siggiewi. After numerous lawsuits, and finally a papal brief, this charity was diverted to the Magdalenes, who looked after girls in danger of falling into prostitution, although eight places were kept for poor Ciantar relations.[20] Exposed children were sent out to be nursed by reliable women and then brought up, the girls eventually being given dowries and the boys trained in a craft for which they were suited.

The patronage of the Sacred Infirmary and its satellite institutions was enormous. Its demands for supplies, its provision of jobs, its political control over the Order's subjects, were far-reaching. The 'gift relationship' – he who gives dominates – was very thoroughly practised in Hospitaller Malta. The date 1631, the last Chapter General before the late eighteenth century, is perhaps a less important date for the hospital than for other Hospitaller institutions. The setting up of charitable foundations and pious gifts by individual members of the Order continued into the eighteenth century. The system extended to the provision of doctors in the villages and a strict enforcement of quarantine to prevent the spread of disease.

But having stressed the political role of the Sacred Infirmary, the Order did continue to treat their lords, the sick. The Knights may have had rather finer bed linen for themselves, but they continued to regard all the patients equally. They still conducted an important military hospital. They had wards for the

---

[18] Malta, Cod. 295, fol. 75v.
[19] Malta, Cod. 1960, fol. 20v.
[20] A. Critien, 'A Convent and a Hospital of the Past', *Archivium Melitense*, **10** (1940), pp. 5–6.

treatment of fevers, for the incurable and for the mentally and physically handicapped. Even those with venereal diseases, rejected in many medical hospitals, were mentioned without judgement. Slaves were also given care. Bribes were strictly forbidden by the Order in the Infirmary, but a preliminary analysis of hospital wills shows that a large number of the sick left a small gift to their carers, very often the ward guardians, for their kindness. Patients, apart from religious, came from all over Europe. The year 1632 saw fifty-five deaths of seculars in the hospital: twenty-one Maltese, two Gozitans, four from various parts of Italy, two from Sicily, five from all over France, six *forçats*, five employees of the Order, five slaves, one with no place mentioned and one bastard infant. A year earlier there was a Fleming, several people from the Spanish kingdoms, a merchant from Aleppo and a freed slave, Theodore de Muscovia.[21]

The great growth in the hospital and charitable work of the Order provided it with a purpose when crusading declined in the late seventeenth century. It was a role in harmony with the teaching of the post-Tridentine Catholic Church and one that therefore kept the bishop and the inquisitor at bay. Politically it ensured a less disrupted state than many secular contemporaries enjoyed. It was a 'medicalization of the state', even if not quite in the terms that Foucault envisaged.

---

[21] Malta, Cod. 1720, fols 209r–210v.

12

Corsairs Parading Crosses: the Hospitallers and Venice, 1530–1798

Victor Mallia-Milanes

This paper concentrates on the often inimical nature of the relationship between the Republic of Venice and the Order of St John between 1530 and 1798. It is intended to propose a plausible explanation for the mutual distrust sustained by the two institutions and to focus attention on why such mutual antipathy was allowed to prevail so long.

The traumatic experience of the loss of Rhodes, the embarrassing eight-year odyssey over warring Christian Europe and the tortuous politics inspired by the Lutheran Reformation were all as threatening to the Order's existence as the ever-expanding power of Islam. To these should be added Venice's direct, public, hostile attitude which posed as dangerous a threat to the Hospitallers and to their beliefs in the sanctity of tradition – to what they claimed to be their right to pursue the *guerre de course*. In the 1580s the Venetian Senate, relieving its feelings against the Order of St John, dubbed the Knights Hospitallers 'corsairs parading crosses'.[1] In the 1660s Mgr Galeazzo Marescotti, the Apostolic Delegate and Roman Inquisitor on Malta, called Venice 'the Order's worst enemy',[2] and in 1716, in one of his despatches to the Senate written shortly after a four-month sojourn on the island, Giacomo Capello, the Venetian resident minister in Naples, confessed that in Hospitaller Malta the very term 'Venetian' was odious.[3]

More often than not, the Venetian Republic's persistent complaints against Hospitaller and Maltese unrestrained disruption of the richest caravan routes

---

[1] A. Tenenti, *Piracy and the Decline of Venice. 1580–1615* (London, 1967), p. 39. For the Order of St John in Malta, *Hospitaller Malta 1530–1798: Studies on Early Modern Malta and the Order of St John of Jerusalem*, ed. V. Mallia-Milanes (Malta, 1993).

[2] E. Schermerhorn, *Malta of the Knights* (Surrey, 1929), p. 201.

[3] Archivio di Stato, Venice (ASV), *Senato, Dispacci da Giacomo Capello, Residente per la Serenissima, Napoli*, 27 May 1716.

in the eastern Mediterranean, turning them into perpetual war zones, would suddenly change into 'real measures of compulsion'. These would have 'greatly accelerated' the Order's 'military decline' had they not been counterpoised by the Venerable Council's retaliatory measures and occasionally by timely papal intervention.

The sixteenth century offers strong evidence of Venice's 'discourtesy' towards the Order in moments when the latter's requests for assistance had been of supreme urgency. The Turkish siege of Rhodes in 1522 is one classic example. On that occasion Venice watched passively the slow fall of 'Christendom's strongest bulwark' in the East, the one 'nearest the confines of the Ottoman Empire'. She even closed her ports in Crete and Cyprus to the Knights of St John and denied, for reasons of state, those 'noble and courageous adventurers' who, on their own initiative, had volunteered to offer their services, the opportunity of going to the aid of the Hospitallers. The case of Malta in 1565 is another example. The Venetians are said to have rejoiced at the fall of Fort St Elmo to the Turkish besiegers on 23 June.

On two occasions – one in the 1580s, the other in the 1740s – the Venetians and the Hospitallers were in a state of near warfare. Both were precipitated by the Hospitallers' piratical activity in the Levant, and on both occasions, the Senate voted for the confiscation of Hospitaller property on Venetian territory. In 1584 the *sequestro* was accompanied by other resolutions, including the dismissal of all Hospitallers on the pay list of the Republic, their immediate expulsion from Venice and the interdiction of trade and all forms of correspondence between the two states. Knights Hospitallers and Maltese subjects of the Order would be treated anywhere as enemy corsairs. In 1741, in addition to the *sequestro*, the Senate ordered the indiscriminate sinking of all ships flying the Hospitaller Cross. In August 1584, barely one month after the *sequestro* had been ordered, Grand Master Hugues de Loubenx de la Verdalle reacted by instructing the Captain-General of the Galleys to sail out in quest of Venetian ships and conduct them to Malta by fair or foul means.[4] In 1742, by now with no hope of a peaceful settlement, Grand Master Emanuel Pinto secured the passage of the *Decreto contro i Veneziani* through his State Council. This embraced, among others, two principal elements. First, it withheld the reception of any Venetian patrician in the Order as long as the *sequestro* remained in force. Second, Hospitaller galleys and Maltese privateers were instructed (perhaps more diplomatically than in 1584) to extend to all ships flying the banner of St Mark the same treatment that they themselves received from the Venetians.

---

[4] Bartholomeo dal Pozzo tells us that no Venetian ship felt secure from plunder, while the Hospitaller galleys never missed the slightest opportunity to inspect and ransack any Venetian vessel that sailed their way, seizing all infidels and infidel goods on board. The Republic proceeded most rigorously against all Hospitallers and Maltese privateers whom storms and other mishaps dragged into Venetian ports.

This feeling of antagonism between the 'noble merchant' and the 'noble pirate' was longstanding, rooted in their attitudinal dispositions, contradistinctive both by vocation and by profession. Venice's privileged geographical location,[5] its mercantile aristocracy's respectable dedication to wholesale trade, its special relationship with the Ottoman Empire and its characteristic tolerance towards non-Christians [6] contrasted as sharply with the Western nobility's innate prejudice against indulgence in any form of commercial activity as with the Hospitallers' own bellicose vocation of inherent hostility towards Islam. The Hospital's professed attitude towards the infidel, its declared enemy with whom it considered itself permanently at war, formed perhaps the only ideological basis for the Hospitallers' persistent endeavour to assert their politico-military relevance to contemporary Christian Europe. Their tireless efforts to justify and conveniently keep alive the idea of the crusade were in themselves a defiance of Venice's overriding political and economic interests. For Venice the Turk was her foremost trading partner with whom she never hesitated to ally herself, pledging to defend his interests, and growing increasingly economically dependent on him, especially after the Ottoman conquest of Syria and Egypt. In this sense, the Hospital's physical presence at the heart of Venice's Stato da Mar posed a direct challenge to the peaceful realization of the Republic's objectives – first through its possession of Rhodes (which Andrea Loredan in 1497 had dubbed 'protectress of corsairs'[7] and which the Venetians themselves had tried but failed to take in 1234)[8] and, after 1530, through its members' relentless privateering warfare in the Levant.

There was another major force of friction. Venice's general ecclesiastical policy, the nature of her traditional relations with the Church of Rome, and her reputed anticlericalism were in many ways reflections of her inherent distrust of the papacy in its 'two-dimensional character'. To Venice, more perhaps than to any other Italian state, the 'temporality' of the pope, the neighbour sovereign whose principality bordered uncomfortably on her own, bred suspicions of his territorial ambitions. His 'spirituality' as head of the universal Latin Church, increasingly exalting in the post-Tridentine period, was equally irritating; his strong endeavour to impose ecclesiastical discipline and conformity in matters of spiritual jurisdiction collided with her traditional policy of Republican liberty, autonomy and religious toleration.

This feeling of aversion towards the 'papal prince' was necessarily extended to the Hospitallers whose ultimate head he was. An exempt Order of the Church, at once noble, regular and military, the Hospital owed no allegiance to either secular sovereignty or diocesan authority. It had its own clergy and

---

[5] B. Pullan, *The Jews of Europe and the Inquisition of Venice 1550–1670* (Totowa, NJ, 1983), p. 3.

[6] Ibid., p. 3.

[7] M. Sanuto, *I Diarii*, ed. R. Fulin et al., 58 vols, **1** (Venice, 1879–1903), p. 770.

[8] A.T. Luttrell, 'Venice and the Knights Hospitallers of Rhodes in the Fourteenth Century', *Papers of the British School at Rome*, **26** (1958), p. 196.

built its own churches. Within this context, the Hospitallers, like the beneficed clergy in general over whom the Council of Ten held tight control, were not among the men whom Venice could comfortably trust. In fact, notwithstanding their noble birth, notwithstanding the hereditary right that every Venetian patrician had, on reaching the age of twenty-five, to enter the Great Council, the beneficed clerics in Venice were excluded from 'magisterial office and from seats in legislative councils'.

A law of 1597 reveals how the Hospitallers were viewed by the Council of Ten, that powerful group of wise men responsible for the integrity and security of the Venetian State. On 13 August that year the Senate decreed that during its discussions on matters concerning the Religion of Malta, the *papalisti* – as the Venetian patricians with close ties with the papal court were known[9] – would be excluded,[10] as they had traditionally been whenever Venetian policy towards Rome was debated.[11] In 1498 the *commenda*, the smallest unit of administration of the Hospitaller estates making up the Grand Priory, had been defined as an ecclesiastical benefice.[12] This distinction was given more focus a century later, suggesting the general direction which the Venetian mind took when it thought of the Hospitallers. The Signory's official hostile attitude towards the papacy was now formally extended to the institution of the Hospitaller Order of St John: like the papacy, the Hospitallers too were, by implication, a foreign political power whose interests were believed to run counter to those of the Republic.

There was nothing, therefore, about the Hospitaller Order that was remarkably attractive to the Venetian patrician. Indeed, the Hospitaller Cross would deprive him of his right of access to 'offices of great honour' (generally assigned to the richer members of the patriciate) or to those of 'profit' (generally reserved for the poorer ones).[13] Few patricians, in fact, were prepared to sacrifice their 'service to the state' in order to join the Hospital. According to a Venetian report drawn up in April 1627, there were thirty-four Hospitallers 'in the State of the Republic of Venice,' of whom only fourteen were Venetians.[14]

Through their sceptical commitment to the Ottoman Porte, the Venetians were generally able to enforce their will upon the principality of Malta, seriously questioning the Hospitallers' right to wage a 'just war' against the infidel, and

---

[9] See P.F. Grendler, *The Roman Inquisition and the Venetian Press 1540–1605* (Princeton, NJ, 1977), pp. 29–30; E. Besta, *Il Senato Veneziano* (Venice, 1899), pp. 214–18; D.E. Queller, *The Venetian Patriciate: Reality versus Myth* (Urbana, 1986), pp. 184, 186, 216, 217, 219.

[10] See A. Sagredo, 'Leggi venete intorno agli ecclesiastici sino al secolo XVIII', *Archivio storico italiano*, 3rd ser., **2**, i (1865), 104; also *Leggi venete intorno agli ecclesiastici sino al secolo XVIII*, ed. A. Papadopoli (Venice, 1864), p. 32.

[11] Ibid., pp. 92–133.

[12] Ibid., p. 104; Papadopoli, p. 32.

[13] See B. Pullan, *Rich and Poor in Renaissance Venice: The Social Institutions of a Catholic State, to 1620* (Oxford, 1971), p. 393.

[14] ASV, *Consultori in Jure, busta* 58, fol. 19r.

demonstrating, in what they believed to have been unmistakeable terms, that the Order's solemn profession of faith in the rectitude of its medieval principles had all along been a perfect example of 'high theory in the service of low cunning'.

Very often drawing the papacy into their own scheme to render the Hospitallers incapable of resistance, the Venetians constituted at least one other powerful force of change whose influence had been as crucial in the general development and decline of the Maltese *corso* as that traditionally attributed to France and Rome.[15] A classic example was the case of 1586, when souring relations between Venice and the Order had culminated in a complete rupture on a scale the two states had never experienced before. On 31 October Cardinal Girolamo Rusticucci, papal Secretary of State, sent Grand Master Verdalle an 'advice' which the Maltese chronicler and conventual chaplain of the Order, Fra Carlo Micallef defined as 'irritating in the extreme' and a 'most damaging pontifical resolution', too prejudicial to the interests of the Hospitallers. The pope had ordained that all vessels proceeding from Christian ports to Turkish lands or vice versa could henceforth trade in all sorts of merchandise, excepting only contraband goods, with no hindrance or interference. Thus, by a stroke of the papal pen, the Order's galleys and Maltese privateers flying the Hospitaller Cross were forbidden to capture or molest 'any vessel navigating Levantine waters, whether belonging to Turks or Jews when charged in Christian ports'. Then, in July 1587, the papal injunctions were further extended, this time in order to protect all Levantine Jews, their ships, and their trade in legitimate commodities. The Order's reluctant submission to the pressure of papal sanctions is best seen in the amendments which the Grand Master and his Venerable Council were forced to make to the conditions inserted in their letters patent to corsairs in order to conform to the new papal ordinances.[16] On another occasion, in 1714, to avoid the escalation of a similar Venetian–Hospitaller crisis, Grand Master Ramon Perellos felt constrained to proclaim the Adriatic, north of Otranto and Capo Santa Maria, and its approaches, out of bounds to the Hospitaller Cross.[17]

Between 1536 and 1741 Venice employed the *sequestro* on eleven occasions. The seizure of Hospitaller lands and revenues, lying within easy grasp of the Signory, offered the Republic the only weapon she believed she could employ in the hope of containing Hospitaller and Maltese privateering in the Levant. In practice, it was a clumsy precaution, which, through its ineffectiveness, continued to provoke Western corsairs far too long.

[15] For Venice, V. Mallia-Milanes, *Venice and Hospitaller Malta 1530–1798: Aspects of a Relationship* (Malta, 1992). For France and Rome, see R.E. Cavaliero, 'The Decline of the Maltese Corso in the Eighteenth Century: A Study in Maritime History', *Melita Historica*, 2, iv (1959), pp. 224–38; P. Earle, *Corsairs of Malta and Barbary* (London, 1970).

[16] See, for example, Malta, Cod. 445, 289r.

[17] V. Mallia-Milanes, *Descrittione di Malta, Anno 1716: A Venetian Account* (Malta, 1988), p. 6.

The frequency with which Venice resorted to the *sequestro* as the sole instrument of her defence policy *vis-à-vis* the Hospitallers points to the hollowness of her approach to a problem which had been scourging her Stato da Mar ever since the Hospitallers had first set foot on the island of Malta (if not for longer). Indeed it is tempting to believe that Venice had never seriously resolved to annihilate it. It is hardly credible, for example, that daring acts of piracy, such as Don Diego Brochero's in the sixteenth century or Captain Grillo's in the eighteenth, could have been allowed to pass unnoticed by the Cretan guards, unless one reads in the Senate's persistent recourse to the *sequestro* a painful awareness of the growing laxity among the Venetian officials entrusted with the naval defence of its Stato da Mar. The question of the *ponentini* was in fact one of the themes which Nicolò Suriano, Provveditor dell'Armada, chose to discuss in his *relatione* of 1583. Privateers 'of the Grand Duke of Florence,' he observed,

> ... were a common sight in the Levant; and so were those of the Hospitallers of Malta; as well as others which set out from Messina, albeit with smaller vessels, *fuste* and *fregate*. The Turks resent them for the harm they inflict on them, no less than they resent the harm inflicted on them by the Uskoks.[18]

A few years earlier, in order to appease or accommodate the Turks, the Signory had resolved to augment the Cretan guards to seven galleys in the hope of rendering their vigilance more effective. Better equipped than they had ever been before, they would be in a stronger position to chase and disarm the *ponentini*. But this was precisely what the Venetian admiral, Suriano, seriously questioned, advocating instead a policy of caution. It should, he said, be the task of every state representative overseas *to scare these corsairs away*: to avoid, in other words, the need to disarm these privateers, with their important connections with the West. The root of the problem, according to Suriano, lay in the natural affection islanders had towards the westerlings, such that no Venetian legislation, however rigid and severe the penalties contemplated by the Signory, could ever hope to eradicate. Like the Uskoks in Dalmatia, these westerlings found the local inhabitants on such Venetian islands as Crete, Cerigo, Zante, Cephalonia, Paxos, Corfu, and others, all too ready to offer them access not only to a safe haven but also to reliable information about the whereabouts of the Cretan guards. The protection extended to the Hospitallers and other westerlings by the local inhabitants of these islands extended even further. Venetian vassals often misled Venetian authorities by providing them with false reports on the movements of these Western privateers. The whole issue, of course, revolved around one crucial factor – *how to scare these corsairs away*. In the admiral's view, the solution rested solely with the Capitani da Mar who

---

[18] Suriano's *relatione* is reproduced in V. Lamansky, *Secrets d'Etat de Venise: Documents, Extraits, Notices et Etudes servant à éclaircir les rapports de la Seigneurie avec les Grecs, les Slavs et la Porte Ottomane à la fin du XVe et au XVIe siècle* (St Petersburg, 1884), pp. 601–3.

should diligently endeavour to keep such privateers away from the islands in the manner described below.

> In the winter, [he suggested] when these vessels set out on the *corso*, the Captain of the Cretan Guards should wait for their arrival between the Garbusce of Crete, San Nicolò di Vlamona on the island of Cerigo, and the Porto delle Quaglie at Cape Matapan. The westerlings generally proceed to these areas on account of the heavy Turkish traffic practised there. And since at the Porto delle Quaglie Venetian vessels had often encountered some antagonism from the Magnotti, it was safer for the Captain of the Guards to stay as far as possible at San Nicolò di Vlamona. Here a strong tower should be constructed to render the place securer, to cover armed vessels, and to deny westerlings access to the port. The Porto delle Garbusce should likewise be made safer ..., Its Provveditor dell'Armada or Governatore delle Galere de Condannati should stay between Paxos, Cephalonia, and Zante to overawe the inhabitants of Thiachi, who are reported to protect the westerlings.[19]

There was another aspect to the question. The Republic's failure to clear the Levant of Western piracy and privateering underscored the growing weakness of her naval organization and the inadequacy of her surveillance. This was partly due to a relaxation of effort. Venetian officials, stationed at strategic bases along her fast diminishing possessions, were either becoming increasingly lax in their vigilance, or the fleet was steadily growing too inefficient to deal with the corsair vessels of the *ponentini*. In 1589, at the end of his mission as Commander of the Cretan fleet, Filippo Pasqualigo attributed the inadequacy of the Venetian squadron to solve the corsair question permanently to a number of factors. Chief of these was 'the striking lack' of sailors and galley commanders, a state of affairs which had only recently, he observed in 1589, become too obvious. This, in turn, he attributed to the poor pay attached to the respective posts (wages were, of course, fixed by the Senate for all categories of naval employees). It was to be expected that a situation like this would inevitably encourage interested persons, including those already engaged on the Venetian fleet, to seek better employment elsewhere, either in the service of foreign states or on vessels other than those of the Republic.[20] Ten years later, Nicolò Donato observed that wages in 1599 stood at the level of 'some 50 or 100 years previously'. Under such discouraging conditions, he continued, those who remained enrolled in active service with the Republic were unavoidably those whom he described as 'miserable, dejected, dispossessed, and utter failures'.[21]

The question of the 'low calibre' of Venetian crews[22] was raised again before the Senate by Giovan Battista Michiel, captain of the Venetian fleet

[19] Ibid., pp. 602–3.

[20] Ibid., pp. 578–9.

[21] Ibid., p. 581. On wages and other conditions of employment of Venetian crews, see F.C. Lane, *Venice: A Maritime Republic* (Baltimore, 1973), pp. 49–51, 168–70, 342–4, 382–4, 414–15.

[22] See *Crisis and Change in the Venetian Economy in the Sixteenth and Seventeenth Centuries*, ed. B. Pullan (London, 1968), p. 8.

against the Uskoks, in his *relatione* of April 1597.[23] Michiel reported that, during his term of office, several 'deserters' had been included among members of the galley crews. On the slightest motive of discontent, these *scapoli* would immediately escape from service and engage with the Uskoks, 'in whose company they commit all sort of crimes'. Then, on finding that such a way of life was not quite to their taste, they would find no difficulty in once more enrolling on Venetian ships and being assigned posts of responsibility. On several occasions, Venetian galleys had been abandoned by whole gangs of these fugitives.[24] Such deplorable conditions rendered any operation against the fully armed and well equipped *ponentini* ludicrous.[25]

The scarce documentation that has survived the *sequestro* of 1741 provides sufficient insight into the methods used by the Republic to confiscate the Order's Venetian estates over the years. That *sequestro* followed an interesting report, drawn up five years earlier, on the Grand Priory of Venice, which, among other issues, provided the Signory with a brief survey of precisely such methods. The *Cinque Savii alla Mercanzia* was the magistracy entrusted with the task of maintaining effective control over the actual execution of the *sequestro*, acting in concert with the rectors and other state representatives to avoid all sorts of fraudulent practices in the confiscation of Hospitaller funds.

In theory, the confiscation of Hospitaller funds should have been a very simple exercise. Every commandery was bound by the statutes to channel one-third of its net income to the receiver, who, in turn, after having had his final statements of account approved at the prioral chapter, would forward them to the Common Treasury in Valletta. If the Venetian authorities confiscated these *responsiones* at the receiver end, all would have been straightforward. But the system adopted by the Republic in 1741, and on many other previous occasions, was different and complicated. The Senate preferred to go to the roots of Hospitaller revenues: the smallest estate holder who owed the Hospital rents in cash, or kind, or both. This approach cannot be categorized as inefficient. It was a question of the end justifying the means. The *sequestro* had developed over the years into a search for the Hospitallers' real sources of income, and this method offered the Republic the opportunity of gaining a more realistic perspective of the scattered nature of Hospitaller holdings in the Veneto. There were, for example, 126 leaseholders, or *livellarij*, most of them Venetians, occupying different portions of what Lodovico Manin, the Podestà and Vice-Capitano of Padua, called three Hospitaller country estates or *ville*, situated

---

[23] Lamansky, p. 580.

[24] On the endemic problem of desertion, G. Parker, *The Military Revolution: Military Innovation and the Rise of the West, 1500–1800* (Cambridge, 1988), pp. 55–8, and corresponding notes; M.E. Mallett and J.R. Hale, *The Military Organization of a Renaissance State: Venice c.1400 to 1617* (Cambridge, 1974), pp. 18–19, 122–3, 293, 348, 371, 390.

[25] See Bernardo Venier's *relatione* of 15 January 1606 in Lamansky, p. 588.

in the city of Padua and its territory.[26] It was through his involvement in the *sequestro* of 1741 as rector in Friuli that Girolamo Gradenigo discovered that the Hospitallers had possessed three commanderies that fell within his jurisdiction.[27] The Senate's method enabled the Signory to assess the true extent of Venetian land owned by the Hospitallers, and what proportion of the revenue produced by these ecclesiastical estates on Venetian soil was channelled into foreign hands – perhaps even to reward the enemies of the Republic.

Judged by its results, however, the *sequestro* of 1741, which dragged on for six whole years, left Venice extremely disillusioned and beginning to lose faith in its effectiveness. When, in the early 1750s, the Republic was again confronted by a new list of grievances against corsairs flying the Hospitaller Cross, she resorted instead to such alternative measures as the suppression of Maltese consulates on Venetian islands, such as Corfu and Zante,[28] where corsairs parading the Hospitaller Cross had sought shelter at the end of their privateering operations. This suggests that the Republic felt a necessity for a change of focus and attitudes, in direct contrast to the prevalent policy of the past 250 years. The suppression of Maltese consulates was perhaps a useful temporary expedient which brought the Republic to a belated awareness of a new reality. There was truly no further point in communicating grievances to either Rome or Valletta, or in trying to coerce the Grand Master into rectifying abuses. The negative approach simply did not work.

The history of the *sequestro* in fact underscores a curious contradiction within Venice's entire approach to the Hospitallers in Malta. The Republic of Venice had been among the very first states in Europe to recognize the importance of resident ambassadors at foreign courts; and their reports to Senate at the end of their mission had often been instrumental in determining the direction of the Republic's foreign policy. Ironically, she was among the last to apply that experience to the central Mediterranean island. It was at this point that Grand Master Pinto's dismissal of his consul in Venice, Gio Batta Zocchi (1752), raised the question first of the Venetian consulate in Malta and subsequently that of establishing a resident Venetian ministry on the island. In fact, on 25 September 1754, Commendatore Massimiliano Buzzaccarini Gonzaga was the first to be accredited *Huomo della Repubblica di Venezia* to the Grand Master's court in Valletta. His mission was to protect and extend help to all Venetian subjects who 'proceeded to Malta for purposes of trade' or who were 'conducted to Malta by shipowners and Christian corsairs'. In the latter case, he was 'to produce ... the immediate release of ships, effects, and persons', and to take cognizance of 'all minute details of the circumstances'

---

[26] ASV, Cinque Savii alla Mercanzia; the archival records of the Venetian Magistracy of Trade (CSM), new ser., *busta* 86, 'Malta', pt. 1, fol. 39r.

[27] Ibid., fol. 35.

[28] Mallia-Milanes, *Venice and Hospitaller Malta*, pp. 207–10.

in which such 'arrests' had occurred. He was assigned an annual stipend of 800 Venetian ducats.[29]

The effects of Venice's changed attitude towards Hospitaller Malta were visible, immediate and durable.[30] From being traditional foes the two states were soon to become trading partners, and, in fact, a lucrative bilateral commercial agreement was concluded between the two in the 1760s and renewed in the 1780s. Nor can the role played by the neutral, central Mediterranean island in the Republic's peace treaties with Algiers and Tunis (1763), Tripoli (1764) and Morocco (1765) be denied, if only as a secure and direct source of intelligence, amply evidenced in Buzzaccarini Gonzaga's voluminous correspondence to the *Cinque Savii alla Mercanzia*. The scale of privateering activity in the Levant and the rhythm with which it was pursued under cover of the Hospitaller Cross, which had given the Venetians so much umbrage in the past, diminished considerably from the 1760s onwards; and although serious, not entirely unsuccessful, attempts were made to revive the 'industry' during Emanuel de Rohan's magistracy, the cases which in the past would have very likely soured relations between the two states were too few and far between to warrant the historian's legitimate attention. The occasional appearance in the Maltese harbours of an insignificant number of Venetian vessels at the turn of the century gave way to the Adriatic Republic's full exploitation of Hospitaller Malta as a naval base in the 1780s when the Signory, at formal war with Tunis, discovered in the island 'another Venice in the Mediterranean'.

---

[29] ASV, CSM, *Diversorum, busta* 403, *fasc.* 76, 'Commissione per l' Huomo della Repubblica di Venezia in Malta', 25 September 1754; ibid., 24 August 1754.

[30] This subject is discussed in detail in Mallia-Milanes, *Venice and Hospitaller Malta*, pp. 221–69.

13

'A Parish at Sea': Spiritual Concerns aboard the Order of St John's Galleys in the Seventeenth and Eighteenth Centuries*

David Allen

Which images evoke today that vanished reality of the religious, military, Hospitaller Order of St John of Jerusalem? Alongside the knights' eight-pointed cross, alongside their buildings in the Near East, Rhodes or Malta, let us consider also some of their votive paintings now hanging in the sanctuary of Our Lady of Graces at Zabbar in Malta. Here the future Pope Alexander VII had often prayed in the 1630s, when he was Inquisitor and Apostolic Delegate, hearing mass in the company of knights who were thanking Our Lady for her intercessions during their recent encounters with the Turks at sea. Votive paintings commemorated her graces as well as gifts to her sanctuary of altar-fronts, chasubles, copes and coats of arms of individual knights.[1] Such paintings delineate the perils of the sea menacing all men aboard the Order of St John's galleys in the early modern period, whether they were knights of noble birth, brother chaplains of respectable family or convicts and slaves chained to their oars.

In calmer moments the Order of St John's galleys could be seen more clearly as 'a parish at sea', a microcosm of that society left behind on *terra ferma* but which was never obscured for too long from the pilot's vision. Aboard, as elsewhere in Christian Europe, Church coexisted with State, the Order's chaplains collaborating with their brother knights in the government of the galley's lower orders, non-commissioned officers, crewmen and the men condemned to their oar. This apostolate of the sea was both distinctive and dangerous, and the various provocations to Christian witness aboard what was both a fighting vessel and prison are described by the unpublished manuscript which is now the focus of my paper.

* I remain grateful to the British Academy for its generous grant in aid of my research at Malta.
[1] See J. Zarb, *Zabbar Sanctuary and the Knights of St John* (Malta, 1969).

Dell'Instruzione per i Cappellani di Galera had been written by Fra Giovanni
Domenico Manso in response to repeated requests from other chaplains that
he should codify, for themselves and their successors, the best pastoral practice
aboard the Order of St John's galleys. Dated 1699, on the eve of the War of
the Spanish Succession, Manso's treatise anticipated Pope Clement XI's brief
of 1704 which would emphasize how the Order of St John's *carovane* in the
Levant afforded equally frequent opportunities both to chaplains and to
knights to die for their faith at the hands of the implacable Turks.[2]

Understandably enough, the knights have been emphasized in the Order
of St John's meagre historiography at the expense of its chaplains. A lower
category in the Order's hierarchy, chaplains were themselves ranked as
conventual chaplains or chaplains of obedience and either rank included
deacons as well as priests. All owed obedience to the Prior of the conventual
church of St John in Valletta, but chaplains of obedience usually resided
outside Malta, ministering to the rural populations of their Order's commanderies in continental Europe.[3] Fewer in number than chaplains of obedience,
conventual chaplains were better educated and of higher calibre. Unlike their
brother knights, conventual chaplains were not required to submit proofs of
nobility for entry to the Order, but they had to be of legitimate birth and
descended from five generations of bourgeois ancestry. Drawn from various
nationalities, conventual chaplains were appointed with the Grand Master's
approval and subject to a two-thirds majority vote in the Order's Venerable
Assembly of Conventual Chaplains. Like their brother knights, conventual
chaplains were assigned to their respective *Langue* and priory within the Order.
Whereas the native Maltese were always excluded from the rank of knight within
the military Order which ruled their islands, they were sometimes allowed in
as conventual chaplains and were usually assigned – in the absence of a Maltese
Langue – to the French and Italian *Langues* of the Order.

It was from among the Order of St John's conventual chaplains that priests
were chosen for the ministry of their 'parish at sea'.[4] Unless a conventual chaplain

---

[2] See National Library of Malta (NLM), Lib.MS.211 and Archives of the Order of Malta (AOM)
1927. I remain grateful to the Librarian and his staff for their unfailing courtesy. Cf. G. Psaila Cumbo,
*La dignità del Priore della Chiesa, la Veneranda Assemblea dei Cappellani Conventuali e i Fratelli Cappellani
dell'Ordine nel Codice Gerosolomitano e alla luce del Diritto Canonico* (Malta, 1938), pp. 24–5.

[3] See J. Chetail, 'Le bas clergé sous l'Ancien Régime: Les Curés de l'Ordre de Malte', *Annales
de l'Ordre Souverain Militaire de Malte*, 1969, pp. 98–9.

[4] The profile of the Order of St John's conventual chaplains relative to their brother knights
was revealed in an estimate of the Order's members in 1631, now preserved in the Vatican
Library as MS.Barb.Lat.5036. 148 conventual chaplains were then distributed among the Order's
Langues: Provence = 47; Auvergne = 20; France = 20; Castile = 25; Italy = 0; Aragon = 30; Germany
(including Bohemia) = 6. By contrast, the Order's knights then numbered 1,755, who were
distributed as follows: Provence = 272; Auvergne = 143; France = 361; Castile = 239; Italy 584;
Aragon = 110; Germany (including Bohemia) = 46. The Order's servants-at-arms numbered 155
and were distributed as follows: Provence = 40; Auvergne = 18; France = 74; Castile = 17; Italy =
0; Aragon = 3 and Germany (including Bohemia) = 3.

made two *carovane* aboard the Order's galleys, he could not be eligible for a pension from the Grand Master; and four *carovane* were necessary if he sought the elusive reward of his commandery. Long before this, he might have been sold into slavery and detained for years before his ransom were arranged. In the earlier seventeenth century, such a fate befell the Maltese conventual chaplain, Fra Fabrizio Cagliola, who was to recall his experiences when writing his picaresque novel or 'tragi-comedy' about Gabriello Pulis from Senglea, *Le Disavventure Marinaresche o sia Gabriello Disavventurato*.[5] Before his death in the 1660s, Cagliola found time also to write a moral tract for the instruction of his fellow chaplains, but his work treated the pastoral challenge aboard his Order's galleys much less immediately than Manso's work a generation later.[6] Even so, both Cagliola and Manso were following the tradition of writing confessors' manuals, though Manso's bellicose context never permitted him the luxury of viewing the sacrament of penance 'in a timeless and bloodless universe', to quote John Bossy's phrase.[7] Manso's penitents were violent fighters and might be Muslim, Catholic, Protestant or Orthodox. Aboard the Order of St John's galleys authoritative and quick responses were expected from the chaplain-confessor, however difficult the challenge to his scruples might be. Besides this tradition of confessors' manuals, other obvious influences on Manso's treatise were his Order's regulations about the galleys, as well as the relevant decrees formulated by his Venerable Assembly of Conventual Chaplains. Probably another influence was the work of navigation published in 1643 by the Jesuit mathematician and naval chaplain to the French fleet, Georges Fournier, *Hydrographie contenant la théorie et la pratique de toutes les parties de la navigation*. This maritime encyclopedia was familiar to many knights of St John and its final section, 'De la dévotion des gens de mer', highlighted St Francis Xavier as the patron saint of all mariners.[8]

Whatever the influences on his treatise, *Dell'Instruzione per i Cappellani de Galera* was especially the product of Manso's own personality and experience, both of which, nevertheless, must now be deduced from his manuscript, since

[5] See NLM, Lib.MS.654, which was published with a preface by I.S. Mifsud as *Disavventure Marinaresche* (Malta, 1929). Other conventual chaplains taken as captive slaves in the seventeenth century included Bartolomeo Scaglia (1626), Giovanni Venier (1627) and Giovanni Columbat. See G. Psaila Cumbo, pp. 19–20, 26.

[6] See AOM 1926 ('Istruzione a'Fra Cappellani Gerosolomitani per poter con faciltà regolare le conscienze di tutti i Cavalieri ed altre persone soggette al Sacro Ordine Gerosolomitano').

[7] J. Bossy, 'The Social History of Confession in the Age of the Reformation', *Transactions of the Royal Historical Society*, 25 (1975), p. 21.

[8] See C. Chabaud-Arnault, 'Un Aumônier de la flotte sous le règne de Louis XIII, le Père Fournier', *L'Université Catholique* (Lyon), 11 (1892), pp. 375–91; F. de Dainville, 'Saint François Xavier, Patron des Gens de Mer', *Archivum Societatis Iesu*, 22 (1953), pp. 107–13; D.F. Allen 'The Social and Religious World of a Knight of Malta in the Caribbean, *c.* 1632–1660', in *Malta, A Case Study in International Cross-Currents*, ed. S. Fiorini and V. Mallia-Milanes (Malta, 1991), pp. 147–57.

he personally remains more anonymous than the novel-writing Cagliola, whom
Manso quotes in his own work.

In the 'parish at sea' about which Manso was so eloquent, his chaplain was
a lonely figure and one dependent upon his inner resources rather than upon
the fluid society of the galley to which he was expected to minister. A landlubber
amidst a crowd of mariners, the chaplain might inspire moral respect from his
'parishioners' only by his character and with benign assistance from the galley's
captain. Noticeable among the chaplain's 'parishioners' were the novice knights
of St John who were then engaged in learning the manoeuvres of naval warfare
for which their Order was long renowned in the Levant. Many of these young
nobles represented families throughout Catholic Europe which numbered
also dukes and cardinals in their senior branches. Back in France, Spain,
Portugal, Italy or Germany, the young knights of St John had been accustomed
to seeing chaplains in their parents' households as ornamental adjuncts to the
daily round of domestic service and as men who might say grace at table or
help with the writing of letters. On the galleys where these *caravanisti* were
now training, their naval instructors were senior knights from their own aris-
tocracies whereas their moral instructors were chaplains from lower down the
scale. This difference in social standing might be bridged by the self-aware
chaplain who possessed personal charisma. Only this latter trait – according
to Manso – not any reliance on his priestly function itself would win the
chaplain respect from the galley's captain, senior knights and novices alike.[9]
Should some of the knights reveal their breeding by condescending to speak
kindly to their chaplain, he should be grateful for this opportunity of civil con-
versation in so limited a society, but he should never mistake such overtures
as invitations to familiarity.[10]

Under cover of familiarity, some knights would attempt to probe their
chaplain in certain generalized cases of conscience but he must tell them, Manso
advised, that the proper forum for such discussion had to be the sacred tribunal
of confession and not the galley's poop. Manso warned also how the chaplain
must be careful not to demean himself nor compromise his ministry by participating in games of dice or cards aboard his galley. Manso quoted St Cyprian
on the distinctive role of the priest's hands in holding the Eucharist and not
dice. Even to watch knights playing dice or cards would certainly draw censure
upon the chaplain, since he could never pass unseen in so observant a parish.[11]
Where other knights might relieve the boredom of some days afloat by reading
books, their chaplain was advised by Manso to ensure that these did not risk
excommunication by reading or possessing books prohibited by the Church.
For a reader's eyes are the windows of his soul and through which poison might

---

[9] St Paul and Gregory the Great were both cited by Manso in support of this observation; see
NLM, MS.211, fols 7–8.

[10] Ibid., fol. 10.

[11] Ibid., fols 10–11; 8.

enter his heart. Manso warned how some *caravanisti* on the galleys would inform
their chaplain that the 'prohibited books' they were detected in reading had
never been condemned by their own bishop back home in France, Spain or
wherever. Manso conceded that not all 'prohibited books' were necessarily
heretical. Even so, Manso urged his chaplain to reply promptly that there was
a ban in Malta on any book condemned by the Tridentine Index of 1564 or
by its revisions (such as Clement VIII's Index of 1596) or on any publication
censured by the papal bull *In Coena Domini*, which was read aloud every year
on Maundy Thursday.[12] The chaplain was not empowered to grant absolution
to any penitent knight who had been found in possession of a heretical book.
First the Inquisitor of Malta had to be informed, after when absolution might
be granted by the chaplain once the penitent had burnt the offending work.
Manso insisted that his chaplain should urge the penitent to denounce to the
Inquisition other knights whom he knew to be reading heretical books.[13]

Besides 'prohibited books' and games of chance, duelling was another
consequence of life aboard the galleys against which Manso directed his pen.
Similarly, as wars between nations might be judged just or unjust, the duel
between two fighters intending to wound or kill the other was allowed by Manso
to be just or unjust according to its original motivation. Manso was necessarily
excluded by birth from that aristocratic code of honour which supported so
distinctive a form of duelling within the Order of St John. He advised his chaplain
by reference to pronouncements made in 1665 against illicit duels by Alexander
VII, sometime Inquisitor of Malta. Also cited by Manso were earlier decrees
against illicit duels by the Council of Trent, by Gregory XIII and by Clement
VIII in 1592.[14]

At this point it is wise to remember that the preacher will always be against
sin! What other evidence exists to corroborate that reality aboard the Order
of St John's galleys against which Manso prescribed the moral influence of his
chaplain-confessor? It was rare for knights to keep diaries of their *carovane* and,
if they wrote letters, they preferred to highlight enemy action rather than
reflecting upon their own behaviour when their galley was becalmed or when
they were in port. Fortunately, however, some relevant testimony from the
knights themselves does survive to corroborate Manso's concerns about gaming,
'prohibited books' and duelling among the *caravanisti*. Such evidence reminds
us that some Knights of St John were committed to keeping their vows of
poverty, chastity and obedience, however demanding their Order's distinctive
spirituality might have been. This had always emphasized the near impossi-
bility of one man's succeeding both as knight and Hospitaller – both as warrior
and carer for the sick and poor.[15]

---

[12] Ibid., fols 128–30.
[13] Ibid., fols 144–7.
[14] Ibid., fols 147–68.
[15] Cf. NLM, Lib.MS.1416, fols 131–2; 93.

The moral dilemmas arising on these galleys as they were to be codified by the chaplain Manso in 1699 would still be present in 1764, when Camillo Spreti, a young Italian knight from Ravenna, wrote his own advisory treatise for novice brethren setting out on their *carovane* for the first time. Spreti had in mind one of his own nephews following himself into the Order of St John. He highlighted the tedium of the galleys, their cramped space and the daily sight of nothing but sky, water and the faces of other *caravanisti*. In such conditions – even more restricting than in Malta itself – Spreti advised his young knight to speak judiciously in so international an assembly. The tedium of the galleys could be relieved not by card-playing, which would only lead to arguments and duels, but by reading a holy book. Above all, the novice knight needed a good friend to keep him out of mischief, but Spreti quoted Ovid on the difficulty ever of finding such a man. Female company, of course, was impossible on the galleys. In any case, Spreti had written a sonnet against women. He warned his young knight of the harpies back in Malta who had ruined many a gullible knight and so cancelled his dream of equipping later his own galley for battle against the Turks. Spreti advised the young knight on the galleys to seek protection from the souls in Purgatory, to attend the chaplain's daily mass and to pray all the time for divine protection against the Devil's guile which would certainly tempt him every waking moment of his *carovane*. Spreti's manuscript dates from his twentieth year and shows one Knight of St John trying to keep his vows in the so-called Age of Enlightenment.[16]

Among Christian powers of the early modern period, the Order of St John did not monopolize the galley as a vessel of regional utility: Mediterranean ports sheltered galleys as often as sailing ships. Comparative questions arise, therefore, about pastoral practices aboard galleys or sailing ships which did not fly the Order of St John's standard in the Mediterranean of this early modern period. First under Richelieu, Colbert, and until its disbandment in 1748, the French galley fleet was officered and trained by Knights of St John, who passed on not only their naval expertise but also their wisdom as prison warders aboard galleys.[17] The Order of St John did not provide chaplains to the French galleys, who were answerable to Vincent de Paul's successors in his *Congrégation de la Mission* and to the bishop of Marseilles. From the 1690s these drew censure from Huguenots condemned to the galleys – more bitter censure indeed than that directed at the Knights of St John often commanding these galleys. Trying to convert these Protestants, Roman Catholic chaplains aboard French galleys could be punitive and vindictive.[18]

---

[16] See NLM, Lib.MS.1202, fols 155–201.

[17] This point is emphasized by P.W. Bamford in his study of Louis XIV's galley fleet, *Fighting Ships and Prisons* (Minneapolis, 1973), p. 26.

[18] See M. Emerit, 'Au temps de Saint Vincent de Paul, la Mission de Savary de Brèves en Afrique du Nord (1606)', *Revue française d'histoire d'outre-mer*, 52 (1965), pp. 297–314; Bamford, pp. 99, 101, 121.

The Jesuits came forward with their mission to mariners aboard sailing ships more often than galleys, although at Naples in the early seventeenth century, a Jesuit sodality called the Holy Mercy cared for convicts who might have been wrongly condemned to their oar.[19] Elsewhere a distinctive and well documented apostolate of the sea was served by those Jesuits aboard the fleet of Flanders between 1623 and 1662. Here they preached and dispensed the sacraments just as, earlier, the Jesuit missionaries Francis Xavier and Matteo Ricci had conducted their ministry similarly during their long sea voyages to the Orient.[20] Much of this detailed testimony from the Jesuits' naval missions aboard sailing ships chimes in with the evidence we have quoted earlier in this paper from the Order of St John's galleys. Liturgical practices were common to both ministries: morning prayers, the *Angelus* at noon and, in the evening, litanies of the saints and preaching the catechism, besides hearing individual confessions. A portable altar was kept in the poop for the daily celebration of mass. Here there were liturgical differences aboard galleys, seldom far from land, and sailing ships on longer sea voyages. When in port or in a sheltered creek, the Order of St John's chaplains could celebrate mass on a portable altar even among fishing boats on the beach. But at sea and two hours before sunrise, they celebrated the so-called dry mass (*messa secca*), which omitted those mass parts between the Offertory and Communion inclusive. This too was the Jesuit practice aboard the fleet of Flanders until 1638, when they were granted permission by the Holy See to celebrate mass at sea, because of the shared desire to see more frequent communions aboard.[21]

Whether in the Indian Ocean, the Atlantic or the Mediterranean, there was always afloat in the early modern period a Counter-Reformation 'parish at sea', which complemented Carlo Borromeo's Counter-Reformation parish on land. Swearing, games of chance, duelling or the reading of prohibited books were all sins targeted by the Jesuit naval chaplains as often as they drew censure from the conventual chaplains aboard the Order of St John's galleys. These latter were offended also by overhearing blasphemy, and Manso advised his chaplain to demand punishment of the offenders: chains for free oarsmen and floggings for those already chained.[22] Yet the effective clerical response always was to show humanity, gentleness and affection, in short to show the Hospitaller character of the Order. This could, indeed, be evidenced even aboard the Order's galleys by the chaplain's nursing aid to wounded men, by his writing down the dictated will of a dying knight or by his receiving into the Church a dying

---

[19] See L. Chatellier, *The Europe of the Devout* (Cambridge, 1989), p. 131.

[20] See E. Hambye, *L'Aumônerie de la Flotte de Flandres au XVIIe siècle. 1623–1662* (Louvain, 1967). I wish to thank Dr R.A. Stradling for drawing my attention to this work. Cf. J.D. Spence, *The Memory Palace of Matteo Ricci* (London, 1985), p. 76.

[21] See G. Psaila Cumbo, pp. 25–6; E. Hambye, pp. 102–6; NLM, Lib.MS.211, fols 275–8. For 'Dry Mass', see *New Catholic Encyclopaedia* (Washington, 1967), 9, p. 414.

[22] Repeated blasphemies against the Catholic faith, the Blessed Virgin and the saints were to be punished back in Malta. See NLM, Lib.MS.211, fols 275–8.

Muslim, Protestant or Orthodox. In such moments the chaplain's role as confessor was paramount and Manso's manual of 1699 covered the extreme contingencies likely to confront his Order's chaplains aboard its galleys.[23] Conventual chaplains aboard the galleys also took turns to attend the sick and dying in their Order's celebrated hospital at Valletta. For almost a century this had its separate ward for galley slaves, long before Vincent de Paul, Gaspard de Simiane and Bishop Gault collaborated with the French Crown to establish a galley hospital at Marseilles in 1646.[24]

Whilst the Order of St John's hospital at Valletta probably looked after its sick galley slaves better than the hospital at Marseilles, the Order remained fatalistic about life aboard its galleys to a greater degree than the Jesuits were ever fatalistic about their mission aboard the sailing ships of the period. From the Order of St John's archives I have not yet found anything so positive as this praise of the ordinary mariner by Fr. Georges Fournier, SJ, in the 1630s:

> It is wrong, even heretical, to assert that a poor man doing his job, a soldier bearing arms or a sailor cannot become perfect. True virtue resides in deeds not words. Usually sailors are better at working than expressing themselves in words; they can save their souls by exemplifying virtue rather than by analysing that same virtue in words.[25]

This difference in tone between a religious order and a religious, military order is probably explained as much by the Jesuits' emphasis on human perfectibility as by the dependence of the Maltese economy on the brutalities of the Order of St John's *corso* in the Levant. And another difference was this. Although the Order of St John's *carovane* embodied the Counter-Reformation 'parish at sea' as authentically as the Jesuit-served sailing ships of the period, the Order of St John's 'parish at sea' was linked with a larger, far-flung parish on land. Prayers for the success of its *carovane* were said in the Order's commanderies throughout Catholic Europe and at the convents of its nuns, *les Dames Hospitalières*, in Spain, Portugal and France. Prominent in this prayerful process at Malta were two churches especially: *Notre Dame de Liesse* on the waterfront at Valletta and, of course, Our Lady of Graces at Zabbar. In this latter sanctuary the reality of the Order's 'parish at sea' was immortalized by some of those votive paintings I mentioned at the beginning of this paper.

---

[23] See NLM, Lib.MS.211, fols 349–96.

[24] See A. Zysberg, *Les Galériens* (Paris, 1987), p. 353; Bamford, p. 215.

[25] My translation is from the French quoted by Chabaud-Arnault, 'Un Aumônier', p. 383. About 1553–54 the Venetian galley captain, Cristoforo Canale, had argued that galleys could be conduits of Christian reformation for convicted criminals sentenced to their oar: 'For blasphemy, gambling, theft, lechery, drunkenness and other vices (if any remain) are strictly forbidden to them. Little by little they are introduced to the virtuous and Christian conduct they are compelled to observe on the galley, and there they are taught the trades most necessary to life, at their own choice, in such a way that on their release from slavery they may be able to earn a living. And all become well versed in nautical affairs. One may conclude, then, that a work so pleasing to God, so advantageous to princes and so beneficial to the prisoners themselves can only be of boundless profit.' See D. Chambers and B. Pullan, *Venice, A Documentary History, 1450–1630* (Oxford, 1992), p. 101. Let me thank Professor Pullan for drawing my attention to this source.

14

The Order of St John in England, 1827–1858

Jonathan Riley-Smith

Like so much of the history of the Military Orders in the nineteenth century, an accurate account of the origins of The Most Venerable Order of St John has never been published. This paper begins and ends with a catastrophe for the English knights, but it should be remembered that thirty years later they were legitimized when Queen Victoria made St John an order of the British Crown.

On 20 December 1858 the lieutenant grand master, the vice-chancellor and the magistral secretary of the Sovereign Military Order of Malta demanded publicly that their names be removed from a work entitled *Synoptical Sketch* and published by 'a respectable society calling itself Sovereign Order of St John of Jerusalem Anglia'. They stated, furthermore, that 'the Order of St John of Jerusalem of which his Excellency (the lieutenant) is the head ... has never been in any organic connexion with the above named society'.[1] They followed this up with a protest to the British Crown.[2] In a storm of publicity,[3] four Catholic knights of St John and one Protestant left the English Order.[4] This is an attempt to sketch in the background to that event.

In the confusion that reigned in the Order of Malta after the loss of its island state in 1798, the French knights arrogated to themselves the right to manage the Order's affairs as a whole through a capitular commission, the powers of

---

[1] Museum and Library of the Most Venerable Order of St John, (hereafter MVO), Historical Memoranda I.38, 107.

[2] Ibid., 1.50.

[3] Library of the British Association of the Sovereign Military Order of Malta (hereafter BASMOM), Letter Book 1.329–31; MVO, Letters of Claudius Shaw (Correspondence bundle 17), William Winthrop and J.O. Woodhouse (Correspondence bundle 18).

[4] MVO, Historical Memoranda 1.128–30; Letters of Walter Strickland, together with a reply, in Correspondence bundle 17.

From *The Military Orders: Fighting for the Faith and Caring for the Sick*, ed. Malcolm Barber. Copyright © 1994 by Malcolm Barber. Published by Variorum, Ashgate Publishing Ltd, Gower House, Croft Road, Aldershot, Hampshire, GU11 3HR, Great Britain.

which they claimed, through a mistranslation of a papal letter, to have been recognized by the pope. They were supported by the French government and, somewhat ambiguously, by the lieutenant.[5] But with the commission's head, the Commander Jean-Louis de Dienne, a very old man – it was later said that he had been 'in his dotage' when he approved the sending of representatives to England in 1826[6] – power fell in 1821 into the hands of the chancellor, the Marquis Pierre-Hippolyte de Sainte-Croix-Molay or of Santa Croce. Sainte-Croix was said to have been secretary to the chancery of the Spanish and Portuguese knights of Malta. His title was dubious. He was rumoured to have been deeply in debt.[7] When, twenty years later, Robert Pearsall referred to him as he described the origins of the English *Langue* to the secretary-general of the Austrian knights of Malta, the secretary broke in:

> What, has Sancta Croce been in England too? I hope he did not get any money out of you. He went to France, and raised there some thousands of francs with which he decamped, but surely the English have had more sense than to let him play the same trick with them.[8]

With Sainte-Croix in charge, the French knights of Malta pursued a heady foreign policy with the aim of restoring the Order's presence in the Mediterranean. The revolt of the Greeks against Ottoman Turkish rule was attracting adventurers from all over Europe, and the Turkish empire seemed to be on the verge of collapse.[9] In July 1823, the capitular commission, apparently with the backing of the French government, entered into an alliance with the leaders of the Greek revolt under Alexander Mavrokordatos. The Greeks recognized the Order's sovereignty over Rhodes and bound themselves to cede two islands as stepping stones to its reconquest. In return the Order would provide troops and 10,000,000 francs for the war.[10] Accordingly, an attempt was made in the following November to raise on the London market £640,000 worth of stock, returning 5 per cent, through the issuing of 5,000 bonds, redeemable after twenty years. In a prospectus the ability of the Order to meet any debt was described in glowing terms.[11]

---

[5] See M.H.T. Michel de Pierredon, *Histoire politique de l'ordre souverain de Saint-Jean de Jérusalem (Ordre de Malte) de 1798 à 1955*, 2nd edn, 3 vols so far (Paris, 1956–), 2, pp. 137–60, esp. pp. 137–48.

[6] MVO, Historical Memoranda 1.98.

[7] R. Woof, *Order of St John of Jerusalem in England* (London, 1872), proof, opp. p. 13; MVO, Historical Memoranda 1.238–9, 243; 3.133; Pierredon, 2, pp. 198–298; cf. BASMOM, Letter Book 1.185.

[8] MVO, Minutes and Deliberations of the Sovereign Order of Saint John Anglia (the minute book of the English *Langue*) (OSJ Anglia Minutes) 107.

[9] For the background, see M.S. Anderson, *The Eastern Question, 1774–1923* (London, 1966), pp. 53–8.

[10] Pierredon, 2, pp. 211–15; and see pp. 205–59, 269. See also MVO, Historical Memoranda 1.105, 242–3; Woof, pp. 6–7; E. Driault and M. L'Héritier, *Histoire diplomatique de la Grèce de 1821 à nos jours*, 5 vols (Paris, 1925–6), 1, pp. 208–15.

[11] MVO, Ms K 8/1 (bonds); Pierredon, 2, pp. 245–6 (extracts from printed prospectus); Historical Memoranda 1.7 (copy of the prospectus), 121 (transcripts of press comment).

The treaty was opposed in Greece by rival liberators and the governments of England, Austria and Russia wrecked it.[12] Meanwhile there were rumours that the money raised in London was being misused. In December 1823 the lieutenant published his disavowal of the loan, and in 1824 he revoked the capitular commission's powers and dissolved it. He sent an agent from Italy to reorganize the French *Langues*. The French government, for its part, withdrew its recognition of knighthoods granted by the commission and acknowledged only those specifically authorized by the lieutenant himself. The capitular commission therefore ceased to have any legal existence.[13]

The decision of the lieutenant and the attitude of the government of France had little effect, however, on the council of the French *Langues* which reconstituted itself under the control of Sainte-Croix, confirming the unlimited powers which had already been conferred on him. It still claimed to enjoy the powers of the capitular commission and was as committed as ever to the Mediterranean adventure. In June 1826 it decided to give *all* Christians the opportunity to contribute to the recovery of an island headquarters in the Mediterranean and the restoration of the Order's ancient naval role. This was a prelude to another appeal to England, and Dienne and Sainte-Croix authorized two emissaries to open negotiations with a Scot called Donald Currie, who lived in London.[14] One of these emissaries was a man called Philippe de Chastelain, a shady character who at times passed himself off as a count and had to be rescued by Currie from a debtor's prison;[15] he ended his days in the 1870s eking out a living in Scotland as a 'Professor of the French Language and Drawing in all its departments in Edinburgh and Peebles'.[16] The French thought that Currie was a Scottish gentleman and the owner of an estate. He was not, but he apparently had respectable connections. He was an army accoutrement maker who, according to Chastelain, was 'of some education, but [of a] very common appearance'. He had become known to the French through his trade, had travelled to France and had met Sainte-Croix.[17]

The agreement made between Currie and the representatives of the French *Langues* was recorded in three Instruments of Convention, together with a further agreement clarifying the terms of payment to Currie on commission. Currie was empowered to raise £240,000 by private subscription. With the money he was to employ men and to buy arms, munitions and vessels for a Mediterranean expedition. The pay and conditions of service of the officers he commissioned

[12] Letter of Chastelain. MVO, Historical Memoranda 1.105, also 242–3; Pierredon, 2, pp. 248–9,255–6.

[13] MVO, Historical Memoranda 1.85–6; BASMOM, Letter Book 1.30. See Pierredon, 2, pp. 257–8, 260–72, 289–90; also MVO, OSJ Anglia Minutes 24, 26.

[14] MVO, First Instrument of Convention. Ms K 32/4 (translation in Historical Memoranda 1.43–9).

[15] MVO, Archives § 57; Copies of Documents 96. See also Bigsby, notes in OSJ Anglia Minutes 386–7.

[16] Visiting Card. MVO, Historical Memoranda 1.244–5, also 75, 101–3, 105, 234–48; 3.226.

[17] MVO, Historical Memoranda 1.243, 247; Bigsby, notes in OSJ Anglia Minutes 377, 384.

were detailed. A 'Gallo-Britannic factory', incorporating a hospital, was to be established to provide a base for merchants in the Levant. Two clauses stipulated that financial subscribers could become members of the Order and that all officers commissioned by Currie would also have the right to join it.[18] The Instruments were soon followed by a Letter of Instruction to Currie, who was appointed the Order's agent-general, empowering him to set up a hospital to be served by brothers of the Anglican rite.[19]

The scheme to raise an expeditionary force in England made some sense in view of the chaos reigning in the Levant, the growing economic importance of Britain, the huge stocks of war surplus that could be bought cheaply and the large number of unemployed English soldiers and sailors who were drifting about the country in the 1820s. The fact that this was to be a private venture, funded by subscription, made it difficult for any government to intervene. The proposal to establish a commercial centre in the eastern Mediterranean answered to the needs of British merchants after the folding of the Levant Company in 1825. But what about the recruitment of non-Catholic knights of Malta? It is clear from the preamble to the Instruments, in which the French council claimed to be acting in the interests of the 'Grand Priories of Brandenburg and the Greek Grand Priories of Russia',[20] that precedents – the Protestant Bailiwick of Brandenburg, which had been encouraged in 1763 to seek closer ties with the Order, had begun to pay responsions and had even agreed to send deputies to the general chapter in Valletta of 1776,[21] and a short-lived non-Catholic grand priory of Russia founded by Tsar Paul I – were very much in mind; it is worth noting that the right extended to Currie's officers to apply for membership of the Order echoed one of the criteria for membership of the Russian grand priory.

Although Currie did not raise much money,[22] he recruited a number of Hospitallers, although he was not too particular whom he enrolled.[23] In February 1830 Sainte-Croix, now dreaming of the establishment of a headquarters for the Order in Algeria, authorized Currie and Chastelain to form a committee to revive the English *Langue*; the French would recognize the knights it nominated and any funds it collected were to be under its own control. This committee, calling itself the Council of the English Language, was formed at

---

[18] MVO, First, Second and Third Instruments of Convention. Mss K 32/4; Historical Memoranda 1.43–9; Copies of Documents 1–9, 82–3; OSJ Anglia Minutes 3, 5–11. See also Pierredon, **2**, pp. 291–3.

[19] Although receptions had to accord with the Order's statutes. MVO, Letter of Instruction. Ms K 32/4; OSJ Anglia Minutes 6–7; Bigsby, notes in OSJ Anglia Minutes 389.

[20] MVO, First Instrument of Convention. Ms K 32/4. See also Sainte-Croix's later letter to Currie in Copies of Documents 74–5.

[21] See R. Cavaliero, *The Last of the Crusaders* (London, 1960), pp. 160, 164.

[22] MVO, OSJ Anglia Minutes 11

[23] For an example, see MVO, Historical Memoranda 1.123.

a special meeting on 12 January 1831[24] and presidential executive power were given to another charlatan who called himself Count Alexander Mortara. Some idea of Mortara's style can be gleaned from a letter he wrote from the 'Auberge of St John, St John's Gate, St John's Square, Clerkenwell' – in other words from the pub that then occupied the Gatehouse of the medieval priory – claiming that he and his *confrères* had opened a hospital.[25]

In the winter of 1830–31 Currie recruited the Reverend Robert Peat, the rector of New Brentford in Middlesex and a former chaplain of King George IV, and John Philippart, a clerk in the War Office.[26] Peat and Philippart soon realized that Mortara was up to no good – they accused him of selling knighthoods[27] – and, with Currie's support, they had set up a rival centre of power within the *Langue* as early as the following April.[28] They expelled Mortara from the Order and Currie followed their example, dismissing him as unworthy and demanding the return of the money and property he held.[29] This made no difference at all to Mortara, who continued to run his own group. In March 1832, Peat and Philippart met Chastelain and persuaded him to take their complaints of corruption and mismanagement to Sainte-Croix in France. To their amazement and anger the French backed not them, but Mortara.[30]

The situation in London in the mid-1830s, therefore, was as follows. There were two English *Langues*, an 'official' one under Mortara, recognized by the French, and an unrecognized one under Peat.[31] The unrecognized group, however, seems to have been much the more respectable of the two: Peat had rescinded the nominations of those individuals who could not prove their right to bear arms[32] and he had recruited some quite influential people. It was probably this that persuaded him to try to take advantage of the fact that the

---

[24] MVO, Copies of Documents 60–71, and see 72–82; OSJ Anglia Minutes 11–12; Bigsby, notes in OSJ Anglia Minutes 383. See also Pierredon, **2**, pp. 295–6.

[25] MVO, Historical Memoranda 1. 75, 125, 243, 245; Ms K 32/4; Bigsby, notes in OSJ Anglia Minutes 390; Archives § 122.

[26] MVO, Historical Memoranda 1.123–4, 247; Ms K 8/6; OSJ Anglia Minutes 12; Bigsby, notes in OSJ Anglia Minutes 383–4; Nominations and Declarations 1–3; Peat's letters in Correspondence bundle 15; Philippart's in Historical Memoranda 3.222–31. For Philippart, see *Dictionary of National Biography* (*DNB*), **15**, p. 1054.

[27] MVO, Archives §§ 4–5, 10, 46.

[28] Ibid., §§ 1–4.

[29] Ibid., §§ 25,52; Historical Memoranda 1.125; Copies of Documents 98–9.

[30] MVO, Archives §§ 39, 51, 54–7, 63, 72, and see 69, 71, 76–7, 85–8, 119–20, 122, 124, 126; Historical Memoranda 1.75, 101–3, 245; 3.248; OSJ Anglia Minutes 6–7; Bigsby, notes in OSJ Anglia Minutes 388–9. See Copies of Documents 99, 101; Peat's letter of 24 July 1832 in Correspondence bundle 15; Bigsby, notes in OSJ Anglia Minutes 385.

[31] Bigsby (notes in MVO, OSJ Anglia Minutes 378, 390) called Peat's group 'that of St Croix'. Sainte-Croix was living in London in 1835 and had attached himself to Peat, but he had lost touch with the French by then. For an attempt to establish the Order in Scotland see Peat's letter of 6 May 1836 in Correspondence bundle 15.

[32] MVO, OSJ Anglia Minutes 20.

Letters Patent of Philip and Mary, which in 1557 had revived the Order in England and restored those estates which had not yet been alienated, had never been repealed. Were they still in force? On 24 February 1834 he took an oath of office as prior before the Lord Chief Justice of England in the Court of King's Bench; the fact that he was allowed to do so was to his *Langue* evidence that the Letters Patent were still valid.[33] And when Mortara disappeared after being challenged to a duel early in 1837 by one of Peat's supporters,[34] the field was left to Peat's *Langue*.

By the time of Peat's death in April 1837,[35] therefore, his party comprised the only English *Langue*. But the English knights were a tiny and disorganized group of men. They had, of course, lost touch with the French, since they had not been recognized by them; they did not even have the address of the French grand secretary.[36] But they now became more active, largely through the enthusiasm of a Scot called Richard Broun, who had been made a knight in 1835 and as registrar and then grand secretary ran the *Langue* from 1837 to his death in December 1858. Broun, who made enormous personal sacrifices for the English Order, was an eccentric individual, 'busily engaged in the projection of a number of schemes, most of them of a somewhat fantastic nature', which led him once into bankruptcy: he died in great distress. He was, for instance, obsessed with extraordinary rights which he believed belonged to the heirs of baronets like himself; and he was satirized by Disraeli in *Sybil* as 'Sir Vavasour Firebrace'.[37]

He and his colleagues wanted to make contact with their *confrères* the knights of Malta abroad and, in July 1837, William Crawford and Robert Lucas Pearsall were sent to France and Germany respectively.[38] Crawford carried a letter asking for protection and assistance. He found the French grand secretary in Paris and brought back to London the news that Sainte-Croix had been engaged in fraud, but also quite erroneous confirmation that the English *Langue*'s origins had been regular.[39] Delighted that contact had been made, the English fired off a series of questions. They were concerned about the legality of their origins and about the terms of the Instruments of Convention of 1827: they very reasonably refused to be bound by the obligation to furnish an expeditionary force. They were also anxious about the prospect of heavy fees and passage money. The English upper classes, they insisted, were not well off. And they were worried about their status; obviously they had not revived the

---

[33] See MVO, Historical Memoranda 1.90; Bigsby, notes in OSJ Anglia Minutes 387–8; Nominations and Declarations 34.

[34] Bigsby, notes in MVO, OSJ Anglia Minutes 390.

[35] MVO, OSJ Anglia Minutes 22.

[36] See Ibid., 25.

[37] BASMOM, Letter Book 1.173; Bigsby, notes in MVO, OSJ Anglia Minutes 379; *DNB*, 2, p. 1377; I. Anstruther, *The Knight and the Umbrella* (London, 1963), pp. 80–81.

[38] MVO, OSJ Anglia Minutes 23.

[39] Ibid., 24–9.

Order in its traditional sense – most of them were, after all, Protestants – but they felt that somehow the Order should adapt to take account of them. They wanted a pluriform, secularized Order; and their ideal was expressed in a very British way.

> The Order could no longer either be Monastic or Celibate. It appeared to the English council however to be extremely desirable that a suitable Edifice as the Chef Lieu of the Order, partaking of the character of a modern Club-House, should be founded at the joint expense of the eight *Langues* in Paris.[40]

The French provided regulations for admission and the scale of fees in use. The English were told that they could only correspond with the grand magistry through the French council; that diplomas or bulls of the lieutenant in favour of Protestants could only be granted if the cases for special dispensation were presented to the Order's sacred council in Italy; that Sainte-Croix was no longer a member of the French council and that the present members did not know if he had received from the sacred council the legal authority to institute the Order in England as a chapter. The French promised to lay the propositions the English had sent before the lieutenant and to transmit his reply, but it seems they never did so.[41]

The emphasis on the powers of the grand magistry over the appointment of knights worried the English; and they were also concerned about the legality of the impending election of Sir Henry Dymoke as their prior.[42] They proposed – and this shows how divorced from reality they were – that a general chapter of representatives of the eight ancient *Langues* should be convoked to adapt the statutes and to delegate to each *Langue* the authority to administer its own affairs.[43] They did not know that there were not eight *Langues* formally in existence. They did not even seem to have realized that they were suggesting an infringement of the prerogatives of the grand magistry. They wrote to the lieutenant in July 1838, asking for confirmation of their revival, ratification of their membership and the general chapter. The French were asked to transmit the letter to Italy, but they do not seem to have wanted to post on something so impertinent and they conveniently mislaid the first copy handed to them; it was not until March 1840 that the French mandatory-general confirmed that he had sent it.[44] By then the English were becoming more intransigent. They would have no interference from Italy on the appointment of their prior;[45] and in April 1839 they had written a second letter to the lieutenant, stating that

---

[40] Ibid., 30–39.

[41] Ibid., 40–41; MVO Historical. Memoranda 1.39–41.

[42] MVO, OSJ Anglia Minutes 53–5, 58, 86.

[43] Ibid., 41; Letter from Sir Joshua Colles Meredyth (20 November 1837) in Correspondence bundle 14.

[44] MVO, OSJ Anglia Minutes 51–5, 57–9, 61, 72–6, 84, 103, 122.

[45] Ibid., 74.

they would continue to run their *Langue* along present lines unless he summoned a general chapter.[46]

Meanwhile, the other emissary, Robert Pearsall, had been sent to Germany, which he knew well, to try to establish links with the German knights of Malta. Pearsall was a composer, very successful in his day, and was one of those sophisticated and snobbish men who knew everyone worth knowing.[47] Crawford had brought back from Paris worrying news about Sainte-Croix's activities. It was more than confirmed by Pearsall in mid-1838.

> The marquis de Santa Croce is perfectly well known to be a person of irrespectable character,... If these circumstances were publicly known in England we would find it difficult to obtain members of that high respectability we need. Allow me to ask whether our *Langue* has been formally recognized by the French *Langues?*[48]

A Frenchman Pearsall knew denied knowledge of any of the figures in the capitular commission who had signed the Instrument of Convention in 1827 and stated that their names were not familiar in the 'best society of Paris'.

> I therefore leave it to you to judge how far it may be safe or prudent for us to have anything more to do with these people until we are satisfied of their respectability from *unquestionable* authority.[49]

A year later, after he had returned to England, Pearsall wrote to protest that, in a publication called *The Hospitallaria*, his mission had been declared to have been

> ... in the highest degree satisfactory. Is this the fact? My mission had no result. I was at first received with much politeness; but owing to the bad character of Santa Croce I experienced afterwards the deepest mortification ... *The Hospitallaria* is avowedly put in circulation for the purpose of gaining recruits ... Now supposing that on the faith of the statements that work any man of angry temperament such as Sir J. Sebright[50] were to become a member and after having paid his money were to find out Santa Croce's character; and that it was known to you [Richard Broun] and that the German-Italian knights refused to join us ... what might be the consequences?[51]

In the aftermath of his experiences, Pearsall's first reaction was to suggest that the English knights find someone of the status 'to maintain our position

---

[46] Ibid., 76–8, 165. See also MVO Historical Memoranda 3.44, 73, 78, 82, 154; OSJ Anglia Minutes 181–2, 186–8, 193.

[47] *DNB*, 15, pp. 603–4. See MVO, Historical Memoranda 3.146–7, 149, 154.

[48] MVO, Historical Memoranda 3.133.

[49] Ibid., 3.134. See also 135; MVO, OSJ Anglia Minutes 45–9, 60, 87–8.

[50] Sir John Sebright, Bart., *DNB*, 17, p. 1108.

[51] MVO, Historical Memoranda 3.139; OSJ Anglia Minutes 60; and see Historical Memoranda 3.146, 147; Letters from Sir Joshua Colles Meredyth in Correspondence bundle 14. Meredyth had been knighted on Malta by Grand Master Hompesch in 1798. Copies of Documents 128; OSJ Anglia Minutes 24.

against the pretensions of the Italians'.[52] That meant a member of the royal family, whom, it was suggested, could take the office of Turcopolier. Pearsall was pressing for this from the middle of 1838, proposing first the duke of Cambridge and then either the duke of Sussex or the king of Hanover.[53]

It was decided to approach the duke of Sussex. It is a measure of the innocence of the leaders of the English *Langue* that they thought that the appointment as their head of an eccentric member of a very eccentric family, who was also the Grand Master of the English freemasons, would somehow enable them to come to terms with the grand magistry in Rome.[54] Sir William Hillary, a member of the *Langue* who had been the duke's equerry, was asked to lend a hand. Hillary had visited Malta in 1797 and had seen Grand Master Hompesch's court in its last days of faded splendour,[55] had raised his own regiment in the Napoleonic War, had founded the Royal National Lifeboat Institution[56] and was obsessed by a plan for the Christian reoccupation of the Holy Land, which would be governed by the Order of Malta.[57] He took to this task with the enthusiasm he showed in everything he did: 'the placing [of] a Prince of the Blood Royal of England at our head is the crowning work', he wrote.[58] But in the summer of 1839 the duke refused.[59] Hillary expressed his disappointment with his usual verve.

> I feel with you, all the difficulties which a Prince of the Blood Royal of England has to encounter in these times, with a Court constituted like ours – with such hostility to the Chartered rights of Aristocrat and Hereditary rank, as those now in power have shewn.[60]

The names of the king of Hanover (again) and Prince Albert[61] were canvassed. By June 1841 it was even being proposed to surrender the English *Langue* into the hands of the queen in the hope of it being re-created as a state Order with Prince Albert as Grand Master – the first sign of something like the solution that was to come in 1888. Pearsall was scathing. Prince Albert, he wrote,

---

[52] MVO, Historical Memoranda 3.138; OSJ Anglia Minutes 60.

[53] MVO, Historical Memoranda 3. 135, 138–9; OSJ Anglia Minutes 101.

[54] See *DNB*, 1, pp. 729–30.

[55] MVO, Historical Memoranda 3.4, 49.

[56] *DNB*, Supplement, pp. 847–8.

[57] MVO, Historical Memoranda 3.1–113 *passim*; OSJ Anglia Minutes 134, 141, 146–9, 154–7, 166–7, 175; *DNB*, Supplement, p. 848; Letters of Arthur Murray in MVO, Correspondence bundle 14. An appeal to the king of Prussia, who was on a visit to England, to support the scheme for the Holy Land was turned down flat. The king was offended by a reference to the Order's sovereignty. Historical Memoranda 3.149–50; OSJ Anglia Minutes 195–9, 202–3. See Bigsby, notes in OSJ Anglia Minutes 391.

[58] MVO, Historical Memoranda 3.18.

[59] Ibid., See 3.13, 16–18, 22, 25–6, 29, 138–9; OSJ Anglia Minutes 64–72, 74, 77, 83, 88–91, 101–2. See also Historical Memoranda 3.98, 102, 104; OSJ Anglia Minutes 232–3, 239, 244, 247–8.

[60] MVO, Historical Memoranda 3.29.

[61] Ibid., 3.33–5, 38; OSJ Anglia Minutes 208.

... comes out of a very slippery family. I knew an aunt of his personally who was as false as a cat. His uncle Leopold is not much better; and his father is one of the greatest rogues that were ever embodied in ermine.[62]

He went on to propose what could be a second way forward.

We ought to endeavour to get hold of some influential Catholics. If we had three or four *important* Catholics in our fraternity I think that I could open a direct communication with Rome through the recently consecrated bishop of Strasbourg who is a particular friend of mine.[63]

Another route was explored in 1841. In September Sir Warwick Tonkin[64] was sent to Paris on a 'special mission' to confer with the French council on the subject of Sir William Hillary's scheme for the Christian reoccupation of the Holy Land. But he also carried with him the Instruments of Convention of 1827 and he thought he had persuaded the French grand secretary to recognize them as being legitimate and correct. In fact, all the French grand secretary had done was to sign the First Instrument and record over his signature that he had taken cognizance of Tonkin's mission,[65] but at least he had put his name, however qualified, to the founding document of the English *Langue*.

The English also decided to approach the grand magistry directly. Sir Robert Chermside, physician to the British Embassy in Paris and the English *Langue*'s representative there, alerted Richard Broun to the fact that the grand bailiff Fra' Cristoforo Ferretti was coming to London and in the spring of 1843 Broun, Tonkin and Ferretti had several meetings. Ferretti was very pleasant and agreed to deliver to the lieutenant and his council a document containing a series of propositions, together with a covering letter and a copy of the Letters Patent of Philip and Mary. The English proposed that 'the *Langue* of England and the *Langue* of Italy' – an insulting start, since the grand magistry was not the *Langue* of Italy – should begin discussions on equal terms, each recognizing the other's authority and membership; that the English would cooperate with the Italians in any plan for the reorganization of the Order; that the administration of the English *Langue* would be vested in the grand prior and his council, together with the right to admit whomsoever they pleased; that the government of the English *Langue* would be in conformity with the

---

[62] MVO, Historical Memoranda 3.144; OSJ Anglia Minutes 160–2. The idea was still being discussed in 1845. Arthur Murray's letter in Correspondence bundle 14. Prince Albert had the cross of Malta. OSJ Anglia Minutes 143–4, 207, 225; BASMOM, Letter Book 1.96.

[63] MVO, Historical Memoranda 3.144; also 156. In fact there were already Catholics in the *Langue*, and of the four who were to resign in 1858, two had been made knights of St John in 1841.

[64] Tonkin had been received into the Anglo-Bavarian and Prussian *Langue* in 1830. MVO, OSJ Anglia Minutes 149, 152.

[65] MVO, First Instrument of Convention. Ms K 32/4; Historical Memoranda 1.42; OSJ Anglia Minutes 168–9, 178–9, 203; for Tonkin's report, see 179–85, and for his letters, see Correspondence bundle 17; also the letters of Meredyth and Perrott in Correspondence bundles 14–15. For a later, inaccurate reference, BASMOM, Letter Book 1.82–5, 88–90.

ancient statutes 'in so far as these statutes are compatible with the existing habits and feelings of British society'; that the English would pay responsions when they were numerous enough, but that as soon as the Holy See recognized their existence a donation would be made to the Order of Malta's hospital in Rome;[66] and that English admissions should comprise Protestants as well as Catholics.[67] Ferretti had these propositions translated into Italian and he forwarded them to the grand magistry through the papal ambassador in Paris.[68] The lieutenant replied on 17 August. He was very polite, but firm.

> Not without real pain, we feel ourselves placed in the impossibility to be able to lend our adhesion to the project, since the statutes of the Order prohibit Protestants, into which Roman Catholics only are admitted.[69]

Broun's reply was touchy – he was offended at not being addressed as grand secretary – and intransigent. He repeated an argument suggested to him by Sir William Hillary:[70] that at a time when Catholics could now sit in Parliament they should not be excluding Protestants from their institutions. Perhaps not surprisingly the lieutenant did not write again.[71]

In the late 1840s the *Langue* nearly died out and Richard Broun became thoroughly disheartened.[72] But after 1855, and particularly from January 1857, there was a resurgence of interest, and the council agreed to print a new edition of Broun's *Synoptical Sketch* of the Order, which he had first published in 1837.[73] Although the *Langue* remained a small body of men,[74] it was not short of grand ideas, such as taking advantage of the close ties between Turkey and Britain in the aftermath of the Crimean War to negotiate the return of Rhodes to the Order.[75]

At this point there developed the kind of approach to the grand magistry suggested by Robert Pearsall twenty years before – the use of a Catholic knight of the *Langue* as an intermediary. John James Watts, a scholarly man whose passion was the Order's history, had been received into the *Langue* in 1832.[76] He had then gone abroad and had rarely been in England for twenty-

---

[66] This followed Pearsall's suggestion (MVO, OSJ Anglia Minutes 177) that the English should contribute to the Pontifical Military Hospital being run by the Order of Malta.

[67] MVO, OSJ Anglia Minutes 218–21; Perrott's letters in Correspondence bundle 15; BASMOM, Letter Book 1. 25.

[68] MVO, OSJ Anglia Minutes 228–9; also 230, 232; and the correspondence of Chermside and Tonkin in Correspondence bundle 17.

[69] MVO, OSJ Anglia Minutes 233–5. Obviously a clumsy translation of an Italian original.

[70] MVO, Historical Memoranda 3.98.

[71] MVO, OSJ Anglia Minutes 235–9, 242, 245, 249, 258.

[72] Bigsby, notes in MVO, OSJ Anglia Minutes 379.

[73] MVO, OSJ Anglia Minutes 280, 291 ff, 297 ff, 311, 314, 321, 347, 351–2.

[74] Ibid., 291 Cf. BASMOM, Letter Book 1.24, 78.

[75] MVO, OSJ Anglia Minutes 294. The membership of the Prince of Wales was already envisaged. Ibid. 322.

[76] MVO, Historical Memoranda 1.129, 225–33; 3.241; BASMOM, Letter Book 1. 138; Letter of Robert Peat in MVO, Correspondence bundle 15. Watts's books are now in the BASMOM Library.

five years: in the late 1850s he was living on Malta. He had, therefore, been completely out of touch with the English.[77] In the summer of 1857 his existence was brought to Broun's attention and he was appointed commissioner to the *Langues* of Italy and Spain with the task of advertising the English to the knights of Malta.[78] Interest in the grand magistry had been rearoused in England by news of its plans to found a hospital in Jerusalem, and the English *Langue* announced publicly that it would support it,[79] although Broun was much more enthusiastic about the idea of reoccupying Rhodes. For him, the establishment of a hospital for pilgrims in Jerusalem was

> ... like a recurrence of the Dark Ages, and savours of monkdom, instead of chivalry. We live in a material age, one of progress and rationality; and the Order of St John must aim at higher things than washing the feet, and healing the sores of the few thousands of persons who may think fit to pay visits to the early scenes of the Christian faith.[80]

In the spring of 1858 Watts told Broun that he was planning to go to Rome for the general chapter to be held on the Order's feast day, 24 June: he did not add that he had already made up his mind that, as a Catholic, he should apply for reception into the Order of Malta.[81] Broun replied with a long letter of instructions, going over the old ground, but admitting that 'we must now, however, through your diplomacy feel our way.' He enclosed a copy of his *Synoptical Sketch* for presentation to the lieutenant.[82] On 17 June Watts visited the officials of the grand priory of Rome. Their reaction was astonishing. The sacred council of the Order was specially convened on the following day and Watts was asked to address it. He gave a short talk on the origins of the English *Langue*, but he was immediately confronted with the true story.

> After this exposé [he wrote] what more could I say? Obviously the question now was, not of a concurrence of the Italian *Langue* to our resuscitation, but whether we had any right to be considered a branch of the ... Order ... at all!'

He battled on, however, stressing that whatever their origins the English had acted in good faith, and drawing attention to the Letters Patent of 1557 and Peat's declaration in the Court of King's Bench in 1834. Count Gozze, the magistral secretary, acknowledged the advantages of cooperating with a go-ahead, practical people like the English, stated that the grand magistry was willing to meet them half-way and promised to prepare a paper on the matter.

---

[77] MVO, OSJ Anglia Minutes 317–18, 320, 323, 325, 328–9, 334–5, 337–8; BASMOM Letter Book 1.132–5, 138.
[78] BASMOM, Letter Book 1.13–15, 138.
[79] Ibid., 1. 54–5. See MVO, OSJ Anglia Minutes 354.
[80] BASMOM, Letter Book 1.18–20, 24; also see 38.
[81] Ibid., 1. 21–7, 36–7; MVO, OSJ Anglia Minutes 337.
[82] BASMOM, Letter Book 1. 21–7.

Watts reported all of this to Broun;[83] he did not add that he had been received into the priory of Rome as a knight of Devotion.[84]

The speed of the sacred council's reaction is proof that something was in the wind. In fact it had already been in touch with two Englishmen, George Bowyer and Edmund Waterton, with a view to the restoration of a Catholic grand priory of England. In a note on the evidence provided by the *Synoptical Sketch* about the English *Langue*, Gozze, who was severely critical of the English attitude to their foundation, drew attention to the Letters Patent of 1557 and stated bluntly that the Order needed an English priory and that Bowyer, Waterton and Watts could provide its nucleus.[85] The English were later convinced that it was the ambiguity surrounding the Letters Patent of 1557 that really mattered to the members of the sacred council, who, in the tradition of all managers of great corporations, at once sat up and responded warmly when they heard of them.[86] This impression may have been gained from Watts's letters, because Watts was himself a great enthusiast for the idea that the *Langue* had been recognized as an existing corporation in 1834.[87] But Gozze and his colleagues seem to have been chiefly concerned with re-establishing the grand priory of England and gaining Catholic support in the richest and most powerful country in Europe.[88] Cooperation with the Protestants of the English *Langue* could be beneficial in this respect.

The paper Gozze had promised Watts was presented on 25 June 1858. His idea, which had been perhaps originally suggested by someone in the Vatican in the 1840s,[89] was that a Catholic priory in England should be formed first. This was to be recognized as a corporation, in order to claim rights under the Letters Patent. Once the Catholic priory had been established, it would announce to the grand magistry the formation of a Protestant branch, which of course already existed. In this way the relations of the grand magistry would be directly with Catholics and only indirectly with Protestants. Gozze waxed lyrical on the union.

> The Protestant branch of the English *Langue* would have to be considered as possessing a distinct interior organization, although bound to the Order by the same chivalric forms, the same exterior symbols, sharing the same illustrious

---

[83] BASMOM, Letter Book 1.28–33.

[84] BASMOM, Letter Book 1.36–7. The lieutenant's letter to Watts of 8 July addressing him as a member of the Order was regarded by the English as a compliment to their *Langue*. Letter Book 1.57, 106–7.

[85] BASMOM, Letter Book 1.40–45. See also the mysterious correspondence in 1857, involving George Bowyer, the grand magistry and a M. de Barnaby in London, in MVO, Correspondence bundle 19.

[86] See the notes in MVO, Historical Memoranda 1.93–9; and the undated brief for counsel, Historical Memoranda 1.109–12.

[87] See, for instance, BASMOM, Letter Book 1.149–50.

[88] Ibid., See 1.57–60.

[89] See Robert Chermside's letter of 22 April 1846. MVO, Historical Memoranda 3.208.

history, ... sympathizing in full reciprocity in respect to all the noble, chivalric, philanthropic and charitable tendencies ... This species of union already exists in the Order with the Protestant branch which represents the ancient Grand Bailiwick of Brandenburg in the German *Langue* ... Such are, Sir and dear Confrère, my ideas on the course to pursue to bring back to the common mother the branch of the Order of St John which has been formed in England; a branch irregular in truth up to the present moment, but in which we recognize with pleasure the germs of the most noble and most legitimate aspirations. You know with what joy this event would be hailed amongst us, and that to render it possible we would sacrifice everything excepting simply those immutable principles from which we cannot detach ourselves without crime.[90]

In a covering letter to Broun, Watts stressed that the Catholics would not interfere with the way the Protestant section was run. 'The pope will have no more to do with the matter from first to last than the Lord Mayor of London.'[91]

On 14 July a chapter general of the English *Langue* welcomed the tone of Gozze's paper. A special committee of five men, to be called The Extension Committee, had been formed to consider relations with other *Langues* and had already drafted a letter to be sent to Rome. As a move to meet Catholic wishes, but perhaps also to retain control, the Catholic members of the *Langue* were to be gathered into a new Catholic Priory of Clerkenwell within the *Langue*, and Watts was made its first prior.[92] The despatch sent to Rome is a remarkable document for its time and place. Although they did not want their origins impugned and were very unhappy about the idea that the Catholics alone would claim rights as a corporation under the Letters Patent of 1557, the English approved of them constituting a distinct class with their own prior, who would have a seat on the Protestant grand council and would act as the channel of communication with Rome and with Cardinal Wiseman, the Catholic archbishop of Westminster. And they stated:

> We are ready to recognize it [the grand magistry] as the supreme authority of the Order, provided it, in return, will meet us at once as brethren, in the position we now stand; receiving our catholics according to the ancient rules, and our protestants on the principles enunciated by your Excellency, in conformity with the precedent already established in the Bailiwick of Brandenburg.[93]

---

[90] BASMOM, Letter Book 1.46–50; MVO, Historical Memoranda 1.78, 82–3, also 76–7, 79–81, 88–9.

[91] BASMOM, Letter Book 1.51–3. Another development, a recommendation by the pope that the Order of Malta should modify its rules to take modern developments into account, delighted the English. Letter Book 1.58, 62–7, 106–7.

[92] MVO, OSJ Anglia Minutes 353–8,361; BASMOM, Letter Book 1.68–75, 77, 98–100. But a list of officers drawn up about this time surprisingly includes the name of Edmund Waterton as prior of Clerkenwell. MVO, Correspondence bundle 18.

[93] BASMOM, Letter Book 1.71–5; and see 120–25.

'We have passed the Rubicon', wrote Broun.[94] English society was very Protestant and the leaders of the English *Langue* were only too conscious that a wave of vehement anti-papist emotion might soon come crashing down on them. They wanted the independence of the Protestant section of the Order to be stressed and they believed that if Wiseman had to be involved he should be involved secretly.[95] Broun was inclined to fuss about details, but everyone agreed that legitimate recognition must come first and as quickly as possible, before the Press heard of the negotiations.[96] On 24 July Watts reported that he had had the Extension Committee's response and was hopeful that it would be well received in the grand magistry.[97]

The officials in Rome did their best to meet English concerns. The Order of Malta could never recognize the original establishment of the English *Langue* as legitimate, but was prepared to admit that the English had acted in good faith; Cardinal Wiseman had no authority over the Order of Malta and could therefore claim no powers over the Order of St John in England.[98] They also pressed Watts on the establishment of the Catholic priory and its acceptance in law as a corporation. They wanted him to go to England to get in touch with Bowyer and Waterton, whom he did not know, since the three of them were to be 'the pivots' of the new foundation.[99] It was now August and there was the usual exodus from Rome. Gozze went on holiday to the Black Forest in Germany. Everything was now hanging on the meeting of the sacred council in late October, but the officials of the Order of Malta were very optimistic.[100]

It is hard to see how the subjection of the English *Langue* to a Catholic grand priory, however autonomously the Protestants were constituted, could have been acceptable in mid-nineteenth-century Britain. But in fact it was Catholics, not Protestants, who destroyed it. On 27 August Watts, who was back in Malta, received the following telegram from Bowyer and Waterton. 'Hold no communication whatever with Brown and his friends till we meet. Do not accept their offer. When will you come?'[101] George Bowyer was a very able academic lawyer and MP in his late forties, who had converted to Catholicism in 1850.[102] Edmund Waterton was a much younger man, still only in his twenties, a

[94] Ibid., 1.79.

[95] Ibid., 1.79–85. For the Order's appeal to Protestants, see the letter from Rev. Gustavus Adolphus Warner (24 February 1858) in MVO, Correspondence bundle 18. See, in general, J. Wolffe, *The Protestant Crusade in Great Britain 1829–1860* (Oxford, 1991).

[96] BASMOM, Letter Book 1.88–97, 103–8.

[97] MVO, OSJ Anglia Minutes 358–60.

[98] BASMOM, Letter Book 1.114–17; MVO, Historical Memoranda 1.76, 88–9; OSJ Anglia Minutes 362–3; Woof, p. 39.

[99] BASMOM, Letter Book 1.101–2, 128–35; MVO, Historical Memoranda 1.87.

[100] BASMOM, Letter Book 1.89, 114–27; MVO, Historical Memoranda 1.76, 88–9.

[101] BASMOM, Letter Book 1.135. Watts's reply, ibid., 137–43.

[102] *DNB*, 2, pp. 989–90. See also D. Heffernan, *Sir George Bowyer, QC., MP., Knight of Malta* (Abingdon, 1983).

devout born Catholic, with romantic antiquarian and genealogical interests.[103] Rumours of their opposition had reached the ears of members of the English *Langue* but it came as a shock to Gozze and Watts. In the middle of August Gozze was still in favour of union, but he now knew of the attitude of Bowyer and Waterton and, although not well, was prepared to go to London to try to win them over.

He had reached London by 26 August, when he, Bowyer and Waterton wrote to Watts, demanding that he break off negotiations and come to England to meet the 'real' English knights.[104] Bowyer and Waterton followed this up with letters, quite violent in tone, in which they threatened to object to Watts's membership of the Order of Malta if he did not at once denounce his former associates, since any half-measures would compromise them and the whole Order.[105]

Bowyer and Waterton had convinced Gozze with three arguments. The first was that Richard Broun was a sham. Bowyer, who was to inherit a baronetcy himself in 1860, was, Waterton wrote,

> ... perfectly well acquainted with the history and character of the person who calls himself Sir R Brown ... Brown is no knight, but a vile imposter. He got served heir, as the Scotch law is, by a process which you will learn when you come to England. He has been concerned in all sorts of transactions, Clubs; Railway Companies; Burial Societies; etc. – but has never been recognized a Sir, or a Baronet ... He is certainly one of the most artful and clever imposters I ever heard of.[106]

Secondly, Broun had so infected the group he led that several other members were also questionable. One, Sir James Burnes – the only other leader referred to – was, they admitted, decent and honest, but was a freemason, which was true.[107] Of the other members, one was 'a swindler', another was 'an insolvent', another was connected 'to Chartists and revolutionists'. Another, who called himself the Baron de Bliss, was 'the son of Aldridge the Omnibus manufacturer and horse-dealer'; and the chaplain had changed his name to Bellew from Huggins or Higgins and 'had been expelled from Cambridge for some bill transaction'.[108] Thirdly, no rights as a corporation could be claimed in law under the Letters Patent, because corporations needed unbroken succession and there was no such succession, particularly in terms of the religious Order which the Hospital of St John had been in 1557.[109]

---

[103] *DNB*, 20, p. 908.
[104] BASMOM, Letter Book 1.144–59. For Gozze's surprise at the turn of events, ibid., 157, 195–6.
[105] BASMOM, Letter Book 1.187–96, 208–13, 223–7. See also 160–65, 170–72, 203–7.
[106] Ibid., 1. 155–7, 208–10; MVO, Historical Memoranda 1. 93–5; Woof, p. 38.
[107] BASMOM, Letter Book 1.156–8, 193, 196, 237, 241. For Burnes, see *DNB*, 3, p. 391. See also notes in MVO, Historical Memoranda 1.93–9.
[108] BASMOM, Letter Book 1.157, 214–15, 224–5.
[109] Ibid., 1.157, 190–91 208–9.

On the last point Bowyer, who was a good lawyer, and Waterton were right: the claim to existence as a corporation had been one of Broun's mirages. On the other hand their accusations against Broun and at least two other members of the English *Langue* – those against Broun astonished Watts, who pointed out that Broun had been secretary to the committee of baronets and appeared in Burke's *Baronetage*[110] – were very unfair. Although the title Broun held had been in abeyance for fifty-two years, it had been claimed, and proved before a jury, not by him, but by his father in 1826. It was true that its validity had been debated: it was one of the Nova Scotian baronetcies and there was a question mark over the succession of the third baronet, who had apparently not used the title. Nevertheless, the title had been acknowledged in all the printed authorities [111] and it still survives. Broun was an eccentric and an enthusiast, but he was not an imposter. Neither was John Bellew, who was indeed the son of a Captain Robert Higgin of the 12th Regiment and had adopted the name of his mother, a co-heiress under the will of her uncle, Major-General Bellew. Ordained in 1848 after being at Oxford, not Cambridge, he was one of the most fashionable preachers in London in the 1850s and 1860s. In 1868 he was to convert to Catholicism: 'His sincerity in thus acting was attested by the circumstance that in doing so he gave up what brought him in, at a moderate computation, £1,000 a year.'[112] Nor was Henry Bliss, whose father James Aldridge, 'the Omnibus Manufacturer and Horse-dealer' cannot have been so very unrespectable since his father was a Hampshire JP and Deputy Lieutenant. Henry Bliss had changed his surname to that of his mother on inheriting Brandon Park in Suffolk from his uncle. He did rather foolishly, though typically for the time, use a title granted him by the kingdom of Portugal in 1855,[113] but any criticism on this score did not come well from Waterton, who used to write the title 'twenty-seventh lord of Walton' on the visiting cards he used abroad.[114]

The zeal of Bowyer and Waterton stemmed from their determination, as 'real knights', to have nothing to do with what they called 'humbug'.[115] Enthusiasts for the restoration of the Catholic Order in England, they saw no reason why they should have anything to do with Protestants. Watts, who had not been to England for years and had, therefore, not a leg to stand on in argument with them,[116] had to give way. And they convinced Gozze, who wrote to Watts that connections should be severed for the time being; the English *Langue* could be recognized in the same way as was the Protestant Bailiwick of Brandenburg

---

[110] Ibid., 1.160–63.

[111] See J. Foster, *Peerage, Baronetage and Knightage of the British Empire* (London, 1882), p. 682.

[112] *DNB*, 2, pp. 192–3.

[113] J.B. Burke, *A Genealogical and heraldic history of the landed gentry of Great Britain and Ireland*, 5th edn, 2 vols (London, 1871), 1, p. 114.

[114] *DNB*, 20, p. 908.

[115] See for instance BASMOM, Letter Book 1.189.

[116] Ibid., 1.155.

only if it got rid of half its members, adopted another method of admission and divested itself of Broun's influence.[117]

Meanwhile in England the news of Gozze's visit and Bowyer and Waterton's objections had leaked from the Catholic community to the English *Langue*.[118] Broun wrote angrily to Watts[119] who, on 1 October, warned him that negotiations were going to be suspended and reported that he had been instructed to resign from the English *Langue* immediately.[120] Watts now sketched out for Gozze a draft of a diplomatically expressed announcement of the withdrawal of the Order of Malta from negotiations,[121] but this was not needed. On the 13th the English council agreed that the earlier response to Rome should be cancelled forthwith, and Broun wrote coldly to Gozze along these lines.[122] Gozze seems to have suggested in reply that Broun had been acting without authority from the English chapter. This occasioned a hysterical letter. The English chapter had withdrawn its agreement to the scheme, Broun assured Gozze, because of the insulting behaviour of the grand magistry, which had offered membership of the Order of Malta to Watts, had sent Gozze himself on a clandestine mission to England to deal with one or two men who were knights of Malta but not in the English *Langue*, and had endorsed a petty intrigue hatched in London by 'a clique of obscure and fanatical individuals'.[123] The English blamed the turn of events on George Bowyer and of course they were right. Watts himself was convinced that the sacred council would never persist against the wishes of two of the three knights on whom it hoped to build the grand priory of England.[124] And although Richard Broun died in early December,[125] his death came too late to be of any use in negotiations. Convinced that the English *Langue* was not respectable, the grand magistry took the step which I described at the start of this paper.

---

[117] Ibid., 1.237–43.

[118] Ibid., 1.173–8.

[119] Ibid., 1.179, 181–6; MVO, OSJ Anglia Minutes 365.

[120] BASMOM, Letter Book 1. 214–7. For Broun's violent reply, ibid. 244–57. In fact Watts, who also wrote that it was something of a relief to have had definite orders (ibid., 216–17), had been forced by Broun's letter to lie: he had not yet had any direct instructions from the Order of Malta, ibid., 217–22.

[121] Ibid., 1.260–61.

[122] MVO, OSJ Anglia Minutes 366–7. Incidentally, the council meeting was chaired by a Catholic, Count de Salis, who was to become chancellor briefly from November 1858. OSJ Anglia Minutes 368. Count de Salis seems also to have been a knight of Malta. See his correspondence in Correspondence bundle 17.

[123] MVO, Historical Memoranda 3.216; BASMOM, Letter Book 1.332–4.

[124] BASMOM, Letter Book 1.200; and see 210–13.

[125] BASMOM, Letter Book 1.329; and see 330–31.

Part II

The Order of the Temple

15

Hugh of Payns and the 1129 Damascus Crusade

Jonathan Phillips*

It is well known that in 1127 Hugh of Payns travelled to the West in order to raise men and to secure papal endorsement for the emerging Order of the Temple. Clearly the rise of the Templars would be highly significant in the development of the Latin East. But, this has meant that historians have ignored the other element of Hugh's embassy: King Baldwin II of Jerusalem sent him to persuade the leading men of the West to help besiege the key Muslim city of Damascus.[1]

By 1127 the settlers' military position was strong enough for them to consider attacking such an important Muslim settlement. This was in stark contrast to the circumstances early on in Baldwin's reign when the Franks had been on the defensive throughout the Latin East. The disaster at *Ager Sanguinis* in 1119 had left Antioch severely weakened and without a leader. The capture of Count Joscelin I of Edessa in September 1122 and, seven months later, the imprisonment of King Baldwin himself, meant that three of the four Latin territories were leaderless.[2] The summer of 1124 marked a turning point for the Franks. The defeat at *Ager Sanguinis* had led to an appeal to the West for help which resulted in the Venetian crusade of 1122. In conjunction with the Venetian fleet the important seaport of Tyre was captured in July 1124.[3] One month later Baldwin was released. He promptly besieged Aleppo – the first evidence

* I would like to thank Professor J.S.C. Riley-Smith for his advice and assistance in preparing this paper.

[1] WT, p. 620.

[2] H.E. Mayer, *The Crusades*, 2nd ed., trans. J.B. Gillingham (Oxford, 1988), pp. 73–5.

[3] J.S.C. Riley-Smith, 'The Venetian Crusade of 1122–24', in *I Comuni italiani nel regno crociato di Gerusalemme: Atti del colloquio 'The Italian Communes in the Crusading Kingdom of Jerusalem'*, ed. G. Airaldi and B.Z. Kedar (Genoa, 1986), pp. 339–50.

that he was prepared to launch an offensive against the Muslim heartlands –
although, in this case, after a four-month siege the Christians were compelled
to retreat. In June 1125 Baldwin achieved his most impressive success to date
with victory over an army from Mosul at the Battle of A'zaz, and, in the autumn
of that same year, he raided the territory of Damascus.[4] It was recorded that
the king utilized all the knights of the realm and gained much plunder.[5] In
early 1126 Baldwin decided to intensify his campaign against the Damascenes
and he ordered a full assembly of the kingdom's military strength. The
Christians marched deep into hostile territory and, after engaging the Muslims
in a gruelling battle, the Franks triumphed.[6] Baldwin did not attempt to
capitalize on his victory and withdrew to his own lands. The earlier successes
at Tyre and A'zaz indicated that the king could defeat the Muslims in both
siege and battle, while the 1125 raid on Damascus had served as a precursor
to the larger invasion of 1126.[7] To achieve more permanent results would require
further planning and additional assistance.

In 1127 the king acted upon two of the key issues in his reign. First, an
embassy led by William of Bures was dispatched to Count Fulk V of Anjou to
convey an offer of marriage to Melisende, heiress to the throne of Jerusalem.
Secondly, at around the same time, the king sent the master of the Templars,
Hugh of Payns, and several other 'men of religion' to the West. William of Tyre
wrote that Hugh was instructed to rouse the people of Europe to assist the
Latin East in an attempt to besiege Damascus.[8] Admittedly, William wrote
his chronicle several decades later but he is the only narrative source to describe
what took place in Jerusalem at this time.[9] When relating the events of 1127
it is noticeable that William did not mention Hugh of Payns' efforts to establish
the Templars; this aspect of his journey only emerges from charter evidence.
Notwithstanding his known commitments to the Templars, the essence of
Hugh's journey appears to have been to persuade people in the West to mount
a new crusade. The campaign against Damascus was of considerable significance for the security of the Holy Land, and the fact that Baldwin entrusted
such an important task to the leader of the Templars only seven years after
their foundation demonstrated great faith in Hugh. If, as it appears, Hugh led
the recruitment for the crusade, then this indicates even further the scale of
the responsibility that he had been given. It was also the first of many occasions
when a member of a military order would be used to convey important

---

[4] Fulcher of Chartres, *Historia Hierosolymitana, (1095–1127)*, ed. H. Hagenmayer (Heidelberg,
1913), pp. 763–9, 772–3.

[5] WT, p. 607.

[6] Fulcher of Chartres, *Historia Hierosolymitana*, pp. 784–95; WT, pp. 608–10; Ibn al-Qalanisi,
The Damascus Chronicles of the Crusades, ed. and trans. H.A.R. Gibb (London, 1932), pp. 176–7.

[7] Fulcher of Chartres, *Historia Hierosolymitana*, pp. 773–4.

[8] WT, pp. 618, 620.

[9] P.W. Edbury and J.G. Rowe, *William of Tyre: Historian of the Latin East* (Cambridge, 1988), p. 26.

diplomatic messages to the West. The fact that William of Bures' embassy was simultaneously engaged in securing a husband for Melisende may not have been a coincidence. This overlap need not have detracted from either project, and conceivably, they could complement one another.

Hugh is first located in Anjou in April 1128.[10] As master of the Templars, Hugh was already acquainted with Fulk, because in 1120, the count had made a pilgrimage to Jerusalem and, during his stay in the East, he became closely connected with the Templars.[11] It has recently been argued that the Order was founded shortly before Fulk arrived in the Latin East in 1120, and by staying with the Templars in Jerusalem the count had demonstrated his support for them at a very early stage in their development.[12] On his return to Anjou he paid the brothers an annual income of thirty livres.[13] Fulk was therefore an appropriate figure for Hugh to approach with regard to his attempts to gain support for the Templars. It is also possible that Hugh intended to try to persuade the count to participate in the planned attack on Damascus. Fulk had shown himself to be a supporter of the settlers during his earlier visit when he had maintained, at his own expense, 100 knights in the kingdom for a year,[14] and this background suggested that it might be worthwhile for Hugh to ask him to help the East again. The envoy seems to have been successful in this aim, for in May 1128 the count took the cross at Le Mans.[15] Early in his mission, therefore, Hugh had gained an important and influential recruit.

Hugh's progress through north-western Europe can be traced primarily by grants of lands and rights to the Templars. He can be found in witness lists from Anjou, Flanders, Grangia (near Troyes) and possibly Avignon.[16] As Templar benefactions none of these documents mentioned the expedition against Damascus, and consequently they can provide a misleading picture of Hugh's journey. Narrative sources indicate a different state of affairs. The *Anglo-Saxon Chronicle* recorded that in 1128 Hugh met Henry I of England in Normandy where the king gave him a sizeable amount of treasure. The Templar continued his travels to England and Scotland where he received great riches apparently designed to be sent to Jerusalem. It is not clear whether this money was to be for the benefit of the Templars or to aid the Christian cause in general. Hugh reportedly managed to recruit the largest number of people

---

[10] CT, no. 8, pp. 5–6; H.E. Mayer, 'The Succession to Baldwin II of Jerusalem: English Impact on the East', *Dumbarton Oaks Papers*, 39 (1985), p. 147.

[11] Orderic Vitalis, *The Ecclesiastical History*, ed. and trans. M. Chibnall, 6 vols (Oxford, 1969–80), 6, pp. 310–11; J.Chartrou, *L'Anjou de 1101 à 1151* (Paris, 1928), pp. 14–15.

[12] R. Hiestand, 'Kardinalbischof Matthäus von Albano, das Konzil von Troyes und die Entstehung des Templerordens', *Zeitschrift für Kirchengeschichte*, 99 (1988), pp. 317–20.

[13] Orderic Vitalis, *Ecclesiastical History*, 6, pp. 310–11.

[14] WT, p. 633.

[15] *CT*, no. 12, p. 9.

[16] *CT*, nos 8, 12, 13, 15, 16, 22, 30, pp. 5–6, 8–10, 10–11, 16, 23.

to travel to Jerusalem since the days of Pope Urban II. Their purpose was clearly to attack Damascus, for Hugh had claimed that there was a great war afoot.[17]

A study of the charter evidence reveals some of the individuals and regions that supported the crusade. For example, it is possible that Hugh's presence in Flanders encouraged people in the vicinity to take the cross. A charter from the Flemish abbey of Eename indicates that Thierry of Chièvres sold his allodial land at Bossuyt to the church in order to finance a journey to Jerusalem.[18] Although this transaction is dated between the years 1128 and 1133, Thierry may have been one of the 'many noblemen' whom William of Tyre claimed came to the Latin East in 1129. Others to take the cross seem to have included Hugh III of Le Puiset, William VI of Montpellier, Henry and Robert Burgundio, Guitier of Rethel and Reynald of Bar-le-Duc.[19] Because it does not appear that anyone other than Hugh of Payns and his colleagues tried to raise men for the crusade it seems that the success of this aspect of the mission was almost entirely the result of their own efforts.

At this early stage in the crusading movement the exact process at the start of such an expedition was not immutably fixed. Certainly there was some papal involvement in the 1122 Venetian crusade.[20] By contrast, there survives no such evidence for the crusade of 1128–29 and there is no record that Hugh of Payns visited the pope on his journey through Europe. Honorius II was not present at the Council of Troyes in January 1129, perhaps the last obvious opportunity to endorse publicly the expedition before it departed, although a papal legate, Matthew of Albano, was in attendance. Nevertheless, Honorius knew that Fulk was considering travelling to the East and marrying Melisende because Archbishop William I of Tyre had visited him in May 1128, and it is not unreasonable to suggest that the crusade against Damascus was also discussed.[21] Although there is no record of any papally organized preaching for the expedition, the presence at Fulk's court of a papal legate, Bishop Gerard of Angoulême, around the time that the count took the cross, may indicate some connection between Honorius and the crusade.[22] Once a person had

---

[17] *Anglo-Saxon Chronicle*, ed. and trans. D. Whitelock (London, 1961), pp. 194–5.

[18] *Cartulaire de l'abbaye d'Eename*, ed. C. Piot (Bruges, 1881), no. 28, p. 29.

[19] WT, p. 620. For Hugh III of Le Puiset see: Suger, Abbot of St Denis, *Vie de Louis VI le Gros*, ed. and trans. H. Waquet (Paris, 1964), pp. 170–71. For William VI of Montpellier, see *Cartulaire des Guillems de Montpellier*, ed. C. Chabeneau (Montpellier, 1884-6), p. 177. For Robert and Henry Burgundio: *RRH*, no. 130, p. 32; H.E. Mayer, 'Angevins *versus* Normans. The New Men of King Fulk of Jerusalem', *Proceedings of the American Philosophical Society*, **133** (1989), pp. 6–7. For Guitier of Rethel: *RRH*, no. 121, p. 30. For Reynald of Bar-le-Duc, *Cartulaire de l'église Saint-Lambert de Liège*, ed. S. Bormans and E. Schoolmeesters, 6 vols (Brussels, 1893-1933) **1**, pp. 58–60.

[20] Calixtus II, *Bullaire*, ed. U. Robert, 2 vols (Paris, 1891), **2**, pp. 266–7; Riley-Smith, 'Venetian Crusade', pp. 340, 345–8.

[21] Honorius II, 'Epistolae', *Patrologia Latina*, **166**, cols 1279–80; Mayer, 'Succession to Baldwin II of Jerusalem', pp. 142–3.

[22] *CT*, no. 12, pp. 8–10.

decided to participate in the crusade some formal ecclesiastical involvement was required to take the cross and it is highly probable that Honorius at least sanctioned this aspect of the crusade, even if we cannot prove that he actively promoted the expedition himself.

The actions of Hugh and his followers constituted a rare example of the Latin settlers conducting recruitment for a crusade through their own agents. All subsequent missions focused upon envoys whose role was to deliver a letter to a major figure and then leave either the pope or local ecclesiastics to arrange the details of recruitment. This was the case in 1146 when Eugenius III delegated responsibility for the Second Crusade to Bernard of Clairvaux.[23] The only parallel example to 1128 was in 1106–7 when Bohemond I of Antioch toured France urging men to join him on crusade. Unlike Hugh, however, Bohemond had the prestige of being a ruling prince in the Latin East and a hero of the First Crusade. He was also accompanied by a papal legate, Bruno of Segni, who formally proclaimed a new crusade.[24]

Although it was reported that Hugh of Payns brought many men with him to the Latin East, relatively few of the leading figures in the West are known to have joined him. Political factors may help to explain this. Flanders was recovering from the murder of Count Charles the Good in March 1127 and the deposition of William Clito in July 1128. These events had also been of concern to Louis VI of France, Henry I of England and Duke Godfrey VII of Lower Lorraine and presumably served to distract them from involvement in the crusade. Likewise, the new ruler of Flanders, Count Thierry, was probably unwilling to leave his lands until he had established some stability, although later events were to demonstrate that he was a highly motivated crusader.[25] In essence, these were not favourable conditions for Hugh to try to recruit leading noblemen or kings for a new crusade. In general terms, however, he appeared to achieve some success, and the contemporary Muslim chronicler Ibn al-Qalanisi noted that the Franks of the East were 'reinforced also from sea by the king Count ... having with him a vast host'.[26] Fulk's decision to participate might have encouraged others, particularly Angevins, to fight in the East. For example, Hugh of Amboise was amongst the many men who took the cross with the count in May 1128.[27] Fulk therefore acted as a figurehead around whom the crusaders could gather.

---

[23] P. Cole, *The Preaching of the Crusades in the Holy Land, 1095–1270* (Cambridge, Mass., 1991), pp. 40–49.

[24] J.S.C. Riley-Smith, *The Crusades: A Short History* (London, 1988), pp. 90–91.

[25] J.P. Phillips, 'Thierry of Flanders and the 1157 Siege of Shaizar', in *New Directions in Crusading Studies*, ed. M. Markowski (forthcoming).

[26] Ibn al-Qalanisi, *Damascus Chronicle*, p. 195.

[27] 'Gesta Ambaziensum Dominorum', *Chroniques des Comtes d'Anjou et des seigneurs d'Amboise*, ed. L. Halphen and G. Poupardin (Paris, 1913), p. 115.

The Franks had recently benefited from the arrival of Bohemond of Taranto which lifted the burden of the Antiochene regency from King Baldwin.[28] In contrast, the Muslims had faced some serious problems. In February 1128 Tughtigin of Damascus finally succumbed after a lengthy illness and was succeeded by his incompetent son, Buri.[29] Baldwin chose not to exploit this – a decision which might add credence to the idea that the king had a long-term plan to attack Damascus, which relied on Western help. He did not wish to endanger this project with an opportunist strike, however favourable the circumstances, and it is noticeable that he engaged in no known military action in 1127 and 1128. When Fulk and the other crusaders arrived in the summer of 1129 Baldwin's patience seemed to be rewarded, for this enhanced the Christians' military strength. To complement this, political good fortune continued to favour the settlers. The Assassins were driven out of Damascus in September 1129 and their panic-stricken leader, Isma'il, offered the Christians the castle of Banyas in return for his safety. The king accepted the offer and took control of the site.[30]

In the autumn of 1129 Baldwin summoned the military strength of the Latin East to attack Damascus. The scale of this force was in contrast to the 1126 expedition which had consisted solely of men from Jerusalem. After the raids of previous years, the aim of the 1129 campaign was to capture the city itself.[31]

Unfortunately for the king his plans failed completely. In November 1129 the Christian forces had advanced to about six miles from Damascus.[32] William of Bures led a large group of knights away on a foraging expedition, a division of the Frankish forces which exposed them to attack. The Muslims discovered this and ambushed the Christian raiders, killing a considerable number of men. An enormous storm prevented the Franks from counterattacking and they were forced to retreat.[33] A measure of the threat that the assembled Christian forces had posed may be gauged by Ibn al-Qalanisi's comment, 'So the hearts of the Muslims were relieved from terror, and restored to security after fear.'[34] Damascus had been spared, and Baldwin's carefully evolved strategy had been ruined by a single tactical misjudgement.

In conclusion, it is evident that there was a distinct overlap between the embassies of Hugh of Payns and William of Bures. Both focused on Fulk V of Anjou, whose position as a potential husband for the heiress of Jerusalem and

---

[28] Fulcher of Chartres, *Historia Hierosolymitana*, pp. 805–9, 819–22.

[29] Ibn al-Qalanisi, *Damascus Chronicle*, pp. 177–84; Ibn al-Athir, 'Kamel Altevarykh' (extract), *RHC Or*, 1, pp. 364–8.

[30] Ibn al-Qalanisi, *Damascus Chronicle*, pp. 189–94.

[31] WT, p. 620.

[32] Ibn al-Qalanisi, *Damascus Chronicle*, p. 196.

[33] Ibn al-Qalanisi, *Damascus Chronicle*, pp. 197–200; WT, pp. 621–2; Ibn al-Athir, 'Kamel Altevarykh', pp. 385–6.

[34] Ibn al-Qalanisi, *Damascus Chronicle*, p. 200.

as a known supporter of the Latin East meant that he was also an appropriate figure to ask to participate in the crusade against Damascus. He acted as a figurehead for others to join the expedition while Hugh recruited men over a wide area of north-west Europe.

Hugh's mission also constituted a very rare embassy to the West for help in a campaign designed to expand Christian territory; almost every other appeal during the twelfth century was sent as a result of a serious military setback.

Finally, in light of the kingdom of Jerusalem's steadily evolving aim to attack Damascus it seems that the primary reason why Hugh was sent to the West was to raise men for a new crusade. In spite of this, the more successful aspect of his mission – securing support for the Templars – has attracted far more attention, presumably because it proved to have a lasting impact on the history of the Latin East, something that his main task had the potential, if not the good fortune, to achieve.

16

Templar Castles on the Road to the Jordan

Denys Pringle

THE ROAD TO THE JORDAN

The road from Jerusalem to Jericho and the sites associated with Christ's Temptation in the Wilderness and Baptism in the River Jordan was being frequented by Christian pilgrims from early in the fourth century.[1] Soon after the fall of Jerusalem to the army of the First Crusade in 1099, Count Raymond of St Gilles, fulfilling the instructions given him by Peter Bartholomew in Antioch, led his men to bathe in the waters of the Jordan near Jericho;[2] and the following Epiphany, his example was followed by other crusading leaders, including Bohemond of Antioch, Baldwin of Edessa (the future Baldwin I), Godfrey of Bouillon and the patriarch, Daimbert of Pisa.[3]

In the twelfth century, the journey to the Jordan and back continued to be a normal feature of Holy Land pilgrimage.[4] Most pilgrims would probably have left Jerusalem through the east (or Jehoshaphat) gate and would have followed the road down through Gethsemane, then up over the Mount of Olives to Bethphage and on to Bethany (see Figure 16.1). Just beyond Bethany, near the place where Mary of Bethany was supposed to have run out to meet Jesus,

[1] *Itinerarium Burdigalense*, ed. P. Geyer and O. Cuntz, Corpus Christianorum, Series Latina, **175** (Turnholt, 1965), pp. 1–16; trans. J. Wilkinson, *Egeria's Travels to the Holy Land*, revised ed. (Jerusalem and Warminster, 1981), pp. 160–61; cf. D. Baldi, *Enchiridion Locorum Sanctorum*, 2nd ed. (Jerusalem, 1955), pp. 345–58; J. Wilkinson, *Jerusalem Pilgrims Before the Crusades* (Warminster, 1977), p. 28, maps 9 and 14.

[2] Raymond of Aguilers, X, *RHC Occid*, **3**, pp. 301–2; WT, IX.3, p. 424; S. Runciman, *A History of the Crusades*, 3 vols. **1** (Cambridge, 1954–55), p. 293.

[3] Fulcher of Chartres, *Historia Hierosolymitana*, I.xxxiii.20, I.xxxiv.l, ed. H. Hagenmeyer (Heidelberg, 1913), pp. 332–4; WT, IX.15, pp. 440–41; Runciman, **1**, p. 307.

[4] J. Wilkinson, J. Hill and W.F. Ryan, *Jerusalem Pilgrimage 1099–1185*, Hakluyt Society, 2s., 167 (London, 1988), pp. 50–55, fig. 11; *The Atlas of the Crusades*, ed. J. Riley-Smith (London, 1990), p. 42.

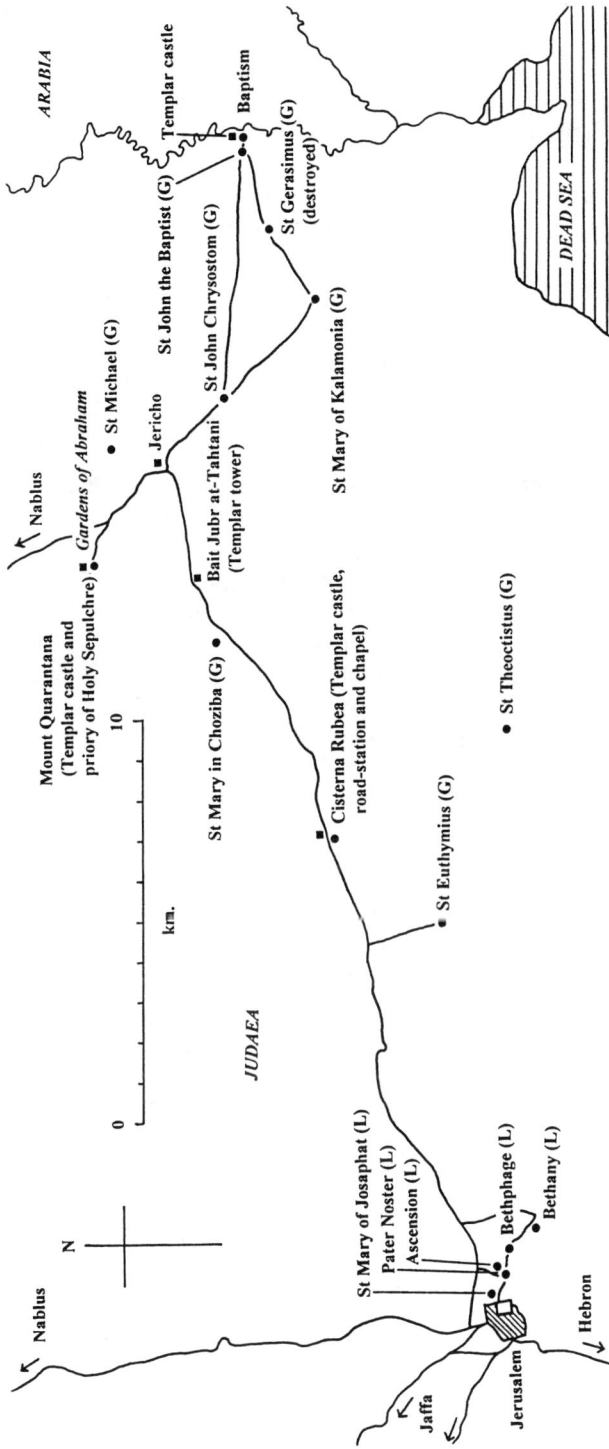

Figure 16.1   Map showing the road from Jerusalem to the Jordan in the twelfth century

Note: G = Greek Orthodox church or monastery   L = Latin church or monastery

the road turned abruptly north and continued downhill for some two km to join the old Roman road, which left Jerusalem from the north (or St Stephen's) gate and ran north-eastward over Mount Scopus.[5]

From the junction of the two roads the Roman road continued to the north-east, descending 350 m in altitude over the next 8–9 km as it followed the course of the Wadi al-Haud. After passing a turn on the right to the Orthodox monastery of St Euthymius (Kh. Khan al-Ahmar), the road proceeded north-eastward again, up the Ascent of Blood (Tal'at ad-Damm in Arabic, Ma'ale Adummim in Hebrew), so named after the red colour of the rocks (Figure 16.2), over a rise, and then down once more to join the Wadi al-Qilt. Half-way down this wadi, clinging to the north wall of the canyon, was the Orthodox monastery of Choziba. 'After this', wrote the Greek pilgrim John Phocas in 1185, 'comes a long, narrow, and very rough road', on which 'there is no stone pavement'. This led down into the plain and oasis of Jericho.[6]

In the twelfth century, benefiting from the relative security afforded by the crusader conquest and from the patronage of Emperor Manuel I Comnenus (1143–80), a number of the Orthodox monasteries around Jericho were rebuilt.[7] There was also a Latin presence in the former Byzantine *lavra* of *Douka*, on the Mount of Temptation (Jabal al-Quruntul), where a priory of the Holy Sepulchre was established in 1133–34.[8] The tithes of Jericho were given to the priory two years later;[9] and in 1143, the lordship, valued at 5,000 *aurei* per year, was granted by Queen Melisende to the sisters of Bethany.[10]

THE PROBLEM OF SECURITY IN THE TWELFTH CENTURY

Although twelfth-century writers extolled the fertility of the oasis of Jericho and marvelled at its exotic plants, they also contrasted the poverty of the Muslim village then existing with what they supposed to have been the size and strength of the city that had fallen to Joshua.[11] Security was a continual problem. All of the monasteries were fortified in some way, either by strong high walls or by the nature of their locations. Theoderic tells us that during a

---

[5] M. Avi-Yonah, *Map of Roman Palestine*, 2nd ed. (Jerusalem, 1940), p. 45.

[6] *Compendiaria Descriptio*, XX, ed. L. Allatius, *Patrologia Graeca*, **133**, col. 949; trans. A. Stewart, *The Pilgrimage of Joannes Phocas in the Holy Land*, PPTS, **5** (London, 1896), p. 26.

[7] A. Augustinović, *Gerico e dintorni: Guida* (Jerusalem, 1951); D. Pringle, *The Churches of the Crusader Kingdom of Jerusalem: A Corpus*, 3 vols. (in progress), **1** (Cambridge, 1993–) no. 39, pp. 108–9; no. 85, pp. 197–202; no. 95, pp. 221–2; pp. 275–6.

[8] Ibid., **1**, nos. 104–7 pp. 252–8.

[9] Ibid.

[10] WT, XI.15, XV.26, pp. 519, 709-10; cf. Theodoric (Theodericus), *Libellus de Locis Sanctis*, XXX, ed. M.L. and W. Bulst, Editiones Heidelbergenses, **18** (Heidelberg, 1976), p. 37; trans A. Stewart, *Theoderich's Description of the Holy Places*, PPTS, **5** (London; 1896), p. 49.

[11] Daniel the Abbot, 'The Life and Journey of Daniel, Abbot of the Russian Land', XXXV, trans. W.F. Ryan, in Wilkinson, Hill and Ryan, p. 138.

raid by Zangī, perhaps that recorded in 1139, six monks of the Orthodox monastery of St John beside the Jordan had been decapitated, and that, even at the time of his visit around 1172, lands in the oasis were left uncultivated on account of the Saracen inroads.[12]

Security was no less a problem on the road from Jerusalem to Jericho. It had always been so, and explains why Jesus chose it as a setting for the parable of the Good Samaritan (Luke 10: 30–37). On the Mount of Olives, the church of the Ascension, served by Augustinian canons, was described by Theoderic as, 'strongly fortified against the infidels with towers both great and small, with walls and battlements and night patrols'.[13] Excavations by the late Fr Virgilio Corbo, OFM, revealed, attached to the octagonal church, the basement of part of the house of the canons, containing stables and a bakery.[14] At Bethphage, the church was likened to a tower by John of Würzburg (c. 1165), a description that is borne out by its excavated ground plan.[15] At Bethany, William of Tyre tells us that Queen Melisende constructed a strongly fortified tower to protect the nuns from the attacks of the Muslims; and investigation of the site shows that, in addition, the convent buildings were surrounded by a strong wall with projecting towers.[16]

Such passive defence, however, was obviously not enough to protect pilgrims travelling on foot from attacks by the local Bedouin. As late as 1767, Giovanni Mariti describes the problems that pilgrims had faced for centuries. Of Adummim he writes:

> This place has been dangerous for travellers in all periods, nor is it less so at present, unless one goes that way in a large company and with a good escort, having always been a place where highway murderers lie in wait.[17]

THE ROLE OF THE TEMPLARS

One of the principal roles that had been envisaged for the Templars by Patriarch Warmund and the other bishops at the time of their formation in 1119 was to 'keep the roads and highways safe from the menace of robbers and

---

[12] Theoderic, XXX, ed. Bulst, p. 37; PPTS, 5, p. 49; cf. WT, XV. 6, pp. 682–4.

[13] Ch. XXVII, ed. Bulst, p. 34; PPTS, 5, p. 44.

[14] V. Corbo, *Ricerche archeologiche al Monte degli Ulivi*, Studium Biblicum Franciscanum, Collectio Maior, 16 (Jerusalem, 1965), pp. 115–25.

[15] *Descriptio Terrae Sanctae*, VI, *Itinera Hierosolymitana Crucesignatorum (saec. XII–XIII)*, ed. S. de Sandoli, Studium Biblicum Franciscanum, Collectio Maior, 24, 4 vols (Jerusalem, 1978–84), 2, p. 248; trans A. Stewart, *The Description of the Holy Land*, PPTS, 5 (London, 1896), p. 24; Pringle, 1, p. 158, fig. 47.

[16] WT, XV.26, pp. 709–10; Pringle, 1, pp. 133–4, figs. 43–4, pl. LXXXII.

[17] *Viaggi per l'isola di Cipro e per la Soria e Palestina … dall'anno 1760 al 1768*, 9 vols, 2 (Florence, 1769–76), p. 95.

highwaymen, with especial regard for the protection of pilgrims'.[18] We may assume that after the road from Jaffa to Jerusalem – which by 1169–71 was protected by major Templar castles at Latrun (*le Toron*) and Yalu (*Castellum Arnaldi*) – [19] the Jerusalem to Jericho road would have assumed a high priority. Indeed, in the Hierarchical Statutes, that were incorporated into the Templars' Rule between *c.* 1165 and 1187, we read:

> The Commander of the City of Jerusalem should have ten knight brothers under his command to lead and guard the pilgrims who come to the river Jordan; ... if he finds a nobleman in need he should take him to his tent and serve him with the alms of the Order; and for this reason he should carry a round tent and food, and lead pack animals and bring back pilgrims on the animals if necessary.[20]

Our principal source of evidence for Templar activity in protecting pilgrims on the Jericho road is the German pilgrim, Theoderic, who probably travelled along the road in 1172.[21] Of the oasis itself, or 'Garden of Abraham', he writes:

> Many towers and large houses are possessed there by the power of the Templars, whose practice, as also that of the Hospitallers, is to escort pilgrims who are going to the Jordan, and to watch that they be not injured by the Saracens either in going or returning, or while passing the night there.[22]

The pilgrims would spend the night camping in the Gardens of Abraham at the foot of the Mount of Temptation.

> They are protected on three sides by the garden itself from the ambuscades of the infidels; on the fourth side they are guarded by patrols of the Hospitallers and Templars.[23]

It is uncertain where exactly the Hospitaller knights were based. The Templars, however, had at least two castles in the immediate vicinity. One was on the summit of the Mount of Temptation itself. Theoderic tells us:

> The crest of Mount Quarantana and its subterranean caves are full of victuals and arms belonging to the Templars, who can have no stronger fortress or one better suited for the annoyance of the infidels.[24]

---

[18] WT, XII.7, p. 554; trans. E.A. Babcock and A.C. Krey, *A History of Deeds Done Beyond the Sea*, Columbia University Records of Civilization, Sources and Studies, 35, 2 vols, **1** (New York, 1943) p. 525.

[19] M. Benvenisti, *The Crusaders in the Holy Land* (Jerusalem, 1970), pp. 281–2, 314–18; D. Pringle, 'Survey of Castles in the Crusader Kingdom of Jerusalem, 1989: Preliminary Report', *Levant*, **23** (1991), pp. 87–91.

[20] *RT*, §121; trans. J.M. Upton-Ward, *The Rule of the Templars*, Studies in the History of Religion, **4** (Woodbridge, 1992), p. 49; cf. M. Barber, 'Supplying the Crusader States: The Role of the Templars', in *The Horns of Ḥaṭṭīn*, ed. B.Z. Kedar, (Jerusalem and London, 1992), pp. 314–26 (at p. 317).

[21] Theodoric, ed. Bulst, pp. 5–6.

[22] Ch. XXXVIII, PPTS, **5**, p. 46; ed. Bulst, p. 35.

[23] Ch. XXIX, PPTS, **5**, p. 48; ed. Bulst, p. 36.

[24] Ch. XXIX, PPTS, **5**, p. 49; ed. Bulst, p. 36.

Rising some 500 m above the plain of Jericho, this lofty plateau (extending some 100 by 40 m) had already been fortified in Hasmonean times, when as the fortress of Dok (or *Dagon*) it was held by Ptolemy, son-in-law of Simon Maccabeus, and was the scene of the latter's assassination in 134 BC (1 Maccabees 16:15).[25] The caves and rock-cut cisterns are still in evidence around the summit (grid ref. 19091423). Traces have also been recorded of an irregularly shaped fortress wall, extending some 30 by 76 m and enclosing a small chapel. But although the officers of the Survey of Western Palestine (SWP) imply that these were both the work of the Templars,[26] the wall seems more likely to be Hasmonean and the chapel Byzantine, though very possibly re-used in the twelfth century, as it was later, by pilgrims visiting the place of Our Lord's Third Temptation.[27] Quite possibly, as Theoderic implies, the natural defensibility of the site required little further enhancement.

The second castle stood at the edge of the Jordan, near the place of Baptism and the Greek church of St John the Baptist. Theoderic gives no details, save that it was 'a strong castle of the Templars'.[28] No trace of it survives.

CISTERNA RUBEA (QAL'AT AD-DAMM)

At a point roughly midway along the road from Jerusalem to the Jordan, Theoderic describes another Templar castle:

> To the eastward, beyond Bethany, at a distance of four miles from Jerusalem, there stands on a mountain the Red Cistern [*cisterna Rubea*], with a chapel attached to it.... Here the Templars have built a strong castle.[29]

The Red Cistern was located at Adummim, on the borders of Judah and Benjamin (Joshua 15:7; 18:17).[30] By AD 331, a fort had been built, and around 395–408 it was being garrisoned by the *Cohors I Salutaris*, an auxiliary unit, whose duty it was to protect travellers on the road.[31] When St Jerome accompanied the worthy Roman matron Paula to Jericho in AD 385, and recalled at this point Jesus' parable of the Good Samaritan, his description of the inn to which the

---

[25] F.M. Abel, *Géographie de la Palestine*, 3rd ed., 2 vols. (Paris, 1967), **1**, pp. 375–6; M. Avi-Yonah, *Gazetteer of Roman Palestine*, Qedem, **5** (Jerusalem, 1976), p. 52.

[26] C.R. Conder and H.H. Kitchener, *The Survey of Western Palestine: Memoirs*, 3 vols, **3** (London, 1881–83), pp. 204–5.

[27] F.M. Abel, 'Topographie des campagnes machabéennes (suite)', *Revue biblique*, **35** (1926), pp. 206–22, 510–33; Pringle, *Churches*, **1**, no. 107, p. 257.

[28] Ch. XXX, PPTS, **5**, p. 49; ed. Bulst, p. 37.

[29] Ch. XXVIII, PPTS, **5**, p. 45; ed. Bulst, p. 35.

[30] Cf. Abel, *Géographie*, **2**, pp. 174, 179; Y. Aharoni, *The Land of the Bible: A Historical Geography*, trans. A.F. Rainey, 2nd edn (London, 1979), p. 59.

[31] Eusebius of Caesarea, *Onomasticon*, ed. E. Klostermann, *Das Onomastikon der Biblischen Ortnamen*, Die griechischen christlichen Schriftsteller der ersten drei Jahrhunderte, 11.1 (Leipzig, 1904), p. 24, lines 9–11; Jerome, *Liber locorum*, ed. Klostermann, loc. cit., p. 25, lines 7–16; *Notitia Dignitatum*, ed. O. Seeck (Berlin, 1876), no. 48, p. 74; cf. Avi-Yonah, *Gazetteer*, p. 78.

Figure 16.2   The Ascent of Blood (Ma'ale Adummim, Tal'at ad-Damm), looking north-east with the Templar castle of the Red Cistern (Castellum Ruge Cisterne, Qal'at ad-Damm) on the horizon; the remains of the khan lie out of sight to the right of it

Figure 16.3   Qal'at ad-Damm: vault 2 from the west, with the rock-cut ditch and entrance (denoted in 9 in Figure 16.4) in the foreground

unfortunate man was carried as *stabulum ecclesiae* seems to suggest that a church and road-station also existed at the site by then. To Jerome is also due the idea, repeated by medieval writers, that Adummim was so called because of the blood shed there by the attacks of robbers.[32]

Pilgrim writers of the twelfth century were familiar with Jerome's account, although the *ascensus ruforum siue rubrantium* of the *Liber locorum* had by then become the *rubea cisterna*.[33] Theoderic is the only pilgrim to offer an explanation for what was probably simply an error of transcription, by suggesting that this was where Joseph had been thrown into a pit by his brothers; but other pilgrim texts place this with more authority in the plain of Dothan.[34]

The Templar castle that Theoderic saw at the Red Cistern around 1172 was already deserted when it was occupied by the Ayyubids after the battle of Hattin in July 1187.[35] It is marked as *cast(ellum) Ruge cist(er)ne*, however, on a map of around 1252 attributed to Matthew Paris;[36] and a French text of around 1228–31 says: 'Between Jericho and Jerusalem there is a place called *le Rouge Cisterne*. There used to be there a hostelry, where those who were going to Jericho and to the river would lodge.' It is not entirely certain, however, whether the writer is describing something that existed before 1187 or at the time of Christ, for he continues, 'And there it was that the Samaritan carried the man ...'[37]

Later medieval pilgrims distinguished the ruined *khan*, in which travellers would stay, from the castle a short distance away, suggesting that they had always been different buildings.[38] Brother Felix Faber, for example, says that the building in which the German pilgrims of 1480–83 lodged had once been a

[32] *Epistula CVIII*, xii.3, ed. I. Hilberg, *Corpus Scriptorum Ecclesiasticorum Latinorum*, 55 (Vienna, 1912), p. 321; trans. Wilkinson, *Jerusalem Pilgrims*, p. 51.

[33] *Descriptio locorum* [1131/43], XLIV, ed. S. de Sandoli, *Itinera*, 2, p. 106 (trans. J.R. MacPherson, *Fretellus*, PPTS. 5 (London 1896), p. 44); Fretellus, *Descriptio de Locis Sanctis* [1137], LXXI, *Rorgo Fretellus de Nazareth et sa Description de la Terre Sainte*, ed. P.C. Boeren (Amsterdam, 1980), p. 40; A. de Marsy, ed., 'Fragment d'un cartulaire de l'ordre de Saint-Lazare en Terre Sainte', *AOL*, 2B (1884), 121–58 (no. 2 [1142], pp. 123–4); *RRH*, no. 210 [1142] p. 53.

[34] Ch. XXVIII, PPTS, 5, p. 45; ed. Bulst, p. 35; cf. *Atlas of the Crusades*, p. 43.

[35] Ralph of Coggeshall, *Chronicon Anglicanum*, ed. de Sandoli, *Itinera*, 3, p. 114; cf. *Gesta Regis Henrici II*, RS, 49.2, p. 24; 'Imād al-Dīn al-Iṣfahānī, *Conquête de la Syrie et de la Palestine par Saladin*, trans. H. Massé, Documents relatifs à l'histoire des croisades, 10 (Paris, 1972), p. 99 [Tall al-Ahmar?]; J. Prawer, *Histoire du royaume latin de Jerusalem*, 2nd edn, 2 vols, 1 (Paris, 1975), p. 664.

[36] K. Nebenzahl, *Maps of the Bible Lands: Images of Terra Sancta through Two Millennia* (London, 1986), no. 13, pp. 38–9; cf. R. Röhricht, 'Karten und Pläne zur Palästinakunde aus dem 7. bis 16. Jahrhundert', *Zeitschrift des Deutschen Palästina-Vereins*, 18 (1895), no. 16, pp. 173–182.

[37] Ernoul, in *Itinéraires à Jérusalem et descriptions de la Terre Sainte redigées en francais aux XIe, XIIe & XIIIe siècles*, ed. H. Michelant and G. Raynaud, Publications de la Société de l'Orient Latin, Série géographique, 3 (Geneva, 1882), p. 70.

[38] Baldi, *Enchiridion*, nos. 562 [1335] and 563 [1345], pp. 353–4; Fra Niccolò da Poggibonsi, *Libro d'Oltramare (1346–1350)*, ed. A. Bacchi della Lega, Studium Biblicum Franciscanum, Collectio Maior, 2 (Jerusalem, 1945), p. 82; T. Bellorini and E. Hoade, trans., *Visit to the Holy Places of Egypt, Sinai, Palestine and Syria in 1384 by Frescobaldi, Gucci & Sigoli*, Studium Biblicum Franciscanum, Collectio Maior, 6 (Jerusalem, 1948), p. 79.

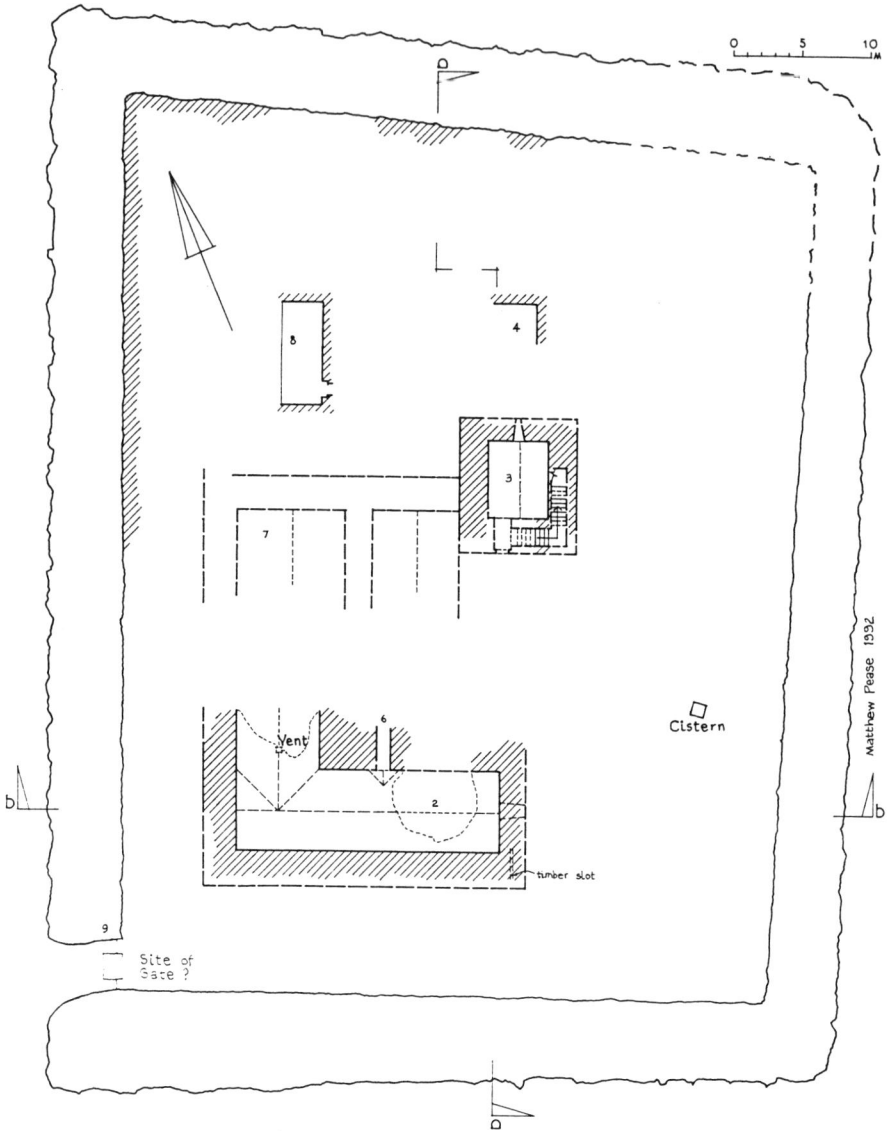

Figure 16.4   Qal'at ad-Damm: plan of the Templar castle (drawn by Matthew Pease, BSAJ Survey 1988)

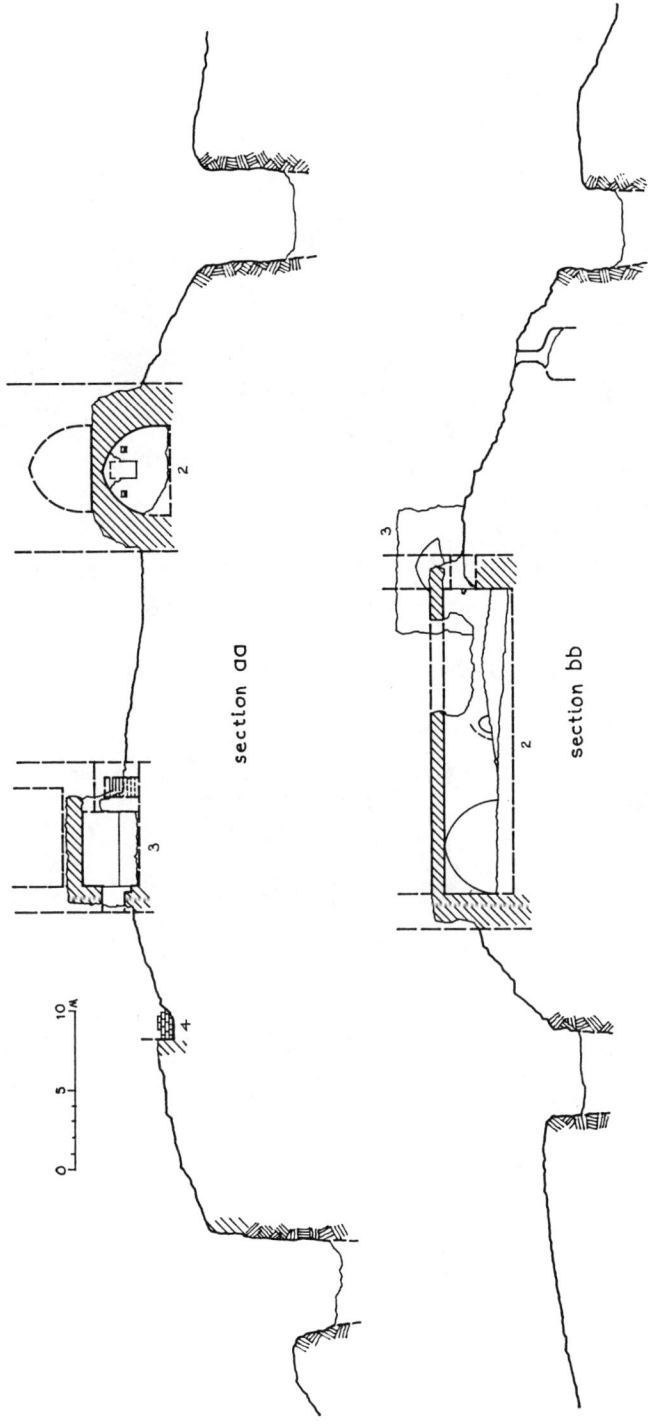

section aa

section bb

Figure 16.5 Qal'at ad-Damm: sections through the Templar castle (drawn by Matthew Pease, BSAJ Survey 1988)

Figure 16.6   Qal'at ad-Damm: the rock-cut ditch at the north corner

*Figure 16.7   Qal'at ad-Damm: tower 3, looking north-east from the top of vault 2,
with the Judaean Wilderness behind*

caravanserai or inn, of which only the four walls were standing, set around a well.[39]

> It was dangerous to sleep in that place ... because the walls were ruinous, and stones detached from the mortar hung above our heads, threatening to fall.[40]

This was evidently not the castle, for Giovanni Mariti in 1767, after first describing the *khan*, in which he also stayed, then continues:

> A little further on, on the left hand, above a hill you see a dismantled castle, which seems once to have been strong and respectable. It is surrounded by a ditch, excavated by dint of chiselling into the living rock. This was a fortress at the time of the Christians, and now it is called the Castle of the Samaritan, after the nearby khan .... There was there a church, but now this too is destroyed [41]

The site was studied by the officers of the SWP in November 1873. From their description and sketch plan it appears that the condition of the building has changed little over the past century apart from the inevitable collapse and robbing of stone from some of the structures.[42] The site has also been described more recently by the late Fr Bellarmino Bagatti.[43]

The castle occupies the summit of a hill on the north side of the road (grid ref. 18411361) (Figures 16.2 and 16.3). It is defined by a rock-cut ditch, 4.5–6.0 m wide and (in its partly filled-in state) between 2 and 8 m deep. Because the ground falls away towards the east, the rectangular area thus enclosed appears irregular on the plans published by the SWP and Bagatti. In fact in horizontal projection it is fairly regular, though slightly truncated at the north-east corner, and measures some 49 m NE–SW by 59–63 m NW–SE (see Figures 16.4 and 16.5). The inside faces of the ditch are in places revetted with masonry towards the top; the build is rough, laid in relatively narrow courses and with most of the facing now missing (Figure 16.6). It is uncertain, however, how high these walls would have stood. At the south end of the north-west side (denoted 9 in Figure 16.4), a causeway with a stone-lined pit (1.8 by 1.6 m) in its centre evidently represents the site of the entrance.

Roughly in the middle of the castle, at its highest point, stand the remains of a tower (denoted 3 in Figure 16.5), which would have measured 9.3 by 8.5 m, with walls 1.4–2.5 m thick (see Figures 16.7–16.10). It was built of roughly squared ashlars of soft yellow sandstone, with window surrounds and vault-springers in a harder grey limestone. The course heights vary from 23 to 36 cm, averaging 27.6 cm. Only the barrel-vaulted basement is left, though most

---

[39] *The Book of the Wanderings*, trans. A. Stewart, PPTS, **7–10**, 2 vols, **2** (London, 1893), pp. 65–70.

[40] Ibid., p. 69.

[41] *Viaggi*, **3**, p. 97.

[42] Conder and Kitchener, **3**, pp. 172, 207–9.

[43] B. Bagatti, *Antichi Villaggi cristiani di Samaria*, Studium Biblicum Franciscanum, Collectio Minor, **19** (Jerusalem, 1979), pp. 75–9, fig. 25, pls. 23–4; cf. Benvenisti, pp. 324–5, pls.pp. 308, 327.

Figure 16.8   Qal'at ad-Damm: the interior of vault 2, looking south-east

Figure 16.9   Qal'at ad-Damm: the interior of vault 2, looking north-west

Figure 16.10   Qal'at ad-Damm: tower 3 from the south-west

of its west wall has gone. Just above the level of the springing, a row of eleven small putlog holes on either side evidently supported the centring during construction. The basement was plastered internally and lit on the east by a splayed slit-window (80 cm wide internally), whose outer surrounds have now been mostly robbed. A number of graffiti of late and post-medieval date, some evidently Christian, are incised on the internal walls.[44] The door, though now missing, was evidently on the west, and to the right-hand side of the entrance passage a stairway led up inside the wall to the now-vanished upper floor.[45] The small size of this tower, with an internal floor area of only 23 m², suggests that it was more probably intended as a look-out and possibly a signalling position than as a place for continuous habitation. Indeed, even though its height is now reduced, it is still possible to see from its first floor the Mount of Olives in one direction and the fortress on the Mount of Temptation in the other.

To the west of the tower lie the remains of an L-shaped structure (denoted 2 in Figure 16.4), barrel-vaulted internally with a span of 5.6 m. The vault has a pointed profile; but during construction the centring appears to have sagged, with the result that it bulges outwards somewhat on the south-west side. In

---

[44] S. de Sandoli, *Corpus Inscriptionum Crucesignatorum Terrae Sanctae (1099–1291)*, Studium Biblicum Franciscanum, Collectio Maior, **21** (Jerusalem, 1974), pp. 334–5, figs. 149–50.

[45] Conder and Kitchener, **3**, pp. 208–9.

the south-east end wall is a splayed window, flanked internally by a pair of cavetto-moulded stone corbels (Figures 16.8 and 16.9). A pointed-arched opening in the north-east wall (1.07 m wide, its jambs robbed) has been interpreted as a stairway to the upper floor,[46] but this has yet to be substantiated by clearance. The walls are of hard grey limestone tuff, while the corbels and window surrounds are of softer yellow sandstone. The pointing is in grey-white lime mortar, spread out over the face of the stones, with herringbone trowel impressions made in the surface. The vault was evidently merely the basement of some more important apartment, of which, however, only part of the stone paving survives. This structure, now very indistinct as a result of collapse and burial, appears to be linked to remains of others (denoted 7 in Figure 16.4), which adjoin the tower on its north-west side. Some indication of these is given on the SWP plan,[47] and a photograph of 1939 shows one of the vaults still standing.[48]

Downhill to the north-east of the tower, remains of two other structures are visible (4 and 8 in Figure 16.4). One of these (4), built in fine ashlar, was possibly a cistern. Bagatti interprets both structures as Byzantine and compares the trowel-impressed pointing on them to that surviving on the Byzantine monastery on Mount Nebo.[49] While this dating is quite possible, however, there seems to be no particular reason, in the absence of excavation, to consider them as necessarily earlier than the other structures of medieval date which bear the same type of pointing. None the less, Byzantine, as well as medieval, pottery litters the site,[50] supporting the idea that the fourth-century fort mentioned by Eusebius would have occupied this position.

Immediately next to the road itself (that is, a little south of the modern road) stands the Inn of the Good Samaritan (Khan Hathrur), a Turkish *khan* built in 1903. In December 1939 Fr Bagatti was able to determine the existence of a Byzantine mosaic beneath one of its rooms, suggesting that it occupied the site of the earlier road-station and *caravanserai* dating from late Roman times.[51]

BAIT JUBR AT-TAHTANI

Some 6.5 km east of Qal'at ad-Damm, at Bait Jubr at-Tahtani, stand the remains of another tower (Figures 16.11 and 16.12). This is set upon a rocky eminence to the right of the road just at the point where it emerges from the Wadi al-Qilt into the plain of Jericho (grid ref. 19051396). To the east there is a suggestion that the rock has been artificially scarped; but modern road-building operations make this hard to verify.

---

[46] Bagatti, p. 78.

[47] Conder and Kitchener, 3, p. 208.

[48] Bagatti, p. 79, fig. 23.1.

[49] Ibid., p. 78, fig. 25.

[50] Ibid., p. 78, fig. 24.3–4.

[51] Ibid., p. 78, pl. 22.2; cf. E. Hoade, *Guide to the Holy Land* (Jerusalem, 1946), pp. 354–7; 9th ed. (Jerusalem, 1978), pp. 473–4.

Figure 16.11   Bait Jubr at-Tahtani: crusader tower, looking east, with the oasis of Jericho behind

Figure 16.12   Bait Jubr at-Tahtani: crusader tower from the south-west

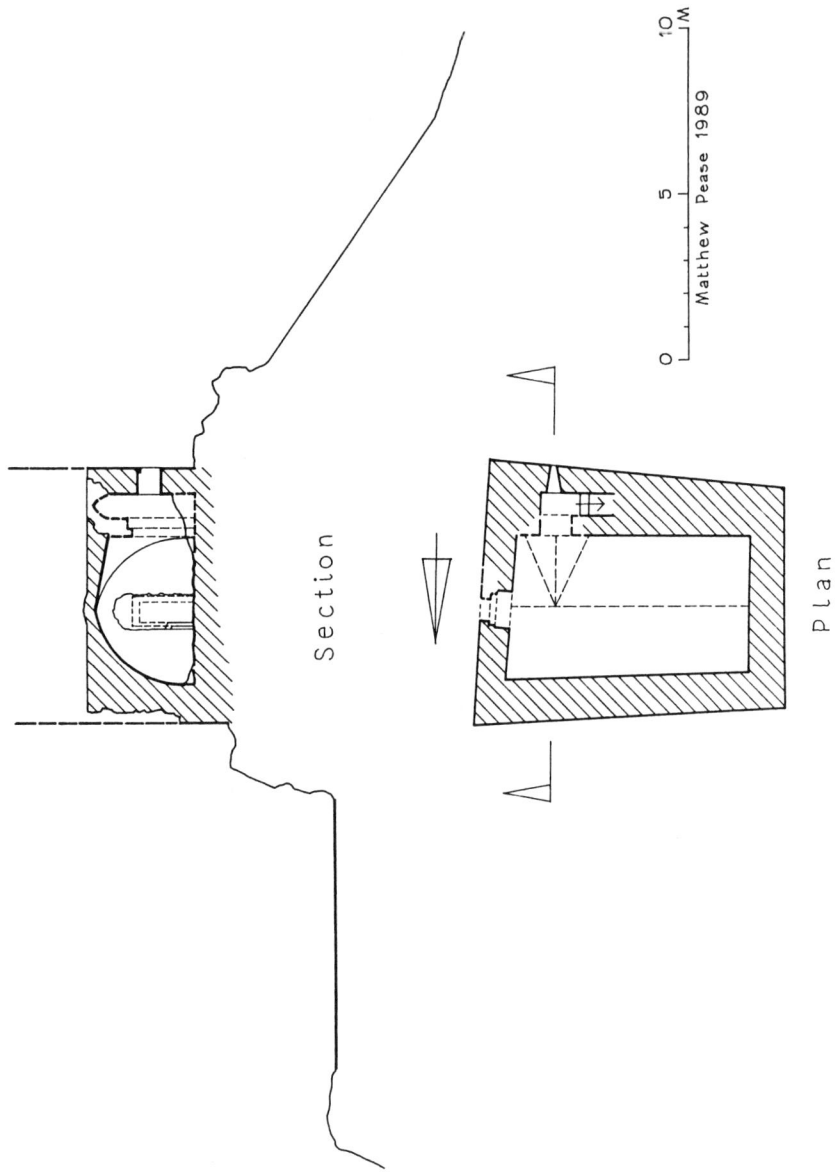

Section

Plan

Matthew Pease 1989

0   5   10
                              M

Figure 16.13   Bait Jubr at-Tahtani: plan and section of the crusader tower (drawn by Matthew Pease, BSAJ Survey 1989)

Figure 16.14   Bait Jubr at-Tahtani; crusader tower, the entrance to the blocked stairway in the south wall

The tower is built with facings of rough irregular blocks, laid in courses 23–25 cm high, set in lime mortar which in places bears the same type of trowel-impressed pointing noted at Qal'at ad-Damm. The wall-cores are largely earth-filled. Most of the quoins have been robbed, though one on the north-east is rusticated.

In plan the tower is quadrangular, measuring c. 9.5 m by 6.6–8.1 m (see Figure 16.13). Only the barrel-vaulted ground floor remains, entered through a door on the east, 0.85 m wide with all but three of its jambs robbed. The vault is rubble-built and plastered. Within the south wall, a stairway to the first floor led off to the right-hand side of an arched recess (Figure 16.14), lit by a splayed lintelled embrasure (11 by 50 cm) with rusticated freestone surrounds on the outside.

This tower is not mentioned specifically by any source of the crusader period. From the late thirteenth century, however, its abandoned remains began to be identified by Western pilgrims as the church of the Miracles of Christ, where Jesus had restored the sight of a blind man (or, according to one evangelist, of two blind men).[52] Its location and method of construction, however, point to a connection with the builders of Qal'at ad-Damm and suggest its identification as a fortified post guarding the Jericho road.[53]

---

[52] Augustinović, pp. 58–60, fig. 13; Pringle, *Churches*, 1 pp. 101–2.

[53] Benvenisti, p. 325; Conder and Kitchener, 3, pp. 190–91; Pringle, 'Survey of Castles', no. 2, p. 88.

DISCUSSION

Without excavation or more precise documentary information, it is difficult to tell exactly how the system of protection offered by the Templars – and to a lesser extent the Hospitallers – operated on the road to the Jordan. The only effective method for protecting travellers would have been a mobile mounted guard, as later pilgrim accounts make clear. All we are left with today, however, are the static remains of buildings.

It may be assumed, however, that a castle such as Qal'at ad-Damm would have been permanently garrisoned. Indeed, the comparable twelfth-century Templar installation at *le Destroit* (Khirbat Dustray), guarding the road between Haifa and Caesarea, consisted of a central fortified tower surrounded by yards containing stables; castle and road-station were there combined in one complex.[54] At Qal'at ad-Damm it seems that the castle and *caravanserai* had always been separate, and that the chapel mentioned by Theodoric and evidently accessible to pilgrims was attached to the latter, as it probably had also been in Byzantine times. The Red Cistern, whose biblical association the Templars had evidently invented, was no doubt the well that Felix Faber saw in the centre of the *caravanserai* in the 1480s.

The purpose of the small isolated towers, of which Bait Jubr at-Tahtani appears to be the only surviving example, is less certain.[55] The restricted internal size of this tower, amounting to only 32 m², and its lack of an outer defensive enclosure suggests that, if it was intended for a permanent garrison, then they and their horses must have been accommodated inside it. In theory a maximum of five horses could have been stabled on the ground floor, with the men quartered on the floor above. There is no direct evidence, however, to indicate the use of the ground floor as a stable; and unless or until it can be tested archaeologically, such an interpretation can therefore be no more than hypothetical.

The survey work in 1988–89 at Qal'at ad-Damm and Bait Jubr at-Tahtani was carried out under the auspices of the British School of Archaeology in Jerusalem and with the support of the Royal Archaeological Institute.

---

[54] C.N. Johns, *Guide to 'Atlit: The Crusader Castle, Town & Surroundings* (Jerusalem, 1947), pp. 15–17, 94–8, figs. 6, 38; A. Ronen and Y. Olami, *'Atlit Map*, Archaeological Survey of Israel, 1 (Jerusalem, 1978), no. 87, pp. 50–52, 13.

[55] A vaulted building at Bait Jubr al-Fauqani (grid ref. 18931389), identified by Benvenisti (p. 325) as another tower, appears to be a Byzantine cistern.

17

The Architecture of the Knights Templars in England*

Pál Ritoók

My subject has not been thoroughly researched by modern scholars,[1] and therefore my aim here is to offer a number of preliminary general observations. First, I am going to give a short account of the sources of Templar architecture, followed by a sketch of an average Templar preceptory using the example of South Witham. Then I am going to make a survey of building types used by the Templars, which will include an analysis of the plan-types of their churches and, finally, an evaluation of the architectural decoration of Templar buildings.

There are three main written sources. First, there is the Inquest of their lands and revenues made between 1185 and c. 1190.[2] This source mentions two types of buildings which belonged to the Templars – namely churches and mills – but does not provide any architectural details. Next there is the collection of inventories made by the sheriffs after the arrests of the Templars in 1308.[3] These include very detailed descriptions of animals and of objects found inside

---

* In preparing this study I have drawn on the advice, knowledge, assistance and financial support of numerous persons and institutions. I am indebted to them all and in particular to The George Soros Foundation, my late Professor Erik Fügedi, Professor Michael Gervers, Pamela Willis and her colleagues at the Museum of the Order of St John, Eric Christiansen, Professor Howard Colvin, Stephen Johnson, Philip Mayes, John Bold, the Hungarian National Board for the Protection of Historic Monuments, Exeter College Oxford, the St John Historical Society and several others. Despite this enormous help my study may contain mistakes, erroneous observations and conclusions, and for these I am solely responsible.

[1] There is only one general survey of Templar architecture, E. Lambert, *L'architecture des Templiers* (Paris, 1955).

[2] *Records of the Templars in England in the Twelfth Century. The Inquest of 1185 with illustrative Charters and Documents*, ed. B. A. Lees, The British Academy Records of the Social and Economic History of England and Wales, 9 (London, 1935).

[3] Examples in Public Record Office, *Extents [Exchequer K.R.]*, nos. 12–19.

buildings, but they do not give descriptions of the buildings themselves. The last major source is the Extent of Hospitaller Lands made in 1338.[4] This contains a special section which deals with former Templar lands given to the Hospitallers after the dissolution of the Order. Again, it provides little direct information about the buildings themselves, but it does contain some details of their condition and the money spent on renovation.

Apart from written sources there is archaeological evidence, or at least information from drawings and records written by antiquaries. As map 1 in Beatrice Lees' edition of the 1185 Inquest shows,[5] within fifty years of their first foundation in the 1130s, the Templars held lands throughout the country, although they did not build on every property recorded on the map. They did not build castles because England served as a source of revenue and not as a battlefield against the infidels. Castles would have been obvious indications of their existence and building activity, but they did leave other architectural remains: semi-fortified or lightly defended rural dwellings, chapels, parish churches, halls, mills, barns and earthworks in the form of moats, dams and fishponds. However, surviving material is extremely patchy. Few Templar sites have been excavated, and the majority of descriptions are largely superficial. Moreover, since there are few examples of existing Templar buildings or even visible ruins, identification is often difficult.

The excavations at South Witham (Lincolnshire)[6] do, however, enable us to form a picture of an average Templar preceptory (see plan in Figure 17.1), especially if supplemented by examples of existing buildings from other Templar sites. The most extensive Templar estates were located in Yorkshire and Lincolnshire, so in this respect South Witham seems to be a good example, although it was the smallest preceptory in the area. Its importance lies in its completeness not only as a preceptory of the Templars, but as an example of an entire farm layout at the end of the period of economic growth in the thirteenth century, yet before the demographic disaster of the Black Death. It was inhabited some time before 1185 until 1313–38, when it was described as a destroyed messuage. There is no evidence that occupation continued after that time. The development of the site consists of three major phases:[7]

Phase 1:   The construction of an aisled hall and two ancillary buildings and a water mill.

---

[4] *The Knights Hospitallers in England*, ed. L.B. Larking and J. M. Kemble, Camden Society, **65** (London, 1855).

[5] *Records of the Templars*, map 1.

[6] P. Mayes, 'Lincolnshire: South Witham', *Medieval Archaeology*, **10** (1966), p. 180; **11** (1967) pp. 274–5; *Current Archaeology*, **9** (1968),pp. 232–7.

[7] My thanks to Philip Mayes and Stephen Johnson for allowing me to read the manuscript of a monograph on South Witham excavation to be published by English Heritage (hereafter SWEH).

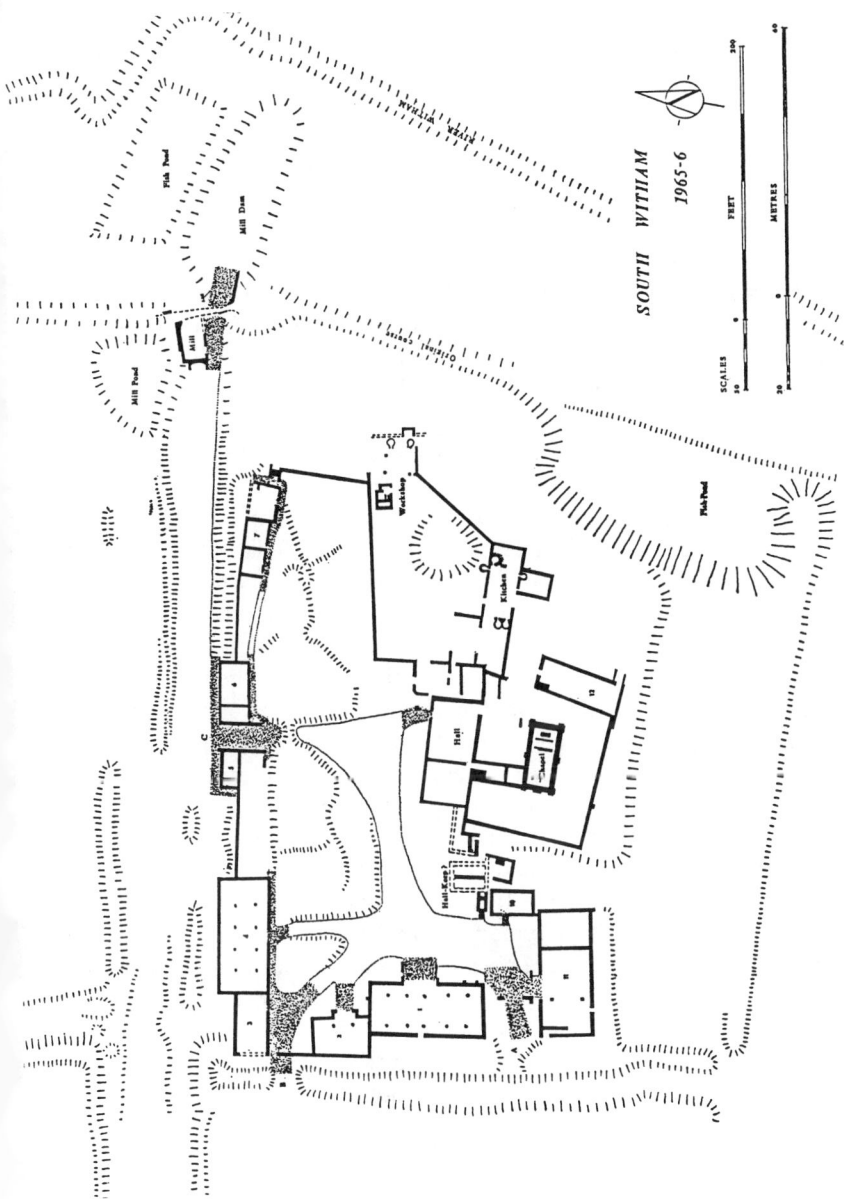

Figure 17.1   Plan of the Templar preceptory at South Witham (© The Society for Medieval Archaeology)

Phase 2:   Former buildings were destroyed except for the water mill and parts
           of walls of the former hall; the construction of a full range of buildings
           took place between *c.* 1220 and 1240: the chapel, hall and the kitchen
           in the centre; the lesser hall and the peripheral buildings: barns, animal
           houses, dairy and brew house and gatehouses.

Phase 3:   The water mill fell into disuse, the lesser hall was demolished, the
           surviving hall was slightly enlarged, minor alterations were made to
           the chapel and to buildings east of the hall.

Construction of South Witham lies in the period when, as a result of the
economic growth of the twelfth and thirteenth centuries, stone replaced the
earlier less durable and cheaper materials.[8] This became familiar all over the
country at just about the time when phase two was constructed. Other examples
include Goltho, Faxton and Seacourt (Oxfordshire).[9]

The first building of special architectural interest is the chapel because its
nave had two storeys and the chancel had one. Although Templar churches and
chapels are commonly thought to have a round nave, there are several rectangular
chapels of which Rothley (Leicestershire) (Figure 17.4) and Balsall (Warwick-
shire) are the best preserved. Rothley is nearly contemporary with South
Witham (*c.* 1240); Balsall is a simple rectangular building dated to *c.* 1290, but
it has been heavily altered. In Balsall the west end of the nave consisted of two
storeys. In South Witham the upper storey was probably intended for the
preceptor and brethren while the lower one was for lay workers of the manor.[10]

After the chapel the second most important building was the hall which was
in the centre of the site. The hall was rectangular with a rectangular cross-wing
to the west of it, which may have been the solar, and there was probably an
upper storey. The larger part to the east formed the hall itself.[11] Standing
Templar halls can be found in Temple Balsall and in Temple Strood (Kent),
and these can help us imagine the main domestic building at South Witham.
The hall in Balsall is included in a later building but at Temple Strood it survives
in a freestanding rectangular form. It had no internal communication between
the storeys. The undercroft is divided into three bays by a ribbed quadripar-
tite vault. The upper storey is approached by an external staircase which has
been reconstructed. In the upper storey the position of a screen or partition is
deducible from the arrangement of the side walls. The most precious parts of
the existing building are the first-floor doorway and the internal wall-arcades.
The building was dated by the excavator to not long before 1241[12] – that is,

---

[8] J. T. Smith, *Interpretation and Significance*, SWEH; C. Platt, *Medieval England: A Social History
and Archaeology from the Conquest to 1600 A.D.* (London, 1978), p. 40.

[9] Platt, p. 41.

[10] Smith, loc. cit.

[11] Mayes, SWEH.

[12] S. E. Rigold, 'Two Camerae of the Military Orders', *Archaeological Journal*, **122** (1965),
pp. 88–9, 93–4, 96.

contemporary with phase two of South Witham, and can serve as a parallel with the western wing of the South Witham hall.

There are no surviving kitchens or workshops on Templar sites, but we are much luckier in the case of barns. There are the remains of barns of great size at South Witham comparable to the famous Templar barns at Cressing,[13] although the most exact parallels of the South Witham barns are those at Great Coxwell.[14] The Cressing barns relate to an earlier phase of construction (1200–c. 1250), so they are more useful in helping to envisage the earlier South Witham barns, built from timber only.[15] These represent not only a fine example of Templar architecture but form an important chapter in the history of carpentry in England.

The excavators of South Witham have not found the remains of a dovecote, but there was possibly one of rectangular plan at Temple Hirst, east of the main domestic building.[16] Probably the best known dovecote relating to the Templars is that at Garway.[17] The actual building is dated by its inscription of 1326 – that is, to the time when the estate already belonged to the Hospitallers – but I think we have good reason to assume that this, or an earlier structure, had already existed before.[18] The 1338 Extent of the lands of the Hospitallers mentions several dovecotes on estates formerly belonging to the Templars, and it is unlikely that all of them were newly built by the Hospitallers.

A water mill belonged to the earliest phase of South Witham. This was a rectangular structure, located at the north-eastern corner of the manor, where it was fed by the River Witham, and some timbers of the mill race have been preserved.[19] The importance of the South Witham water mill lies in the fact that, apart from a middle-Saxon water mill at Old Windsor, it is the only fully excavated medieval water mill.[20] There are many Templar estates listed in the 1185 Inquest as having mills, although it does not generally make a distinction between water and windmills, with a few exceptions such as Dunwich in Suffolk and Weedley in Yorkshire.[21] It was quite usual to use both

[13] C.A. Hewett, 'Structural Carpentry in Medieval Essex', *Medieval Archaeology*, 6–7 (1962–63), pp. 241–2; idem, *The Development of Carpentry, 1200–170. An Essex Study* (Newton Abbot, 1969), pp. 22–3, 40–46.

[14] Platt, pp. 47–8.

[15] Hewett, *Development*, loc. cit.

[16] H. E. Chetwynd-Stapylton, 'The Templars at Templehurst', *Yorkshire Archaeological Journal*, **10** (1887–89), pp. 431–3.

[17] J. Webb, 'Notes on a Preceptory at Garway, in the County of Hereford', *Archaeologia*, **31** (1846), pp. 183–97; The Royal Commission on Historical Monuments, England [hereafter RCHM], *An Inventory of Historical Monuments in Herefordshire*, **1**, South-West (London, 1931), p. 72.

[18] Webb, pp. 191, 195.

[19] Mayes, SWEH.

[20] J. G. Hurst, 'A Review of Archaeological Research (to 1968)', in *Deserted Medieval Villages, Studies*, ed. M. Beresford and J.G. Hurst (London, 1971), p. 141 n. 130.

[21] J. M. Steane, *The Archaeology of Medieval England and Wales* (Beckenham, 1985), p. 170; E.J. Kealey, *Harvesting the Air. Windmill Pioneers in Twelfth-Century England* (Bury St Edmunds, 1987), pp. 41, 57, 230–31, 248–9, 261–2.

types as alternative sources of power, since streams were not always strong enough. In the last phase of South Witham the water mill fell into disuse and was replaced by a windmill for this reason.[22] The windmills were post-mills whose mounds can be detected through aerial photographs, but I have not seen any showing soil marks of possible Templar windmills. Mills were often donated, but the Templars also built many of their own, a typical example being that in the hamlet of Temple Guiting, in Barton.[23] Temple Strood had a water mill fed by the River Medway which must have been a tide mill.[24] One of the Barton mills is described as a fulling mill, which suggests that the others were probably corn mills, but generally it is difficult to identify their precise functions. The introduction of windmills to England is often attributed to the military orders but, important as these were to the orders' economy, there is no definite evidence for this view.[25]

Fishponds are usually closely related to watermills, and in South Witham there were two. More complex series had auxiliary breeding chambers and separate ponds for different types of fish. The most fully developed series can be seen at Harrington in Northamptonshire near a preceptory of the Templars, where it consisted of a battery of different shaped embanked ponds in a shallow valley, with deep supply channels, all linked by a complex system of overflow channels, leats and sluices.[26] Moats, needed both for drainage and for defence as in South Witham, required similar earthworks. Other examples are Temple Hirst, Fenwick, Whitley and Faxfleet.[27]

There are some Templar analogies to the preceptory of South Witham which have been excavated, such as those at Whitfield and Temple Ewell in Kent.[28] The general characteristic of Templar farms was a well organized ground plan of the manor which shows similarities with lay and monastic practice. The closest parallels to the Templars can be found on Hospitaller estates and on Cistercian granges where an inner and outer court preserved privacy and isolated *famuli* from brethren,[29] a pattern which can be seen in phases two and three at South Witham. Manor houses of landlords rich enough to have their own chapel also closely resemble Templar preceptories.[30] Examples which could be quoted include Weoley near Birmingham (1260), Penhalam

---

[22] Mayes, SWEH.

[23] R. H. Hilton, *The West Midlands at the End of the Thirteenth Century* (London, 1967), pp. 209–10.

[24] Rigold, 88.

[25] Kealey, pp. 40–41.

[26] Steane, pp. 171–2.

[27] J. E. Le Patourel, *The Moated Sites of Yorkshire*, The Society for Medieval Archaeology. Monograph Series, 5 (London, 1973), pp. 111, 124, 129; Chetwynd-Stapylton, loc. cit.

[28] F.L. Page, 'Whitfield Preceptory. A Report on the Excavations from 1964 to 1966 by the Duke of York's Royal Military School Archaeological Society', *Kent Archaeological Review*, 3 (1967), pp. 186–91; A.C. Hogarth, 'Temple Ewell', *Kent Archaeological Review*, 1 (1965), pp. 5–6.

[29] Platt, p. 61.

[30] Smith, SWEH.

at Jacobstow, Cornwall (c. 1200–1300), the bishop of Hereford's manor house at Prestbury, Gloucestershire (thirteenth–fourteenth century),[31] and the manorial complex at Cuxham, Oxfordshire (c. 1315).[32]

Little can be said about town houses and inns, because there are few buildings which can be identified as Templar houses. We know that the Angel Inn in Grantham apparently belonged to the Templars in 1291.[33] Houses in towns were marked with crosses showing that the owner of the building was exempt from taxation, and there are two Templar examples of this at Canterbury and Rochester.[34]

In the case of standing village churches, it is not possible to attribute them to the Templars without a minute study of documents and without archaeological investigation. Many existing churches (and, as we have seen, other buildings such as mills, barns, and town houses) were given to the Templars. Moreover, in some cases, the Templars received only a half or a quarter of a church or they held only the altar dues, making evaluation of the style of the building even more problematical. In these cases the Templars probably did not pay attention to the structure or decoration, and left maintenance to the villagers. Sompting (c. 1180–90) is a good example of the re-use and rebuilding of an earlier existing church by the Templars. The plan shows that the Saxon tower was retained as well as the proportions of the Saxon nave, without aisles, which the Templars extended towards the east without a chancel arch. On the north side they provided a transept with a two-bay eastern aisle including two chapels. On the southern side of the nave the Templars built a chapel for their own use, completely isolated from the nave.[35]

More is known about Templar churches with circular naves, or rotundas, which have been surveyed by Michael Gervers.[36] Since his survey we can add a seventh rotunda to the six studied by him, but four of them cannot be evaluated in detail owing to lack of information. The earliest is the Old Temple in Holborn, built around 1135, which we know, both from sixteenth-century accounts and 1875 excavations, had a circular form.[37] The remains of the rotunda in Dover, built before 1185, suggest that it had no internal arcade and

---

[31] Platt, pp. 58, 59, 82.

[32] T. Rowley, *The High Middle Ages 1200–1550*, The Making of Britain (London, 1986), p. 70.

[33] W.A. Pantin, 'Medieval Inns', in *Studies in Building History: Essays in recognition of the work of B.H. St. J. O'Neil*, ed. E.M. Jope (London, 1961), p. 190.

[34] C. Perkins, 'The Knights Templars in the British Isles', *English Historical Review*, 98 (1910), p. 218.

[35] I. Nairn and N. Pevsner, *The Buildings of England. Sussex* (Harmondsworth, 1965), pp. 330–32; P. Excell, *A Brief Guide to Sompting Parish Church* (1979); *Guide to the Church of St Mary Sompting*, ed. W.H. Godfrey (Sompting, 1970?).

[36] M. Gervers, 'Rotundae Anglicanae', in *Actes du XXIIe Congrés international d'Histoire de l'Art* (Budapest, 1972), pp. 359–76.

[37] Ibid., p. 365.

that its chancel was not apsidal but tapered.[38] We know little more about the rotunda of the Templars at Bristol other than that it also had a circular nave and that it was built after 1150, probably with an inner arcade.[39] In Camden's *Britannia* it is claimed that there was a round Templar church at Aslackby,[40] which was rebuilt as a farmhouse much later. It is not known whether the square tower still visible as part of the farmhouse before 1892 was built together with the round church in 1164 or whether it was a later addition.[41]

More attention has been paid by architectural historians to the New Temple (see Figures 17.2 and 17.3), Garway, and Temple Bruer (see Figure 17.5) which are all dated around 1180. Each of them originally had a circular nave with a chancel with an apsidal ending. All were rebuilt or extended during the twelfth and thirteenth centuries and changed and ruined in later centuries. They all display interesting features such as a tower, or towers, connected to the rotunda. At Garway a detached tower was built early in the thirteenth century, which served both as a keep on the Welsh border and as a treasury.[42] The towers at Aslackby and Temple Bruer might have performed similar functions. The Temple Bruer towers, north and south of the chancel, were built one after the other at the very end of the twelfth century,[43] and are reminiscent of the Caesar tower and the so-called Great Tower of the Paris Temple complex, also located north and south of the original rotunda.[44] These served as massive donjons and were safe places for storing the treasure of the French Templars. It is likely that there was a similar structure at the London Temple, but there is no direct evidence for this. At Garway, structural problems seem to have led to the replacement of the rotunda by a rectangular nave, for the chancel, although part of its northern wall was preserved, received a new eastern end. A southern chapel was added to the chancel, possibly in the thirteenth century, and then in the sixteenth century its walls were replaced by a new southern chapel.[45] At Temple Bruer, apart from the two towers, the church did not need enlargement until it became the property of the Hospitallers. The London Temple was enlarged by the Chapel of St Ann in about 1200. Later on the Templars built a three-aisled choir of five bays, replacing the apsidal chancel. This building was consecrated in 1240.[46] These additions show that the original rotundas did not meet the later needs of the Templars.

---

[38] Ibid., p. 366.

[39] Pevsner, *The Buildings of England. North Somerset and Bristol* (Harmondsworth, 1973), p. 409.

[40] Gervers, pp. 366–7.

[41] The Order of St John in Lincolnshire, *Yearbook* (1973), pp. 20–21.

[42] RCHM, *Herefordshire*, loc. cit.

[43] St. J. Hope, 'The Round Church of the Knights Templars at Temple Bruer', *Lincolnshire Archaeologia*, 61 (1908), pp. 177–98.

[44] Lambert, pp. 158–9.

[45] RCHM, *Herefordshire*, 1, South-West, pp. 70–72.

[46] W.H. Godfrey, 'Recent Discoveries at the Temple, London, and Notes on the Topography of the Site', *Archaeologia*, 95 (1953), pp. 123–40.

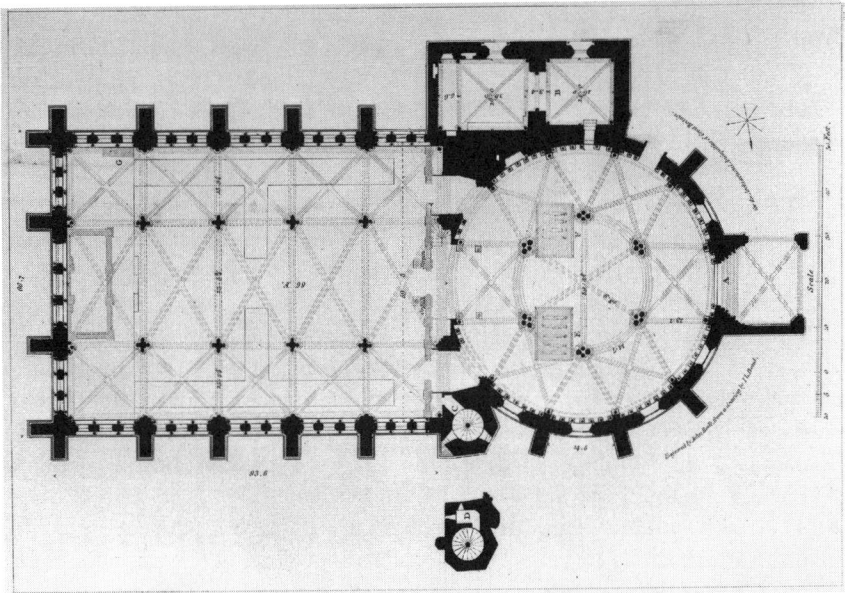

Figure 17.2   Plan of the Temple Church, London (© Museum and Library of the Order of St John, Clerkenwell)

Figure 17.3   West doorway, Temple Church, London. Engraving of 1807 (© Museum and Library of the Order of St John, Clerkenwell)

There is therefore clearly a connection between rotundas and the Templars in England, but a rotunda in itself does not indicate a Templar church. Sometimes this form was used by the Hospitallers and other religious orders related to the Holy Land and to the crusades or in churches built by persons who were connected to these orders or who took part in the crusades. In the case of the Templars the circular form was considered to be either a copy of the Temple of Solomon or of the Church of the Holy Sepulchre in Jerusalem. The latter example is the much more likely model because the former would presumably have produced imitations which were polygonal, rather than circular, in form.

It is no easier to identify a specifically Templar iconography than it is to find a characteristically Templar church. Corbels with grotesque or animal heads can be found reset on the ground floor of the tower at Temple Bruer, on the corbel table in the chancel at Temple Guiting, and in churches at Shipley, Tickencote and Sompting, where the bosses also deserve further study.[47] There is a peculiar head at Garway on the northern side of the chancel arch. At Temple Bruer on the ground floor of the tower, the walls are covered with blank arcading: shafts are missing and capitals are worn, but leaves can be seen. There is also a defaced effigy in a sunk-pointed trefoil, and the intersecting small-scale arcading is an interesting reset fragment. However, no-one could argue that such decoration was exclusively Templar. Nor are crosses seen in Templar churches of special significance. Crosses can be seen on one of the corbels at Temple Guiting and on the remains of the preceptory at Sandford-on-Thames, as well as on the beautiful church of Birkin which is thought to have been influenced by the Templars (although it did not belong to them). However, it would be difficult to argue that these crosses exhibit any great differences from those displayed by other lay or ecclesiastical communities. The one church which might be expected to have exhibited a special iconography is the Temple Church in London. Various attempts have been made to identify the figures on the western doorway either with Henry II and three Templars or Patriarch Heraclius with three attendant clergy, and George Zarnecki tends to accept the possibility that the busts on the doorway represent the Infidels.[48] I have to leave the question open.

My conclusion is that it is not possible to identify a specifically Templar architecture in England. The architecture of their rural dwellings did not differ from manors of wealthy landlords or monastic granges such as those of the Cistercians. Nor was the circular plan of some of their churches an exclusive feature, since

[47] R. Gem, 'An Early Church of the Knights Templars at Shipley, Sussex', in *Anglo-Norman Studies VI, Proceedings of the Battle Conference 1983*, ed. R. Allen Brown (Woodbridge, Suffolk, 1984), pp. 238–46; W. St. G. Coldwell, *Notes on St Peter's Church, Tickencote* (Tickencote, 1943); for Sompting, see note 35.

[48] G. Zarnecki, 'The West Doorway of the Temple Church in London', in *Studies in Romanesque Sculpture* (London, 1979), pp. 245–53.

Figure 17.4   Rothley, Leics. Thirteenth-century Templar chapel (© Museum and Library of the Order of St John, Clerkenwell)

Figure 17.5   Temple Bruer, Lincs. Engraving of 1726 (© Museum and Library of the Order of St John, Clerkenwell)

this form was preferred in some cases by the Hospitallers and by some founders of churches or chapels who either took part in, or were somehow linked to, the crusades or who just wanted to commemorate the Holy Sepulchre. It can be said that the masonry was generally of high quality, but the present state of research gives no grounds for believing in any special Templar iconography.

18

The Surrender of Gaston and the Rule of the Templars

Judi Upton-Ward

'The Templars abandoned two castles, Gaston and Roche La Roussel': so the continuator of William of Tyre tells us.[1] And it is all he tells us of the surrender of Gaston – one of the most important Templar strongholds in the Principality of Antioch – in 1268, to the Mamluk sultan, Baybars. Other Western sources are no more informative except, that is, the account written by the Templars themselves and contained in the Barcelona manuscript of their Rule. After a description of the castle's geographical location, its strategic importance to all parties in the region and a brief history from the time Gaston was granted to the Templars up to 1268, this paper will examine the major contemporary Arabic sources in conjunction with the Rule of the Templars, and attempt to indicate the importance of this often-neglected source not only to the history of the crusades in general, but also to an understanding of the military order itself.

The Amanus mountain range runs to the north and west of Antioch and marks the frontier between Asia Minor and Syria. North of the Belen Pass, or Syrian Gates, it is orientated almost north–south. It is narrow, varying from 20 to 40 km, and rises rapidly on both sides, several peaks reaching 2,000 or 3,000 m and remaining snow-covered until early summer, while the lower slopes are clad with pine and oak forests. On the western side, the mountains are penetrated by valleys, but on the eastern side they form an uninterrupted barrier. South of the Belen Pass, the orientation changes to north-east–south-west, the peaks are lower, reaching only 1,200 to 1,700 m, and the slopes more gentle. Where the mountains reach the coast, they separate the Bay of Antioch from the Gulf of Alexandretta, and north of this point lies Arsuz, which the Franks called Port-Bonnel. Approximately 20 km north of the Belen Pass lies that of Hajar Shughlan. The Belen Pass provides the easier crossing as the mountain

---

[1] *Eracles*, **2**, p. 457.

From *The Military Orders: Fighting for the Faith and Caring for the Sick*, ed. Malcolm Barber. Copyright © 1994 by Malcolm Barber. Published by Variorum, Ashgate Publishing Ltd, Gower House, Croft Road, Aldershot, Hampshire, GU11 3HR, Great Britain.

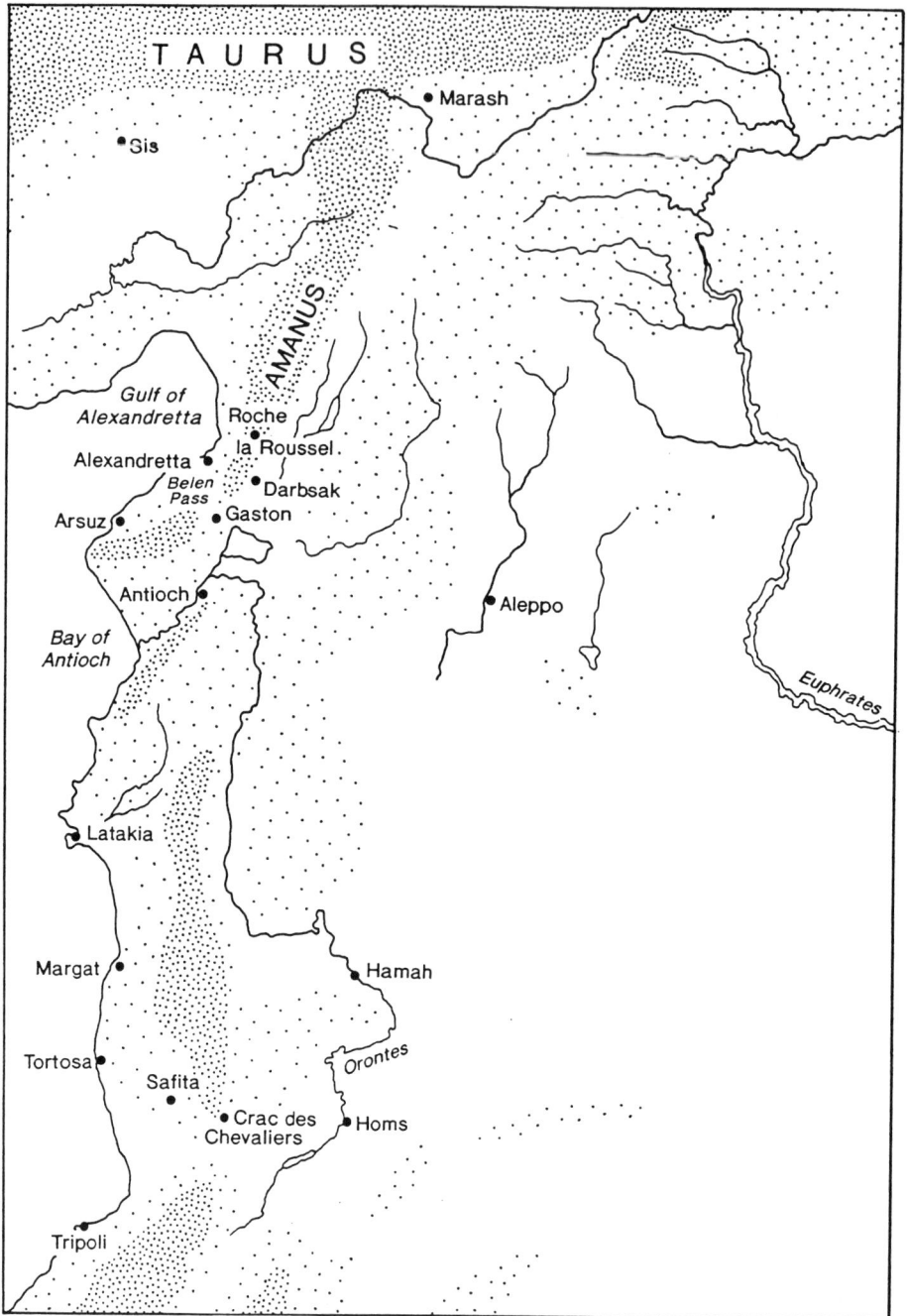

Figure 18.1   Map showing the strategic positions of Gaston and neighbouring castles

range is narrower and the altitude well below 1,000 m. It is on this pass that the important fortress of Baghras, which the Franks called Gaston, is situated, on a rocky outcrop whose eastern side overlooks the plain of Aleppo. The route to Antioch along the Pass of Hajar Shughlan is longer, but it provides a more direct road to Aleppo. It also has the advantage that it could be entered from the west even when the Portella, a strip of land between the Amanus and the sea, was in enemy hands. Halfway down this pass, the castle of Roche La Roussel overlooked a crossroads, while the fortress of Darbsac controlled its eastern entrance. The nearby site of the castle of Roche Guillaume has, as far as I know, so far not been identified.[2]

The only contemporary Western description of Gaston is that of Wilbrand of Oldenburg, who visited it in 1211 while it was held by the Armenians. Wilbrand tells us that Gaston was

> ... a very strong castle, with three very strong towered walls round it, situated in the last mountains of Armenia. It diligently watches the entrances and paths to that land .... Antioch is overlooked from it direct and from the neighbourhood; it is four leagues away.[3]

We have a very vivid description of the castle by the Arab historian, Imad ad-Din, who took part in the siege of Gaston by Saladin's forces in 1188. In his elaborate prose he tells us:

> We saw it [the castle] towering on an impenetrable summit, rising on an impregnable rock, its foundations touching the sky ...; penetrating the ravines, it climbed the mountains, it flaunted its walls in the clouds, shrouded in fog, inseparable from the clouds, suspended from the sun and the moon; ... no-one would have aspired to climb up there; whoever coveted it had no means of getting there; whoever raised his eyes to it could not fix his gaze.[4]

However, the fortress is not of the scale which one would expect from its historical importance, for the rocky outcrop on which it is built limits its dimensions.

To control this area, a march was created in the twelfth century and the Templars were established there in the 1130s. Thoros of Armenia temporarily occupied the castles in the middle of the century, but was forced to return them to the Order; they were in Templar hands when Gaston and Darbsac fell to Saladin in 1188. The Muslims later abandoned Gaston and, together with Port-

---

[2] The geographical description is taken from C. Cahen, *La Syrie du Nord au temps des Croisades* (Paris, 1940), pp. 140–45; and J. Riley-Smith, 'The Templars and the Teutonic Knights in Cilician Armenia', in *The Cilician Kingdom of Armenia*, ed. T.S.R. Boase (Edinburgh: Scottish Academic Press, 1978), p. 92.

[3] *Peregrinatores*, ed. Laurent, p. 174, quoted by A.W. Lawrence, 'The Castle of Baghras', in Boase, p. 45.

[4] Imad ad-Din al-Isfahani, *Conquête de la Syrie et de la Palestine par Saladin*, trans. H. Massé (Paris, 1972), p. 142 (my translation).

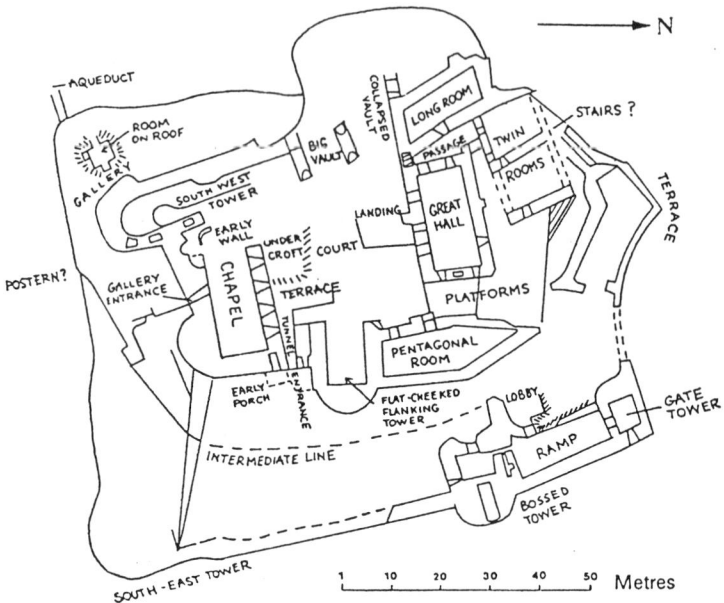

Figure 18.2   Plan of the Castle of Gaston
From A.W. Lawrence, 'The Castle of Baghras', in *The Cilician Kingdom of Armenia*, ed. T.S.R. Boase (Edinburgh: Scottish Academic Press, 1978), p. 48.

Bonnel, it was seized (probably in 1191) by Leon of Armenia who set about establishing a permanent occupation. He rebuilt and garrisoned Gaston and then granted it in fief to his seneschal, Adam, who held it from at least 1198 to 1215. Occupation of Gaston considerably strengthened the Armenians' position, as it threatened both Antioch and Aleppo and opened the way to northern Syria. The struggle over possession of the fortress lasted over twenty years until Leon occupied Antioch, and Gaston lost some of its strategic importance for him. The Templars then occupied the castle until 1268.

There are three contemporary, or near-contemporary, Arabic biographies of Baybars extant. Firstly, that of Ibn 'Abd al-Zāhir (1223–92) who was the court biographer.[5] An abridged version by his maternal nephew, Shafi b. 'Ali (1252–1330) was completed, according to the colophon, in 1316.[6] The biography by 'Izz al-Din Ibn Shaddad (1217–85)[7] was written between 1277 and 1279, shortly after the sultan's death. Unfortunately, only the second volume of this work, containing annals covering the period 1271–77, is extant. For this reason I have chosen Ibn 'Abd al-Zāhir's work as the main Arabic source for the

---

[5] Ibn 'Abd al-Zāhir, *al-Rawd al-zāhir fī sīrat al-Malik al-Ẓāhir*, ed. 'Abd al-'Azīz al-Khuwayṭir (Riyyad, 1976).

[6] Shafi b. 'Ali, *Kitāb ḥusn al-manāqib al-sirriyya al-muntaza'a min al-sīra al-Ẓahiriyya*, ed. 'Abd al-'Azīz b. 'Abdallāh al-Khuwayṭir (Riyyad, 1976).

[7] Edirne, *Selimiye* ms 2306.

surrender of Gaston in 1268. In addition I have studied the accounts of later Arab historians, namely Abu'l Fida (1273–1331),[8] Ibn al-Furat (1334–1405),[9] al-Maqrizi (1364–1442)[10] and al-'Aini (1360–1451).[11]

Ibn 'Abd al-Zāhir tells us:

> ... the Sultan captured Antakya [Antioch] and Dar Kush and other castles, and there remained in that region only Bagras. The inhabitants of the last place, the Templars, felt threatened, especially after the recapture of Sis, and later its inhabitants left the place. The Emir, Shams ad-Din Eksanker ... took possession of it on Saturday, the 13th day of Ramadan, and he found only an old woman. The place was strongly fortified and well-equipped, and became part of Islamic territory without difficulty.[12]

Abu'l Fida's account is less detailed, but follows Zahir in broad terms. In addition, we are told that 'the garrison retreated in great haste'. Al-Maqrizi provides no new information, while al-'Aini goes on to compare this incident favourably with the unsuccessful seven-month siege by Saladin's son, al-Malik al-Zāhir Ghazi and the army of Aleppo. His account ends with the eulogy:

> ... Baybars became master of it easily and without being obliged to lay a siege. The sultan occupied yet many more fortresses and castles, then returned to his estates covered in glory and triumphant.[13]

Our Templar source for the surrender of Gaston is the Catalan manuscript of the Order's Rule – an incomplete version held in the Archivo de la Corona de Aragón in Barcelona, which Delaville Le Roulx dates to the last years of the thirteenth century.[14] He suggests that it was probably used by the Masters of the Temple in Aragon and Catalonia, for copies were restricted to the higher officials of the Order, and the pages dealing with the procedures for receiving a brother are more worn than others, indicating that they were used by the Master at receptions. In its original state the document most probably also contained the Primitive Rule and the Hierarchical Statutes, although the part that has come down to us consists of only some of the procedures for the Holding of Ordinary Chapters, Details on Penances and Reception into the Order of a non-combatant brother.

---

[8] Abu'l Fida, 'Annales', *RHC Or*, 1, p. 152.

[9] Ibn al-Furat, *Tarikh al-Duwal wa'l-Muluk*, trans. in U. & M.C. Lyons, *Ayyubids, Mamlukes and Crusaders*, 2 (Cambridge, 1971), p. 127.

[10] Al-Maqrizi, trans. Quatremère as *Histoire des Sultans Mamlouks de l'Egypte*, 1,2, p. 56.

[11] *RHC Or*, 2, pp. 234–5.

[12] Ibn 'Abdal Zahir, pp. 325–7. I am indebted to Dr Kemal Çiçek of Trabzon University, Turkey, for his translation of this passage.

[13] *RHC Or*, 2, p. 235.

[14] J. Delaville le Roulx, 'Un nouveau manuscrit de la Règle du Temple', *Annuaire-Bulletin de la Société de l'Histoire de France*, 26, 2 (1889), pp. 185–214.

Figure 18.3   The ascent to Gaston, from the east

Figure 18.4   Gallery hall, from the north

Figure 18.5   Hall and platform, from the south-east

It is in the second section that the greatest interest lies, for the examples of infringements of the Rule and their consequent penances differ considerably from those given in the French manuscripts. The surrender of Gaston is just one example that is included in the Barcelona manuscript but not in those of Paris and Rome. The narrative takes up four folios,[15] with approximately two-thirds of a page illegible. The account may be said to consist of two parts: the events of the surrender itself, and the consequences of it to the brothers concerned. We are told that the events took place while Guerant of Sauzet was Commander of the Land of Antioch. When news came to him that Baybars was on his way to Antioch with his army, Guerant asked the Master to send men and 'other things' to Gaston which he needed to garrison the castle. Baybars took Antioch in two days, and the brothers at Gaston were in despair, not knowing what to do because they had no arms with which to defend the castle. Then, while the brothers were eating, one of their number named Guis de Belin took the keys of the castle, rode out to Baybars and offered them to him, saying that the brothers wanted to surrender. Upon hearing this, the sultan sent for large numbers of men, and the brothers subsequently told their commander that they did not think they could defend the castle against them. The commander maintained that he would defend it as best he could, but while the brothers agreed to do as he commanded, the sergeants told him they would leave because they did not wish to die. Consequently, the other brothers and the commander then agreed that, because they had no arms and the Master could not help them, and because the sultan knew their situation, it would be better to retreat to La Roche Guillaume, another of their castles nearby, taking with them what they could, and destroying the rest. This is the course of action they eventually took, except that, the Rule tells us, they did not destroy everything they left behind. Meanwhile, the Master had heard that Antioch had been taken and knew that the brothers could not defend Gaston, nor could he send help. Instead, he sent a messenger, Brother Pelestort, to collect together the brothers if they had surrendered and left Gaston, and, if they had not, to instruct them to surrender the castle and go to La Roche Guillaume, taking with them what they could and destroying what they could not. Of course, when Brother Pelestort reached Gaston, he found that the brothers had surrendered it and left.

The commander and brothers of Gaston later went to Acre, the Templars' headquarters, to confess to having surrendered the castle without permission, and this led to a division among the brothers when it came to deciding upon the appropriate punishment. Some brothers favoured their expulsion from the Order because they had surrendered a border castle without the permission of the Master and the Convent; others felt that expulsion was inappropriate because the brothers had taken the action agreed upon by the Convent, even

---

[15] Archivo de la Corona de Aragón, Barcelona, *Cartas Reales*, ms. 344, fols 53a–57b.

though they had surrendered before they had actually received the Master's instructions. Finally, they were allowed to remain in the Order for this reason, and because the situation was a new one. However, because they had not destroyed everything in the castle, it was suggested that they should lose their habits for a year and a day, the next most severe punishment to being expelled. The Master informed the Convent of this suggestion and they agreed to it.

The Templars' own account, then, while providing us with 'inside' information, in broad lines corroborates the accounts we have studied in the Arabic sources. All are agreed that Baybars took possession of the castle without difficulty, that the Templars departed in some haste, and that they did not destroy everything left in the castle. It also raises some interesting points concerning the Order's system for judging infringements of the Rule.

The Barcelona manuscript gives a ruling which was designed to provide guidance on just such an incident as happened at Gaston: 'And whoever surrenders a castle in march lands may not remain in the house if he has done it without permission.'[16] In other words, the punishment was expulsion from the Order, with no possibility of readmission. The case of Gaston was controversial in that the local commander had given the same order as the Master, but, in fact, anticipated it by surrendering the castle before the messenger had arrived and made known those instructions.

The discussion in Acre is one of several examples showing the deliberations of the elders of the Order on difficult points of discipline. The French Rule dictates that:

> ... the brothers of the Temple should know that when any failing comes to chapter, and the failing touches on the habit, or if it is new, or if it is serious, or if it is such that the brothers are not certain what they should do about it, they should defer judgement, until it is brought before the Master or before such other worthy brother of the house who has the authority and the knowledge to address it....[17]

In fact, there is great emphasis in the Rule on the opinion of the Orders' elders with regard to sentencing; and established custom and memory played a part in the construction of those sections of the Rule dealing with penances. The maintenance of discipline was extremely important within the Order, for it was the application of the discipline of monastic life to the battlefield which made the Templars invaluable to the crusading armies of the West. However, extenuating circumstances were always taken into account, and if a brother was generally of good behaviour, he would be judged less harshly than an habitual offender, even if his offence was more serious.

---

[16] Ibid., fol. 35.
[17] *The Rule of the Templars*, trans. J.M. Upton-Ward (Woodbridge, 1992), § 527, pp. 140–41.

At his reception, a brother was asked: 'Do you ... promise to God and to Lady St Mary that you, all the remaining days of your life, will help to conquer, with the strength and power that God has given you, the Holy Land of Jerusalem; and that which Christians hold you will help to keep and save within your power?'[18]

In 1188 Gaston had withstood a siege of several weeks until Saladin's troops were beginning to lose heart. The Templars had defended the castle well, and Imad ad-Din informs us that 'the submission of these intractable men surprised us: they surrendered it although they had been jealous even of the sun which penetrated it.'[19] Eighty years later, one Templar gave up heart and offered the keys of the castle to Baybars before the sultan had attempted to take it. It was only after this, the Rule tells us, that he sent for large numbers of men, and the sergeants threatened to leave 'because they did not wish to die'. The commander, despite his desire to defend the castle in accordance with his vows, had to bow to pressure from the sergeants and retreat.

The castle of Gaston appears to have been the Templars' first important marcher lordship, before that of Gaza, which was granted to them in 1149. Its strategic importance can be seen in the long and bitter struggle they fought against Leon of Armenia for it. However, in the 1260s the situation in the East was extremely difficult, and many appeals were made to the West for help. Morale was obviously at a very low ebb in 1268, and this may be at least partly explained by the fact that Antioch had just fallen. This had been the first Syrian city to be taken by the Christians, in 1098, and they had held it without interruption for 170 years. It is not surprising, therefore, that this event plunged the brothers into low spirits, or even desperation. If the Mamluk sultan had taken a city as important as Antioch so easily, how could they be expected to hold out against him? They had no arms and the Master was not in a position to send reinforcements from Acre.

Thus the episode of the surrender of Gaston demonstrates the value of this Templar source to supplement the chronicles. Where Western chronicles fail to provide anything but the minimum of information, the Rule of the Templars not only gives a detailed account of the surrender, but also an insight into the procedures for sentencing and punishing brothers who transgressed the regulations.

---

[18] Ibid., § 676, p. 174.
[19] Imad ad-Din, p. 143.

19

The Templars in Cyprus

Peter Edbury

Our knowledge of Templar activity in Cyprus between the Latin conquest in 1191 and the suppression of the Order in the years 1307–12 is, to say the least, patchy. Templars feature in comparatively few episodes: they purchased the island from King Richard of England in 1191 and ruled it until the early months of 1192; in the 1270s they quarrelled with the king of Cyprus, Hugh III, over their recognition of his rival, Charles of Anjou, as King of Jerusalem, and Hugh confiscated their Cypriot lands; they participated in some Cyprus-based military operations around the year 1300 which culminated in their occupation of Ruad; and, finally, there exists some interesting material from Cyprus on the circumstances of the suppression of the Order.

Moving from political and military activities to the question of endowments, we find that the evidence is even thinner: not a single charter or confirmation recording grants of property has survived. However, it is possible from the sources at our disposal to obtain an impression of the significance of what must have been one of the wealthiest and most powerful corporations on the island.

Richard the Lionheart conquered Cyprus in May 1191 en route for Palestine and the siege of Acre. Scholars disagree as to whether his conquest was premeditated or more a matter of opportunism,[1] but there is little doubt that the English king was not interested in acquiring the island for its own sake but merely wanted to raid the island for supplies and as much cash as possible to help pay for his campaign in the Holy Land. Having seized what he could at the time of the invasion, he quickly sold Cyprus to the Templars for 100,000 gold dinars, of which 40,000 were paid immediately. But the Templars either underestimated the resources that were needed to administer the island or simply

---

[1] P.W. Edbury, *The Kingdom of Cyprus and the Crusades, 1191–1374* (Cambridge, 1991), p. 8 and n. 17.

From *The Military Orders: Fighting for the Faith and Caring for the Sick*, ed. Malcolm Barber. Copyright © 1994 by Malcolm Barber. Published by Variorum, Ashgate Publishing Ltd, Gower House, Croft Road, Aldershot, Hampshire, GU11 3HR, Great Britain.

lacked the manpower to do so. According to one version of the French Continuation of William of Tyre, they

> ... wanted to rule the people of the island of Cyprus as they would the people in a village in the land of Jerusalem. They wanted to rob, beat and ill-treat them, and they aimed to control the island of Cyprus through twenty brother knights....

At Easter 1191 the people of Nicosia rose in revolt. Another version of the same narrative tells us that the Templars mustered all the available Latins and that the total came to fourteen knights, twenty-nine other mounted men and seventy-four foot soldiers. They sallied forth from their stronghold and butchered large numbers of insurgents.[2]

The Order had clearly taken on more than it could manage. Had it succeeded in turning Cyprus into a Templar sovereign state, its subsequent history would have been very different. But it was not to be. The Templars found that they could neither govern the island nor pay their debt to King Richard. The answer to their difficulties lay in the politics of Latin Syria. To cut a long story short, Richard decided that Conrad of Montferrat should rule the remnants of the kingdom of Jerusalem while the King of Jerusalem, Guy of Lusignan, should have Cyprus. The Templars seem to have been happy to fall in with this solution to what had become an extremely fraught political conflict. Unfortunately the fullest accounts of the transaction concerning Cyprus contradict each other at vital points. One version of the *Continuation* of William of Tyre states that Guy reimbursed the Templars the 40,000 dinars they had paid Richard and accepted responsibility for the balance of 60,000 still owed.[3] But another version – the one which is probably closest to the events and which also gives some plausible circumstantial details – claims that Guy paid Richard 60,000 dinars and that, although he owed a further 40,000, the king did not insist on payment; this version makes no mention of Guy paying the Templars anything.[4]

These two accounts cannot both be right. Elsewhere I have followed the second,[5] but on reflection I am no longer sure. The English sources claim that Richard gave Cyprus to Guy, and this would seem to be more in keeping with the implication of the first version that Guy paid Richard nothing. The *Itinerarium peregrinorum* speaks of the 'condition of the Templar sale having been exchanged', and this too would appear to support the first account. What may have happened is that Guy compensated the Templars for their outlay, accepted that he now owed Richard the balance, but then succeeded in avoiding having to make any payments.[6]

---

[2] *Cont WT*, pp. 135, 137; *Eracles*, 2, pp. 189–91.

[3] *Eracles*, p. 191.

[4] *Cont WT*, pp. 137, 139, cf. pp. 136, 143. The later versions (*Eracles*, pp. 187–8 var. CG; *Ernoul-Bernard*, p. 286) say that Guy bought Cyprus from Richard.

[5] Edbury, p. 9.

[6] 'Itinerarium Peregrinorum et Gesta Regis Ricardi' in *Chronicles and Memorials of the Reign of Richard I*, ed. W. Stubbs (RS 38), 1, p. 351.

In the light of the circumstances in which he had acquired the island, it is possible that Guy found himself under moral, and perhaps financial, obligation to the Templars and that his indebtedness to the Order was one reason for its generous endowment there. Unfortunately, we do not know the full extent of the Templars' holdings in the island, although we can identify some of their estates. Still less do we know when they obtained them. What is certain, however, is that almost all their properties passed to the Hospitallers in the second decade of the fourteenth century after the Order's suppression, and we do have a fairly accurate idea of the extent of the Hospitaller estates in Cyprus after the transfer. In the fourteenth century the Knights of Saint John held a number of properties that are not attributable to either Order in the thirteenth. Whereas it is possible that some may have been fresh acquisitions, the probability is that almost all the fourteenth-century Hospitaller estates had been obtained before the end of the thirteenth by one or other of the two Orders. As some of the documentation recording gifts to the Hospitallers in Cyprus survives, and so our knowledge of the thirteenth-century Hospitaller estates seems likely to be more complete, it may well be that a majority of these unattributable estates had in fact belonged to the Templars.[7]

If I am right, then it is probable that the Templars would have been among the richest landholders in Cyprus after the Crown. Apart from the Hospitallers, only the archbishop of Nicosia and the greatest of the lay lords such as John of Ibelin, Count of Jaffa, who in the mid-thirteenth century is known to have held Episkopi and Peristerona, can have had comparable incomes. Whether the Templars were wealthier than the Hospitallers is hard to judge. In the mid-thirteenth century the archbishop of Nicosia made agreements with both Orders in respect of the tithes they owed. In 1255 the Hospitallers undertook to pay the archbishop 300 white besants annually in lieu of tithe, plus a silver mark for their cemetery rights, while in 1261 the Templars agreed to pay 190

---

[7] Known Templar estates: Khirokitia, Yermasoyia, Phasouri, Psimolophou (and the dependent settlements at Tripi and Kato Deftera), Gastria and Temblos, together with properties in Limassol, Nicosia, Paphos and Famagusta. Known Hospitaller estates from before 1300: Kolossi, Plataniskia, Monagroulli, Phinikas, Palekhori, Kellaki, Louvaras and Trakhoni, together with properties at Nicosia, Limassol and Mora, and unidentified localities: *Esteriga*, Nostra Dame de *Combos* and St George. Additional estates in the possession of the Hospitallers by 1319–20: *Mons Esquillate*, Apsiou, Yerasa, Paramytha, Mathikoloni, *Sirincocie* (= Syrianokhori?), Sanidha, Anoyira, Akoursos, Ayios Konstantinos, *Androclio*. J. Richard, *Chypre sous les Lusignans. Documents chypriotes des archives du Vatican (XIVe et XVe siècles)* (Paris, 1962), pp. 111–20, cf. p. 68; J. Riley-Smith, *The Knights of St John in Jerusalem and Cyprus, c. 1050–1310* (London, 1967), p. 505; Edbury, pp. 77–8. *Mons Esquillati*, unidentified by Richard, could be an attempt at Latinizing 'the Mountain of Kellaki'; if so, it presumably denotes a group of Hospitaller estates in the Troodos to the north of Kellaki (see the map in Richard, p. 71). Later medieval lists name many more Hospitaller properties, some of which, however, were probably settlements dependent on the estates mentioned in this note. L. de Mas Latrie, *Histoire de l'île de Chypre sous le règne des princes de la maison de Lusignan*, 3 (Paris, 1852–61), pp. 502–3; Florio Bustron, 'Chronique de l'île de Chypre' ed. R. de Mas Latrie, in *Collection des documents inédits sur l'histoire de France: Mélanges historiques*, 5 (1886), pp. 170–71, 246–7.

besants as tithe and, again, a silver mark for cemetery rights. These settlements provide the only indications of the relative wealth of the Orders of which I am aware, but they raise more problems than they solve. Although at first sight, they might seem to indicate that the Hospitallers were wealthier, the Templars may have driven a harder bargain. In any case, both Orders seem to have held most of their possessions outside the Nicosia diocese.[8]

Although they were richly endowed, the Templars are unlikely to have maintained a substantial military establishment in Cyprus before 1291. They had acquired the fort at Gastria to the north of Famagusta by 1210, but from the little known of its structure it would not appear to have required a substantial garrison.[9] The same would have been true of the fortified towers they owned at Limassol, Yermasoyia and Khirokitia. They would have used the income from their estates to help support their obligations in Syria rather than assist in the defence of the island. By the same token, an absence of Templar military strength in Cyprus would have meant that the Order played little part in the politics of the Lusignan kingdom, and so would have tended to obviate the danger of confrontation with the secular authorities.

It is with this thought in mind that we come to the breach between King Hugh III and the Templars in the mid-1270s. Hitherto there had been no recorded conflict between the Order and the royal dynasty. Although it is true that, in 1210, the disgraced regent of Cyprus, Walter of Montbéliard, had sought refuge with the Templars, and it may be significant that Hugh I, who came into his inheritance at this time, is known to have been a patron of the rival Order, the Hospitallers,[10] there is no evidence that any coolness that may have developed at that time amounted to anything. Indeed, a few years later the Templars and the Ibelin-dominated regime in Cyprus united in opposition to the Emperor Frederick II and his officers.[11]

In the 1270s King Hugh III of Cyprus and Charles of Anjou, King of Sicily, were both laying claim to the kingdom of Jerusalem. Hugh had possession of Acre, the one remaining royal city, and in 1269 had been crowned and anointed king. But as his reign progressed and dissatisfaction grew in various quarters, so the fact that his title was disputed came to acquire greater significance. Initially he seems to have had Templar support, but, with the election of William of Beaujeu as master in 1273, the Order moved decisively into Charles's camp. So far as is known, Hugh had done nothing in particular to antagonize the Templars, but William was a relative of the Angevin royal house and, before

---

[8] *CH*, no. 2762; J.L. La Monte, 'A Register of the Cartulary of the Cathedral of Santa Sophia of Nicosia', *Byzantion*, 5 (1930), nos. 90, 92. Cf. Riley-Smith, pp. 432–3.

[9] *Eracles*, p. 316; C. Enlart, *Gothic Art and the Renaissance in Cyprus*, tr. and ed. D. Hunt (London, 1987), pp. 473–5.

[10] Edbury, pp. 44, 46.

[11] A. Demurger, *Vie et mort de l'ordre du Temple*, 2nd ed. (Paris, 1989), pp. 235–6. Cf. Pope Gregory IX, *Registres*, ed. L. Auvray (Paris, 1890-1955), no. 1037.

his election, had been Templar commander in Apulia. It is also worth noting that many Templars were from France, where Charles's brother, and now his nephew, had each ruled as king, and so there may well have been a natural sympathy for his claims, and it was also true that the Templar establishments in the East had come to depend heavily on the ports of Charles's kingdom for their supplies of food, arms and horses. In 1276, with both the Templars and the Venetians, who had their own reasons for disaffection, ranged against him, Hugh found that his authority in Syria was undermined to such an extent that he retired to Cyprus, leaving Acre to fall into the hands of Charles's officers. Later he regretted his surrender and, in 1279 and again in 1283–84, vainly attempted to re-establish his position. William of Beaujeu had eased the Angevin assumption of power in Acre and continued to give Charles's agents his full support.[12] Not surprisingly, Hugh retaliated by taking reprisals on the Templars' Cypriot properties. In the aftermath of his first abortive attempt to re-occupy Acre in 1279, he ordered the confiscation of their estates and the destruction of their house at Limassol.[13] How long this confiscation lasted is not clear: in the early 1280s Pope Martin IV ordered Hugh to stop harming the Templars and not to touch their possessions, and it may have been at about the same time that the pope had the archdeacon of Tortosa and the bishop of Sidon, both of whom, incidentally, were beneficed in Templar-controlled cities, pronounce sentence against him.[14]

The antipathy between the Templars and the Lusignan kings continued until the Order's suppression. With the fall of Acre in 1291 the Templars moved their headquarters to Cyprus, and henceforth the number of Templars stationed on the island would have been far greater than before. A Chapter General held in Nicosia in 1291 is said to have been attended by 400 brothers of the Order; in 1300 the Order was able to send 120 knights, 500 archers and 400 servants to garrison the island of Ruad; one deposition made at the Templar trial mentions an assembly of 120 brothers or more held at Limassol in 1304; in 1308, 38 brother knights and 35 sergeants are reported to have been arrested when the members of the Order were rounded up.[15] With far larger forces now in the island, tension apparently remained high. Early in his reign, King Henry II sent an embassy to the pope to complain about the Order, and in 1298 the pope

---

[12] Edbury, pp. 93–6; A. Forey, *The Military Orders from the Twelfth to the Early Fourteenth Centuries* (Basingstoke and London, 1992), p. 133; M. Barber, 'Supplying the Crusader States: The Role of the Templars', in *The Horns of Ḥaṭṭīn*, ed. B.Z. Kedar (Jerusalem and London, 1992), pp. 325–6.

[13] 'Annales de Terre Sainte', ed. R. Röhricht and G. Raynaud, *AOL*, 2 (1884), p. 457, cf. p. 456; 'Les Gestes des Chiprois', *RHC DArm*, 2, p. 784.

[14] *Veterum Scriptorum et Monumentorum ... Amplissima Collectio*, ed. F. Martène and U. Durand (Paris, 1727–33), 2, col. 1300; L. de Mas Latrie, 2, p. 109.

[15] *Procès*, 1, p. 562; 2, p. 139; 'Chronique d'Amadi', in *Chroniques d'Amadi et de Strambaldi*, ed. R. de Mas-Latrie, 1 (Paris, 1891–93), pp. 239, 286. At the Templar trial in Cyprus 76 members of the Order, of whom at least 38 were brothers, were examined. M. Barber, *The Trial of the Templars* (Cambridge, 1978), p. 219.

told the king and the Master, James of Molay, to resolve their differences. Continued Templar contacts with the Sicilian Angevins may have contributed to the difficulties; disputes over the right of the Order to acquire property and claim exemption from taxes further soured relations; and there is evidence, too, to suggest that disagreements between the king and the military orders impaired the effectiveness of the Christian response to the Mongol invasion of Syria in 1299. In 1306, when the Cypriot nobles forced King Henry to relinquish his authority to his brother, Amaury, lord of Tyre, the Templars gave them strong support, and, even after their arrest two years later, members of the Order persisted in expressing their hostility towards the king.[16]

It would, however, be misleading to give the impression that, after the retreat from mainland Syria in 1291, the Templars did little in Cyprus other than quarrel with the king. For example, in 1302 the Master, James of Molay, acted decisively in ransoming the count of Jaffa and members of his family who were seized by Greek pirates from his estate at Episkopi.[17] In 1300 the Templars joined the Cypriots and Hospitallers in a naval raid on Egypt and Syria, and the following year they participated in the occupation of the island of Ruad, remaining there in force, after the Cypriot and Hospitaller withdrawal, until the Egyptian sultan moved against them in 1302, and most of the Templar garrison was killed or taken captive.[18] Futile as these military actions may seem in retrospect, the Order's commitment to the recovery of the Holy Land was none the less very real. In about 1305 James of Molay submitted a proposal to the pope calling for a full-scale crusade to win back Jerusalem in which he envisaged that Cyprus would be used as a forward base.[19] At the same time the Order had been building up its fleet, and the surviving registers of a Genoese notary working in Famagusta at this period provide evidence for Templar involvement in the vigorous commercial life of that city.[20] Furthermore, despite the Order's constant arguments with the Crown, the people of Cyprus themselves evidently held them in high regard, for, when Cypriot lay witnesses were called to testify in the Templar trial, not one of them was prepared to condemn the Order, and many spoke openly in its favour. Even those nobles – such men as the seneschal Philip of Ibelin, Baldwin of Ibelin, Rupen of

---

[16] L. de Mas Latrie, 2, pp. 108–9; Boniface VIII, *Registres*, ed. G. Digard et al. (Paris, 1884–1939), nos. 2438–9, 2609, 3060–62; *Notai genovesi in Oltremare: Atti rogati a Cipro da Lamberto di Samuceto*, ed. R. Pavoni (C[ollana] S[torica di] F[onti e] S[tudi]) 49 (Genoa, 1987), no. 202; Edbury, pp. 111–13, 121.

[17] 'Amadi', p. 238.

[18] M. Barber, 'James of Molay, the Last Grand Master of the Temple', *Studia Monastica*, 14 (1972), pp. 98–9; Edbury, pp. 105–6.

[19] S. Schein, *Fideles Crucis: The Papacy, the West and the Recovery of the Holy Land. 1274–1314* (Oxford, 1991), pp. 201–2.

[20] *Notai genovesi in Oltremare: Atti rogati a Cipro da Lamberto di Sambuceto*, ed. V. Polonio (CSFS 31) (Genoa, 1982), nos 148, 166, 171, 219, 258, 413; ed. R. Pavoni, (CSFS 32) (Genoa, 1982), no. 206; ed. Pavoni (CSFS 49) (Genoa, 1987), nos 104, 150, 155, 162.

Montfort and Aygue of Bethsan – who had been close to the king and so might have been tempted to avenge themselves on the Templars for their support of Amaury of Tyre, chose not to do so.[21]

I should like to conclude by offering some hypotheses. It is my belief, although there is insufficient evidence to prove it, that the Templars received most of their lands in Cyprus in the immediate aftermath of the Lusignan establishment in the 1190s. So long as the Order was content to transfer the income from its estates to Latin Syria and not involve itself in the island's politics, all went well – or at least nothing happened that was sufficiently dramatic to leave a mark on the sources. However, in the 1270s the Order's espousal of Charles of Anjou's claims brought it into conflict with the Lusignans, and the lingering ill-will thus generated came to acquire greater significance when, after 1291, the Templars moved their headquarters to Cyprus and thereby increased their numbers on the island. In Cyprus they never managed to acquire the sort of autonomy they had enjoyed in their lordships at Sidon, Tortosa, Château Pèlerin and elsewhere in Syria, and in all probability successive kings tried to keep them at arm's length and to prevent them from having influence in the affairs of their realm. Rich, militarily powerful and yet constricted by royal authority, Templar relations with the Crown remained poor. In 1295 Pope Boniface VIII issued a bull stating that they were to enjoy the same privileges in Cyprus as they had had in the Holy Land.[22] What exactly that meant is not clear, but almost certainly it should be taken as evidence of Templar aspirations to free themselves from both secular and ecclesiastical jurisdiction. Maybe a desire for greater freedom also lay behind their support for the 1306 revolution. Old habits die hard. Just as James of Molay, in 1305, could advocate a type of crusade which arguably was already anachronistic, so, too, may he have been striving for the sort of role in Cypriot political affairs that his predecessors had played in the kingdom of Jerusalem as far back as the third quarter of the twelfth century.

---

[21] Barber, *Trial of Templars*, pp. 218–19; Edbury, p. 125 n. 94.
[22] Boniface VIII, nos. 487, 1937.

20

Towards a Profile of the Templars in the Early Fourteenth Century

Alan Forey

The testimonies of the Templars during their trial are perhaps more interesting for the incidental information they provide about the brethren and the Order than for their direct answers to the articles of accusation. The records of the trial can be used to discuss a variety of topics, including recruitment[1] and literacy, but this paper will consider briefly the age-ranges of brethren, their length of service, and mobility of brothers within the Order.

Most sets of testimonies provide evidence about length of service, and a number also include information about the ages of brethren. That the figures given are no more than approximate is at once apparent from a rapid perusal of the testimonies: ages, for example, are often recorded in round numbers, especially for the older brethren. The testimonies of those who were interrogated more than once reveal numerous discrepancies, as does the evidence of brethren who were admitted to the Order on the same occasion but who claimed to have served for differing lengths of time. Allowance must also be made for errors in transcription. It would therefore be unwise to attempt to use evidence about ages or length of service in too precise a manner. But the brethren's responses are not to be rejected altogether, and they do of course indicate the perceptions of the brothers themselves. The information given in Tables 20.1 and 20.2 relates to the time when Templars were questioned, not when they were arrested, and was therefore, in some cases, provided several years after recruitment had stopped.[2] But to amend this evidence in order to indicate the situation in 1307 would tend to increase error, and those who had died between 1307 and the time when interrogations took place

---

[1] A.J. Forey, 'Recruitment to the Military Orders (Twelfth to Mid-Fourteenth Centuries)', *Viator*, **17** (1986), especially pp. 144–7, 150–51.

[2] The following sets of testimonies have been used: Paris, 1307 and 1310–11: *Procès*: Poitiers, 1308: K. Schottmüller, *Der Untergang des Templer-Ordens*, **2** (Berlin, 1887), pp. 13–71; H. Finke, *Papsttum und Untergang des Templerordens*, **2** (Münster, 1907), doc. 155, pp. 329–42; Clermont, 1309:

would be left out of account. Only the earliest testimony of those who were questioned on more than one occasion is used for the purposes of calculation.

Table 20.1   Ages of Templars at time of interrogation

	Paris 1307	Paris 1310–11	Lérida 1310	Total	Hospitallers 1373
Below 20	3 (2.4%)	–	–	3 (0.8)	–
20–29	25 (20.2)	14 (7.0)	4 (12.9)	43 (12.1)	9 (5.1)
30–39	23 (18.5)	48 (24.1)	10 (32.3)	81 (22.9)	36 (20.2)
40–49	24 (19.4)	59 (29.6)	8 (25.8)	91 (25.7)	49 (27.5)
50–59	33 (26.6)	45 (22.6)	7 (22.6)	85 (24.0)	46 (25.8)
60–69	10 (8.1)	25 (12.6)	2 (6.5)	37 (10.5)	27 (15.2)
70–79	5 (4.0)	5 (2.5)	–	10 (2.8)	9 (5.1)
80 and over	1 (0.8)	3 (1.5)	–	4 (1.1)	2 (1.1)
Total	124	199	31	354	178

	Paris 1307	Paris 1310–11	Lérida 1310	Total	Hospitallers 1373
Below 30	28 (22.6)	14 (7.0)	4 (12.9)	46 (13.0)	9 (5.1)
Below 40	51 (41.1)	62 (31.2)	14 (45.2)	127 (35.9)	45 (25.3)
Over 40	73 (58.9)	137 (68.8)	17 (54.8)	227 (64.1)	133 (74.7)
Over 50	49 (39.5)	78 (39.2)	9 (29.0)	136 (38.4)	84 (47.2)
Over 60	16 (12.9)	33 (16.6)	2 (6.5)	51 (14.4)	38 (21.3)

The ages of Templars at the time of the trial have already been investigated by Anne Gilmour-Bryson,[3] but she was contributing to a discussion of ageing and the aged in medieval Europe, and was primarily concerned with brethren who were over fifty years old. There is therefore scope for adding to what she has written, although the calculations given in Table 20.1 are based only on the direct evidence about ages provided in the proceedings, whereas she also sought to calculate the ages of brethren whose length of service alone is known: the validity of the latter procedure is not altogether free from doubt. For comparison, information is given in Table 20.1 about the ages of Hospitallers in the priory of France in 1373.[4]

Le Procès des Templiers d'Auvergne, 1309–1311, ed. R. Sève and A.M. Chagny-Sève (Paris, 1986); ? Provence: Finke, **2**, doc. 156, pp. 342–64; British Isles, 1309–11: D. Wilkins, *Concilia Magnae Britanniae et Hiberniae*, **2** (London, 1737), pp. 329–401; Mas-Deu, 1310: *Procès*, **2**, pp. 423–515; Lérida, 1310: Finke, **2**, doc. 157, pp. 364–78; Cyprus, 1310: Schottmüller, **2**, pp. 143–400; Alès, 1310: L. Ménard, *Histoire civile, ecclésiastique et littéraire de la ville de Nismes* (Paris, 1750–58), **1**, Preuves, doc. 136, pp. 172–95.

[3] A. Gilmour-Bryson, 'Age-Related Data from the Templar Trials', in *Aging and the Aged in Medieval Europe*, ed. M.M. Sheehan (Toronto, 1990), pp. 129–42.

[4] A.M. Legras, 'Les effectifs de l'ordre des Hospitaliers de Saint-Jean de Jérusalem dans le prieuré

Table 20.2   Templars' length of service at time of interrogation

	Paris 1307		Poitou 1308		Clermont 1309	
Under 10 years	64	(47.8)	11	(34.4)	20	(29.8)
10–19 years	25	(18.7)	12	(37.5)	13	(19.4)
20–29 years	28	(20.9)	5	(15.6)	18	(26.9)
30–39 years	9	(6.7)	3	(9.4)	13	(19.4)
40–49 years	8	(6.0)	–		3	(4.5)
50–59 years	–		1	(3.1)	–	
60–69 years	–		–		–	
Total	134		32		67	

	Provence?		British Isles 1309–11		Mas Deu 1310	
Under 10 years	7	(29.2)	33	(36.3)	5	(20)
10–19 years	8	(33.3)	23	(25.3)	13	(52)
20–29 years	3	(12.5)	21	(23.1)	2	(8)
30–39 years	4	(16.7)	11	(12.1)	5	(20)
40–49 years	2	(8.3)	3	(3.3)	–	
50–59 years	–		–		–	
60–69 years	–		–		–	
Total	24		91		25	

	Lérida 1310		Cyprus 1310		Cyprus: knights without office	
Under 10 years	8	(25.8)	46	(63.9)	31	(81.6)
10–19 years	9	(29.0)	17	(23.6)	6	(15.8)
20–29 years	12	(38.7)	6	(8.3)	–	
30–39 years	2	(6.5)	2	(2.8)	–	
40–49 years	–		1	(1.4)	1	(2.6)
50–59 years	–		–		–	
60–69 years	–		–		–	
Total	31		72		38	

	Alès 1310		Paris 1310–11		Total	
Under 10 years	6	(20.0)	63	(36.0)	263	(38.6)
10–19 years	12	(40.0)	57	(32.6)	189	(27.8)
20–29 years	3	(10.0)	39	(22.3)	137	(20.1)
30–39 years	4	(13.3)	11	(6.3)	64	(9.4)
40–49 years	5	(16.7)	3	(1.7)	25	(3.7)
50–59 years	–		1	(0.6)	2	(0.3)
60–69 years	–		1	(0.6)	1	(0.1)
Total	30		175		681	

de France en 1373', *Revue Mabillon*, **60** (1984), pp. 368–9; *L'enquête pontificale de 1373 sur l'ordre des Hospitaliers de Saint-Jean de Jérusalem*, ed. A.M. Legras, I (Paris, 1987), p. 105.

The proportion of brethren in the upper age groups was clearly smaller in the Temple than in the Hospital in 1373: in the Hospital the over-forty and over-fifty age groups were proportionately about 10 per cent larger than in the Temple, whereas in the below-forty group the situation was reversed. In explanation of the high percentage of older Hospitallers, it has been suggested that, during the decades preceding the 1373 enquiries, recruitment had been restricted for economic reasons, and that the supply of knightly recruits may have diminished.[5] Yet, although there was also a higher proportion of Templars than of Hospitallers below thirty, the Templars in that age group comprised a relatively small percentage of the overall membership: even if the figures for Paris in 1310–11 were crudely adjusted to indicate the situation in 1307, the numbers in their twenties would still be considerably smaller than of those in their thirties or forties; and although the records of the interrogations in Paris in 1307 mention twenty-eight brothers under thirty, only fourteen were under twenty-five. All these figures relate to western Europe, where most Templars resided, and – as will be seen – there may have been a somewhat higher proportion of young brethren at the Order's headquarters in Cyprus; but as the average age of recruitment was the mid- to later twenties,[6] a very large group below thirty would not be expected.

The majority of the Templars appear to have been in their thirties, forties and fifties. As the numbers in their fifties are usually not strikingly smaller than those in their thirties or forties, while brethren in their sixties are noticeably fewer (the Hospitaller figures are similar in this respect), it would seem – assuming that recruitment patterns had not markedly changed in the decades preceding the trial – that while many Templars survived their fifties, there was a high mortality rate amongst those in their sixties. There were, however, a few Templars who claimed to have passed eighty, and one Templar in Navarre was said to have been one hundred years old.[7]

To modern eyes, the Templars in western Europe would seem to have been predominantly middle-aged, but it may be asked how contemporaries would have regarded them. There are, of course, numerous medieval sources which seek to divide a man's life into stages, although the number of stages varies, as does the length of each stage.[8] Nor is it clear that the Templars themselves would have been aware of such views: these were the product of the literate element of society, and were scarcely based on observation. But, among these sources, it was common for *adolescentia* to be seen to end between twenty-five and thirty, with twenty-eight as the figure commonly given. On this calculation,

---

[5] Legras, 'Effectifs', pp. 362–4.

[6] Forey, p. 150.

[7] Finke, 2, doc. 158, p. 379.

[8] For recent discussions, see J.A. Burrow, *The Ages of Man: A Study of Medieval Writing and Thought* (Oxford, 1986), and E. Sears, *The Ages of Man: Medieval Interpretations of the Life Cycle* (Princeton, 1986).

therefore, few Templars in western Europe would have been classified as *adolescentes*. Most would have been regarded as having reached maturity and to be in the prime of their life – a stage which was commonly seen to last until forty-five or fifty – or to be beyond that stage, although only a few reached the upper age limits given in medieval schemes.

Length of service was obviously related to some extent to age. Figures for length of service in western Europe (see Table 20.2) do not present an altogether uniform pattern, but overall the largest group comprised those who had been Templars for less than ten years, even though many of the testimonies were given several years after recruitment had stopped. The group with 10–19 years' service is approximately 72 per cent of that with less than ten years' service, and the ratio between brethren with 20–29 years' service and those with 10–19 years' service is similar, although the difference between the first two groups would presumably have been greater if recruitment had continued after 1307. If the assumption is again made that recruiting patterns had not markedly changed in the decades before the trial, this evidence would suggest that a significant number of Templars did not serve more than ten years, either because of death – some recruits were of a fairly advanced age – [9] or apostasy, which was most likely to occur within a few years of recruitment. It is, however, among brothers with more than thirty years' service that a noticeably sharper fall in numbers is apparent: the group which had been in the Order for 30–39 years is less than half the size of that with 20–29 years' service; and hardly any brethren were Templars for half a century. Given the average age of recruitment, a large number of brothers with service of much more than 30–35 years would not be expected. By comparison, recruits entering Christ Church, Canterbury, in the late thirteenth and early fourteenth centuries had a career in the monastery which lasted on average 30.6 years, and a quarter of them were monks for forty or more years; and at the Dominican convent of Santa Maria Novella in Florence, in the later thirteenth century, friars served on average for thirty-two years.[10]

The most striking feature of the figures for length of service, however, is the contrast between western Europe and Cyprus. Of those interrogated in western Europe between 1309 and 1311, the highest percentage of brethren who had served for less than ten years occurs in the British Isles, where just over 36 per cent fell into this category. In Cyprus the figure is nearly 64 per cent. Forty-six out of seventy-two Templars questioned in Cyprus in 1310 had joined the Order since the beginning of the fourteenth century. Most of these were knights, and of the brothers in this category who did not hold office, over 80 per cent had less than ten years' service when they were interrogated.

[9] Forey, p. 150.

[10] J.C. Russell, *British Medieval Population* (Albuquerque, 1948), pp. 189–92; D. Herlihy, 'The Generation in Medieval History', *Viator*, 5 (1974), pp. 354–5.

It appears, therefore, to have been the practice to dispatch knightly recruits quickly to the East, where they usually served for only a limited term. This custom is also apparent from comments made by individual brethren during interrogation. The knight William of Reses, for example, who appeared before the pope in June 1308, said that he had been sent out to the East immediately after he had been received into the Order, and that he had served there for three years; and another knight, William of Torrage, told the papal commissioners in Paris that he had been dispatched to the East in his first year as a Templar, and had remained there for a year and a half.[11] The ages of the brethren in Cyprus is not recorded, but evidence from the West suggests that knights tended to join the Order at a lower age than recruits to other ranks.[12] It seems, therefore, that young knightly brethren who were capable of fighting were commonly stationed in the East, whereas in Western countries the membership, which was usually engaged in administration or agricultural work, included a larger proportion of older brethren.

The presence at the Order's headquarters of a large group of young knights with only limited experience probably influenced the way in which decisions were made there, for senior officials in the East were much older and had usually served for many years. In 1307 the Grand Master, James of Molay, stated that he had been a Templar for forty-two years, and Raimbaud of Caron, the Preceptor of Cyprus, who at the time of the trial was some sixty years old, had been in the Order for a similar length of time.[13] In 1310 the marshal of the Order said that he had joined 34 years earlier.[14] That there was a difference of outlook between the two groups is indicated by James of Molay's testimony in 1309, when he told the papal commissioners that, in the time of the Grand Master William of Beaujeu,

... he, James, and many other brothers of the convent of the said Templars, young men, eager for war, as is the way with young knights who want to participate in deeds of arms,[15] ... grumbled against the said master because, during a truce which the former king of England had made between the Christians and Saracens, the master showed respect to the sultan and remained on good terms with him.[16]

At this stage James of Molay had been in the Order for only a few years. This criticism was, of course, similar to that voiced by some crusaders, who felt that the military orders were not sufficiently aggressive towards Islam, but who had

---

[11] Schottmüller, **2**, p. 19; *Procès*, **2**, p. 12.

[12] Forey, p. 150.

[13] *Procès*, **2**, pp. 305, 374; cf. Finke, **2**, doc. 154, pp. 324, 328.

[14] Schottmüller, **2**, p. 167.

[15] Cf. G. Duby, 'Dans la France du Nord-Ouest au XIIe siècle: Les "jeunes" dans la société aristocratique', *Annales. Economies, Sociétés, Civilisations*, **19** (1964), pp. 835–46.

[16] *Procès*, **1**, pp. 44–5.

little knowledge of the political situation in the East.[17] Yet James went on to tell the commissioners that

> ... in the end he, brother James, and others of the convent of the said Templars accepted the situation, realising that the said master could not have done anything else, because the Order then had under its authority and in its custody many cities and strongholds near the borders of the sultan's land, and these could not have been protected in any other way, and would indeed have been lost at that time, if the said king of England had not sent supplies.

The young knights deferred to the wisdom of their more experienced superiors. The incident suggests that, although according to Templar regulations the Master was under an obligation to consult his chapter and even to accept a majority decision on some issues,[18] the influence of the rank-and-file knights at the central Convent was limited by their youth and inexperience, and that central government was under the control of the Master and leading officials, who were older and usually had many years of service.

Most Templars, however, joined the Order in the West and spent the whole of their careers there, in some cases serving in the same house for long periods of time: Simon of Elne, who was questioned in Roussillon in 1310, stated that he had spent all his 36 years in the Order at the house of Mas-Deu;[19] and of the twenty-five brethren of that convent interrogated in 1310, eighteen had been admitted to the Order there. But Templars joined an Order rather than a house, and there was more mobility within the Temple than among Cluniacs or Cistercians; in this respect the Templars and members of other military orders were more comparable with friars. Templar houses in the West did not consist of large communities, devoted primarily to a contemplative life: they usually comprised a mere handful of brethren, who were much involved in working the land and running estates; and brothers were transferred from one place to another as the needs of each house demanded. In the Templar testimonies, mobility is suggested first by references to receptions of recruits which a brother had witnessed in various places, although he may not always have been resident in houses where he attended admission ceremonies. Mobility is further implied by the formula adopted in some sets of answers to questions about alms-giving: these commonly refer to alms-giving 'in the houses' (in the plural) in which a brother had resided. Many individual testimonies, however, provide more precise evidence. Robert le Verrier, for example, who was from the diocese of Rouen, told the papal commissioners in Paris that he had held the office of *claviger* in four houses, even though he had been a Templar for

---

[17] For example, Otto of St Blasien, *Chronica*, ed. A. Hofmeister, *MGH, Scriptores rerum germanicarum*, **47** (1912), p. 68; 'Continuation de Guillaume de Tyr de 1229 à 1261, dite du manuscrit de Rothelin', *RHC Occid*, **2**, p. 549.

[18] *RT*, caps 85, 87, 92, 97, 390–91, 520, 657, pp. 79–80, 82–3, 85, 217–18, 273–4, 337.

[19] *Procès*, **2**, p. 511.

just over four years before his arrest; and Walter of Clifton, who was arrested in Scotland, reported that he had spent three years at Temple Newsam in Yorkshire, one in London, three at Rockley in Wiltshire and at Aslackby in Lincolnshire, and three at Balantrodoch in Scotland.[20]

Yet, although some who joined the Order in western Europe were sent out to the East and vice versa, there appears to have been limited mobility between provinces in the West: movement was usually within provinces. In this the Temple did differ to some extent from the orders of friars.[21] All Templars of the Convent of Mas-Deu who were questioned in 1310 had been received into the Order in the Aragonese province, as had all those interrogated at Lérida in 1310. A few years earlier, when James II was besieging the castles of the Aragonese Templars, the latter had reminded him that 'all of us are your natural subjects (*naturals*)', and the same point was made by the king himself when he was later negotiating about the fate of Templar property in his kingdoms.[22] Of those questioned in the British Isles, only half a dozen had been recruited abroad, and these – to judge by names – were men of English origin, most of whom had joined the Order in the East. Similarly the majority of those questioned at Clermont in 1309 had entered the Order in the province of Auvergne and, of the remainder, some had clearly returned to their native district after recruitment elsewhere: Bertrand of Sartiges, for example, who had been admitted at Tortosa in the county of Tripoli, belonged to a well known family in the Auvergne.[23] There were some brethren who had joined the Order in one French province and who appear to have been serving in another; and the preceptor of the house of Rué, in the diocese of Fréjus, at the time of the arrests, had been received in Castelo Branco in Portugal.[24] But these were exceptions. Whereas, in the Franciscan and Dominican orders, transfers to other provinces were made partly for the purposes of study, in the Temple there was little need for frequent interchange of personnel between Western provinces. Numerous transfers would have merely made for greater administrative complexity and would, in many instances, have occasioned language difficulties.

This situation tended to make provinces more inward-looking and self-contained, and there was the danger that local ties and loyalties would become of overriding significance. Thus when James II was taking action against the Aragonese Templars at the end of 1307, they reminded him of the military assistance they had given to Pedro III when the French had invaded in 1285.[25]

---

[20] Ibid., **2**, pp. 41–3; Wilkins, **2**, pp. 380–81.

[21] J.R.H. Moorman, 'The Foreign Element among the English Franciscans', *English Historical Review*, **62** (1947), pp. 289–303; A.B. Emden, *Survey of the Dominicans in England* (Rome, 1967), pp. 22–5.

[22] Finke, **2**, docs 48, 125, 134, pp. 71, 233, 267.

[23] *Procès d'Auvergne*, pp. 220, 295.

[24] Finke, **2**, doc. 156, p. 352.

[25] Ibid., **2**, doc. 48, p. 72.

Yet, if there were dangers, there is little sign of a significant trend towards a provincial independence of the kind visible in the Order of Santiago in Portugal at the turn of the thirteenth and fourteenth centuries.[26] As far as can be discerned from the sparse surviving evidence, attempts to weaken links between provinces and the Order's headquarters appear to have been made by kings – for financial reasons – rather than by the brethren of a province.[27]

[26] D.W. Lomax, 'El rey Don Diniz de Portugal y la orden de Santiago', *Hidalguía*, 30 (1982), pp. 477–87.

[27] H. Finke, *Acta Aragonensia*, 1 (Berlin, 1908), doc. 108, p. 158; V. Salavert y Roca, *Cerdeña y la expansión mediterránea de la Corona de Aragón 1297–1314*, 2 (Madrid, 1956), doc. 72, p. 102; J. Petit, 'Mémoire de Foulques de Villaret sur la croisade', *Bibliothèque de l'Ecole des Chartes*, 60 (1899), p. 607.

21

Testimony of Non-Templar Witnesses in Cyprus

Anne Gilmour-Bryson

The first problem concerning the trial, or hearing, of Templar prisoners in Cyprus relates to the dating of the interrogations themselves.[1] Some scholars assert that they took place in May 1310; others prefer the more logical date of May 1311, eleven months after King Henry II had returned from exile in Armenia.[2] On the other hand, the testimony is resolutely in favour of the Order and its members – which leads to the supposition that the earlier date may be more plausible since Amaury of Lusignan, the regent, allegedly favoured the Templars while the king was opposed to them, since he blamed them for complicity in his downfall.[3] In addition, several noble witnesses had accompanied the king into exile, and, hence logically should not have been in Cyprus in May–June 1310.[4] Rudt de Collenberg, who cites references to the Templar inquisition in Cyprus in 1311 in several places, mistakenly refers to Vat. Arch. AA D-224,

---

[1] K. Schottmüller, *Der Untergang des Templer-Ordens*, **2** (Berlin, 1887, repr.; New York, 1970), pp. 143–400.

[2] See for example, P. Edbury, *The Kingdom of Cyprus and the Crusades, 1191–1374* (Cambridge, 1991), pp. 122–36; M. Barber, *The Trial of the Templars* (Cambridge, 1978), pp. 216–20; F.-J.-M. Raynouard, *Monumens historiques* (Paris, 1813), p. 285; G. Hill, *The History of Cyprus*, **2** (Cambridge, 1940–1952), pp. 270–73. *Regestum Clementis Papae V* (Rome, 1887), year 6, part 2, no. 7599, indicates that a trial ought to have occurred in late 1311. A bull of 13 August 1311 delegates Dominic of Palestrina, who was sent to Cyprus to enquire about the Templars, as receiving a stipend to come from Templar 'biens'. *Reg. Clem.*, no. 7603, suggests he should use torture if need be.

[3] Edbury, pp. 113–27.

[4] Philip and Balian of Ibelin, among others. See *RHC DArm*, **2**, p. 922 and W.H. Rudt de Collenberg, 'Les Ibelin aux XIIIe et XIVe siècles. Généalogie compilée principalement selon les registres du Vatican', reprinted in his *Familles de l'Orient latin XIIe–XIVe siècles* (London, 1983), p. 191.

which is in fact an inventory made of Templar property in June of that year, and not one of the trial manuscripts in the Archives' possession.[5]

The testimony heard in Cyprus is particularly significant for three reasons. Firstly, the witnesses all maintained their complete innocence, unlike most Templars elsewhere, but similar to those heard in the Iberian peninsula and, on the whole, in England.[6] Secondly, because Cyprus was the overseas head-quarters at the time, a higher percentage of important members testified there than elsewhere. Thirdly, a wide range of non-Templar witnesses also testified as they did in London – although in the latter trial the evidence could scarcely be described as credible.[7]

In this paper, I am discussing only the evidence of non-Templars. The rank of many of these witnesses,[8] and their connection to the deposed king, would have led one to expect that their testimony would have been damaging to the Order, yet it was not. These men appeared in two groups. From 1–4 May twenty-one appeared, mostly of high social status but with only two definitely identifiable clerics, both abbots. The second group includes twenty clerics, both regular and secular. The two inquisitors were the bishops of Famagusta and Nimosia or Limassol, since at the time Nicosia was without a bishop.[9]

Philip of Ibelin,[10] the first witness,[11] seneschal of Cyprus and Jerusalem 1302–18, was possibly the most credible lay witness – and certainly the most important. He was the leader of the group of barons who remained faithful to the king. His principal statement, like all the rest given under oath, was that

---

[5] Rudt de Collenberg, 'Les Ibelin', p. 191, and his 'Etat et origine du haut clergé de Chypre avant le Grand Schisme d'après les registres des papes du XIIIe et du XIVe siècles', in *Mélanges de l'Ecole Française de Rome*, **91** (Rome, 1979), pp. 292, 299 *et passim*. Cyprus trial mss: Vatican Archives D-223 and D-228; D-229 is missing. D-224 is in fact an inventory of Templar property on Cyprus made on 26 June 1311.

[6] For the Iberian peninsula see H. Finke, *Papsttum und Untergang des Templerordens*, 2 vols, **2** (Munich, 1907), and his *Acta Aragonensia* (Berlin, 1908–1923), 3 vols, *passim*; A. Mercati, 'L'inter-rogatorio de Templari a Barcellona (1311)', *Gesammelte Aufsätze zur Kulturgeschichte Spaniens*, 6, 1937, pp. 240–51. The English interrogations are in D. Wilkins, *Concilia Magnae Britanniae et Hiberniae, A.D. 446–1718* (London, 1797), pp. 329–401.

[7] See Wilkins, *Concilia*, pp. 358 ff. and A. Gilmour-Bryson, 'The London Templar Trial Testimony: Truth, Myth, or Fable', in *The World Explored. Essays in Honour of Laurie Gardiner*, Melbourne Department of History Monograph Series (Melbourne, 1993), pp. 44–61.

[8] Further information on these witnesses may be found in W.H. Rudt de Collenberg, 'Les dispenses matrimoniales accordées a l'Orient Latin selon les registres du Vatican d'Honorius III à Clément VII (1223–1385)', *Mélanges de l'Ecole française de Rome Moyen Age Temps Modernes*, **89** (Rome, 1977) and L. de Mas Latrie, *Trésor de Chronologie d'histoire et de géographie* (Paris, 1889).

[9] Rudt de Collenberg, 'Etat et origine', p. 278; Hill, *History of Cyprus*, **2**, p. 271.

[10] See Rudt de Collenberg, 'Les Ibelin', on this family and E.G. Rey, *Les Familles d'Outre-Mer de Du Cange* (Paris, 1869), on most of the noble families mentioned. See also Edbury, *passim*.

[11] Schottmüller, **2**, pp. 152–3.

the secrecy of Templar receptions led to suspicion of evil-doing. This statement was certainly borne out by evidence heard everywhere in Christendom.[12]

Baldwin of Ibelin, another supporter of the king, appeared next.[13] He was an important functionary but added no new evidence. He merely supported the Order.

The king's marshal in Cyprus, Reynald of Seisson (or Soissons),[14] added in his statement that the Templars did believe in the sacraments and conduct their religious ceremonies correctly, a statement echoed by many subsequent witnesses.

Aigue (Agua or Ague) of Bessan (Bethsan) testified next but without disclosing new evidence.[15] He was loyal to the king and married to Eschive of Mongisart, connecting him to the higher nobility.[16]

James of Plany, a knight, spoke eloquently about Templars who shed their blood for Christ and the Christian faith, insisting that they were as good and as honest men of religion as one could find in any religious order.[17]

Raymond Bentho, custodian of the imprisoned Templars in Nicosia, stated that he had attended many Templar services and found their religious practices exemplary. He told of a giant Host which appeared at a Templar mass, insisting that it was a miraculous occurrence.[18] This story contrasts with the various instances of diabolical intervention described in French Templar testimony and that of certain English lay witnesses [19]

Lord Perceval of Mar of Genoa, described only as a citizen of Nicosia, told of a group of Templars languishing in a Saracen prison who chose decapitation rather than deny their faith.[20]

In contrast to the many allegations that the Rule was dishonourable, Balian of Mongisart, a knight, said that he had seen the Rule itself and 'everything written in that book was good, efficacious, and useful, nor was there any Christian in the world, who having heard these words, would consider this rule anything but saintly and good'.[21]

The second, and mainly less important group, was presumably assembled out of frustration since, by the time they appeared, all seventy-six Templar witnesses had testified without admitting any guilt whatever. The testimony of these witnesses is recorded only briefly, in summary form,[22] but could

---

[12] See answers to allegations numbers 36, 37, 70, 71, 106, 119 in the standard list concerning secrecy of receptions and resulting suspicion, *Procès*, 1, pp. 89–96.

[13] Schottmüller, 2, p. 153.

[14] Ibid., 2, pp. 153–4.

[15] Ibid., 2, p. 154.

[16] Rey, pp. 69, 249; Edbury, pp. 127–8.

[17] Schottmüller, 2, p. 155.

[18] Ibid., 2, p. 157.

[19] The two largest French trials, both held in or near Paris, are in *Procès*, 1 and 2.

[20] Schottmüller, 2, pp. 160–61.

[21] Ibid., 2, p. 163.

[22] Ibid., 2, pp. 376–400.

hardly have been deemed satisfactory if guilt were the desired outcome. The major faults alleged against Templars remained the same – secrecy of receptions and the possible acquisition of goods and money by improper means – but no statements even remotely imply heresy or grave misconduct. Given their depressing lack of success with their previous round of ninety-seven witnesses, the inquisitors now changed their approach, concentrating instead on religious offences, non-consecration of the Host and other liturgical errors.

The first important witness was Robert, Bishop of Beirut, who appeared eighth, on 2 June.[23] He most certainly ought to have been well informed about members of the Order as he declared that he had spent forty years among them. Since the Templars often had secular priests operating within, but not attached to, the Order, this statement does not imply that he had ever been a Templar himself. Nevertheless, this long association with the Order might, of course, have made him reluctant to speak out against them, even if he had wanted to, for fear he might have appeared guilty by association. His testimony emphasized the religious regularity of Templar religious offices and Eucharistic practices.

The tenth witness, a certain Lawrence of Beirut, assessor of the church at Nicosia, had also spent time with the Templar Order – eighteen years in fact. In his testimony he mentioned that he had heard the confessions of sixty Templars, implying that he, too, was one of the many non-Templar priests serving with the Order. He also praised Templar religious practices and gave no condemnatory testimony. Several other clerical witnesses[24] mentioned having heard Templar confessions over a long period of years. Given that in other trials – such as most of those held in France – witnesses admitting the performance of illicit acts also stated that they had confessed to priests and been absolved, the non-guilty testimony given here by several clerics tends to add to the impression that the guilty acts had never taken place.[25]

The predominantly clerical nature of the second set of non-Templar witnesses has provided a rare opportunity to gather information on early fourteenth-century religious practices. For eight years John Frisoni, a priest of Nicosia, had been chaplain to a Templar who had communicated and confessed at least four times a year – rather more often than usual at the time. In fact he sometimes communicated daily, and every day heard the divine office. At a time of very infrequent religious observances, it is surprising that Cypriot Templars seem to have been so faithful in performance of their religious duties. Testimony given here also confirmed what many Templars had said

---

[23] Ibid., 2, pp. 378–9. *GC*, p. 862, note 3, confirms that Robert was bishop of Beirut as at 1291.

[24] See, for example, witness Jacobus Symeonis in Schottmüller, 2, p. 380.

[25] Admittedly, maintaining the secrecy of the confessional would not allow the priest to discuss Templar offences communicated to him. However, the priest would certainly be able to make remarks detrimental to the Order without betraying his sacramental office.

elsewhere: they could, and did, make their confessions to Dominicans, Franciscans, secular priests, and those of other orders, not only to their own chaplains.[26] William of Biblio, a priest, had the unusual experience of serving as a deacon under a Templar chaplain before becoming a priest himself. He was able to testify with fifteen years' experience as a chaplain to the Order that there were no faults whatever in Templar religious practices.[27]

After hearing fifteen clerical witnesses and one knight, eight more knights took their place on the witness stand, interspersed with eight more clerics, and three burghers or merchants. The witness with the most notorious name was most certainly Simon of Montolif[28] who shared his name with that of the murderer of Amaury, although in fact this man was another member of the family, and brother of the bishop of Paphos.[29] Balian of Saxony (or de Soissons), a knight, provided eye-witness information of the religious devotion of James of Molay whom he had often seen attending services in Nicosia.[30] John Lombard, a knight and viscount of Nicosia, testified that William of Beaujeu,[31] the Templar Grand Master who died in the fall of Acre in 1291, confessed to a Franciscan priest.[32] Since Beaujeu would normally have had his own chaplain,[33] his confession to someone outside the Order might seem odd, but it is evident that the Templars suffered a continuing shortage of chaplains within the Order. The witness had heard that James of Molay had confessed but only through fear of torture,[34] a probable reality given the Grand Master's various and differing confessions between 1307 and the end in 1314.[35] Bernard, Prior

---

[26] This testimony was confirmed by many others in this trial; see for example the marshal of the Order, Schottmüller, 2, p. 221: ... *lic[uit] eis confiteri et aliis religiosis et minoribus et predicatoribus, et per manus eorum communicaverunt, et hoc etiam fecerunt [pluries]* and the testimony of witnesses 3, 13–34, 36, 39–44, 46, 63–64, 75, ibid., pp. 225–372. None of the other witnesses denied the possibility of confession to non-Templar priests, but I have omitted them because they gave no definite information on the subject or because the answer to that allegation was not transcribed by the notary.

[27] Schottmüller, 2, p. 383.

[28] Ibid., 2, pp. 385–6.

[29] Edbury, p. 126, note 97. See also Rudt de Collenberg, *Les grâces papales autres que les dispenses matrimoniales accordées a Chypre de 1305–1378 selon les Archives du Vatican, Epeteris tou Kentrou Epistimonikon Erevnon*, 8 (Nicosia, 1975/1977), p. 193, who lists twelve papal privileges received by this family.

[30] Schottmüller, 2, p. 386.

[31] On this man see Rey, pp. 890–91.

[32] Schottmüller, 2, p. 388. Other testimony on Beaujeu's devotion to religious observance is given by a knight, Bernard of Aquilano, ibid., p. 390. In the *GC*, p. 871, John the Lombard was sent as ambassador to the king of France by Amaury in 1307, which would appear to indicate that he was on Amaury's side. On this matter, see also Edbury, p. 119.

[33] L. Dailliez, *Les Templiers et les règles de l'ordre du Temple* (Paris, 1972), in one of the 'statuts hiérarchiques', no. 77, believed to have been written prior to 1187, says: 'The master must have 4 horses [bêtes], a chaplain, a clerk ... a sergeant, a valet ...' (p. 65).

[34] Schottmüller, 2, p. 388.

[35] See Molay's first confession in *Procès*, 2, pp. 305–6. Later interrogations appear in *Procès*, 1, pp. 32–5, 42–5, 87–8.

of St George's church in Nicosia, after giving the usual response to the items of accusation, added the information that seventy-two Templars, including the Grand Master, had confessed before the pope.[36] It is surprising with what accuracy this information was disseminated to Templars everywhere. It might not be improper to suggest, however, that the witness was not offering this information from his own knowledge but responding to information provided by the inquisitors.[37]

Brother Francis, Prior of St Julian of Nicosia, the Teutonic church, was one of the most important witnesses of this group.[38] The Teutonic Knights might have been jealous of the Templars, but in this case the prior had nothing injurious to say. He declared himself ignorant as to whether or not the Templars believed in the sacraments. He leapt to their defence when it came to accusations concerning their alleged lack of charitable work, insisting that, on the contrary, they gave out bread, meat, and sometimes money to the needy every week, including gifts of that sort to his own hospital.

The next two witnesses were burghers and merchants, appearing for no stated reason.[39] The first one praised the Order and its religious practices. The second told a tale about a Templar priest and chaplain who exorcised a woman by casting out demons residing within her.

Henry of Bibbio,[40] a knight, gave precise testimony concerning Templar bravery while fighting in Acre and Tripoli against the Saracens. While he had heard some stories in Syria regarding the secrecy of Templar receptions, he added nothing new. Bibbio gave the most complete testimony of any witness concerning the Order's charitable activities towards the poor in Acre, stating that 'bread and meat were given out and sometimes clothing and robes, and sometimes money, to poor knights, widows, maidens and others'.[41] The Temple also acted as a hostel for poor pilgrims and other needy persons. He had heard from a local lord who had been held captive in Babylon that two former Templar brothers he met there had been converted to the Muslim faith. Even these men said that no errors against the Christian faith had existed within the Templar Order.[42]

Another Philip of Ibelin appeared next, son of Balian.[43] He had nothing new to add, except that he himself had received hospitality from the Templars, when

---

[36] Schottmüller, **2**, p. 389.

[37] See *Procès*, **1**, p. 96.

[38] Referred to in the text as *de ordine cruciferorum*, Schottmüller, **2**, p. 391. On the Teutonic Knights on Cyprus, see Edbury, pp. 78–9.

[39] Guido de Bandes Acconensis and Perocius, son of lord George, Schottmüller, **2**, pp. 392–3.

[40] Ibid., **2**, pp. 393–5.

[41] Ibid., **2**, p. 394.

[42] Ibid., **2**, p. 395.

[43] His father Balian was a partisan of Amaury – see the *RHC DArm*, p. 921. Philip too may have been one of the partisans of Amaury referred to by Edbury, p. 129.

he lodged with them as did other travellers.[44] The next knight's testimony conformed to the generally favourable picture painted by his predecessors on the stand.

Since the following witness was Baldwin of *Villaganti*, Prior of the Dominican Order in Nicosia, and there was considerable ill-will between Franciscans, Dominicans, and Templars, his testimony would be expected to highlight unfavourable aspects of Templar behaviour. Indeed, several Franciscans gave the most damning testimony against the Order in London.[45] The prior had been misinformed by Dominican brothers who had come from overseas to Nicosia that the Grand Master and others had confessed in Paris, Apulia and Aigues-Mortes to most of the errors alleged against them.[46] While he admitted that Templars confessed to Dominican priests, he said nothing about the nature of the confessed sins. He too had been offered hospitality by the Order and had stayed on Templar premises. He offered no evidence of illicit acts at all except hearsay remarks he had heard from returned Dominicans. The subsequent Dominican witness had nothing to add to preceding testimony.[47]

The most potentially interesting witness appeared last: Simon of Sarezariis, Prior of the Hospital of St John of Jerusalem in Nicosia.[48] He had been informed by the Hospitaller prior for France of the confessions made by the Grand Master and others. Hostile from the start, and in opposition to the preceding witnesses, the prior said that he had heard that the Templars did not believe in the sacraments of the Church. In fact he stated in response to each allegation that he believed the accusation to be true, but when asked for evidence could only allude to vague conversations with unknown persons at some time in the past. Although the prior made no definitive statement he is the only witness at this hearing to leave an impression of potential guilt. This should not be surprising, considering the rivalry between the two military orders in Cyprus – a rivalry which sometimes erupted in outright fighting and bloodshed.

It is perfectly evident that most of the noble witnesses came from well known powerful Cypriot families – in most cases partisans of Henry II. Despite this, their testimony resolutely favoured the Order. Whatever its date, the evidence itself is particularly rich in details about the Templars' lives as fighting men in the field, as givers of hospitality and charity and as faithful Christians.

---

[44] Schottmüller, **2**, p. 396.

[45] Wilkins, *Concilia*, **2**, p. 359.

[46] Schottmüller, **2**, p. 397.

[47] Nicholas of *Marsiliaco*, ibid., **2**, p. 398.

[48] Ibid., **2**, pp. 398–9.

22

The Suppression of the Templars in Cyprus according to the Chronicle of Leontios Makhairas

Annetta Iliéva

In recent years there have been some successful attempts to rehabilitate the Templars by considering *de novo* the evidence for the prehistory and development of the trial of their Order in 1308–11. An important element in these arguments is the nature of the testimonies submitted during the hearing in Cyprus where the Order established its headquarters after the fall of Acre in 1291. It is well known that all seventy-six extant Templar depositions from the inquiry in Nicosia rejected the accusations against the Order and that, from a total of fifty-six witnesses – knights, abbots, priests, canons, friars, monks, burghers – only the prior of the Hospital challenged this assertion of innocence. This data derives from the inquiries conducted in May–June 1310 and in 1311.[1] Malcolm Barber has suggested that a new trial, following Clement V's letters of August 1311, found against the Templars on the island, but it should be emphasized that no documentary evidence survives to prove this.[2] Yet there is one piece of evidence, also of Cypriot provenance, which offers some support for the Hospitaller prior's observations. Admittedly it is not contemporary, but it is nevertheless important since the author, Leontios Makhairas, is generally impartial when dealing with the Latins and their religious beliefs. Its importance

---

[1] K. Schottmüller, *Der Untergang des Templer-Ordens*, 2 (Berlin, 1887), pp. 147–218, 376–400. The hearings hitherto dated to 1–5 May 1310 have recently been redated to 1–5 May 1311, P. Edbury, *The Kingdom of Cyprus and the Crusades, 1191–1374* (Cambridge, 1991), p. 125 n. 94. Cf. M. Barber, *The Trial of the Templars* (Cambridge, 1978), pp. 218 ff.; A. Gilmour-Bryson, *The Trial of the Templars in the Papal State and the Abruzzi* (Città del Vaticano, 1982), pp. 20–23, J. Riley-Smith, *The Knights of St John in Jerusalem and Cyprus c. 1050-1310* (London and New York, 1967), pp. 219–20; A. Luttrell, 'The Hospitallers in Cyprus after 1291', in idem, *The Hospitallers in Cyprus, Rhodes, Greece and the West, 1291–1440* (London, 1978), no. II, p. 167.

[2] P. Partner, *The Murdered Magicians. The Templars and their Myth* (Oxford, 1981), p. 81; Edbury, p. 136.

appears to be even greater in view of the absence of this evidence from both the *Chronique d'Amadi* and Florio Bustron.

Notably, Makhairas does not associate the Templars with Amaury's coup against Henry II on 26 April 1306, although he is definitely on the side of the king. But several historians claim that the Master of the Order, James of Molay, supported the rebels, while later, in 1310, the Hospital – the Temple's rival – played a prominent role in Henry's restoration.[3] In contrast to 'Amadi' and Bustron, however, in § 47 of his *Chronicle*, Leontios Makhairas names James of Molay as the Master of the Hospital and further continues to speak only of τοῦ Σπιταλλίου. In my opinion, the problem is not solved if we simply assume that Makhairas was unaware of the real events and is mistaken in his identification.[4] When reading his chronicle we must not forget that earlier, in §§ 13–17, he had already related the story of the suppression of the Templars in a rather interesting way.

A lacuna at the end of § 10 prevents us from learning how Makhairas described the events which led to the Easter revolt against the Templars in 1192. Another gap in *V* (Venice: Marciana: Ms. gr. VII, 16), which is a little smaller in *O* (Oxford: Bodleian: Selden supra 14), also prevents the reader from gaining a clear impression of our chronicler's view of events comprising this important episode. However, it would seem that Makhairas did write a full description of the Templar sally from the castle of Nicosia at Easter, but then, instead of going on to describe the bargain by which Guy of Lusignan came to be involved in Cypriot affairs (which does not appear until § 20) he gives in §§ 13–17, a unique account of why and how the Templars in the island were all put to death.

Makhairas presents the reasons clearly and explicitly, stating that the punishment was a divine judgement carried out through 'the most holy pope'.[5] The chronicler is deeply convinced that the brethren have committed deadly sins and his charges – the principal one being that of apostasy – are identical to those levelled against them everywhere in the course of the inquiries.[6] The

---

[3] Luttrell, 'The Hospitallers in Cyprus after 1291', pp. 166–7; idem, 'The Hospitallers at Rhodes: 1306–1421', in *Crusades*, 3, p. 286; idem, 'The Hospitallers' Interventions in Cilician Armenia: 1291–1375', in idem, *Latin Greece, the Hospitallers and the Crusades, 1291–1440*, (London, 1982), pp. 124–5; idem, 'The Hospitallers in Cyprus: 1310–1378', Κυπριακαὶ σπουδαί, 50 (1986), p.156; G. Hill, *History of Cyprus*, 2 (Cambridge, 1948), p. 219 n. 2; Riley-Smith, pp. 210, 212; H. Luke, 'The Kingdom of Cyprus, 1291–1369', in *Crusades*, 3, p. 343.

[4] Leontios Makhairas, *Recital Concerning the Sweet Land of Cyprus Entitled 'Chronicle'*, 1 (Oxford, 1932). The second volume (introduction and commentary) is referred to as Dawkins, 2. His comment on § 47 is on p.47 n. 1.

[5] Makhairas, *Recital*, § 13.

[6] Dawkins, 2, p. 50; Barber, *passim*; S. Menache, 'Contemporary Attitudes Concerning the Templars' Affair: Propaganda's Fiasco?', *Journal of Medieval History*, 8 (1982), p. 136. Cf. Gilmour-Bryson, p. 79, §§ 78–9 (pronounced in Rome's Templar church of S. Maria sull' Aventino in 1309): '*Item, quod aliquando predicta abnegatio Christi fiebant in presentia magistri et conv[entus predictorum]. Item, quod predicta fiebant et servabantur in Cipro*'.

story related by Makhairas oscillates between some knowledge of the real events and complete invention. As Makhairas describes it, the pope, displeased with the secret ceremony of admission into the Order, summoned the Grand Master of the Hospital and bade him administer the same ceremony.

> Then was the pope very well pleased, when he saw that they of the Hospital were good Christians.... Then he bade his secretary write two letters to every ruler in the world where there were Templars, their houses and holdings ...[7]

René de Mas Latrie was convinced of the 'entière fausseté de ces prétendues lettres apostoliques'.[8] A more careful examination, however, discloses an interesting mixture of fantasy and reality. It is known that the bull *Pastoralis praeeminentiae* issued on 22 November 1307 'ordered all the monarchs of Christendom to arrest the Templars and sequester their lands in the name of the papacy; the rulers were ordered to do that "prudently, discreetly and secretly"'.[9] The beginning of Makhairas's version of the papal letter is almost identical to that of Clement V's epistle of 20 August 1308 to King Philip IV of France. This epistle was accompanied by a 'copy of a letter which he had received from Amalric, lord of Tyre', written in response to the pope's letters on the question of the Templars, the latter having been brought to Cyprus by Hethum, lord of Gorhigos. Carrying the papal orders to arrest the Templars – and, possibly, even *Pastoralis praeeminentiae* – Hethum had reached Famagusta on 6 May 1308.[10]

The pope's letter, as presented in Makhairas's *Chronicle* then goes on to inform the ruler that he should 'guard well' the second, sealed letter, 'in a fit place' until 'the coming day of Pentecost'. 'And when you go to church, when the first mass ends, before the people leave the church, open the sealed letter, and what it commands do forthwith, and this on pain of excommunication.'[11] This sealed letter is then quoted as saying:

> ... before the hour comes to dinner, you command that they all be put to death ... and that you have mercy on no one of them ... all their goods and their heritages, which lie in your country, [should] be handed over to the control of the Hospitallers.

---

[7] Makhairas, *Recital*, S. 14.

[8] Diomède Strambaldi, 'Chronica del regno di Cypro', in *Chroniques d'Amadi et de Strambaldi*, ed. R. de Mas Latrie, 2 (Paris, 1891–93), p. 6 n. 2.

[9] Barber, pp. 2, 73, 74. Cf. Menache, p. 139.

[10] Edbury, p. 121. The beginning of the pope's letter in Makhairas (§ 15, lines 28–9): 'Our well-beloved son, greeting and archiepiscopal blessing.' Clement V's epistle as in E. Baluze, *Vitae paparum Avenionensium hoc est Historia pontificium Romanorum ...*, ed. G. Mollat, 3 (Paris, 1921), p. 84: *Clemens, episcopus, servus servorum Dei, carrissimo in Christo filio Philippo, regi Francorum illustri, salutem et apostolicam benedictionem.*

[11] Makhairas, *Recital*, § 15, lines 30–36. Cf. a passage in Amaury's response as in Baluze, *Vitae paparum*, p. 85: *... sicque oportuit in hujusmodi complendo negotio cum multa deliberatione, studio, et cautela procedere, secundum quod paterne litte continebant ...*

God's wrath is then invoked upon any disobedient ruler who ignores the papal command.[12]

The ruler of Cyprus carried out the pope's orders to the letter. It is difficult to say why the chronicler does not mention his name, although Makhairas seems to have been aware that he was Amaury of Lusignan, the lord of Tyre. He gives no particular reason for the executions, other than that God

> ... was sorely angered with them because of their sins: and it was for this reason they were all destroyed in one day, and not one of them escaped; and if God had to deal with clean men, he would have saved them: and this was the wrath of God.[13]

Now, let us briefly compare Makhairas's account with what actually happened after Hethum delivered the papal orders to Amaury.[14] Since on 13 October 1307 James of Molay, the Grand Master, and Hugh of Pairaud, the Visitor were arrested together with the other Templars in France, the chief official of the Order left in Cyprus was Ayme d'Oselier, the Marshal. On 27 May he and some fourteen brethren presented themselves before Amaury in Nicosia. There they read a public statement of belief before an assembly of clergy and people. However, Amaury had already secretly sent an armed force to Limassol and on the night of 28 May gathered a second assembly of clergy, knights and people, at which the papal letters concerning the trial in France and the accusations against the Order were read. The Templars were besieged at Limassol and surrendered on 1 June – the Saturday preceding Whit Sunday.[15] Amaury then informed the pope by letter that he had fulfilled the prescriptions concerning the Templars' property.[16] The hearings were to start two years later, and it was only by the bull *Ad providam* of 2 May 1312 that their property was granted to the Hospital.[17]

Clearly, the elements of secrecy, papal letters and Whit Sunday were not simple inventions in Makhairas's narrative. What is falsely presented as truth, however, is the extermination of all the Templars in Cyprus on just one day – that of Whit Sunday – after the first mass but before the dinner hour, plus the simultaneous order by the pope that their property should be given to the

---

[12] Makhairas, *Recital*, § 15, lines 37–end.

[13] Makhairas, *Recital*, § 16.

[14] On what follows, see Baluze, *Vitae paparum*, pp. 85–6 (Clement V's letter mentioned above); Cf. Chronique d'Amadi, in *Chroniques d'Amadi et de Strambaldi*, 1, pp. 283 ff.; Florio Bustron, *Chronique de 'ile de Chypre*, ed. R. de Mas Latrie, in *Mélanges historiques. Choix de documents*, Collections de documents inédits sur l'histoire de France, 5 (Paris, 1886), pp. 164 ff.; Barber, pp. 217–18; N. Housley, *The Avignon Papacy and the Crusades, 1305–1378* (Oxford, 1986), pp. 262–5.

[15] Cf. 'Amadi', p. 289:... *sabato poi, che era primo di de zugno et vigilia de la Pentecoste, li Templieri hanno mandato le sue arme et cavalli ne la casa del re a Limisso*; Bustron, 'Chronique', p. 169.

[16] Baluze, *Vitae paparum*, p. 86.

[17] Barber, pp. 3, 238; Menache, p. 143; Luttrell, 'The Hospitallers in Cyprus: 1310–1378', p. 156; Edbury, p. 136.

'good Christians' of the Hospital.[18] Particularly interesting is the first distortion. In Catholicism, Whit Sunday is of equal rank to Easter Sunday, and at Pentecost salvation is realized in the messianic blessings of the forgiveness of one's sins and the gift of the Holy Spirit. In the Orthodox Church the liturgy is followed by vespers which are distinguished by the service of genuflection when the prayers mark a shift from the mystery of the Spirit to the mystery of the Trinity. Here, Pentecost is considered as 'the final event in the history of our salvation', as 'the Easter of the Spirit'.[19] The Templars slaughtered the Cypriots in Nicosia on Easter Sunday and since they were subsequently arrested on the eve of Pentecost, it was convenient for Makhairas (or his source) to make them all perish on that great church holiday. The moral addressed to both Catholics and Orthodox is clear: the Templars' sins were not remitted and they were not saved on Whit Sunday. The divine judgement was sweeping and final; none was able to escape it.

Why did our chronicler relate this story if, as modern scholarship concludes, the Templars in Cyprus were innocent?[20] Was he moved by the crushing of the uprising against the Templars as described in an earlier source and decided to falsify the evidence of the source at his disposal concerning the trial of the Templars? Or was the distortion already present in his source(s)? Finally, is he simply inserting a legendary story current among the inhabitants of Nicosia in his own day and ignored by 'Amadi' and Bustron? A definite answer to all these questions is hardly possible, but investigation into Makhairas's version of the events of 26 April 1306 and of the following two years may be of some help.

This investigation shows that Makhairas (or his source) knew both the original French text of the declaration presented to Henry II on 26 April 1306 by Amaury and his party and of the agreement drafted between the king and his brother on 14 May 1306. The date of the latter appears only in its Latin translation discussed by C. Kohler, together with the Latin translation of the declaration. Kohler gave a résumé of those parts of the translations (executed from the French originals) which were omitted in the French version of the original texts that has survived.[21] The manuscript in which the declaration is immediately followed by the agreement had been prepared c. 1307 and was discovered by Abbot Giraudin in the 1880s. It has been published several times.[22]

---

[18] Cf. Bustron, 'Chronique', pp. 170–1 for the same error which, however, is corrected later (pp. 246–7).

[19] *The Year of Grace of the Lord. A Scriptural and Liturgical Commentary on the Calendar of the Orthodox Church by a Monk of the Eastern Church*, trans. D. Cowen (Crestwood, N.Y., 1980), pp. 216, 246 n. 1.

[20] Barber, pp. 220 ff.

[21] C. Kohler, 'Documents chypriotes du début du XIVe siècle', *ROL*, **11** (1905–8), p. 440 ff.

[22] By L. de Mas Latrie in 'Texte officiel de l'allocution adressée par les barons de Chypre au roi Henri II de Lusignan pour lui notifier sa déchéance', *Revue des questions historiques*, **43** (1888), pp. 534–41; by R. de Mas Latrie as a note to 'Amadi' (pp. 242–8); by G. Paris and L. de Mas Latrie as a note to *Les Gestes des Chiprois*, RHC DArm, **2**, pp. 858–62. Another, unpublished, version of the May agreement, dated 31 January 1307, is noted by Luttrell, 'The Hospitallers in Cyprus after 1291', p. 166 n. 4. Cf. Edbury, p. 119.

L. de Mas Latrie was aware of Giraudin's correct observations concerning these documents but nevertheless suggested that the second document was a royal charter produced on the same day as the declaration: Henry II caused it to be read out before the assembly of 26 April 1306, thus confirming the first agreement between the two parties. L. de Mas Latrie also postulated the drafting of a second agreement in the middle of 1307.[23] Although there is no ground for such duplication, it has been accepted by most authorities on Cypriot history.[24]

It is only in the Latin translation that Hugh of Ibelin's name appears in connection with the declaration and it would seem significant that Makhairas too refers to this man in the same context.[25] Makhairas's details of the agreement are also correct, and it seems that he (or his source) had the second document before him.[26] Makhairas is closer to the truth than 'Amadi' and Bustron when he claims that 'for fifteen days' (after 29 April) mediators between the king and Amaury tried hard to reconcile the two parties.[27] And in the next paragraph he evidently describes the agreement of 14 May.[28]

Thus, the evidence in Makhairas concerning Amaury's coup seems generally trustworthy except for just one element: as was pointed out above, until the death of Henry II, there is no mention of the Templars. Bustron, however, claims that James of Molay and the bishop of Limassol, Peter of Erlant, were the men responsible for the drafting of the charter by which Amaury was proclaimed governor of Cyprus.[29] But the charter does not bear the seal of the Grand Master.[30] Indeed, Barber asserts that James of Molay was in the list of signatories to the charter/declaration of Amaury's complaints against the king.[31] This claim can be understood only if we assume that, like other scholars before him, Barber takes the second document in the copy discovered by Giraudin to have been drafted on 26 April 1306. As for the first document there, it is only the Latin translation that has the names of all the barons who *appendirent leur sceau à la sommation* but this does not include *Jacobus de*

---

[23] L. de Mas Latrie, 'Texte officiel', pp. 524–5 n. 1, 531, especially 532. He was followed by the younger Mas Latrie, 'Amadi', pp. 251–2 n. 3; cf. Bustron, 'Chronique', p. 139 n. 2.

[24] Contra: Luttrell, 'The Hospitallers in Cyprus after 1291', p. 166 n. 4; Edbury, pp. 117, 119.

[25] Makhairas, *Recital*, § 49. Kohler, 'Documents chypriotes', p. 442.

[26] Makhairas, *Recital*, § 57. 'Amadi', p. 251; Bustron, 'Chronique', p. 140. Cf. the beginning and the end of the document in the French copy as in 'Amadi', p. 245 n. 8: *Henri, XIII, roy de Jerusalem latin et roy de Chipre, et nous la communauté des hommes du dit royaume de Chipre, faisons assavoir à touz ceaus qui cest present escript liront ou orront que nous ... ce contient, sommes en tel manière en accort.*

[27] Makhairas, *Recital*, § 55.; 'Amadi' (p. 251) has [più] *che XX giorni*, counting from 29 April. Cf. Bustron, 'Chronique', p. 139.

[28] Makhairas, *Recital*, § 56.

[29] Bustron, 'Chronique', p. 138.

[30] Kohler, 'Documents chypriotes', p. 452. Cf. M. Barber, 'James of Molay, the Last Grand Master of the Order of the Temple', *Studia Monastica*, **14** (1972), p. 102.

[31] Barber, 'James of Molay', p. 103. Cf. idem, *Trial*, p. 285 n. 1.

Mollayo.[32] On the other hand, all three chroniclers say that James of Molay was a creditor of Amaury; it is here that Makhairas makes him 'Master of the Hospital'. Both manuscripts of Makhairas's chronicle, as well as Strambaldi's Italian translation, contain the same error, although the correct identification is given in both 'Amadi' and Bustron.[33] Again, when 'Amadi' and Bustron describe the Masters of both the Temple and the Hospital as mediators between the two parties in the days following the coup, Makhairas prefers to speak only of the Hospital.[34] The agreement of 14 May was signed by both Masters but here Makhairas refers to the suspect 'two seals of the Commander of the Hospital'.[35]

Moreover, 'Amadi' and Bustron accuse James of Molay of trying to profit from the strife between the two brothers in the interest of his Order.[36] Nor do the Italian texts ignore the Templars' attempt to seize the king's palace on 17–21 January 1308; they represent the Marshal of the Temple as a bitter enemy of Henry II, claiming also that the Templars had an interest in ensuring that the quarrels continued, and that they wished to weaken the kingdom.[37] In this respect, it seems strange that they do not mention the trial of the Order in Cyprus.

It seems, then, that one important conclusion is plausible: the Templars were deliberately denied the role they had in the events of 26 April 1306 and later. Since this distortion is common for the manuscript tradition of Makhairas's chronicle,[38] but is lacking both in 'Amadi' and Florio Bustron whose longer narratives, though similar overall to the former, are sometimes wrong in the details, several explanations are possible.

The most straight forward explanation is to attribute the distortion to Makhairas himself. As a native patriot, he chose to relate the story he knew about the trial and the end of the Templars immediately after the Cypriot uprising against them in 1192, and then decided to keep silent about Amaury's relations with the Order – on the grounds that this treacherous baron could not have been the instrument of divine judgement. This view must assume that Makhairas knew that it had been Amaury who had arrested the Templars on the eve of Pentecost, 1 June 1308. Conversely, the distortion could be attributed to an earlier source, or sources, used by Makhairas. This is thrown into doubt by the fact that almost all the dates in Makhairas's narrative on Henry

---

[32] Kohler, 'Documents chypriotes', p. 443.

[33] Makhairas, *Recital*, § 47; 'Amadi', p. 248; Bustron, 'Chronique', p. 138.

[34] 'Amadi', p. 251; Bustron, 'Chronique', p. 139; Makhairas, *Recital*, § 55.

[35] Makhairas, *Recital*, § 56. Cf. the end of the French copy as printed in 'Amadi', p. 247 n. 8. The corresponding text of 'Amadi' runs (p. 251): *Et fu fatto tra loro scritto de nodaro sigilato col bollo de li doi maestri et de tutti li vescovi, priori et abbati et altri capi religiosi.*

[36] 'Amadi', p. 261; Bustron, 'Chronique', p. 149.

[37] 'Amadi', pp. 260–62, 266; Bustron, 'Chronique', pp. 149–51, 153–5. Cf. Hill, pp. 228 ff.; Riley-Smith, p. 211; Luke, p. 344 (as in n. 3 above).

[38] However, I was not able to consult *Cod. Ravenna Clas. 187* containing a third version of the chronicle, closer to that in *O*.

II's reign are completely wrong. A third explanation is to suggest that the substitution of the Temple for the Hospital in §§ 47, 55 and 56 is due to the intervention of a later, ignorant copyist of the chronicle. To him, it would have seemed illogical that the Templars who had all apparently perished in a single day, as related previously, could reappear in the narrative later on. The weak point in this proposition is the necessity of postulating a common prototype which already had the correction for both (*V* and *O*) versions of the chronicle. However, prior to a new critical edition of the text, the existence of this prototype remains highly problematical. Whatever the real motivation behind this distortion may have been, it is obvious that some members of Cypriot society – Latins or Greeks – were convinced that the Order of the Templars had committed great sins and was subsequently justly punished.

Part III

The Teutonic Order

23

Eight Hundred Years of the Teutonic Order

Udo Arnold

In the twelfth century the most important orders of knighthood were the Templars and the Knights of St John, both centred on Jerusalem. In about 1120, at about the same time as the Templars were founded, a German hospital was also established in the city.[1] However, all this was lost when Jerusalem fell in 1187 – the event which precipitated the Third Crusade. Unprecedented numbers of Germans participated in this crusade, many drawn from areas not previously affected by crusading enthusiasm. The Low Germans and the Flemings went by sea, others overland. Between 1189 and 1191 many took part in the siege of Acre, but the besiegers were unaccustomed to the climate and epidemics raged amongst them. In response to this, in 1190 crusaders from Bremen and Lübeck built a hospital from the sails of their ships, and a hospital brotherhood was established just as it had been a century before with the Hospital of St John. Imbued with the desire to reconquer Jerusalem, its members adopted the name of the city for their new brotherhood. This is the origin of the Teutonic Order; it has no connection with the older German hospital in Jerusalem.[2]

---

[1] There is no complete history of the Teutonic Order in English. In German: H. Boockmann, *Der Deutsche Orden. Zwölf Kapitel aus seiner Geschichte*, 3rd edn (Munich, 1989); M. Tumler and U. Arnold, *Der Deutsche Orden. Von seinem Ursprung bis zur Gegenwart*, 5th edn (Bad Münstereifel, 1992); *800 Jahre Deutscher Orden*, ed. G. Bott and U. Arnold (Gütersloh and Munich, 1990) (catalogue of an international exhibition); only up to 1400, M. Tumler, *Der Deutsche Orden im Werden. Wachsen und Wirken bis 1400* (Vienna, 1955).

[2] See U. Arnold, 'Entstehung und Frühzeit des Deutschen Ordens. Zu Gründung und innerer Struktur des deutschen Hospitals von Akkon und des Ritterordens', in *Die geistlichen Ritterorden Europas*, ed. J. Fleckenstein and M. Hellmann (Sigmaringen, 1980), pp. 81–107; U. Arnold, 'Vom Feldspital zum Ritterorden. Militarisierung und Territorialisierung des Deutschen Ordens (1190–c. 1240)', in *Balticum. Studia z dziejów Polityki, gospodarki i kultury XII–XVII wieku, ofiarowane Marianowi Biskupowi*, ed. Z.H. Nowak (Toruń, 1992), pp. 25–36.

The Teutonic Order never forgot its origins in the Third Crusade: the ideology of Jerusalem, the provision of medical care, and the connection with the Empire of the Staufen were engraved in its consciousness for centuries. After the conquest of Acre the brothers received a house in the city and built a hospital, a chapel and dwellings. The Germans used this hospital, and its position was confirmed by Duke Frederick of Swabia, son of the late emperor, Frederick I. This strong connection with the Roman emperors was instrumental in promoting the Order's position during the following decades: Henry VI and Frederick II gave their support, as did the Staufen party in the Empire. After the marriage between Henry VI and Constance of Sicily, the Staufen increased their interest in Mediterranean politics, and the Emperor decided to make his presence felt in the Holy Land. Thus, in 1198, the German hospital – the only German settlement in the Mediterranean area – was transformed into an order of knighthood modelled on the Templars and the Knights of St John and founded upon the twin elements of knighthood and medical care. Papal confirmation followed and, within three decades of its genesis as a field hospital, the Teutonic Order had acquired the same rights as the Templars and the Hospitallers.

Marked progress was made in the time of the Grand Master Hermann of Salza (1209–39), who was one of the famous diplomatists of the thirteenth century.[3] It was his successful intercession in the conflict between the pope and the emperor, following the Hohenstaufen intervention into Mediterranean politics, which particularly assisted the Order. Both the pope and emperor granted gifts and privileges during this period, and their example inspired many nobles and townsmen to follow suit. Gratitude for medical care and military action in the Holy Land, or for the establishment of hospitals in the Empire, persuaded many to make donations which they hoped would ensure their future spiritual welfare.

By about 1200 the Order had gained properties in Styria (today northern Slovenia), in Thuringia and in the southern part of the Tyrol. Some time later, houses in Prague and Vienna, Hesse, Franconia, Bavaria, parts of Greece and the Burzenland (in present-day Rumania) followed. By about 1220 the first settlements in the Low Countries appeared, followed, a few years later, by others in present-day Switzerland and France. In 1230 the Order entered Prussia and Spain. By 1237, when it absorbed the Order of the Swordbrothers in Livonia, it was established from the Atlantic to the Gulf of Finland.

Many of its acquisitions were made with the higher goal of the Holy Land in mind. In the Alps and in Austria the Order preferred possessions near the roads and passes to the south, and in Italy the Order's houses were often established in the important ports of embarkation for crusaders – from Venice in the north to Barletta in Apulia – and in Sicily, the fulcrum of Mediterranean

---

[3] H. Kluger, *Hochmeister Hermann von Salza und Kaiser Friedrich II.* (Marburg, 1987).

communications. The Order also tried to obtain a seat in Cyprus, so conveniently near the Holy Land. Except for Venice, all these areas fell within the Staufen sphere of influence.

New brothers entered the Order – both nobles and townsmen – especially from the German-speaking areas of the Empire. In its early decades the Order seemed to develop in connection with the houses of Staufen and Thuringia, with an ideal centre in the Holy Land and another centre at Marburg, at the sepulchre of Saint Elizabeth. Elizabeth's brother-in-law, Conrad of Thuringia, obtained her canonization in 1235 thereby emphasizing her connection with the Order, since after the death of Hermann of Salza, Conrad became the next Grand Master. However, during the great conflict between the emperor and the pope, the young Order became more independent.[4]

A principal reason for this independence was the Order's determination to build up its own state[5] – a policy quite distinct from the other knightly orders. Its first opportunity arose in the Burzenland, belonging to Hungary. King Andrew II gave the territory to the Order in 1211 – in the same year as his daughter Elizabeth went to Thuringia – with the intention that the Knights should fight against the pagan Cumans. The Order's successes in these wars led to the acquisition of new lands on the Hungarian frontier, which it united with its existing territory in the Burzenland. In short, it became a state within a state, a situation which, in 1225, led to its expulsion by King Andrew.

At the same time the Order received a privilege from the Emperor Frederick II, which removed its possessions in the Holy Land from local secular jurisdiction, thus complementing the papal exemption of 1216. These possessions were on the frontier to the north and east of Acre, near the seat of the Grand Master at Montfort, and thus opened up the prospect of building up its own territory by expanding into Muslim lands. Under Hermann of Salza, this policy of seeking to establish an independent territory characterized the Order; it can be seen in the Burzenland, in the Holy Land, in Armenia, in Spain, in Prussia and in Livonia. In every region it adopted the same system: acquisition of possessions on the Christian frontier, subjugation of the neighbouring pagans, the building up of an independent territory based upon the original gift, and then new conquests unconnected to the old hierarchy. Although exiled from Hungary, and unsuccessful in the Holy Land, the Order achieved its aim with spectacular success in Prussia.

Thereafter the Order wavered between the poles of the Holy Land and Prussia – a problem which can be seen very clearly at the end of the thirteenth and the beginning of the fourteenth centuries.[6] Jerusalem was the centre of the

---

[4] U. Arnold, 'Der Deutsche Orden zwischen Kaiser und Papst im 13. Jahrhundert' in *Die Ritterorden zwischen geistlicher und weltlicher Macht im Mittelalter*, ed. Z.H. Nowak. Ordines militares 5 (Toruń, 1990), pp. 57–70.

[5] Arnold, 'Feldspital'.

[6] U. Arnold, 'Konrad von Feuchtwangen', *Preussenland*, 13 (1975), pp. 2–34; U. Arnold,

Christian world, despite its fall in 1244, and even after losing all its possessions in the Holy Land in 1291, a strong party in the Order remained in the Mediterranean area, as did the Templars and the Hospitallers. However, the destruction of the Templars helped the Prussian party in the Order: in 1309 the seat of the Grand Master was transferred from Venice, where it had been since 1291, to Marienburg in Prussia.

The Order created its central territory around the Baltic between 1230 and 1309. The Polish dukes of Masovia and Silesia, fighting for predominance in Poland, had called upon its support against the Prussian pagans and, over a fifty-year period, the Order subjugated the Prussians. With the incorporation of the Livonian Swordbrothers in 1237 it took on the conflict with Russian Novgorod in addition,[7] but the defeat on the ice of Lake Peipus in 1242 put an end to this advance and established a frontier with Russia which remained for 300 years. In Prussia the Order built up an independent, sovereign state, which was governed not as a missionary venture, but in a spirit of *Realpolitik*. The subsequent conquest in 1309 of Pomerelia, a Christian territory to the west of the Vistula, demonstrated to the whole of Europe that there had grown up in Prussia an independent power which commanded the respect of other states, especially those in the Baltic region. It was governed not by a king, but by a religious Order – an Order which now became increasingly noble in its composition, turning its back on townsmen, and which emphasized its role in the battle against the pagans to the detriment of its function as a hospital. The crusades against the Lithuanians made Prussia a crusading centre in the fourteenth century, and nobles from the whole of Europe – even from England and Scotland – came there.[8] The fourteenth century was the heyday of the Prussian state of the Teutonic Order.

After the subjugation of the Prussian territories, the Order established its castles (which are still well known today) and settled Prussians, Poles and Germans in villages and towns. These, by a process of assimilation, became a new people – the Prussians – who lived in that region until 1945. Missionary work was usually undertaken by Dominicans and Franciscans. Originally, the territory of Prussia was divided – two parts to the Order, one part to the bishoprics, but the Teutonic Order incorporated three of the four bishoprics thereby enabling it to become the sole sovereign power in foreign politics. It built up a very effective administration, dependent not on one leader such as a king, but upon the whole Order with its system of convents located in castles all over the country. This was a completely new form of government in Europe at that time and, until the later struggle with Poland, was more effective than

'Deutschmeister Konrad von Feuchtwangen und die "preussische Partei" im Deutschen Orden am Ende des 13. und zu Beginn des 14. Jahrhunderts', in *Aspekte der Geschichte. Festschrift für Peter Gerrit Thielen*, ed. U. Arnold (Göttingen, 1990), pp. 22–42.

[7] F. Benninghoven, *Der Orden der Schwertbrüder* (Cologne, 1965).

[8] W. Paravicini, *Die Preussenreisen des europäischen Adels*, 1 (Sigmaringen, 1989).

any other governmental administration. The Order possessed many large farms, and became rich. The large cities, such as Elbing, Thorn, Königsberg and Danzig, were members of the Hanse and traded all over the Baltic and the North Seas. Many English and Scottish traders came to Prussia too. Using the Hanse privileges, the Order built up its own trading organization from Prussia to western Europe, and in this way rivalled the cities. However, although this was successful in the thirteenth and fourteenth centuries, it became a problem in the fifteenth century.

After the conquest of Pomerelia in 1309 a state of opposition developed between Prussia and Poland, which had also wanted Pomerelia. When, in 1385–86, Poland and Lithuania were united, it was only a question of time before it became a struggle between the Order in Prussia and the new Polish–Lithuanian state. This is not the place to analyse the political situation in the Baltic area around 1400, but it is clear that the so-called modern state of the Order of the thirteenth and fourteenth centuries then lost not only its powerful position but its inner purpose too. This was, of course, a problem for all orders of knighthood at this time but it can be seen most clearly in Prussia.

The beginning of the end of the state came with its defeat by Poland and Lithuania at battle of Tannenberg (Grunwald) in 1410.[9] In the First Treaty of Thorn in 1411 the Order retained its landholdings, but had to pay such a huge indemnity that its wealth was severely undermined. Attempts to raise the money were thwarted by the inter-city rivalry – a problem which characterized politics throughout Europe in the fourteenth and fifteen centuries. Prussia may have been affected a little later than most countries on account of her better economic situation, but after 1410 this became the Order's principal problem in the state. In 1454 the cities and a large proportion of the rural population revolted and a thirteen-year struggle ensued. At its end, in the Second Treaty of Thorn in 1466, the Order lost the western parts of its territory, including all the large and wealthy cities except for Königsberg. It also lost Marienburg – the seat of the Grand Master and the largest castle in Europe – and it had to swear an oath of fealty to the Polish king.

The Order in the Empire and in Livonia did not accept this treaty, but in Prussia the Grand Master could do little else than try to mitigate its effects. At the beginning of the sixteenth century the Order in Prussia hoped to defy Poland by choosing a duke of the Empire as Grand Master – Frederick of Saxony refused the oath to the Polish king, while Albert of Brandenburg-Ansbach tried to struggle against Poland. Finding no help from either his own Order or the Empire, he sought a political solution: in 1525, in the Treaty of Cracow, Albert became the first hereditary duke of Prussia, holding it as a fief of the king of Poland, and then resigned from the Order and became a Lutheran. The Teutonic Order had lost both its Grand Master and its most important territory.

[9] M. Burleigh, *Prussian Society and the German Order. An Aristocratic Corporation in Crisis c. 1410–1466* (Cambridge, 1984).

The history of the Teutonic Order in Livonia differed from that in Prussia.[10] After the incorporation of the Swordbrothers in 1237, it tried to achieve the same position as it had in Prussia, but this proved impossible. The bishoprics, especially the archbishopric of Riga, were too strong and, except for the southern bishopric of Kurland, the Order was unable to incorporate them. With its territories in the south and the middle of the country, and the purchase of the northern part – Estonia – from Denmark in 1346, the Order possessed the greater part of the country, but power was divided between the Order, the bishops of Riga, Dorpat and Oesel-Wiek, and the city of Riga. This form of government persisted until the end of the Livonian confederation in 1561. The Order established castles as it had in Prussia, but no new German settlers came to farm the land; the only immigrants were nobles, who held the land as fiefs, and traders and craftsmen who came to the towns. Most of the inhabitants were therefore indigenous – a situation which has persisted until the present day. Moreover, the Order had few large farms and, unlike in Prussia, played little part in trade which was largely controlled by the townsmen. Domestic problems, such as the rivalry with the towns which characterized the Order's rule in Prussia, were therefore absent. However, Livonia's foreign policy included an alliance with Poland and Lithuania against Moscow which was trying to conquer the countries to the west, including Livonia itself. The Order's allies in Livonia were therefore its enemies in Prussia.

Thus, the Order's problems arose not from its function as a monastic community, but rather from its role as governor of a state. The end of the Order in Livonia was due partly to external pressure and partly to the country's internal structure rather than to the Order's own internal condition. Walter of Plettenberg, the Master of Livonia (1494–1534),[11] defeated the Russians and tolerated the Reformation, thereby permitting Catholics and Lutherans to live together in the Livonian branch of the Order – the great conflict between the confessions was non-existent until the confederation of Livonia broke down under Russian assault. The result of that struggle was almost identical to that in Prussia: the southern part of Livonia became a dukedom in Kurland under the last Master, Gotthard of Ketteler, while the other parts of the Order's possessions fell to Poland and Sweden. Four hundred years after conquering Prussia and Livonia the Order had lost everything – territory, wealth, knights and reputation. What remained was a German imprint, the Lutheran confession, and links to the culture of western Europe which have endured over the centuries, including the Communist era, until the present day.

---

[10] Old, but good: L. Arbusow, *Grundriss der Geschichte Liv-, Est- und Kurlands*, 4th edn (Riga, 1918); W. Urban, *The Baltic Crusade* (DeKalb, Ill., 1975).

[11] *Wolter von Plettenberg. Der grösste Ordensmeister Livlands*, ed. N. Angermann (Lüneburg, 1985).

The transfer of the Grand Master's seat to the Baltic rendered the Mediterranean region peripheral. Distance means estrangement, and by the middle of the sixteenth century the Order had lost most of its Mediterranean possessions. Powers as diverse as the Turks and the Papal Curia took the opportunity to enrich themselves, a situation sometimes compounded by the administration of the Order. In the south of France its possessions had been lost even earlier – in the fourteenth century.[12]

The losses in the Mediterranean area increased the significance of the Order's possessions to the north of the Alps in Germany. Here was the centre of the Empire, where, since the beginning of the thirteenth century, the Order had acquired so many possessions: houses, meadows, fields, vineyards, forests, as well as existing hospitals and churches. Here, medical care, the care of souls, and agriculture were the functions of the Order. The properties yielded rents and, through this economic base, the means for fighting against the pagans were acquired; but the care of souls and the medical responsibilities had direct effects at a local level.[13]

The branch of the Order in the Empire must not therefore only be seen from the viewpoint of the war against the pagans, but also as an entity in itself,[14] since it was from this that it acquired its importance inside the Empire. Its possessions derived mostly from the Staufen party. We can differentiate groups of donors: on the one hand, the higher nobility, who gave significant properties; on the other, the lower nobility and ministerial class who donated possessions in their homelands. Often the donations were tied to entrance into the Order, so that the donations provided simultaneous subsistence for the new brothers. An intimate connection therefore remained between the donor's family and the Order, for the family lived near the commandery, and sometimes continued to use the donations, thus creating strong links between the Order and the lesser nobility. It is often argued that the Order served as a hospital for the noble class in the fifteenth and sixteenth centuries, the basis of which was laid in the thirteenth century. But this branch of the Order was integrated in the surrounding society and was a part of the Church in the Empire, just like the large chapters of convents or cathedrals. Consequently there was an almost complete absence of non-German brethren; they were only found on the fringes of the Order's sphere of influence, for example in Italy. This has given the erroneous impression that the Order admitted only Germans, but the contraction into a national Order only came with the economic crisis of the fifteenth century, which hit the lesser nobility hard and caused them to try to ensure their own subsistence by this means.

---

[12] K. Forstreuter, *Der Deutsche Orden am Mittelmeer* (Bonn, 1967).

[13] K. Militzer, *Die Entstehung der Deutschordensballeien im Deutschen Reich*, 2nd edn (Marburg, 1981).

[14] *Kreuz und Schwert. Der Deutsche Orden in Südwestdeutschland, in der Schweiz und im Elsass*, ed. U. Arnold (Mainau, 1991); *Ritter und Priester. Acht Jahrhunderte Deutscher Orden in Nordwesteuropa*, ed. U. Arnold (Alden Biesen, 1992) (catalogues of international exhibitions).

The Order's possessions in the Empire were scattered, rather than being formed into territories as in Prussia, Livonia or the Holy Land. They were governed by a hierarchy comprising a commander, a land-commander, and a Deutschmeister.[15] The land-commanders' regions differed in size and wealth and their function varied with the changes in emphasis in the Order's activities. The most important regions were in the Rhine-Maas area and in Franconia. However, as the jurisdictions of the bishoprics and cities became increasingly territorial, the Order's exemptions began to cause friction. Thus, in 1494, the Deutschmeister became a prince of the Empire, in contravention of the papal privilege of the thirteenth century, while at the same time the Order tried to territorialize its own possessions. Thus it made the region of Mergentheim in Franconia into an almost self-contained entity.[16]

However, before this, the agrarian crisis of the fourteenth century had led to a fall in agricultural production,[17] and this had affected the Order's economic base. One solution was to reduce the number of members: from the end of the fourteenth century until the beginning of the sixteenth century, the membership of the Order's branch in the Empire fell by two-thirds. At the same time it halted the admission of townsmen into the ranks of the knights, and the Order's ethos consequently changed to that of the noble knight rather than of the monk: the *miles* displaced the *monachus*. The Reformation had contributed to this process but was not the most significant influence. The fundamental causes were the losses of Prussia and, four decades later, of Livonia.

After the Treaty of Cracow in 1525, the Deutschmeister became head of the Order.[18] Thereafter the centre of the Teutonic Order was located in the Empire, and the Order became very closely involved in the politics of the Empire under the house of Habsburg. Indeed, the links were so strong that, from the end of the sixteenth century until the end of the First World War, the Grand Master was a prince of the house of Habsburg or of related houses.

Next in importance to this consolidation of the Order in Germany were the problems caused by the Reformation during which the Order lost most of its priests. In Franconia, in 1513, 68 per cent of the brethren were priests, but in 1577 this had fallen to only 6 per cent, which in practice meant that there were only two. The knights, however, did not lose their central position during the Reformation, for the Order remained as a 'Hospital of the German nobles'.

---

[15] See diagram, *Ritter und Priester*, p. 13.

[16] B. Demel, 'Mergentheim – Residenz des Deutschen Ordens', *Zeitschrift für Württembergische Landesgeschichte*, **34/35** (1975/76), pp. 142–212.

[17] K. Militzer, 'Auswirkungen der spätmittelalterlichen Agrardepression auf die Deutschordensballeien', in *Von Akkon bis Wien. Studien zur Deutschordensgeschichte vom 13. bis zum 20. Jahrhundert. Festschrift zum 90. Geburtstag von Althochmeister P. Dr. Marian Tumler O.T.*, ed. U. Arnold (Marburg, 1978), pp. 62–75.

[18] B. Demel, 'Der Deutsche Orden zwischen Bauernkrieg (1525) und Napoleon (1809). Ein Beitrag zur neuzeitlichen Deutschordensgeschichte', in *Von Akkon bis Wien*, pp. 177–207.

Only the confession of the knight changed, where the principality itself changed its confession. So we find not only Catholics in the Order, but Lutherans and Calvinists too, who, after 1648, received equal rights. For nearly 300 years the Order was a triconfessional institution, bound together by its possessions. Thus, the non-Catholics had their seat and vote in the General Chapter of the Order just like the Catholics, and only the Grand Master consistently has been a Catholic throughout the Order's entire history – a circumstance that is unique in the history of the modern Empire.

After 1525 two lines can be discerned in the Order's politics. The first is the attempt to regain Prussia,[19] a policy which continued until the era of Napoleon and his reorganization of Europe. The other is the reform of the Order in accordance with contemporary needs. In 1606 Grand Master Maximilian of Austria promulgated a new Rule.[20] At its centre was the knight, once more imbued with the ideal of fighting against the pagans, in this case the Turks. At the same time the position of the priests was enhanced because the Order needed them both for itself and for its many rectories. These changes were seen as the way forward.

The connection to the house of Habsburg gave the Order necessary support, as well as a new prominence, since the Order's leaders were not only Grand Masters, but also governors of the Netherlands, archbishops or bishops. Similarly, for the bishops and archbishops, the post of Grand Master was particularly attractive. After all, there were many bishops, but only one Grand Master! Moreover, the post brought with it the role of fighter against the pagans. Thus, in 1696, the emperor, his brother-in-law, the Bavarian prince of Pfalz-Neuburg and the Grand Master of the same house built up their own regiment, known as the 'Hoch- und Deutschmeister', which still exists today.[21] One problem remained, that of the Order's formation of territorial units, a trend which had been most extensive in Utrecht in the Netherlands. From the end of the sixteenth century, Spain fought to preserve its rule in the northern parts of the Netherlands. It was a political battle, but also a confessional one, from which the Calvinistic provinces emerged victorious. Thus in 1637 the brothers in Utrecht broke away from the Teutonic Order and integrated themselves into the Netherlands in the same way as the Order of St John had done in Brandenburg. As *Ridderlijke Duitsche Orde, Ballij van Utrecht* they still exist today.[22]

In the same epoch the Order experienced an economic recovery – the first since the late medieval agrarian crisis. This is still evident today in the archi-

---

[19] U. Arnold, 'Mergentheim und Königsberg/Berlin – die Rekuperationsbemühungen des Deutschen Ordens auf Preussen', *Württembergisch Franken*, 60 (1976), pp. 14–54.

[20] H. Noflatscher, *Glaube, Reich und Dynastie. Maximilian der Deutschmeister (1558–1618)* (Marburg, 1987).

[21] E. Finke, *K.(u.)k. Hoch- und Deutschmeister. 222 Jahre für Kaiser und Reich* (Graz, 1978).

[22] J.H. de Vey Mestdagh, *De Utrechtse Balije der Duitse Orde ruim 750 jaar geschiedenis v/d Orde in de Nederlanden* (Utrecht and Alden Biesen, 1988); *Ritter und Priester*, pp. 90–96, 256–7.

tecture, for the Grand Masters, the land-commanders and the commanders built new palaces and churches, or rebuilt the old ones. Knights now lived in accordance with their rank. Priests remained necessary, but they had almost no say in the Order.

At the same time, however, the Order was deeply affected by wider political changes. After the Habsburg retreat in the treaty of 1648, there followed a systematic extension of French influence towards the east, while at the same time the old Romano–German Empire began to fall into ruin. The upheavals of the late eighteenth century were even more profound: the establishment of a new constitutional model in America, the French Revolution, and the rise to power of Napoleon Bonaparte.[23] Napoleon's seizure of clerical possessions was a signal for many German princes to follow suit. France confiscated the Order's possessions to the west of the Rhine, and Napoleon's allies did likewise: the rulers of Württemberg, Bavaria, Prussia, Saxony, Hesse and others participated in the expropriation and the expulsion of the Order. After 1809, the priests were allowed to stay in their rectories, but they had to resign from the Order. Only the emperor of Austria, the adversary of France, stayed his hand. Ultimately, after 1809, the Order survived only in the Habsburg territories with a centre in Austrian Silesia.[24]

Initially, this did not result in reorganization. Although the Austrian emperor nominated the Grand Master, he provided no new basis for the Order, so that its membership dwindled until only the Grand Master and four knights were left. Then, in 1839, the emperor agreed to a new form of organization for the Order, so that it could regenerate itself. However, the basis had changed. In the thirteenth century the Order had existed throughout Europe, and from the sixteenth century over the whole of the Romano–German Empire: now it survived only in the Austrian Empire. Moreover, the Order's triconfession status was lost, for it reverted to Catholicism exclusively. This was the background to the reorganization, which must be seen too within the political context of nineteenth-century Austria: revolution, industrialization, pauperism and wars in the Balkans were the dominant features of the period.

Nevertheless, on the basis of its knightly and charitable tradition, the Order was able to make a fresh start. The branch of sisters, which had existed down to the end of the Middle Ages, was renewed and soon developed an excellent reputation in the charitable and educational fields.[25] In order to produce a better educated priesthood, the Grand Master built convents; brotherly consciousness was henceforth the guiding theological principle.[26] At the time when the

---

[23] F. Täubl, *Der Deutsche Orden im Zeitalter Napoleons* (Bonn, 1966).

[24] W. Irgang, *Freudenthal als Herrschaft des Deutschen Ordens 1621–1725* (Bonn, 1971).

[25] E. Gruber, *Deutschordensschwestern im 19. und 20. Jahrhundert. Wiederbelebung, Ausbreitung und Tätigkeit 1837–1971* (Bonn, 1971).

[26] U. Gasser, *Die Priesterkonvente des Deutschen Ordens. Peter Rigler und ihre Wiedererrichtung 1854–1897* (Bonn, 1973).

Red Cross was created, the knights of the Order developed war hospitals which have played a meritorious role in Austria's wars. In order to finance itself, the Order founded two institutions: the knights of honour and the Marianer. Laymen received the cloak of the Order or a special cross, and they supported the hospitals.[27] The knights themselves were mostly officers in the Austrian army. From these new impulses there developed a living Order, centred on the Austrian part of Silesia and the southern part of the Tyrol. Care of souls in the rectories, work in schools and other pedagogical fields, and in the hospitals of the Order were the main spheres of action for the priests and the sisters, while the knights expanded the hospitals in both war and peace, and served the Austrian state as officers and diplomats. The Grand Masters were archdukes of the Habsburg house.

After the First World War the Austrian state broke down, the Habsburgs had to renounce the throne, and the Order – perceived as an Order of the Habsburg house – was expropriated. However, after it proved its independence in ecclesiastical law, the new states of Austria, Czechoslovakia, Yugoslavia and Italy recognized the Order, and Rome gave it a new Rule, based on the new ecclesiastical law. No knights were admitted, the last dying in 1970. In 1923, Archduke Eugen of Austria resigned from his function as Grand Master and opened the way to the direction of the Order by the priests. This made it the only clerical Order with a branch of priests and a branch of sisters under the leadership of priests. Knights, knights of honour, and the Marianer became remnants of the past, condemned to die out. This was difficult for the knights to accept, for they had led the Order since 1198, but Rome no longer wanted the Order in that form. In a sense, Rome took over its functions and not its history, making it just another ecclesiastical order.

But there is another point of interest in the history of the Teutonic Order in the nineteenth and twentieth centuries.[28] In the former Holy Roman Empire we see a dualism between Prussia and Austria, both of which aspired to leadership, resolved ultimately by the war of 1866 and the victory of Prussia over France. From then on, the newly-founded empire of 1871 was dominated by Prussia, and needed a tradition different from that of the medieval empire. In this context, the Teutonic Order, so strongly identified with Prussia in the past, proved serviceable, and a new tradition was created which, although founded on fiction rather than truth, has since become embedded in the popular mind. In the wars of liberation against Napoleon, the Iron Cross, which was created in 1813, was modelled upon the cross of the Order; thus the medieval history of the Order was at Prussia's disposal. Writers and poets, such as Joseph von Eichendorff and Gustav Freitag followed, as did historians, such as the Prussian Heinrich von Treitschke in the mid-nineteenth century. The castle of Marienburg became the symbol of a new Prussian–German

---

[27] G. Müller, *Die Familiaren des Deutschen Ordens* (Marburg, 1980).

[28] For the following see *800 Jahre Deutscher Orden*, pp. 437–505.

nationalism. In the nineteenth century Prussia created a tradition which did not correspond to historical reality, but the contemporary Order found it impossible to defend itself, or, indeed, to correct this distortion of its history. It is therefore not surprising that this 'fabricated tradition' of the nineteenth century has remained in the common consciousness, in the empire of 1871, in the Republic of Weimar, in the 'Third Reich', and sometimes even today. It can be seen in the use of the terms and emblems of the Order, as well as in historiography, where it is not confined to schoolbooks but can be found even in the works of good historians. The medieval history of the Order in Prussia is a typical example of a politically motivated abuse of the past.

It is very interesting to find the same process in Poland, only with the premises reversed. Poland was partitioned by Russia, Austria and Prussia and, just as Prussia took a positive view of the Teutonic Order's tradition, Poland viewed that same tradition very negatively. So Poland fought a historiographical battle against the contemporary enemy, the kingdom of Prussia, within which the former lands of the Order lay. This Prussian–Polish dichotomy which, after the foundation of the new empire in 1871, became a German–Polish dichotomy, is still politically exploited today. Only in recent years has historiography become less biased, but there is still a long way to go.

After the First World War the Order was able to reorganize itself. Its administrative centre was at Vienna, its economic centre in Czechoslovakia, and there were operational centres there and in Yugoslavia and Italy – that is, in the southern part of the Tyrol. This, however, all came to an abrupt end when, in 1938, the German Reich occupied Austria. National Socialism had its own plans for a German Order and dissolved the Teutonic Order in Austria in 1938 and in Czechoslovakia in 1939. In Yugoslavia and in Italy the Order was bound to suffer because it had been identified so extensively with Germanism. The events which followed in Germany abused the history of the Teutonic Order and its name, but had no connection with the real Order.

After the Second World War most members of the Order were expelled from Czechoslovakia. However, they were able to start afresh in Germany; Austria returned its confiscated possessions; and in Italy the Order survived almost undamaged. The members found plenty of work in caring for souls and in charitable and pedagogical fields, especially in Germany and Austria, but they had lost their economic support in the former Austrian Silesia, so the definitive incorporation into the structures of the Roman Church presented no problem. The Order now revived the old structure of three branches: brethren, sisters and associates, led by the Grand Master as before. This is a special case because male and female orders are separated in the Roman Church. The associates are made up of laymen and priests working in their professions who support the Order's duties[29] of caring for souls and social–charitable work.

---

[29] Müller, *Familiaren*; M. Reiss, *Deutschordensfamiliaren in Deutschland in drei Jahrzehnten (1957–1988). Eine Bildmonographie* (Marburg, 1991).

Moreover, by means of a critical examination of the past, it is increasingly clarifying its own history. The Order's work can be seen in Austria, Italy, Germany, Slovenia, the Czech Republic, Slovakia and Belgium; there are also some associates living in other countries, for instance in England.

If we look back at the 800 years of the Teutonic Order, there remains the question of a balance-sheet. It is not easy to draw up. In each era of the Order's existence contemporaries searched for answers to the problems of their own times. In the Middle Ages, the answer had been sought in the juxtaposition of the cross and the sword. Fighting against the pagans, subjugation and mission, building a territory and settlement, political conflict and charitable and hospital work were interconnected through the dual role of knight and monk. The creation of the Order's own state through the subjugation of Prussia and the development of a Christian and Germanic 'Prussian' people is surely a lasting legacy, still evident today, as it is in a weaker form in Livonia too. Prussia and Livonia were added to the cultural family of middle Europe, formed by the Roman Church and further influenced by the Reformation. This happened because the Order in the Middle Ages had the power to mould its own history, but the more it became an object of history, especially in modern times, the smaller was its influence. Thus, as its political importance diminished, it was increasingly integrated into general political and ecclesiastical developments, and its military and religio-charitable achievements became mere stones in a mosaic planned outside the Order, as for example in its contribution to the fight against the Turks or its work as a bulwark of Catholicism within a Protestant setting. So extensively has the Order's history been manipulated that it was used as an element in the political propaganda of its enemies, against which the Order has been unable to defend itself.

Today the Teutonic Order has no political importance, and its clerical and charitable work is no better than that of other orders. It is now attempting to find a new role in modern times, but one which does not renounce its own history. This history has lessons for us today: the need to surmount national, confessional and ethical frontiers, to think in terms of the whole of Europe, and to reflect upon one's obligations not only to oneself as an individual but also to mankind as a whole. Thus the present-day Order is trying to find a way forward by looking back into its own history – a triconfessional history which in turn has reflected that of the whole of Europe.

24

Frederick II, the Hohenstaufen, and the Teutonic Order in the Kingdom of Sicily

James M. Powell

The origins and the early history of the Teutonic Order have been the subject of numerous studies, including recent work by Marie-Luise Favreau-Lilie, Dieter Wojtecki, and Udo Arnold. Their attention has been attracted by the difficult problem of the connections between the Order and the German hospitals in Jerusalem and Acre, the constitutional development of the Order, and its growth in Germany.[1] Although Kurt Forstreuter has written extensively on the Order in the Mediterranean, like them, he has given relatively little attention to relations between Frederick II and the Teutonic Order in the kingdom of Sicily. Even the biographers of Frederick, who have dealt in detail with the relationship between Frederick II and the Master of the Order, Hermann of Salza, have been chiefly content to describe the importance of Hermann's role in Frederick's crusade and in his relations with the papacy without focusing directly on the kingdom of Sicily.[2]

Yet this neglect does not arise from the unimportance of the Order in the kingdom nor of the kingdom in the history of the Order. On the contrary, there is ample evidence in Mongitore's classic work on the Church of the Magione in Palermo, one of the most important houses of the Order in Sicily,[3] the Order's

---

[1] M.-L. Favreau, *Studien des Frühgeschichte des deutschen Ordens* (Stuttgart, 1974); D. Wojteckl, 'Der deutschen Orden unter Friedrich II', in *Probleme um Friedrich II*, ed. J. Fleckenstein (Sigmaringen, 1974), pp. 187–224. In this article, Wojtecki focuses on the development of the Order in Germany. More recently, Udo Arnold has discussed the origin and early history of the Order in 'Entstehung und Fruhzeit des Deutschenordens', in *Die geistlichen Ritterorden Europas*, ed. by J. Fleckenstein and M. Hellmann (Sigmaringen, 1980), pp. 81–107. These works are also valuable for their extensive bibliographical notes.

[2] K. Forstreuter, *Der deutsche Orden am Mittelmeer* (Bonn, 1967).

[3] A. Mongitore, *Monumenta Historica Sacrae Domus Mansionis SS Trinitatis Militaris Ordinis Theutonicorum Urbis Panormi* (Palermo, 1721). Forstreuter, p. 110, characterizes the list of charters of the Magione by V. Mortillaro, *Elenco cronologico delle antiche pergamene pertinenti al reale chiesa della*

central role in the life of the kingdom. Likewise, on the mainland, the Order centred its activities initially on its house in Barletta, under a grant from the Emperor Henry VI, but spread to other places soon after.[4] In order to explain the growth of the Order in Sicily, there has been a general tendency to combine evidence of Hermann of Salza's relations with Frederick with a general impression that the prosperity of the Order in the kingdom of Sicily was a product of this personal tie. On the basis of a study of materials relating to the kingdom, the present paper suggests that this view is too facile. It distorts the position of the Order and its Master and ignores the circumstances that obtained in the kingdom in the period prior to Frederick II's crusade.

Within the kingdom of Sicily, it has been argued, the Order benefited from strong support by the Emperor Henry VI and the Empress Constance. In a charter of 20 May 1197, Henry VI granted and confirmed the hospital of St Thomas, which had been built by the Order, to the brethren of the Hospital of the Germans in Jerusalem.[5] In July, Henry and Constance granted the church of Santa Trinità in Palermo, with all its properties and other rights, to the brethren of the Teutonic Order.[6] This church, popularly known as the Magione, had been endowed by Matthew of Ajello, the Chancellor of King William II, for the Cistercians. Mongitore indicates that the Cistercians were ejected from the church by Henry VI for favouring Tancred against the claims of his wife, Constance.[7] His charter, however, makes it clear that the grant to the Teutonic Order was made at its request. Moreover, Henry's chancery inserted into the grant the phrase *salvo mandato et ordinatione nostra et heredum nostrorum*, which made it contingent on a possible future decision by the Crown. While it is clear that Henry and Constance were favourably disposed to the Teutonic Order, these two grants do not justify the view that they took the initiative in supporting it. On the contrary, the evidence shows that the leaders of the Order in Barletta and in Palermo seized the initiative to secure royal support. The Order also sought and obtained support from the burghers of Palermo, as grants by *Constantinus dictus marmorarius* and *Robertus quidam Faber* indicate. These were both made to Gerard, Master of the house of the Teutonic Order at Santa Trinità. Constantine had two houses and a business, whose accounts he made over to the Order for collection.[8] Robert seems to have been a man of considerable wealth, with houses and property in Palermo

---

Magione (Palermo, 1858) as almost unusable owing to numerous gaps in the documentation and other errors. Mongitore drew on the archives of the Magione and also used two manuscripts now in the Archivio di Stato della Catena, Palermo, Ms 6, fourteenth century, papal privileges for the Teutonic Order, and Ms 7, seventeenth century, chiefly royal and papal privileges for the Magione. Each bears the title, *Tabulario della Magione*, assigned by the archivist.

[4] *Regesta Imperii* IV, new edn (Graz and Cologne, 1951–53), no. 593, p. 240; Forstreuter, pp. 124–6.

[5] *Regesta Imperii* IV, 3, no. 593, p. 240; no. 601, p. 243; no. 709, p. 272; no. 707, p. 276.

[6] Mongitore, pp. 13–14; *Regesta Imperii* IV, no. 601, p. 243.

[7] Mongitore, p. 12.

[8] Ibid., pp. 16–17.

and in the country.[9] Neither had heirs. These charters provide evidence that
Gerard as Master of the Order in Palermo was very active in promoting the
interests of the Magione.

Moreover, the leadership of the Order at Palermo and Barletta pursued their
interests with the same vigour during the minority of Frederick II, not only
seeking confirmation of earlier grants but obtaining additional gifts. In a word,
the activities of the Teutonic Order in the kingdom of Sicily during the
minority of Frederick were similar to those of other ecclesiastical institutions,
seeking to ensure their possessions during a period of instability and even trying
to gain some advantage from the circumstances of the period. Thus, Frederick's
charter of December 1202, commemorates the generosity of his parents and
makes a grant of the *casale Meserelle in tenimentis cephale cum molendino et perti-
nentiis suis* ... in consideration of the honesty and religion of the Holy Hospital
of St Mary of the Germans in Jerusalem *pro animabus felicium parentuum nostrum
domini imperatoris et domine imperatricis bone memorie.*[10] However, the same
formula is found in a renewal of a privilege for the Hospitallers in October 1209
– a good indication that the formulae in these charters were typical products
of the chancery during Frederick's minority.[11] The number of grants to the
Teutonic Order, however, does seem to have exceeded that to the Hospitallers
and the Templars. The former had enjoyed considerable support from the
Normans and had their privileges confirmed by Constance and later by
Frederick, but there is little evidence of additional support for them, or for
the Templars, during the minority. On the other hand, the grant to the
Teutonic Order discussed above added a provision for a tax exemption on goods
imported, sold or exported from the kingdom by the Order. This grant was
not unusual – the other Orders had it – but it shows that the Teutonic Order
continued to pursue its interests aggressively and had, perhaps already during
the minority of Frederick, developed a policy of seeking parity with the Hospitallers and Templars in the kingdom of Sicily.

That this was the case seems to be confirmed from a renewal of another charter
of Henry VI in October 1204, for the brethren of the Hospital of St Thomas
of Barletta, to which lands from the royal domain were added.[12] Another
renewal for the Magione, in 1205, of the charter *Dignitas regia*, already renewed
in 1202, contained an added grant of

*omnes villanos casalis Politii ubicumque sunt et terram que est prope domum Sancte Trinitatis
que dicitur Hartilgidie et aliam terram in qua fuit Masara, que est inter jardinum predicte
Sancte Trinitatis et murum civitatis nostri Panormi in loco qui dicitur Alza.*

[9] Ibid., pp. 17–18.

[10] *Historia diplomatica Friderici II*, ed. J.L.A. Huillard-Bréholles, 6 vols in 12 with Introduction,
1 (Paris, 1852–61); repr. Turin, 1963, pp. 95–7.

[11] *Acta Imperii*, ed. G. Winkelmann, 2 vols, **1** (Innsbruck, 1880–85), no. 134, p. 112; see, also,
no. 95, p. 85, June 1206.

[12] *Historia diplomatica*, **1**, pp. 110–12

In this instance, the Order was taking the opportunity to round out its holdings near the church.[13] In September 1206, when Frederick was still only twelve years old, Gerard, Master of the *domus Sancte Trinitatis* in Palermo secured the right to a fishing boat for use in the port of Palermo and the surrounding sea without payment of taxes.[14] This mention of Gerard provides further evidence that these grants were not merely the result of royal favour but were actively sought. Frederick was not in control of his own chancery at this time. Whatever favour the Order may have enjoyed at this time from the Hohenstaufen in Germany, it is difficult to make the case that its growth in the kingdom of Sicily during the minority of Frederick was the result of ties to the ruling house.

Even after Frederick left the kingdom of Sicily in 1212 to obtain the German crown, he granted a charter that had been requested by the hospital of St Thomas in Barletta.[15] In a grant made at Nuremberg in December 1216, he granted the Order a house in Brindisi that had once belonged to Admiral Margaritus who had led the Sicilian fleet in the defence of Tyre at the time of the Third Crusade.[16] But the strongest evidence that the Order had been pursuing a deliberate policy of seeking parity with the other Orders comes from a charter granted by Frederick on 24 June 1217. Its opening words are revealing.

> By the devoted petitions of Master Hermann and the Brethren of the Hospital of St Mary and the house of the Germans in Jerusalem, approving by the royal clemency, in support and to the profit of the same house and brethren, [we concede] the liberties, customs, and all the rights, to which the Knights of the Temple and the Hospital of St John in Jerusalem have been privileged in our kingdom of Sicily.[17]

Up to this time, the Teutonic Order had contented itself with improving its economic position. Now, it attained, at least in general terms, a similar status to the other Orders. This concession was especially valuable given the strong favour which had been shown to the Hospitallers under the Norman kings.

There is a possible explanation for the willingness of Frederick to accede to Hermann's petition. Following his attendance at the Fourth Lateran Council in 1215, Hermann journeyed to Palermo, where he met Frederick's queen, Constance of Aragon, and escorted her, with their son Henry, to Germany.[18] It was in December 1216, that Frederick first mentioned Hermann in a charter in which he granted the Order 150 ounces of gold *tari* a year from the income of Brindisi *in excambium cujusdam tenimenti* that Frederick had received from the Order in Germany. Most probably, this exchange was undertaken at the

---

[13] Ibid., 1, pp. 95–7.
[14] Ibid., 1, pp. 121–2.
[15] *Acta Imperii*, 1, no. 121 pp. 106–7.
[16] Ibid., 1, no. 141, pp. 119.
[17] Ibid., 1, no. 145, pp. 121–2.
[18] W. Cohn, *Hermann von Salza* (Bresslau, 1930), pp. 19–21.

request of Hermann and was in the interest of the Order.[19] The importance
of this charter is strongly suggested by the fact that the Order took the trouble
to have it confirmed by Pope Honorius III in March 1218.[20] At the same time,
the brethren secured confirmation of another charter of Frederick, which had
granted the Order 200 ounces of *tari* from the income of Messina.[21] These confirmations are noteworthy because they represent substantial incomes and they
are among the very few grants to the Order that appear in the register of Pope
Honorius III.[22] This is surprising given the very large number of papal privileges
obtained from Honorius by the Order.[23] While the role of Hermann of Salza
in securing these grants can certainly be used to sustain the argument that he
was a personage of increasing influence at the imperial court, his desire for papal
confirmations of these charters raises a question about the degree of trust that
existed in the relationship between Frederick and the Order.[24] The very
magnitude of these grants, combined with a concern that Frederick might alter
his policy toward the Order in the future, may well have persuaded Hermann
of Salza to seek support from the papal curia.

In fact, there are signs that 1219 marked a change in the relations between
Frederick and the military orders in the kingdom of Sicily. The Teutonic Order
joined others from the Kingdom of Sicily in seeking re-confirmations of charters
that Frederick had confirmed during his minority and of grants he had made
during his minority. Hermann of Salza had already departed on crusade to the
East by this time. Whether his absence affected the concerns of his brethren
in Italy is impossible to say. What is evident is that, beginning in February
1219, a number of charters from the Order in the kingdom were presented for
confirmation. There is no indication that these were anything but routine acts
of the imperial chancery. Nor is there any explanation of why they were
presented to the court at this time. The charters in question were *Dignitas regia*,
now swelled with the grants made during the minority, namely *Meserella* and

---

[19] *Historia diplomatica*, 1, pp. 488–90. Hermann is mentioned but his role is not clear.

[20] *Regesta Honorii III*, ed. P. Pressutti, 2 vols, 1 (Rome, 1888–95), no. 1173, pp. 195–6, 22 March, 1218.

[21] *Historia diplomatica*, 1, pp. 510–11. This grant was also confirmed by Honorius III, *Reg. Hon. III*, 1, no. 1172, p. 195, 21 March, 1218.

[22] For another confirmation of a charter of Frederick II, see *Reg. Hon. III*, 1, no. 2123, p. 351, 25 June, 1219. On 1 February 1220 the Master and brethren obtained a confirmation of Frederick II's earlier confirmation of the grant of the church of the Magione in Palermo to the Order by Henry VI and Constance. *Reg. Hon. III*, 1, no. 2318, p. 385, 1 February 1220. However, this document was not put into Honorius's register. It is printed in Mongitore, p. 30.

[23] Most of these were granted between late 1220 and early 1222. *Reg. Hon. III*, 1, no. 2440, pp. 491–565. These documents form the bulk of the letters of Honorius III in Palermo. Archivio di Stato della Catena, Ms 6 and most have been printed in *Tabulae Ordinis Teutonici*, ed. E. Strehlke (Berlin, 1869; repr. Toronto, 1975), pp. 272–340.

[24] Cohn, pp. 26–7.

Meserella and the *villanos Politii*, *Quod sacrosanctis ecclesiis*, which granted freedom from taxes for a single fishing boat in Palermo, and *Cum ad nostre cumulum*, which entrusted the leper hospital of St John in Palermo to the *domus Sancte Trinitatis* in Palermo.[25] This last grant was made specifically to Brother Gerard, Master of the Magione. This mention of Gerard, who had played a leading role in securing grants for the Magione during Frederick's minority, suggests he was still active in protecting his house from loss.[26]

Perhaps Gerard also figured in a more significant effort undertaken at Goslar in July 1219. The imperial chancery issued a confirmation of the charter of Henry VI and Constance, *Ad eterni regni*, which had granted possession of the Magione and exemption from port taxes to the Teutonic Order.[27] As we have already noted, the charter granted by Henry and Constance had contained a clause of reservation, *salvo mandato et ordinatione nostra et heredum nostrorum*, perhaps arising from the manner in which the church had been taken from the Cistercians. Frederick's confirmation did not take the form of a re-issue of *Ad eterni regni*. The new charter, *Regia serenitas clementia*, contained, however, the same clause of reservation that had been in the original.[28] The reason for seeking this confirmation is evident since, later in the same month, the Palermitan brethren obtained a charter to protect them against the molestations of royal tax collectors in Palermo.[29] This letter refers to these acts as taken contrary to the grant made by Henry VI and Constance and confirmed by Frederick, which seems to refer to *Ad eterni regni*.[30] In fact, however, there is no evidence of any previous confirmation of *Ad eterni regni* by Frederick before July 1219. On the other hand, there had been efforts to protect the privileges of the Order which did not refer to this grant in specific terms.[31] The degree of concern within the Order at this time may also be measured by the fact that it sought and obtained a papal confirmation of *Regia serenitas clementia* on 1 February 1220.[32] Clearly, there were uncertainties in the minds of the members of the Order and they resolved these by waging a campaign for protection of their position on two fronts. As

---

[25] For *Dignitas regia*, see *Historia diplomatica*, **1**, 586–8, Hagenau, February 1219; for *Quod sacrosanctis ecclesiis*, see ibid., **1**, 588–90, Hagenau, February 1219; for *Cum ad nostre cumulum*, see ibid., **1**, 590–91, Hagenau, February 1219.

[26] Ibid., **1**, pp. 590–91.

[27] Mongitore, pp. 13–14; Huillard-Bréholles, **1**, pp. 651–3.

[28] *Historia diplomatica*, **1**, p. 652: ... *salvo mandato et ordinatione nostra et heredum nostrorum* ...

[29] Ibid., **1**, pp. 653–4.

[30] Ibid., **1**, p. 653: *Fratres ... conquesti sunt quod doanerii et cabelloti contra privilegia domini imperatoris felicis memorie patris nostri sibi indulta et a nobis confirmata, frequenter in civitate nostra Panormi [ipsos] indebite molestant.*

[31] See, for example, the charter of 24 June 1217 which granted the Teutonic Order the same privileges in the kingdom as those possessed already by the Templars and Hospitallers: (*Acta Imperii*, **1**, no. 145, pp. 121–2.

[32] *Reg. Hon. III*, **1**, no. 2318, p. 385; Mongitore, p. 30.

the date for Frederick II's imperial coronation loomed closer, there seems to have been mounting pressure to secure confirmations of earlier charters.[33]

Frederick's return to the kingdom of Sicily in November 1220 and his summons of the Diet of Capua in December provides a probable explanation for the events of the preceding year. The decisions taken at Capua, particularly the *Lex de resignandis privilegiis*, must have required a period of preparation, and rumours about the actions to be taken on Frederick's return to the kingdom probably aroused the concerns of his south Italian subjects. The *Lex de resignandis privilegiis* was directed against those who had used the turmoils of the late Norman period and the minority to enhance their positions at the expense of the Crown. It affected not only the nobility and the Italian maritime powers that had grown strong in the kingdom in the late twelfth and early thirteenth centuries, but the large ecclesiastical landholders as well. As one of the major beneficiaries of royal largess under Henry VI and Constance, as well as during Frederick's minority, the Teutonic Order faced a potentially difficult situation.

The law on the revocation of privileges set the Order on a course of renewed negotiations, made difficult to follow because of the absence of clues found in others of Frederick's charters at this time. The charters of the Order confirmed in Germany were not burdened with the clause, *salvo mandato et ordinatione nostra*, and the brethren in the Kingdom of Sicily did not present charters for reconfirmation immediately on Frederick's return to Sicily. In the case of the Abbey of Montevergine, on the other hand, it has been easy to trace the path of negotiations because of the royal chancery's employment of the reservation clause in its charters.[34] Likewise, in a charter confirmed on 11 June 1221 for the monastery of S. Maria de Valle Josaphat, which had close ties to Jerusalem and the crusade, there is a specific mention that the charter had been presented in accordance with the requirements of the law on privileges.[35] However, when the Teutonic Order presented a series of charters for confirmation in April 1221, no clauses of reservation were inserted, although the timing indicates that they were being handed in as a result of this legislation.

The privileges presented for confirmation in Otranto at this time were not merely for the Magione, but for the Order as a whole. Moreover, Hermann of Salza and the pope were involved in these negotiations. In *Per presens scriptum*, Frederick noted the special relationship of the Teutonic Order to his parents and took it fully under his imperial protection, confirming all the privileges it held from his parents and from himself.[36] With this letter, Frederick in effect

---

[33] See the charter of Montevergine, May 1219 in *Historia diplomatica*, 1, pp. 631–3, which shows that the concerns of the Teutonic Order were shared by the monks and Abbot of Montevergine. See, also, J.M. Powell, 'Frederick II and the Church in the Kingdom of Sicily', *Church History*, 30 (1961), pp. 28–34.

[34] Powell, 'Frederick II', pp. 28–34.

[35] *Acta Imperii*, 1, no. 228, pp. 210–11.

[36] *Historia diplomatica*, 2, 156–7.

exempted the Order from the *Lex de resignandis privilegiis*. He also confirmed various other grants. In one of several versions of *Inter alia pietatis*, granted to the Order in April 1221, he confirmed Henry VI's grant of Mesagne at the request of Hermann.[37] One of the most interesting of the new charters was a new issue of *Cum ad nostre cumulum*, which had been granted to Gerard in 1219 at Hagenau, but was now specifically granted to Hermann and the Order.[38] This charter, which had turned the leprosarium of St John in Palermo over to the Order, was actually a new grant containing no mention of the grant to Gerard, suggesting that it was the product of the negotiations we have been attempting to trace. In another issue of a charter *Inter alia pietatis*, at this time, Frederick confirmed the possessions, rights, and liberties of the Teutonic Order in the kingdom.[39] Again, this was done at the behest of Hermann of Salza. He also secured the confirmation of the charter which had granted the house of Margaritus in Brindisi to the Order.[40]

At Catania, in December 1221, the process culminated in the grant of two charters specifically for the Teutonic Order, one employing the formula *Inter alia pietatis*, which clarified and reconfirmed all the grants of Frederick's predecessors and which settled the issue of port taxes; and the other, by which Frederick petitioned Honorius III to grant the Order the same status as that given to the Hospitallers and the Templars.[41] In fact, the papacy was already moving in this direction. In January 1221, Honorius III had granted the Teutonic Order the same liberties and immunities accorded to the other two orders. Throughout this period, privilege after privilege flowed from the papal chancery to implement this decision.[42]

Gone now were the days of uncertainty and hesitation that had marked the early years of the Order in the kingdom of Sicily and threatened its position even after the influence of Hermann of Salza began to make itself felt at the imperial court. The efforts of Gerard, Master of the house of Sancta Trinità in Palermo, had played a critical role in developing the position of the Order in Sicily, just as others had worked at Brindisi to ensure a foundation for its work there. Certainly, we cannot detract from the importance of Hermann of Salza, whose interventions on behalf of the Order in 1219 and later were crucial to the success of the negotiations that won Frederick's warm support for it by 1221. But that achievement was the culmination of years of labour by others on behalf of the Order in the kingdom of Sicily, during which some of the risks taken might well have led to a different outcome. The traditional view of the Hohenstaufen as patrons of the Order has much truth in it, but it seems

---

[37] *Ibid.*, 2, pp. 163–5.

[38] *Ibid.*, 2, pp. 165–6.

[39] *Acta Imperii*, 1, no. 219, pp. 202–3.

[40] Ibid., 1, no. 220, pp. 204–5.

[41] *Historia diplomatica*, 2, pp. 226–8; 224–5.

[42] *Tabulae Ordinis Teutonici*, pp. 272–340; Favreau, pp. 81–82.

also to have been carefully fostered by the Order in its own interest. Frederick himself undoubtedly knew even before 1221, however, that he was not so much erecting a monument to his ancestors as he was recognizing valuable services rendered to him by Hermann of Salza.

25

Patronage of Elizabeth in the High Middle Ages in Hospitals of the Teutonic Order in the Bailiwick of Franconia

Klaus Guth

PATRON SAINTS OF THE TEUTONIC ORDER

The Teutonic Order has had three principal patrons: Mary as the mother of God, St Elizabeth of Thuringia and St George. The inauguration of the Teutonic Order at Acre (1189–90) is celebrated on 6 February as the solemn Feast of Our Dear Lady of the Teutonic House of Jerusalem, and is followed in the hierarchy of feasts by the Feast of St Elizabeth (19 November), the first female patron, and the Feast of St George (23 April). According to Udo Arnold's research into the liturgical manuscripts of the Middle Ages,[1] the Feast of St Elizabeth had a higher status (*totum duplex*, with octave and nine lessons), than St George's Day with only nine lessons. These liturgical-historical facts are only true, however, for the second half of the thirteenth century, after Elizabeth had been canonized in 1235 by Pope Gregory IX, only four years after her death. At that time, the Teutonic Order celebrated the feast of St Elizabeth in the same way as Epiphany and the Feasts of the Assumption and the Nativity of the Virgin. However, towards the end of the thirteenth century, and during the fourteenth century, the status of St George began to rise within the Teutonic Order, when, particularly in Prussia, his feast was celebrated as equal to that of St Elizabeth. The circumstances of the conquest of Prussia and the advance towards Latvia and Livonia (after 1283) benefited the celebration of the martial George, and his banner was carried first in front of the army into battle. It was followed by the flag with the image of the Madonna

---

[1] U. Arnold, 'Elisabeth und Georg als Pfarrpatrone im Deutschordensland Preussen. Zum Selbst-verständnis des Deutschen Ordens', in *Festschrift zur 700 jährigen Wiederkehr der Weihe der Elisabethkirche*, ed. U. Arnold and H. Liebing (Marburg, 1983), pp. 164–70. See also O. Reber, *Die Gestaltung des Kultes weiblicher Heiliger im Spätmittelalter. Die Verehrung der Heiligen Elisabeth, Klara, Hedwig und Birgitta* (Hersbruck, 1963).

and the flag of the Order with the eagle and cross. The connection between the Order's Eastern policy and its increasing interest in the patronage of St George cannot be explored further here; instead, this paper will concentrate upon the bailiwick of Franconia, where the Order's preference for St Elizabeth was strongly connected with the founding of hospitals in the region.

EARLY ELIZABETH-HOSPITALS IN THE BAILIWICK OF FRANCONIA

The origin and expansion of the bailiwick of Franconia in the high Middle Ages is controversial. It is argued by Klaus Militzer (who places its origins in 1268) and Christian Tenner,[2] that it developed from the gradual amalgamation of the houses of the Teutonic Order in southern Germany to form an independent bailiwick, covering a large area from the Inn in the east and south to beyond the Rhine in the west, and to Thuringia and Hesse in the north.[3] Christian Tenner identifies eight houses of the Order as possessing hospitals in this area. They were located in Speyer, Ellingen, Öttingen, Frankfurt-Sachsenhausen, Neubrunn-Prozelten, Donauwörth, Nuremberg and Mergentheim. The most recent history by Dieter J. Weiss, however, restricts the origins of the bailiwick of Franconia to the southern German area, comprising Franconia, Bavaria and Swabia, within which the Order had founded hospitals in Nuremberg, Donauwörth, Ellingen, Mergentheim, Öttingen, Münnerstadt and Speyer.[4] Reliable evidence concerning the hospitals is, however, only available from the late thirteenth century onwards, even though in the course of the thirteenth century it is possible to identify twenty prebends acquired by the Order in Franconia and the surrounding areas.[5] Elizabeth can be shown to be the hospital patron saint in Nuremberg and the patron of the altar in Donauwörth, Ellingen and Mergentheim. The research of Christian Tenner, Klaus Militzer and Dieter J. Weiss has shown that the origins of the hospitals belonging to the Order in the bailiwick of Franconia, and therefore their patrons, can only be partially determined. The clearest case is that of Nuremberg, where the patronage of St Elizabeth is mentioned in a charter for the hospital in 1277 but, although the houses in Donauwörth, Ellingen and Mergentheim owned several hospitals in the high Middle Ages, their patronage cannot be clearly determined.

In Donauwörth,[6] a central point on the medieval pilgrims' way which came from the south from Augsburg and extended to Denmark, there were long-

---

[2] K. Militzer, *Die Entstehung der Deutschordensballeien im Deutschen Reich* (Marburg, 1981), p. 136; C. Tenner, *Die Ritterordensspitäler im süddeutschen Raum (Ballei Franken). Ein Beitrag zum frühesten Gesundheitswesen*, Ph.D. thesis (Munich, 1969), pp. 52–8.

[3] See map, Militzer, p. 218.

[4] J. Weiss, *Die Geschichte der Deutschordens-Ballei Franken im Mittelalter* (Neustadt and Aisch, 1991), pp. 28–38. The sources for hospitals in the last three places on the list are very meagre.

[5] Ibid., p. 133.

[6] Ibid., pp. 54–6; Tenner, pp. 50–52; Militzer, pp. 111 ff.

standing imperial possessions. On 27 June 1214 Frederick II made a gift of the chapel which lay at the head of the Danube Bridge to the Hospital of the Germans of Jerusalem, placed the chapel and all its possessions under his protection, and obliged all his followers to make gifts to it. There is no evidence as yet of a hospital there;[7] it is not referred to in the sources until the late thirteenth century at which time its capacity was small – for only three beds are mentioned. By the mid-fourteenth century, through gifts from citizens of Donauwörth,[8] ten beds were available for clergymen and five beds for the acutely ill. A hospital patronage is not mentioned for the early years of the *Jakobskapelle* (Jacob's Chapel), but an Elizabeth-patronage occurs in the consecration of the altar in 1343. After the Trinity altar and the altar to the Virgin Mary, in second place in the hierarchy are St George, Mary Magdalene and Elizabeth, and in third place the angels and the other saints. Up to the Reformation, the hospital in Donauwörth remained more a refuge for incurables than a clerical institution.[9]

Around 1180, in Ellingen, north of the town of Weissenburg, there was a hospital which had been donated by Walter and Kunigunde from the family von Ellingen.[10] On 8 September 1216, Frederick II transferred this hospital to the Teutonic Order and placed it under the protection of the ruling king or emperor. This grant engendered a longrunning conflict between the original owner of the hospital, the wealthy canon chapter of Berchtesgaden, in Nordgau, and the Teutonic Order; and the Grand Master, Hermann of Salza, was obliged to obtain a further imperial confirmation. A convent of the Teutonic Order is not in fact mentioned until 1253. Soon after, in 1255, there is explicit reference to a hospital of St Maria of Ellingen,[11] but whether hospital patronage is meant here remains open to conjecture.

Mergentheim, the later centre of the Teutonic Order, achieved its early peak in the high Middle Ages through the Hohenlohe family line. In 1208 the crusader, Albert of Hohenlohe, transferred the parish church in Mergentheim to the Hospitallers. When his nephew, Andreas of Hohenlohe, joined the Teutonic Order in 1219, his lands and possessions in Mergentheim and the surrounding area came into the Order's possession. Two further brothers, Henry and Frederick followed his example, and in 1220 Frederick II confirmed their grants to the Teutonic Order.[12] Henry of Hohenlohe quickly advanced through the Order's ranks; already by 1221 he had become the first commander of Mergentheim. From 1232 he held office as German Master three times, and from 1244 to his death in 1249 he was Grand Master. It seems likely that an

---

[7] Tenner, p. 52.

[8] Weiss, p. 249.

[9] Ibid., pp. 343, 54–6, 312.

[10] Ibid., pp. 57–64.

[11] Ibid., pp. 60, 343: Bayer. Haupstaatsarchiv München, Geistliche Ritterorden, Urkunden (M-RO), 1916, 1372.

[12] Ibid., p. 74.

institution for the care of the old and sick was established by the Order at Mergentheim. In 1246 seven lay brothers are recorded in the house, although there is no documentary evidence to support the claim of a memorial plate on the hospital building that a hospital fund was set up by the German Master, Wolfram of Nellenburg in 1340.[13] As the earliest patron of the house, the knight and saint, Pancras, is mentioned in a letter of indulgence of 1285, and this indulgence was supposed to be obtainable on all the usual feasts, including those of the Virgin Mary and St Elizabeth, as well as on the day of the church's consecration and on that of its patron.[14] Mary, George and Elizabeth are named as further patrons in the late Middle Ages, together with a George brotherhood from 1446.[15] In the late Middle Ages a priest from the Order was responsible as hospital master for the liturgy and pastoral care (1478).[16]

THE ELIZABETH-HOSPITALS IN MARBURG AND NUREMBERG

According to the research of Udo Arnold on the parish patron saints, Elizabeth and George, in the lands held by the Teutonic Order in Prussia,[17] Elizabeth-patronage can only be found in three or four churches there (Königsberg in the bishopric of Samland, Reichenberg in the bishopric of Ermland and Ladenburg, in the bishopric of Pomesain) in the period 1325–42. Even altars were rarely consecrated to her. Parishes dedicated to George, however, occur three times as frequently. The reasons for this seem to lie in the function of George as a knightly and courageous examplar. The Teutonic knights had, since their foundation, remained a hospitaller order, but the ideal of caring servants who carried out their duties in the hospitals was hardly encouraged or needed[18] as an example at a time when the expansion of the state of the Teutonic Order against heathen forces was the paramount consideration.

As countess, simple hospital sister, and later saint, Elizabeth of Thuringia exemplified the caring ideal of the Order through her service to the old, sick, poor and those with wasting diseases. Thuringia and Franconia, Marburg[19] and

---

[13] Tenner, p. 59; Weiss, p. 223.

[14] Weiss, p. 344.

[15] G. Zimmermann, 'Patrozinienwahl und Frömmigkeitswandel im Mittelalter, dargestellt an Beispielen aus dem alten Bistum Würzburg', *Würzburger Diözesangeschichtesblätter*, 21 (1959), p. 49, n. 67.

[16] Weiss, p. 331: Staatsarchiv Ludwigsburg, B 250, Urkunden no. 156; Schönhuth, Urkunden, Hospital, pp. 351–4.

[17] Arnold, 'Elisabeth und Georg', particularly pp. 177 ff.

[18] Ibid., particularly p. 183; K. Guth, 'Hochmittelalterlicher Humanismus als Lebensform. Ein Beitrag zum Standesethos des westeuropäischen Weltklerus nach Johann von Salisbury', in *The World of John of Salisbury*, ed. M. Wilks (Oxford, 1984), pp. 63–76.

[19] W. Moritz, 'Das Hospital der heiligen Elisabeth in seinem Verhältnis zum Hospitalwesen des früheren 13. Jahrhunderts', in *Sankt Elisabeth. Fürstin Dienerin, Heilige. Aufsätze, Dokumentation, Katalog* (Sigmaringen, 1981), pp. 101–16; Militzer, pp. 94–100.

Bamberg/Nuremberg[20] were regions to which the countess was closely connected through her marriage, relatives and, later, banishment. After her exile from Wartburg, near Eisenach, her uncle, Bishop Eckbert of Bamberg (from the family of Andechs-Meranier), attempted to arrange for her remarriage, but Elizabeth already had other plans for her life. Inspired by the example of St Francis, she served the sick as a religious nurse in the hospital she had founded at Marburg until her death in 1231, aged twenty-four. After her death, the relatives of her husband, Count Louis IV of Thuringia, who had died on Frederick II's crusade to the Holy Land in 1227, handed over the hospital, which was part of the widow's inheritance, to the Teutonic Order (1234).[21] Count Conrad IV, Elizabeth's brother-in-law, achieved her canonization in 1235 before entering the Teutonic Order himself. Elizabeth's own exemplary charitable work in Marburg, her burial place in the hospital church there, and her patronage as countess promoted her celebration as the hospital-saint thereafter.

The example of Marburg in adopting the patronage of St Elizabeth was followed by the Teutonic Order in Nuremberg which had rapidly become an important base for the Order in the bailiwick of Franconia. As early as 1209 King Otto IV had granted the *Jakobskirche* with all its goods and, in 1216, Frederick II had conceded the *Burgkapelle*. King Henry VII and many German nobles added to the patrimony with generous donations.[22] By 1236 at the latest the Order had established a hospital there with its own custodian, independent of the commander. Witnesses of a gift of property to the Order in Horbach, near Langenzenn, include the priest brothers Bernolf, the commander Arnold, the custodian of the hospital, Conrad and the cellarer, Hermann.[23] The charter speaks of a Conrad *provisor hospitalis*, although at this time there is no record of a patron.

Gifts, purchases by the Order and letters of indulgence expanded the landed power of the prebend of Nuremberg in the following years. 'Up to the end of the thirteenth century, the Order was able to secure at least twelve indulgences for the Nuremberg settlement, mostly from bishops who were passing through.'[24] In one of these letters, the earliest reference occurs to the patronage of the hospital: *ut pauperes domus hospitalis sancte Elizabeth in Nurenberch nostris elemosinis*

---

[20] A. Wendenhorst, *Das Bistum Bamberg*, 2, *Die Pfarreiorganisation* (Berlin, 1966), p. 345; O. Reber, *Die heilige Elisabeth – Leben und Legende* (St Ottilien, 1982).

[21] H. Boockmann, *Der Deutsche Orden. Zwölf Kapitel aus seiner Geschichte* (Munich, 1981), pp. 46–65; M. Werner, 'Die heilige Elisabeth und die Anfänge des Deutschen Ordens in Marburg', in *Marburger Geschichte*, ed. E. Dettmering and R. Grenz (Marburg, 1980), pp. 121–66.

[22] Weiss, pp. 33 ff.; Tenner, pp. 105 ff., Militzer, pp. 116–37.

[23] Staatsarchiv Nürnberg, Repertorium, 59, no. 131, fol. 145 (*c.* 1236); Nürnberger Urkundenbuch (NUB), 284, p. 168.

[24] Weiss, p. 35.

et impendiis adiuventur, ut illis ad sustentacionem.[25] This letter of 18 August 1262 refers to the great number of poor inhabitants of the hospital. A later letter from of 1274 [26] complains of the meagre means available for the sustenance of the numerous sick people in the city. Up to the founding of the *Heilig-Geist-Spital* (Holy Spirit Hospital) by Conrad Gross in 1339[27] the Elizabeth-hospital, situated in front of the city walls about two km from the castle, next to special houses for lepers, remained the only hospital in Nuremberg.[28]

In the long term, it could only maintain its function as a hospital for the city population by means of gifts from rich families, and by buying land and collecting gifts with the help of 'messengers' of the hospital. Originally, the land owned by the Teutonic Order and its hospital lay outside the Nuremberg walls in front of the West Gate to the southern part of the city – the so-called Lorenzer city, named after the Lorenz church, south of the River Pegnitz. The value of this land increased as the city expanded.

However, the erection of a second, larger wall to protect the city's wealth and industry in front of the gates of the first ring, enclosed the prebend, the hospital of the Teutonic Order and its area of fertile land and pasture in the area in front of the city. Following the erection of the *Spittler Tor* (Hospital Gate) in 1356, about 250 m west of the Order's hospital, conflict between the imperial city and the settlement of the Teutonic Order became inevitable. Claims for religious immunity on lands owned by the Order, the contributions of the citizens there to the Order, the city's jurisdiction over the inhabitants and demands for contributions to the building of the city wall ensured there would be friction. Hartmut Boockmann[29] has calculated that, in this period, the Teutonic Order held the rights to 368 sites in the city as well as the land belonging to the hospital. Thus, in *c.* 1400, approximately 1,472 people in Nuremberg had financial obligations to the Order. With around 20,000 inhabitants in Nuremberg at this time, this in itself was sufficient reason for conflict in the eyes of the city fathers. However, the sale of all rights to land in the city in 1419 ended the immunities which were the cause of the trouble. Half of the sum of 9,231 guilders which was realized by this sale flowed into Prussia which, under Grand Master Michael Küchenmeister, had been in a state of financial need since the first Thorn peace.[30] After this time, up to the Reformation, the Elizabeth-hospital in Nuremberg changed from a hospital for the poor, the sick and those with wasting diseases to an institution caring

[25] Tenner, p. 107. Source in: M-RO, 3472; NUB, 396, p. 241.

[26] M-RO, 3462; NUB, 502, p. 309.

[27] U. Knefelkamp, *Das Heilig-Geist-Spital in Nürnberg vom 14.–17. Jahrhundert* (Nuremberg, 1989).

[28] H. Boockmann, 'Der Deutsch Orden in Nürnberg', in *Die Rolle des Ritterordens in der mittelalterlichen Kultur*, ed. Z.H. Nowak (Toruń, 1985), pp. 89–104, particularly pp. 92–9.

[29] Ibid, particularly pp. 97–9.

[30] Boockmann, *Der Deutsche Orden. Zwölf kapitel aus seiner Geschichte*, pp. 192 ff.

for the younger sons of noble families.[31] Since the fourteenth century other institutions had been available for the city population.[32]

In the thirteenth century the Elizabeth-hospital was the only hospital in the city, closely connected, through donations, with the rich families of the city and its surrounding area.[33] At the same time, the bishops responsible for jurisdiction – Arnold, Count of Solms, Bishop of Bamberg (1286–1296) and Leopold I of Gründlach (1296–1303) – confirmed the position of the Teutonic Order in their dioceses (1287, 1289).[34] The fresco cycle depicting the legend of St Elizabeth of Thuringia in the chancel on the north side of the Teutonic Order's church of St Jacob in Nuremberg, which is dated around 1330–40, seems to confirm the introduction of the saint from Thuringia approximately 100 years after her death.[35] The Order, the city and the Emperor Louis the Bavarian (1294–1347) were all involved with this building, which, as its statues show, strongly reflects noble piety.[36] Is it chance that the fresco cycle of Elizabeth's life was completed just at the time when Nuremberg received a new hospital, donated by a patrician (Conrad Gross), under a new patron? The new Holy Spirit Hospital in Nuremberg took over the function of the city hospital from the Teutonic Order, leaving the Order's hospital largely to the lesser German nobility.

In the German Empire, however, the examples of Marburg[37] and Nuremberg led numerous towns and cities to introduce the patronage of Elizabeth for subsequent hospital foundations.[38] Siegfried Reicke's research into the hospitals of the Middle Ages[39] has shown that there were fifteen Elizabeth-hospitals outside Hesse, while a further eight hospitals possessing the patronage of Elizabeth are known to have existed in the Middle Ages, although, of course, this does not cover all Elizabeth-hospitals in the German Empire. In Franconia, in particular, the memory of Elizabeth remains alive even today.[40] Pictorial

[31] H. Boockmann, *Johannes Falkenberg, der Deutsche Orden und die polnische Politik* (Göttingen, 1975), p. 89, n. 157.

[32] K. Guth, 'Spitäler in Bamberg und Nürnberg als bürgerliche Sozialeinrichtungen der mittelalterlichen Stadt', *Jahrbuch für fränkische Landesforschung*, 38, (1978), pp. 39–53.

[33] Cf. Salbuch der Deutschordenskommende Nürnberg, 1343; Staatsarchiv Nürnberg, Reichsstadt Nürnberg, Salbücher 134; Salbuch des Elisabethspitals 1394–1397, Nürnberg, Stadtarchiv, D 11, esp. no. 1.

[34] Weiss, p. 35; NUB, 743, pp. 433 ff.; NUB, 942, pp. 564

[35] *800 Jahre Deutscher Orden. Austellung des Germanisches Nationalmuseum, Nürnberg, Katalog*, ed. G. Bott and U. Arnold (Gütersloh and Munich, 1990), pp. 533–4.

[36] Ibid., pp. 532 ff.: Three Kings, various apostles, Bartholomew (as patron of the Frankfurter Kaiserwahlkirche and also Saint of the Empire), and finally Jacob.

[37] Moritz, 'Das Hospital', p. 113.

[38] Reber, *Die Gestaltung*; E. Roth, 'Sankt Elisabeth. Leber und Verehrung in Franken' in *Volkskultur in Franken*, 1: *Kult und Kunst*, ed. K. Guth (Bamberg and Würzburg, 1990), pp. 26–40.

[39] S. Reicke, *Das deutsche Spital und sein Recht im Mittelalter*, 2 vols (Stuttgart, 1932, repr. Amsterdam, 1970).

[40] Cf. Wendehorst, *Das Bistum Bamberg*, 2, *Die Pfarreiorganisation (see register: Elisabeth); Bayrische Kunstdenkmale (Kurzinventare)*, ed. M. Petzet and T. Breuer, Bayerischen Landesamt für Denkmalpflege (Munich, 1958 ff.) (see register: Elisabeth); *Die Kunstdenkmäler Bayerns* (Munich, 1895 ff.) (cf. register: Elisabeth).

representations in churches and museums, statues, panels, fountains, hospitals, names and legends commemorate a noble life in the service of the poor and sick – a life which was prematurely ended.

26

The Teutonic Order confronts Mongols and Turks

Jürgen Sarnowsky

When German crusaders joined the siege of Acre after the fall of Jerusalem in 1187, they felt the necessity of caring for their sick and founded (in about 1190) a field hospital near the churchyard of St Nicholas outside the walls of the town. After the conquest of Acre, the hospital acquired a house and a piece of land in the city near the gate of St Nicholas. By then, a small fraternity of brethren had gathered at the hospital which was transformed into a military order in 1198, at the time when the early death of Henry VI and the double election in Germany had caused political problems for the Staufen party.[1]

Little is known about the expansion of the Order up to the beginning of the thirteenth century, but after Hermann of Salza succeeded as Master in 1209–10, his close relationship to the Popes Honorius III and Gregory IX, and especially to Emperor Frederick II, soon opened the way for a rapid development of the youngest of the greater military orders. In 1220, the Order bought the so-called *Seigneurie de Joscelin* in the Holy Land and, within a few years, had begun the construction of its main castle, Montfort.[2] In the Golden Bull of Rimini

---

[1] For an overall history of the Teutonic Order see H. Boockmann, *Der Deutsche Orden. Zwölf Kapitel aus seiner Geschichte*, 2nd edn (Munich, 1982); for its early history see M.-L. Favreau, *Studien zur Frühgeschichte des Deutschen Ordens*, Kieler Historische Studien, 21 (Stuttgart, 1974); U. Arnold, 'Entstehung und Frühzeit des Deutschen Ordens', in *Die geistlichen Ritterorden Europas*, ed. J. Fleckenstein and M. Hellmann, Vorträge und Forschungen, 26 (Sigmaringen, 1980), pp. 81–107; H. Kluger, *Hochmeister Hermann von Salza und Kaiser Friedrich II*, Quellen und Studien zur Geschichte des Deutschen Ordens, 37 (Marburg, 1987). I wish to thank Mrs Cornelia Oefelein and Miss Claudia Rosenhan, Berlin, for correcting the first English version of this paper. The faults that remain are mine.

[2] Cf. Kluger, pp. 48–9; H.E. Mayer, 'Die Seigneurie de Joscelin und der Deutsche Orden', in *Die geistlichen Ritterorden Europas*, pp. 171–216; W. Hubatsch, *Montfort und die Bildung des Deutschordensstaats im Heiligen Lande* (Göttingen, 1966); K. Forstreuter, *Der Deutsche Orden am Mittelmeer*, Quellen und Studien zur Geschichte des Deutschen Ordens 2 (Bonn, 1967), esp. pp. 41–9.

From *The Military Orders: Fighting for the Faith and Caring for the Sick*, ed. Malcolm Barber. Copyright © 1994 by Malcolm Barber. Published by Variorum, Ashgate Publishing Ltd, Gower House, Croft Road, Aldershot, Hampshire, GU11 3HR, Great Britain.

of 1226, Frederick II granted the Order the rights of a prince of the Empire for the territories to be conquered from the heathen Prussians. Hermann of Salza had received a call for help from Conrad, Duke of Mazovia, and after 1230 the Order became increasingly involved in the crusading activities in the Baltic.[3] In 1237, after it was united with the Swordbrothers, it acquired Livonia.[4] After the fall of Montfort in 1271 and of Acre in 1291 the Order concentrated on the Baltic, where its principal opponents were the pagan Lithuanians. In the battles against them, the Order received help from crusaders from all over Christian Europe.[5]

Thus the Teutonic Order had its main battlefields in the Holy Land and the Baltic, but throughout its medieval history it was also involved in plans and combined efforts for the defence of Christianity against Mongols and Turks. This paper aims to give a short survey of this part of the Order's activities, from its alleged participation in the battle of Liegnitz (Legnica) in 1241 to the failure of its employment against Mongols and Turks in the fifteenth century.

THE TEUTONIC ORDER AND THE MONGOL THREAT

It was not until the 1220s that Christian Europe learned of the threat of an attack by the Mongols.[6] In 1237 they began with a campaign in the West and, after conquering and destroying Kiev in 1240, they turned towards Hungary and Poland. In March 1241 one of the Mongol armies burned down Cracow and marched into Silesia, where they met resistance from Duke Henry II. He and his nobility were defeated in the battle of Liegnitz on 9 April 1241.[7] According to later traditions, a contingent of the Teutonic Order participated in these conflicts, headed by the Prussian Master, or even Grand Master Poppo of Osterna

---

[3] Cf. Boockmann, pp. 70–93; M. Biskup and G. Labuda, *Dzieje Zakonu Krzyzackiego w Prusach*, 2nd edn (Gdańsk, 1986), pp. 96–133; B. Schumacher, *Geschichte Ost- und Westpreussens*, 6th edn (Würzburg, 1977), pp. 31–3.

[4] For them see F. Benninghoven, *Der Orden der Schwertbrüder, Fratres Milicie Christi de Livonia*, Ostmitteleuropa in Vergangenheit und Gegenwart, 9 (Cologne and Graz, 1965).

[5] Cf. W. Paravicini, *Die Preussenreisen des europäischen Adels*, 1, Beihefte der Francia, 17/1 (Sigmaringen, 1989), with further literature.

[6] For early knowledge of the expansion of the Mongols cf. *Der Mongolensturm, Berichte von Augenzeugen und Zeitgenossen, 1235–1250*, ed. H. Göckenjan and J.R. Sweeney, Ungarns Geschichtsschreiber, 3 (Graz-Vienna-Cologne, 1985), pp. 28–38 (from the introduction). For European knowledge of and attitudes towards the Mongols see J. Fried, 'Auf der Suche nach der Wirklichkeit. Die Mongolen und die europäische Erfahrungswissenschaft im 13. Jahrhundert', *Historische Zeitschrift*, **243** (1986), pp. 287–332.

[7] For extracts from the sources for the Mongol campaign in Poland and Hungary see: *Schlesisches Urkundenbuch*, 2, 1231–1250, ed. W. Irgang (Vienna-Cologne-Graz, 1977), nos. 198, 202, 204, 206, 208, 211–22, pp. 125–34; for the battle of Liegnitz: *Vita sanctae Hedwigis ducissae Silesiae*, ed. A. Semkowicz, *Monumenta Poloniae Historica -Pomniki Dziejowe Polski*, 4 (Lwów, 1884, repr. Warsaw, 1961), pp. 501–655, here pp. 559–70; *Scriptores rerum Silesiacarum oder Sammlung schlesischer Geschichtsschreiber*, ed. G.A. Stenzel, 1 (Breslau (Wrocław), 1835), pp. 106–8 (*Chronica*

who is said to have been killed and buried together with Duke Henry.[8] However, Poppo became Prussian Master in 1244 and Grand Master in about 1253,[9] and contemporary sources do not mention the Order's participation.[10] On the other hand, we do know of Templars who possibly died in the battle,[11] and so it is also possible that members of the Teutonic Order formed part of Duke Henry's army, although only a few could have been there in time.[12]

Setting aside the problem of its support for Silesia, the Order played an important role in the papal plans for the defence of Christianity against the Mongols.[13] In November 1247 the Franciscan John of Pian Carpini returned from his missions to the Russian princes and to the Mongol Khan, bringing with him the information that the Mongols again planned to attack the West, Hungary, Poland, Prussia and Livonia. In January 1248, Pope Innocent IV renewed contact with the most important Russian princes, Daniel of Halic and Alexander Nevsky of Susdal, and asked them to inform the Order of the approach of the Mongol armies.[14] As early as late November 1247 the pope

---

Principum Poloniae); *SRP*, **3**, p. 59 (*Annalista Thorunensis*). For the events of 1241 see L. Petry, *1241. Schlesien und der Mongolensturm* (Breslau (Wrocław), 1938); J. Matuszewski, *Relacja Długosza o najeździe tatarskim w 1241 roku* (The Report of Długosz on the Tartar Invasion in 1241) (Lódz, 1980); *Wahlstatt 1241, Beiträge zur Mongolenschlacht bei Liegnitz und zu ihren Nachwirkungen*, ed. U. Schmilewski, Beiträge zur Liegnitzer Geschichte, 21 (Würzburg, 1991).

[8] Johannis Dlugossi, *Annales seu Cronicae incliti Regni Poloniae*, lib. 7–8 (Warsaw, 1975), p. 25; *SRP*, **3**, p. 390 (list of masters in Johannes de Posilge); ibid., **4**, pp. 367–70 (*Danziger Ordenschronik*), closely related to the narration in the Life of St Hedwig in German in: *Vita sanctae Hedwigis*, pp. 569–70. All sources date from the later fifteenth century or the first half of the sixteenth century.

[9] K.H. Lampe, 'von Osterna, Poppo' *Altpreussische Biographie*, **2**, ed. C. Krollmann, K. Forstreuter and F. Gause (Marburg, 1967), p. 485.

[10] See the remarks of J. Voigt, *Geschichte Preussens von den ältesten Zeiten bis zum Untergange der Herrschaft des Deutschen Ordens*, 9 vols (Königsberg, 1827–1839, repr. Hildesheim, 1968), **2**, pp. 414–15 and 660–65; cf. H. Patze, Der Frieden von Christburg vom Jahre 1249', *Jahrbuch für die Geschichte Mittel- und Ostdeutschlands*, 7 (1958), 39–91, here p. 77, n. 152. Lampe, 'Poppo', on the contrary, does not exclude Poppo's participation, while it is wrongly described as a fact e.g. in *Geschichte Schlesiens*, **1**, 5th edn, ed. L. Petry, J.J. Menzel and W. Irgang (Sigmaringen, 1988), pp. 108–10. For the latest treatment of the problem see T. Jasinski, 'Zur Frage der Teilnahme des Deutschen Ordens an der Schlacht von Wahlstatt', in *Wahlstatt 1241*, pp. 117–27, who is very careful in assessing the likelihood of the Order's participation.

[11] See the letter wrongly dated 1236 incorporated in the continuation of the *Historia Regum Francorum*, ed. O. Holder-Egger, *MGH SS*, 26 (Hanover, 1882, repr. Stuttgart and New York, 1964), pp. 604–5. According to the letter, six brothers, three knights, two sergeants and 500 men were killed in the battle; three brothers escaped. The authenticity of this letter has recently been doubted.

[12] The later reports on the participation of the Order seem to rest on local traditions. Cf. Voigt, *Geschichte Preussens*, **2**, p. 664; *SRP*, **3**, p. 390, n. 3. Duke Henry received help from Bohemia, so that members of the Order may have come from the houses in Bohemia, e.g. from Troppau, which had been confirmed to the Order by Innocent III as early as in 1204 (for the early history of the bailiwick of Bohemia see K. Militzer, *Die Entstehung der Deutschordensballeien im Deutschen Reich*, Quellen und Studien zur Geschichte des Deutschen Ordens, 16, 2nd edn (Marburg, 1981), pp. 57–63).

[13] Cf. Patze especially pp. 84–9.

[14] *Preussisches Urkundenbuch*, ed. R. Philippi, A. Seraphim, M. Hein, E. Maschke, H. Koeppen

had sent a new mediator to establish peace between the Order and the rebellious Prussians who had risen against Christianization.[15] It seems that he intended to use the Order as his military force in the East and, for that, it was necessary for its war with the Prussians to come to an end. This was achieved in 1249, in the treaty of Christburg (Dzierzgoń), but the Order escaped the impending battles against the Mongols when two of their Grand Khans died in 1248 and 1251 respectively.[16] In 1254, when the Mongols invaded Hungary again, Innocent anticipated an attack on the Order's territories and ordered the preaching of the Cross in Prussia and Livonia.[17] The plan for a crusade against the Mongols was renewed in 1258, after they had invaded Poland. In July, the new pope, Alexander IV, instructed the Mendicants, whom he had commissioned to preach, not to neglect the preaching for the crusades in Prussia and Livonia, especially since the Teutonic Order itself was preparing defensive measures against the enemies.[18] Throughout 1259 the threat of an attack by the Mongols continued and, in December, the pope advised the Order to cooperate with its Christian neighbours.[19] This seems to have included even the Orthodox Russians, for in January 1260 Alexander took under papal protection all territories that the Order had received, or would receive, as a donation from the Russians or, upon success, might conquer from the Mongols, provided that it received the consent of the former Christian proprietors.[20] Perhaps, by organizing the defence against the Mongols, the pope intended to unite the Russians with the Roman Church, planning that the Order should play a leading role in this scheme.

By March 1260 the preparations for a crusade against the Mongols had obviously become even more concrete. The crusaders who had gathered in Prussia were instructed to follow the advice of the brethren of the Teutonic Order because of their experience in the fight against the pagans. The Prussian Master, Hartmann of Grumbach, was made captain and principal leader

---

and K. Conrad, 1–6 (Königsberg and Marburg, 1882–1986), 1, no. 204, p. 142. For the Prussian relations with the Russian princes see K. Forstreuter, *Preussen und Russland von den Anfägen des Deutschen Ordens bis zu Peter dem Grossen*, Göttinger Bausteine zur Geschichtswissenschaft 23 (Göttingen, 1955), pp. 24–6; idem, 'Der Deutsche Orden und Südosteuropa', *Kyrios-Vierteljahrsschrift für Kirchen-und Geistesgeschichte Osteuropas*, 1, (1936), pp. 245–72, here p. 257.

[15] Schumacher, p. 40; Biskup and Labuda, pp. 143–7; Boockmann, pp. 97–8.

[16] Patze, pp. 86–7.

[17] *Preussisches Urkundenbuch*, 1, no. 289, pp. 216–17: letter of the pope to the clergy in Prussia and Livonia.

[18] ... *Predicti fratres hospitalis euisdem (tanquam) veri Christi pugiles animam suam pro impugnatione Tartarorum ipsorum oportuno loco et tempore affectu promptissimo et corde imperrito ponere sint parati*, *Preussisches Urkundenbuch*, 1, 2, no. 61, pp. 55–6; cf. Patze, p. 87; Voigt, 3, pp. 150–51. The first instruction for the Mendicants in *Preussisches Urkundenbuch*, 1, 2, no. 59, pp. 51–3.

[19] *Preussisches Urkundenbuch*, 1, 2, no. 82, pp. 73–4.

[20] Ibid., no. 89, pp. 80–81, cf. Voigt, 3, p. 163; Forstreuter, *Preussen*, p. 27; idem, 'Orden-Südosteuropa', 257.

(*capitaneus et dux principalis*) of the crusading army, which might have been encamped at the southern borders of the Order's territories.[21] But it seems that the army was not large enough to sustain more than defensive operations and, in September 1260, the pope had to admonish King Ottokar of Bohemia and the Margrave of Brandenburg not to hinder the Mendicants and the priests of the Teutonic Order when preaching the Cross for the crusade in Prussia and Livonia.[22] At the same time, when Alexander also appealed to the German archbishops not to neglect the crusade in Prussia and Livonia,[23] tension was growing between the Order and the newly converted Prussians. Soon the Prussians initiated their second rebellion, even more intense than the first in the 1240s.[24] This outbreak forced the pope to redirect the crusaders, who had come to fight the Mongols, against the rebellious Prussians.[25]

This seems to have been the end of the papal plans. Time and again the danger of an attack by the Mongols recurred, as in 1286, when, according to the report of the *Annalista Thorunensis*, the Order evacuated four castles in the south of its territory because it had received news of the approach of a Mongol army.[26] But by the beginning of the fourteenth century the Order's main opponents were the heathen Lithuanians, who succeeded in establishing their rule over large territories south-east of Prussia.[27] It was only after their Christianization and the marriage of their Grand Duke Jagiełło with the heiress of Poland in 1386, that the Order again participated in battles against the Mongols.

The Order was now surrounded by the union of Poland and Lithuania. It tried to maintain its position by denying the success of the Christianization of Lithuania or, alternatively, by separating King Władisław Jagiełło of Poland and the Lithuanian Grand Duke Witold (Vytautas).[28] It was part of the latter

---

[21] *Preussisches Urkundenbuch*, **1, 2**, nos 98–9, pp. 84–6, also cited by Patze, p. 88. For the possibility of the protection of the southern borders of Prussia by the crusaders see Voigt, 3, p. 167. Those operations are probably the basis of the remarks of the bishop of Padua who stated in 1263 that the brothers *nuper Tartaros sunt invasi*, *Preussisches Urkundenbuch*, **1,2**, no. 207, p. 160.

[22] *Preussisches Urkundenbuch*, **1, 2**, nos 111–12, pp. 101–2. The pope forbade the king of Bohemia to come to Prussia or Livonia without the Order's prior consent. For possible reasons see Patze, p. 87, Voigt, 3, p. 171; he also repeated his statement on the readiness of the Order to fight the Mongols.

[23] *Preussisches Urkundenbuch*, **1, 2**, 113, pp. 102–3, cf. Voigt, 3, p. 171.

[24] For the second rebellion see Boockmann, pp. 100–1; Biskup and Labuda, pp. 180–85, Schumacher, pp. 42–3. It was probably caused by a defeat the Order suffered by the Lithuanians.

[25] *Preussisches Urkundenbuch*, **1, 2**, no. 134, p. 111, cf. Voigt, 3, pp. 174–5.

[26] *Anno 1286 Culmeze. Schoneze, Grudentz, Reden derelicte sunt ad preceptum dominorum, quia Tartari venire dicebantur*, *SRP*, 3, p. 62 (*Annalista Thorunensis*). In 1340, the Prussian bishops again reported the danger of an attack by the Mongols, see *Preussisches Urkundenbuch*, 3, no. 345, pp. 240–41.

[27] For the expansion of Lithuania especially under Gedimin, Olgerd and Kynstute, see M. Hellmann, *Gründzuge der Geschichte Litauens und des litauischen Volkes*, Grundzüge, 5 (Darmstadt, 1976), pp. 20–32; for the conflict with the Lithuanians, cf. Boockmann, pp. 151–69.

[28] Boockmann, pp. 172–4.

strategy when, in October 1398, the Order made peace with Witold.[29] The grand duke wanted to turn towards the territories of the Golden Horde in the south and south-east, and probably received a promise of help from the Order; indeed, it seems that, even before this, the Order had despatched small forces to help Witold in his campaigns, and it is possible that in 1398 sixty men fought against the Mongols under Eberhard of Wallenfels, former adjutant (Kompan) of the Grand Master.[30]

Now, having concluded the compact, the way was open for official support by the Order. When Witold prepared for a large-scale campaign against the Mongols, the Order sent the commander of Ragnit, Marquard of Salzbach, with some knights and more than 300 men[31] who came from different parts of Prussia.[32] The commander received 425 marks in Bohemian money as financial aid.[33] The Polish contingent was four times larger than that of the Order, but Witold was also supported by Orthodox Christians and by Mongol dissidents, so that the army also consisted of schismatics and pagans. Even so, Pope Boniface IX thought it necessary to issue a crusade encyclical.[34] The campaign failed completely. The army moved into an area near one of the tributaries of the Dnjepr, the Vorskla. When Witold withdrew his troops from a Mongolian fortification, they followed and defeated the Christian army in a bloody slaughter. Witold and his brother narrowly escaped, as did Marquard of Salzbach, but many Lithuanians, Poles and Prussians died, and with them nine Teutonic Knights.[35]

---

[29] The treaty of Sallinwerder (12 October, 1398) gave Samogitia to the Order, defined the border lines between Prussia and Lithuania and the spheres of influence; see the German text of Witold's charter in *Die Staatsverträge des Deutschen Ordens in Preussen im 15. Jahrhundert*, ed. E. Weise, **1**, 1398–1437 (Königsberg, 1939, repr. Marburg, 1970), pp. 9–12.

[30] *SRP*, 5, p. 226 (a fragment of 1412–13 preserved in the chronicle of Paul Pole). The employment of Prussian contingents in 1398 is confirmed by Johannes von Posilge, *SRP*, 3, p. 222. For the career of Eberhard of Wallenfels cf. G.A. von Mülverstedt, 'Die Beamten und Conventsmitglieder in den Verwaltungs-Districten des Deutschen Ordens innerhalb des Regierungsbezirks Marienwerder', *Zeitschrift des Historischen Vereins für den Regierungsbezirk Marienwerder*, 8 (1883), pp. 1–48, here p. 33.

[31] According to Johannes von Posilge, the Order sent *hundert glenyen* (*SRP*, 3, p. 230) or *Spiesse* which probably meant groups of three to four men armed with crossbows (see *Das Soldbuch des Deutschen Ordens 1410/11*, ed. S. Ekdahl, Veröffentlichungen aus den Archiven Preussischer Kulturbesitz, 23/I (Cologne and Vienna, 1988), pp. 19 and 26, n. 12; Voigt, 6, p. 168, on the contrary, thought that there was a contingent of five hundred men; the fragment of 1412–13, *SRP*, 5, p. 226, speaks of 1,600 horses and many good men, which makes it possible that the Order's contingent was even larger.

[32] When, in 1400, money was paid for the losses of the defeat at the Vorskla, it went to people in the area of Danzig (Gdańsk), Königsberg, Elbing (Elbląg), Balga, Brandenburg, Christburg (Dzierzgoń) and Osterode (Ostróda), see *Das Marienburger Tresslerbuch der Jahre 1399–1409*, ed. E. Joachim (Königsberg, 1896, repr. Bremerhaven, 1973), pp. 69, 75 and 79.

[33] Ibid., p. 34.

[34] Cf. Hellmann, p. 41; Boockmann, p. 175.

[35] See the accounts of Johann von Posilge, the *Annalista Thorunensis* and the continuation of Detmar *SRP*, 3, pp. 229–31.

This marked the end of the Order's cooperation with the Lithuanians in driving back the Mongols, although it supported Witold again between 1406 and 1409 in his campaigns against the principalities of Pskow and Moscow.[36] On the whole, the Order was not very successful in its combats against the Mongols.

THE TEUTONIC ORDER AND THE TURKS

A lack of success also holds true for the plans to employ the Teutonic Order in the defence of Christianity against the Turks. The only area in which the Order itself was threatened by the rise of Ottoman power was Greece. Since 1209, following the establishment of the Latin Empire of Constantinople, it had had some possessions in the west and south of the Peloponnese.[37] The Order's houses in Greece formed the bailiwick of Romania under a provincial commander who had his residence in Mosteniza in the mountains in the north of the Peloponnese. When the Order's headquarters had been moved to Prussia, these convents became even more remote. After its defeat at Tannenberg (Grunwald) in 1410 it tried to sell the bailiwick to Venice, but the Republic was apparently not interested.[38] Although the Order participated in the payment of a tribute to the Turks between 1397 and 1402, the prime enemies there were the Byzantines of Mistra who conquered the north-west of the Peloponnese between 1422 and 1432. In these conflicts the Order's principal convent in Mostenitsa and other possessions were lost. Only the house in the Venetian Modon (Methone) in the south remained in the hands of the Order until 1500, when the city was taken by the Turks. But even before 1432 the Order's position in Greece was too weak to offer any effective resistance against the Turkish advance.[39]

It was in the context of criticism of the Order's policies that plans were developed for its transfer to the borders of Christendom to fight against Mongols and Turks. The first proposal to shift the Order's base to the south or south-east was made by the Lithuanians in 1358. When Emperor Charles IV appealed to them to convert to Christianity, they demanded that the Order should be transferred to their deserted border areas and that they then take over the larger parts of the Order's territories in Prussia and Livonia.[40] Similar

---

[36] Forstreuter, *Preussen*, pp. 46–7; cf. *SRP*, 3, pp. 282–3 (continuation of Johann von Posilge, for 1406).

[37] See Forstreuter, *Orden-Mittelmeer*, pp. 71–86; idem, 'Orden-Südosteuropa', 247–55.

[38] See the report of the Order's official at the papal court, Peter of Wormditt, in *Die Berichte der Generalprokuratoren des Deutschen Ordens an der Kurie*, 1–4, 2, ed. K. Forstreuter and H. Koeppen, Veröffentlichungen der Niedersächsischen Archivverwaltung, 12, 13, 21, 29, 32, 37 (Göttingen, 1961–1976), 2, no. 61, pp. 125–6; cf. Forstreuter, *Orden-Mittelmeer*, p. 79.

[39] See Forstreuter, *Orden-Mittelmeer*, pp. 75–6, 81–2 and 238–9, for the internal developments in the bailiwick.

[40] The letter of Charles in *Preussisches Urkundenbuch*, 5, no. 642, pp. 361–2; the demands of the Lithuanians are related by Hermann von Wartberge, *SRP*, 2, pp. 79–80. Cf. Forstreuter, 'Orden-Südosteuropa', pp. 258–9; H. Grundmann, 'Das Schreiben Kaiser Karls IV. an die heidnischen Litauer-Fürsten 1358', *Folia Diplomatica*, 1, ed. S. Dušková, (Brno, 1971), pp. 89–103, here especially pp. 96–9.

plans were developed after the Order's defeat against Poland and Lithuania. For example, in February 1414, the Polish ambassadors to the Council of Constance proposed that the brethren should follow the original aims of the Order and turn against Mongols and Turks, and, in October 1418, one of the officials of the Order informed the Grand Master that the Polish king, Władisław Jagiełło, had begun secret negotiations with Denmark concerning the Order's transfer to an area near to the king of Cyprus and the Master of the Hospitallers on Rhodes.[41] Obviously, the Order's enemies were planning to deprive it of its base in Prussia and the Order was unable to rise to the challenge. This led to repeated criticism which culminated in 1455, after the beginning of the Thirteen Years' War, when the Polish king, Kasimierz IV, accused the Order of having hindered the Poles from fighting the Turks and other pagans by attacking them.[42]

It was far more difficult for the Order to evade the appeals to defend Christianity when they emanated from its allies. Since 1426, Sigismund, King of Hungary and King of the Romans, had repeatedly considered inviting the Order into Hungary (as in 1397).[43] After some delays caused by Turkish attacks and negotiations in which Sigismund made various promises concerning the New Mark (the eastern part of Brandenburg which the Order held in pawn), the Grand Master, Paul of Rusdorf, finally agreed to send out a contingent of six brothers under Nicholas of Redwitz, who had been with the king for some time. The members of the Order were probably accompanied by Prussian craftsmen, civilians and military.[44] The main task of this small group was to organize the

[41] Jagiełło and the king of Denmark discussed the possibility '*das sie den orden zcu Prussen welden uffnemen unde welden in seczen bii den koning von Cypern unde by den meister von Roddys ...*': *Berichte der Generalprokuratoren*, **2**, no. 300, p. 576 n. 5, partly edits the document in *Regesta Historico-diplomatica Ordinis S. Mariae Theutonicorum 1198–1525*, ed. E. Joachim and W. Hubatsch, **1**, 1–3, **2** and index (Göttingen, 1948–1973), here **1**, 1, no. 2807, p. 176; letter of Sander von Machwitz, *Vogt* of the New Mark, to the Grand Master, of 2 October, 1418; cf. Forstreuter, *Orden-Mittelmeer*, p. 221; idem, *Preussen*, p. 37, n. 19; K.H. Lampe, 'Die europäische Bedeutung des Deutschen Ordens', *Blätter für deutsche Landesgeschichte*, **88** (1951), pp. 110–49, here. p. 118.

[42] During negotiations with officials of the Order he is reported to have said that the brethren *haben aber in 200 iaren und doboben weynigk gefochten und gestreten widder dy uncristen. Sunder wor dy crone von Polen widder dy Turken unde uncristen gestreten haben, so haben dy creuzciger sy vorhyndert, und in dy lant zcu Polen gezcogen mit unrechte, sy vorbrant und vorheret und groslich geschwechet ... SRP*, **4**, p. 439 (*Danziger Chronik vom Bunde*).

[43] See the instruction of the Commander of Rheden, Count Rudolf of Kyburg, for his mission to Hungary which concerns also the restitution of the *Worczlant* (*Burzenland*) and the gift of other territories, in *Codex diplomaticus Prussicus, Urkunden-Sammlung zur älteren Geschichte Preussens*, ed. J. Voigt, **4–6** (1853–61, repr. Osnabrück, 1965), **6**, no. xlix, p. 53; cf. E. Joachim, 'König Sigmund und der Deutsche Ritterorden in Ungarn 1429–1432', *Mitteilungen des Instituts für Österreichische Geschichtsforschung*, **33** (1912), pp. 87–119, here pp. 88–9.

[44] Joachim, p. 98; Forstreuter, *Orden-Mittelmeer*, p. 222; Lampe, 'Bedeutung', p. 119. For their supply of money see the letter to the officials of the Order in Prussia in *Acten der Ständetage Preussens unter der Herrschaft des Deutschen Ordens*, ed. M. Toeppen, **1** (Leipzig, 1878, repr. Aalen, 1973), no. 389, pp. 516–18; for the brethren see the document described in *Regesta Historico-Diplomatica*, **1**, 1, no. 5096, p. 318.

defence of the border region at the Danube, close to the 'Iron Gate', since the Order had contributed to the colonization and defence of south-east Hungary 200 years previously.[45] In July 1429 they reached Bratislava, in October Buda. Finally they came to the territories around Severin (Szörényvár), with which they had been endowed by Sigismund.[46] In May 1430 the Order's official at the papal court was informed that the Order was well established in Hungary.[47] But soon many problems arose and, by March 1432, the situation had greatly deteriorated. According to a report, Nicolas of Redwitz and the other members of the Order wrote to the Grand Master, stating that they had virtually no income and had been prevented by the Hungarian nobility from fortifying their castles. When attacked by the Turks they had received no help from the Hungarians.[48] The stability of the peace which Sigismund had established with the Turks in 1429 was the most important condition for the success of the whole enterprise, but in the summer of 1432 the Turks devastated Vallachia and southern Hungary. During this campaign nearly all the Order's castles were lost and many of its men must have died. The remainder were able to maintain the Order's position in three castles, under very poor conditions, until 1434, at which time the Grand Master finally decided to withdraw his halfhearted support.[49] The Order's difficult situation in Prussia and its inability to organize the supplies for a contingent of brethren far away from its territories contributed to the failure of this plan to employ it for the defence of Christendom against the Turks.

After 1466, when the Order had lost two-thirds of its Prussian territories to Poland, it was too weak to initiate attacks on any pagan enemies on its own. However, because it was now obliged to perform military service for the Polish kings, it was involved in the Polish campaigns against the Turks. In 1485, the Turks devastated Vallachia again, and when Kasimierz IV summoned his

---

[45] Cf. Boockmann, pp. 68–9; H. Zimmermann, 'Der Deutsche Ritterorden in Siebenbürgen', in Fleckenstein and Hellmann, *Die geistlichen Ritterorden Europas*, pp. 267–98.

[46] Sigismund informed the Grand Master on 30 July, 1429 that the brethren had arrived in Bratislava, and on 9 October Nicolaus von Redwitz wrote from Hungary, *Regesta Historico-Diplomatica*, 1, 1, nos. 5148 and 5197, pp. 322 and 325. For the endowment (and first problems) see Joachim, pp. 99–101 and 108–13 (documents on the castles and incomes received by the Order and on the costs for the defence of the castles).

[47] See the letter to the Procurator in Rome, dated 26 May, 1430, in *Berichte der Generalprokuratoren*, 4, 1, no. 131, pp. 174–6: ... *Dominus Claus Redevicz semper est cum rege et bene stat et omnes alii domini de ordine sunt potentes, et dedit eis adhuc unum novum dominium magnum cum multis vilis, silvis, pratis, terris et aquis et muneribus, et sunt in magna gracia regis* ...; cf. Joachim, p. 101. About this time Nicholas of Redwitz even hoped to establish a friendly relationship with the Turkish 'emperor' because he asked the Grand Master for dogs to be sent to him: cf. his letter of 14 May, 1430, partly edited in *Liv-, Est- und Curländisches Urkundenbuch*, 8, ed. H. Hildebrand, (Riga and Moscow, 1884, repr. Aalen, 1974), no. 208, pp. 124–5.

[48] The letter is edited in Joachim, pp. 116–18; cf. *Regesta Historico-Diplomatica*, 1, 1, no. 5999, p. 373.

[49] See Joachim, pp. 103–5 and 118–19 (letter of the Master Paul of Rusdorf to Nicholas of Redwitz, 2 January, 1434). For the reasons for the failure of the enterprise, cf. Forstreuter, *Orden-Mittelmeer*, p. 222.

army, Grand Master Martin Truchseß of Wetzhausen came in person, together
with 500 men. But, according to a chronicle from Danzig (Gdańsk), the Order's
contingent was too small to offer any substantial help, and the king sent them
back.[50] Twelve years later, in 1497, King John Albert compelled Grand Master
Hans of Tiefen to participate in another campaign against the Turks. The
depressing journey of the ageing master is described in his secretary's diary.[51]
The Order's contingent consisted of about 1,500 men with horses and their
attendants – altogether about 4,000 men. The Grand Master was accompanied
by several of the Order's officials and other men from Prussia. They started
on 1 June and crossed through Poland until they reached Lemberg (Lwów)
by the end of August. By then the Grand Master had fallen seriously ill, and
he died on 25 August. Some of the Order's officials decided to bring his body
back to Prussia, so that their participation in the campaign came to an end even
before it had really started; but many of their men subsequently died in John
Albert's defeat by the Turks.[52] Although plans for the Order's participation
in the defence of Christianity continued even after the Reformation and the
loss of Prussia and Livonia,[53] this was the last of the Order's larger medieval
operations against the pagans.

   Thus, when, in one of the late medieval death-dance scenes, a brother of the
Teutonic Order turns to Death saying that he had fought Turks and pagans
but had been defeated only by death,[54] this is, at best, only part of the truth.
It was not against Mongols and Turks that the Order played its most important
role, although the series of events which have been presented here show that
it never completely lost the original idea which was fundamental to its foundation.

[50] *SRP*, **4**, pp. 687–8 (*Danziger Chronik vom Pfaffenkriege*), where the Polish army is estimated
at 600,000 men (!).
   [51] Liborius Naker's *Tagebuch* in *SRP*, **5**, pp. 289–314; for the events cf. ibid., **4**, pp. 445 (continuation of the *Danziger Chronik vom Bunde)* and 689 *(Danziger Chronik vom Pfaffenkriege)*; also
Forstreuter, *Orden-Mittelmeer*, p. 223; idem, 'Orden-Südosteuropa', p. 261.
   [52] For the journey back see again the diary, *SRP*, **5**, pp. 312–13; for the Prussians who died in
the campaign see ibid., p. 314, also **5**, p. 498 (*Bernt Stegmann's Hanseatische Chronik*).
   [53] Forstreuter, 'Orden-Südosteuropa', pp. 261–6. For the Grand Master Maximilian of Austria
(1585/90–1618), who was a leading figure in the Habsburg campaigns against the Turks, see
H. Noflatscher, *Glaube, Reich und Dynastie. Maximilian der Deutschmeister (1558–1618)*, Quellen und
Studien zur Geschichte des Deutschen Ordens, **11** (Marburg, 1987).
   [54] *Mit Türcken und heyden han ich gestritten, von unglöubig vil erlitten, aber mit keinem sterckeren han
ich grungen, der mich alls der tod hab betzwungen*, *SRP*, **2**, p. 178, from a death-dance scene on a wall
in the house of the Dominicans in Berne, Switzerland, now lost.

27

The Treatment of Prisoners of War during the Fighting between the Teutonic Order and Lithuania

Sven Ekdahl

The last of the Baltic crusades – a subject about which noteworthy books have been written by Eric Christiansen,[1] William Urban[2] and Norman Housley[3] – was the conflict between the Teutonic Order in Prussia–Livonia and Lithuania. It lasted over a century, until the heathens converted in 1387. In his chronicle, Peter of Dusburg entitled one chapter, which concerns developments in 1283 on the occasion of the suppression of the final important uprising of the oppressed native Prussians, 'Here the Prussian war ends and the war against the Lithuanians begins' (*Explicit bellum Prussie, incipit bellum Lethowinorum*).[4] Thenceforth, the Teutonic Order was only able to fulfil the mission, 'Fighting for the Faith', that had been bestowed upon it by the pope and the emperor, by means of war with its eastern neighbour, Lithuania.

However, the Order failed to accomplish its aim of conquering and Christianizing Lithuania. On the contrary, it was the Lithuanians who were eventually victorious at the end of this long and bitterly fought military campaign. After the adoption of the Christian faith by Grand Prince Jogaila (later King Jagiełło of Poland) and the union with the kingdom of Poland (1385–86),[5] the Polish and Lithuanian armies succeeded in subduing the might of the Teutonic

[1] E. Christiansen, *The Northern Crusades. The Baltic and the Catholic Frontier 1100–1525* (London and Basingstoke, 1980).

[2] W. Urban, *The Baltic Crusade* (DeKalb, Ill., 1975, 2nd edn, Chicago, 1994); idem, *The Prussian Crusade* (Lanham, 1980); *The Livonian Crusade* (Washington, 1981); *The Samogitian Crusade* (Chicago, 1989).

[3] N. Housley, *The Later Crusades, 1274–1580. From Lyons to Alcazar* (Oxford, 1992), pp. 322–75.

[4] *SRP*, **1**, p. 146.

[5] *La cristianizzazione della Lituania. Atti del colloquio internazionale di storia ecclesiastica in occasione del VI centenario della Lituania cristiana (1387–1987)*, ed. P. Rabikauskas. Pontificio comitato di scienze storiche, Atti e documenti, **2** (Città del Vaticano, 1989). Cf. S.C. Rowell, *Lithuania Ascending. A Pagan Empire within East-Central Europe, 1295–1345* (Cambridge, 1994).

Order in the famous battle at Tannenberg/Grunwald/Žalgiris in 1410.[6] After
a second victory against the Order in 1422, the border between Prussia and
Lithuania was fixed and was to remain thus until 1919. Consequently, the
expansion of the Teutonic Knights stagnated, and its decline became a foregone
conclusion. Its Prussian history ends in 1525, the history of its Livonian branch
terminating in 1561. In the *Reich*, however, the Order continued to exist.

Notwithstanding the fact that, towards the end of the fourteenth century,
both emperors and popes had forbidden the Order to wage war against the then
Christianized Lithuania, the Grand Masters continued their military efforts
unabated, albeit now without the massive support previously rendered by
crusaders from central and western Europe. This shows how closely the Order
had identified itself with its military mission and how sensitively it would react
to anything that might jeopardize the legitimacy of its existence. There was
now talk of a transfer of the Order to alternative theatres of war within
Christendom.

During the many years of my research into the history of the Teutonic Order
in Prussia, I have become convinced that topics relating to the
crusades–mission–settlement theme need to be reappraised and examined in
the context of a comparison with similar phenomena in the Spanish *Reconquista*
and other crusades. In previous research each case was, more or less, observed
and examined in isolation; it is my view that a comprehensive synthesis of these
complex events is lacking.

It is my aim to present a concise summary of my ideas. The settlement of
Prussia by the Teutonic Order may be likened to a forward-moving 'frontier'.
New tracts of land were gradually conquered, protected by fortresses and
were cultivated by the remaining native population, as well by incoming
settlers from the West. In order to maintain its power and to establish a
territorial state – an objective the Teutonic Order doubtlessly strove to realise
– the demand for human labour was very great. This was also the case after
the campaign against Lithuania had begun and enemy invasions had caused
severe devastation and gaps in their own population. As long as the fighting
was commissioned by the pope and emperor against heathens, military support
from the ranks of central and western European nobility was assured, as
Werner Paravicini has pointed out in his excellent work on the Prussian
campaigns of European nobility.[7] The campaigners in Prussia brought large

---

[6] S. Ekdahl, *Die Schlacht bei Tannenberg 1410. Quellenkritische Untersuchungen. Bd. 1: Einführung
und Quellenlage*, Berliner Historische Studien, **8** (Berlin, 1982). As for the captured banners of the
Teutonic Order, see S. Ekdahl, *Die 'Banderia Prutenorum' des Jan Długosz – eine Quelle zur Schlacht
bei Tannenberg 1410*, Abhandlungen der Akademie der Wissenschaften in Göttingen, Philologisch-
Historische Klasse, Dritte Folge **104** (Göttingen, 1976); Lithuanian edn, S. Ekdahl, *Jono Dlugošo
'Prūsų vėliavos' Žalgirio mūšio šaltinis* (Vilnius, 1992).

[7] W. Paravicini, *Die Preussenreisen des europäischen Adels*, 1. Beihefte der Francia, **17/1** (Sigmaringen,
1989) (vols 2 and 3 are in progress).

amounts of money into the country and stimulated the economy, especially in the large centres such as Danzig and Königsberg.

The military campaigns against Lithuania, generally referred to in the German literature as the *Litauerreisen*, were not, in principle, very different from the usual method of waging wars in the Europe of that time: the strategy was generally that of rapid devastation with the aim of weakening the enemy and then returning home with the booty, hopefully unharmed. However, there were two deviations from the strategies that were practised in central and western Europe: firstly, the extreme severity and brutality employed by both sides, which had been the rule of the day even before the arrival of the Teutonic Order in the whole of the Baltic area, as has been demonstrated impressively by Astaf von Transehe;[8] secondly, the custom of enslaving prisoners of war if captives were taken. The Order was seen to be on the side of justice, but only as long as it was fighting heathens. According to the schoolmen and canonists it was permissible to enslave heathens but not Christians. Thomas Aquinas wrote, 'Christians may keep non-Christian slaves [*infideles*], whether they be Jews, heathens or Saracens'.[9]

There is no doubt that, on each side – among the Teutonic Order as much as the Lithuanians – human beings were considered the most important and valuable 'booty' from military ventures. Strangely enough, little significance has so far been attached to this aspect of the history of the Teutonic Order, even in otherwise remarkable analyses such as that of Henryk Łowmianski.[10] A good exception is an article by Friedrich Benninghoven, where reference is made not only to various material goods, horses and cattle, but also to captives.[11] In fact, the chronicles abound with details about military campaigns on both sides where hundreds or thousands of people were abducted to Prussia, Livonia or Lithuania.[12] Those who were captured by the Lithuanians could expect, according to the chroniclers of the Order, 'permanent slavery' (*ewige Sklaverei*) abroad: by contrast, there is very little mention of the fate of Lithuanians or Russians abducted to Prussia or Livonia. It is our aim here to shed some light on this grey area.

Firstly, however, it should be demonstrated that captives were not always taken. Occasionally, one reads that each and every enemy was killed, male and female, young and old. This was most likely the practice in circumstances where a lack of time or other complications made it impossible to take captives. If

---

[8] A. von Transehe, 'Die Eingeborenen Alt-Livlands im 13. Jahrhundert', *Baltische Monatsschrift*, **43** (1896), pp. 219–43, 289–315, 347–75.

[9] *Summa theologica*, **II**, II q. 10 art. 9,3.

[10] H. Łowmiański, 'Agresja zakonu krzyżackiego na Litwę w wiekach XII–XV', *Przegląd Historyczny*, **45** (1954), pp. 338–71.

[11] F. Benninghoven 'Zur Technik spätmittelalterlicher Feldzüge im Ostbaltikum', *Zeitschrift für Ostforschung*, **19**, (1970), pp. 631–51.

[12] See *SRP*, **1–3**.

problems were encountered on the journey home, such as very deep snow in winter, the captives, who were loaded on to sledges, were run through by the sword (*durch das Schwert laufen*), as the killing of captives was frequently paraphrased. In most cases, however, it was sufficient to kill the men and abduct only women and children as valuable booty. The men were killed as a safety precaution against insurgence in captivity.

Devoid of any sentimentality, the Austrian heraldic poet, Peter Suchenwirt, depicts the details of such human abduction during the Prussian campaign of Duke Albert III of Austria in the year 1377:

> Women and children were taken captive;
> What a jolly medley could be seen:
> Many a woman could be seen,
> Two children tied to her body,
> One behind and one in front;
> On a horse without spurs
> Barefoot had they ridden here,
> The heathens were made to suffer:
> Many were captured and in every case,
> Were their hands tied together
> They were led off, all tied up –
> Just like hunting dogs.[13]

I believe that the majority of these countless thousands of captives were put into slavery in Prussia, in cities and fortresses as well as on the estates and farmsteads of the Order and the rural nobility. They were thus capable of fulfilling a multitude of needs, especially in agriculture, where there was always a very high demand for human labour. Tilling the soil, sowing, harvesting and threshing were some of their duties as well as herding, feeding and milking cattle and also operating the hand mill.

The sources back up my second assertion to an even greater degree, namely that Lithuanian prisoners of war, in this case including males, were settled in Prussia to fill the gaps in the native population. This would have been most likely after the mid-fourteenth century, when the influx of settlers from the West had declined due to the plague and other reasons. The *Litauerreisen* were now undertaken with greater intensity to compensate for the population deficit and to promote colonization despite difficulties. For security reasons it was easier to exercise control more efficiently in several smaller settlements in the interior of the country, rather than in larger, closed settlements. Thus in 1382 the commander of Balga spent the princely sum of 4,000 marks on the settlement of prisoners of war.[14] On the occasion of the handing over of the commandery of Ragnit to a new *Komtur*, in 1392, there were thirty-five captives

---

[13] *SRP*, 2, p. 166.

[14] *Das grosse Ämterbuch des deutschen Ordens*, ed. W. Ziesemer (Danzig, 1921), p. 150.

in the fortress;[15] in 1396 there were seventy-three.[16] Periodically, mention is made of the Order purchasing a wife for a settler;[17] in such cases the settler need not, of course, have been a prisoner of war.

In the Order's official inventory books 'iron' is often listed in connection with prisoners of war, although no details could be found about its intended use.[18] I think it means some sort of handcuffs or fetters. In the fortress of Ragnit in 1416 there were '6 hantgefengnisse' in the saddle-house and '26 ysen czu gefengnisse' in the forge.[19] It does, however, seem apparent that chains listed under warfare equipment were intended for prisoners of war. Such a chain existed in 1440 for twenty-three captives in the fortress of Preussisch-Holland: *Item eyne kethe czu gefangenen czu 23 mannen'*.[20]

Reference is occasionally made to the sale of Lithuanian captives. This can be deduced from a statement made by the Grand Master in 1325,[21] and it is given open expression in a letter of the Master of Livonia in 1411.[22] The advocate (*Vogt*) of Rossitten in Livonia is said to have profited from the sale of captive Lithuanians to the Russians.[23] During his Prussian campaign in 1390, the earl of Derby bought captive Lithuanian princes and then apparently took them back to England.[24] Other sources report on how the crusaders brought back captives to western Europe.[25]

Early evidence for the payment of ransom money for captives dates from the year 1369;[26] in later times it became more common, on both sides, for captives to be bought freely. Similarly, captives were exchanged, if some prior agreement had been reached. It was quite common, after significant peace treaties, such as Sallinwerder in 1398 and Thorn in 1411 (after the battle at Tannenberg), to discuss the issue of prisoners of war in lengthy negotiations and finally arrive at satisfactory solutions.[27] The latter phenomena will not be dealt with in detail here since they are well known in other parts of Europe.

---

[15] Ibid., p. 261.

[16] Ibid., p. 263.

[17] *Das Marienburger Tresslerbuch der Jahre 1399–1409*, ed. E. Joachim (Königsberg, 1896; repr. Bremerhaven, 1973), pp. 317–18.

[18] *Das grosse Ämterbuch*, pp. 30, 32, 35, 41, 43, 173, 222, 266, 274, 280, 284.

[19] Ibid., p. 274.

[20] Ibid.,p. 98; also see p. 157.

[21] *Preussisches Urkundenbuch*, 2 (1309–35), ed. M. Hein and E. Maschke (Königsberg, 1932–39), no. 536.

[22] *Liv-. Esth- und Curländisches Urkundenbuch nebst Regesten*, ed. F.G. von Bunge, 4 (Reval, 1859), no. 1872.

[23] L. Weber, *Preussen vor 500 Jahren in cultur-historischer, statistischer und militairischer Beziehung nebst Special-Geographie* (Danzig, 1878), p. 637. See also the books by Christiansen, Urban and Housley cited in note 1 above.

[24] *SRP*, 2, pp. 642, 791–3.

[25] *SRP*, 2, pp. 107, 741; *SRP*, 3, p. 598.

[26] *SRP*, 2, p. 95. Cf. *SRP*, 3, p. 610, n. 5.

[27] As for the ransom of the prisoners from the 'Great War' of 1409–11 by the Teutonic Order, see M. Pelech, 'W sprawie okupu za jeńców krzyżackich z Wielkiej Wojny (1409–1411)', *Zapiski Historyczne*, 52, (1987), pp. 131–52, 327–44.

To avoid creating an unbalanced picture, I would like to re-emphasize that the Lithuanians behaved no differently from the Teutonic Order. The crusaders captured by them might await death by fire or other forms of martyrdom; for example, they might be sacrificed to the heathen gods.[28] Eric Christiansen's book quotes examples of the Lithuanians selling captive Poles to the Russians.[29] If the captive was not bought freely or exchanged, various forms of slavery would be resorted to. Polish chroniclers, as well as those of the Order, repeatedly tell us how the Lithuanians used their prisoners of war to settle their lands.[30] According to a remark from the year 1420, it was considered a tradition that captives who had already been settled could no longer be made to return to their own lands.[31]

To conclude, it seems important to question the extent to which the Teutonic Order was seriously interested in the Christianization of the Lithuanians, except on its own terms. Its opponents denied any such interest and have strongly maintained instead that the Order's primary objective was oppression through military means.[32] Given that the Order ignored the conversion of the heathens in 1387, there is some substance to this assertion. We have also seen that, according to the laws of Christendom, only Jews, heathens or Saracens could be subjected to slavery and that settlement and colonization in Prussia was partly maintained by means of prisoners of war, especially in the second half of the fourteenth century. These captives who were abducted during repeated *Litauerreisen* were an important prerequisite for the advance of the Christian 'frontier'. When this human reservoir was no longer available, the dynamic of the Order weakened.

The above hypotheses may seem exaggerated, but they should stimulate discussion, not only of the Teutonic Order, but also of the military orders and the crusades in general. For this reason there is a final question that I believe should be considered. That is, how were such affairs managed during the Spanish *Reconquista* and the other crusades? Were the conditions prevalent there not similar? The work of Verlinden,[33] as well as that of several other historians, has informed us of the developments in Spain and the Latin East to a greater degree than in Prussia–Livonia and Lithuania – at least on this particular

---

[28] *SRP*, **2**, pp. 496, 554, 596, 638.

[29] Christiansen, p. 146.

[30] See also Geheimes Staatsarchiv Preussischer Kulturbesitz, Berlin, XX. Hauptabteilung (Historisches Staatsarchiv Königsberg), Ordensbriefarchiv no. 4503 from 1425. The enemies had made prisoners in Prussia '*und furten sy us dem lande und besatczten ir lant domethe*'.

[31] *Codex epistolaris Vitoldi, magni ducis Lithuaniae, 1376–1430*, ed. A. Prochaska. Monumenta medii aevi historica res gestas Poloniae illustrantia, 6 (Cracow, 1882), p. 471.

[32] Cf. M. Hellmann, 'Die Päpste und Litauen', in *La cristianizzazione della Lituania*, p. 60.

[33] C. Verlinden, *L'esclavage dans l'Europe médiévale*, **1**, *Péninsule Ibérique-France*; **2**, *Italie, Colonies italiennes du Levant, Levant Latin, Empire Byzantin*, Rijksuniversiteit te Gent. Werken uitg, door de Faculteit van de Letteren en Wijsbegeerte, **119**, **162** (Bruges and Ghent, 1955, 1977).

issue. In fact, Acre was Holy Land's largest slave market at the time of the crusades. With so many questions remaining unanswered, I believe that this phenomenon warrants comprehensive international research.[34]

---

[34] Cf. Ekdahl, *Die Schlacht bei Tannenberg*, p. 5 n. 16. Some of these problems will be dealt with in the second volume of W. Paravicini's book *Die Preussenreisen des europäischen Adels*.

28

The Recruitment of Brethren for the Teutonic Order in Livonia, 1237–1562

Klaus Militzer

Although, throughout its history, the Teutonic Order received both non-Germans and non-nobles, from its beginnings it was dominated by the lower aristocracy or gentry.[1] Despite the fact that the Rule of the Order, which dates from the mid-thirteenth century, places no restrictions on recruitment, at the beginning of the fourteenth century (or perhaps even a few years earlier) the Grand Master Dietrich of Altenburg demanded, for the first time, that candidates for reception should be of noble birth, although he did admit exceptions. Subsequently, during the fourteenth and fifteenth centuries, the Teutonic Order made the recruitment of non-noblemen more difficult and, by the end of the fifteenth century, was demanding proof of four noble ancestors.[2] These rules applied to the entire Order and were accordingly followed by the masters of Livonia in the reception of brethren for their branch of the Teutonic Order.

Apart from the knights – the most important group in the Order – there were also ordained priests and the so-called *Graumäntler* – sergeants who wore grey coats, and who performed subordinate functions. Priests lived as brothers in the Livonian branch of the Order, and were often of burgher origin. In the fourteenth and fifteenth centuries some of them were born in Prussia and even in Livonia. A priest brother could not become master or commander of a house, or even vice-commander, either in Livonia or in Prussia, although he could, however, become a commander of a house in the German Empire.[3] We know little about the recruitment of the *Graumäntler*. Some may have been

---

[1] H. Boockmann, *Der Deutsche Orden. Zwölf Kapitel aus seiner Geschichte* (Munich, 1981), pp. 58–65.

[2] K. Militzer, 'Die Aufnahme von Ritterbrüdern in den Deutschen Orden. Ausbildungsstand und Aufnahmevoraustsetzung', *Das Kriegswesen der Ritterorden im Mittelalter. Ordines militares, Colloquia Torunensia Historica*, 6, (1991), pp. 7–10.

[3] R. Wenskus, 'Das Ordensland Preussen als Territorialstaat des 14. Jahrhunderts', *Der deutsche Territorialstaat im 14. Jahrhundert I, Vorträge und Forschungen*, 13 (1970), p. 370.

sons of German-speaking families in Livonia or Prussia or may have been drawn from indigenous tribes,[4] but our knowledge of this subject is insufficient and this paper will therefore focus upon the knight brothers.

It is possible to distinguish four principal periods in the recruitment of the knight brothers.[5] The first period extended from the incorporation of the Order of the Swordbrothers – the predecessor of the Teutonic Order in Livonia – into the Teutonic Order on 12 May 1237 until 1309. The Order of the Swordbrothers had originally been founded by the Cistercian monk Theoderic (later abbot of Dünamünde) and, since 1207, had acted as the military arm of the bishop and archbishop of Riga. During this time it had developed independently and had built up its own power and territory in Livonia and Estonia. However, in the battle at the Saule on 22 September 1236, the Order had suffered a rout by a Lithuanian army in which about fifty knight brothers, amongst them the Master Volkwin, were killed. Since the Order had only between 120 and 180 knights at that time, the loss of between 28 and 42 per cent (perhaps a third of the knights) weakened it to such an extent that its whole position in Livonia and the Baltic was threatened. Its incorporation into the Teutonic Order guaranteed the survival of the remaining Swordbrothers and saved their position in the Baltic world – although the pope laid down certain conditions before incorporation was allowed. These conditions were contained in the Treaty of Stensby on 7 June 1238, under which the Teutonic Order ceded Harrien and Wierland to the Danish king, so that the northern part of Estonia, including the important town of Reval which had been held by the Swordbrothers, was returned to Denmark.

The loss of northern Estonia provoked the surviving Swordbrothers to rebellion. Hermann Balk, the first Master of Livonia, who had negotiated the treaty, was forced to resign and left Livonia. Moreover, the Teutonic Order had not only to face the opposition of the former Swordbrothers, the incorporation also led to a strained relationship with the archbishop of Riga and his suffragans as well. According to the Order's mission and ethos it had to struggle against the pagans – that is, against the Lithuanians – and also against schismatics and heretics – that is, against the orthodox principalities of Polock and Novgorod, including Pskow. The war against the Orthodox principalities was waged with the same brutality as against the pagans. The problems which caused the failure of the Swordbrothers remained unresolved and were aggravated by internal conflicts. Therefore, during this period, the Teutonic Order first had to consolidate its government in Livonia.[6]

---

[4] B. Jähnig, 'Verwaltung und Personal des Deutschen Ordens in Preussen, insbesondere an Danziger Beispielen', *Deutsche Ostkunde*, **35** (1989), pp. 88–9.

[5] The following statements are a summary of my detailed research in L. Fenske and K. Militzer, 'Ritterbrüder im livländischen Zweig des Deutschen Ordens', *Quellen und Studien zur baltischen Geschichte*, **12** (1993), especially pp. 11–70.

[6] F. Benninghoven, 'Der Orden der Schwertbrüder', *Ostmitteleuropa in Vergangenheit und Gegenwart*, **9** (1965), *passim*.

In the first period, between 1237 and 1309, about 200 knight brothers were living in the castles in Livonia each year, and therefore we can assume that the Livonian branch of the Order may have had a membership of between 1,200 and 1,400 knight brothers. However, we only know the names of 215 of them and can identify just 85, which means that we can assign only 6–7 per cent of the knight brothers of this period to a particular family or to a region in which he was probably born. Nearly all the persons we can identify were masters, marshals or commanders in Livonia; mere knight brothers without functions are mostly unknown. Sometimes we do know their forenames but, in nearly all cases, brethren with forenames, but without any other characteristics, cannot be securely identified. Although this is a small database, it does permit some conclusions to be drawn. Three masters of Livonia came from southern Germany, namely Franconia and the archbishopric of Salzburg. Two masters and seven commanders and four knight brothers originated in the low plains of northern Germany. These thirteen comprise 15 per cent of all identified brothers. Only a few brothers came from the Rhineland – some from the areas north of Cologne, towards the Netherlands and Belgium, but more from the Middle Rhine, from Hesse and territories near to southern Germany. The proportion of Westphalians, who made up less than 20 per cent of the identified brothers, was relatively small, and for this period we know of no knight brother coming from the County of Mark, the heart of Westphalia, although later on, sons of families from this county dominated the Teutonic Order in Livonia. The proportion of masters from families from middle and eastern Germany – that is, from territories around the Harz mountains, from Thuringia and territories along the coast of the Baltic Sea east of the Elbe – was conspicuously high.

Later on the proportion of recruits from the territories mentioned above who joined the Livonian branch of the Order fell markedly. The first brother from Westphalia, later the principal region of recruitment, to become Master of Livonia was Henry of Dincklage (1295–1296), who, although born in the bishopric of Münster, grew up in a region on the borders of Westphalia and not at its core. The majority of the first masters, vice-masters, marshals and commanders of the first period came from Thuringia, Saxony, Hesse or south Germany, precisely those regions in which the Order already held territories, had founded commanderies and had recruited brothers. Therefore, after the incorporation of the Swordbrothers, the Teutonic Order filled the leading positions with brothers from bailiwicks in the German Empire, from Prussia or even from Palestine, rather than use surviving Swordbrothers, most of whom came from different regions. Nor did they recruit from the local population, for during this period there is only one known native, a Livonian called Ykemele, and he did not become a commander but remained a simple brother. Although other natives may have been recruited, we do not have any more information and, even if they did exist, none became a commander, let alone marshal or master. The offices were reserved for Germans, most of whom were aristocrats. In this first period, however, few of the high functionaries, the masters and the marshals, remained in Livonia for long. Most of them came from the bailiwicks in the German Empire, Prussia or Palestine, stayed for a few years in Livonia as master, marshal or commander and then returned. This pattern was also evident in the Order's other branches in Prussia, Palestine, and even in the bailiwicks in the German Empire during the thirteenth century.[7]

In the second period, the so-called golden age of the Teutonic Order (1310–1410), the structure of the Livonian branch changed. Westphalians now comprised 36 per cent of all identified brethren, more than double the level of the former period; brothers from the Rhineland reached 28 per cent, also double the level of the former period; Saxons and brothers from territories along the coast of the Baltic Sea maintained the same proportions; while brothers from south Germany and Thuringia virtually disappeared. In this period we can identify a Scandinavian brother, Otto, a son of the Danish king, and a brother from a German-speaking noble family which had settled in Livonia. Although in comparison with the first period, the proportion of identifiable brothers diminished, we can nevertheless see that the Livonian branch of the Teutonic Order had now found a regional basis for recruitment. This basis was Westphalia, together with the Rhineland and the contiguous territories in the north and east. Forty per cent of all commanders, marshals and masters now originated in this region, and a master from the County of Mark is identifiable for the first time, Goswin of Herreke, born in Opherdicke near Unna or Dortmund, and Master between 1341 and 1359. Although the Westphalian brethren produced most of the identified commanders, they did not produce most of the masters, who were more commonly Rhinelanders.

Despite the wars with the neighbouring territories and the disputes with the archbishop of Riga, his suffragans and the town of Riga, this second period also saw the consolidation of the Order's government in Livonia, with masters holding office for much longer periods. Now it became usual for a Master of Livonia to be elected or appointed by the Grand Master for life and not just for a few years as in the past. He did not resign after a short term of office, and it was no longer usual for commanders from the bailiwicks in the German Empire, or from Prussia, to be sent to Livonia to take up offices for short terms. If a member of a family in Low Germany decided to enter the Livonian branch of the Teutonic Order, he remained a brother of this branch until death, unless unusual circumstances forced a rotation.[8]

In the third period, from the battle of Tannenberg in 1410 until the death of the Master, Walter of Plettenberg, in 1535, the Westphalians consolidated their dominance of the Livonian branch. They now comprised more than half

---

[7] Fenske and Militzer, pp. 32–4.

[8] Ibid., pp. 35–7.

of all identified brethren, and sometimes more than 60 per cent. The number of Rhinelanders reached 30 per cent. In contrast, families settled along the coast of the Baltic Sea sent only a few recruits to Livonia, while the number of Saxons was reduced, with few holding office. An exception is the Thuringian, Henry of Notleben, who became marshal and for a time was the candidate for master of a faction inside the Order, the so-called Rhenish party, which was supported by the Grand Master in Prussia, but was eventually defeated by the Westphalian majority. It is possible, too, in this period to identify thirteen brothers from Livonia itself, although these were sons of German-speaking noblemen settled in Livonia and were often affiliated to Westphalian noble families. At this time, also, some brothers from southern Germany belonged to the Livonian branch only in a limited sense, in that most of them were transferred by the Grand Master for disciplinary reasons, could not obtain important offices in Livonia, and often left the country after a few years.

A protocol of visitation, initiated by the Grand Master, survives for the year 1451. In this protocol the visitors recorded the castles in which the brethren lived, together with comments about their origins. There are a few omissions, but the gaps do not affect the conclusions which can be drawn. According to the protocol the Westphalians accounted for more than 60 per cent of all known brethren, while the Rhinelanders and Hessians made up just over 30 per cent. Saxons and families from territories along the Baltic Sea were not represented. The Westphalians accounted for more than two-thirds of all officials – that is, of commanders and so-called advocats of the same rank. Among the Westphalians 48 per cent came from families originating in the Mark, a figure which rose to 56.3 per cent among Westphalian commanders and advocats.

The third period is therefore characterized by the dominance of the Westphalians, who occupied most of the offices and provided most of the masters. In this the Livonian branch differed from the Prussian branch, where most of the officials were derived from Thuringia, southern Germany and the Rhineland. The efforts of some Grand Masters, such as Paul of Rusdorf, to strengthen their influence in Livonia with the help of Rhenish brothers and their partisans, were doomed to failure because of this built-in Westphalian majority, and the politics of these Grand Masters led to unnecessary friction. The struggle among the factions in the Livonian branch ended with victory for the Westphalians, who escaped from the regimentation imposed from Marienburg when the Grand Masters lost the right, established in the mid-fifteenth century, to appoint the master from two candidates proposed by the Westphalian brothers and instead had to appoint the only candidate elected by the Livonian brethren.[9]

---

[9] Ibid., pp. 37–46.

The final period, which extended from 1536 until the end of the Order's government in Livonia in 1562, was characterized by the progressive domination of the Westphalians who now comprised nearly 60 per cent of all identified brothers. The proportion of Rhinelanders reached nearly 40 per cent, while the numbers of brothers from the other regions were negligible. Only two members of Livonian noble families can be identified from 168 knight brothers. The Westphalians raised their proportion of officials to nearly 70 per cent, with the Rhinelanders making up less than 30 per cent. Only one commander came from a noble German-speaking family of Livonia. Among the Westphalians, the brothers from the Mark had now gained a dominant position, making up more than half of all Westphalians and 30 per cent of all identified knight brothers, as well as a third of all officials (advocats, commanders, marshals and masters), while three of the five masters in this period came from the Mark. In short, the Livonian branch of the Teutonic Order was close to becoming an Order of the Mark and its noble families.[10]

Brethren from Low Germany were thus always dominant in the Livonian branch of the Teutonic Order. It is true that in the first period of consolidation knight brothers originating in other regions had had leading positions, but they could not change the regional composition of the brethren. Probably the surviving Swordbrothers – the majority of whom came from Low Germany and who had entered the Teutonic Order in 1237 – maintained their tradition that members of families from Low Germany had to serve in the Order in Livonia. It may be that the German-speaking noble families in Livonia supported the idea because they came from Low Germany too, and often still had relations there.

In the following years the Westphalian brethren pushed out all non-Westphalians, and even the Rhinelanders ended up in second place. Finally, the sons of families from the Mark got the upper hand. Native Livonians could not place their sons in the Order; throughout the entire period we know of only one example. The German-speaking noble families in Livonia were represented by only a few knight brothers despite their relationship with families from Low Germany, and even from Westphalia, which had sent sons into the Order. The brethren and the officials, commanders, marshals and masters remained foreigners, who progressively lost any connection with the noble families in Livonia. The gap between the interests of the settled noble families on the one side and the brethren on the other was one of the causes for the decay of the Order's power in Livonia and its secularization in 1562, parallelling the situation which had developed some generations before in Prussia.

The Teutonic Order had always been a corporation which was dominated by the ministerial nobility deriving from serfdom, and later on by the gentry. In the first period – the time of consolidation until 1309 – only 12 of 75

---

[10] Ibid., pp. 46–9.

identified brothers, or 16 per cent, can be assigned to German dynasts and families of the high nobility. The Livonian branch of the Teutonic Order was dominated at all times by the small propertied gentry or low nobility. Nor did many brothers derive from urban patrician families; in the first period only 12 per cent came from this type of background. Three of 18 identified masters came from dynastic families, only one from a patrician family. Most of the masters in the first period were descended from the low nobility, the so-called ministeriality. In the following periods no member of the high nobility became master, and by the end of the Order's reign in Livonia, this group had even been pushed out of the ranks of commanders. After 1536, in the last period, only one member of a high noble family can be identified. He became vice-commander in Livonia, but failed to become commander, and eventually returned to his native Brabant, where, with the assistance of his relatives, he rose to a be land-commander of the bailiwick of Aldenbiezen.

It is true that the low nobility, the ministeriality, and later on the gentry, dominated the Livonian branch of the Teutonic Order and that the members of this group pushed members of other groups out of the offices, especially out of the important ranks of masters, marshals and commanders. Nevertheless, there is no doubt that the sons of families of the high nobility had better opportunities for promotion than did the members of the lesser nobility or of the urban patriciate. Sons of men belonging to the dynasts and the high nobility held a disproportionate percentage of the leading positions, although from the fourteenth century onwards they could no longer become master. There are differences in the brethren deriving from the gentry too. Members of important families advanced more quickly than did other brethren, while sons of urban patricians had scarcely any chance of becoming commander, especially in the later periods.[11]

When the Order of the Swordbrothers was incorporated into the Teutonic Order, the Grand Master, Hermann of Salza, had given his agent and first Master of Livonia, Hermann Balk, sixty knight brothers to accompany and help him. These brothers were drawn from the bailiwicks in the Empire or from Prussia, and most of them were probably Thuringians, Hessians and Franconians, but this situation was to prove the exception rather than the rule. According to the mid-thirteenth century Rule of the Order, the Grand Master had to receive candidates in a ceremony held during a chapter meeting. However, at the same time, the ritual of reception suggests that other brothers could be authorized by the Grand Masters to receive candidates, who had to take a special oath to the Grand Master. Therefore, from the middle of the thirteenth century or even before, the Livonian masters would themselves have recruited brothers. In the early fifteenth century we have our first information on how this process of recruitment worked in the Livonian branch. In 1411 the land-commander

---

[11] Ibid., pp. 50–60.

of Westphalia recruited thirty-three noblemen for Livonia on the orders of the Livonian Master. The candidates went to Lübeck and from there by ship to Livonia, their passage and the equipment with horses and weapons partially financed by the land-commander, who was never repaid. In 1434 the land-commander of Utrecht recruited knight brothers and sent them to Livonia, and the next year the same land-commander sent knight brothers by ship from Kampen in the Netherlands to Livonia. In addition to these newly recruited candidates, the Grand Master sometimes transferred brothers from Prussia and from the bailiwicks in the Empire for disciplinary reasons, but such brothers remained outsiders in Livonia; most of the brethren in Livonia were received in the German Empire specifically for Livonia.[12] The ideal knight brother, requested in Prussia as well as in Livonia, was a young, healthy and fit nobleman, who, from the fourteenth century, should also originate from a German-speaking noble family. Such recruits – trained to fight and born to rule – accorded with the conceptions of the time and with the ideas of their own class.[13]

---

[12] Ibid., pp. 60–64.
[13] Militzer, 'Aufnahme', pp. 10–13.

29

Hospitality and Chivalry in the Teutonic Order*

Bernhard Demel O.T.

Since its inception in 1190 as a *Deutsche Hospitalbruderschaft*, located beside the harbour at Acre, the history of the Teutonic Order can be seen to have developed in three stages: as a hospital brotherhood from 1190 until 1198–99, formed to care for sick pilgrims and injured crusaders during and after the Third Crusade; as a spiritual order of knighthood of the Roman Church from 1199 to 1929; and, since 1929, as a purely spiritual order, without the chivalrous element, but as a modern association of lay persons and clergy, the *Familiaren* and the *Oblaten*. Throughout these phases hospitality has remained the primary focus of the Order's mission. Even during its period as an order of knighthood, with a membership largely drawn from the aristocracy of the Empire, the brothers continued to maintain their provision of shelter, care and support for the sick and aged, as well as their responsibilities towards their own members and servants. Both aspects of their role – hospitality and chivalry – are examined in this paper.

Extensive research into the Order's history in both eastern and western Europe, and in the Mediterranean, has produced important information about these two components of the Order's mission. Examination of the personal histories of knights and clergy as well as nuns, particularly in the early sixteenth century and in 1837–41 in the Austrian Empire, and for the period since 1918 in the countries which succeeded the Empire (Austria, Italy, the former Yugoslavia and Czechoslovakia), has made it possible to arrive at certain conclusions. These are that the original aim of providing hospitality has always been maintained, from the shelter for pilgrims, the sick, the old, and others

---

* This is a summary of the paper delivered at the conference. The full version appears in *Schriften des Alemannischen Instituts der Universität Freiburg im Breisgau*, 1994, under the title: 'Der Deutsche Orden am Oberrhein, im Elsaß und der Schweiz'.

in need offered in the medieval period down to the modern hospitals and the general and specialized nursing homes operated today. For example, during the 'new age', the electoral Grand Master, Franz Ludwig von Pfalz-Neuburg (1694–1732), ensured that the concept of caring for the old, sick and needy was fully incorporated into new measures and initiatives being taken.

Currently, the Teutonic Order is running only one hospital (in Friesach in Kaernten, Austria) with its own nuns, together with a priest who performs pastoral duties for the sick there. However, the Order, which has sisters and priests specially trained for the purpose, is represented in other hospitals (such as Bad Mergentheim, Germany), while it has its own nursing home at Cologne, as well as an important role in nursing homes initiated by the Order at Regensburg and Nuremberg, and in municipal institutions (for example, at Lana in the south Tyrol).

Part IV

The Spanish Orders

30

Possessions and Incomes of the Order of Calatrava in the Kingdom of León in the Twelfth and Thirteenth Centuries

Carlos de Ayala Martínez

This paper is an attempt to analyse the role and position which the brothers of Calatrava wished to create in the territories of the Galicio–Leonese kingdom. It is not a topic of major importance, but we believe we have filled a gap in the extensive historiography of the Order of Calatrava. There is an ample, up-to-date bibliography on the Order's presence in Castile, and there is no lack of related studies of its activities in Aragon and Valencia. Its limited presence in Navarre and in Portugal is also well known, and there is some scanty information on its activities in the remote Baltic lands bordering Prussia. What has been lacking is a monographic study on the Leonese knights of Calatrava which would complement the work of the late Professor Derek Lomax on *Las milicias cistercienses en el reino de León*.[1]

My original study collected together the different acquisitions of the Order of Calatrava in Leonese territory – mainly *fundiarias* properties and incomes – and analysed their nature and function as far as possible in an attempt to establish their consequent relative worth. However, here we will limit ourselves to one approach: the study of the origin, development and disappearance of the complex and diversified estate of the Order of Calatrava in León. This falls into three clearly distinct periods.

THE FIRST PHASE: *c.* 1170–1217

The first phase begins with the Order's first appearance in the kingdom – probably in about 1170 when it received two Asturian estates – and continues until 1218, when the Order formally relinquished its material presence in Leonese lands. These fifty years saw the unsuccessful attempt by the Calatravan leaders to establish the Order within the Leonese political sphere. Prior to 1218,

---

[1] D.W. Lomax, 'Las milicias cistercienses en el reino de León', *Hispania*, 23 (1963), pp. 29–42.

From *The Military Orders: Fighting for the Faith and Caring for the Sick*, ed. Malcolm Barber. Copyright © 1994 by Malcolm Barber. Published by Variorum, Ashgate Publishing Ltd, Gower House, Croft Road, Aldershot, Hampshire, GU11 3HR, Great Britain.

it acquired a total of three certain *villas* or villages[2] and five probable ones,[3] in addition to an unknown royal possession and some estates,[4] several groups of houses,[5] at least three churches[6] and a castle.[7] It seems, however, that this firm resolve, which stemmed from the Order's initially powerful vocation,[8] soon weakened, anticipating its resounding failure in the middle term. We do not know exactly which properties, apart from the castle and *villa* of Alcántara, passed to the Order of the *Pereiro* in 1218, but from the more or less direct information available to us, little more than 50 per cent of the initial possessions of Calatrava existed beyond the date of the transfer, or at least they do not appear to be documented under the new Alcántaran jurisdiction.

There are other indicators of the insignificance of the Order's base in León. It is evident, for example, that the economic potential of the Order's possessions was quite limited, since, of the Order's twelve acquisitions for which we have information on the original source of the possession, only five came from the monarchy. This is an unusually low proportion for the development phase of a military order: royal endowments obviously tend to be more significant than those from individuals.

---

[2] These were: the *villa* of Pinos, in the Leonese mountains, D. Lomax, pp. 38–9; the *villa* of Alcántara conceded to the Order of Calatrava immediately before the 'refounding' of Alcántara, L. Martin Martin, *Documentación medieval de la Iglesia Catedral de Coria* (Salamanca, 1989), pp. 37–8 and Aldeanueva de Campomojado, *BC*, p. 450.

[3] They are probably *Cougeli* and *Frigerum* in Galicia, Caso in Asturias, the Pereiro, and Valde-sandinas with their houses, *BC*, pp. 23, 33, 44.

[4] The *realengo* of Nava included certain estates: Castromilanos, Tejeros and Valdelobón; *Bullarium Ordinis Militiae de Alcantara*, ed. I.J. Ortega y Cotes, J. Fernández de Brizuela and P. de Ortega Zuñiga y Aranda (Madrid, 1759) (hereafter *BA*), pp. 5–6. The Order's first two Asturian possessions are designated as estates situated in the *villas* of Santa Marina and Villaverde: AHN, OO.MM, Calatrava, carp. 455, no. 14; *BC*, p. 10. The estate of Valle, *BA*, pp. 9–10, had a distinct population centre which, with inhabitants and farms, had been associated with the repopulation of Mansilla, according to its charter granted by Ferdinand II in 1181, two years before Valle was integrated into the Order, J. Rodríguez, *Los Fueros del Reino de León*, 2 (León, 1981), p. 131. Less important were the estate of Penedo in Orense, and the Villa de Elgon, both objects of an exchange which the Order of Calatrava confirmed with the bishop of Orense in 1215, *BA*, p. 19.

[5] From very early on the Order had associated houses with vineyards and orchards, together with land for repopulation, in Allarix, AHN, OO.MM, Calatrava, carp. 455, no. 23; *BC*, p. 18. It also held houses, vineyards and land in Troncoso, *BC*, pp. 23, 33, 44. A *domum* is documented in Benavente in 1187, to which undefined appertinences were attached, as in many other *villas* and places, ibid. More definite are the *tiendas* and vineyards which appear near the houses of Segovia in Salamanca, ibid. In addition, the Order had other houses in present-day Salamanca, *BA*, p. 16.

[6] One in Caso, *BC*, pp. 23, 33, 44, another in Zamora, A. Torres y Tapia, *Crónica de la Orden de Alcántara*, 1 (Madrid, 1763), p. 216, and a third in Mayorga, *BC*, pp. 23, 33, 44, which had houses and other appertinences.

[7] The donation of the castle of Alcántara, was accompanied by important rights associated with the *villa* and including tolls, mills, and fisheries.

[8] The Order, founded in Calatrava in 1158, was already established in Navarre in 1163, in Portugal around 1175, a little earlier in León, and in 1179 in Aragon.

The insignificance of the properties held by the Order of Calatrava in León before 1218, and the relatively small involvement of the monarchy in their acquisition, confirm the initial lack of Calatravan presence in the kingdom. Closely linked to this is its marginal position in commercial centres and along lines of communication. As is well known, the kingdom of León is formed around two great routes which bisect each other at right angles: the old *guineana* road and the prosperous *Camino de Santiago*. The various manifestations of the kingdom's economic vitality depend on these two basic reference points, but the Order of Calatrava did not acquire prime locations within this framework, nor did it establish itself in the principal cities and their immediate surroundings. This absence was not compensated for by the Order's meagre presence in Benavente, Zamora and Salamanca. Moreover, there were few jurisdictional disputes with churches and monasteries which suggests that, even in rural areas, the Order's lands were not bordered by the lordships of institutions with well-established jurisdictional powers. A scattered patrimony, separated from the kingdom's principal economic centres constitutes, then, the second indicator of the small role which the Order played there.

The disappearance of Calatrava in the Kingdom of León in these early years cannot, however, be explained solely by economic weaknesses, for it was also closely bound up with the political relations between Castile and León in the second half of the twelfth century and the beginning of the thirteenth century. The date of the foundation of the Order of Calatrava cannot be attributed exclusively to the Templars' abandonment of the original stronghold in La Mancha. No sooner was the first Spanish military order founded in Castile than its Leonese division appeared, founded as the monarchy's instrument of power to play a key role in the uniting of the kingdom following the death of Alfonso VII and the failure of the concept of empire. The early 'export' of the Order beyond the borders of Castile sprang indirectly from the attempts of the most powerful kingdom in the peninsular to achieve supremacy. Unsurprisingly, under these circumstances the Order of Calatrava was less than well received in León, whose monarchy, which would never abandon the legitimate imperial inheritance, wished to maintain its sovereign independence at all costs.

The Order of Calatrava was introduced into León during a hiatus in the strained relations between Castile and León, which preceded the confrontation which was finally brought to an end by the treaties of Medina de Rioseco (1181), Fresno-Lavandera (1183), and Tordehumos (1194). Frontier difficulties served as a pretext for mutual suspicion, and it is significant that in the last of these treaties, that of Tordehumos, the Order of Calatrava took charge of the castles which Alfonso VIII pledged in the agreements adopted with Alfonso IX.[9] Later disputes and temporary agreements did little to help create

---

[9] Cubillas de Duero, Villanueva, Santibáñez de Resova, San Román de Entrepeñas and Tremaya. Alfonso IX was doing the same with Castrotierra, Herrera de Riaño, Almanza, Peña Ramir and Colle, which all remained in the custody of the Templars, J. González, *Alfonso IX*, 2 (Madrid, 1944), pp. 116–19, no. 79.

the desired climate for peace until finally, in 1217 – the same year as the royal donation of Alcántara to the Order of Calatrava – the kings of Castile and León reached a firm basis for future understanding.

THE SECOND PHASE: 1218–30

The second phase runs from the agreement between Calatrava and Alcántara in 1218, and the year 1230, which saw the definitive union of Castile and León. Some of the factors which contributed to the failure of the Calatravan presence in the preceding period continued, though abated, throughout the second decade of the thirteenth century. Although it is clear that, in 1217, a new process was begun which, in the middle term, would result in peaceful coexistence between the kingdoms of Castile and León nevertheless, while Alfonso IX lived, the struggle for the succession continued. Ultimately, one of the solutions to this – the elevation to the Leonese throne of his son Ferdinand – would lead to the end of the independent existence of the kingdom of León.

Therefore, in the course of this period, during which the dominant sectors of feudal society still continued to acquire new powers and property, the Order tried out new ways of procuring revenue through a scrupulous, if not exhaustive, application of religious criteria which made it not only the Order of Alcántara's superior authority in disciplinary matters, but also gave it ecclesiastical control as well. The renunciation of revenues of an economic and political nature opened the way for the exploitation of ecclesiastical revenues alone.

The 1218 agreement on the transfer of Calatravan possessions to the reconstituted Order of Alcántara is the principal manifestation of the impracticality of the Order of Calatrava's initial project in León. When Alfonso IX had conceded the castle of Alcántara to the Order the previous year, he had done so with the clear intention of establishing there a major monastery and master's headquarters independent of the Castilian institutions. Since the Order was unwilling to accept this solution, it finally negotiated a revitalization of the Calatravan dependency of the *Pereiro* in exchange for the transfer in its favour of the castle of Alcántara and the rest of its possessions in the kingdom. If it was impossible to establish a fully Calatravan project in León, under its master's authority, it was preferable to strengthen the jurisdictional dependency of an already existing affiliated institution which could not fail to be grateful for the Order's obvious generosity.

The Order's leaders certainly took very seriously their protective role towards Alcántara after 1218. There is evidence that both masters led several apparently joint initiatives; we also know of the friction caused by such initiatives at certain times. What can also be clearly seen is that in this new period, with one exception,[10] Calatrava's income in León was reduced almost exclusively to tracts of land derived from the control of ecclesiastical revenues.

---

[10] The donation of Bolaños, on the frontier, defined and confirmed by the queen of Castile: J. González, *Reinado y Diplomas de Fernando III*, 2 (Còrdoba, 1983), pp. 291–3; *BC*, p. 61.

THIRD PHASE: 1230–1300

The third phase runs from 1230 to the end of the century, and could even be extended to the first decades of the fourteenth century. The political distrust which contributed decisively to the failure of the Calatravan project in León had disappeared, or at least had greatly diminished, and the Order initiated a halfhearted recovery of possessions in the kingdom. However, it did so under extremely adverse conditions, for the process of allocating Leonese land was in an advanced stage, and the well established feudal powers in the region were not willing to share material wealth already threatened by the first signs of economic recession.

In effect, when in the final months of 1230 Alfonso IX died and the struggle for the succession was predictably resolved in favour of Ferdinand III, the Order's leaders seem to have changed their attitude towards the kingdom of León. It was symptomatic that one of the first decisions of the new king of León was the concession to the Order of Calatrava of certain possessions in Benavente.[11] Nevertheless, the newly acquired possessions were not numerous,[12] and perhaps lacked any real potential; thereafter the Order's activity in the kingdom can be seen to have as its principal aim the preservation and increase of ecclesiastical possessions and revenues. In this way, in the course of the fourteenth century, the Order of Calatrava gradually discarded its actual and potential interests in the territories of the Leonese monarchy.

[11] J. González, *Fernando III*, 2, pp. 318–19.
[12] The Asturian estate of *Planni*, AHN, OO.MM, Calatrava, carp. 459, no. 112; *BC*, pp. 114–15 or the village of *Cenestriel* in Salamanca, AHN, OO.MM, *Registro de Escrituras de Calatrava*, 2, sign. 1342-C, fol. 141, and 6, sign. 1346-C, fols 38–9.

31

Agrarian Structure in the Calatravan Lordships of the Southern Meseta of Castile in the Twelfth and Thirteenth Centuries*

Enrique Rodríguez-Picavea Matilla

After livestock rearing, agriculture was the basic economic activity in the Calatravan estates of the Castilian southern tableland. However, it was clearly dependent upon the practice of livestock rearing, which was essential to the feudal economy of the Order of Calatrava, except in very localized areas where it concentrated on more specialized crop production. To analyse the level of importance attained by agriculture in the economic structure of the Calatravan domains, it is necessary first to ascertain the types of crop which existed, then the techniques used to harvest them, and finally to study the organization of the agricultural landscape and the forms of ownership and land exploitation.

TYPES OF CROP

Cereals

The cultivation of cereals extended, to a greater or lesser degree, over the whole area of the Calatravan possessions. In much of the twelfth-century Calatravan documentation there are general references to cereals as opposed to vineyards. Since the majority of these instances refer to the fertile Tagus valley or to its northern tributaries, it must be concluded that in that area there already existed the classic dual system of crops based on cereals and vines. South of the Tagus these crops appear less frequently, at least during the twelfth century.

However, documentation referring specifically to the types of cereal cultivated and the techniques used is scarce. José María Mínguez has postulated that this lack of precision in the documentation reflects an agrarian structure in which the rearing of livestock was characteristic and there was little rational organi-

---

* Dedicated to the memory of Derek Lomax

From *The Military Orders: Fighting for the Faith and Caring for the Sick*, ed. Malcolm Barber. Copyright © 1994 by Malcolm Barber. Published by Variorum, Ashgate Publishing Ltd, Gower House, Croft Road, Aldershot, Hampshire, GU11 3HR, Great Britain.

zation of the land,[1] just as happened, in fact, in the Calatravan estates that we are analysing. Nevertheless, as Mínguez has also pointed out, in the case of the monastery of Sahagún, when references are made to livestock, the species tend to be clearly identified, distinguishing between oxen, cows, ewes, mares, mules and pigs, and male or female. This reinforces the hypothesis that livestock rearing predominated on the Calatravan estates.

The predominant cereals were wheat and barley. The existence of rye is also documented, albeit far less frequently, and occasionally its production surpassed that of barley, even reaching quantities close to those of wheat. We know nothing about the cultivation of other cereals such as oats, or of vegetables such as chick-peas, which are later documented in the *Campo de Calatrava* for the fifteenth century.[2]

Thus, the surviving documentation generally implies a clear prelevance of wheat and barley cultivation on the Calatravan estates of the southern plateau. This predominance was prolonged, as is confirmed by more precise documentation from the fifteenth century.[3] The cultivation of these two cereal crops answered two needs: the production of bread for human consumption, deriving principally, but not exclusively, from wheat flour; and the provision of the necessary feedstuff for the livestock, essential to an agrarian economy clearly oriented in that direction.

The cultivation of these cereals was organized and controlled by the Order of Calatrava with the dual aim of channelling the rural surpluses in the form of feudal revenue and securing feedstuff for the ever-increasing livestock herds. While the soil type and the prevailing economic structure certainly favoured the spread of wheat and barley crops, the Calatravans evidently channelled and directed these crops to their own advantage.

Vineyards

Vineyards came next in importance to cereals in the Calatravan agricultural framework of the southern plateau. We have already seen how the general references to vineyards are documented in practically all the Calatravan estates connected to the Tagus river and its tributaries, even in some locations in the *Campo de Calatrava*.

The existence of numerous vineyards is documented in the Tagus valley almost from the beginning of Christian control, and their cultivation was

---

[1] J.M. Mínguez, *El dominio del monasterio de Sahagún en el siglo X. Paisajes agrarios, producción y explotación económica* (Salamanca, 1980), p. 155.

[2] E. Solano, *La Orden de Calatrava en el siglo XV. Los señoríos castellanos de la Orden al fin de la Edad Media* (Seville, 1978), pp. 225, 234.

[3] Ibid., pp. 332–3.

probably previously linked to the Mozarabs. They are also related, to a large extent, to the provisioning of urban markets, especially that of Toledo.[4]

Another region with a relative abundance of vineyards is that adjacent to the lands of Maqueda and Santa Olalla. Further east, in the present-day province of Guadalajara, the Order of Calatrava held several vineyards in the diocese of Sigüenza[5] and connected with the *encomienda* of Medinaceli.[6] In addition, it had at least six *aranzadas* of vineyard in Fuentelaencina[7] and several lands also dedicated to the vine belonging to the *encomiendas* of Zorita[8] and Cogolludo.[9] There are even vineyards belonging to the Order documented on the boundary at Cuenca, Albadalejo, Cañete[10] and Moya[11] and, at the opposite extreme, corresponding ones in the *encomienda* of Plasencia.[12]

Finally, in the *Campo de Calatrava*, some vineyards had already been planted in the Muslim period. In this region the Order initiated the planting of new vineyards – a policy which sometimes became a heavy burden for the inhabitants. The *fuero* of Miguelturra, dated to the 1230s,[13] even agreed to the development of the estate by planting not cereals – undoubtedly the most extensively planted crop – but vines, which thus became the crop most heavily promoted by the Order. This also occurred in Almodóvar in 1260, making it easier to sell their products in the local fairs.[14]

However, undoubtedly the promotion of the vine by the Order of Calatrava was primarily undertaken because surplus crops could more easily be converted into income. Consequently, the Order of Calatrava initiated a process of the patrimonial accumulation of vineyards, through gifts or purchases, accompanied

---

[4] See the vineyards documented in Aceca and its surroundings in the Archivo Histórico Nacional, Ordenes Militares (hereafter AHN, OO.MM), carp. 455, no. 18 and sign. 1342-C, fol. 42; R. Menéndez Pidal, *Documentos lingüísticos de España, 1: Reino de Castilla* (Madrid, 1919), pp. 375–6; A. González Palencia, *Los mozárabes de Toledo en los siglos XII-XIII*, 4 vols, 1 (Madrid, 1926–1930), no. 244; J. González, *El Reino de Castilla en la época de Alfonso VIII*, 3 vols, 2 (Madrid, 1960), pp. 201–3, 514–15.

[5] AHN, OO.MM, carp. 442, no. 32.

[6] In particular, various vineyards in the *villa* of Medinaceli and the villages of Huerta, Padilla, Torralba and Capris passed into the hands of the Order in 1223. See AHN, OO.MM, carp. 458, no. 87, in *Bullarium ordinis militiae de Calatrava*, ed. J. Ortega y Cotes, J.F. Alvarez de Baquedano and P. de Ortega Zuñiga y Aranda (Madrid, 1761) (hereafter *BC*), pp. 57–8.

[7] AHN, OO.MM, sign. 1343-C, fol. 8.

[8] AHN, OO.MM, carp. 460, no. 127.

[9] AHN, OO.MM, carp. 458, nos 88, 89.

[10] AHN, OO.MM, carp. 456, no. 27, in L. Salazar y Castro, *Pruebas para la Historia de la Casa de Lara* (Madrid, 1694), p. 15; *BC*, p. 449.

[11] Published in González, *Alfonso VIII*, 3, pp. 665–6.

[12] From 1218 they are documented as appertinences of the Order of Mountjoy (Menéndez Pidal, *Documentos*, pp. 439–40), a little later they passed into the hands of the Order of Calatrava under whose control they remained at least until 1291. See AHN, OO.MM, carp. 426, no. 148.

[13] Published in E. Hinojosa, *Documentos para la Historia de las instituciones de León y Castilla (siglos X–XIII* (Madrid, 1919), p. 150.

[14] E. Agostini Banus, *Historia de Almódovar del Campo*, fasc. ed. (Ciudad Real, 1990), p. 63.

by protection measures and the promotion of new plantations not only in the *Campo de Calatrava*, as we have already seen, but also in the Alcarria and in the region of Toledo.

Olives

Among the other crops grown on the Calatravan estates, it is worth emphasizing the few documentary references to the existence of olives. The greater concentration of olive groves on the southern plateau was around Talavera. The Order had olive groves in this *villa* from 1172,[15] but their existence is also confirmed in the lands of Maqueda and Zorita.

Vegetable Gardens

In contrast to the few references in the sources to olive groves, there is great emphasis on the vegetable gardens which are sometimes interspersed with olive groves, vineyards and barley fields. However, the strictly horticultural crops were fruit trees, flax, hemp, *sumach*, mulberries, roses and other flowers.

The best and largest vegetable gardens were to be found in the Tagus basin, since their existence was closely connected with the greater or lesser abundance of water and with the systems of irrigation. The best systems of vegetable garden irrigation in the southern plateau were those built by the Muslims, using water from the Tagus. Although it is not documented, it is possible that, as in other areas of Andalucía, the Christian feudal powers adapted to these complex hydraulic systems which assured the maintenance of the technological level in the cultivation of irrigated crops and guaranteed the organization of the social distribution of the water.[16] But, as Barceló indicates, in those places, mainly to the south of the Tagus, where no previous infrastructure had been organized for the irrigation of land, the Order of Calatrava had to create its own hydraulic system based on the mill, so that the irrigation of land remained somewhat subsidiary to, and dependent on, the water left over from the working of the mill itself. The same author argues that this was done for economic, rather than technical reasons, since the mills secured an important portion of income, and this factor reduced the importance of irrigated crops in the feudal economy.[17]

The existence in the Calatravan documentation of a greater number of mills compared to vegetable gardens may support the above hypothesis. In this way, irrigation farming, like dry farming, was controlled by the Order of Calatrava and organized to its own advantage. The logic of the feudal system,

---

[15] J. González, *Alfonso VIII*, 2, pp. 281–3.

[16] See M. Barceló, 'La arqueología extensiva y el estudio de la creación del espacio rural', in M. Barceló *et al*, *Arqueología Medieval. En las afueras del 'medievalismo'* (Barcelona, 1988), p. 239. The reference to *almunias* in the sources could be to vegetable gardens of Muslim origin. See, for example, J. González, *Alfonso VIII*, 2, p. 868.

[17] Barceló, 'La arqueología', pp. 241–3.

as it was established in the southern plateau – streamlined and free from the strong internal contradictions present to the north of the Sistema Central – permitted the seigneurial powers to organize and control production.

CULTIVATION TECHNIQUES AND SYSTEMS

The cereal lands were developed basically with the plough, which was drawn by a pair of oxen held by a yoke and made effective largely by the efforts of the peasant handling it. Not all farmers had the good fortune to own an ox yoke; some ploughed their lands with a single ox, thus having to make do with cultivating half the area of land ploughed by a pair of oxen, as well as exerting greater human effort in the process.

Although oxen were undoubtedly the best animals used for ploughing the land, the *fuero* of Miguelturra alludes also to mule yokes, and even to mixed pairs of oxen and mules – although this seems to be more the exception than the rule. Elsewhere only ox yokes are recorded. In addition to ox yokes, there are references to the thresher and the plough – which was symmetrical and of the Mediterranean type, with the ploughshare toughened by fire, but without an iron coating, and also to the hoe and the sickle for harvesting.

There were three fundamental agricultural tasks that had to be accomplished in the cereal lands: sowing, ploughing and reaping. The vineyards also required three basic annual tasks: digging, pruning and dressing.[18] All these tasks were undertaken manually with the mattock, which appears in the documents for breaking up and digging the land. Pruning was carried out with sickles, while the knife served to cut the grape clusters during the autumn harvest.

Apart from the work connected with the care of the vegetable gardens and irrigated crops, the principal task was first to construct the irrigation system and then to maintain it in perfect condition. The sources show a great preoccupation with the maintenance of the irrigation systems for the vegetable gardens in good condition without at the same time depriving the mill of the supply of water necessary to turn its wheels, which were the central element of the hydraulic system.

We cannot provide much information on the rotation of crops. The only well documented system is that of *año y vez* – that is, a continual biennial rotation of one year of crop and the next fallow. However, since we have only two examples of this type, it cannot be proved that this was a widespread system of cultivation rather than a mere exception. It would be safer to conclude that, in a region where there was no strong pressure on the land, there was more extensive cultivation, with a third, a quarter or an even greater proportion left fallow.[19] Conversely, in extensive cultivation fallow land meant more pasture

---

[18] AHN, OO.MM, carp. 459, no. 110.

[19] This idea is put forward in A. Barrios, *Estructuras agrarias y de poder en Castilla. El ejemplo de Ávila*, 2 vols, 2 (Salamanca, 1983), pp. 116–18.

for the animals – fundamental to a livestock economy – and their excrement would have completed the cycle by providing fertilizer, which was indispensable in an agriculture with little technological development. Pigeon droppings were also very valuable for the fertilization of fields, not only for cereals but also vineyards and vegetable gardens.

ORGANIZATION OF AGRARIAN LAND AND TYPES OF LAND OWNERSHIP

In the Calatravan estates of New Castile, the organization of agricultural land was closely linked to the type of land ownership, and was therefore the result of a series of geographical factors – such as soil fertility and abundance of water – and historical factors – such as the economic orientation of the land and its organization by the dominant class.

The seigneurial domain of the Order of Calatrava is proof that the structure of land ownership conditioned the type of agricultural landscape, since it is undeniable that the Calatravans reserved for themselves, on all their estates, the development of the best and most extensive areas of cultivation. All this demonstrates a certain importance for the Calatravan 'reserve'.

At the opposite end of the land development system found on the Calatravan estates, the *quiñón* was the basic unit of rural development. It related to the area of land given to each peasant with the ability to work one pair of oxen. In general terms, it was equivalent to one yoke of land or the area of land that could be worked by a team of oxen under the *año y vez* system.[20] The *quiñón* was essentially devoted to the cultivation of cereal and, in this sense, was distinct from the land devoted to vineyards.

Parallel to the process of the division of arable land, symbolized by the *quiñón* and realized together with repopulation and the social organization of land for the benefit of the feudal powers, there was also a process of concentration of territory into the hands of the Order of Calatrava. This started in the twelfth century and is especially evident in the area around Toledo, where the Order's estate had to superimpose itself on to an already existing structure of land ownership.

At this point it is fitting to ask what was the relationship between cereal cultivation and vineyards. We can provide little information on this subject, but it seems possible to establish a provisional and approximate ratio of one yoke of cereal for each *aranzada* of vineyard. Nor is it surprising to find that grapes fetched a higher price, in both absolute and relative terms, than cereals since cereal lands were more extensive than vineyards.

Information on vegetable gardens is even more scarce. The general impression is that there were fewer of these than the vineyards, and that their area was also smaller.

---

[20] On this, see especially J. González, *Repoblación de Castilla la Nueva*, 2 vols, 2 (Madrid, 1975–1976), pp. 184–5.

Having analysed the relationship existing between the three principal crops – cereals, vines and vegetables – on the Calatravan estates, it remains now to comment on their specific arrangement in the agrarian landscape and their distribution with regard to population centres and uncultivated land.

Land began to be organized for agriculture on the outskirts of the villages, and even within the villages themselves in the case of vegetable gardens and barley fields which were frequently adjacent to the houses. From the same centre of population emerged a radial network of roads which had a dual purpose: to link the centres of population and to permit access to the crops in the surrounding areas. At the same time they fulfilled the function of delimiting the cultivated plots.

In the first strip of land – the one nearest to the village or *villa* – we frequently find, next to the orchards, *herrenes* and barley fields where gramineous plants were grown and cut whilst still green to feed to the livestock. They were connected to the orchards by small paths which also led to the threshing floors, where the grain was separated from the straw using a thresher.

In the second strip of land there were mainly vineyards and cereals. Between the cereal plots, each village had large meadows which were devoted to pasture for the livestock, whose number multiplied in proportion to the importance of the livestock economy. In any case, the areas of cereal cultivation were always located in the area furthest from the centre of population, bordering on to waste land and natural forest vegetation.

However, it seems that, in some cases, the plots – vegetable gardens as well as olive groves, vineyards and cereal fields – were gradually fenced in. The immense threat which the herds of livestock posed to the crops in a clearly livestock-oriented economy gave rise to numerous fines and other means to prevent animal damage to crops.

To conclude our analysis we should consider whether the agricultural system differed between regions – that is whether each region of Calatravan possession had a particular organization of agricultural land and a specific landscape. Firstly, there is a difference between the *Campo de Calatrava* and the other Calatravan estates. The central nucleus of the Order's lands lacked a developed agrarian structure as a result of their geo-strategic position which transformed them into a territory linking Toledo and Andalucía, and into an area suitable for the practice of transhumance, while at the same time its border location meant that continued cultivation was constantly threatened by mounted Christians and Muslims. These circumstances dictated the maintenance of a livestock-oriented economy and the slow progress of agriculture, which was cereal in character, despite the Calatravan efforts to plant vineyards.

On the other hand, in the lands north of the Tagus, even in the most northern sector of the Toledan Sisla, the situation was slightly different. Before the beginning of Calatravan control, there existed an agricultural tradition from the Muslim period which had been continued by the Christians. The problem in these areas was not so much the ploughing of new land for agriculture as the control of land already under cultivation. This prompted the great eccle-siastical powers of the southern plateau, namely the Church of Toledo and the military orders – to initiate a process of patrimonial accumulation.

In any case, the fundamental economic orientation of these territories was the rearing of livestock, and the Order of Calatrava made this economic activity possible, raising it to the highest level of development. Thus, we can say that generally there were no great regional differences in the organization of the agrarian landscape on the Calatravan estates, the organization of land being largely for livestock in all of them. Perhaps there may have been some slight differences, ranging from the absolute prevalence of livestock-rearing in the *Campo de Calatrava* to its absence in the urban *encomiendas* of Toledo, Talavera and Madrid, while there was a certain emphasis on agriculture in some possessions in the Tagus basin, such as Aceca and Polán. But such nuances did not arise from the overall economic structuring of the landscape, but from specific, local circumstances such as the fertility provided by the waters of the Tagus, or the Order of Calatrava's need to establish itself in the principal Royal Councils of the southern Castilian plateau. Although this gradation meant a contrast between intensive areas (the Tagus) and extensive areas (La Mancha) of cultivation, in the framework of Calatravan possessions the former had a definite character and cannot be considered as truly representative of the Order's agricultural landscape as a whole.

32

Organization of Land in the Peninsular South-East: the Commandery of Segura de la Sierra of the Order of Santiago, 1246–1350*

José Vicente Matellanes Merchán

Our objective is to ascertain, as far as possible, the possessions under the jurisdiction of Segura de la Sierra which, for various reasons split into distinct smaller commanderies.[1] This frontier enclave became the basis for a vast group of commanderies in Andalucía and Murcia.

The division of its sphere of influence led Segura to hold properties in the present-day provinces of Jaén, Granada, Murcia and Albacete, and to possess an extensive network of castles which were decisive in the taking of the kingdom of Murcia,[2] and which assumed a leading role against the kingdom of Granada.

Prior to the gift of Segura, the Order of Santiago already had some possessions in the region, which later formed part of the commandery. In May 1235, Ferdinand III donated the *villa* of Torres, near Segura, with its outposts

---

* To Derek Lomax, with deep respect and admiration

[1] There are several opinions on the progressive division of the outposts of Segura into independent commanderies. Peinado Santaella states that the transfer of the main commandery of Castile to Segura in 1245 meant a restructuring of its estates in the region of Alta Segura in order to improve its control and defence of the territory, 'Un señorío en la frontera del reino de Granada: la Encomienda Socovosa finales de la Edad Media (1468–1526)', *Congreso de Historia de Albacete*, 2 (Albacete, 1984). Also in connection with the transfer of the main commandery in 1245, M. Rodríguez Llopis states that the extensive commandery was impossible to control and defend, and this led to is subdivision into smaller and defensible centres, in *Conflictos fronterizos y dependencia señorial, la Encomienda de Yeste y Taibilla (s. XIII–XV)*, IEA (Albacete, 1982), p. 37. Other possibilities are those outlined in 'Repoblación y Organización del espacio en los señoríos santiaguistas del reino de Murcia (1235–1350)', *Murgetana*, 70 (1986).

[2] *Desde Segura se extendió el Señorío de la Orden en la Sierra, incluso en su vertiente oriental; con tal base era fácil la penetración en el reino de Murcia y la expansión hasta Huéscar*, J. González, *Reinado y diplomas de Fernando III*, 1 (Cordoba, 1980), p. 184.

From *The Military Orders: Fighting for the Faith and Caring for the Sick*, ed. Malcolm Barber. Copyright © 1994 by Malcolm Barber. Published by Variorum, Ashgate Publishing Ltd, Gower House, Croft Road, Aldershot, Hampshire, GU11 3HR, Great Britain.

(Albanchez, Beas, Canena, Cotiellas), a grant which included grazing rights.[3] The king followed this up in 1239 with a donation of the *villa* and castle of Hornos, near the border of Segura.[4] In the same year, Juan, Bishop of Osma, exchanged with the Order the *villa* of Veas for various properties,[5] an exchange which was confirmed by Ferdinand III.[6]

On 21 August 1242 Ferdinand III gave to the Order the *villa* of Segura de la Sierra with its castles and outposts, excluding the pertinences of the kingdom of Murcia, at the Councils of Riópar and Alcaraz, and those of the kingdom of Jaén at the Councils of Baeza and Ubeda.[7] This grant was confirmed by his son, the *Infante* Alfonso,[8] on 5 July 1243, who also listed the castles belonging to the *villa*: Moratalla, Socovos, Vicorto (a hamlet next to Elche de la Sierra), Goutar (at the foot of the Peñas del Molino), Letur, Pliego (MTN no. 889, particularly near the present-day toponyms of Casa de Requena, and Cortijo de Pliego in Arroya de los Frailes), Feréz, Abejuela, Benizar (7 km from Socovos, MTN, 889) Nerpio, Taibilla, Yeste, Graya (present-day la Graya), Burgueya (near Huéscar),[9] Catena, Albanchez, Huéscar, Miravetes, Volteruela[10] and Aznar (identifiable with the meadow of Itnar, to the south-west of Letur, MTN 867).[11]

In 1243 the *Infante* Alfonso who, because of his father's illness had taken on the task of capturing Murcia, gave to the Order, for its good services in the

---

[3] AHN, OO.MM, Uclés, carp. 311, nos 2 and 3, in Innocent IV's confirmation of 15 September 1245; González, *Fernando III*, 3, no. 554, pp. 71–3. On the boundaries of Torres see B. Chaves, *Apuntamiento legal sobre el dominio solar de la Orden de Santiago en todos sus pueblos*, fasc. edn (Barcelona, 1975), fol. 195.

[4] AHN, OO.MM, Uclés, carp. 311, nos 4 and 5, in Innocent IV's confirmation of 5 September 1245; J. González, *Fernando III*, 3, no. 657, pp. 197–9,

[5] AHN, OO.MM, Uclés, carp. 357, no. 1.

[6] J. González, *Fernando III*, 3, no. 658, p. 199.

[7] As can be seen here, the king was pursuing a well defined policy in Andalucía by removing the Order from the cities and protecting the Royal Councils from any possible interference from the Order: AHN, OO.MM, Uclés, carp. 311, nos 6, 7, 8 and 9 (in Innocent IV's bull of 1245), *Bullarium Equestris Ordinis Sancti Jacobi de Spatha*, ed. A.F. Aguado de Córdoba, A.A. Alexán y Rosaes and J. Lópe Agurleta (Madrid, 1719), p. 153; J. González, *Fernando III*, 3, no. 700, pp. 248–50.

[8] M. Rivera Garretas, *La encomienda, el priorato y la villa de Uclés en la Edad Media, Formación de un señorío de la Orden de Santiago*, CSIC (Madrid and Barcelona, 1985), no. 190, pp. 396–7.

[9] This place is the one cited in a document dated 2 July 1331 as *encima del camp de Borgeia, aprop d'Osca. terra del dit rey de Granada*, M. Rodríguez Llopis, *Documentos de los Siglos XIV ~ XV Señoríos de la Orden de Santiago* (Murcia, 1991), pp. 6–8 (this information is on p. 7).

[10] M. Rodríguez Llopis, *Conflictos y dependencia señorial*, p. 28, identifies Volteruela with the future Puebla de D. Fadrique.

[11] In the identification of places, we have followed *Colección de Documentos para la Historia del Reino de Murcia*, ed. J. Torres Fontes et al. 3 (Murcia, 1963) (hereafter *CODOM*), pp. 24–5. Alternative locations for the places in the donation are proposed by J. Rodríguez Llopis, *Conflictos y dependencia señorial*, p. 53, where, for example, Goutar is identified with Villares on the boundary of Segura de la Sierra. Catena is situated a league from Segura and Aznar is identified with the meadow of Itnar (n. 53). He equates Volteruela with the future Puebla de D. Fadrique, p. 28.

taking of Chinchilla, the *villa* of Galera, near Huéscar in the present-day province of Granada, and its villages and towers: Orce, Caztalla, Itur, Las Cuevas de Almizra and Color.[12]

Undoubtedly the Order intended to consolidate its frontier possessions even at the cost of having to cede, at least temporarily, more northerly possessions, for also in 1243 it exchanged, with Gil Gómez, the *villa* and castle of Paracuellos and its possessions in Segovia for Hijar and three castles in Segura: Vicorto, Villares and Abejuela, together with whatever arms and *maravedís* this lord possessed.[13]

As previously mentioned, the commandery's possessions became fairly scattered; this is illustrated by the donation, in 1245, of the castle of Elda from Guillen el Aleman.[14] In August 1253 this castle was subsequently handed over to Sancho Sánchez of Mazuelos by the Master, Pelay Pérez, with the permission of Pedro Fernández, knight commander of Segura, in exchange for a very important grant of properties in the kingdom of Murcia and others to the north of the Duero.[15]

On 12 February 1246, Pelayo Pérez, Master of the Order, confirmed the *fuero* at the Council of Segur;[16] this confirmed a previous *fuero* whose date and donor are unknown. However, it seems to be an extension of the *fuero* of Alcaraz conceded by Alfonso VIII in 1213.[17] This document is interesting, moreover, because it contains the division of the commandery already referred to, and the presence of a knight commander of Moratalla – a fact which seems to confirm the opinion of Miguel Rodríguez Llopis on the disintegration of the main commandery.[18] Furthermore, in this confirmation there appear new possessions linked to Segura, such as Chiclana, Beas and Castril.

---

[12] AHN, OO.MM, Uclés, carp. 311; no. 10 and AHN, OO.MM, Uclés, carp. 2, vol. 1, no. 10, (in Alfonso X's confirmation of 7 April 1254); M. Rivera Garretas, no. 110, pp. 396–7; *CODOM*, 3, no. 2, pp. 2–3.

[13] Rivera Garretas, *La encomienda*, no. 193, p. 401.

[14] AHN, sellos 63/2, *CODOM*, 3, no. 6, p. 6. J. Torres Fontes informs us that, upon hearing of the death of Guillen el Aleman, the king and the Master of the Order gave his son four horses, five mules and money so that he could return to his lands in exchange for renunciation of his rights, *CODOM*, 3, p. 52, n. 46.

[15] *BC*, p. 189 and *CODOM*, 3, no. 17, pp. 15-16. The latter document shows how properties belonging to Segura served as a base for the creation of other commanderies in Andalucía, since Sánchez Mazuelos left to the Order Las Peñas de San Pedro, the two *Caudetes* and Torre de Regim which would be the basis of the future commandery of Seville.

[16] Rodríguez Llopis, 'La evolución del poblamiento en las sierras de Segura (provincias de Albacete y Jaén), durante la Edad Media', *Al-Basit*, 19 (1986), pp. 5–32, here p. 7, n. 5.

[17] L.R. Villegas Díaz 'Sobre el fuero de Segura y otros documentos medievales jienenses', *Actas I coloquio de Historia de Andalucía Medieval* (Córdoba, 1982), p. 427.

[18] He states that in 1245 the commanderies of Moratalla, Yeste and Taibilla were created, *Conflictos y dependencia señorial*, p. 53, n. 56, although it should be added that the first documented commander of Yeste was Suer Flores in 1331 (p. 107).

Continuing with the possessions of Segura, a document exists in which properties are conceded to the Order in Jaén, an area excluded from the grant of Segura, and which confirms the royal policy in Andalucía of removing from the orders cities and areas under the control of the Royal Councils, and centring gifts in frontier and mountain areas.[19] This grant, made in February 1246, transferred to the commandery of Segura several houses in Jaén belonging to Rabif Zulema, fifteen *aranzadas* of vineyard and four *aranzadas* of vegetable garden, the tower of Mezquinel and two adjacent windmills, in addition to the tower of Maquif and estates of fifteen *yugadas*. There is no mention of the transfer of jurisdiction.[20]

Donations were not always confined to territorial property; some served to provide the Order with a substantial disposable income. This is the case with Ferdinand III's gift of 1246, which conceded to the monastery of Segura an annual rent of 2,000 *maravedís* in the saltworks of Belinchón,[21] which was independent of the tithes which the Order already had from Alfonso VIII.[22]

Information on the Order's possessions does not always appear in a concise form. For example, Chiclana appears as a possession of the commandery in the naming of parties in the litigation brought against the archbishop of Toledo dated 1 April 1253, in which Pedro Fernández participated. This, together with the reference in the *fuero*, identifies it as a possession of the commandery of Segura, relating it to Ferdinand III's gift to the Order of nine *yugadas* of estate in Santiesteban, nine *aranzadas* of vineyard, one *aranzada* of vegetable garden and a pair of houses in Linares.[23]

As previously noted, the grants sometimes appear to be removed from the centre of the border region of Segura and are located in La Mancha which had economic links to the area rather than any direct connection with the repopulation and defence of the frontier. One example is the donation made by Alfonso X in July 1256 to the knight commander of Segura, Pedro Fernández, of the farm

---

[19] C. Segura Graiño, 'La formación del patrimonio territorial de las Ordenes Militares en el Alto Valle del Guadalquivir en el s. XIII', *Anuario de Estudios Medievales*, 11 (Barcelona, 1981), p. 110; M.A. Ladero Quesada, 'La Orden de Santiago en Andalucía, bienes, rentas y vasallos a finales del siglo XV', *Historia, Instituciones y Documentos*, 2 (1970), pp. 329–82, here p. 332.

[20] González, *Fernando III*, 3, no. 735, pp. 301–3. This grant, together with Albanchez, Canena and various possessions in Ubeda and Baeza, formed part of the commandery of Bedmar in the fifteenth century (Ladero Quesada, 'La Orden', pp. 343–4). As can be seen, time and again, the territorial base of the commandery of Segura served to form a vast complex of commanderies which the Order had in Andalucía.

[21] González, *Fernando III*, 3, no. 745, pp. 310–11.

[22] On 10 April 1178 Alfonso VIII donated the tithes of the saltworks of Belinchón, González, *El reino de Castilla en la época de Alfonso VIII*, 2 (Madrid, 1961), pp. 491–2.

[23] González, *Fernando III*, no. 717, pp. 276–7. In the fifteenth century these possessions formed part of the commandery of Montizón, Ladero Quesada, 'La Orden', p. 349. They appear as one unit together with Chiclana, Chaves, *Apuntamiento*, fol. 185.

of Abeiazat in La Mancha; this served as a reward for the support lent by the Order in the taking of Orihuela.[24]

However, if these grants were important in what may be called the rearguard, even more important were those properties which the commandery received in regions bordering the kingdom of Granada, and which are today located in the province of the same name. Here, we refer specifically to Sancho IV's grants of Castril and Orcera, which both formed part of an exchange with lands further north, implying a premeditated policy, on the Order's part, of grouping together possessions in the south where land was cheaper and still to be populated. Castril was given to the Order by Sancho IV when he was still *Infante*, in April 1282, in exchange for Libriella,[25] which already appeared as part of the boundary of Segura and assumed an important position on the frontier with Granada, being situated geographically between Huéscar and Quesada.[26] Orcera, also granted by Sancho IV, in November 1285, was exchanged with the *villa* of Amusco near Monzón.[27]

Finally let us analyse two possessions which highlight the Order's role in repopulation. The first is the donation made by Ferdinand IV in December 1307 of Yechar, Fortuna and the *real* of el Pino and the mayoralty of the suburb of Moros del Arrabal de Arrixaca in Murcia,[28] which is related to the Christian repopulation of Murcia to the detriment of the still theoretical authority of the Muslim king of Arrixaca.[29] The second of these documents, concerning

[24] *CODOM*, **3**, no. 26, pp. 36–8; C. de Ayala Martínez, 'La Orden de Santiago en la evolución política de Alfonso X', *Cuadernos de Historia Medieval*, **4** (Madrid, 1983). This place is identified as Socuellanos, Chaves, *Apuntamiento*, fol. 194 and A. Madrid y Medina, 'Alfonso X El Sabio y la Mancha Santiaguista', *Espacio, tiempo y forma*, ser. 3, Historia Medieval, **2** (1989), pp. 205–18, and was very important in the repopulation of what are nowadays the border towns of Socuellanos, Tomelloso and part of the Campo de Criptana, M. Corchado Soriano, *El priorato de Uclés, iniciación al estudio geográfico-histórico del Priorato de Uclés en la Mancha* (Madrid, 1965), p. 19).

[25] AHN, OO.MM, Uclés, carp. 311, no. 14. It was confirmed on 20 November 1285 when Sancho IV acceded to the throne: AAHN, OO.MM, Uclés, carp. 311, No. 15, confirmed later by Alfonso XI on 8 April 1329 in Alcalá de Henares; AHN, OO.MM, Uclés, carp. 311, no. 16. Sancho IV's document is published in J. Torres Fontes, *Documentos de Sancho IV* (Murcia, 1977), no. II, doc. 29 April 1282, p. 2, and the confirmation of 20 November 1285 in ibid., no. LV, pp. 47–50.

[26] Ladero Quesada, p. 333.

[27] AHN sellos caja 13, no. 1, previously in Uclés, carp. 311, no. 17. This place appears together with La Puerta, Benatave, Torres de Albanchez, Genave, Villa Rodrigo, Siles, Santiago and Hornos as possessions of the commandery of Segura at the end of the fifteenth century, Chaves, *Apuntamiento*, fol. 195.

[28] J. Torres Fontes, 'Los mudéjares murcianos en el siglo XIII', *Separata de Murgetana*, Acad. Alfonso X el Sabio, 17 (Murcia, 1961), pp. 57–90 (pp. 34–6).

[29] Torres Fontes, 'Los mudéjares', p. 25, asserts that the grant to the Order of Santiago is conclusive evidence of the erosion of the power which the Moorish king of Arrixaca had exercised until then. However, this grant was fiercely contested by the Murcian council which did not consider the Order's establishment in the city as favourable to its interests, and succeeded in having this gift revoked on 4 June 1308, J. Torres Fontes, *Privilegios de Fernando IX a Murcia*, no. 4, p. 13, and returned to its previous owner, Pedro Gueralt, who was entrusted with its repopulation, Torres Fontes, 'Los mudéjares', doc. IV, pp. 36–7.

Salfaraz, a church which already belonged to the Order around 1217,[30] is dated 11 July 1335. In it Pedro García and Pedro Gil acknowledge receipt from the Order of the house, tower and farmhouse of *Fas-Alfaraz*, situated near Segura, and agree to develop it as well as pay the tithe to the knight commander of Segura.[31]

As can be seen, the estate of the commandery of Segura de la Sierra was sufficiently extensive and heterogeneous for smaller commanderies to emerge from it. This process underlines its territorial and economic importance which made it, for a long time, the major commandery in Castile.

---

[30] In fact, the case brought by the Church of Toledo against the Order of Santiago over the jurisdiction of certain churches in the Campo de Montiel and the mountains of Segura predates the building of some of them (Salfaraz, Albanchez and La Puerta) in the years following 1217, Rodríguez Llopis, 'La evolución del poblamiento', 7, n. 5.

[31] AHN, OO.MM, Uclés, carp. 311, no. 51

33

Architecture and Power: the Seats of the Priories of the Order of Santiago

Aurora Ruiz Mateos, Jesús Espino Nuño and Olga Pérez Monzón

In the late Middle Ages the Order of Santiago became a 'feudal' institution with great economic and political power, control of which was desired by nobles as well as kings. These same nobles and kings were the patrons of important artistic undertakings aimed at the greater glory of the Order and themselves. Taking advantage of a period of economic prosperity, the Order's officials decided to carry out ambitious architectural programmes in some of their most symbolic buildings: Uclés, San Marcos and Calera de León. We have chosen these buildings because they express simultaneously a triple architectural concept: they reflect the power and prestige of the Order of Santiago; they demonstrate their hierarchical significance; and they show the importance of the place in which they were erected. Because of the Order's long architectural history, the present research is centred on the period of the last two-thirds of the fifteenth century and the sixteenth century.

From the architectural point of view, the period studied is a complex one in the peninsula, during which a revitalized gothic style co-existed with surviving mudejar elements on the one hand, and an emergent renaissance style on the other. In this setting the Santiago monasteries studied reproduce the same cloister plan, around which are arranged the conventual outbuildings, with the church against one of its galleries. Nor can we ignore the symbolic value of these buildings where, in addition to general references to the Order (scallopshells, coats of arms and images of the patron saint commemorate the benefactors), individual masters and priors left reminders of themselves through the building of funerary chapels, donations and heraldic emblems. The difference in importance between the three monasteries is essentially reflected in the greater or lesser presence of these 'personal expressions'.

From *The Military Orders: Fighting for the Faith and Caring for the Sick*, ed. Malcolm Barber. Copyright © 1994 by Malcolm Barber. Published by Variorum, Ashgate Publishing Ltd, Gower House, Croft Road, Aldershot, Hampshire, GU11 3HR, Great Britain.

SANTIAGO DE UCLÉS

The work carried out in the Santiago buildings at Uclés during the sixteenth century definitively transformed the military stronghold[1] into a notable conventual complex erected on the foundations of the Order's earlier religio-military centre.

The Order's new aristocratic–feudal interests, together with the architectural shortcomings of the original centre, minutely detailed by the 'masters of geometry', Antón Egas and Alonso de Covarrubias,[2] brought about a remodelling and complete alteration in the Santiago building. It was begun in 1529 by Francisco de Luna, a master in the renaissance tradition who was active in the region of Cuenca,[3] and finished in the following century by artists trained in the El Escorial and baroque traditions.[4]

The new complex retains the classical cloister arrangement with its communal buildings (of special interest are the chapel of San Agustín and the refectory on the ground floor and the cells on the upper floor), meeting rooms and lodgings (an infirmary and a fine inn connected to the so-called 'courtyard of the Knights'), and storage buildings (wine cellars, warehouses and stables are distributed around the complex), an arrangement which turned it into an autonomous and independent entity.

The church of Santiago,[5] located on the north side of the cloister, deserves special mention. The ground-plan of the nave incorporates the sacristy and treasury[6] and, on the Gospel side, the various funerary chapels belonging to Juan Hurtada de Mendoza, the governor of Cazorla, the count of Paredes, and the priors Juan de Velasco and Hernando Santoyo.[7] These funerary chapels,

---

[1] This *villa*, dominated by the castle of Almohad origin, was given to the Order of Santiago by Alfonso VIII on 9 January 1174. See M. Rivera Garreta, *La encomienda, el priorato y la villa de Uclés en la Edad Media. Formación de un señorío de la Orden de Santiago* (Madrid and Barcelona, 1985), pp. 34–8.

[2] The report of these masters in 1525 emphasizes the architectural shortcomings of the buildings: its narrow rooms, the lack of essential rooms such as chapter house, infirmary, library and main cells, and the shortage of water. Archivo Histórico Nacional (hereafter AHN), Archivo Judicial de Toledo, leg. 22.444.

[3] This new building was part of the Santiago priory's programme of construction of the first half of the sixteenth century, reflecting the soundness of the economy and the increase in population in the region at this time. See J.M. de Azcarate, 'El convento de Uclés y Francisco de Luna, maestro de cantería', *Archivo Español de Arte*, 29 (1956), pp. 183–5; M.L. Rokiski Lazaro, *Arquitectura del XVI en Cuenca* (Cuenca, 1985), pp. 116–20.

[4] The economic crisis of the middle of the century prolonged the work with the result that several artistic styles co-exist here. Luis de Vega, Gaspar de Vega, Pedro de Tolosa, Diego de Alcántara and Francisco de Mora were outstanding among the new masters. See J.M. de Azcarate, 'El oinvento', p. 187; Rokiski Lazaro, *Arquitectura*, pp. 302–3.

[5] The present church, begun by Luna and finished in the sixteenth century, is characterized by the influence of the El Escorial tradition.

[6] The monastery's numerous ornaments and jewels were kept in these rooms AHN, OO.MM, libro 1086-C, fol. 153.

[7] The alabaster tomb of the Master Jorge Manrique projected out into the centre of the main chapel, AHN, OO.MM, libro 1067-C, fol. 107.

Figure 33.1   The sacristy of Uclés (Cuenca)

Figure 33.2   Exterior of Uclés (Cuenca)

together with others in the cloister,[8] are clear evidence of the symbolic significance of Uclés because of its role as the Order's principal monastery.

From an artistic perspective, the participation of outstanding contemporary masters (Egas, Covarrubias, Luna), and the adoption of the prevailing artistic styles in accordance with the innovative taste of the nobility, reflect the importance of this complex. Nevertheless, the long duration of the work determined the eclectic character of the building of Uclés, where elements of the gothic (ribbed vaults), mudejar (wooden ceilings and plasterwork) and renaissance (*a candilieri* decoration in the sacristy (see Figure 33.1) and treasury, coffered ceiling in the great hall, and façades and finials in the El Escorial tradition) (Figure 33.2)[9] coexist.

SAN MARCOS DE LEÓN

In 1172, before coming a brother, Suero Rodríguez founded, together with other nobles, a monastery in the city of León consecrated to San Marcos.[10] Although this was originally a dependency of Uclés, in time it attained a similar importance in the territory of León. Proof of this can be seen in the presence, in the cloister of the old monastery, of the chapel of San Agustín, seat of the conventual chapters, and of the tomb of the first Master, Don Pedro Fernández de Fuentencalada.[11]

The earliest information on the building comes from a report arising from a visitation made in 1442, when the buildings were in a neglected state. This would explain the modifications carried out to the church and most of the cloister buildings at the end of the century by the prior, García Ramírez. The work was fairly well advanced in 1494 and practically finished in 1498; from the documents we can deduce that the plans were traditional, combining gothic and mudejar elements.

However, before the whole building was completed, the Visitors of 1503 and 1508 indicated the need to reconstruct the main chapel[12] and the monastery cloister[13] respectively. These initiatives caused King Ferdinand to order, in

---

[8] The documents refer to the so-called Old Masters' or San Agustín chapel, the graves of Alonso and Juan Díaz Coronado and the tombstones of numerous knights of Santiago, AHN, OO.MM, libro 1067-C, fol. 108.

[9] These rooms are described in AHN, OO.MM: libro 1086-C, fol. 5; libro 1067-C, fol. 107; libro 1084-C, fol. 425v.

[10] This foundation was made on lands donated by the *infanta* doña Sancha in 1152 for the construction of a pilgrims' hospital. See D.W. Lomax, *La Orden de Santiago (1170–1275)* (Madrid, 1965), pp. 69 ff.

[11] Although the complex of San Marcos was conceived in relation to the pilgrimages to Compostela, the documents of the sixteenth century seem to indicate a dual aim: while the hospital, retained its original function serving pilgrims, the monastery looked more towards the Order's possessions in Extremadura and the kingdom of León.

[12] *A causa de que la capilla que agora está no es para se dexar en una aldea*, AHN, OO.MM, libro 1093-C, fol. 277.

[13] AHN, OO.MM, libro 1094-C, fol. 306.

Figure 33.4   Detail of the façade of San Marcos (León)

Figure 33.3   Interior of the church of San Marcos (León)

Figure 33.5   Cloister walk of Calera de León (Badajoz)

Figure 33.6   Cloister of Calera de León (Badajoz)

the Chapter of Valladolid in 1513, the complete reconstruction of the complex,[14] entrusting the design to Pedro de Larrea, an architect who was at that time working on the monastery of San Benito of the Order of Alcántara.

Although the work did not begin immediately, we know that in 1528 the main chapel had already been demolished and that the present church was being built close to the monastery.[15] Ten years later the new church, the façade up to the present doorway, two of the cloister walks, the chapter house and the laundry were almost finished,[16] – that is, practically everything that was built in the sixteenth century. The towers and the upper section of the facade were never completed.[17]

The reason for such large-scale improvements to San Marcos after the alterations carried out by García Ramírez was not so much the poor maintenance of the monastery as the need to create an architecture appropriate to a building of this importance. Elements of the two aesthetic trends which, without being mutually exclusive, were expressions of modernity, were used to make it 'representative' – late gothic and renaissance, both understood in the broadest sense (see Figures 33.3 and 33.4) This makes the building a very clear example of the use of an architectural style as a symbolic reference to the power of the institution to which the building belongs.

SANTIAGO DE CALERA DE LEÓN

The monastery of Calera de León (Badajoz) was built between the 1550s and 1570s because the symbolic monastery of Tudía, situated as it was in the mountains of Tudía, was considered insalubrious and unhealthy. The speed of construction gave the whole complex great stylistic homogeneity within the context of sixteenth-century Extramadura.[18]

In accordance with the mudejar tradition, the exterior of Calera is austere, with plain, closed walls with hardly any decoration. The richness of the work is inside, in the magnificent gothic ribbed vaults to all the walks and rooms (see Figure 33.5); and in the renaissance purism of the cloister arcades[19] (Figure 33.6). The decorative elements make constant references to the building's patron saint: Santiago crosses, scallops and the lion of San Marcos.

---

[14] *Porque ese dicho convento es casa vieja y mal edificada e no está echa y ordenada según e como conviene para casa de Religión especialmente siendo tan principal y teniendo tan buena renta como tiene*, cited in W. Merino Rubio, *Arquitectura Hispano Flamenca en León* (León, 1974), p. 200.

[15] AHN, OO.MM, libro 1098-C, fol. 419.

[16] AHN, OO.MM, libro 1099-C, fol. 416.

[17] On the phases and the masters in charge of the work, see M. Gomez Moreno, *Catálogo Monumental de León* (Madrid, 1925), pp. 293–8; V. Nieto Alcaide, A.J. Morales and F. Checa, *Arquitectura del Renacimiento en España, 1488–1599* (Madrid, 1989), pp. 187–90.

[18] See A. de la Banda y Vargas, 'Arquitectura del Renacimiento y Barroco', *Historia de la Baja Extremadura*, 2 (Badajoz, 1986), pp. 547–56.

[19] AHN, OO.MM, libro 1012-C, fol. 1307v.

The rooms of the monastery of Calera are organized round a central courtyard in the classic manner; on the ground floor the refectory, kitchen, laundry, sacristy, treasury and chapter house are noteworthy, and on the upper floor the guest room and brothers' cells.

The church is located against the north side of the cloister. It joins the main chapel of a previous religious building which existed at least to the end of the fifteenth century, and the single aisle of a church built about the middle of the sixteenth century,[20] thus providing the extra space needed by the resident community of the new monastery. A characteristic element of its ground plan are the niche chapels on the Epistle side which, in contrast to Uclés, do not have a funerary function. No official of the Order of Santiago chose the church of Calera as his burial place for one obvious reason: the proximity of the charismatic monastery of Tudía, where the Masters Pelayo Pérez Correa, Gonzalo Mejía and Fernando Ozores are buried.

.

---

[20] I. Fronton Simon, F.J. Pérez Carrasco, O. Pérez Monzón and A. Ruiz Mateos, 'La Iglesia del Conventual Santiaguista de Calera de León', *Revista de Estudios Extremeños*, 48 (1992), 1, pp. 73–113.

Part V

The Perceptions and Role of
the Military Orders

34

The Confraternity of La Sauve-Majeure: a Foreshadowing of the Military Order?*

Marcus Bull

The emergence of the military orders was intimately connected to crusading thought and practices. The Templars and their imitators were not technically crusaders, being differentiated by the nature of their votive obligations and the duration of their service. But the physical setting in which the earliest brethren operated was one created by crusading; and brethren and crusaders alike bore witness to the particular ways in which, by the end of the eleventh century and the early decades of the twelfth, the Latin world approached the concept that violence could be used in the service of the Church and in the hope of spiritual gain.

The question therefore arises whether the search for the orders' origins can usefully be pushed back before the launching of the First Crusade in November 1095. When Pope Urban II issued his crusade appeal at the Council of Clermont, were there already present within western European society ideas and institutions which not only touch on the broad problem of the antecedents of crusading but also anticipate the distinctive characteristics of the military orders? The fact that observers were impressed by the novelty of the brethren's synthesis of military activity and patterns of behaviour associated with professed religion suggests that close analogues had not existed in the recent past.[1] Consequently we need to expand our terms of reference when exploring possible precedents.

It would be of limited value simply to isolate collectivities which were more than transitory and pursued ends considered to be laudable. This formulation

---

* I would like to thank Dr Jane Martindale for her assistance in clarifying a number of points.

[1] Bernard of Clairvaux, 'Liber ad milites Templi de laude novae militiae', *Sancti Bernardi Opera*, ed. J. Leclercq, C. H. Talbot and H. M. Rochais, 8 vols, 3 (Rome, 1957–77), pp. 214, 215, 219–21; J. Leclercq, 'Un document sur les débuts des Templiers', *Revue d'histoire ecclésiastique*, 52 (1957), pp. 86–9.

would include kinsmen engaged together in a vendetta or bodies of household knights grouped around their lord. Both types of relationship, the familial and the feudal, could exert a powerful hold on warriors' imaginations; and both had resonances in the crusaders' and the military orders' vocations. But this observation does not get us far along the road to the military orders themselves, beyond the general point that lords and knights in the years around 1100 were comfortable with the idea of solemnly binding themselves to communal acts and investing those acts with deep emotional significance. A more realistically precise search for analogues of the orders must first introduce the Church as an indispensable and formative influence. Second, it must single out any group capable of enjoying a sense of institutional identity – as instilled by such means as initiation ceremonies and modes of prescribed conduct – which was detached from the normal run of conventions governing relationships among Europe's warrior classes.

It is within these parameters that attention has sometimes been drawn to a collection of laymen associated with the abbey of La Sauve-Majeure in the late eleventh century. This group, or 'confraternity', has been supposed to have been licensed by the monastery to use force in order to protect the monks themselves as well as pilgrims and merchants; it thus represented one attempt by the Church, shortly before the First Crusade, to invest the profession of arms with an ethically positive purpose within a framework of regulated communal endeavour.[2] A re-examination of the evidence, however, suggests that the experience of La Sauve did not anticipate the military orders in such a direct way.

La Sauve-Majeure was situated in Entre-Deux-Mers. The abbey's founding father was St Gerard of Corbie, who led an assorted group of monks and lay followers from north-eastern France to Aquitaine in 1079 and established the monastery in woodland fifteen miles east of Bordeaux.[3] About sixty years of age, Gerard had had a long, but chequered, monastic career. He had entered Corbie as an oblate and had risen to positions of authority as the close associate of Abbot Fulk I.[4] Later, however, he had experienced bitter failure as abbot of Saint-Vincent, Laon, and Saint-Médard, Soissons.[5] In seeking out a distant spot to pursue his vocation afresh, Gerard may be said to have anticipated the methods of later reforming monastic movements. But neither in his own spir-

---

[2] C. Erdmann, *The Origin of the Idea of Crusade*, trans. M. W. Baldwin and W. Goffart (Princeton, 1977), p. 272; H. Hoffmann, *Gottesfriede und Treuga Dei*. Monumenta Germaniae Historica Schriften, 20 (Stuttgart, 1964), p. 105; A. J. Forey, 'The Emergence of the Military Order in the Twelfth Century', *Journal of Ecclesiastical History*, 36 (1985), p. 189; D. W. Lomax, 'Las dependencias hispánicas de Santa María de la Selva Mayor', *Príncipe de Viana*, 47 (1986), p. 498.

[3] 'Vita S. Geraldi abbatis', *Acta Sanctorum Bollandiana* (*AASS*), April, pp. 419–21; 'Notitia de fundatione monasterii Silvae-majoris', *RHGF*, 14, p. 46.

[4] 'Vita S. Geraldi', pp. 414–18; G. M. Oury, 'Gérard de Corbie avant son arrivée à la Sauve-Majeure', *Revue bénédictine*, 90 (1980), pp. 307–11.

[5] 'Vita S. Geraldi', p. 419; 'Notitia de fundatione', pp. 45–6; Oury, 'Gérard', pp. 311–12.

ituality nor in the regime he instigated at La Sauve can Gerard be described as a mould-breaker. He had evangelical leanings and was influenced by recluses,[6] but broadly his background was in the mainstream of French Benedictinism around the middle years of the eleventh century. His surviving writings and his later reputation at La Sauve do not point to a man with progressive ideas about the spiritual value of violence or the function of warriors within Christian society.[7] Indeed, one of the critical phases in the sequence of events which led to the foundation of the abbey was Gerard's perfectly conventional encouragement of five northern knights to pursue their search for penitence by means of a pilgrimage to Compostela and then the taking of the habit.[8]

The significance of Gerard's career before he moved to Aquitaine lies in his experience of the inability of a monastic community to function properly if the external influences on it were not carefully controlled. During his time at Corbie, the abbey's properties were threatened by its advocate and the count of Amiens, and its exemptions from episcopal jurisdiction were repeatedly challenged by the bishops of Amiens.[9] When, later, Gerard quarrelled with the brethren of Saint-Vincent about their lax communal routine, the local bishop intervened on the monks' behalf and made his position untenable; similarly, his authority at Saint-Médard was undermined by the intervention of King Philip I in support of an earlier abbot, the queen's protégé Pons, who had been deposed for simony.[10] While Gerard's actions at La Sauve suggest that he was by no means hostile in principle to the patronage of secular and ecclesiastical authorities, it is clear that he intended that such patronage could not translate itself into interference.

On their arrival in Aquitaine, Gerard and his party received a favourable reception from Duke William VIII, who encouraged the creation of a new monastery and supported the fledgling community at a legatine council held at Bordeaux in October 1080.[11] William became an enthusiastic benefactor, granting properties and rights of hospitality to the monks and permitting them to hold markets. His most significant contribution was to free the abbey and its possessions from ducal jurisdiction and exactions, thereby creating what some

---

[6] 'Vita S. Geraldi', pp. 418, 419, 421; Hariulf, 'Vita S. Arnulfi confessoris', *AASS*, Aug. 3, p. 237.

[7] G. M. Oury, 'La spiritualité du fondateur de La Sauve-Majeure, saint Gérard (v. 1020–1095)', *Revue historique de Bordeaux et du Département de la Gironde*, new ser. 29 (1982), pp. 5–19, esp. p. 8.

[8] 'Vita S. Geraldi', pp. 419, 420.

[9] R. Bonnaud-Delamare, 'La paix d'Amiens et de Corbie au XIe siècle', *Revue du Nord*, 38 (1956), pp. 175–7; Oury, 'Gérard', pp. 308, 309.

[10] 'Vita S. Geraldi', p. 419; 'Notitia de fundatione', pp. 45–6; Hariulf, 'Vita S. Arnulfi', p. 237; Oury, 'Gérard', p. 312.

[11] 'Notitia de fundatione', p. 46; 'Grand Cartulaire de La Sauve-Majeure', Bibliothèque Municipale, Bordeaux, ms. 769 [= Archives Départementales de la Gironde, H 1-2], pp. 8–10: this document is edited in J. Mabillon, *De Re Diplomatica* (Paris, 1681), pp. 586–7.

of La Sauve's early charters variously term a state of *securitas*, *salvamentum* and *salvitas*.[12] *Salvitates* were zones of immunity – associated with churches and stages on the roads taken by pilgrims to Spain – which had been emerging in southern France since the end of the tenth century. The principle involved was simple: within boundaries established by crosses or marker-stones, areas were created within which the regular exercise of secular authority was wholly or partly suspended.[13] When combined with exemptions from episcopal juris-diction, such as were proposed for La Sauve at the Council of Bordeaux, *salvitates* allowed religious communities a significant level of independence in their legal and economic dealings with the outside world.

Both Gerard's first *Vita* (*c.* 1140) and some of the first entries in La Sauve's twelfth-century cartulary emphasize the role played by William in putting the abbey on its feet.[14] The acknowledgement of this debt is a valuable indication that the *salvitas* was treated as the fundamental institution governing the monastery's relationships with its neighbours. In particular it was the *salvitas* which informed the creation and activity of the so-called confraternity. The dynamics at work become clear when it is considered that La Sauve was both a foreign implantation staffed by men with no familial or linguistic roots in the region and an institution insisting on considerable autonomy as a matter of principle. A source of Benedictine communities' strength was their ability to create a nexus of intimate ties with the local laity by providing liturgical inter-cession and stimulating family traditions of benefaction and recruitment. Ultimately a community's position was underwritten by its locality's instinctive respect for it and the value attached to its spiritual power: immunities, exemptions and pure economic power could seldom guarantee monasteries continued prosperity if the pious enthusiasms of their lay constituencies were diverted to other, more fashionable, expressions of the religious life. The onus was consequently on Gerard and his followers to manufacture affective support-mechanisms in order to recreate a situation which in most instances evolved over generations.

One technique adopted was to broaden the range of persons who were formally committed to respecting the abbey's *salvitas*. Viscount Peter of Gavarret, for example, was invited to acknowledge La Sauve's *libertas*, as was William Amanieu of Benauges, the single most influential lord in the abbey's immediate vicinity.[15] One document in the abbey's cartulary records that

---

[12] 'Cartulaire', pp. 8–9, 10, 12. Cf. ibid., pp. 13–14, 14–15, 78, 170, 215.

[13] See C. Higounet, 'Les chemins de Saint-Jacques et Les sauvetés de Gascogne', *Annales du Midi*, 63 (1951), pp. 293–304; E. Magnou-Nortier, *La société laïque et l'église dans la province ecclési-astique de Narbonne (zone cispyrénéene) de la fin du VIIIe à la fin du XIe siècle.* Publications de l'Université de Toulouse-Le Mirail, **A 20** (Toulouse, 1974), pp. 293–8.

[14] 'Vita S. Geraldi', p. 419; 'Cartulaire', pp. 4, 8–9, 11–13, 111, 114. See also 'Notitia de fundatione', p. 46; Hariulf, 'Vita S. Arnulfi', p. 237.

[15] 'Cartulaire', pp. 10, 12, 14.

Arnald of Blanquefort and others swore to become *defensores et aduocatos*; another powerful lord, Raymond of Gensac, styled himself the monks' *frater et amicus ... defensor et aduocatus*.[16] No surviving document precisely defines the role such men were expected to play, but it was broadly understood that they were meant to act against all those *tam amicos quam inimicos* who unjustly seized or claimed the abbey's property or inflicted injury on the monks and their dependants.[17]

On the face of it, this obligation might seem to relate to some form of military body devised to protect La Sauve's interests, and as such a foreshadowing of the military orders. Such an interpretation appears unwarranted, however, for it is based on an inaccurate reading of La Sauve's early documents by the abbey's mid-nineteenth-century historian, the Abbé Cirot de la Ville, who envisaged the creation of a standing force in a sanctifying ceremony held in the abbey church and characterized by the blessing of swords.[18] While tenth- and eleventh-century pontificals suggest that it is not impossible that swords could have been blessed in the context of the designation of important lords as *defensores*[19] – especially given Gerard's roots in north-eastern France, close to the Empire – Cirot de la Ville's failure to identify his source precisely, the absence of such a document from the cartulary, and the fact that the names of his ten-man 'Société pour la défense de l'abbaye' can be taken from unrelated early charters (in some instances so early that La Sauve's church was not yet built), all suggest that he simply assumed that such a ceremony took place on the basis of later chivalric rites.[20] That rights of *aduocatio* were among those expressly negated by the *salvitas* supports this view.[21] In reality, the attraction of the *defensores* for the monks was not their warrior expertise as such, but their capacity to judge and their authority over kinsfolk and vassals. The *defensores* were consequently of elevated social status, men described as *proceres*, *principes et nobiles regionis*, *nobiles milites* and *principes castella tenentes*.[22] When, most probably in 1120, the abbey's *salvitas* was rehearsed in the presence of

---

[16] Ibid., pp. 11, 165.

[17] Ibid., p. 11.

[18] Abbé Cirot de la Ville, *Histoire de l'abbaye et congrégation de Notre-Dame de la Grande-Sauve*, 2 vols, 1 (Paris and Bordeaux, 1844–5), pp. 297–8.

[19] See J. Flori, 'Chevalerie et liturgie: remise des armes et vocabulaire "chevaleresque" dans les sources liturgiques du IXe au XIVe siècle', *Le moyen âge*, 84 (1978), pp. 266–78, 423–6, 434–8; idem, *L'essor de la chevalerie XIe–XIIe siècles*. Travaux d'histoire éthico-politique, 46 (Geneva, 1986), pp. 81–111.

[20] Cirot de la Ville's supporting document, *Histoire*, 1, pp. 497–8, simply reproduces a later copy of 'Cartulaire', p. 11 referring to an oath taken by Arnald of Blanquefort and others to become *defensores et aduocati* and outlining their duties.

[21] 'Cartulaire', p. 10.

[22] Ibid., pp. 10, 11, 12, 14. See C. Higounet, 'En Bordelais: "Principes castella tenentes"', *La noblesse au moyen âge XIe–XVe siècles: Essais à la mémoire de Robert Boutruche*, ed. P. Contamine (Paris, 1976), pp. 97–104.

Duke William IX and a large aristocratic gathering, those present were described as *barones ac principes* whose predecessors had first sworn to uphold the monastery's security.[23]

The enforcing of judgements and the exercise of authority carried with them the possibility of violence; one document speaks of *ultio* and *uindicta* against persistent opponents of the abbey.[24] But direct force was only one aspect of the judicial procedures which the monks wished to operate for their benefit, and one which they intended should be marginalized. In at least one case they exerted themselves to prevent a property dispute between two laymen, which had a bearing on the abbey's interests, from being resolved by judicial duel: this was done, they said, so that blood would not be shed on their account.[25] Some of La Sauve's earliest documents insist that tenurial patterns in the abbey's vicinity were very complex, consisting of a patchwork of allods and fiefs spread among a number of kindreds.[26] It was therefore useful to secure the good offices of those lords and dynasts who could supervise the reshuffling of rights and properties as grants to the abbey were made or contested. Typical of what the monks had in mind was the resolution *interuenientibus proceribus* of a long dispute between the abbey and a kinsman of one of its first and most generous benefactors.[27]

Apart from respect for ducal authority – to which the monks appealed regularly – what could have induced the lords of the Bordelais to swear to protect La Sauve's rights? The answer to this reveals the true significance of the abbey's experience, for the lure attracting the powerful laymen, and what turned *defensores* into *confratres*, was the provision of intercession. The connection was probably first made in relation to Duke William VIII, who was granted a weekly mass and the benefit of daily alms-giving in return for his generosity to the abbey.[28] Similarly, the document recording that Arnald of Blanquefort and other nobles had become *defensores* refers to their receipt of the 'benefits of the church', defined as the celebration of a weekly mass by each ordained monk, special prayers, association with alms-giving, a burst of liturgical commemoration after death and 'honourable' – that is, quasi-monastic – burial rites *ut confratrem decet*.[29] This generous package must be seen in the context of Gerard's well documented interest in establishing ties of confraternity with religious houses. Prestigious abbeys such as Saint-Jean-d'Angély, Conques and Brantôme were among the first to agree with La Sauve a sequence of bell-tolling, offices, masses, psalms and alms whenever news of the death of a monk from

---

[23] 'Cartulaire', p. 22.
[24] Ibid., p. 11.
[25] Ibid., pp. 4–5.
[26] Ibid., pp. 3, 4, 5, 12, 110–11. Cf. 'Vita S. Geraldi', p. 419.
[27] 'Cartulaire', p. 52. Cf. ibid., pp. 4, 5, 6–8, 11, 16, 18–19, 21, 36, 49, 142, 145, 166.
[28] Ibid., p. 13.
[29] Ibid., p. 11.

the other house reached them.[30] The abbey of Maillezais entered into a similar arrangement, and may have done so as early as 1080 with the resolution of a dispute about the eviction of one of their number who had been living as a hermit near the site of La Sauve.[31] Gerard was thus an abbot attuned to the power of intercession in creating and perpetuating stable relationships. The liturgical and extra-liturgical services offered to La Sauve's lay *confratres* did not fully match those of monastic and clerical associates in their solemnity and duration, but they were fair approximations in harmony with, for example, the wish expressed by a benefactor of another Aquitanian abbey that provision be made for his soul 'as if he were a monk'.[32]

It is impossible to gauge the effectiveness of La Sauve's *defensores* and their commitment to their obligations, but the simple fact that Abbot Gerard chose to exploit the provision of generous spiritual services in order to attract loyalty is itself striking. The confraternity of La Sauve was not a holy militia mandated by the Church to conduct meritorious violence, nor a body with any strong sense of communal identity, ritualized behaviour and horizontal ties governing relations between its members. To this extent it is unreasonable to treat the group as a direct anticipation of the military orders. The abbey's experience is simply an unusually clear (because formally institutionalized) expression of laymen's willingness to act in pursuit of spiritual benefits, and their impulse to share as far as possible monks' ability to increase their own chances of salvation. Monastic role models were crucial in shaping both the ideas of crusaders and the vocation of the military orders. The interest of the confraternity of La Sauve therefore lies in its forming part of a much broader, Europe-wide picture which forms the background to the response to the First Crusade and thus indirectly – but only indirectly – helps to account for the emergence of the military orders.

---

[30] J–L. Lemaître, 'Les confraternités de La Sauve-Majeure', *Revue historique de Bordeaux et du Département de la Gironde*, new ser. **28** (1981), 9–13, 29–30, 32–4.

[31] Ibid., p. 31; 'Cartulaire', pp. 3–4, which is edited in R. Boutruche, *Une société provinciale en lutte contre le régime féodal: l'alleu en Bordelais et en Bazadais du XIe au XVIIIe siècle*. Publications de la Faculté des Lettres de l'Université de Strasbourg, fasc. **100** (Rodez, 1943), pp. 208–10.

[32] *Cartulaire des abbayes de Tulle et de Roc-Amadour*, ed. J-B. Champeval (Brive, 1903), no. 180, p. 112.

35

Medical Knowledge in the Crusading Armies: the Evidence of Albert of Aachen and Others

Susan Edgington

My object in this paper is to establish the ideas about illness and treatment that the crusaders brought with them from the West. There is a tendency, illustrated in the later sources,[1] to assume that they acquired such worthwhile practices from natives in the East. It is of particular interest whether magico-religious beliefs, such as in relics and miracles – a feature of European medicine at this exact time – also dominated medical practice on the First Crusade, which was after all a pilgrimage of unprecedented size to a land whose very earth was a relic.[2]

I am therefore discussing medical knowledge and practice among the first generation of crusaders: that is, my principal sources are the Latin chroniclers, and the period under study is 1095 to about 1120.

The chief eye-witness accounts yield little information.[3] There is little useful for this purpose in the *Gesta Francorum* or the crusaders' letters. Likewise,

---

[1] Ousamah ibn Mounkidh, *Autobiography*, trans. G.R. Potter (London, 1929); *Assises de la cour des Bourgeois*, *RHC Lois*, **2**, pp. 164–9; A.F. Woodings, 'The Medical Resources and Practice of the Crusader States in Syria and Palestine 1096–1193', *Medical History*, **15** (1971), pp. 268–77; R. Hiestand, 'König Balduin und sein Tanzbär', *Archiv für Kulturgeschichte*, **70** (1988), pp. 343–60.

[2] J. Riley-Smith, 'Peace never established: the case of the kingdom of Jerusalem', *Transactions of the Royal Historical Society*, 5th series, **28** (1978), 87–102.

[3] Editions and translations used: Anonymous, *Gesta Francorum*, ed. and trans. R. Hill (London, 1962); *Kreuzzugsbriefe aus den Jahren 1088–1100*, ed. H. Hagenmeyer (Innsbruck, 1902); Raymond of Aguilers, *Liber*, ed. J.H. and L.L. Hill (Paris, 1969) trans. J.H. and L.L. Hill, Philadelphia, 1968; Fulcher of Chartres, *Gesta Francorum Iherusalem Peregrinantium*, ed. H. Hagenmeyer (Heidelberg, 1913), trans. H. Fink and F.R. Ryan (Tennessee, 1969); Robert the Monk, *Historia Hierosolymitana*, *RHC Occid*, **3**, pp. 717–882; Albert of Aachen, *Historia Iherosolimitana*, my edn (PhD London, 1991) and trans.; Guibert of Nogent, *Gesta Dei per Francos*, *RHC Occid*, **4**, pp. 113–263/my trans.; Baudri of Dol, *Historia Jerosolimitana*, *RHC Occid*, **5**, pp. 1–111; Orderic Vitalis, *Historia Ecclesiastica*, ed. and trans. M. Chibnall (Oxford, 1969–1980); Radulf of Caen, *Gesta Tancredi*, *RHC Occid*, **3**, pp. 587–716; Ekkehard of Aura, *Frutolfi et Ekkehardi Chronica*, ed. F.J. Schmale and I. Schmale-Ott (Darmstadt, 1972); William of Tyre, *Chronicon*, ed. R.B.C. Huygens (Turnhout, 1986), trans. E.A. Babcock and A.C. Krey (New York, 1943).

Raymond of Aguilers characteristically ascribes Peter Bartholomew's illness on the one hand, and Count Raymond's cure on the other, each to divine intervention.[4] Fulcher of Chartres, who so often digresses informatively, shows little interest in this subject. His chapter on native cures, including a medicine made of bedbugs and the use of snake poison as its own antidote, seems to derive ultimately from Pliny.[5]

Such a silence among the most valuable sources begs questions: most importantly, how trustworthy are the rest? For instance, when Robert the Monk mentions the activity of doctors after the battle of Nicaea he may be elaborating the *Gesta* from other sources (perhaps oral), from his imagination, or by drawing on his knowledge of battles in the West.[6] Nevertheless, 'secondary' chroniclers may be valuable for their unwitting testimony of attitudes and assumptions among the people of western Europe, and hence the crusaders.

My principal sources are therefore contemporaries writing at varying distances from the action, but incorporating interesting information on medical practice: Albert of Aachen, Guibert of Nogent, Baudri of Dol, Orderic Vitalis, Radulf of Caen and Ekkehard of Aura. William of Tyre wrote at a yet further remove in time.

All of the writers distinguish between wounds, whose cause was known and which were often curable by empirical methods, and disease, the cause of which was not understood and which was the subject of much speculation.

It is well known that Duke Godfrey was wounded in a fight with a bear in Syria in the summer of 1097.[7] In fact he sustained less damage from the claws and teeth of the 'bloodthirsty beast' than he did from getting his legs entangled with his own sword. The result was 'an unstaunchable stream of blood' (probably from the femoral artery) and he collapsed. He was brought into the camp on a litter and there he was treated by, according to Albert, 'very skilled doctors' (*medici peritissimi*). William of Tyre calls them surgeons (*cirurgici*) and adds 'it was hoped that through their zealous efforts and the use of proper remedies he might be restored to health'.[8] Unfortunately neither writer describes the 'proper remedies', for Godfrey's recovery from an apparently mortal wound does seem remarkable.

However, this incident puts Guibert of Nogent in mind of a second case involving a bear, and this is more informative. He writes:

And as we have once mentioned a bear, we should like to take out of turn something Baldwin his brother also did, who now rules Jerusalem, since perhaps

---

[4] Raymond, *Liber*, ch. 5, edn p. 46/trans. pp. 28–9, see below, and ch. 10, pp. 70–77 /p. 53: Peter Bartholomew is visited with blindness by St Andrew.

[5] Fulcher, *Gesta*, III, p. 59, edn p. 814/trans. p. 300; cf. Pliny, *Hist. Nat.* XXIX, 17.61–2, edn W.H.S. Jones, vol. 8 (London, 1963), pp. 222–5.

[6] Robert, *Historia*, III, p. 5, p. 764.

[7] Albert, *Historia*, III, 4; Guibert, *Gesta Dei*, XII, p. 230.

[8] WT, III, 18 (17), edn p. 220/trans. p. 176.

no other more suitable place will occur for reporting it. For the sake of rescuing one of his footsoldiers ... he likewise sustained a very severe wound in battle. The doctor whom he had summoned made a diagnosis, but he feared to cover the wound outside by applying poultices, knowing that the wound had reached the insides of the body quite deeply, and while the surface of the skin might heal smoothly, on the inside a build-up of pus would be encouraged. So he proposed a wonderful expedient from his praiseworthy opinion and experience. He asked the king that he might order one of the Saracens he was holding in custody (for it would be wicked to ask for a Christian), to be wounded in that position and in such a place as the king himself had been wounded, and then to order him to be killed, so that the doctor might investigate freely on the dead body and examine certainly from looking at it what the royal wound was like on its inside. The pious prince was utterly horrified at this ... saying he was not going to be the cause of anybody's death whatsoever, even a person of the worst sort, for the sake of so small a thing as his health, when even that was dubious. Then the doctor said: 'If you draw a line at depriving anyone of life for the sake of repairing your own health, then at least order the bear, which is useless enough except as a sideshow, to be brought; command that it be killed with a weapon when it is upright with its front paws stretched out on high; and when I examine the dead beast's internal organs afterwards, I shall be able to make a sound judgement in one way or another from how far it has penetrated, how great also is your wound.' The king said to him: 'Since it is necessary, the beast is no problem; consider it done.' Therefore, when the experiment had been carried out on the wild beast to please the doctor, he ascertained that, as we have hinted above, it would be troublesome to the king; if a covering was applied too quickly to the wound without the pus being drained first and the torn part brought together.[9]

It would be satisfying if we could be sure that this wound was the one sustained by Baldwin in an ambush in 1103, for we have more than one detailed description of this. According to Albert, Baldwin

... was pierced through the thigh and kidneys ... streams of blood poured forth ... he was thought to have died ... He was able to recover thanks to the skill and experience of very able doctors.[10]

Fulcher recounts that the missile

... injured the king most severely, in the back near the heart. By this stroke he wounded the king nigh unto death. But because Baldwin afterwards sought to have himself carefully treated, after an incision he at length recovered from his troublesome wound.[11]

While William says:

---

[9] Guibert, *Gesta Die*, XIII, pp. 230–31; Hiestand has an excellent discussion of this incident, see fn. 1.

[10] Albert, *Historia*, IX, 22.

[11] Fulcher, *Gesta*, II, 24, edn pp. 460–61/trans. pp. 175–6.

... a javelin struck the King. It entered from behind through the ribs near the heart and just missed dealing a fatal blow. The care of physicians, however, with their use of incisions and cautery, at length restored Baldwin to some degree of health....[12]

In brief, they agree on little, except that a severe wound was successfully treated. Furthermore, the above cases both refer to leaders and to treatment that was unlikely to be available to the average infantryman. There is some evidence that wounded soldiers received care on the battle-field, besides Robert the Monk, mentioned above. William of Tyre says that after the battle of Dorylaeum the army was granted a short rest to care for the wounded.[13] Albert tells how after a sea-battle the wounded Christians were shipped to Acre along with the prisoners of war.[14] We can only guess, or hope, that these wounded received the sort of practical care which cured their leaders.

When the chroniclers are faced with disease they are at a loss to understand its causes, let alone to describe ways of countering it. When pestilence first appeared Albert reports that a conference of leaders thought the 'devastating mortality' had arisen among the people because of their 'great number of sins'.[15] The response was to forbid sinful practices and to decree that anyone who disobeyed was to be punished 'and thus God's people would be sanctified from filth and impurity'. William has a similar passage, adding that the princes decreed a fast – rather odd as he has said that the illness resulted from famine and cold and heavy rainfall, but conceivably a case of making a virtue out of a necessity.[16]

However, when a second epidemic struck in Antioch the crusaders did not put it down to sin, but looked for other causes. Its extent awed them: Albert says that almost daily for six months the death toll was thirty to a hundred, and included every rank, even women, totalling over 100,000.[17] William embellishes the account, saying that 'women in particular were the victims ... nearly 50,000 perishing within a few days'.[18] According to Albert, Godfrey feared 'this was the same illness which he remembered had afflicted Rome long ago with a very similar disaster when he was on an expedition with Emperor Henry IV'.[19] He also reports that 1,500 German crusaders who arrived to reinforce the army were wiped out to a man. Possible explanations are offered: 'some claimed this mortality arose from the unhealthiness of the place, others from the plague-bearing month of August'.[20] William has this report:

[12] WT, X, 25 (26), edn p. 485/trans. p. 453; cf. Matthew of Edessa (*RHC DArm*, 1, p. 68), who says the wound was punishment for the false celebration of Easter.
[13] WT, III, 16 (15), edn p. 217/trans. p. 173.
[14] Albert, *Historia*, XII, 17.
[15] Ibid., III, 57.
[16] I thank Rosalind Hill for the last observation. WT, IV, 22, edn p. 264/trans. p. 220.
[17] Albert, *Historia*, V, 4.
[18] WT, VII, 1, edn p. 344/trans. 299.
[19] Albert, *Historia*, V, 13. The expedition was in 1083.
[20] Ibid., V, 24.

Those who have had the curiosity to investigate this subject in the hope of ascer-
taining the causes of this terrible scourge have arrived at varying conclusions. Some
say that it arose from seeds of disease that were latent in the air. Others believe
that when the people, so long victims of cruel hunger, finally obtained an
abundance of food, they were overeager to eat in order to make up for their
privations. Thus their unrestrained gluttony was the cause of their death.[21]

Radulf of Caen – writing at length and in verse – blames the poisonous
foodstuffs which famine had driven the crusaders to eat.[22] In Guibert's account
of an earlier epidemic in Apulia he cites as possible causes the unaccustomed
heat, corruption of the air and food the crusaders were not used to.[23] Ekkehard,
writing of an epidemic in 1100, suggests first the heat, then the stink of corpses
corrupting the air. He goes on: 'There are also some who say the springs had
been poisoned by the barbarians, or the cisterns by the diseased blood of the
killed....'[24] Quite overwhelmingly, however, the writers seek natural causes
for the plague.

The leaders' response to the Antioch epidemic was likewise pragmatic.
Godfrey left the plague-stricken city for the mountainous region around Edessa
and many others left for the port of St Symeon. They also decided to defer
the army's departure for Jerusalem to allow the people to be restored by rest
and food.[25] Baudri of Dol elaborates:

> Let us rest quietly while our sick and wounded recuperate, and meanwhile let
> us relieve the poor among us. Let us wait for the autumn rains and avoid the harmful
> influences of the Crab and the Lion. In November the temperature will fall; then
> let us assemble and set out again together along the chosen road. Otherwise all
> our people will be prostrated with the untimely heat.... If any poor man is
> physically fit, let him join our forces and we will pay out wages to every one for
> his maintenance. The sick shall be supported by a public dole until they have
> recovered.[26]

Whether such a scheme of public assistance ever really existed cannot be
established; nor to what extent at this time the well known 'hospital' in
Jerusalem provided care for the sick, and how far it functioned solely as a pilgrim
hostel.[27] Daimbert's letter to the pope recounts that during the battle of
Ascalon the crusaders left their baggage and their sick in the city with a

---

[21] WT, VII, 1, edn p. 344/trans. p. 299. See also VII, 11, edn p. 357/trans. p. 314 where the 'unclean
and noxious food' is blamed.

[22] Radulf, *Gesta Tancredi*, LXXX, p. 633.

[23] Guibert, *Gesta Dei*, II, 18, p. 150.

[24] Ekkehard, *Frutolfi*, XX, p. 160.

[25] Albert, *Historia*, V, 13 and 24; WT, VII, 2, edn p. 344/trans. p. 299.

[26] Baudri, *Historia*, III, 20, p. 80, quoted almost verbatim by Orderic, *Historia*, IX, 12 (Chibnall,
V, pp. 130–31). Both develop the account in *Gesta Francorum* which mentions the able-bodied
poor. but not the sick and wounded (pp. 72–3).

[27] WT, I, 10, edn p. 123/trans. p. 80.

garrison.[28] Albert details, *apropos* the quarrel between King Baldwin and Patriarch Daimbert in 1101, a gift of 1,000 gold bezants from Roger of Sicily, one-third of which was 'for the support of the hospital, the feeble and other sick'.[29] There is practically no information about treatment of the sick, other than a belief in 'R and R' – rest and recreation.[30] One could see the influence of the great medical school at Salerno in this approach, noting in passing that Bohemond himself had been treated there, so he at least knew of Salernitan beliefs.[31]

Two authors mention bathing: Albert tells how 'needy and fever-stricken pilgrims were bathing in warm springs to cure their weak bodies'. Unfortunately they were massacred by the Turks, so we do not know if the hydrotherapy worked.[32] William describes a spring near Nicopolis (Emaus):

> Here the ills of men are washed away and the various diseases to which the lower animals are subject are likewise cured. In explanation of this belief, tradition says that ... Christ appeared to His disciples at that same spring and himself bathed their feet in its waters; hence from that time on it became a cure from all ailments.

But he is quoting here explicitly from Sozomenus.[33]

And this, in William, writing so much later and not reporting his own beliefs, is the only instance which even hints at the use of relics to treat the sick in the Holy Land.[34] The only other mention of supernatural healing is found in Raymond of Aguilers who describes how Count Raymond's recovery from illness was miraculously foretold.[35] (William of Tyre seems to suspect him of malingering.)[36] Stephen of Blois' (probably) feigned illness is given short shrift by the chroniclers.[37] Tancred's dysentery is treated most matter-of-factly by Radulf of Caen: the difficulties of reconnaissance are described with sympathy and some humour, and the only miracle attaches to his discovery of

---

[28] Hagenmeyer, *Kreuzzugsbriefe*, XVIII, p. 171.

[29] Albert, *Historia*, VII, 62.

[30] For example, ibid., VII, 12 and X, 51; WT, III, 16 (15), edn p. 217/trans. p. 173; Baudri, *Historia*, II, 4, p. 37 and II, 7, p. 40.

[31] Orderic, *Historia*, VII, 7 (Chibnall, IV, pp. 28–9). His stepmother Sichelgaita acquired her skill in poisons there too (pp. 30–31); cf. William of Apulia, *Gesta Roberti Wiscardi*, ed. M. Mathieu (Palermo, 1961), pp. 248–9. The second important hospital in the eleventh century was at Montpellier – home of eminent crusaders.

[32] Albert, *Historia*, III, 54.

[33] WT, VII, 24, edn p. 376/trans. p. 335.

[34] Orderic (*Historia*, IX, 15) tells how Ilger Bigod took back to France 'a little ball of the hair of Mary' which he distributed there and which healed many sick people (Chibnall, V, pp. 170–71).

[35] Raymond, *Liber*, III, edn p. 46/trans. pp. 28–9.

[36] WT, V, 7, edn p. 280/trans. pp. 235–6.

[37] For example, Raymond, *Liber*, ch. 10, edn p. 77; Anon, *Gesta Francorum*, IX, 27, p. 63; Fulcher, *Gesta*, I, 16, edn p. 228; Baudri, *Historia*, III, 12, p. 71; Guibert, *Gesta Dei*, XXV, pp. 199–200.

a cache of 400 ready-hewn timbers while squatting in the bushes.[38] Godfrey's
last illness is generally treated as simply that, although Orderic accuses the
citizens of Jaffa of poisoning him.[39] When Baldwin dies in 1118 his last hours
are described, including a fish breakfast and the pain from his old wound, but
no desperate remedies are resorted to.[40] He called on his cook, not his doctor,
to embalm him.[41] Even in the case of these heroes, there seems to have been
a real appreciation of the inevitability of disease and death and the limitations
of medical knowledge and ability.

Thus the first generation of crusaders seems to have approached medicine
in a very practical way, and may have had less to learn from the native practitioners than has been assumed. To underline this I offer an example from Albert
– his only one – of a native cure:

> In this region of Sidon, while many were in danger from the fiery snakes ... and
> there was great weeping and wailing over those dying, the people were taught
> this medicine by the natives: that anyone who was bitten by a snake should go
> up to one of the nobler and more eminent people in the army, and if the wound
> of the sting was touched and embraced by that man's right hand the poison
> spread through the limbs would be seen to do no more harm. In the same way
> also they were taught another medicine, that a man who was bitten should lie at
> once with a woman, a woman with a man, and thus they would be released from
> all the swelling and heat of the poison.[42]

If the natives were serious (and perhaps they were not) then the first 'cure'
was simply thaumaturgy, and unlikely to be of use, while the second would
do more harm than good, by speeding the flow of the poisoned blood around
the body.

To summarize, the evidence is fragmentary and sometimes contradictory,
and little of it comes from eye-witness accounts. The crusaders had a clear understanding of wounds and treated them empirically. They understood the need
to drain the infection and used bandages, incisions and cautery as appropriate.
In the cases of Godfrey and Baldwin they were successful.

The first epidemic was greeted by religious hysteria, but the subsequent,
more serious one elicited a more rational response (perhaps because prayers
and penance had not worked), with the chroniclers proposing natural causes
and describing sensible reactions.

There is little evidence about remedies, but a notable absence of the magico-
religious ones which are a feature of Western medicine at this time.

This practical approach may explain why the crusaders learnt so readily from
medical practice in the East.

---

[38] Radulf, *Gesta Tancredi*, CXX, pp. 689–90.

[39] Orderic, *Historia*, X, 21 (Chibnall, V, pp. 340–41); cf. Matthew of Edessa (*RHC DArm*, 1, pp. 49–50). Matthew also claims Tancred was poisoned (p. 103).

[40] Fulcher, *Gesta*, II, edn pp. 609–13/trans. pp. 221–2: WT, XI, 31, edn p. 544/trans. p. 515.

[41] Albert, *Historia*, XII, 26–7.

[42] Ibid., V, 40.

36

Crusaders and Patrons: the Influence of the Crusades on the Patronage of the Order of St Lazarus in England

John Walker

In his book, *England and the Crusades*, Christopher Tyerman suggested that, 'the spread of pious and charitable grants to the new, specifically crusading orders and others associated with the Holy Land confirms a general interest in the crusade and Outremer'.[1] Indeed, it seems reasonable to assume that, with the growth of interest in the crusades in England, crusading orders might expect to receive patronage from people who either physically participated in expeditions to the Holy Land or who were simply influenced by events in that area. Support for this view comes from Janet Burton's study of the Yorkshire Templars in which she shows that the increase in the foundation of Templar preceptories in the county coincided with the Second and Third Crusades.[2] It is the aim of this paper to consider the hypothesis that the crusades acted as a stimulus to the patronage of crusading orders, using evidence from the patronage of the Order of St Lazarus which settled in England in the twelfth century.

The Order of St Lazarus was founded in Jerusalem in the early decades of the twelfth century.[3] It seems to have developed out of a situation whereby knights who contracted the disease of leprosy entered a hospital in Jerusalem which was originally run by Armenian monks following the Rule of St Basil. The membership of the Order comprised a master, leprous and healthy knights, clerics and brethren to look after the sick. From an early date these members

---

[1] C. Tyerman, *England and the Crusades 1095–1588* (Chicago, 1988), p. 31.

[2] J.E. Burton, 'The Knights Templar in Yorkshire in the Twelfth Century: A Reassessment', *Northern History*, 27 (1991), pp. 31–5.

[3] For the Order of St Lazarus see S. Shahar, 'Des Lepreux pas comme les autres', *Revue Historique*, 267 (1982), pp. 19–41. Other works on the history of the Order include R. Pétiet, *Contribution à l'histoire de l'Ordre de Saint Lazare de Jérusalem en France* (Paris, 1914); P.B. de la Grassière, *L'ordre militaire et hospitalier de Saint Lazare de Jérusalem* (Paris, 1962).

From *The Military Orders: Fighting for the Faith and Caring for the Sick*, ed. Malcolm Barber. Copyright © 1994 by Malcolm Barber. Published by Variorum, Ashgate Publishing Ltd, Gower House, Croft Road, Aldershot, Hampshire, GU11 3HR, Great Britain.

evidently adopted the Rule of St Augustine which was already followed by most hospitaller organizations in the West. At first, the Order's principal function was in the realm of hospital care, especially in the care of lepers – a function which distinguished it from the other larger military orders. However, by the thirteenth century, with the increasing need for manpower in the Holy Land, members of the Order became involved in limited military action. Most of the information relating to the Order's possessions comes from a cartulary fragment of the Jerusalem hospital.[4] This shows that the Order owned hospitals in Jerusalem and Acre, and small-scale lands and rents largely concentrated in the southern part of the kingdom of Jerusalem. These possessions were given by royal and noble patrons, as well as members of the lower social classes.

From the mid-twelfth century the Order also began to receive benefactions in Europe, and was established in France following Louis VII's grant of land at Boigny near Orléans.[5] In addition, the Order was also given possessions in Italy, the Empire, Spain, parts of eastern Europe[6] and England. The establishment in England can be dated from c. 1150, when Roger I of Mowbray founded the hospital of Burton Lazars in Leicestershire, which became the chief house of the English branch of the Order of St Lazarus.[7] As in the Holy Land, the Order's English members were subject to the rule of a master, who in turn was subject to the Grand Master of the Order in the Holy Land and, after the loss of the Christian possessions there, to the Master of Boigny. The other members included lepers, brethren to care for the sick and clerics; the functions of the English branch were chiefly concerned with the care of lepers and the collection of alms for the Holy Land.

The most important evidence relating to the Order's English activities is the cartulary of Burton Lazars, drawn up in 1404 by order of the then Master, Walter of Lynton.[8] The document contains little in the way of internal evidence, but a great deal of information concerning the possessions and patrons of the English Order. Its possessions were concentrated in eastern England, particularly in Leicestershire where, in addition to the hospital of Burton Lazars, the Order also owned a hospital at Tilton, the advowson of two churches, and c. 3,000 acres of land.[9] The Order was also given eleven other hospitals, including St Giles at Holborn, granted in 1299 by Edward I, and Holy

[4] A. de Marsy, 'Fragment d'un Cartulaire de l'Ordre de Saint Lazare, en Terre-Sainte', *AOL*, 2 (1884), pp. 121–57.

[5] *Etudes sur les Actes de Louis VII*, ed. A. Luchaire (Paris, 1885), p. 208.

[6] Pétiet, pp. 99–148.

[7] BL, Cotton ms. Nero CXII, fol. 3. For the English branch of the Order see *The Victoria History of the County of Leicester*, 2, ed. W.G. Hoskins (London, 1954), pp. 36–8; *The Burton Lazars Cartulary: A Medieval Leicestershire Estate*, ed. T. Bourne and D. Marcombe (Nottingham, 1987); J. Walker, *The Patronage of the Templars and of the Order of St Lazarus in England in the Twelfth and Thirteenth Centuries*, unpublished PhD thesis (St Andrews, 1990).

[8] BL, Cotton ms. Nero CXII.

[9] Walker, pp. 269–77.

Innocents at Lincoln, granted in 1461 by Edward IV.[10] As in the Holy Land, the patrons of the English branch of the Order were drawn from a wide range of social backgrounds, although the majority of donations were made by members of local county families and the knightly classes.[11]

In order to assess the importance of the crusading influence on the patronage of the Order of St Lazarus it is obviously important to be able to assess the number of patrons who went on crusade. The evidence for the participation of Englishmen in crusades has been studied by several historians, including Beatrice Siedschlag, Bruce Beebe and Simon Lloyd who have produced lists of English crusaders using evidence including the grants of protection made for crusaders' lands and the appointment of crusaders' attorneys.[12] Of course these records take no account of those who might have made arrangements to go on crusade then actually failed to fulfil their vows, nor of those private pilgrims or crusaders from the lower classes who had no reason, or were unable, to ask for protection or to appoint an attorney in their absence.[13] Nevertheless, the available evidence does provide the names of a considerable number of English crusaders and forms the basis for this study.

From the list of known crusaders, several patrons of the Order of St Lazarus have been identified. Two of the most important were Roger I of Mowbray and William I Burdet. Roger I of Mowbray was the son of Nigel of Aubigny who had been granted large estates in Yorkshire and Leicestershire by Henry I in the early twelfth century.[14] It is possible that Roger participated in four expeditions to the Holy Land. He certainly took part in the Second Crusade, and was in the Holy Land again in 1164, where he witnessed a charter of King Amaury to the Order of St Lazarus.[15] In addition, he may have joined the count of Flanders' expedition in 1177. Ten years later, as part of the Christian force defeated at Hattin in 1187, he was captured by the Muslim forces and subsequently ransomed by the Templars and Hospitallers. He died soon afterwards and was buried in the Holy Land. Roger I was a generous patron of several religious orders including the Templars, and was largely responsible for the establishment of the Order of St Lazarus in England, to whom he gave rents from his mills in Yorkshire and several small grants in eastern Leices-

---

[10] *Calendar of the Patent Rolls preserved in the Public Record Office*, 1292–1301, p. 404; 1461–67, p. 123.

[11] Walker, p. 246.

[12] B. Siedschlag, *English Participation in the Crusades 1150–1220* (Bryn Mawr, 1939), pp. 107–44; B. Beebe, 'The English Baronage and the Crusade of 1270', *Bulletin of the Institute of Historical Research*, 48 (1975), pp. 143–8; S. Lloyd, *English Society and the Crusade 1216–1307* (Oxford, 1988), appendix 4.

[13] Beebe, p. 131; Burton, pp. 31–2.

[14] *Charters of the Honour of Mowbray 1107–1191*, ed. D.E. Greenway (London, 1972), pp. xvii–xxii.

[15] Marsy, p. 140.

tershire.[16] However, his most important grant was made *c.* 1150 and comprised two carucates of land, a messuage, and the site of a mill in Burton Lazars.[17] This donation constituted one of the largest made to the Order in England, and was probably given soon after Roger's return from the Second Crusade. The importance of this particular grant is heightened by the fact that it is generally assumed to be the foundation charter of the hospital of Burton Lazars.[18]

William I Burdet was from a branch of the Burdet family which held land in Cold Newton, Lowesby and Burton Lazars in Leicestershire.[19] He was descended from Robert Burdet (died by 1086) and was a steward of King Malcolm IV of Scotland, and a member of the court of Robert II Beaumont, Earl of Leicester. Although there is no contemporary evidence for William's crusading activity, two English antiquarians, John Nichols and William Dugdale, have suggested that he did go to the Holy Land in the twelfth century. Nichols suggested that

> ... in the latter end of the reign of King henry II, Sir William Burdet undertook a voyage to the Holy Land; whither the king and the king of France intended to have gone with an army royl to the assistance o Guy de Lusignania king of jerusalem, who was then taken prisoner by Salaine souldan of Aegypt, who had taken Jerusalem and all the holy Land in 1187; ...[20]

In fact, Nichols' suggestion can be immediately discounted, as Burdet was dead by 1184.[21] The reference given by William Dugdale appears to be better founded. He describes Burdet as '... both a valiant and devout man [who] made a journey to the Holy Land, for subduing of the infidels in those parts ...'.[22] He suggests that William was on crusade in the mid-twelfth century, possibly as a participant on the Second Crusade. It was presumably after his return that he gave the Order the advowson of the Leicestershire hospital of Tilton, the churches of Galby and Lowesby (Leicestershire), and Haselbeech (Northamptonshire), and a carucate of land in Cold Newton (Leicestershire).[23] This grant was second only to that of Roger of Mowbray in terms of size and importance.

---

[16] BL, Cotton ms. Nero CXII, fols 3v, 4, 4v; Greenway, p. 182; B.A. Lees, *Records of the Templars in England in the Twelfth Century. The Inquest of 1185* (London, 1935), pp. 33–5, 78, 111, 125, 132, 254–8, 269–70.

[17] BL, Cotton ms. Nero CXII, fol. 3.

[18] For discussion of this point see Walker, pp. 119–21.

[19] D. Crouch, *The Beaumont Twins* (Cambridge, 1986), p. 127; K.J. Stringer, *Earl David of Huntingdon* (Edinburgh, 1985), pp. 159–60.

[20] J. Nichols, *The History and Antiquities of the County of Leicester*, 4 vols in 9, 3, i, (Leicester, 1795–1815), p. 337.

[21] *Pipe Roll 31 Henry II*, Pipe Roll Society, xxxiv, (1913), p. 104.

[22] W. Dugdale, *Monasticon Anglicanum*, revised edition, J. Caley, H. Ellis and R. Bandinel, 6 vols in 8, 3 (London, 1817–30), p. 455.

[23] BL, Cotton ms. Nero CXII, fol. 98.

Leaving aside the activities of Roger of Mowbray and William Burdet, the evidence for other patrons of the Order having been on crusade is slight. In the twelfth century only five other patrons are known to have gone to the Holy Land. These included King Richard I, who confirmed Henry II's grant of forty marks; Robert III, Earl of Leicester, who gave a rent of ten shillings in Leicester; and William I, Earl of Derby, and Henry of Lacy, who gave the advowsons of the churches of Spondon (Derbyshire) and Castleford (Yorkshire) respectively.[24] In the thirteenth century only three patrons can be identified. These were King Edward I, Simon de Montfort, who confirmed Robert III's grant, and William II, Earl of Derby, who confirmed the grant of his father, William I.[25] In addition, Nigel Amundeville went to the Holy Land in the late twelfth or early thirteenth century,[26] while a further three patrons, Warin fitz Simon, Geoffrey Hay and William of Mowbray, may have been crusaders.[27]

In total, therefore, only fourteen (or 7 per cent) of the 200 patrons of the Order of St Lazarus in England may have been involved in crusading activity, suggesting that the influence of the crusades on patronage was relatively slight. An assessment of the timing of some of the grants made by crusaders further strengthens this argument. Thus Robert III, Earl of Leicester's grant of a rent in Leicester was made at least four years before he went on the Third Crusade, while Simon de Montfort's confirmation of the same grant was made six years before he went on crusade in the 1240s. Furthermore, if physical participation in the crusades did not significantly influence patronage, nor apparently were events in the Holy Land of great influence on the many benefactors who stayed at home. The cartulary of Burton Lazars includes only two references to the Holy Land. The first is contained in a grant made in the early thirteenth century by William fitz William fitz Hugh of Burton, who gave a small amount of land in Burton Lazars *in subsidium terre sancte*.[28] The second reference occurs in a charter of Nigel Amundeville, who ordered his son Robert to allow the Order full possession of a half bovate of land in Carlton le Moorland (Lincolnshire) *quod fratres predicti in partibus transmari-*

---

[24] For their crusading activity see Siedschlag, pp. 123, 128; W.E. Wightman, *The Lacy Family in England and Normandy 1066–1194* (Oxford, 1966), pp. 83–5; J. Gillingham, *Richard the Lionheart*, 2nd edn (London, 1989), pp. 125–216. For their patronage see BL, Cotton ms. Nero CXII, fol. 110; BL Harleian ms. 3868, fol. 15v; *Calendar of the Charter Rolls preserved in the Public Record Office*, 4, p. 77; T. Rymer, ed., *Foedera, conventiones, litterae et cuiusunque generis acta publica inter regis Angliae*, new ed., ed. A. Clarke *et al*, 4 vols in 7 parts, I.i (London, 1816–69), p. 49.

[25] For their crusading activity see M. Prestwich, *Edward I* (London, 1988), pp. 66–85; F.M. Powicke, *King Henry III and the Lord Edward* (Oxford, 1947), p. 205; Siedschlag, p. 143. For their patronage see BL, Cotton ms. Nero CXII, fol. 110; BL Harleian ms. 3868, fol. 15v; *Calendar of Patent Rolls*, 1292–1301, p. 404.

[26] BL, Cotton ms. Nero CXII, fol. 118.

[27] For their possible crusading activity see *Complete Peerage*, 9, p. 373; Siedschlag, pp. 115, 127. For their patronage see BL, Cotton ms. Nero CXII, fols 3v, 28, 44, 84.

[28] BL, Cotton ms. Nero CXII, fol. 19.

nis tantos mihi fecerunt.[29] This lack of apparent concern for the Holy Land is repeated in the cartulary of the Templar preceptory of Sandford in Oxfordshire, which contains only two charters (out of nearly 500) which refer to grants being made in aid of the Holy Land.[30]

Although the evidence which has been considered suggests that the crusades had little effect on patronage, several final points must be emphasized. In the first place it is possible that many patrons may have made benefactions to the Order, and to other religious orders in general, as a means of salving their consciences for not participating in the crusading movement. Secondly, not all the crusaders' grants were made at some time removed from the crusades in which they participated. Thus both Roger of Mowbray and William Burdet appear to have made their donations on their return from the Second Crusade, while King Richard I's confirmation of Henry II's grant of forty marks was made just before his departure on the Third Crusade. Finally, and most importantly, the nature of the crusader-patrons' grants should be seen in its proper context. Although it is true that only a small proportion of donors were crusaders, it is clear that it was their donations which were particularly significant. In fact, crusaders were responsible for the donation of three of the Order's thirteen English hospitals, including the two most important houses at Burton Lazars and St Giles at Holborn; five of their nine churches; as well as relatively large landed endowments in Leicestershire. Indeed, the patronage of the two patrons considered in detail – Roger of Mowbray and William Burdet – was of the utmost importance in the Order's development not only in eastern Leicestershire but for the English Order in general. Their benefactions came at a crucial time for the Order, being made at an early stage in its development in England, and their patronage encouraged other members of their families to follow suit: in the twelfth and thirteenth centuries four other Mowbrays and nine other Burdets made benefactions to the Order which consolidated the grants of their crusading forebears.[31]

Any study of the motivation behind religious donations reveals a complex combination of influences at work and, in terms of the Order of St Lazarus, family, feudal and geographical ties can be traced to a varying degree among its benefactors. Nevertheless, although many factors were at work, it is evident that those patrons who made the most important grants were those who were closely linked to the crusading movement. Quality rather than quantity is the key to understanding the influence of the crusades on the patronage of the Order of St Lazarus in England. While the majority of patrons were seemingly unaffected by events in the Holy Land, without the donations of such crusaders as Roger of Mowbray and William Burdet the development of the Order of St Lazarus in England would have been a much slower process.

---

[29] Ibid., fol. 118.

[30] A.M. Leys, 'The Sandford Cartulary', *Oxfordshire Record Society*, **19** (1937), pp. 3, 67.

[31] BL, Cotton ms. Nero CXII, fols 3, 3v, 4, 12, 13, 24v, 25, 25v, 36, 39, 40, 41v, 44, 45, 81, 98, 98v; Walker, pp. 116–34.

37

The Military Orders in Mainland Greece

Peter Lock

Material and documentary evidence for the deeds of the three great international military orders in mainland Greece is not abundant for the thirteenth and fourteenth centuries. It is, however, sufficient for certain hypotheses to be advanced. We know that the Templars took an active role in conquest of central Greece in 1205–10 and that the Hospitallers, as allies and rivals of the Venetians, tried in vain to stem the Turkish advance around 1400. Paradoxically the Teutonic Order has left the best documented, yet most elusive, sites for archaeological fieldwork.

During the thirteenth century the orders seemed content to use their Greek estates as sources of endowment. In the fourteenth century the Teutonic Order, and more especially the Hospitallers, took an active role against the Greeks of Mistra and then the Turks and their involvement became more overtly political. In both these activities they received considerable backing from popes and publicists in the West. Their mode of operation was not dissimilar to that of the Venetians in protecting their colonial possessions in the Aegean, in that Frankish and Greek potentates were prepared to make considerable concessions to both the Hospitallers and the Venetians, but both were selective in what territories they took over and concerned to mount a common Christian front with the Greeks. In this both groups failed, and by 1500 the whole Balkan peninsula was in Turkish hands. The material remains of the orders quickly disappeared: the names of their churches were changed, and few traces of their *casals* and castles remain today.

On the face of it, the three military orders seem to have played little part in the planning and execution of the Fourth Crusade. Villehardouin ignored the Orders and Robert of Clari mentioned them only once, but in connection with the story of Conrad of Montferrat and events in Jerusalem in 1185.[1] Not surprisingly this silence extends to modern historical works on the Crusade, none of which mention the military orders.[2] Whilst this absence of evidence need not amount to evidence of absence, it does permit two hypotheses to be considered.

The first theory is that the orders took no hand in the Crusade and such endowments as they received in Greece between 1206 and 1210 came as pious gifts in support of their work in the Holy Land with such members as were present in the new Latin states arriving with the influx of Latins from the Holy Land in or soon after November 1204. Yet this is unlikely, judging from the strong Lombard connections evident in the early days of the orders in Latin Greece. There is strong circumstantial evidence that the military orders, especially the Templars, played a considerable role in the conquest of Greece and that their members hailed mainly from northern Italy. In addition to Clari's narrative, which linked the orders with the interests of the House of Montferrat, three other points must be considered: namely the presence of Barozzi, a Venetian and the Master of the Temple in Lombardy, in Constantinople in May 1204, to whom the task of announcing the coronation of Baldwin of Flanders and presenting precious gifts to Innocent III was entrusted;[3] the support which the Templars were to give to the legitimist Lombard faction in Thessaly in 1208–9;[4] and above all the active acquisition of estates in central Greece and Thessaly – the very areas over which Boniface of Montferrat, as ruler of Thessalonika, claimed suzerainty.

The source for these land grants is the Registers of Innocent III. In the middle of September 1210 the Templars sought papal confirmation of various grants that had been made to them since 1205. This action was prompted by the political embarrassment caused by their unsuccessful support of the Lombard faction in Thessalonika in 1207–8.

In early 1209 the Order had lost both Ravennika, where there seems to have been some sort of repaired Byzantine fortification, and 'Sydonius', or Lamia, where they had spent heavily on the construction of a castle.[5] Ravennika had been granted to the Templars by Boniface himself and Lamia had been a joint grant by his constable Amedeus of Pofoy and Guido Pelavicino, both landowners needing assistance against the Greeks of Epiros, as Pofoy's crucifixion in 1210 was to demonstrate. The Emperor Henry, who confiscated the properties, seems

---

[1] Robert of Clari, *The Conquest of Constantinople*, trans. E.H. McNeal (New York, 1936), pp. 61–2.

[2] See for example D.E. Queller, *The Fourth Crusade* (Philadelphia, 1977); J. Godfrey, *1204. The Unholy Crusade* (Oxford, 1980); J. Longnon, *Les Compagnons de Villehardouin* (Paris, 1978); and *Crusades*, 2, pp. 153–85.

[3] Innocent III, *PL*, **215**, cols 447–54.

[4] Henri de Valenciennes, *Histoire de L'Empereur Henri de Constantinople*, ed. J. Longnon (Paris, 1948), para. 671 strongly identified the Templar strongholds with the Lombard cause.

[5] Innocent III, *PL*, **216**: 323–4.

to have asserted his rights as overlord and perhaps chose to make an example
of a military order to emphasize his point more widely. No doubt he was
spurred on by the presence of fortifications in these places but, whatever his
fears, the Templars resorted to appeals to the Papal Curia rather than to arms.
With this example before her and with imperial backing, Margaret of Hungary
disputed certain unnamed rights and possessions in the kingdom of Thessalonika granted to the Templars by her dead husband before September 1207.[6]
These grants belonged to the very early days of the conquest as did the other
grants for which confirmation was sought in September 1210. The Papal
Legate Benedict of Santa Susana had granted them the house of Philokalia in
Thessalonika and the church of Fota, or Fotini, outside the walls of Thebes.[7]
This church had been renamed Santa Lucia – an example of a Latin name encap-
sulating the meaning of the Greek dedication. Rolandino and Albertino da
Canossa had granted them 'de Rupo', presumably Sykamino near Oropos on
the Attic coast, where a Templar castle was taken over by the Hospitallers in
1314.[8] The late archbishop of Thebes had given them a garden in Thebes 'when
he had been archbishop elect' – that is, in August 1206 – and James of Avesnes,
who was dead by 1210, had conceded various estates and rights on Euboea.[9]
Some of these grants, like the house of Lagnan and the *casal* of Oizparis, had
been confirmed by the new ruler of the island, Ravanno dalle Carceri, but other
rights which he sought to retain for himself were now a matter of dispute. It
would appear that the initial grants to the Templars were considered over-
generous by the second generation of settlers who perhaps did not look to
Templar support as their immediate predecessors had done.

In the Peloponnese the Templars received the *casal* of Pasalin from William
of Resi, the *casal* of Palaiopolin from Hugh of Besançon and that of Luffestan
from William of Champlitte; all of these grants were confirmed in 1210 by
Geoffrey of Villehardouin who, at that time or fairly soon after, granted them
four knights' fees as he did the Teutonic Knights and the Hospitallers.[10] In
Achaia there were disputes with the archbishop of Patras over the monastery
of Provata and the house of Gerocomita.[11]

The fortification of some of these sites suggests that the Templars were
actively involved in the subjugation of Greece. Given the state of the evidence
this can be no more than an hypothesis but it seems to hold good. In 1206 the
Latin emperor had granted Satalia to the Templars.[12] On the strength of the

---

[6] Ibid., **216**: 230–31.

[7] Ibid., **216**: 327–8 (docs CXLIII, CXLV).

[8] Ibid., **216**: 328 (doc. CXLIV); *ROL*, 3 (1895), 655.

[9] Innocent III, *PL*, **216**: 329 & 331.

[10] Ibid., **216**: 329–30; *Chronique de Morea [L de C]*, ed. J. Longnon (Paris, 1911), para. 121; *Libro
de los Fechos*, ed. A. Morel-Fatio (Geneva, 1885), para. 131; *Chronicle of the Morea [X t M]*, ed.
J. Schmitt (London, 1904), lines 1951–3.

[11] Innocent III, *PL*, **216**: 331–2.

[12] Ibid., **216**: 1019.

concentration of Templar lands in central Greece, Dr Hendrickx has identified this with the area of Satalia near Chalkis in Euboea. However, it is more likely to have been Satalia in western Turkey and to have formed one with the ambitious grants of yet unconquered lands which had been made to Renier of Trit, Louis of Blois and Stephen of Perche as Dukes of Philippopolis, Nicaea and Philadelphia respectively and to the Hospitallers at Pergamum.[13] If this identification is correct it certainly places the Templars in the context of conquest.

The same can be said, on a limited scale, for both the Hospitallers and the Teutonic Knights, although the latter, as a relatively new and poor Order, played a more constrained role. In 1210 the Knights of St John had seized the castle of Gardiki from the Latin diocesan. Gardiki in the Pindos Mountains was a precarious outpost of Latin rule and the town must have been lost by June 1212 when Larissa was reoccupied by the Greeks.[14] The Teutonic Order did not enjoy the same freedom of action for many decades. Certainly it received four fees in Messenia soon after 1210, but as late as 1237 its resources were considered only sufficient to defend Chlemoutsi castle.[15]

After the first four years of conquest, the sources suggest a passive role for the orders in Greece. In the *Chronicle of the Morea* they appear to have played no significant part in the defence of either Thebes or Constantinople in the mid-1230s, nor to have participated in the Pelagonia campaign of 1259. The specific locations of the properties of the orders in the Peloponnese are not definitely known.[16] They seem to have been either in north-west Messenia around Kalamata or in Elis.[17] However, they were certainly not in Skorta, which was the area in which conquests were to be made up to 1249. Indeed, the Greek version of the *Chronicle*, in explaining the conflict between Villehardouin and the Church in 1219, suggests that neither the Templars nor the Hospitallers were prepared to help in any way in the subjection of the area.[18] The three orders do not seem to have offered much hope of assistance to the Latin Empire either. In 1246 Emperor Baldwin II approached the Spanish Order of

---

[13] B. Hendrickx, 'Régestes des Empereurs Latins de Constantinople (1204–1261/72)', *Byzantina*, **14** (1985), p. 37; Villehardouin, *La Conquête de Constantinople*, ed. E. Faral, 2 vols (Paris, 1939), paras 304–5, 311, 316; R. Rodd, *The Princes of Achaia and the Chronicles of the Morea*, 2 vols, **1**, (London, 1908), p. 65.

[14] Innocent III, *PL*, **216**: 304, 307–8; D.M. Nicol, *The Despotate of Epiros* (Oxford, 1957), pp. 36–7.

[15] *Tabulae ordinis Theutonici*, ed. E. Strehlke, (Berlin, 1860), no. 133, p. 134; A. Forey, *The Military Orders* (London, 1992), p. 39.

[16] A. Bon, *La Morée Franque* (Paris, 1969), p. 100.

[17] W. Miller, *The Latins in the Levant* (London, 1908), p. 52; C. Hodgetts and P. Lock, 'The Topography of Venetian Messenia', in *Essays on the Medieval Archaeology of Greece*, ed. P. Lock and G. Sanders, Oxbow Monographs (Oxford: forthcoming). I owe information on the German investigations near Olympia regarding Mostenitsa to verbal communication from Col. Erhard P. Opsahl.

[18] *X t M*, lines 2631–2720; Bon, p. 95.

Santiago to provide a force of 1,500 warriors for two years in return for land in Constantinople and 40,000 marks.[19] The scheme never materialized, but it does show a disinclination on the part of the orders to become involved militarily in the Aegean in the mid-thirteenth century.

After 1312 the Hospitallers became the most powerful order in Greece when they acquired all former Templar property in Achaia and Crete. Lands seem to have changed hands whilst enquiries into Templar activities, begun in August 1308, were still in progress. The Hospitallers received charge of the Hospital of Saint Sampson in Corinth in 1309 together with the *casal* of Palaiopolis,[20] and in November 1310 all proceeds from the Templar lands in central Greece were to be handed over to Duke Walter I of Brienne to resist the frequent incursions ... *a graecis scismaticis de imperio Romanie* ....[21] In 1310 and 1311 the inquisition and torture of the Templars proceeded only in Achaia and Crete.[22] Presumably the disturbed nature of central Greece made it difficult to gain custody of the Templars and their lands there, but what about Euboea where the Venetian bailie exercised reasonable control? The actual fate of the Templars in Greece is unknown, but presumably it was no different from that of Templars elsewhere. However, they were probably few in number and they had greater opportunity to avoid detention than in western Europe.

In 1314 the former Templar lands in central Greece did not pass to the Hospitallers as did the lands in the Morea and Crete. Instead they were assigned to Walter of Châtillon, the Constable of France and grandfather and guardian of Walter II of Brienne, the infant Duke of Athens whose father had been killed by the Catalan Company near Halmyros in March 1311. None the less, the Hospitallers acquired the former Templar stronghold at Sykamino in Attica, perhaps by agreement with the Briennists to give the Order a material interest in their cause.[23]

During the fourteenth century the attitude of the orders in Greece changed from one of economic exploitation to one of active defence.[24] The brethren are recorded as taking part in battles. For example, the *Libros de los Fechos* noted the death of the preceptor of the Teutonic Order during the defence of the castle of St George in Elis about 1320.[25] The campaigns of Andronikos Asen in the

---

[19] Forey, p. 39.

[20] Clement V. (1885–92), *Registum Clementis Papae V ... nunc primum editum cura et studio Monachorum Ordinis S. Benedicti*, 1–9 (Rome, 1885–92), 3, nos 3401, 3415, 3515; 4, no. 1000; *Librode los Fechos*, para. 588. See Innocent III, *PL*, 216: 329–30 for Templar possessions at Picotin near Palaiopolis.

[21] Clement V, *Reg. Clem.* V, 5, no. 5768.

[22] Ibid., V, 6, nos 7597, 7600, 7606.

[23] A. Rubió i LLuch, *Diplomatari de l'Orient Català* (Barcelona, 1947), doc. LXIII, pp. 78–9; J. Delaville le Roulx, *Les Hospitaliers à Rhodes* (Paris, 1913), p. 201 attests the existence of two commanders, one for the Morea and one for the Duchy of Athens in late 1330. See also Bon, p. 243, note 6 and Miller, p. 239.

[24] A. Luttrell, 'The Crusade in the Fourteenth Century', in *Europe in the Late Middle Ages*, ed. J.R. Hale, J.R.L. Highfield and B. Smalley (London, 1965), p. 129, 139–44.

[25] *Libro de los Fechos*, para 652.

Alpheios valley after 1316 seemed to have provoked a reaction amongst the Teutonic Knights which previous Greek campaigns in the same valley in 1262–63 had failed to do.[26] The loss of Acre in 1291 may have increased their interest in their Greek lands, at a time when Greek raids threatened those interests and inclined them to shoulder their feudal obligations to the princes of Achaia and their *baillies*. In June and July 1324 Nicholas, the Preceptor of the Teutonic Knights at Mostenitsa, and John of Baux, the Commander of the Hospital, were ordered, along with fourteen other liege vassals of the principality, to appear at Glarentza ready for a campaign against the Greeks of Mistra.[27]

Just as warfare had wiped out the Templar properties in central Greece as a source of re-endowment after 1311, so ten years later endemic raids and official wars threatened the substance and the safety of the orders and their neighbours in the Morea. In addition to Greek campaigns from Mistra, the Catalans and their Turkish auxiliaries raided for slaves along the Corinthian Gulf. Prior to the 1370s the Hospitallers, preoccupied with Rhodes, seemed disinclined to follow up the numerous papal directives to move against the Catalans and content to leave the defence of the Morea to the Venetians. Indeed, one of the principals in the negotiations in 1321 to turn the Morea into a Venetian protectorate was John of Baux.[28] However, the advance of the Turks in the southern Balkans brought the frontier to the Morea and from the early 1340s, as Professor Housley has noted, the Turk became the main foe of crusading activity, the naval league its main expression and Romania the front line.[29]

Within Greece the task of defence fell to the Hospitallers and the Venetians. Both parties took a more active role in the diplomacy and administration of Romania and were prepared to create protectorates over territories no longer governable or defensible by their rulers.[30] Dr Luttrell has examined the chronology and the pitfalls of the leasing of the principality of Achaia by the Hospital in 1377.[31] In 1399 the Greek governor of the Morea ceded Corinth and Mistra to the Knights for a year because of the invasion of Yakoub Pasha.[32] The *Chronicle of Galaxeidi*, written in 1703, gives an account of an abortive three-month naval operation in the Gulf of Itea in 1404 mounted by the Knights from three *galeotes* and intended to capture Salona.[33] The Knights provided funding to the inhabitants of Galaxeidi for a church of St John of Jerusalem, which was built and renamed Panteleimon on their evacuation, and substantial financial

---

[26] Note the silence of *L de C*, paras 320–46.

[27] Rodd, 2, p. 157.

[28] *Reg. Clem. V*, 7, nos 72–3, 125, 338; 8, nos 14, 131–2; 9, nos 44–7; Rodd, 2, p. 157.

[29] N. Housley, *The Later Crusades* (Oxford, 1992), p. 59.

[30] R.J. Loenertz, *Byzantina et Franco-Graeca*, 1 (Rome, 1970), pp. 21–2 and 329–69.

[31] A. Luttrell, 'The Principality of Achaea in 1377', *Byzantinische Zeitschrift*, **57** (1964), pp. 342–7.

[32] Loenertz, pp. 21–2.

[33] C.N. Sathas, *Chronikon anekdoton Galaxeidiou* (Athens, 1865), pp. 208–9. See J. Rosser in *Essays on Medieval Archaeology*, ed. Lock and Sanders (forthcoming).

aid to the villagers of Loidoriki and Vitrinitsa to revolt against the Turks. Church construction as a means of cementing a Latino–Greek front against the Turks might also explain the construction of the church of the Chora in Corinth which has recently been redated to the time that the Knights occupied that city.[34]

The archaeological record of the military orders in Greece is elusive.[35] We really know nothing of the whereabouts of the fiefs granted at various times to the three orders. Even a relatively well documented site such as the head-quarters of the Teutonic Order at Mostenitsa has been sought in Messenia and in Elis and may point to relocation of the Order between 1220 and 1320.[36] Toponyms are rare and sherding can only point to a period rather than to a century. Even the frequently mentioned 'German House' at Modon lies unrecognized in the grid of streets awaiting excavation.[37] Perhaps this is a good point to stop in our consideration of the military orders in Greece – we have the street plan but not yet the directory.

---

[34] I am indebted to Mr Eric Ivison of the British School at Athens for information on the redating of the Chora church.

[35] B.K. Panagopoulos, *Cistercian and Mendicant Monasteries in Medieval Greece* (Chicago, 1979), p. 66; S. Symeonoglou, *The Topography of Thebes* (Princeton, 1985), p. 167; W. Leake, *Travels in the Morea*, 2 (London, 1830), pp. 103–5; Rodd, 1, pp. 163–4 for some of the problems.

[36] *X t M*, line 1955; section 48 of the Assize of Romania; Miller, pp. 52, 392; Bon, p. 243.

[37] Miller, pp. 344, 495.

38

Knights and Lovers: the Military Orders in the Romantic Literature of the Thirteenth Century

Helen Nicholson

Religious orders made frequent appearances in the romantic and epic literature of the Middle Ages, as well as in other literary genres which I shall not discuss here. In the thirteenth century their most frequent role was giving hospitality to travelling knights. In the Grail romances in particular, hermits and Cistercians gave spiritual advice to knights. Yet romances seldom depict religious persons in association with romantic love.

I have traced around twenty epics, romances and love songs of the thirteenth century in which the military orders appear. Around half of their appearances are in a military role, while the rest are in charitable roles, supporting and lodging poor knights, burying the dead, or providing a place of penance, retirement or refuge.

By the third decade of the thirteenth century the Templars were being depicted as the allies of lovers, at first aiding them in their grief, and eventually giving them active assistance in their love affairs. The Hospitallers also appeared briefly in this role. I shall examine the course of this development and then consider why these two orders in particular were depicted in such a role by romanciers, more often than any other religious order.

The most extreme development of the military orders' romantic image appeared in the French verse romance *Sone de Nausay*, written in the second half of the thirteenth century, possibly in the 1270s. The following extract illustrates their role here. The scene is the major house of the Temple in Ireland; the queen of Ireland and the master of the Temple in Ireland are discussing Sone de Nausay.

> ... The queen rose, sick with the pain that grieved her. She led the Templar to counsel, not concealing her desire from him. She said to him: 'Master, I have loved you in good faith and have shown it. Now it seems to me that I have fallen into

From *The Military Orders: Fighting for the Faith and Caring for the Sick*, ed. Malcolm Barber. Copyright © 1994 by Malcolm Barber. Published by Variorum, Ashgate Publishing Ltd, Gower House, Croft Road, Aldershot, Hampshire, GU11 3HR, Great Britain.

misfortune. I shall never conceal this from you, for I have great faith in you. I have fallen in love with this knight, from which my heart is greatly troubled. If I see him leave me, I could well go mad. Show me how you love me; help me with your advice.'

The Templar said: 'I will give you the best advice that I know. You have a fine hall here which was built a long time ago by the kings. Go and eat there now and stay there tonight. When it gets dark, have your bed made up in such a place that no one knows where it is except the one commanded to make it. I will bring this knight in by a wicket gate, but first I will inform him.'

This is exactly what the Templar does, and, after urging Sone to kiss the queen twice, leaves the couple together.

> But I cannot tell you whether they played together or whether he talked of love; but they didn't make much noise.[1]

The result of this liaison is a son, which the master Templar brings to Sone in Norway, after Sone has married his Norwegian sweetheart and the queen of Ireland, in her grief, has driven the Templars out of Ireland.

Sone survives in a single manuscript, and the names of the author and patron are unknown. Yet, although no other surviving romance goes so far in associating the religious knights and lovers, *Sone* is firmly set in literary tradition.

It is difficult to pinpoint the military orders' first appearance in a romantic role in fiction, partly because the dating of fictional literature is usually uncertain, and partly because one can never be sure that one has found everything. The earliest example I have found occurs in a love song by Gontier de Soignies, a poet from Hainaut or north-eastern France, probably writing in the first two decades of the thirteenth century. Depicting himself as disappointed in love, Gontier declares that, to escape love's pangs and to avoid hearing about love, he will leave the world, go overseas for God's sake and join the Order of the Temple.[2]

In making this declaration, Gontier was merely exploiting a familiar literary theme. For around fifty years, the writers of epics had been depicting knights joining or proposing to join the Order of the Temple, or the Temple and Hospital, in penance for murder[3] – a theme which reflected real life. Around 1228, the writer Jean Renart adapted this theme in his verse romance *Guillaume de Dole*: here the crime is not murder, but obstructing true love.[4] Jean's use of

---

[1] *Sone von Nausay*, ed. M. Goldschmidt, Bibliothek des Literarischen Vereins in Stuttgart (BLVS) **216** (Tübingen,1899), lines 6541–68, 6731–4.

[2] *Gontiers de Soignies: il canzoniere*, ed. L. Formisano (Milan and Naples, 1980), no. XVIII, 'Lan quant voi esclarcir,' p. 130, lines 63–4, and pp. lx–lxii.

[3] *Raoul de Cambrai, chanson de geste*, ed. P. Meyer and A. Longnon, Société des anciens textes français (SATF) (Paris, 1882), lines 3427–8; *Orson de Beauvais, chanson de geste du XII siècle*, ed. G. Paris, SATF (Paris, 1899), lines 3319–21; *La chevalerie Ogier de Danemarche*, ed. M. Eusebi (Milan and Varese, 1953), line 10427; *Renaus de Montauban, oder die Haimonskinder, Altfranzsisches Gedicht*, ed. H. Michelant, BLVS 67 (Stuttgart, 1862), p. 337 line 10.

[4] Jean Renart, *Le Roman de la Rose ou Guillaume de Dole*, ed. F. Lecoy, Classiques Français du moyen âge (CFMA) **91** (Paris, 1962), line 5589.

342 HELEN NICHOLSON

this theme suggests that the association between the Order of the Temple and romantic love in literature was well established by 1228.

From being a place of penance, the Order of the Temple became depicted as a place of escape. Again, this was a theme which reflected real life.[5] The first accounts of a man joining the Order to escape a broken heart appeared in chronicles at the beginning of the thirteenth century. The chronicle attributed to Ernoul, written in the late 1190s, recounts that Gerard of Ridefort, Master of the Temple from 1185 to 1189, had joined the Order of the Temple during a severe illness. Shortly before, he had failed in a bid to win the hand of the heiress of Botron, so the story grew up that Brother Gerard had joined the Templars as a result of his broken heart. A Genoese writer recorded this tale at the beginning of the thirteenth century, as did a later version of Ernoul's chronicle.[6]

The theme was then taken up by romantic writers. Probably its best known appearance was in the immensely popular poem *La chastelaine de Vergi*. The date of this is unknown, although it was written before 1288. The story ends with the death of the lovers and their betrayer, while the remorseful duke enters a military order. In most of the manuscripts he enters the Order of the Temple, but in two he enters the Order of the Hospital. One of these dates from the thirteenth century and the other from the fourteenth century.[7]

The theme reappeared in an early fourteenth-century version of the Crusade Cycle, where one of the major characters, Harpin de Bourges, enters the Order of the Temple on the death of his wife, the queen of Nubia.[8] The familiarity of this theme was underlined in *Sone de Nausay*. Rebuking Sone's childhood sweetheart, Ydain, for refusing Sone's love, her nurse Sabine declares that he will go overseas and give himself to the Temple, as if this were an act expected from disappointed young lovers.[9]

Another important charitable role for the military orders both in real life and in romances and epics was the burial of the dead. By the mid-thirteenth

---

[5] For example, Aubrey of Trois Fontaines, 'Chronica,' ed. P. Scheffer-Boichorst, *MGH SS*, 23, p. 826, cf. M. Barber, 'The Origins of the Order of the Temple,' *Studia monastica*, 12, (1970), p. 223; *CT*, no. 27 (c. 1129–32); *Codex diplomaticus Brandenburgensis. Sammlung der Urkunden. Chronicken und sonstigen Geschichtsquellen für die Geschichte der Mark Brandenburg und ihrer Regenten*, ed. A.F. Riedel, 41 vols. (Berlin, 1838–69), D p. 15 (under 1268).

[6] *Cont WT*, p. 46 paragraph 33; 'Regni Iherosolynmitani Brevis Historia,' in *Annali Genovesi di Caffaro e de'suoi continuatori dal MXCIX al MCCXCIII*, ed. L.T. Belgrano and C.I. di Sant'Angelo, new ed., 5 vols., Fonti per la Storia Italia, 11–14 *bis*, 1 (Rome, 1890–1929), pp. 137–8; *Ernoul-Bernard*, p. 114.

[7] *La chastelaine de Vergi, poème du XIII siècle*, ed. G. Raynaud, 2nd ed. revue par L. Foulet, CFMA 1 (Paris, 1912), p. iii and lines 941–3, pp. iv–v, 35.

[8] *The Old French crusade cycle vol. VII: the Jérusalem continuations, part 1: la chrétienté Corbaran*, ed. P.R. Grillo (Alabama, 1984), p. xxi, note 24; S. Duparc-Quioc, *La chanson d'Antioche – étude critique* (Paris, 1978), pp. 67–8 on ms. T, also pp. 63–4 and note 76 on manuscript L.

[9] *Sone*, lines 8705–6.

century the romantic role of the Order of the Temple had developed from being a place of refuge for lovers to being their last resting place. In the fictional 'Life' of the troubadour Jaufré Rudel, written a little before 1250, Jaufré takes the cross and goes overseas in order to set eyes on the countess of Tripoli, whom he has loved without ever seeing her. Becoming ill on the voyage, he has one glimpse of her beauty before expiring in her arms. Heartbroken, she has him buried in the house of the Temple of Tripoli and becomes a nun.[10]

The Order reappeared in this role in the Arthurian verse romance *Claris et Laris*, written between 1261 and 1268, probably before 1263. It survives in only one manuscript. The author places the Templars in the role of hosts and undertakers for wandering knights, a role usually performed in Arthurian romance by hermits. But they do not take on the hermit's other role – that of spiritual advisers to wandering knights.

The Templars appear in connection with the adventures of the *Lai Hardi*, the bold-ugly knight, who has promised to avenge a young lady whose lover has been murdered. The Templars bury the dead man and lodge the *Lai Hardi* and the lady. When her lover's murderers have been killed, the lady falls dead on her lover's grave and the Templars bury her alongside him.[11]

Another real-life role frequently assigned to the Templars, Hospitallers or Teutonic knights in romances was hospitality to travellers. Only the Templars, however, were depicted lodging lovers or those on missions of love, and they did not appear in this role until after 1250. In *Sone de Nausay*, the Templars of Ireland take in the fugitive Sone, his Norwegian sweetheart Odee and his horse Morel, and subsequently ensure their guests' safe escape from the country without the knowledge of the amorous queen.[12] Sone eventually marries Odee. In *Le Roman de Laurin*, written in prose by an anonymous writer in the 1250s or 1260s and surviving in eight manuscripts, a house of the Temple lodges the count of Provence on his way to ask for the hand in marriage of Dyogenne, daughter of the king of Aragon. In this case, however, the count fails in his suit.[13]

The military orders repeatedly appear in epic and romance advising the king of Jerusalem and his barons on the defence of the Holy Land. The role of counsellor was also adapted to fit a romantic theme, as we have seen above in the extract from *Sone de Nausay*. As *Sone* also featured the Temple as a place of refuge for a broken heart and as a place of lodging for lovers, the extension to the role of counsellor may have seemed natural to this writer and his patron.

---

[10] *Les chansons de Jaufré Rudel*, ed. A. Jeanroy, CFMA **15** (Paris, 1924), p. 21; for date see p. vii note 1.

[11] *Li romans de Claris et Laris*, ed. J. Alton, BLVS 169 (Tübingen, 1884, repr. Amsterdam, 1966), lines 9863–71, 9907–22.

[12] *Sone*, lines 5995–6916.

[13] *Le roman de Laurin, fils de Marques le sénéchal*, ed. L. Thorpe (Cambridge, 1958), p. 111, lines 4613–4.

All these examples come from French romances. In German works, the orders'
image was very different. The earliest reference to a military order in a German
romance of undisputed date is in Wolfram von Eschenbach's *Parzifal*, written
for Hermann, landgrave of Thuringia, between 1200 and 1210. It was an
immensely popular poem: eighty-six manuscripts survive, and there are
numerous references to it in other works.[14] Perhaps because of the great
interest which Wolfram and his patron had in the mysterious East, Wolfram
named the chaste brotherhood of knights which guarded his Grâl Castle from
impure persons after the Templars.

It seems that Wolfram's chaste knights came to dominate the literary image
of the real order among German-speakers, for I have found no references to
the Templars as supporters of lovers in German romances. However, chastity
was a desirable quality in romantic lovers, and the author of the verse romance
Reinfrid von Braunschweig, written at the end of the thirteenth century, refers
to the chaste 'Templars' who guarded the Grail as an example for his lovers.[15]

I have only found one other romantic reference to the Templars in a German
work, and none at all to the Hospitallers or Teutonic knights, although all three
orders appear in other roles. The other romantic reference is in *Orendal*, a verse
romance of highly disputed date. Here their role is obstructive to love rather
than supportive. As this runs counter to all the other instances we have
examined, it is likely that the present form of this poem dates from after our
period.[16]

We must now consider why two military orders should be associated with
romantic love more than any other religious order.

The Order of the Temple had a unique claim to knighthood.[17] It was the
only international military order which had never been a hospital, and as such
was untouched by the respectable, colourless image of the traditional religious
life. Contemporaries usually referred to the brothers as knights, even when
the Order had become a part of the established religious landscape and the
brothers in Europe seem to have been regarded exactly like those of other
religious orders. Knights who were also religious men held a great attraction
for the inventiveness of chroniclers and romanciers alike. In the didactic
chronicles they formed a useful focus for moralizing tales. In epics and romances
they were brave and amenable to love, as knights should be.

---

[14] Wolfram von Eschenbach, *Parzifal*, ed. K. Lachmann and W. Spiewok, 2 vols. (Stuttgart, 1981);
B. Schirok, *Parzifalrezeption im Mittelalter* (Darmstadt, 1982), esp. p. 57.

[15] *Reinfrid von Braunschweig*, ed. K. Bartsch, BLVS **109** (Tübingen, 1871), lines 780–91.

[16] *Orendal*, ed. H. Steiner, Altdeutsche Textbibliothek 36 (Halle, 1935); F.W. Wentzlaff-
Eggebert, *Kreuzzugsdictung des Mittelalters. Studien zu ihrer Geschichtlichen und Dichterischen Wirklichkeit*
(Berlin, 1960), pp. 379–80.

[17] Humbert of Romans, ' "De eruditione praedictorum", Liber III: de modo prompte cudiendi
sermones ad omne hominum et negotiorum genus,' in *Maxima bibliotheca veterum patrum et
antiquorum scriptorum ecclesiasticorum*, ed. M. de la Bigne, 27 vols (Lyons, 1677), **25**, p. 472, ch. 36.

In real life, the clergy were as least as much involved in the business of romantic love as knights, and appear as lovers in *fabliaux* and *jeux partis*. However, different literary genres had different rules, for in the romances knights are associated with romantic love, while priests, monks and hermits are generally hostile towards lovers. The knights of the Temple fitted more naturally into the romance genre as supporters of lovers than other religious orders. Possibly the Templars, as knights of the Temple of Solomon, connected in the minds of romance writers with King Solomon's reputation as a lover of women, but I have found no evidence for this.

As the Templars became associated with romantic love, the Hospitallers followed. This is not surprising, for as the Hospital became militarized, and certainly by the time of the Third Crusade, contemporaries usually set the Orders of the Temple and Hospital together. What is surprising is that it should only appear in connection with one tale, and in so few manuscripts.

I would suggest that, because the Hospital always emphasized its image as a hospital and its work for the poor, it managed to suppress 'scandalous' and romantic stories which damaged its serious charitable image. Hardly any legends were told of the Hospital alone during the twelfth and thirteenth centuries; it was only in connection with the Order of the Temple. It does appear in a legend of Saladin, but as a charitable order.[18]

There is some evidence that romancers preferred to use the Templars to assist their lovers when they, or their patrons, had an interest in the Holy Land or crusading. The bishop of Beauvais, patron of Jean Renart, had a traditional connection with crusading. The writer of *Claris et Laris* has a good deal to say about the poor state of the Holy Land in the introduction to his poem. The writer of *Sone de Nausay* claims to be writing for the lady of Beirut. Audiences of the Crusade Cycle would obviously be interested in the Holy Land. The writer of the *Roman de Laurin* had some interest in the Holy Land. However, there is too little evidence to be certain.

The Templars' and Hospitallers' romantic image developed from their other literary images. But whereas their other roles were all firmly based in fact, the brothers' connection with lovers seems to have been more the product of romantic imagination. The Templars make only scattered appearances in such roles, the Hospitallers appear only once, and few of the romances in which they appeared were very well known. Yet their connection with lovers seems to have been well known and well established, for it persists throughout the thirteenth century, in a wide variety of works.

---

[18] *Récits d'un ménestrel de Reims du treizième siècle*, ed. N. du Wailly, Société de l'histoire de France (Paris, 1878), pp. 104–9, 112, paragraphs 198–208, 213.

39

The Lawyers of the Military Orders

James Brundage

Medieval military orders, like religious communities and other corporate bodies at any time and anywhere, constantly needed expert legal advice and assistance in the conduct of their affairs. Although individual members of the group surrendered their personal property upon entrance, the military orders, as collective entities, needed expert help to acquire, defend and dispose of the joint assets they held in common. By 1200 the aggregate assets of the Templars and Hospitallers had become very sizeable indeed and continued to grow in value through most of the thirteenth century, while the Teutonic Knights, although founded only at the very end of the twelfth century, amassed both wealth and power, not only in the Levant but in central and northern Europe as well.[1]

Like other religious houses or communities, the military orders, moreover, wanted recognition, approval of their way of life and special privileges from ecclesiastical authorities and especially from the papacy.[2] By the latter part of the twelfth century, the mounting legalism of ecclesiastical administration made it imperative for religious communities of all kinds to have available the

---

[1] See generally H. Prutz, *Die geistlichen Ritterorden: Ihre Stellung zur kirchlichen, politischen, gesellschaftlichen und wirtschaftlichen Entwicklung des Mittelalters* (Berlin, 1908); *Die geistlichen Ritterorden Europas*, ed. J. Fleckenstein and M. Hellmann, Konstanzer Arbeitskreis für mittelalterliche Geschichte, Vorträge und Forschungen, 26 (Sigmaringen, 1980). For individual orders and regions see also the relevant entries in the 'Select bibliography of the crusades', comp. H.E. Mayer and J. McLellan, in *Crusades*, 6, pp. 511–664.

[2] Both *CH* and *CT* abound in grants of privileges, as does the *Tabulae ordinis Theutonici*, ed. E. Strehlke, 2nd ed. (Toronto, 1975); note also *PUTJ*, no. 77, p. 135. For some legal insights into the application of such privileges see J.A. Brundage, 'A Twelfth-century Oxford Disputation Concerning the Privileges of the Knights Hospitallers', *Mediaeval Studies*, 24 (1962), pp. 153–60, reprinted with original pagination and corrections in *The Crusades, Holy War and Canon Law* XII, (London, 1991).

services of men trained in Romano-canonical procedures[3] in order to process their petitions at the curia and to keep vigilant watch lest those privileges be infringed or even withdrawn. In addition, both religious orders and individual religious houses, found it advantageous, and often indispensable, to secure the favour of at least one permanent, high-ranking member of the curia, usually a cardinal, who served as protector of the institution's interests at the curia, usually in return for annual gifts and subsidies.[4] In the language of legal practice this amounted to giving an influential curial officer a watching brief and rewarding him with an annual retainer in return for his vigilance in guarding the institution's well-being.

It was further necessary, moreover, for the military orders, as for other religious orders, to keep one or more permanent proctors at the papal court.[5] Proctors *ad litem* were essentially litigation agents, whose closest analogues in common-law countries were attornies-at-law.[6] These men managed the legal affairs of the principals who employed them: they represented clients before the courts, spoke on their behalf, and often had the power to negotiate and make commitments that bound the client legally. Medieval lawyers commonly referred to each party's proctor in litigation as *dominus litis*, since the courts regarded proctors quite literally as the 'masters (or, one might even say, the 'owners') of the lawsuit' before them.[7]

---

[3] Members of the military orders were, to be sure, likely to have some skill in the customary law of the regions from which they came, since forensic skills were normally considered part of the essential equipment of men of noble or knightly standing. Note the remarks of Philippe de Novarre in *RHC, Lois*, **1**, p. 569; and see also H. Prutz, *Kulturgeschichte der Kreuzzüge* (Berlin, 1883; repr. Hildesheim, 1964), pp. 213–15; J.S.C. Riley-Smith, *The Feudal Nobility and the Kingdom of Jerusalem, 1174–1277* (London, 1973), pp. 124, 128; R.V. Turner, *The English Judiciary in the Age of Glanvill and Bracton, c. 1176 1239* (Cambridge, 1985), pp. 34–5; R.C. Palmer, 'The origins of the legal profession in England', *Irish Jurist*, **11** (1976), pp. 128, 142–4.

[4] L.-R. Misserey 'Cardinal protecteur', in *Dictionnaire de droit canonique*, ed. R. Naz, 7 vols, **2**, (Paris, 1935–65), pp. 1339–44; W. Maleczek, 'Ein Kardinalprotektor im Kreuzherrenorden um 1213/1214?', *Zeitschrift der Savigny-Stiftung für Rechtsgeschichte*, Kanonistische Abteilung 60 (1974) pp. 365–74; P. Hofmeister, 'Die Kardinalprotektoren der Ordensleute', *Theologische Quartalschrift*, **142** (1962), pp. 425–74.

[5] R. von Heckel, 'Das Aufkommen der ständigen Prokuratoren an der päpstlichen Kurie im 13. Jahrhundert', in *Miscellanea Francesco Ehrle*, 6 vols, **2**,Studi e testi (Rome, 1924), pp. 290–321; R. Brentano, *Two Churches: England and Italy in the Thirteenth Century* (Berkeley and Los Angeles, 1968; repr. 1988), pp. 29–39.

[6] In addition to proctors *ad litem* medieval practice made much use of procuratores *ad impetrandum*, who acted as agents for processing petitions and other non-contentious business at the Roman curia; see generally P. Herde, *Beiträge zum papstlichen Kanzlei- und Urkundenwesen im 13. Jahrhundert*, 2nd ed. (Kallmünz, 1967), pp. 125–30.

[7] Bernard of Pavia, *Summa decretalium* 1.28.7, ed. E.A.T. Laspeyres (Regensburg, 1960; repr. Graz, 1956), p. 24; Johannes Teutonicus, *Apparatus glossarum in Compilationem Tertiam* 1.22.1 v. *litteras reuocatorias*, ed. K. Pennington, *Monumenta iuris canonici* (cited hereafter as MIC), Corpus glossatorum, **3** (Vatican City, 1981), pp. 143–4; Geoffrey of Trani, *Summa super titulis decretalium* 1.38.18 (Lyon, 1519; repr. Aalen, 1968), fol. 64ra, 66vb; Hostiensis, *Summa aurea*, lib. 1, tit. *De procuratoribus* §14 (Lyon, 1547; repr. Aalen, 1962), fol. 64vb–65ra.

Above and beyond all this, the military orders, like other organized religious groups, often required the service of one or more advocates at the papal courts. Medieval religious communities had a well earned reputation for litigiousness, in which the military orders fully shared.[8] Virtually any gift to a religious community was apt to provoke lawsuits by the donor's heirs who wished to recover the property and resistance from the religious, who were naturally inclined to defend their title to the contested property as a sacred trust that they held for God and their successors in the community.[9] Thus religious communities, including the military orders, were a dependable source of employment for advocates, who, unlike most proctors, were technical experts in the subtleties of Romano-canonical substantive law. By the second half of the twelfth century litigants before the papal courts almost invariably employed one or more advocates to assure effective presentation of their legal arguments.[10]

In addition to disputes that made their way to the papal courts, the military orders were also involved quite regularly in legal business before the courts of bishops, archdeacons and lesser prelates throughout the length and breadth of western Europe. These local and regional courts became increasingly sophisticated during the latter part of the twelfth century and, by the beginning of the thirteenth century, bishops and other prelates were beginning to appoint full-time judges with formal legal training to preside over them.[11] In consequence, the military orders, like other religious communities, also needed to engage trained advocates and experienced proctors to represent their interests before these courts, as well as at the papal court.

A further consequence of all these developments was that religious communities everywhere, including the military orders, faced a constantly

---

[8] G.G. Coulton, *Five Centuries of Religion*, 4 vols, 3 (Cambridge, 1927–50), pp. 509–11, brings together a mass of complaints on this score and, although allowance must be made for Coulton's well known biases, monastic historians generally agree that legal expenses constituted a significant drain on the revenues of late medieval monasteries. Even so well disposed a historian as Dom David Knowles found it necessary to devote many more pages than he might have wished to discussions of monastic litigation, *The Monastic Order in England* (Cambridge, 1949), pp. 272–6, 302–3, 331–45, 630–31, 685–6. See further Brentano, pp. 132, 246; J.E. Sayers, *Papal Judges Delegate in the Province of Canterbury, 1198–1254: A Study in Ecclesiastical Jurisdiction and Administration*, Oxford Historical Monographs (London, 1971), p. 212.

[9] C.R. Cheney, *From Becket to Langton: English Church Government, 1170–1213* (Manchester, 1956; repr. 1965), p. 50; R. Graham, *S. Gilbert of Sempringham and the Gilbertines: A History of the Only English Monastic order* (London, 1903), p. 132.

[10] J.E. Sayers, 'Canterbury Proctors at the Court of "Audientia litterarum contradictarum"', *Traditio*, 22 (1966), pp. 311–45, and 'Proctors Representing British Interests at the Papal Court, 1198–1415', in *Proceedings of the third international congress of medieval canon law*, ed. S. Kuttner, MIC, Subsidia, 4 (Città del Vaticano, 1971), pp. 143–63; W. Stelzer, 'Beiträge zur Geschichte der Kurienprokuratoren im 13. Jahrhundert', *Archivum historiae pontificiae*, 8 (1970), pp. 113–38.

[11] P. Fournier, *Les officialités au moyen âge: Etude sur l'organisation, la compétence et la procédure des tribunaux ecclésiastiques ordinaires en France de 1180 à 1328* (Paris, 1880; repr. Aalen, 1984).

mounting need to find legal advisers and litigation agents to guard their interests at every level of the church structure.

Two basic strategies were available to meet this need. One was to hire proctors and advocates from outside the Order to manage the expanding volume of legal business. Several considerations made this alternative desirable: lawyers experienced and trained in the learned laws were rapidly becoming available nearly everywhere and their numbers increased steadily in response to the growing demand for legal services. Individual houses of the military orders who experienced a regular demand for legal advice might find it advantageous to put one or more proctors and advocates from their region on retainer, so that help would be available when the need arose. This gave the community a degree of security for, at a relatively modest cost, it ensured that counsel would be at hand when they required it, and the retainer itself constituted at least a partial hedge against the potentially ruinous costs of protracted litigation.[12] If the house and its superiors were lucky and chose shrewdly, its retained counsel might be experienced men with influential contacts in local legal circles, which might help to contain litigation costs or, even better, might sometimes make litigation unnecessary.

On the other hand, outside counsel not only tended to be expensive, but might also not be fully committed to the interests of the religious community. Since legal advisers, and especially the more desirable and successful ones, were apt to be in high demand, the possibility that some conflict might arise between the interests of the religious community and the interests of one or more of the advocate's, or proctor's, other clients was an ever-present worry. Although the papal curia perennially attracted a generous supply of proctors and advocates – complaints about their excessive numbers and the volume of litigation at the curia began to appear as early as the mid-twelfth century[13] –

---

[12] One well known example of how much litigation expense might cost a monastic community emerges from the struggle between the English monastery of Evesham and the bishop of Worcester, during which gifts to judges amounted to £160 and lawyers' fees at times came to 50s per day. To meet these and other expenses the monastery had to sequester the funds normally allocated to buy wine and to repair the fabric of the church; in addition, expenditures on both the monks' meals and charitable works were cut. Despite these sacrifices, Evesham's proctor, Thomas of Marlborough, eventually had to slip away secretly from Rome one night in order to evade his creditors, *Chronicon abbatiae de Evesham ad annum 1418*, ed. W.D. Macray, RS, 29 (London, 1863), pp. 121–2, 200. See likewise the detailed account of the expenditures that Richard of Anstey incurred in his suit against Mabel de Francheville, in *English Lawsuits from William I to Richard I*, ed. and trans. R.C. Van Caenegem, 2 vols, Selden Society Publications, 106–7, 2 (London, 1990–91), pp. 397–404. Further examples may be found in G. Dolezalek, *Das Imbreviaturbuch des erzbischöflichen Gerichtsnotars Hubaldus aus Pisa, Mai bis August 1230* (Cologne, 1969), pp. 41–3, and D.M. Owen, 'Ecclesiastical Jurisdiction in England, 1300–1550: The Records and their Interpretation', in *Studies in Church History*, 11 (Oxford, 1975), pp. 199–221 at p. 221.

[13] For example, Peter the Venerable, *Letters*, Epist. 8, ed. G. Constable, 2 vols (Cambridge, Mass., 1967), 1, p. 14; Peter the Chanter, *Verbum abbreviatum*, ch. 51–52, in *PL* 205, pp. 159–62; Gautier de Coinci, 'Vie de Seinte Léocad', lines 1107–16, 1123–46, in *Fabliaux et contes des poètes françois*

the numbers of trained practitioners available at local courts in the more remote districts of Christendom were usually quite modest.[14] In such courts it was possible for an unscrupulous litigant with ample means to engage the services of the entire local bar, thus leaving his opponent unable to secure local counsel or representation in his lawsuit. Canon law provided a remedy for such situations: it is known as distribution of counsel and involved a court order requiring one or more advocates of the local bar to foresake other commitments in order to assist the litigant who came to court without an advocate or proctor.[15]

Important corporate bodies, such as the military orders, were merely acting prudently when they took steps to engage the services of legal counsel and representatives on a long-term basis – at least if they relied upon outside counsel for legal assistance.

An alternative to that sort of arrangement was also open to large and relatively prosperous corporate entities such as the Hospitallers, Templars and Teutonic Knights: this strategy was, so to speak, to grow their own lawyers. The Order could seek to guarantee itself a ready supply of legal advice – what a modern corporation would call house counsel – by attracting legally trained men to join the Order. However, the military orders, unlike some other religious communities, were able to do this only rarely. Perhaps lawyers who were

---

des XI, XII, XIII XIVe et XVe siècles, 2nd ed. by D.M. Méon, 4 vols (Paris, 1808), 1, pp. 306–7. For the views of St Bernard of Clairvaux see the passages cited in J.A. Brundage, 'St Bernard and the Jurists', in *The Second Crusade and the Cistercians*, ed. M. Gervers (New York, 1991), pp. 25–32 at pp. 25–6.

[14] Thus, for example, nine advocates and eight or nine proctors-general practised (though not all at the same time) at the consistory court of the bishop of Ely between 1373 and 1382, while a half-century earlier, in 1322–23, the Exeter consistory court had five advocates and eight proctors, and at Lincoln a statute limited the number of advocates to twelve and proctors to sixteen. See J.A. Brundage, 'The Bar of the Ely Consistory Court in the Fourteenth Century: Advocates, Proctors and Others', *The Journal of Ecclesiastical History*, 43 (1992), pp. 541–60; *The Register of Walter de Stapledon, Bishop of Exeter (A.D. 1307–1326)*, ed. F.C. Hingeston-Randolph (London and Exeter, 1892), pp. 116–17; and C. Morris, 'A Consistory Court in the Middle Ages', *Journal of Ecclesiastical History*, **14**, (1963), pp. 150–59. The *Acta* of the bishop's consistory court in the diocese of Rochester for 1347–48 show only five professional proctors and no advocates; *Registrum Hamonis Hethe, diocesis Roffensis, A.D. 1319–1352*, ed. C. Johnson, 2 vols, Canterbury and York Society, Publications, 48–9, 2 (Oxford, 1914–48), pp. 911–1043. Preliminary soundings in the records of civil litigation of the consistory court of the bishop of Paris for the years 1384–85 indicate that at least eight professional proctors and eight advocates were in regular practice there; *Registre des causes civiles de l'officialité épiscopale de Paris, 1384–1387*, ed. J. Petit, Collection de documents inédits sur l'histoire de France (Paris, 1919).

[15] An undated decretal of Pope Honorius III (1216–27) incorporated into the *Liber Extra* as X 1.32.1, authorized ecclesiastical judges to do this. This policy followed well known precedents in Roman civil law; see Cod. 2.6.7.1 and Dig. 3.1.1.4; see further W. Lyndwood, *Provinciale* 1.13 v. *ad pauperes audiendos* (Oxford, 1679), p. 68. Canon law texts are cited throughout from the standard edition of the *Corpus iuris canonici* by E. Friedberg, 2 vols (Leipzig, 1879; repr. Graz, 1959), while the texts of the *Corpus iuris civilis* are cited from the critical edition by P. Krueger, T. Mommsen, R. Schoell and W. Kroll, 3 vols (Berlin, 1872–95; often reprinted).

attracted to the spiritual values of religious life simply found the military orders less appealing than the mendicant orders or traditional monastic groups, such as the Cistercians and Benedictines.

Another alternative was to train existing members of the military orders in law, so that they would be able to furnish legal services when required. Again, there were a few precedents among traditional religious communities for this approach, most notably the canons of St Ruf, who, unlikely as it may seem, had made the practice of law their special apostolate.[16]

Significant differences emerged among the military orders in the extent of their investment in legal training for their members. The Knights Templars seem to have made little effort either to recruit lawyers or to raise up legal experts from within their own ranks. Still, like many other religious communities, Templar commanderies, as perhaps befitted houses of a military order, were aggressive in pursuit of what they saw as their legal rights and actively pursued litigation against those who threatened them.[17] The Order as a whole, moreover, secured from the papacy a steady stream of privileges and immunities – grants that seldom represented spontaneous favours, but rather materialized as the result of sustained and calculated campaigns waged at the curia, often with the assistance of proctors and legal advisers. The Templar documents in the Archivo de la Corona de Aragón, for example, as A.J. Forey has shown, inform us that houses of the Order regularly paid retainer fees (styled 'pensions') to *legistres*, or lawyers, at the royal court, plus additional sums for the costs of documents drawn up on the Order's behalf.[18] This pattern was not peculiar to Aragon, and documents from other regions similarly show that the Order regularly engaged in the pursuit of privileges and their defence once obtained.[19] The Templars apparently relied primarily upon outside experts for counsel and representation in these proceedings, as well as in lawsuits.[20] Certainly, when the Order was dissolved only a handful of its members had any professional legal qualifications,[21] and Luttrell has correctly observed that most of them made a remarkably inept job of defending themselves when they came to trial.[22]

---

[16] J.-P. Poly, 'Les maîtres de Saint-Ruf: Pratique et enseignement du droit dans la France méridionale au XIIe siècle, *Annales de la Faculté de droit de l'Université de Bordeaux*, 2 (1978), pp. 183–203.

[17] For example, *PUTJ*, 2, pp. 219–21, 250–51, 284–5, 297–8, among many others.

[18] A.J. Forey, *The Templars in the Corona de Aragón* (London, 1973), pp. 320, 416–18.

[19] For example, the papal privileges granted to the Templars by *Omne datum optimum*, originally issued 29 March 1139 and subsequently reissued in 1154, 1163 (twice), 1173, 1179 (twice), 1180, 1182, 1183, 1186, 1188, 1189, and 1194; *PUTJ*, 2, pp. 96–103.

[20] For example, *PUTJ*, 2, pp. 219–21, 250–51, 284–5, 297–8.

[21] Three Templars are identified in the trial proceedings as having studied law, and all of them had completed their legal qualifications before entering the order; *Procès*, 1, p. 185 (Hugh de Marchant), p. 379 (Geraldus de Causso), pp. 422, 598 (Johannes de Folhayo). I am grateful to Dr A.J. Forey for bringing these references to my attention.

[22] A. Luttrell, 'Fourteenth-Century Hospitaller Lawyers', *Traditio*, 21 (1965), pp. 449–56 at p. 450, reprinted with original pagination in his *Hospitallers in Cyprus, Rhodes, Greece and the West, 1291–1440* (London, 1978).

In short, the Templars seem to have opted out of the legal culture that had begun to dominate Western Christendom by the beginning of the thirteenth century, and it may not be exaggeration to suggest that ultimately some of them paid for this with their lives.

The Hospitallers, in contrast, seem to have adjusted much more comfortably than did the Templars to the legalism of the age, and that may in part help to account for their ability to survive, and even to profit from, the demise of the Templar Order. Thus, for example, while Pope Innocent IV (1243–54) authorized both the Hospitallers and the Templars (as well as other religious communities) to let rooms to students in their houses at Paris, the Hospitallers soon began to do so, while the Templars apparently did not.[23] Since the Knights of St John, moreover, owned a number of houses near the Clos Brunel, where the Paris Schools of Canon Law were situated, not only did the Knights soon become the landlords for colleges and hostels that catered to canon lawyers,[24] but they also permitted the Faculty of Canon Law to hold its meetings, elections and examinations in their church.[25]

Luttrell argues that, from around 1380, one can even begin to speak of an informal Hospitaller *studium* of canon law at Paris.[26] Even before that time, the Hospitallers had petitioned for, and received, from Pope Innocent VI (1352–62) permission for their members to study canon law,[27] and, earlier still, at least a few members of the Order had taken law degrees, while a handful of men who had already completed their legal training enlisted in the Order's ranks.[28] Between 1371 and the end of the fourteenth century nearly a dozen Hospitallers are known to have taken degrees in canon law; and they are unlikely to be the only ones who studied law.[29]

The Hospitallers, moreover, unlike the Templars, attracted patronage from lawyers who, while not members themselves, gave financial and other assistance

---

[23] *Chartularium Universitatis Parisiensis*, ed. H. Denifle and Emile Chatelain, 4 vols (Paris, 1889–97; repr. Brussels, 1964), 1, p. 232.

[24] Luttrell, pp. 455–6.

[25] *Chartularium Universitatis Parisiensis*, 3, nos. 1486, 1488, 1535, pp. 321, 328, 443.

[26] Luttrell, 456.

[27] *Chartularium Universitatis Parisiensis*, 3, no. 1230, pp. 40–41.

[28] Luttrell, pp. 450–2, notes that a Hospitaller brother, Beltran of Tarragona, had taken his doctorate in canon law at Lérida in 1349 and was soon appointed a royal counsellor; likewise a legally-trained kinsman of the prior of the conventual church of St John on the island of Rhodes became a knight-brother of the Order in 1346, while the redactor of the systematic collection of the Order's statutes (dated between 1287 and 1303), Brother William of San Stefano, seems very likely to have had some substantial legal training, whether or not he had taken a law degree. A century earlier the Master of the Hospitallers designated Brother Marquisius, rector of the Hospital of St Sigismund, as a proctor and syndic to deal with the Order's litigation at the Roman curia; *RRH*, no. 1029 (1231); J.S.C. Riley-Smith, *The Knights of St John in Jerusalem and Cyprus, 1050–1310* (London, 1967), pp. 379–80, also names several additional legal representatives of the Hospitaller Order.

[29] *Chartularium Universitatis Parisiensis*, 3, nos. 1539, 1549, pp. 448, 480; Luttrell, pp. 452–5.

to the Order.[30] In part this patronage, to be sure, may represent repayment by practising lawyers either for the business that the Hospitallers sent their way, or perhaps also for subsidies that they may have received from the Order while they were studying law.[31]

In any event, although the Order began to train some of its own legal experts and subsidize others, they were not nearly numerous enough to satisfy all the Hospitallers' needs. The Order employed numerous lawyers and notaries: for example, in its administration of Rhodes and its estates in Cyprus,[32] as well as in regions remote from its Mediterranean theatre of operations as England and Ireland.[33]

Like the Templars, the Hospitallers, too, regularly sought and received exemptions and privileges of numerous sorts from the papacy.[34] Petitions for these grants required skilled legal advice, for each petition normally specified in detail the precise mixture of favours and the specific terms of the privileges desired. Petitions contained, in effect, a rough draft of the document that the petitioner sought, and drawing up these statements, which were often quite technical, was no work for amateurs. Moreover, once the petition had been framed to the petitioner's satisfaction, the services of proctors and notaries were essential both to submit the document in proper form and to oversee its safe passage through the labyrinthine corridors of the curial bureaucracy.[35] The management of this whole business formed a significant part of the duties of the Order's proctors-general at the papal court. Prior to 1374 the Hospitallers' proctors-general were members of the Order without legal training and would regularly employ outside professionals to carry out the numerous legal tasks involved in securing privileges and otherwise protecting the Order's interests

---

[30] Luttrell, p. 454.

[31] The Order is known to have provided subsidies – in effect scholarships of a sort – to a handful of law students during the fourteenth century and it is likely that in return the Order expected to receive some legal services from those who had benefited from its support; Luttrell, p. 451.

[32] Ibid., pp. 450–52; P.W. Edbury, *The Kingdom of Cyprus and the Crusades, 1191–1374* (Cambridge, 1991), pp. 77–8.

[33] Thus, for example, *The Cartulary of the Knights of St John of Jerusalem in England, Secunda Camera, Essex*, ed. M. Gervers, Records of Social and Economic History, n.s., vol. 6 (London, 1982), whose index s.v. 'Attorneys' mentions numerous lawyers, both secular and ecclesiastical, employed by the Hospitallers in Essex alone; see also *The Knights Hospitallers in England, being the Report of Prior Philip de Thame to the Grand Master Elyan de Villanova for A.D. 1338*, ed. L.B. Larking and J.M. Kemble, Camden Society, Old Series, 65 (London, 1857), pp. xl–xliii, 101, 178, 210, 218, 219; P. Brand, 'The Early History of the Legal Profession of the Lordship of Ireland, 1250–1350', in *Brehons, Serjeants and Attorneys: Studies in the History of the Irish Legal Profession*, ed. D. Hogan and W.N. Oxborough (Dublin, 1991), pp. 15–50 at p. 41.

[34] The texts of some of the principal grants of privilege may be found in *PUTJ*, 2, pp. 130–35, 159–62, 194–201. See also Riley-Smith, *Knights of St John*, pp. 375–89.

[35] For a lucid and succinct description of the workings of the papal chancery in the early thirteenth century see J.E. Sayers, *Papal Government and England during the Pontificate of Honorius III (1216–1227)*, Cambridge Studies in Medieval Life and Thought, 3rd ser., 21 (Cambridge, 1984), pp. 15–49.

at the curia.[36] In 1374, however, the Master appointed as a proctor-general, one of his relatives, Ferry Cassinel, who was not a member of the Order, but a Professor of Civil and Canon Law. In 1379 the next Master appointed a Hospitaller brother who held a degree in canon law as one of the Order's four proctors-general. From that time forward at least one of the proctors-general was always both a member of the Order and a trained canonist.[37]

The Teutonic Knights, the last of the big three military orders to be founded, adjusted to the new legalism of the thirteenth century even more readily than the Hospitallers had done.[38] In part this reflected, no doubt, the German Order's delicate dual allegiance to the opposing forces of empire and papacy, which forced it to pay continual heed to the legal niceties of its position. Also the fact that the Teutonic Knights, unlike the older military orders, became the rulers of a vast domain in northern Europe no doubt helped to make the Order's leadership keenly aware of the need for able legal counsel in negotiations with their subject populations and with the neighbouring princes of Lithuania and Poland, as well as with the political and religious authorities of Western Christendom.[39] Furthermore, in addition to the legal requirements of the German Order as a whole, individual houses often had their own business to conduct at the Roman curia and needed proctors to attend to these matters.[40]

Given these circumstances, then, it is no surprise to find that the Teutonic Knights, even more than the Hospitallers, perhaps recruited and certainly subsidized law students whose services they subsequently expected to call upon.[41] Hartmut Boockmann has identified forty-four law students, mainly in the fifteenth century, whose education was assisted by Teutonic Order.[42] Only six of these students were actually members of the Order, but the

---

[36] Riley-Smith, *Knights of St John*, pp. 379–80.

[37] Luttrell, p. 453.

[38] On the circumstances of their foundation see esp. U. Arnold, 'Entstehung und Frühzeit des Deutschen Ordens', in *Die geistlichen Ritterorden Europas* (above, n. 1), pp. 81–107.

[39] For an overview of the complex political and diplomatic issues that the Knights faced in the Baltic, see E. Christiansen, *The Northern Crusades* (Minneapolis, 1980). Further details may be found in a series of monographs by W. Urban, beginning with *The Baltic Crusade* (DeKalb, IL, 1975) and continuing in *The Livonian Crusade* (Washington, DC, 1981), *The Prussian Crusade* (Lanham, MD, 1980), and *The Samogitian Crusade* (Chicago, 1989).

[40] Thus, for example, as early as 1248 the house of the Teutonic Order at Nuremberg had engaged Master John of Sancto Germano, a well connected papal notary and curial proctor, to act on its behalf at Rome; W. Stelzer, 'Aus der päpstlichen Kanzlei des 13. Jahrhunderts: Magister Johannes de Sancto Germano, Kurienprokuratur und päpstlicher Notar', *Römische historische Mitteilungen*, 11 (1969), pp. 213, 220.

[41] The French and English monarchs adopted this practice of subsidizng the education of students who would then be expected to give their services in return during the thirteenth century as a more-or-less routine policy of royal administration; F. Pegues, 'Royal Support of Students in the Thirteenth Century', *Speculum*, 31 (1956), pp. 454–62.

[42] H. Boockmann, 'Die Rechtsstudenten des Deutschen Ordens: Studium, Studien förderung und gelehrter Beruf im späten Mittelalter', in *Festschrift für Hermann Heimpel zum 70. Geburtstag*, 3 vols, Veröffentlichungen des Max-Planck-Instituts für Geschichte, 36, **2** (Göttingen, 1972), pp. 313–75.

majority came from regions that the Knights governed in Livonia or Prussia. Some received direct grants outright from the Order's funds, but about a quarter of them had income from ecclesiastical benefices that the Order had bestowed upon them. Most of the students subsidized by the Knights studied in central European universities – mainly Leipzig, Vienna and Rostock – only one studied in France and the remainder attended universities in Italy, predominantly Bologna or Padua.[43] Even while they were still students, several recipients of the Knights' largesse also acted as representatives or agents of the Order, and nearly all of them made careers in activities that one way or another, supported the Knights' interests. Two became the Order's proctors-general in Rome, one became the legal adviser to the Master-General in Prussia, three others became his legal counsellors in Livonia, while another three became the officials-principal, or presiding judges, in bishops' courts, and seven others became bishops themselves in Livonia or Prussia.[44] Hence the Teutonic Order's *Landmeister* in Livonia, Wennemar of Bruggenoy, could boast in a letter to Nicholas of Danzig:

> We want you to know that we and our fellow-preceptors in Livonia are not inclined to call in legal experts from outside [for assistance] in our case, nor would our order in any way require them, for, by the grace of God, our General and the order in Prussia have numerous reputable and well-known men for such affairs and we shall be well content with most of them in the aforesaid matter, since, as we hope, they will not neglect the order's rights.[45]

Although some of the Teutonic Order's own proctors-general in Rome were legally trained, their primary task was not to conduct litigation in person. Their legal training was used in the choosing of advocates to present the Order's case, providing them with instructions on its conduct and defining the position that the Order wished to take in the matter.[46] Names of advocates admitted to practise in the curial courts were kept on file at the *Audientia Sacri Palatii*, and only those listed were eligible to conduct cases there. The records do not make it entirely clear whether the Teutonic Knights kept any Roman advocates on long-term retainers, or whether they engaged their services on a case-by-case basis. Certainly some consistorial advocates worked with remarkable regularity for the Knights, as did local advocates elsewhere. Already in the late thirteenth century one Master Accursus of Arezzo, described as

---

[43] Ibid., pp. 364–5.

[44] Ibid., pp. 370–72.

[45] K. Forstreuter, *Die Berichte der Generalprokuratoren des Deutschen Ordens an der Kurie*, 6 vols, **1**, Veröffentlichen der Niedersächsischen Archivverwaltung, nos. 12, 13, 21, 19, 32, 37 (Göttingen, 1961–), no. 209, pp. 315–16: *Unde scire vos cupimus, quod nos et conpreceptores nostri in Lyvonia ad tales iurisperitos ab extra ad causam nostram vocandos inclinati non sumus, nec aliquo modo per ipsos ordini nostro cautum esset, sed gracia Dei generalis noster et ordo in Pruscia quamplures habet sollempnes ac famosos viros ad talia et quevis majora de quibus suo tempore in premissis bene contentaremur, qui eciam, ut speramus, ordinem in suo iure non negligerent.*

[46] Forstreuter, *Berichte*, **1**, pp. 160–61.

iurisperitus, seems to have acted with some regularity for the Teutonic Order in the Latin Kingdom of Jerusalem.[47] At the beginning of the fourteenth century the Knights repeatedly employed a Roman advocate named Porrina Casoli,[48] and a few years later another advocate named Reinher acted for them in several cases.[49] The consistorial advocate most clearly associated with the Order's interests on a regular basis, Bartholomew of Novaria, was engaged in work on the Knights' behalf repeatedly from the late 1380s until his death in 1405.[50] The Order's proctor-general, Nicholas of Danzig, referred to him as *her Bartholomeus, unsir advocat* in a letter to Hochmeister Conrad of Wallenrode in 1392, which certainly seems to imply that the connection was regular and on going.[51] Bartholomew more than once advanced some of his own money to the Medici bank and other creditors on the Order's behalf in the expectation that the knights would reimburse him in due course, and this, too, strongly implies a long-term, trusting relationship between the advocate (who, given his long experience and the nature of his calling, was not likely to be naive or credulous) and these particular clients.[52]

In summary, then, we have seen that the Templars made few efforts to accommodate themselves to the growing legalism that began to become such a prominent feature of Western society in the late twelfth century. They apparently made no attempt either to train their own members in law or to recruit men who had completed a legal education and instead relied almost entirely upon outside counsel for legal services. The Hospitallers, on the other hand, occasionally underwrote the expenses of legal training for one or another of their members, but this practice seems to have been sporadic and presumably fluctuated according to current perceptions of need, as well as the interests and abilities of the Order's members at any given time. The Hospitallers, in addition, formed close connections with the Canon Law faculty at Paris – a step that may well have stood them in good stead when they needed to engage legal assistance. The Teutonic Knights, more consistently than either of the two older military orders, adopted a long-term policy of subsidizing law students, both members of the Order and others who had close connections with it, for the express purpose of cultivating legal experts whose services would be available as required. In addition, the German Order, assiduously cultivated

---

[47] *RRH*, nos. 1373 (1271), 1384 (1272), 1390 (1273), 1413 (1277). In no. 1467 J. de Wacholt also appeared as a proctor for the German Order in 1286.

[48] Forstreuter, *Berichte*, 1, pp. 74, 160.

[49] Ibid., 1, pp. 81–2, 160, 210 (no. 51).

[50] Ibid., 1, pp. 139, 303–6 (no. 197), 307 (no. 199), 308 (no. 202), 311 (no. 206), 322 (no. 211), 327 (no. 214), 333 (no. 221), 347 (no. 233), 352–4 (no. 242), 367 (no. 258), 370 (no. 263), 340 (no. 225).

[51] Ibid., 1, pp. 82, 160 and 311 (no. 206).

[52] E. Göller, 'Aus der Camera Apostolica der Schismapäpste', *Römische Quartalschrift*, 32, (1924), pp. 97, 128; Fostreuter, *Berichte*, 1, p. 308 (no. 202).

long-term relationships with outside counsel – a practice that tended to work to the Order's advantage.

Neither the armed prowess nor the pious objectives of the medieval military orders could protect them from what Shakespeare called those 'nice sharp quillets of the law' (*Henry VI*, Pt. 1 II.iv.17). Against such weapons the knights, like it or not, required the services of lawyers for the protection, and even the salvation, of their fortunes in this world, if not necessarily in the next.

40

Philippe de Mézières and the Idea of Crusade

Joan Williamson

The collection of essays *Journeys Towards God: Pilgrimage and Crusade* shows, as its title indicates, the interconnectedness of pilgrimage and its 'younger but close relation, crusade'.[1] It is particularly in reading the late J.G. Davies' article in this collection, which reminds us that crusaders were identified as pilgrims, with the crusades considered to be pilgrimages of the Cross,[2] that we are led to consider the nature of the self-chosen pseudonym, *vieil pelerin*, of the greatest crusade propagandist of the second half of the fourteenth century, Philippe de Mézières, and to examine whether his frequent use of the words 'pilgrim' and 'pilgrimage' contains the connotation of armed journey to Jerusalem, thus reflecting his unflagging enthusiasm for the idea of crusade.

In his series of writings composed principally between 1367 and 1396, one of Philippe de Mézières' most constant references to himself is as a pilgrim. He writes of pilgrimage in his narration of how he received, in Jerusalem, a mandate from God to found his chivalric Order.[3] However the meaning here is literal: he was on a pilgrimage to the Holy City, a reading confirmed by his statement elsewhere that it was in the Church of the Holy Sepulchre itself in Jerusalem that he received his inspirational vision.[4] It is as a pilgrim, but literally so, that he presents himself in *Le Songe du vieil pelerin*,[5] as he travels

---

[1] *Journeys Towards God: Pilgrimage and Crusade*, ed. B.N. Sargent-Baur. Studies in Medieval Culture, 30, and Occasional Studies Series of the Medieval and Renaissance Studies Program of the University of Pittsburgh, 5 (Kalamazoo, Mich. 1992), p. vii.

[2] J.G. Davies, 'Pilgrimage and Crusade Literature', in *Journeys Towards God*, pp. 1–30.

[3] Philippe de Mézières, *Nova religio Milicie Passionis Jhesu Christi pro acquisicione Sancte Civitatis Jherusalem et Terre Sancte*, 2nd redaction, Paris, Bibliothèque Mazarine, Paris, ms. 1943, pt. 2, fol. 45v.

[4] Philippe de Mézières, *De la Chevallerie de la Passion de Jhesu Crist*, Bibliothèque de l'Arsenal, Paris, ms. 2251, Ars. ms. 2251, fols 10–12v.

[5] Philippe de Mézières, *Le Songe du vieil pelerin*, ed. G.W. Coopland, 2 vols (Cambridge, 1969), 1, pp. 84, 85, 91.

the world in search of a place where the virtues might dwell. Philippe also incorporates in this allegorical journey accounts of real pilgrimages, such as the pilgrim party's worship at the Church of St James the Apostle in Compostela,[6] and the compulsory stops of all visitors to Paris at Notre Dame and the Sainte Chapelle.[7]

On the other hand, Philippe also uses these words in a metaphorical sense, but not to make of the crusader a special sort of pilgrim. Philippe was greatly influenced by Guillaume de Deguilleville and he uses Guillaume's meaning of 'pilgrim' and 'pilgrimage' as a metaphor for human life, with the mortal world not our true home but a pilgrim place – *Qui est la maison propre en ce monde pelerin de nostre doulz Espous de l'ame?*[8] – and the desired end of the journey arrival at the holy city of Jerusalem Triumphant.[9] Thus, while Philippe incorporates the earlier penitential connection with pilgrimage of earlier writers,[10] the idea of crusade as a superior pilgrimage is not explicit in his works, and we must conclude that 'pilgrim' and 'pilgrimage' did not have the significance of 'crusader' and 'crusade' for him.

However, let us note in this introductory examination of Philippe de Mézières' ideas on crusade that the connection between crusading and the Crucifixion, such as that indicated by James of Vitry,[11] is vividly retained by Philippe in the very name of his military order – the Order of the Chivalry of the Passion of Jesus Christ. Philippe also incorporates other traditional ideas on crusade in his writings. What our author sought was the fulfilment of the prayer of the Pater Noster – 'Thy Kingdom come, thy will be done on earth as it is in Heaven' – symbolized by the recovery of Jerusalem. The recovery of Jerusalem was of the utmost importance to him because he saw this city as the very foundation of the faith: '*Quel merveille! La dicte cite de Jherusalem et le royaume, commencement et fondement de la foy, et royaume singulier, tout autour avironne des anemis de la foy*',[12] thus restating the position which this city had

---

[6] *Le Songe*, **1**, p. 391.

[7] Ibid., **1**, pp. 445–6.

[8] Philippe de Mézières, *Le Livre de la vertu du sacrement de mariage*, Paris, Bibliothèque Nationale, ms. fr. 1175, fol. 39v.

[9] '*Le Testament* de Philippe de Mézières', ed. A. Guillemain, in *Mélanges Jeanne Lods du moyen âge au XXe siècle*. Collection de l'Ecole Normale Superieure de Jeunes Filles **10**, 2 (Paris, 1978), p. 302.

[10] Sermon on the crusade attributed in Oxford, Bodleian Library, ms. Hatton 37, fols 279vb–280vb, to Roger of Salisbury; a sermon preached to Benedictine nuns in Elstow, near Bedford, on the fourth Sunday of Lent, 28 March 1283, in M. O'Carroll, *A Thirteenth Century Preacher's Handbook: Studies in MS. Laud. Misc. 511* (PhD Diss., U. London, 1983); and Humbert of Romans, 'Sermon ad crucesignatos', *Sermones ad diversos status* (Hagenow, 1508). See P.J. Cole, *The Preaching of the Crusades to the Holy Land, 1095–1270*. Medieval Academy Books, **98** (Cambridge, Mass., 1991), pp. 167–72, 174–5.

[11] Jacques de Vitry, 'Ad cruce signatos', in *Analecta novissima spicilegii Solesmensis: Altera continuatio*, ed. J.B. Pitra, **2** (Paris, 1888; repr. Farnborough, 1967), pp. 421–30, 423. See Cole, p. 136'.

[12] Philippe de Mézières, *Letter to King Richard II*, ed. and trans. G.W. Coopland (Liverpool, 1975), p. 99.

earlier held in crusade propaganda, such as that of James of Vitry and Henry of Albano.[13]

Philippe also depicts the exploits of biblical and other warriors for the faith,[14] in the manner of earlier crusading propagandists such as Humbert of Romans, as James A. Brundage has pointed out.[15] Philippe recalls earlier successful Christian soldiers, such as Godfrey of Bouillon and Charlemagne, for which the *Gesta Karoli* of Turpin was a rich source, as Cole recalls,[16] continuing what Brundage has termed Humbert of Romans' 'principle of emulation'.[17] Philippe includes a history of the crusades, listing the chiefs of Jerusalem, from Godfrey to Baldwin II, and providing precise figures for the numbers of soldiers involved in the various battles, all, he says, with the purpose of reviving the old prowess.[18] He particularly echoes Urban II's plea to the French chivalry in 1095 to cease fighting among themselves and to unite against the Turkish conquerors of the Holy Land[19] when, in *Le Songe du vieil pelerin*, he criticizes the countries of the West and offers the young French king, Charles VI, instruction on how to govern his realm and live in peace with his neighbours, so that a new crusade might have a chance of success.[20]

Joshua Prawer has observed that there was a feeling throughout the fourteenth century that a new crusade would work, that 'this confidence was strengthened and reinforced by a new literary genre: *De recuperatione Terrae Sanctae*', and that 'a bountiful crop of such plans poured into the Roman curia and royal chanceries throughout Europe'.[21] Philippe, however, had been a crusader. It was after the successful attack on the Turks at Smyrna in 1346, undertaken by the League of 1344, allying the papacy, Venetians and Hugh IV of Cyprus, that he was knighted;[22] he also fought in other crusades, such as those of Satalia

---

[13] Henry of Albano, *Tractatus de peregrinante civitate Dei*, PL **204**: cols 251–402, 13th tract; Jacques de Vitry, 'Ad cruce signatos', in Pitra, *Analecta*, **2**, p. 422. See Cole, pp. 68–9, 134–6.

[14] Philippe de Mézières, *Epistre lamentable et consolatoire sur le fait de la desconfiture lacrimable du noble et vaillant roy de Honguerie par les turcs devant la ville de Nicopoli*, Bibliothèque Royale, Brussels, ms. 10846, fols 8–10 (some of this depiction is included in the partial publication of the *Epistre* in *Oeuvres de Froissart: Chroniques*, ed. K. de Lettenhove, **16** (Brussels, 1872), pp. 449–51), and fols 25v–27.

[15] J.A. Brundage, 'Humbert of Romans and the Legitimacy of Crusader Conquests', in *The Horns of Hattin*, ed. B. Z. Kedar (Jerusalem, 1992), p. 305.

[16] Cole, pp. 214–15.

[17] Brundage, p. 305.

[18] Philippe de Mézières, *La Sustance de la Chevalerie de la Passion de Jhesu Crist en francois*, pt. 3 of *Philippe de Mézières and the New Order of the Passion*, ed. A.H. Hamdy, repr. from Bulletin of the Faculty of Arts, Alexandria University, **18**, 1964 (Alexandria, 1965), pp. 92, 94–7.

[19] See Cole, pp. 1–25, for a summary of Urban II's ideas.

[20] Mézières, *Le Songe*, **2**, pp. 292–3.

[21] J. Prawer, *The World of the Crusaders* (London, 1972), p. 149.

[22] Mézières, *De la Chevallerie*, fols 13–13v, and *Oratio tragedica seu declamatorio cujusdam veterani solitarii Celestinorum, indigni nomine, in Passionem Domini Jhesu Christi*, Bibliothèque Mazarine, Paris, ms. 1651, fol. 129v.

and Alexandria, to the extent that Thomas J. Hatton was able to suggest, with a degree of credibility although not proof, that Philippe de Mézières could have been a model for Chaucer's crusading 'verray, parfit gentil knyght' of the *Canterbury Tales*.[23] His Rule was therefore based on experience and was considerably less chimeric than many others composed during this century. He himself stresses the serious origin of his ideas, assuring his readers that they were not hastily put together in a tavern in London or Paris;[24] and, in confirmation of the respectability of his Order, he names the first two adherents: Albert Pachost (a great Polish baron) and Monseigneur Estienne de Lessinge (chamberlain of Humbert II, the dauphin of Vienne).[25]

Philippe's texts reveal a man who knows the Orient. We see this indirectly from comments such as when he says he bowed his head to touch the ground in the manner of men of the Orient.[26] He also informs us of his direct knowledge of the Orient, as when he states that he has dealt with the Turks and Saracens for thirty years and knows that they follow or ignore Muhammad as it suits them and that they are therefore not to be trusted.[27] He writes from experience, showing that he knows the routes for crusaders to travel, as when he writes that the 100,000 combatants of his Order should go directly by sea to Jerusalem, parts of the Orient, Turkey, Egypt, and Syria;[28] and when he indicates routes for the different groups of crusaders to take: England, Scotland and Italy will make up one group of knights; German and Prussian knights will go to Constantinople and the Bosporus; knights from Spain and other southern regions will make war on the king of Granada and the Saracens of Bellemarine, so that these will not invade Europe; while the knights from France should sail from Venice.[29] Such knowledge of the Orient is vital for the success of an expedition, he argues, citing the case of St Louis who was defeated at Damietta because he listened to the advice of his Western lords and barons, instead of to that of the Christians of Syria, descendants of the first crusaders, who knew the language of the Saracens, the conditions of the sultan, and the timing of the flooding of the Nile, and whose advice was therefore more trustworthy.[30]

Philippe ascribes the failure of the crusades to pride, avarice and luxury[31] – a criticism which had a long history. These vices were cited as the cause of

---

[23] T.J. Hatton, 'Chaucer's Crusading Knight, a Slanted Ideal', *Chaucer Review*, **3**, no. 2 (1968), pp. 77–87.

[24] Mézières, *De la Chevallerie*, fol. 13v, and idem, *Epistre lamentable*, fol. 56v (K. de Lettenhove, p. 507).

[25] Mézières, *De la Chevallerie*, fol. 13. For identifications see N. Iorga, *Philippe de Mézières (1327–1405) et la croisade au XIVe siècle*. Bibliothèque de l'Ecole des Hautes Etudes, Sciences Philologiques et Historiques, **110** (Paris, 1896; repr. Geneva, 1976), p. 76.

[26] *De la Chevallerie*, fols 11v and 18v.

[27] *Epistre lamentable*, fol. 37v (K. de Lettenhove, p. 478).

[28] *De la Chevallerie*, fol. 36v.

[29] *Epistre lamentable*, fols 45–45v (fol. 45v only in K. de Lettenhove, p. 493).

[30] Ibid., fols 21v–22 (K. de Lettenhove, pp. 471–2).

[31] *De la Chevallerie*, fols 44v–46, and idem, *Epistre lamentable*, fols 5–5v (K. de Lettenhove, pp. 447–49).

the failure of the crusades by the early chroniclers, who transposed St Augustine's analysis of the downfall of Rome in *De civitate Dei* (1.23), an attribution to be repeated in the Middle Ages in *Li Fet des Romains*.[32] As Jeanette Beer comments on Caesar's gradual destruction in this work, taking the man as representative of the state: 'Pride of life, lusts of the flesh, dominion and power were the reasons for his success that contained within themselves the germs of his failure.'[33]

The nefarious consequences of such vices were intensely personal issues for Philippe. Explicitly promised one-third of the revenues of Alexandria at the siege of 1365 to establish his Order,[34] which at this point he was to administer himself,[35] he saw his dream evaporate with the Western knights' insistence on a withdrawal two days after the capture of this richest of cities.[36] Further, the looting and plundering of the Western knights, who filled seventy of their ships with the spoils of Alexandria before sailing for home[37] surely generated his Rule's prohibition against pillage or sacking of captured places for personal gain, with the taking of booty to be organized and distributed according to determined merit and need.[38]

Philippe observes that finances and love of wife, children and their own kingdoms called Western chivalry back to the West, citing, among others, Philip of France and Richard of England who, with badly regulated armies at Acre, returned home too soon.[39] Philippe was not the first to note the drawbacks of temporary expeditions to the Orient because of such lures.[40] He sees, however, the short stays in the Orient of earlier crusaders as one of the principal reasons why these crusades failed, pointing out that when the princes and lords of the West returned home to run their estates, they left the Holy Land worse off than before, because the Saracens vengefully returned to attack the Eastern Christians who remained, weakened now that they were on their own.[41]

Therefore, he seeks to change radically the conditions of Western expeditions to the Orient. His remedy is to decree that knights in his Order of the Chivalry of the Passion of Jesus Christ should not return after six or eight months, but stay for two years, he initially says, later extending this period to three or five years. This is to be a period of probation, after which members will enrol for

---

[32] L.F. Flutre and K. Sneyders de Vogel, *Li Fet des Romains. compilé ensemble de Saluste et de Suetone et de Lucan*, **1** (Paris, 1937–38; repr. Geneva, 1977), bk. 1, prologue, para. 2, and chap. 8, para. 42; bk. 4, chap. 2, paras 5–7 and 32.

[33] J.M.A. Beer, *A Medieval Caesar*. Etudes de Philologie et d'Histoire, **30** (Geneva, 1976), p. 193.

[34] *De la Chevallerie*, fol. 17.

[35] *Oratio tragedica*, fols 194–94v.

[36] Ibid., fol. 73.

[37] H. Luke, *Cyprus: A Portrait and an Appreciation* (London, 1957), p. 49.

[38] *De la Chevallerie*, fol. 89.

[39] *Epistre lamentable*, fol. 21v. (K. de Lettenhove, p. 471)

[40] For example, Humbert de Romans, *De predicacione crucis*, as summarized in Cole, pp. 209–10.

[41] *De la Chevallerie*, fols 31v–32.

life and live in the Orient permanently, freed of the temptation to go back home to oversee the running of their estates.[42] With this end in view Philippe decrees that knights take their wives with them. Abstinence will not be expected of them, particularly in the hot East, which he thinks encourages lust, from which vice conjugal chastity will protect them.[43] All may remarry, and the children should be married off also.[44] He makes detailed arrangements for the accommodation of these families, deciding where the wives, and ultimately widows, will live and what occupations they will engage in: there are to be hospices and hospitals, where orphans will be cared for, the sick tended, and widows housed.[45] While the needs of women, both as wives and widows, will be met, the regimen he proposes for them is much more severe than that for the men of the Order. The women are to maintain silence, not be idle, breastfeed their children and live sequestered lives (as do Oriental women), going out only to visit the sick.[46]

Since the families will accompany the knights and their wives, he arranges for the care of children, for they will also live permanently in the Orient. Therefore, he makes arrangements for the establishment of schools, in which civil and canon law, theology and vocal and instrumental music will be taught[47] – a curriculum quite closely implementing the knowledge of the Bible, geography, canon law, Muhammad and Islamic law which Humbert of Romans said that a man of learning, engaged in crusade sermonizing, needed to know.[48] Although Philippe sees his knights as being of seven languages or nationalities, Latin will be the only language spoken, to ensure a common language. However, Arabic, Tartar, Greek and Armenian will also be taught. Eight (unspecified) Oriental languages will be taught, but only for aural comprehension and oral expression. While of interest, his insistence on Oriental languages marks no innovation. Joshua Prawer, making the point that there was a school of thought which recommended winning back the Holy Land by conversion and that knowing the texts of the infidels would help, recalls that

> ...as far back as the middle of the twelfth century, the great abbot of Cluny, Peter the Venerable, had the Koran translated into Latin and so made it accessible to the West so as to serve the understanding of Islam as a solid basis of anti-Islamic polemics.... Under the influence of Ramon Lull the Council of Vienne (1311) decided to establish six schools of Oriental languages to train the future propagandists and missionaries.[49]

---

[42] Ibid., fols 37v–40.
[43] Ibid., fol. 46v.
[44] Ibid., fols 82v and 86v.
[45] *Nova religio*, 2nd redaction (bk 5), fols 64–5.
[46] Ibid., 2nd redaction (bk 21), fols 105–6v.
[47] Ibid., 2nd redaction (bk. 20), fol. 103.
[48] Humbert of Romans, *De predicacione crucis*, as summarized in Cole, p. 213.
[49] Prawer, pp. 150–51.

Philippe's reasoning is more bellicose than devout: he says that since one cannot trust the Turks and therefore their interpreters,[50] one must oneself learn their language and customs.[51]

Philippe considers the financial consequences of the permanent relocation in the Orient of entire families Knights should give their Western properties to the Order so that they will not be tempted to return.[52] But, before they join, they must draw up wills, making restitution of anything they have unlawfully taken from another, to ensure that money paid into the common purse by a member and that brought with him for his own use will be legitimately acquired and rightfully his.[53] Philippe bids that, this done, all be held in common, with each to receive according to need, in order to avoid avarice.[54] He insists on justice in these arrangements for the financing of his Order: children who do not wish to join the Order when their fathers do will receive their due portion;[55] and while members will thus distribute their possessions between the Order and those of their children who choose not to join the Order, inheritances can be accepted and retained.[56]

Philippe appeals to Christians to eschew pride, avarice and lust,[57] offering his members the three vows of obedience, poverty of spirit and conjugal chastity.[58] Thus his Order will combat pride and ingratitude with true obedience and modesty; lust with temperance and conjugal fidelity; and avarice with the love of God and the revival of Christ's passion, the symbol of the Order.[59]

---

[50] *Epistre lamentable*, fol. 37v (K. de Lettenhove, p. 478), and *De la Chevallerie*, fol. 88v.

[51] *Nova religio*, 2nd redaction (bk. 20), fol. 103.

[52] *De la Chevallerie*, fol. 83v.

[53] Ibid., fols 39–39v.

[54] Ibid., fols 46v and 83.

[55] Ibid., fol. 90.

[56] Ibid., fols 46v and 90.

[57] Ibid., fols 44v–46.

[58] Ibid., fol. 82v.

[59] Ibid., fols 46v–50.

41

Victorian Perceptions of the Military Orders

Elizabeth Siberry

There are two different ways of approaching the subject of Victorian perceptions of the military orders: the image and the reality. This paper seeks to cover not only the Victorian manifestations of the military orders, but also how they were portrayed by contemporaries in literature, music and art. My main focus will be Britain, but to provide some context I will draw parallels from elsewhere in Europe.

What do we mean by the military orders in the Victorian era? After the loss of Malta in 1798, the affairs of the knights of the Sovereign Military Order of Malta were in some chaos.[1] In 1871, however, a new constitution was drawn up for the (non-Catholic) Order of St John of Jerusalem in England. In 1888 the Order was granted a Royal Charter, and Queen Victoria became its sovereign head. Through the St John Ambulance Division and Brigade, the Order saw noble service in the First World War and, rather appropriately, the then Grand Prior, the Duke of Connaught, conferred the Grand Cross of the Order of St John on General Allenby in Jerusalem in 1919.[2] The Sovereign Order, known from 1876 as the British Association, also had a small group of Catholic members during the Victorian period.

The Victorian Order of St John seems to have been very conscious of its history and, in 1926, members of the Order went on a pilgrimage to the Holy Land, visiting Jerusalem and notable crusader sites such as the battlefield of

---

[1] For the story of the attempt by a group of Victorian eccentrics to revive the English *Langue*, see J.S.C. Riley-Smith, 'The Order of St John in England, 1827–58', chapter 14 above.

[2] E.J. King (rev. H. Luke), *The Knights of St John in the British Realm* (London, 1967), p. 166; L. Thomas, *With Lawrence in Arabia* (London, 1925), p. 242. The Grand Cross was also to be conferred upon T.E. Lawrence, but, averse to decorations and military honours, he left Jerusalem for Cairo. Examples of the use of crusader imagery by the St John Ambulance Brigade and Association before and during the First World War can be seen at the museum in Clerkenwell.

the Horns of Hattin. On their voyage from Venice to Jaffa they had lectures on the crusades and the Order's librarian, Edwin King, noted that the parade service at the Anglican Cathedral in Jerusalem in March 1926 was the first time that Knights of St John had marched in the Holy City since it had been captured by Saladin in 1187.[3]

The nineteenth century also witnessed an attempt to revive the Order of Knights Templar in England, the key figures being George III's son, Augustus, Duke of Sussex, Charles Tennyson d'Eyncourt and Admiral Sir Sidney Smith. The last rose to fame when, in 1799, as a naval captain, he joined forces with the Turks to repulse Napoleon's attack on Acre.[4] Sir Sidney clearly saw himself as a Christian knight in the tradition of the military orders. He traced this association back to his intervention in an insurrection of Janissaries in Cyprus in 1799. As a reward for his services he was apparently given a cross worn by Richard I on his crusade. He described the incident in a letter as follows:

> On visiting the venerable Greek Archbishop afterwards ... he embraced me paternally and, at the same moment, adroitly threw the Templar's Cross, which he wore as an episcopal decoration on his breast, around the neck of his English guest, saying, 'This belonged to an Englishman formerly and I now restore it .... It belonged to Saint Richard, surnamed Coeur de Lion, who left it in this church at his departure and it has been preserved in our treasury ever since .... I now make it over to you, in token of our gratitude for saving all our lives.

According to his biographer, it became apparent during Sir Sidney's last illness that this cross had never left his person – that he had constantly worn it under his waistcoat and next to his heart. And when he died in May 1840, he bequeathed the Templar Cross (also confusingly described as the Cross of St John) to the Order of the Templars 'to be kept in deposit in the treasury thereof, from whence it originally came into King Richard's hands and to be worn by the Grand Master and his successors in perpetuity'.[5]

---

[3] E.J. King, *The Pilgrimage of 1926 – Being the Official Journal of the Knights of St John* (London, 1926), pp. 35, 37, 43–5, 48, 69.

[4] For accounts of Sir Sidney Smith's varied career, see Lord Russell of Liverpool, *Knight of the Sword. The Life and Letters of Admiral Sir Sidney Smith* (London, 1964); J. Barrow, *Life and Correspondence of Admiral Sir William Sidney Smith*, 2 vols (London, 1848). Sir Sidney Smith's coat of arms commemorated his famous victory. The shield itself depicted the breach in the walls of Acre, with the standards of the Ottoman Empire and Great Britain; one supporter was a lamb with an olive branch supporting the banner of Jerusalem, the other a tiger with a palm branch, supporting the Union Flag of Britain, with the inscription Jerusalem 1799 upon a cross of St George. See J.B. Burke, *General Armoury of England, Scotland, Ireland and Wales* (London, 1884).

[5] Barrow, *Life and Correspondence*, pp. 409–11. G. Hill, *History of Cyprus*, 4 (Cambridge, 1952), pp. 100–3, plates VII, VIII, published a drawing of the cross made by a Captain Algernon Langton. He noted that the Association Française of the Order of Malta had no record of the original and that it would therefore seem to be lost.

After a career as naval officer and plenipotentiary, Sir Sidney settled in Paris in 1815. There his cross from Cyprus stood him in good stead with the French Neo-Templar Order which had close links with the Freemasons:[6]

> The Grand Master and his Council recognising me as a new Knight Templar elect, duly received me and voting me to be qualified by the above antecedents, recorded me as Grand Prior of England, an authority which Richard I exercised after he had become the purchaser of the land of the Order in Cyprus.[7]

It is at this point that Charles Tennyson d'Eyncourt, a notable Victorian romantic and uncle of the poet Alfred Tennyson, enters the story.[8] He corresponded with a representative of the Freemasons in Paris, Sir John Byerley, and Sir Sidney Smith about the creation of an English branch of the Order of the Temple.

In order to keep his options open, Tennyson d'Eyncourt also tried the Order of Malta, but found 'it could not be had without paying far too dear for the whistle'. The Templars were much more obliging, the Grand Master commenting to Byerley that 'he considered England as the cradle of the Order and you [Tennyson d'Eyncourt] as its founder'.[9] Sir Sidney seems to have ceded his title of Grand Prior to the Duke of Sussex and, in February 1830, wrote to him outlining a plan involving the neo-Templars and the pacification and settlement of Greece.

> A circumstance not to be lost sight of in contemplating the consequences of the resurrection of the Order in the Levant, is that its existence as a Christian military power is not now to be established in the sultan's mind, but is necessarily in the knowledge of the historian and men of suitable education in all the public offices of the Porte, by oral tradition and official documents in their archives.[10]

In February 1838 on the death of the Grand Master, Fabre de Palaprat, Sir Sidney was elected Regent of the Order and wrote to Tennyson d'Eyncourt, encouraging him 'to increase the ranks of the Order from respectable Christian knights in the United Kingdom, known to him as worthy, enlightened and respectable'. Sir Sidney envisaged the knights as 'armed mediators and pacificators, supporters of lawful authority and of charitable institutions, protectors of the weak, the helpless and the oppressed, particularly females, orphans and the aged'. He also had ideas of the Order establishing a convent in Malta, helping to liberate slaves and put down piracy.

---

[6] P. Partner, *The Murdered Magicians: The Templars and their Myth* (Oxford, 1981), pp. 139–40, 149.

[7] Barrow, p. 410.

[8] C. Tennyson and H. Dyson, *The Tennysons: Background to Genius* (London, 1974), pp. 184–7; M. Girouard, *The Return to Camelot: Chivalry and the English Gentleman* (New Haven and London, 1981), pp. 71, 86.

[9] The Tennyson d'Eyncourt papers (TDE) are now housed in the Lincolnshire Archives in Lincoln. I am grateful for the latter's permission to quote from these documents here. See TDE H 8/22, 24, 31, 36, 39, 40.

[10] Barrow, pp. 414–16.

So much for the theory. In practice the English branch of the Order of the Temple had a short life. Sir Sidney died in 1840 and the Duke of Sussex in 1843. Their French brethren sent condolences on the loss of the Grand Prior, expressing the hope that a worthy successor could be identified, but this does not seem to have proved possible.[11] Even d'Eyncourt lost interest and resigned from the Order in 1849.

There was also what might be described as an attempt to launch a crusade, albeit peaceful, in the 1840s. The chief protagonist was Sir William Hillary (1771–1847), who numbered amongst his achievements the establishment of what is now known as the Royal National Lifeboat Institution. In 1797 he had visited Malta where he witnessed the inauguration of the Grand Master of the Sovereign Order and, throughout his life, he was a loyal promoter of attempts to revive the English *Langue*.[12]

In 1840 Acre was freed from the control of the Egyptian Ibrahim Pasha and returned to the Sultan of Turkey, then in alliance with the Christian powers of Europe. This turn of events prompted Hillary to consider the prospects for long-term reoccupation of the Holy Land. On 5 December 1840 he wrote to Sir Richard Broun, Grand Secretary and registrar of the English *Langue*:

> Let then the Order of St John of Jerusalem be patronized and supported by all the Christian powers and remodelled where necessary and practicable, to suit the occasion and let the Paschalics of Gaza and Acre be placed under their sovereign rule paying only a stipulated annual revenue to the Sultan; the perpetual neutrality and possession to be guaranteed to the Order, both by the Christian and Mohammedan powers.

Hillary's letter was duly read out at a Chapter of Council meeting on 18 December and, with their support, he published a pamphlet entitled *Suggestions for the Christian occupation of the Holy Land as a Sovereign State by the Order of St John of Jerusalem* in 1841. In this pamphlet Hillary expounded his ideas in more detail, recalling the role played by the military orders during the crusades and stressing the opportunity now presented for the restoration of the Order of St

---

[11] TDE H/62; TDE H 8/43; 2 TDE H 38/42. J. Burnes, *History of the Knights Templars* (Edinburgh, 1837), p. 53, noted that 'scattered over the mighty empire of Great Britain there are not forty subjects of His Majesty who are Knights Templar and the whole members of the Order probably do not at the moment exceed 300', although there were a number of distinguished associates.

[12] For a summary of Hillary's career, see *Dictionary of National Biography Supplement*, **22** (repr. London, 1921–2), pp. 847–8. Sadly, Hillary's family papers do not appear to have survived, but his correspondence on matters affecting the Order of St John can be found in the Order's Archives at Clerkenwell. I am grateful to Professor Riley-Smith for drawing my attention to the *Minute Book of the English Langue* (1837–58) (*OSJ Anglia Minutes*) and three volumes of letters (*Historical Memoranda*); to the staff of the museum and library at Clerkenwell for their assistance and for permission to quote from these papers.

John to its original splendour. He envisaged a state wherein both Christian and Muslim would enjoy religious freedom and commercial prosperity.[13]

In August 1841 Hillary also published an address to the Knights of St John on the Christian occupation of the Holy Land, concluding:

> It only remains for me, with all deference, to entreat my brother knights of every grade and nation, to recruit their scattered ranks from the nobless, the ancient Chivalric Institutions, and the gentry of the United Kingdom, and of Christendom, to concentrate all their energies for the restoration of their dilapidated Grand Priories and commanderies throughout their various langues – to form a new crusade, not as in days of yore, to convert the Holy Land into a field of carnage and of bloodshed, but a Crusade of Peace – to restore to Palestine that lofty and glorious pre-eminence from which she has long fallen and again to plant the banner of the cross in the land of the redeemer.

Hillary remained indefatigable in his promotion of the crusade, but despite of his efforts it all came to nothing.[14]

So much for the reality. What of the popular image in literature? The obvious starting point is Sir Walter Scott and his novel *Ivanhoe*, published in 1819. The villain of the piece is undoubtedly the Templar, Sir Brian de Bois Guilbert, and at various points in the text Scott makes it clear that his views of the Order of the Temple were unfavourable. For example, Bois Guilbert is described by the Saxon lord Cedric as follows:

> ... they say that he is as valiant as the bravest of his order, but stained with their usual vices, pride, arrogance, cruelty and voluptuousness, a hard hearted man, who knows neither fear of earth, nor awe of heaven.[15]

There is a brief reference to the military orders in Scott's *Essay on Chivalry*, published in the *Encyclopaedia Britannica* in 1818, where they seem to have fallen under his general condemnation of the crusading movement, as 'founded on the spirit of chivalry and on the restless and intolerant zeal which was blended by the churchmen with this military establishment'.[16]

It is perhaps less well known that Scott also wrote a novel about the Knights of St John. It was the product of his journey in 1831 to Malta, but also seems to have been the fulfilment of a lifelong interest in the Hospitallers: one of the books which Scott took with him was a well thumbed copy of Vertot's history of the Order, published in 1819, and Scott wrote that the more he saw of the

---

[13] *Historical Memoranda*, **1**, no. 47; *OSJ Anglia Minutes*, p. 134. Hillary's pamphlet was published in London in 1841. A copy can be found in the British Library. For newspaper reports of Hillary's scheme, see *The Morning Herald*, 27 March 1841, p. 6; *The Argus*, 28 March 1841, p. 196.

[14] *Historical Memoranda*, **1**, nos. 48–54 83; *OSJ Anglia Minutes*, pp. 141, 153–6, 166, 175–6, 196. A copy of the address can also be found in the British Library.

[15] W. Scott, *Ivanhoe* (1819), p. 53. See also p. 244. For evidence of *Ivanhoe's* popularity, see R. Ford, *Dramatisations of Scott's Novels: A Catalogue* (Oxford, 1979), pp. 20–27.

[16] W. Scott, *Essay on Chivalry* (repr. London, 1870), p. 169.

Knights of Malta, the more astonished he was 'at what a gorgeous generation the Order must have been of old'. The novel, *The Siege of Malta*, has only recently been published, because Scott's biographer and son-in-law, Lockhart, was apparently concerned that its quality would detract from Scott's reputation and that he would be accused of plagiarizing Vertot. The plot deals with the siege of Malta by the Turks in 1565, the hero is a Spanish knight, Don Manuel de Vilheyna and, of course, there are frequent references to the Grand Master Jean de la Valette.[17] Scott therefore seems to have had mixed views about the military orders, favouring the Hospitallers far more than the Templars.

Scott apart, the Reverend Frederick Faber, author of a number of devotional books and much attracted by the idea of the Middle Ages and the medieval Church in particular, composed a poem, *Knights of St John*, in which he gave a romanticized view of the Hospitallers, the 'holiest of Knighthood's gallant sons'.[18] But in *The Romany Rye*, published in 1857, George Borrow was less sympathetic, attacking the military orders as a manifestation of the English zeal for gentility rather than as representatives of the simple faith of the early Church.[19]

The military orders also appealed to writers of adventure stories. The prolific popular historian G.A. Henty, for example, published *Knight of the White Cross* in 1896. Although a story of the gallant defence of Rhodes against the Turks and the heroism of one English knight, Sir Gervaise Tresham, Henty repeated criticism of the Hospitallers. He wrote of knights who passed their lives 'in slothful ease at their commanderies' and described the lax way in which they maintained their vow of poverty.[20] Sir Arthur Conan Doyle also painted an unfavourable picture in his novel *The White Company*, published in 1891:

> Knights of St John, having come into large part of the riches of the ill fated Templars, were very much too comfortable to think of exchanging their palace for a tent, or the cellars of England for the thirsty deserts of Syria ... the Hospitallers' mind ran more upon malmsey than Mamelukes and on venison rather than victories.[21]

Turning to music, the French composer Litolff's opera *Les Templiers* was performed in 1886, and Bizet is known to have planned an opera on the same theme in *c.* 1868, but for some reason the project was aborted. The Knights of Rhodes featured in an opera by the German composer Meyerbeer, entitled *Il Crociato in Egitto*, first performed in 1824. The story, which is very loosely connected with Louis IX's Egyptian crusade, is more reminiscent of the

---

[17] See D.E. Sultana, *The Siege of Malta Rediscovered: An Account of Sir Walter Scott's Mediterranean Journey and His Last Novel* (Edinburgh, 1977).

[18] F. Faber, *Poems* (London, 1857), pp. 115–25.

[19] G. Borrow, *The Romany Rye* (repr. London, 1948), Appendix, p. 363.

[20] G.A. Henty, *Knight of the White Cross: A Tale of the Siege of Rhodes* (London, 1896), pp. 33, 188. See also Lt. F.S. Brereton, *Knight of St John: A Tale of the Siege of Malta* (London, 1905).

[21] A. Conan Doyle, *The White Company* (London, 1891), p. 92.

chansons de geste than of Joinville. Its hero is Armando d'Orville, a knight of Provence and nephew of Adriano, Grand Master of the Order of Rhodes, who was left for dead after a surprise Muslim attack. Regaining consciousness, he assumed the clothes of a dead Egyptian soldier, took the name Elmireno and settled in Damietta, then ruled by Sultan Aladino. The action centres on the arrival of a band of Knights of Rhodes in Damietta, to negotiate a peace with the sultan and to find out if Armando is still alive, with the latter's romantic entanglements adding further complexity to the story.

The only other operas which have any connection with the military orders which I have been able to track down are the eleven based on Scott's novel, *Ivanhoe*.[22] In fact, Scott himself attended a performance of Rossini's *Ivanhoe* on 31 October, 1826.

Moving on from music to art, *Ivanhoe* again proved a fertile ground for the artistic imagination. At the novel's peak of popularity at least two *Ivanhoe* paintings were apparently exhibited in galleries every year.[23] There were also, of course, the formal paintings of Grand Priors and dignitaries of the Order of St John, many of which are now displayed at the Order's headquarters in Clerkenwell. In France, episodes and individuals from the history of the military orders were depicted in *Les Salles des croisades*, which formed part of Louis Philippe's scheme of redecoration of the Palace of Versailles in the 1830s[24]

Outside formal ceremonies of the Order of St John, there may even have been a Victorian fashion for dressing up as a Templar or Hospitaller. For example, a J.W. Dunlop wrote that he and his three friends from Edinburgh would be 'happy to appear in our Knight Templar dresses' at the ill-fated Eglington tournament in 1839.[25] The Grand Prior of the Order of St John, Edward, Prince of Wales and later King Edward VII, apparently attended the Duke and Duchess of Devonshire's Diamond Jubilee fancy dress ball as a

---

[22] See J. Mitchell, *The Walter Scott Operas* (Alabama, 1977), pp. 145–200.

[23] I. Anstruther, *The Knight and the Umbrella: An Account of the Eglington Tournament 1839* (repr. Gloucester, 1986), p. 110. For other examples of Ivanhoe paintings, see A. Graves, *The Royal Academy of Arts: A Complete Dictionary of Contributors and their work from its foundation in 1769 to 1904*, 8 vols (London, 1905).

[24] *Notice du Musée Impérial de Versailles*, ed. E. Soulié, 2 vols (Paris, 1859–80), pp. 83–122. In the 1930s, Richard Hollins Murray, the inventor of the road safety feature 'cat's eyes', who had purchased that estate of Dinmore in Herefordshire, a former commandery of the Knights Hospitaller, built a music room and cloisters, which are in effect a memorial to the crusades and the Hospitallers. See R. Hollins Murray, *Dinmore Manor*, Notes, rev. and repr. 1991. The Grand Priory Church at Clerkenwell, with a stained glass window in the crypt dating from 1914 and depicting Raymond du Puy, second Master of the Hospitallers in Jerusalem and the Priory Chapel at the Parish Church of St John in Cardiff are also of interest.

[25] Anstruther, p. 168. Graves also lists a painting by Samuel Drummond, entitled 'Dorset Fellowes Esq. in the costume of a Knight Templar' (1826).

renaissance knight of St John and claimed that he had a silken cross of the Order sewn inside the breast pocket of all his evening coats.[26]

In short, the concept of the military orders, both Templar and Hospitaller, seems to have enjoyed a revival in the Victorian era, manifested by revivals of the orders themselves and the use of their image in literature, music and art. They did not always enjoy a good press, but they were perceived as part of the romantic age of chivalry, of campaigns against the infidel and of Christian heroism, and were thus attractive to a Victorian audience.

---

[26] King, *Knights of St John*, p. 149 n.2.

Select Bibliography

U. Arnold, ed., *Von Akkon bis Wien. Studien zur Deutschordensgeschichte vom 13. bis zum 20. Jahrhundert. Festschrift zum 90. Geburtstag von Althochmeister P. Dr. Marian Tumler O.T* (Marburg, 1978).

U. Arnold, ed., *Zur Wirtschaftsentwicklung des Deutschen Ordens im Mittelalter* (Marburg, 1989).

U. Arnold and M. Tumler, *Der Deutsche Orden. Von seinem Ursprung bis zur Gegenwart* (Bad Münstereifel, 1992).

M. Barber, *The Trial of the Templars* (Cambridge, 1978).

M. Barber, *The New Knighthood. A History of the Order of the Temple* (Cambridge, 1994).

F. Benninghoven, *Der Orden der Schwertbrüder* (Cologne, 1965).

H. Boockmann, *Der Deutsche Orden. Zwölf Kapitel aus seiner Geschichte* (Munich, 1989).

F. Bramato, *Storia dell'ordine dei Templari in Italia* (Rome, 1991).

E. Brockman, *The Two Sieges of Rhodes: 1480–1522* (London, 1969).

M.L. Bulst-Thiele, *Sacrae Domus Militiae Templi Hierosolymitani Magistri: Untersuchungen zur Geschichte des Templeordens 1118/9–1314* (Göttingen, 1974).

M. Burleigh, *Prussian Society and the German Order. An Aristocratic Corporation in Crisis c. 1410–1466* (Cambridge, 1984).

F. Cardini, *Poveri Cavalieri del Cristo. San Bernardo e la Fondazione dell'Ordine Templare* (Rimini, 1992).

I.B. Cowan, P.H.R. Mackay and A. Macquarrie, eds., *The Knights of St John of Jerusalem in Scotland* (Edinburgh, 1983).

A. Demurger, *Vie et mort de l'ordre du Temple*, 2nd ed. (Paris, 1989).

S. Ekdahl, *Die Schlacht bei Tannenberg 1410. Quellenkritische Untersuchungen*, 1, *Einführung und Quellenlage* (Berlin, 1982).

M.-L. Favreau, *Studien zur Frühgeschichte des Deutschen Ordens* (Stuttgart, 1974).

J. Fleckenstein and M. Hellmann, eds., *Die geistlichen Ritterorden Europas* (Sigmaringen, 1980).

A.J. Forey, *The Templars in the Corona de Aragón* (London, 1973).

373

A.J. Forey, *The Military Orders. From the Twelfth to the Early Fourteenth Centuries* (London, 1992).

A.J. Forey, *Military Orders and Crusades* (London, 1994).

K. Forstreuter, *Der Deutsche Orden am Mittelmeer* (Bonn, 1967).

M. Gervers, *The Hospitaller Cartulary in the British Library (Cotton ms. Nero E VI)* (Toronto, 1981).

Z. Goldmann, *Akko in the Time of the Crusades. The Convent of the Order of St John* (Acre, 1987).

E. Gruber, *Deutschordensschwestern im 19. und 20. Jahrhundert. Wiederbelebung, Ausbreitung und Tätigkeit 1837–1971* (Bonn, 1971).

E. Grunsky, *Doppelgeschossige Johanniterkirchen und verwandte Bauten* (Düsseldorf, 1970).

N. von Holst, *Der Deutsche Ritterorden und seine Bauten von Jerusalem bis Sevilla von Thorn bis Narva* (Berlin, 1981).

A. Hoppen, *The Fortification of Malta by the Order of St John, 1530–1798* (Edinburgh, 1979).

W. Hubatsch, *Montfort und die Bildung des Deutschordensstaats im Heiligen Lande* (Göttingen, 1966).

W. Irgang, *Freudenthal als Herrschaft des Deutschen Ordens 1621–1725* (Bonn, 1971).

H. Kluger, *Hochmeister Hermann von Salza und Kaiser Friedrich II* (Marburg, 1987).

E. Kollias, *The City of Rhodes and the Palace of the Grand Master: From the Early Christian Period to the Conquest by the Turks (1522)* (Athens, 1988).

E. Kollias, *The Knights of Rhodes: The Palace and the City* (Athens, 1991).

M.L. Lesesma Rubio, *Templarios y Hospitalarios en el reino de Aragón* (Zaragoza, 1982).

A.M. Legras, *Les commanderies des Templiers et des Hospitaliers de Saint-Jean de Jérusalem en Saintonge et en Aunis* (Paris, 1983).

D.W. Lomax, *La orden de Santiago, 1170–1275* (Madrid, 1965).

A. Luttrell, *The Hospitallers in Cyprus, Rhodes, Greece and the West: 1291–1440* (London, 1978).

A. Luttrell, *Latin Greece, the Hospitallers and the Crusade: 1291–1400* (London, 1982).

A. Luttrell, *The Hospitallers of Rhodes and their Mediterranean World* (London, 1992).

V. Mallia-Milanes, *Venice and Hospitaller Malta, 1530–1798: Aspects of a Relationship* (Malta, 1992).

V. Mallia-Milanes, ed., *Hospitaller Malta 1530–1798: Studies on Early Modern Malta and the Order of St John of Jerusalem* (Malta, 1993).

J.L. Martín, *Orígines de la orden militar de Santiago (1170–1195)* (Barcelona, 1974).

K. Militzer, *Die Entstehung der Deutschordensballeien im Deutschen Reich* (Marburg, 1981).

G. Minnucci and F. Sardi, eds., *I Templari: Mito e Storia. Atti del Convegno Internazionale di Studi alla Magione Templare di Poggibonsi-Siena, 29–31 Maggio 1987* (Siena, 1989).

G. Müller, *Die Familiaren des Deutschen Ordens* (Marburg, 1980).

H. Nicholson, *Templars, Hospitallers and Teutonic Knights. Images of the Military Orders, 1128–1291* (London, 1993).

Z.N. Nowak, ed., *Die Rolle der Ritterorden in der Christianisierung und Kolonisierung des Ostseegebiets* (Toruń, 1983).

Z.N. Nowak ed., *Die Ritterorden zwischen geistlicher und weltlicher Macht in Mittelalter* (Toruń, 1990).

J.F. O'Callaghan, *The Spanish Military Order of Calatrava and its Affiliates* (London, 1975).

Les ordres militaires, la vie rurale et le peuplement en Europe occidentale (XIIe-XVIIIe siècles) (Auch, 1986).

W. Paravicini, *Die Preussenreisen des europaïschen Adels*, 1 (Sigmaringen, 1989).

P. Partner, *The Murdered Magicians. The Templars and their Myth* (Oxford, 1981).

C. Probst, *Der Deutsche Orden und sein Medizinalwesen in Preussen: Hospital, Firmarie und Artz bis 1525* (Bad Godesberg, 1969).

J. Riley-Smith, *The Knights of St John in Jerusalem and Cyprus, c. 1050–1310* (London, 1967).

W.G. Rödel, *Das Grosspriorat Deutschland des Johanniter- Ordens im Übergang vom Mittelalter zur Reformation*, 2nd ed. (Cologne, 1972).

M. Roncetti, P. Scarpellini and F. Tommasi, *Templari e Ospiotalieri in Italia. La chiesa di San Bevignate a Perugia* (Milan, 1987).

R. Sáinz de la Maza Lasoli, *La orden de Santiago en la Corona de Aragón: La encomienda de Montalbán (1210–1327)* (Zaragoza, 1980).

J. Sarnowsky, *Die Wirtschaftsführung des Deutschen Ordens in Preussen (1382–1454)* (Cologne, 1993)

K. Scholz, *Beiträge zur Personengeschichte des Deutschen Ordens in der ersten Hälfte des 14. Jahrhunderts: Untersuchungen zur Herkunft livlandischer und preussischer Deutschordensbrüder* (Münster, 1971).

H.J.A. Sire, *The Knights of Malta* (London and New Haven, 1994).

H. Solano, *La Orden de Calatrava en el siglo XV. Los señoríos castellanos de la Orden al fin de la Edad Media* (Seville, 1978).

F. Täubl, *Der Deutsche Orden im Zeitalter Napoleons* (Bonn, 1966).

J.H. de Vey Mestdagh, *De Utrechtse Balije der Duitse Orde ruim 750 jaar geschiedenis v/d Orde in de Nederlanden* (Utrecht/Alden Beisen, 1988).

B. Waldstein-Wartenberg, *Rechtsgeschichte des Malteserordens* (Vienna, 1969).

B. Waldstein-Wartenberg, *Die Vassallen Christi: Kulturgeschichte des Johanniterordens im Mittelalter* (Vienna, 1988).

A. Wienand, ed., *Der Johanniterorden/Der Maltesenorden: Der ritterliche Orden des hl. Johannes vom Spital zu Jerusalem. Seine Geschichte, seine Aufgaben*, 3rd edn (Cologne, 1988).

A. Wildermann, *Die Beurteilung des Templerprozesses bis zum 17. Jahrhundert* (Freiburg, 1971).

D. Wojtecki, *Studien zur Personengeschichte des Deutschen Ordens im 13. Jahrhundert* (Wiesbaden, 1971).

Index

INDEX OF PLACES